VOL 1

Experience Chemistry

SAVVAS
LEARNING COMPANY

FLINN SCIENTIFIC

We are excited and proud to partner with Flinn Scientific in the development of this highly innovative program. Flinn Scientific supports science educators in opening young minds to the challenges and joys of scientific discovery.

The cover shows bismuth, a commonly used, naturally occurring metal that has some unique properties. The layered, hollowed-out shape of crystallized bismuth is typical of "hopper crystals." The multiple colors of a bismuth crystal are caused by differences in the oxide layer that forms on its surface. Sebastian Janicki/Shutterstock; Bkgd: Sylverarts Vectors/Shutterstock

Savvas Learning Company LLC, 15 East Midland Avenue, Paramus, NJ 07652

Teacher Guide credits: T3 (T,C): Up Late Creative; (B): Kai Kiefer; T4: Tanya Katovich; T13: Steven Errico/Compassionate Eye Foundation/Getty Images; T14: Monkey Business Images/Shutterstock; T16: Mint Images RF/Getty Images; T17: Savvas Learning Company LLC; T18: kali9/Getty Images; T19: lightfieldstudios/123RF; T20: Hero Images/Getty Images; T21: Ian Lishman/Juice Images/Getty Images; T22: Ferrantraite/Getty Images; T24: Monkey Business Images/Shutterstock.

ISBN-13: 978-1-4183-2720-0
ISBN-10: 1-4183-2720-4

SAVVAS
LEARNING COMPANY

1 20

PROGRAM AUTHORS

Christopher Moore, Ph.D. is the Dr. George F. Haddix Community Chair in Physical Science at the University of Nebraska Omaha, where he directs programs for pre- and in-service secondary chemistry and physics teachers. Holding an M.S. in applied physics and a Ph.D. in chemistry from Virginia Commonwealth University, Dr. Moore has worked as a physical science teacher at several secondary schools in Virginia, as a professional materials scientist, and as a scholar of and consultant on science education. His education research focuses on the development of scientific reasoning and expert-like science practice abilities, and his materials science research focuses on electronic materials for devices. He is the author of the books *Teaching Science Thinking: Using Scientific Reasoning in the Classroom* and *Creating Scientists: Teaching and Assessing Science Practice for the NGSS.*

Michael Wysession, Ph.D. is a Professor of Earth and Planetary Sciences at Washington University in St. Louis and Executive Director of The Teaching Center. Author of more than 100 science and science education publications, Dr. Wysession was awarded the prestigious National Science Foundation Presidential Faculty Fellowship and Packard Foundation Fellowship for his research in geophysics, primarily focused on using seismic tomography to determine the forces driving plate tectonics. Dr. Wysession is also a leader in geoscience literacy and education; he is the chair of the Earth Science Literacy Initiative, author of several popular video lectures on geoscience in The Great Courses series, and a lead writer of the Next Generation Science Standards.

Consulting Author

Bryn Lutes, Ph.D. is a chemist, technology translator, and educator. Holding a Ph.D. in organometallic chemistry, Dr. Lutes has worked both in and out of the classroom to help faculty incorporate active-learning techniques and technology to support student learning. She currently teaches General Chemistry for post-baccalaureate premedical students, Quantitative Reasoning, and Inorganic Chemistry Laboratory, where she continues to explore and incorporate active-learning and technology-assisted pedagogies.

CONSULTANT AND REVIEWERS

Program Consultant

Tanya Katovich is a chemistry educator and consultant. In 2015, she received the Davidson Award, presented annually by the Chemical Industry Council of Illinois to an outstanding chemistry teacher in Illinois. In 2017, Tanya became an Illinois finalist for the Presidential Award for Excellence in Mathematics and Science Teaching (PAEMST). She currently serves as the Vice-President and a member of the board of directors for the nonprofit organization Northern Illinois Science Educators (NISE).

Academic Reviewers

Aida Awad
Adjunct Instructor
American Intercontinental University
Buckeye, AZ

Nicole Bouvier-Brown, Ph.D.
Associate Professor of Chemistry & Biochemistry
Loyola Marymount University
Los Angeles, CA

Drew Budner, Ph.D.
Assistant Professor of Chemistry
Coastal Carolina University
Conway, SC

Thomas Bussey, Ph.D.
Assistant Teaching Professor
Department of Chemistry & Biochemistry
University of California, San Diego
La Jolla, CA

Stephen Contakes, Ph.D.
Associate Professor of Chemistry
Westmont College
Santa Barbara, CA

Michael Everest, Ph.D.
Professor of Chemistry
Westmont College
Santa Barbara, CA

Alison J. Frontier, Ph.D.
Professor of Chemistry
University of Rochester
Rochester, NY

Tiffany Hayden, Ph.D.
Associate Professor of Chemistry
Erskine College
Due West, SC

Hasan Palandoken, Ph.D.
Associate Professor
Department of Chemistry & Biochemistry
California Polytechnic State University
San Luis Obispo, CA

Robert Senter, Ph.D.
Instructor and Lab Coordinator
Department of Chemistry and Biochemistry
Loyola Marymount University
Los Angeles, CA

Amanda Silberstein, Ph.D.
Assistant Professor of Chemistry
Westmont College
Santa Barbara, CA

Harry A. Stern, Ph.D.
Center for Integrated Research Computing
University of Rochester
Rochester, NY

Shanju Zhang, Ph.D.
Associate Professor
Department of Chemistry & Biochemistry
California Polytechnic State University
San Luis Obispo, CA

Teacher Reviewers

Scot Abel
Science Curriculum Coordinator
DC Everest Area School District
Weston, WI

Gregory Aniol
Chemistry Teacher
Riverside Unified School District
Riverside, CA

Ed Bolton
Chemistry Teacher
Marquette High School
Chesterfield, MO

Manny Colon
Science Department Chair/
Science and Engineering
Teacher
University Preparatory School
Victorville, CA

Jenn M. Corcoran
Chemistry Teacher
Naugatuck High School
Naugatuck, CT

Karl Craddock
Science Department Chair
William Fremd High School
Palatine, IL

Stephanie Farmer
Chemistry Teacher
Dougherty Valley High School
San Ramon, CA

Jodi Fertoli
Chemistry Teacher
Staten Island Technical High
School
Staten Island, NY

Rhonda Frohn
Chemistry Teacher
Conejo Valley Unified School
District
Thousand Oaks, CA

Sean Gilbert
Chemistry Teacher
Leuzinger High School
Lawndale, CA

Martin Goldman
Chemistry Teacher
Edison High School
Edison, NJ

Rodger Golgart
Chemistry Teacher
Grand Terrace High School
Grand Terrace, CA

Ricardo Gutierrez
Biology/Earth Science Teacher
Temescal Canyon High School
Lake Elsinore, CA

Ava Hughes
Chemistry Teacher
Northwest High School
Cedar Hill, MO

Jessica Johnson
Chemistry Teacher
Jackson Public Schools
Jackson, MS

Brittney Kang
Science Teacher
Portola High School
Irvine, CA

Katie Keeler
Chemistry Teacher
Newbury Park High School
Newbury Park, CA

Kathryn Nelson, MEd, NBCT
Science Department Chair
Sylvania Northview High School
Sylvania, OH

Natalie Nevi
Chemistry Teacher
Norwin High School
North Huntingdon, PA

Ayanna Pantallion
Chemistry Teacher
Santa Monica-Malibu Unified
School District
Santa Monica, CA

Kurt Rogers
Chemistry Teacher
Northern Highlands High
School
Allendale, NJ

Michelle Tindall
K–12 Curriculum Coordinator
Birmingham Public Schools
Birmingham, MI

Susan Todd
Chemistry Teacher
Claxton High School
Claxton, Georgia

Dawn Toth
Chemistry Teacher
Redlands Unified School District
Redlands, CA

Amanda Waterfield
Chemistry Teacher
Victor Valley Unified School
District
Victorville, CA

Lab Review

All labs in the program were developed and tested by FLINN SCIENTIFIC

PROGRAM CONTENTS

VOLUME 1
TABLE OF CONTENTS

Teacher Guide Planning Resources

STORYLINE 1

ENCOUNTER
ANCHORING PHENOMENON What distinguishes the minerals in this mountain?

ENCOUNTER
INVESTIGATIVE PHENOMENON What causes the colors in a fireworks display?

STORYLINE 1 continued

INVESTIGATION 2 The Periodic Table 42

INVESTIGATION 3 Chemical Bonding 66

STORYLINE 2

ENCOUNTER

ANCHORING PHENOMENON How can we produce better foods?

STORYLINE 2 continued

INVESTIGATION 5 Chemical Quantities 152

ENCOUNTER
INVESTIGATIVE PHENOMENON Why do we quantify matter in different ways?

INVESTIGATION 6 Chemical Reactions 182

ENCOUNTER
INVESTIGATIVE PHENOMENON How is energy obtained from chemical reactions?

Resources

Experience Chemistry

Meet *Experience Chemistry*–an exciting, innovative way to teach chemistry. Featuring thought-provoking phenomena that will engage students, *Experience Chemistry* is a curriculum in which student learning is based on **doing science**.

This new program implements a learning model that:

- Organizes learning around Anchoring, Investigative, and Everyday Phenomena, giving students an authentic, real-world experience.
- Immerses students in the doing of science with a variety of hands-on and digital activities designed to reach every learner.
- Partners with Flinn Scientific to deliver high-quality inquiry labs, virtual reality, and performance assessments.
- Allows instructors to personalize their course with additional activities or embed their own.

New Instructional Model

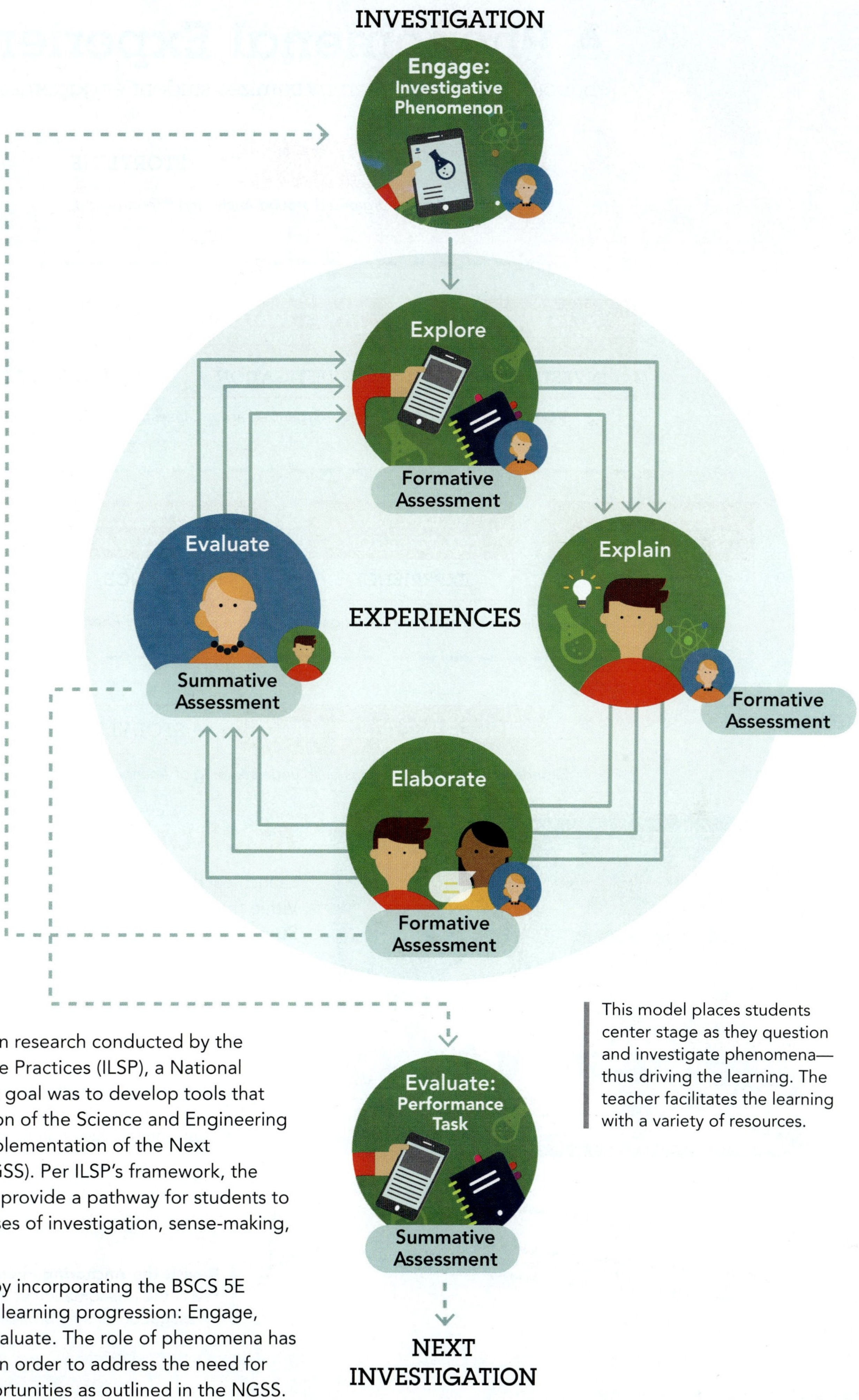

Research

The instructional model is based on research conducted by the Instructional Leadership for Science Practices (ILSP), a National Science Foundation project whose goal was to develop tools that support educators in the integration of the Science and Engineering Practices (SEPs) along with the implementation of the Next Generation Science Standards (NGSS). Per ILSP's framework, the science and engineering practices provide a pathway for students to engage sequentially in the processes of investigation, sense-making, and critique.

This approach has been adapted by incorporating the BSCS 5E Model to round out the five-stage learning progression: Engage, Explore, Explain, Elaborate and Evaluate. The role of phenomena has been intensified in the pedagogy in order to address the need for phenomenon-based learning opportunities as outlined in the NGSS.

This model places students center stage as they question and investigate phenomena—thus driving the learning. The teacher facilitates the learning with a variety of resources.

A Phenomenal Experience

Phenomena organization maximizes student engagement.

ANCHORING PHENOMENON | STORYLINE

5 Storylines—Organized around Anchoring Phenomena

INVESTIGATIVE PHENOMENON | INVESTIGATION

INVESTIGATIVE PHENOMENON | INVESTIGATION

INVESTIGATIVE PHENOMENON | INVESTIGATION

3–5 Investigations per Storyline—Organized around Investigative Phenomena

EVERYDAY PHENOMENON | EXPERIENCE

EVERYDAY PHENOMENON | EXPERIENCE

EVERYDAY PHENOMENON | EXPERIENCE

EVERYDAY PHENOMENON | EXPERIENCE

3–6 Experiences per Investigation—Experience Everyday Phenomena

ANCHORING PHENOMENON | STORYLINE

Experiences and Investigations build understanding of Anchoring Phenomenon

Anchoring Phenomena

Launch each Storyline with an engaging Anchoring Phenomenon Video that introduces and unifies the upcoming chemistry concepts. Students ask questions and gather evidence about the phenomenon on their sense-making journey. At the end of the Storyline, students solidify their mastery of the concepts behind the Anchoring Phenomenon.

Anchoring Phenomenon Video
The Anchoring Phenomenon sets a clear storyline for studying the core concept.

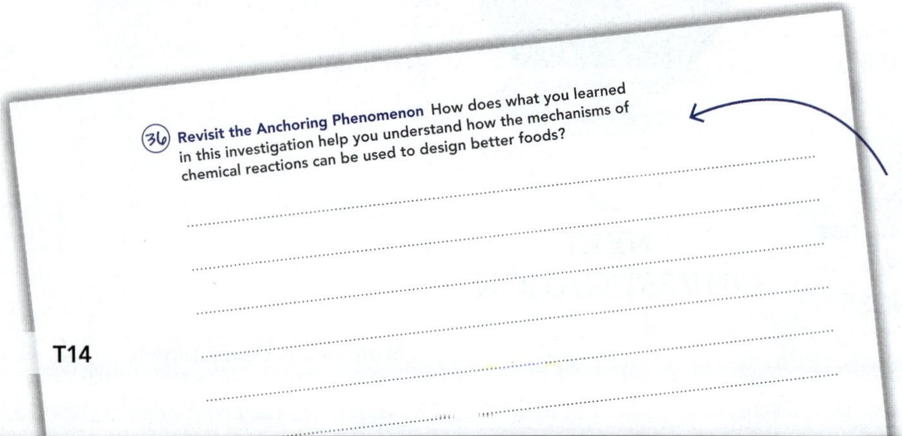
(36) **Revisit the Anchoring Phenomenon** How does what you learned in this investigation help you understand how the mechanisms of chemical reactions can be used to design better foods?

Revisit the Anchoring Phenomenon Students revisit the phenomenon at the end of every Investigation as they broaden their understanding.

Investigative Phenomena

Introduce every Investigation with an Investigative Phenomenon that provides another opportunity for students to interact with an engaging event and gather the knowledge necessary to make sense of the Anchoring Phenomenon.

Investigative Phenomenon Videos spark student curiosity and ground the Investigation in the real world.

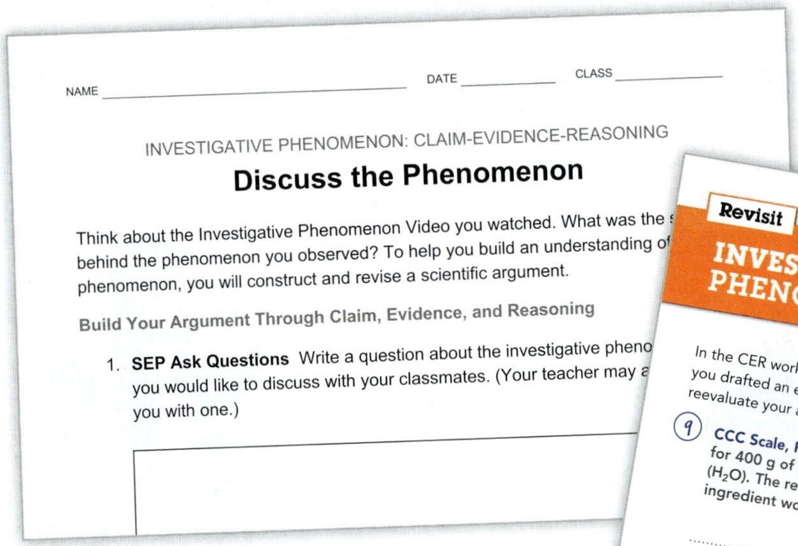

NAME ____________ DATE ________ CLASS ________

INVESTIGATIVE PHENOMENON: CLAIM-EVIDENCE-REASONING

Discuss the Phenomenon

Think about the Investigative Phenomenon Video you watched. What was the
behind the phenomenon you observed? To help you build an understanding of
phenomenon, you will construct and revise a scientific argument.

Build Your Argument Through Claim, Evidence, and Reasoning

1. **SEP Ask Questions** Write a question about the investigative pheno
you would like to discuss with your classmates. (Your teacher may
you with one.)

Revisit the Investigative Phenomenon prompts at the end of every Experience help students refine their understanding as they uncover more knowledge.

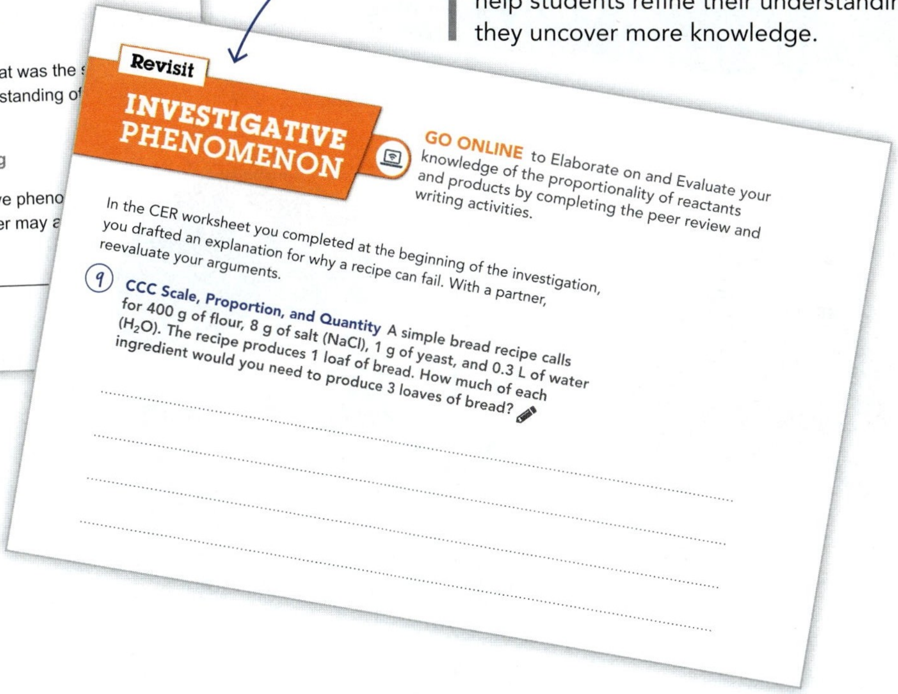

Revisit

INVESTIGATIVE PHENOMENON

GO ONLINE to Elaborate on and Evaluate your knowledge of the proportionality of reactants and products by completing the peer review and writing activities.

In the CER worksheet you completed at the beginning of the investigation, you drafted an explanation for why a recipe can fail. With a partner, reevaluate your arguments.

9 **CCC Scale, Proportion, and Quantity** A simple bread recipe calls for 400 g of flour, 8 g of salt (NaCl), 1 g of yeast, and 0.3 L of water (H_2O). The recipe produces 1 loaf of bread. How much of each ingredient would you need to produce 3 loaves of bread?

Students track their understanding in a **Claim-Evidence-Reasoning** or a **Modeling Worksheet** as they learn more about the phenomenon.

Everyday Phenomena

Students relate Anchoring and Investigative experiences to Everyday Phenomena. From **Flinn Scientific** inquiry lab activities to animations, mathematical modeling, virtual reality and more, students are motivated to figure out *why* and *how* a phenomenon happens. Ongoing exposure to Everyday Phenomena encourages students to apply the science and engineering practices in every lesson.

RELATED PHENOMENA

Want more ideas? The Teacher Guide offers alternative suggestions for Anchoring, Investigative, and Everyday Phenomena.

FLINN SCIENTIFIC

Our partner in Inquiry

Experience Chemistry is the science of doing. An exclusive partnership with **Flinn Scientific**, the leading classroom lab solution provider, embeds engaging **Flinn Scientific Labs** and activities directly into the program.

Inquiry Labs

- Explore concepts with an inquiry lab in every learning experience (over seventy hands-on inquiry labs in the program).
- Differentiate instruction with **four (4) versions of every lab**: Open-Ended, Guided, Shortened, and Advanced.
- Customize the labs on Realize to fit your unique classroom needs.

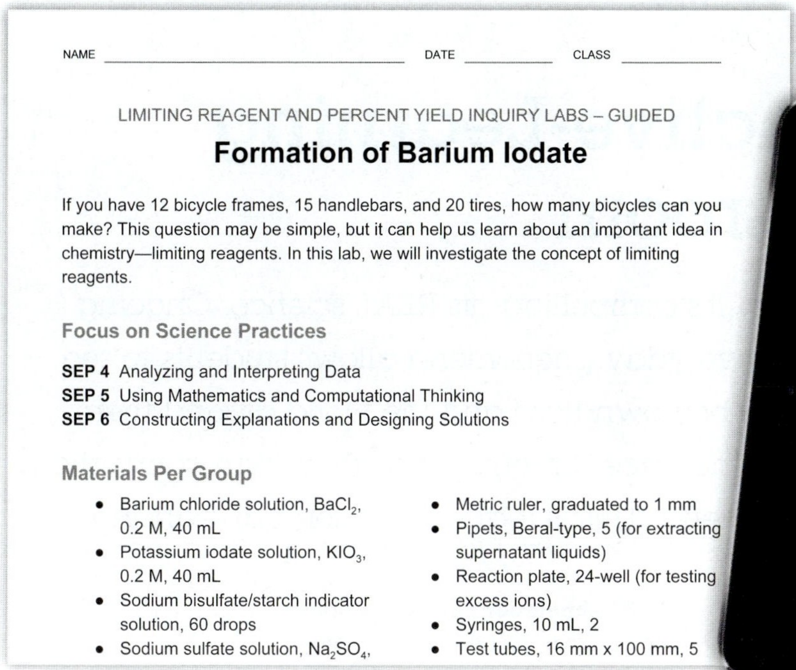
NAME ____________________ DATE __________ CLASS __________

LIMITING REAGENT AND PERCENT YIELD INQUIRY LABS – GUIDED

Formation of Barium Iodate

If you have 12 bicycle frames, 15 handlebars, and 20 tires, how many bicycles can you make? This question may be simple, but it can help us learn about an important idea in chemistry—limiting reagents. In this lab, we will investigate the concept of limiting reagents.

Focus on Science Practices

SEP 4 Analyzing and Interpreting Data
SEP 5 Using Mathematics and Computational Thinking
SEP 6 Constructing Explanations and Designing Solutions

Materials Per Group

- Barium chloride solution, $BaCl_2$, 0.2 M, 40 mL
- Potassium iodate solution, KIO_3, 0.2 M, 40 mL
- Sodium bisulfate/starch indicator solution, 60 drops
- Sodium sulfate solution, Na_2SO_4,
- Metric ruler, graduated to 1 mm
- Pipets, Beral-type, 5 (for extracting supernatant liquids)
- Reaction plate, 24-well (for testing excess ions)
- Syringes, 10 mL, 2
- Test tubes, 16 mm x 100 mm, 5

Differentiate your lessons with four versions of every lab, including: Open-Ended, Guided, Shortened, and Advanced.

Engineering Design Challenges

- Students design, test, and evaluate solutions that mimic the real-world activities of engineers and strengthen their science and engineering skills.

Lab Kits

- Simplify lab setup and solution preparation with readily accessible kits aligned to Flinn labs, activities and assessments.

Performance-Based Assessments

- Students demonstrate NGSS mastery by applying their understanding to a new situation at the end of every Investigation.

Videos

- Engaging Overview and Summary Videos introduce the lab and connect to phenomena.

Virtual Reality Simulations

- Immersive learning in 360° simulations brings chemistry to life with an accessible interface.

Immerse your students in 360° simulations that bring chemistry to life.

An Active-Learning Classroom

It's authentic...it's compelling...its REAL science. Ongoing exposure to everyday phenomena allows students to see chemistry in their own lives and the world around them. Students use the three dimensions as they form connections to the Phenomena. This is real science for real learning.

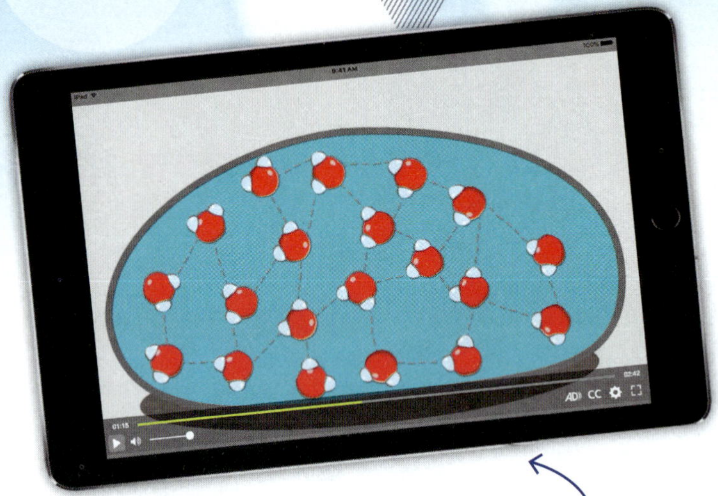

Students improve visual and media literacy while watching **Animations** that explain complex topics.

PhET | **PhET simulations** engage students in an intuitive, game-like environment.

VirtualNerd™ | **Virtual Nerd Tutorial Videos** offer approachable mathematics explanations delivered by on-screen instructors.

Define problems and propose design solutions in **Problem-Based Learning Experiences**.

Modeling Activities provide opportunities for students to model, describe, and predict the behavior of a range of different phenomena.

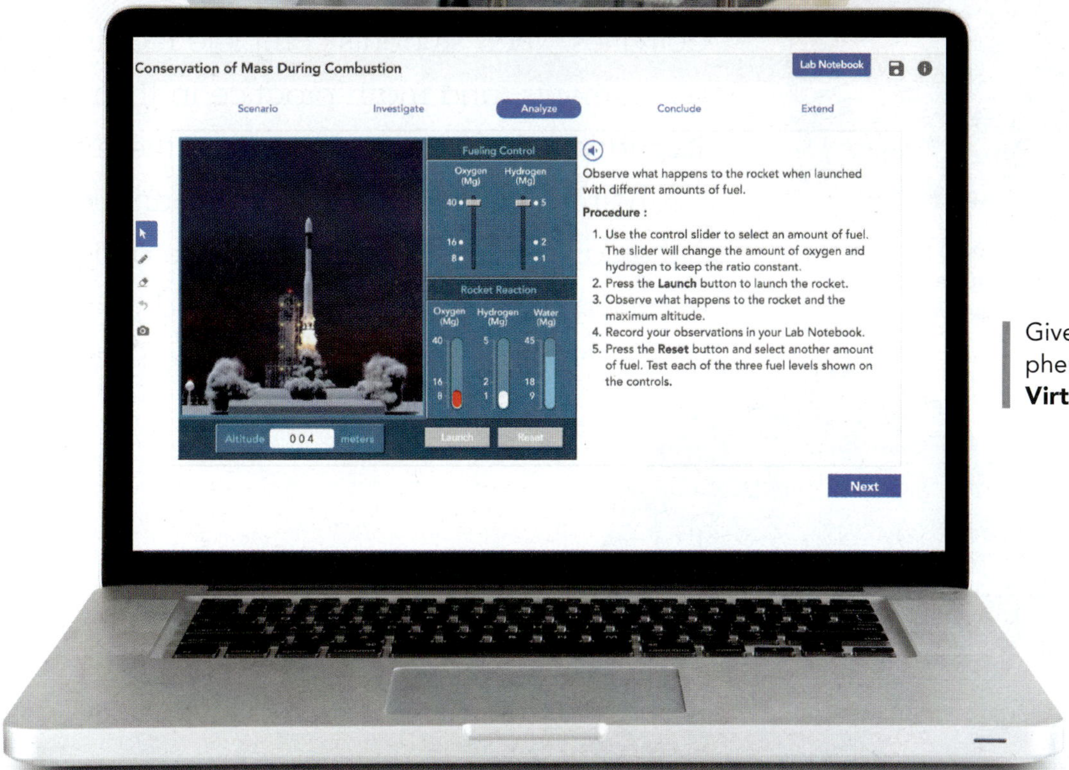

Give all students access to phenomena in compelling **Virtual Labs.**

Students write, defend, and revisit arguments in **Claim-Evidence-Reasoning** activities.

Students improve science literacy skills with **Authentic Readings, Analyzing Data,** and **Writing About Science** activities.

Promote collaboration and engage students in science discourse with **Peer Review** and **Discussion Rubrics**.

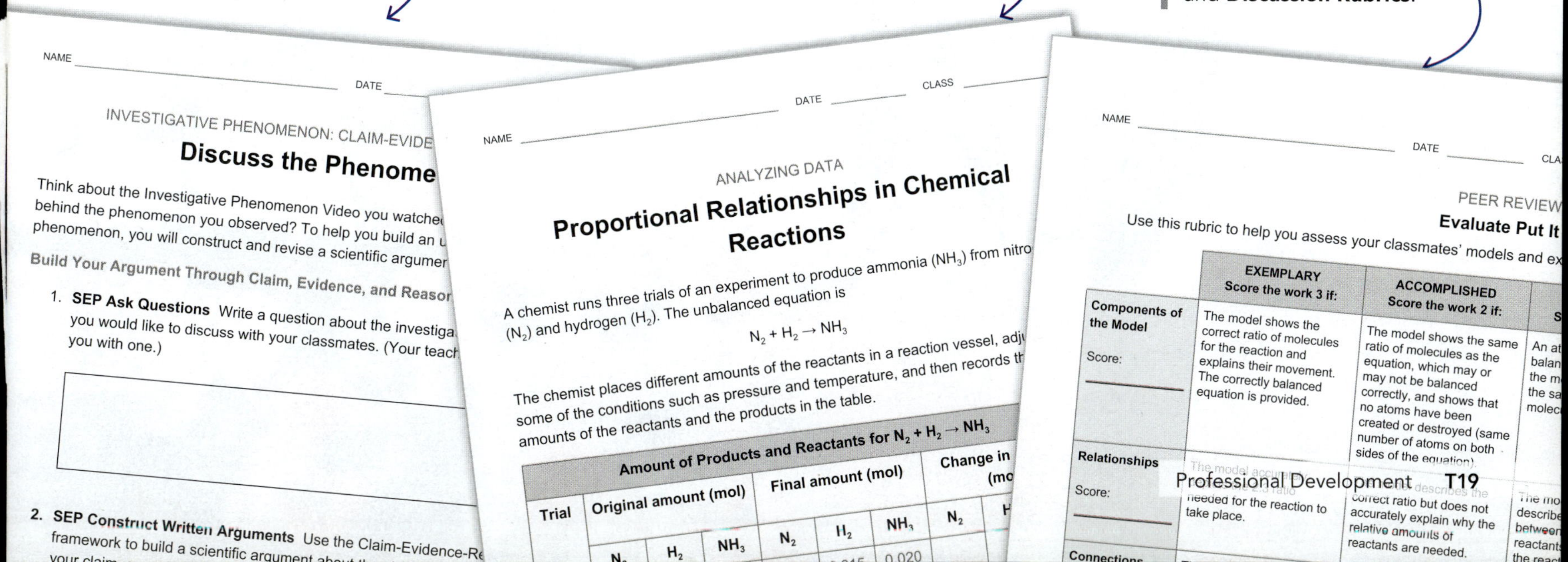

Research shows that students who use science notebooks develop a deeper understanding of science. To learn more visit savvas.com/experiencechemistry

An interactive tool that promotes scientific understanding

With *Experience Chemistry*, we've transformed the traditional textbook into a modern interactive notebook. Students DO chemistry first—by interacting with phenomena and completing hands-on inquiry labs and activities. Then students complete readings, formative assessments, and math practice in their **Student Experience Notebooks**. This gives them real-world context for their readings and the background knowledge necessary to tackle more elaborate activities such as engineering design challenges and peer review.

Percent Yield

Success Stats In the average professional hockey game, a team will make thirty shots at the goal. Theoretically, every shot could result in a score. However, this outcome does not occur. The average professional team scores fewer than two goals per game. The success percentage is the ratio of the actual score to the theoretical score expressed as a percent:

$$\text{Percent Success} = \frac{\text{actual score}}{\text{theoretical score}} \times 100\%$$

Percent Success A hockey team may score on less than 7% of the shots that they make on the goal.

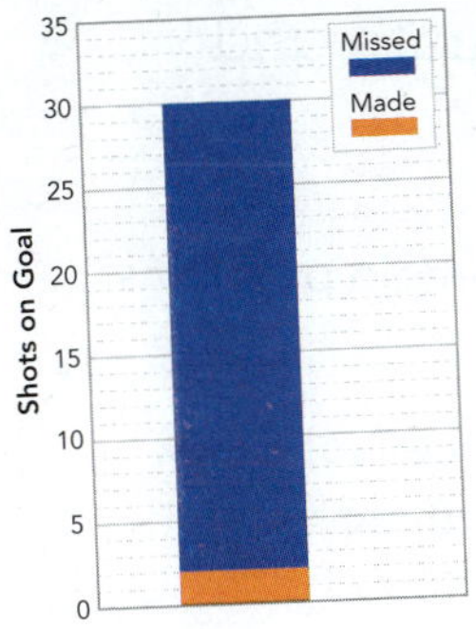

Improving the Score To improve, the team could either try to make more shots on the goal during a game or increase their percent success by making more of the shots they attempt.

(25) **SEP Define a Problem** Grades on tests can also be thought of as a success statistic. How would you define the actual score and theoretical score on an exam, and how would you calculate the percent success?

Percent Yield in Reactions When a balanced chemical equation is used to calculate the amount of product of a reaction, the calculated value represents the **theoretical yield**. It is the maximum amount of product that can be formed. The actual amount of product made during a real reaction is called the **actual yield**. You can measure the mass of the product of a laboratory experiment to find the actual yield. The **percent yield** is the ratio of the actual to the theoretical yield expressed as a percent, and represents the efficiency of a reaction:

$$\text{Percent Yield} = \frac{\text{actual yield}}{\text{theoretical yield}} \times 100\%$$

Theoretical Yield The balanced chemical equation for the formation of ammonia can be used to determine the theoretical yield. Theoretical yield assumes that all of the reactants are used to make the product.

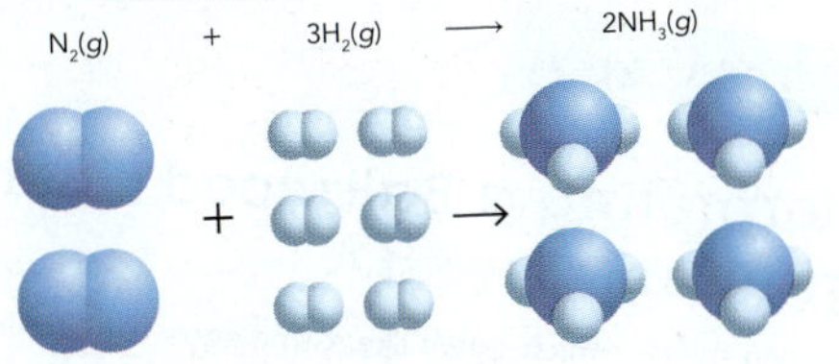

Side Reactions and Actual Yield Often, side reactions reduce the yield of a reaction. In this case, only 50% of the possible ammonia was produced because oxygen caused a side reaction. The oxygen may have been introduced from an impure gas source.

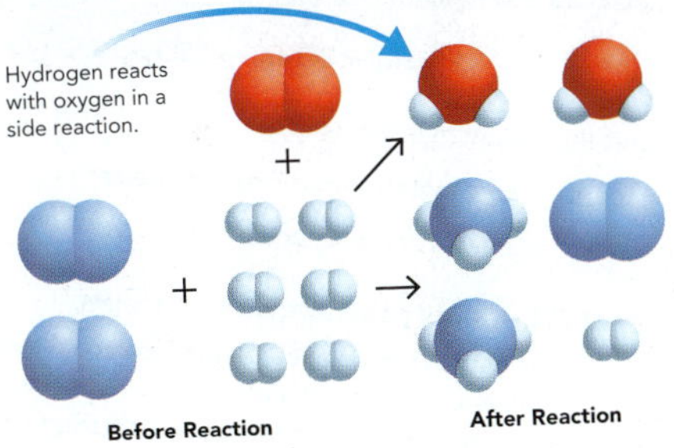

(26) **SEP Construct an Explanation** Imagine you are a chemical engineer at a chemical plant. One day the air conditioning in the plant stops working, resulting in high humidity. The percent yield for a chemical you produce drops significantly. Construct an explanation for the decrease in yield.

Advance Student Thinking and Curiosity

Students use the *Student Experience Notebook* to write and sketch observations, generate questions and ideas, gather data, and engage in argument. Through targeted question prompts in the notebook, students will:

- Propose and develop explanations of the phenomena under study.
- Integrate science and engineering practices and crosscutting concepts in their writings, discussions, analyses, and computations.
- Apply a claim-evidence-reasoning framework to build and refine scientific arguments and explanations.
- Be inspired to carefully observe the phenomena around them and make sense of them.
- Engage in repeated data analysis, reflection, and revision of ideas while uncovering new information.
- Synthesize ideas and conclusions using evidence.

Write and Talk About Science

The interactive *Student Experience Notebook* helps learners strengthen their literacy and communication skills. As students read and engage with the text, they will:

- Practice various forms of nonfiction writing—descriptive, labeling, procedural, explanatory, and narrative.
- Cultivate important skills of data fluency and critical thinking in the contexts of problem solving and scientific investigation.
- Grow more comfortable with academic language.

College and Career Readiness

The ability to reason, research, and analyze logically is a critical piece of the skill set needed in both college and careers. Using a science journal builds the following attributes in learners: reflection, curiosity, openness, internal motivation, persistence, resilience, and flexibility. The practice of documenting and reevaluating their work in the *Experience Notebook* will help students find success in future endeavors.

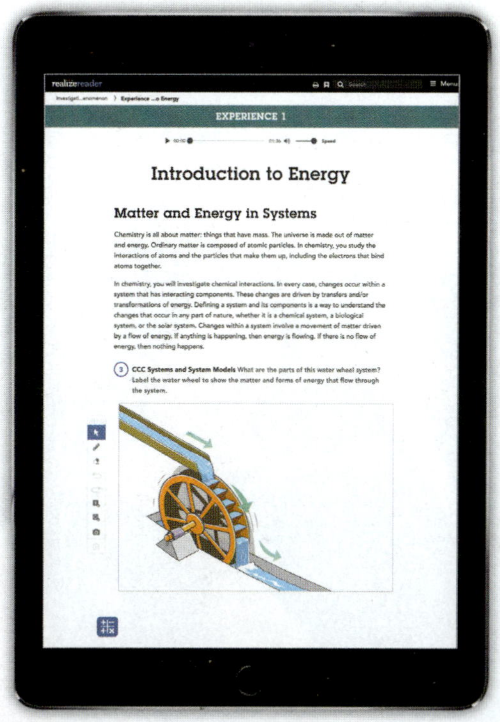

More Math Practice

Students interact with math problems, math-related science, and engineering practices to become more proficient with math and chemistry concepts.

Stepped-out examples break down sample problems for clarity and process guidance.

Problem Banks in the *Student Experience Notebook* and on Savvas Realize provide students with additional problems to build mathematical fluency.

Analyzing Data Activities provide opportunities for students to apply mathematical concepts in real-world contexts.

Lab analysis puts science and engineering skills into practice using collected data and mathematical models.

Virtual Nerd Math Support Videos reinforce mathematical processes, making them perfect for remediation and differentiating instruction.

Integrating Math prompts guide instructors with practical tips for supporting students with mathematics.

SAMPLE PROBLEM

Interpreting a Balanced Chemical Equation

Hydrogen sulfide, which smells like rotten eggs, is found in volcanic gases. The balanced equation for the burning of hydrogen sulfide is

$$2H_2S(g) + 3O_2(g) \rightarrow 2SO_2(g) + 2H_2O(g)$$

Interpret this equation in terms of

a. numbers of representative particles and moles.

b. masses of reactants and products.

ANALYZE **Identify the relevant concepts.**

The coefficients in the balanced equation give the relative number of representative particles and moles of reactants and products. A balanced chemical equation obeys the law of conservation of mass.

SOLVE **Apply the concepts to the situation.**

Use the coefficients in the balanced equation to identify the number of representative particles and moles.

a. 2 molecules H_2S + 3 molecules $O_2 \rightarrow$ 2 molecules SO_2 + 2 molecules H_2O, or
$2\text{ mol } H_2S + 3\text{ mol } O_2 \rightarrow 2\text{ mol } SO_2 + 2\text{ mol } H_2O$

Use the periodic table to determine the molar mass of each substance.

b. 1 mol H_2S = 34.1 g H_2S, 1 mol O_2 = 32.0 g O_2,
1 mol SO_2 = 64.1 g SO_2, 1 mol H_2O = 18.0 g H_2O

Multiply the number of moles of each reactant and product by its molar mass.

$2\text{ mol } H_2S + 3\text{ mol } O_2 \rightarrow 2\text{ mol } SO_2 + 2\text{ mol } H_2O$

$\left(2\text{ mol} \times 34.1 \frac{g}{mol}\right) + \left(3\text{ mol} \times 32.0 \frac{g}{mol}\right) \rightarrow \left(2\text{ mol} \times 64.1 \frac{g}{mol}\right) + \left(2\text{ mol} \times 18.0 \frac{g}{mol}\right)$

$68.2\text{ g } H_2S + 96.0\text{ g } O_2 \rightarrow 128.2\text{ g } SO_2 + 36.0\text{ g } H_2O$

Add the mass... and on...

164.2 g = 164.2 g

...rmation of ... moles, and

SAMPLE PROBLEM SUPPORT

Help students with calculating moles of a product by walking through question 12, part b, on page 349 in the Experience Notebook. The amount of Al_2O_3 is given as 3.7 mol, so that is what you start with. The mole ratio can be found from the balanced equation.

$$3.7\text{ mol } Al_2O_3 \times \frac{4\text{ mol Al}}{2\text{ mol } Al_2O_3} = 7.4\text{ mol Al}$$

Assist students with calculating the mass of a product by walking through question 14 on page 351. Start with 5.00 g CaC_2 (given). Fin... how many grams of C_2H_2 and CaC_2 equal ... ole by looking at the atomic mass on ... ...dic table.

Instructors can encourage the development of math skills with suggestions and strategies to help students work through the sample problems.

Students Demonstrate Understanding

Multiple modes of assessment make it easier for students to demonstrate understanding of the chemistry concepts.

Storyline Assessment

- In the **Problem-Based Learning Experience** students obtain and evaluate information about a related phenomenon and communicate their findings in a written report.
- **Benchmark 3-D Assessments** work well for midterm and final exams.

Investigation-Level Assessment

- **Performance-Based Assessments** measure students' mastery of the science and engineering practices.
- For a summative assessment of the Investigation, assign customizable **3-Dimensional Assessments** in Realize.
- Students **revisit the Anchoring Phenomenon** multiple times as they make sense of the topic.
- **Problem banks** in the *Student Experience Notebook* and in the digital course provide opportunities for students to refine math and analytical skills.

Experience-Level Assessment

- Customizable **interactive online quizzes** conclude every Experience.
- **Assess-on-the-Spot** ideas in the *Teacher Guide* provide quick formative assessments.
- **Revisit Investigative Phenomena** prompts at the end of every Experience tie lesson content to the overarching question.

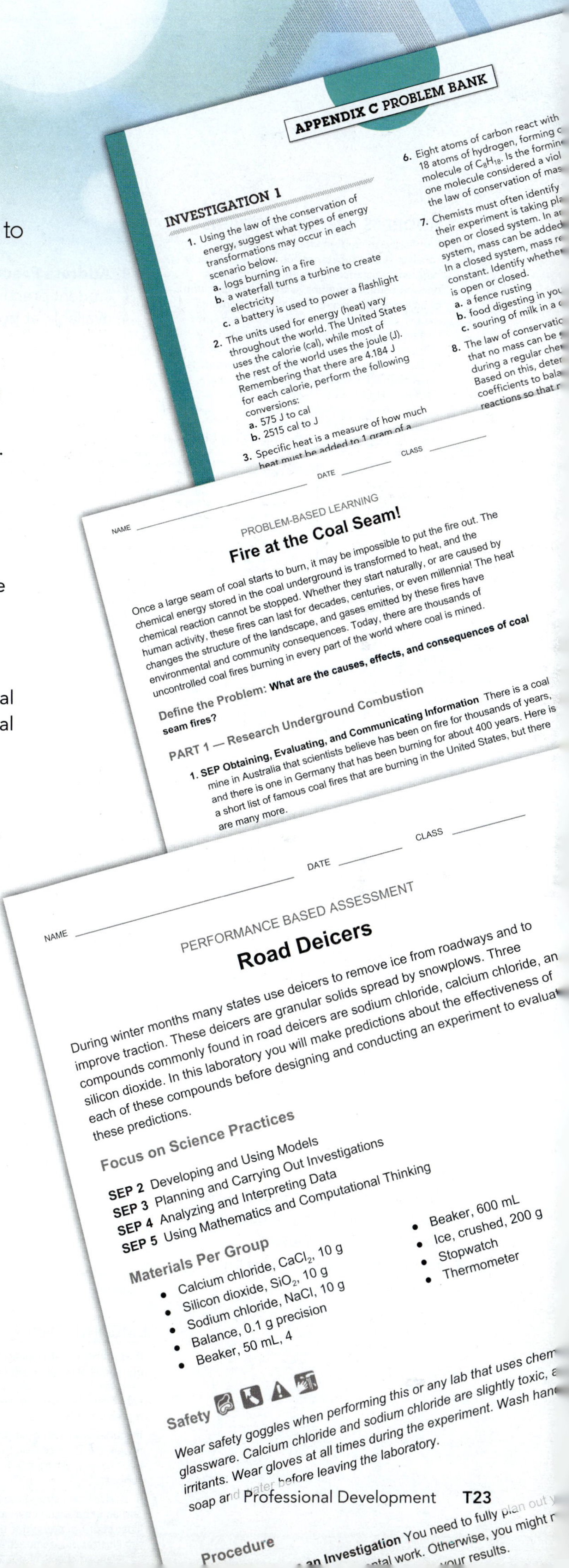

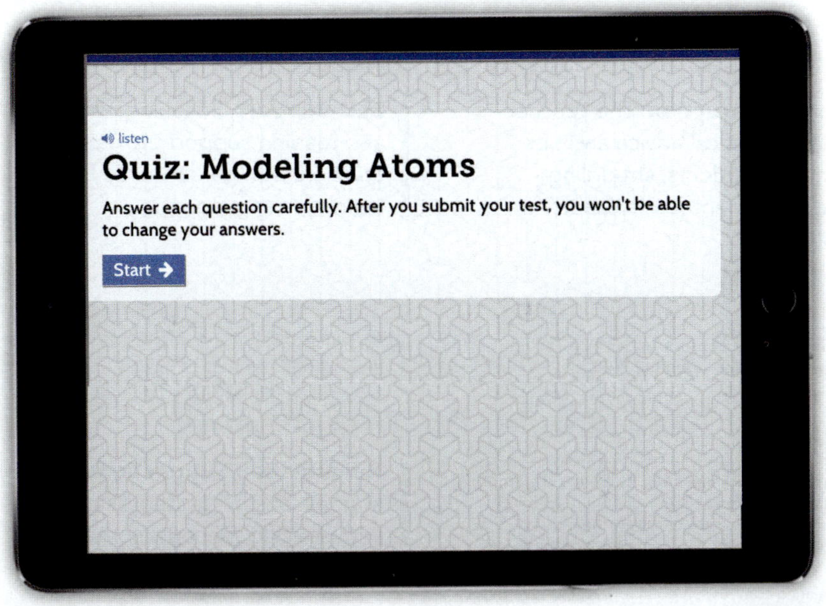

Reinforce Learning

Support all learners in the chemistry classroom.
Look for the following tools within the program.

ADDRESS PRECONCEPTIONS

Emphasize to students that decomposition consists of one substance forming two or more *different* substances. Students tend to limit decomposition reactions to the decomposition of a compound into its component elements. Explain that a compound can also break down into an element and a compound or two or more compounds. Provide examples of decomposition reaction that result in products other than elements: $2H_2O_2 \rightarrow 2H_2O + O_2$ and $H_2CO_3 \rightarrow H_2O + CO_2$.

Address Preconceptions Ideas to address common student preconceptions with tips and explanations are available at point-of-use in the Teacher Guide.

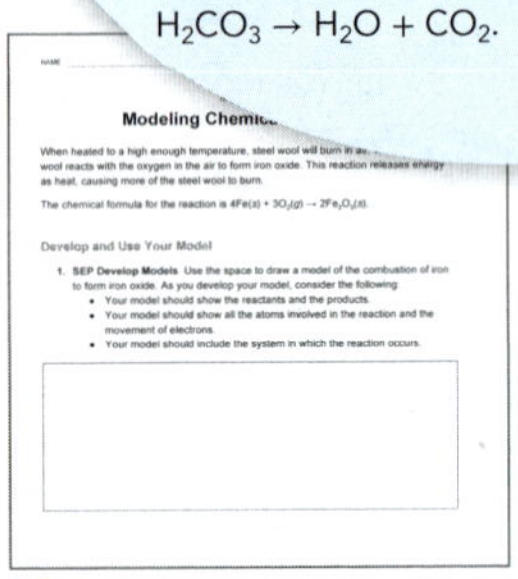

Modeling Interactive Worksheet

INTEGRATE THE THREE DIMENSIONS

In the modeling activity, students demonstrate their knowledge of what happens during a chemical reaction [PS1.B] by making a model [SEP-2] in which they identify and describe the relevant components of the reaction. They evaluate [SEP-8] their own models and the model of a classmate. Students also identify changes of energy [CCC-5] within the systems they model.

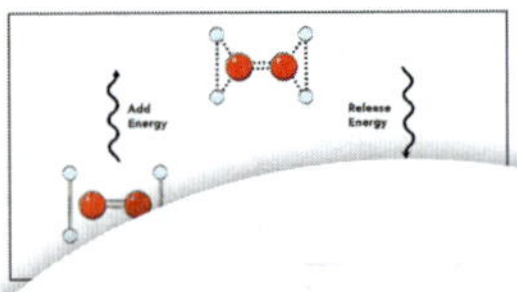

…AIN

…odeling Chemical Reactions

Modeling Use this activity after students have completed the Inquiry Lab in the Explore section of this experience. In this activity, students develop models [SEP-2] to show the chemical reaction [PS1.B] that takes place when steel wool combusts. Their models should show the molecules involved and the movement of electrons. They evaluate [SEP-8] the limitations and strengths of their own models and those of a partner's model.

- Students may choose different formats for their models. Some may choose to make labeled diagrams. Others may make three-dimensional models. Tell students to identify what each part of the model represents.
- After students complete the activity, have them write a short description of the relationship between components, including changes in energy [CCC-5] within the system.

Bonds Breaking and Forming

Animation In this animation, students investigate how a chemical reaction [PS1.B] involves chemical bonds breaking and forming. Students observe a model [SEP-2] of the reaction of hydrogen and oxygen to form water to explore how atoms in reactant molecules rearrange to form product molecules. Students determine that an energy input is required to break bonds in the reactants, and energy is released when new bonds form in the products. Choose among these strategies as you use the animation.

- Make sure that students understand that the rods in the diagrams represent bonds. Point out that some bonds are single bonds and others are double bonds.
- **Ask** What is required to break bonds in the reactants? (an energy input) Reinforce that energy is needed in the breaking and forming bonds.

How Do You Determine if a Graph Represents a Linear, Exponential, or Quadratic Function?

Virtual Nerd Video Use this video tutorial to reinforce whether a graph represents a linear, quadratic, or exponential function.

Modeling Chemical Reactions

Experience Notebook Ideally, assign the Experience Notebook or Realize Reader the day before and then follow up with any of the following suggested instructional strategies to fill in knowledge gaps and deepen understanding. Alternatively, assign it alongside the Modeling Chemical Reactions activity as …ort for the activity.

- …uations (p. 304) Point out that reactants are like the ingredients …d together to make bread. Bread is the product. **Ask** What does …rd equation mean? (yields or produces) Write this reaction …ave students copy it into their science notebooks: Fe_2O_3 …en invite a volunteer to label the reactants and products …board. Keep this equation on the board for additional …t the equation is not currently balanced, but it will …order to balance it.
- …05–306) Write the word *skeleton* on the board. …t in which students are most familiar with the …in their science notebooks why an equation …uld be a skeleton equation. Point out that the …eleton equation. **Ask** How does a skeleton …equation? (A skeleton equation uses chemical
- **Balancing Equations** (pp. 308–310) Refer to the equation on the board. **Ask** Does this equation follow the law of conservation of mass? (no) Why not? (The number of each kind of atom is not the same on both sides of the equation.) Challenge students to balance to equation in their notebooks. ($Fe_2O_3 + 3H_2 \rightarrow 2Fe + 3H_2O$) Then have students work with partners to take turns writing equations for each other to balance. Encourage pairs to challenge another pair to balance the equations they write and vice versa. The pair that correctly balances the most equations wins.
- **Energy of Reactions** (pp. 311–312) Challenge small groups of students to make a concept map with the phrase *Energy of Reactions* in the center. Allow 5 to 10 minutes for groups to complete their maps. Then have one person from each group communicate [SEP-8] the relationships in their group's map.
- Direct student's attention to the table Average Bond Energies on page 311. **Ask** Which two bonds in the table are strongest? (N triple bond to N, N double bond to O) Which two bonds are weakest? (I single bond to I, H single bond to I)
- **What Causes Reactions?** (p. 313) Remind students that they previously learned about the kinetic theory. Ask volunteers to identify parts of the kinetic theory. Then have student pairs communicate [SEP-8] to each other how the kinetic theory relates to the cause [CCC-2] of a chemical reaction [PS1.B].
- On the board write: *10^{-6} seconds to 10^6 years*. Ask students what they think the time span refers to. Then tell them that the time required for chemical change to take place may be less than 10^{-6} seconds or more than 10^6 years. Draw three columns on the board with these headings: *Very fast*, *Average*, and *Very slow*. Call on students to go to the board and add examples of reactions to the columns [CCC-3]. (Examples: Very fast—bleach on a stain; Average—milk spoiling in heat; Very slow—fossilization)

What is a Coefficient?

Virtual Nerd Video Use this video tutorial to reinforce the definition and use of coefficients.

ASSESS ON THE SPOT

Ask students to write a sentence to answer this question: Why do chemical equations have to be balanced when representing a chemical reaction? (Atoms cannot be created or destroyed, so any atom that is present in the reactants must also be present in the products.)

DIFFERENTIATED INSTRUCTION

- **Support Special Needs Students** Students with visual impairment or who are more tactile learners may benefit from using molecular model kits or foam balls of different sizes to represent atoms of different kinds when they practice balancing equations. Provide a few simple, unbalanced chemical equations and have students use the balls to model balancing the equations.

INTEGRATE MATH

Equality Write on the board a simple math equation without coefficients, such as $20 + 10 = 25 + 5$. **Ask** What does the equal sign tell you about the equation? (The sum of the numbers on one side of the equal sign are the same as the sum of the numbers on the opposite side.) Explain that the arrow in a chemical equation is similar. The mass of matter on one side of the arrow must be the same as the mass on the other side.

Now write a math equation with coefficients; for example, $5x^2 + x = 3x^2 + 2x + 2x^2 - x$. Combine them to show that $5x^2 + x = 5x^2 + x$. Point out that the exponents were not altered; only the coefficients were combined. Explain that, likewise, in a chemical equation, only the coefficient in front of a reactant or product can be changed when balancing an equation.

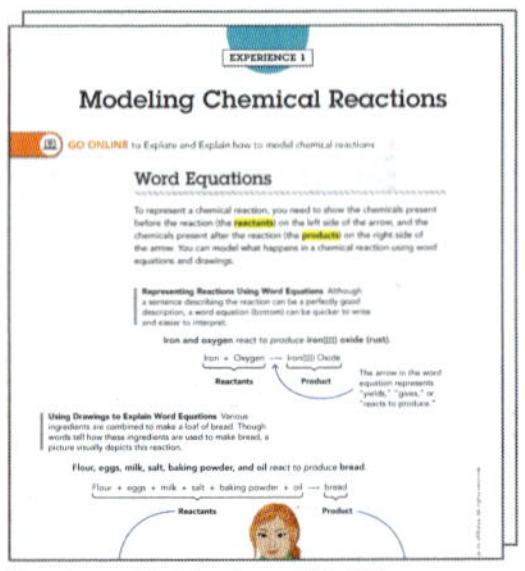

Experience Notebook, pp. 304–313

eTEXT

SAMPLE PROBLEM SUPPORT

To give students practice with writing word and skeleton equations, write this information on the board:

Sulfuric acid reacts with solid sulfur to form sulfur dioxide gas and water.

Call on volunteers to go to the board and write a word equation and a skeleton equation for the reaction. (sulfuric acid (aq) + sulfur (s) → sulfur dioxide (g) + water (l); $H_2SO_4(aq) + S(s) \rightarrow SO_2(g) + H_2O(l)$)

Virtual Nerd Video: What is a Coefficient?

ELD SUPPORT

Reading/Viewing Closely Use the following strategies to help students use knowledge of morphology to determine meanings of *endothermic* and *exothermic* on page 312 of the Experience Notebook.

- **Emerging** Have students draw pictures to illustrate the meaning of the two words. Then ask them to use their pictures to tell a partner in English or their home language what each word means.
- **Expanding** Have student pairs write two sentences for each word—one sentence to explain what it means and another to give an example.
- **Bridging** Have pairs write a paragraph that explains how the two terms relate to chemical reactions.

1 Modeling Chemical Reactions 25…

CLASSROOM MODIFICATIONS

Based on your students' abilities and your schedule, you may choose the Inquiry Lab to be more advanced or more guided.

- **Advanced Inquiry Lab** Students investigate the identity of an unknown Group 1 metal carbonate through gas evolution and titration.
- **Guided Inquiry Lab** Students investigate the identity of an unknown Group 1 metal carbonate through titration.

Differentiated Instruction The Teacher Guide includes practical advice and tips for special needs students, struggling students, less-proficient readers, and advanced students.

ELD Support Speaking, writing and reading support boxes advise teachers with guidance for English Learners Language.

Classroom Modifications Tips to make activities more open-ended or guided allows instructors to adjust based on students' abilities.

…ine to assess students' responses … …or each item to remediate well before assigning th… …ssment.

REMEDIATION SUGGESTIONS

- **If** students are struggling to model chemical reactions by writing skeleton equations and balancing equations, **then** have them write the reaction as a word equation first. Students may also want to review the Inquiry Lab, Evaluate Chemical Reactions, to review how chemical reactions are represented.
- **If** students are struggling to balance combustion equations, **then** have them review the Balance Combustion Equations worksheet. Students may also want to reread pages 308–310 in their Experience Notebooks for additional support.
- **If** students are struggling to identify the differences between a balanced and an unbalanced chemical equation, **then** guide students to examine th… illustrations of equations throughout the lesson. Have students explain… the illustrations demonstrate the differences between a balanced a… …anced chemical equation. Review with students the key …

Remediation Suggestions Multiple suggestions for students struggling with specific concepts complement Experience Level Assessment.

Save time and meet instructional Goals

Experience Chemistry offers a simple framework for teaching chemistry. An **innovative Teacher Guide** provides the resources you need to facilitate an authentic and exciting instructional experience.

Instructional planner Snapshot of upcoming Storylines, Investigations and Experiences with connections to phenomena, standards, and assessments makes planning a breeze.

Got more Time Personalize and enhance instructional plans by assigning the activities with the Got-More-Time icon, as time allows.

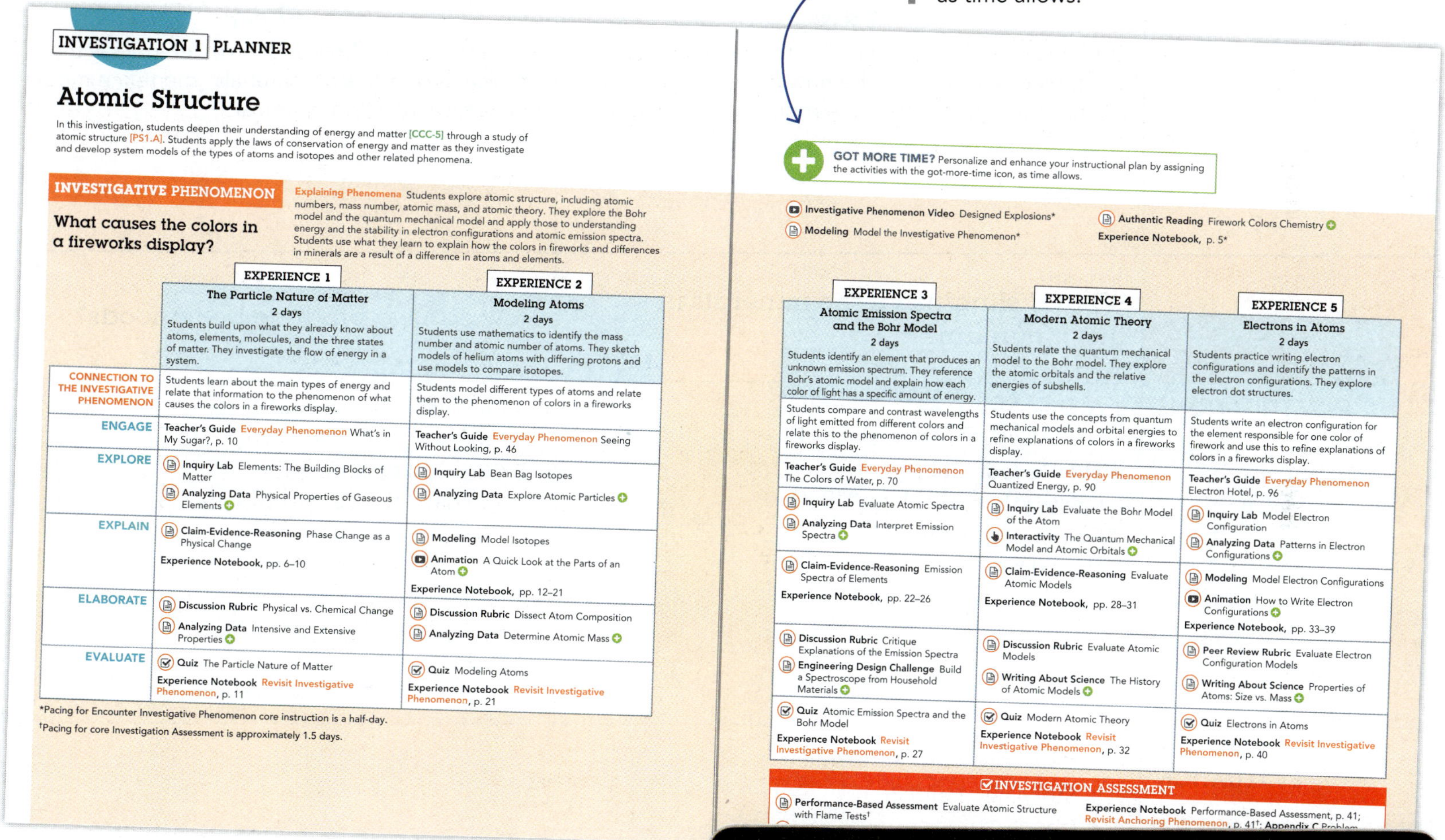

INVESTIGATION 1 PLANNER

Atomic Structure

In this investigation, students deepen their understanding of energy and matter [CCC-5] through a study of atomic structure [PS1.A]. Students apply the laws of conservation of energy and matter as they investigate and develop system models of the types of atoms and isotopes and other related phenomena.

INVESTIGATIVE PHENOMENON

What causes the colors in a fireworks display?

Explaining Phenomena Students explore atomic structure, including atomic numbers, mass number, atomic mass, and atomic theory. They explore the Bohr model and the quantum mechanical model and apply those to understanding energy and the stability in electron configurations and atomic emission spectra. Students use what they learn to explain how the colors in fireworks and differences in minerals are a result of a difference in atoms and elements.

	EXPERIENCE 1 The Particle Nature of Matter 2 days Students build upon what they already know about atoms, elements, molecules, and the three states of matter. They investigate the flow of energy in a system.	EXPERIENCE 2 Modeling Atoms 2 days Students use mathematics to identify the mass number and atomic number of atoms. They sketch models of helium atoms with differing protons and use models to compare isotopes.
CONNECTION TO THE INVESTIGATIVE PHENOMENON	Students learn about the main types of energy and relate that information to the phenomenon of what causes the colors in a fireworks display.	Students model different types of atoms and relate them to the phenomenon of colors in a fireworks display.
ENGAGE	**Teacher's Guide** Everyday Phenomenon What's in My Sugar?, p. 10	**Teacher's Guide** Everyday Phenomenon Seeing Without Looking, p. 46
EXPLORE	**Inquiry Lab** Elements: The Building Blocks of Matter **Analyzing Data** Physical Properties of Gaseous Elements	**Inquiry Lab** Bean Bag Isotopes **Analyzing Data** Explore Atomic Particles
EXPLAIN	**Claim-Evidence-Reasoning** Phase Change as a Physical Change **Experience Notebook,** pp. 6–10	**Modeling** Model Isotopes **Animation** A Quick Look at the Parts of an Atom **Experience Notebook,** pp. 12–21
ELABORATE	**Discussion Rubric** Physical vs. Chemical Change **Analyzing Data** Intensive and Extensive Properties	**Discussion Rubric** Dissect Atom Composition **Analyzing Data** Determine Atomic Mass
EVALUATE	**Quiz** The Particle Nature of Matter **Experience Notebook** Revisit Investigative Phenomenon, p. 11	**Quiz** Modeling Atoms **Experience Notebook** Revisit Investigative Phenomenon, p. 21

*Pacing for Encounter Investigative Phenomenon core instruction is a half-day.

†Pacing for core Investigation Assessment is approximately 1.5 days.

GOT MORE TIME? Personalize and enhance your instructional plan by assigning the activities with the got-more-time icon, as time allows.

Investigative Phenomenon Video Designed Explosions*

Modeling Model the Investigative Phenomenon*

Authentic Reading Firework Colors Chemistry

Experience Notebook, p. 5*

EXPERIENCE 3 Atomic Emission Spectra and the Bohr Model 2 days Students identify an element that produces an unknown emission spectrum. They reference Bohr's atomic model and explain how each color of light has a specific amount of energy.	EXPERIENCE 4 Modern Atomic Theory 2 days Students relate the quantum mechanical model to the Bohr model. They explore the atomic orbitals and the relative energies of subshells.	EXPERIENCE 5 Electrons in Atoms 2 days Students practice writing electron configurations and identify the patterns in the electron configurations. They explore electron dot structures.
Students compare and contrast wavelengths of light emitted from different colors and relate this to the phenomenon of colors in a fireworks display.	Students use the concepts from quantum mechanical models and orbital energies to refine explanations of colors in a fireworks display.	Students write an electron configuration for the element responsible for one color of firework and use this to refine explanations of colors in a fireworks display.
Teacher's Guide Everyday Phenomenon The Colors of Water, p. 70	**Teacher's Guide** Everyday Phenomenon Quantized Energy, p. 90	**Teacher's Guide** Everyday Phenomenon Electron Hotel, p. 96
Inquiry Lab Evaluate Atomic Spectra **Analyzing Data** Interpret Emission Spectra	**Inquiry Lab** Evaluate the Bohr Model of the Atom **Interactivity** The Quantum Mechanical Model and Atomic Orbitals	**Inquiry Lab** Model Electron Configuration **Analyzing Data** Patterns in Electron Configurations
Claim-Evidence-Reasoning Emission Spectra of Elements **Experience Notebook,** pp. 22–26	**Claim-Evidence-Reasoning** Evaluate Atomic Models **Experience Notebook,** pp. 28–31	**Modeling** Model Electron Configurations **Animation** How to Write Electron Configurations **Experience Notebook,** pp. 33–39
Discussion Rubric Critique Explanations of the Emission Spectra **Engineering Design Challenge** Build a Spectroscope from Household Materials	**Discussion Rubric** Evaluate Atomic Models **Writing About Science** The History of Atomic Models	**Peer Review Rubric** Evaluate Electron Configuration Models **Writing About Science** Properties of Atoms: Size vs. Mass
Quiz Atomic Emission Spectra and the Bohr Model **Experience Notebook** Revisit Investigative Phenomenon, p. 27	**Quiz** Modern Atomic Theory **Experience Notebook** Revisit Investigative Phenomenon, p. 32	**Quiz** Electrons in Atoms **Experience Notebook** Revisit Investigative Phenomenon, p. 40

INVESTIGATION ASSESSMENT

Performance-Based Assessment Evaluate Atomic Structure with Flame Tests†

Experience Notebook Performance-Based Assessment, p. 41; Revisit Anchoring Phenomenon, p. 41†; Appendix C Problem

OpenEd Resources

Search and assign OpenEd resources, making it quick and easy to add thousands of reliable, vetted resources.

Partner

Google for Education

Google Partnership

Realize is a partner with Google Classroom. Sharing content, assessments, and rosters is now easier than ever when working with both Realize and Google G Suite for Education.

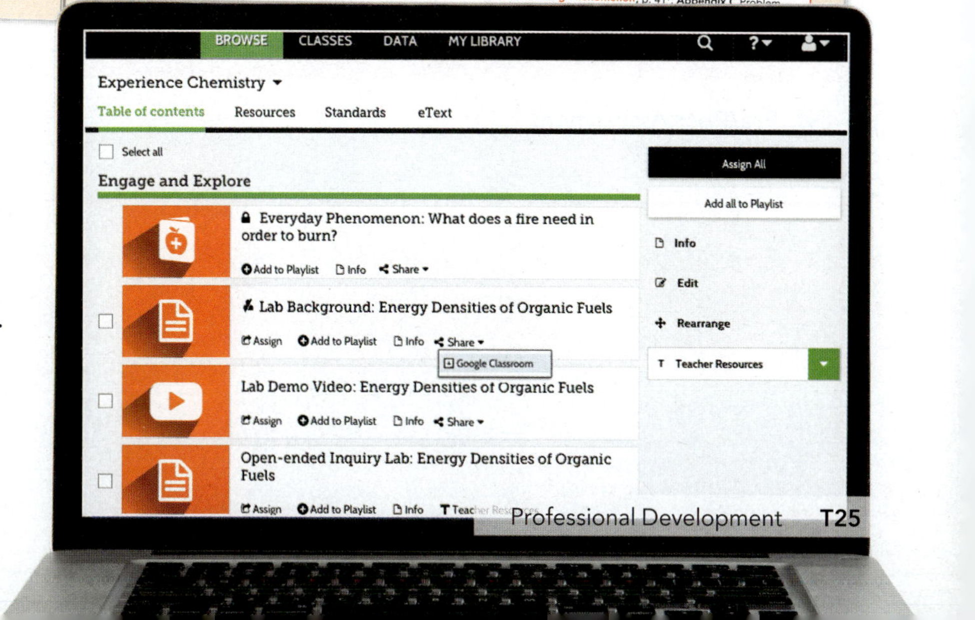

Experience Chemistry

The *Experience Chemistry* program integrates physical science, Earth and space science, and engineering design across five units of instruction called storylines. Each storyline is launched with an Anchoring Phenomenon that is revisited in the Investigations comprising the storyline. *Experience Chemistry* is a blended and integrated approach that optimizes teaching time and student mastery through student-driven digital and hands-on activities. Each learning experience is designed to integrate the three dimensions of science instruction: disciplinary core ideas, science and engineering practices, and crosscutting concepts.

	STORYLINE 1	STORYLINE 2
OVERVIEW	**ATOMS, ELEMENTS, AND MOLECULES** **31 days** Students identify properties of atoms, elements, and molecules and describe how different types of chemical bonds influence the properties of matter.	**UNDERSTANDING CHEMICAL REACTIONS** **47 days** Students explore how structure determines the physical properties of materials, and refine models of chemical reaction systems.
ANCHORING PHENOMENON	What distinguishes the minerals in this mountain?	How can we produce better foods?
INVESTIGATIONS	**1 Atomic Structure** (11.5 days), SE Vol. 1, pp. 4–41 **2 The Periodic Table** (7.5 days), SE Vol. 1, pp. 42–65 **3 Chemical Bonding** (11.5 days), SE Vol. 1, pp. 66–107	**4 Physical Properties of Materials** (13.5 days), SE Vol. 1, pp. 110–171 **5 Chemical Quantities** (9.5 days), SE Vol. 1, pp. 172–213 **6 Chemical Reactions** (7.5 days), SE Vol. 1, pp. 214–249 **7 Stoichiometry** (8 days), SE Vol. 1, pp. 250–279 **8 Thermochemistry** (8 days), SE Vol. 1, pp. 280–307
STORYLINE EVALUATION	**Benchmark 3-D Assessment** Storylines 1 and 2	

COURSE-LEVEL ASSESSMENT

Pre/Post Assessment

STORYLINE 3	STORYLINE 4	STORYLINE 5
THE CHEMISTRY OF CLIMATE CHANGE **36.5 days** Students analyze the connections between chemistry and changes in weather and climate and identify how these changes impact global climate.	**THE DYNAMICS OF CHEMICAL REACTIONS AND OCEAN ACIDIFICATION** **31 days** Students connect how their everyday activities impact Earth by investigating the relationships among reaction rates and equilibrium, acid–base equilibria, and ocean acidification.	**INDUSTRIAL APPLICATIONS** **31 days** Students investigate the transfer of energy, nuclear processes, and green chemistry to develop ideas about meeting the world's energy needs.
Why are we seeing more extreme weather?	How do our everyday activities impact Earth?	How can we sustainably meet the world's energy needs?
9 The Behavior of Gases (9.5 days), SE Vol. 2, pp. 4–41 **10 Weather and Climate** (12 days), SE Vol. 2, pp. 42–97 **11 Global Climate Change** (14.5 days), SE Vol. 2, pp. 98–155	**12 Reaction Rates and Equilibrium** (10.5 days), SE Vol. 2, pp. 158–191 **13 Acid–Base Equilibria** (10 days), SE Vol. 2, pp. 192–227 **14 Ocean Acidification** (10 days), SE Vol. 2, pp. 228–271	**15 Oxidation-Reduction Reactions** (7.5 days), SE Vol. 2, pp. 274–309 **16 Organic Chemistry** (7.5 days), SE Vol. 2, pp. 310–355 **17 Nuclear Processes** (7.5 days), SE Vol. 2, pp. 356–401 **18 Green Chemistry** (8 days), SE Vol. 2, pp. 402–439
Benchmark 3-D Assessment Storylines 3 and 4		**Benchmark 3-D Assessment** Storyline 5

COURSE-LEVEL ASSESSMENT

Pre/Post Assessment

End-of-Course Assessment

PACING GUIDE

The guide on these pages suggests time allocations for the core activities in each experience, investigation, and storyline (including labs). These allotments exclude "Got More Time" activities or projects you may choose to add.

SECTION	Days
STORYLINE 1 Atoms, Elements, and Molecules	**31**
Encounter Anchoring Phenomenon	0.5
INVESTIGATION 1 Atomic Structure	**11.5**
Encounter Investigative Phenomenon	0.5
1 The Particle Nature of Matter	2
2 Modeling Atoms	2
3 Atomic Emission Spectra and the Bohr Model	2
4 Modern Atomic Theory	2
5 Electrons in Atoms	2
Investigation Assessment*	1
GOT MORE TIME Activities	+5.5
INVESTIGATION 2 The Periodic Table	**7.5**
Encounter Investigative Phenomenon	0.5
1 The Periodic Table: An Overview	2
2 The Periodic Table and Atomic Structure	2
3 Periodic Trends	2
Investigation Assessment*	1
GOT MORE TIME Activities	+4.5
INVESTIGATION 3 Chemical Bonding	**11.5**
Encounter Invsestigative Phenomenon	0.5
1 Ionic Bonds	2
2 Metallic Bonds	2
3 Covalent Bonds	2
4 Intermolecular Attractions	2
5 Names and Formulas of Compounds	2
Investigation Assessment*	1
GOT MORE TIME Activities	+6

SECTION	Days
STORYLINE 2 Understanding Chemical Reactions	**47**
Encounter Anchoring Phenomenon	0.5
INVESTIGATION 4 Physical Properties of Materials	**13.5**
Encounter Investigative Phenomenon	0.5
1 States of Matter	2
2 Modeling Phase Changes	2
3 Comparing Ionic and Molecular Compounds	2
4 Comparing Metals and Nonmetals	2
5 Water and Aqueous Systems	2
6 Properties of Solutions	2
Investigation Assessment*	1
GOT MORE TIME Activities	+6.5
INVESTIGATION 5 Chemical Quantities	**9.5**
Encounter Investigative Phenomenon	0.5
1 The Mole Concept	2
2 Molar Relationships	2
3 Percent Composition and Empirical Formulas	2
4 Concentrations of Solutions	2
Investigation Assessment*	1
GOT MORE TIME Activities	+4.5
INVESTIGATION 6 Chemical Reactions	**7.5**
Encounter Investigative Phenomenon	0.5
1 Modeling Chemical Reactions	2
2 Predicting Outcomes of Chemical Reactions	2
3 Reactions in Aqueous Solution	2
Investigation Assessment*	1
GOT MORE TIME Activities	+4.5

SECTION	Days
STORYLINE 2 continued	
INVESTIGATION 7 Stoichiometry	8
Encounter Investigative Phenomenon	0.5
1 Quantifying Reactants and Products	2
2 Chemical Calculations	2.5
3 Limiting Reagent and Percent Yield	2
Investigation Assessment*	1
GOT MORE TIME Activities	+4
INVESTIGATION 8 Thermochemistry	8
Encounter Investigative Phenomenon	0.5
1 Energy in Chemical Bonds	2.5
2 Enthalpies of Formation and Reaction	2
3 Enthalpy in Changes of State	2
Investigation Assessment*	1
GOT MORE TIME Activities	+4.5

*Investigation Assessment includes Performance-Based Assessment, 3-D Assessment, and Revisit Anchoring Phenomenon.

GOT MORE TIME?

If time allows, personalize and enhance your instructional plan by assigning the activities with the Got-More-Time icon in the planners.

Activities include: Analyzing Data, Animation, Authentic Reading, Engineering Design Challenge, Interactivity, Problem-Based Learning, Virtual Reality Experience, and Writing About Science.

LAB SAFETY

When it comes to laboratories in the chemistry classroom, the safety of students and teachers is the primary concern of Savvas. To that end, all versions of the lab investigations give detailed safety information for the student and the teacher at the beginning of each lab.

Safety in the Chemistry Laboratory

The following information about safety issues in the high school chemistry laboratory is intended to be used by classroom chemistry teachers. This reference section is intended to be accessible to the teacher for planning demonstrations and preparing for lab. The material included here is by no means comprehensive. Savvas takes no responsibility for the completeness of this information or for the implementation of these suggestions.

The safety of the students in a high school laboratory is traditionally assigned to the teacher. But the teacher teaches safety awareness by holding each student accountable for the safety of all other participants in the lab, including the teacher. Have students sign a safety contract at the beginning of the year. There is a sample contract in each laboratory manual. Of course, the teacher will most effectively teach safety awareness by modeling safe practices and by making a discussion of safety conerns the first priority for all lab activities. The following suggestions are intended to help you establish a program of safety awareness for staff and students.

Education

- Put together a safety committee for your school. Include faculty, students, and administrators.
- Schedule regular meetings of the safety committee to discuss issues, accident reports, and the results of lab inspections.
- Implement a safety education program for staff and students.
- Require students to know the lab safety rules; assess this by giving a safety quiz; and have the students sign a safety contract to acknowledge that they know the rules and will comply with them. Send the contract home with a set of rules and require that one parent or guardian sign the contract, having read the rules.
- Give a safety grade with each lab, based on each student's behavior during the lab. Penalize unsafe behavior by removing students from the lab.
- Encourage school staff to become certified in CPR and first aid.
- Require that science staff read any of several publications on safety in the high school science classroom.

Management

- Report all accidents to the safety committee.
- Periodically inspect laboratories and report findings to the safety committee.
- Establish an emergency plan and review it periodically with students and staff.
- Keep phone numbers for the fire department, police department, local ambulance, and poison control center next to every phone in a lab or stockroom.
- Display warning signs and safety posters.
- Prohibit student access to stockrooms.
- Require students to keep aisles clear and counters clean. There should be two exits in a laboratory or stockroom, and they should be kept free of obstacles.
- Keep a current chemical inventory. Update the chemical inventory often. Include a Material Safety Data Sheet (MSDS) for each chemical.
- Label all chemicals with the date and possible hazards. Establish a policy for disposing of and buying chemicals.
- In prelab discussions, stress safety issues relevant to each specific lab.

Lab Techniques

- Do not allow any student or staff member to work alone in the laboratory.
- Do not leave any experiment unattended.
- Do not eat, smoke, or drink in the lab.
- Do not store food in chemical refrigerators. Store chemicals only in chemical refrigerators.
- Never taste a chemical in the laboratory.
- Always add acids to water, never water to acids.
- When pipetting, use a suction bulb. Never use your mouth.
- When heating the contents of a test tube, direct the mouth of the test tube away from yourself and away from others.

Personal Safety

- Always wear goggles in the lab. Require students and anyone entering the lab to wear goggles.
- Provide lab coats and aprons for all participants in the lab.
- Take into account student health problems such as allergies or asthma.
- Do not allow untied long hair, loose clothing, bare feet, open-toed or -heeled shoes, or dangling jewelry to be worn in the lab.
- Strongly discourage the wearing of contact lenses in lab. In the event of a chemical splash into the eye, the lenses may hold chemicals in contact with the eye, potentially causing greater injury.

Equipment

- Make available the following items in all labs and demonstration areas: an ABC fire extinguisher, a smoke alarm, a safety shower, an eye-wash faucet, a fume hood.
- Maintain and check all safety equipment regularly.
- Keep a first-aid kit stocked and available.
- Keep flammable chemicals in an approved fireproof cabinet.
- Attach compressed gas cylinders to counters or walls. Move them on dollies on which they are secured.
- Use safety shields when there is a possibility of explosion, implosion, chemical splashing, or fire.
- Use hot plates in lieu of open flames as often as possible.
- Use dispensing devices such as syringes, spigots, or droppers, rather than having students pour chemicals from their containers.
- Be prepared for spills, especially acid spills. Spill-control devices are available from suppliers. To avoid mercury spills, use alcohol thermometers.

Storing Chemicals

- Store chemicals in stockrooms, not in the lab.
- Do not store chemicals alphabetically. Use an approved system of chemical storage, and post legends in the stockroom.
- Store only the chemicals you will use during a school year.

Disposal

- Dispose of broken glass in a dedicated container kept out of the way and clearly labeled.
- Dispose of chemicals in the following ways:
    - Neutralize acids and bases and flush down the drain.
    - Flush light metal salts and their solutions down the drain with excess water.
    - Precipitate and filter heavy metals. Evaporate heavy metal solutions down to salt. Keep heavy metals salts in labeled containers and dispose of them by following local regulations.
    - When in doubt, check with local authorities about local regulations.
- Have a disposal plan for each lab, and include directions for disposal in your prelab discussion.

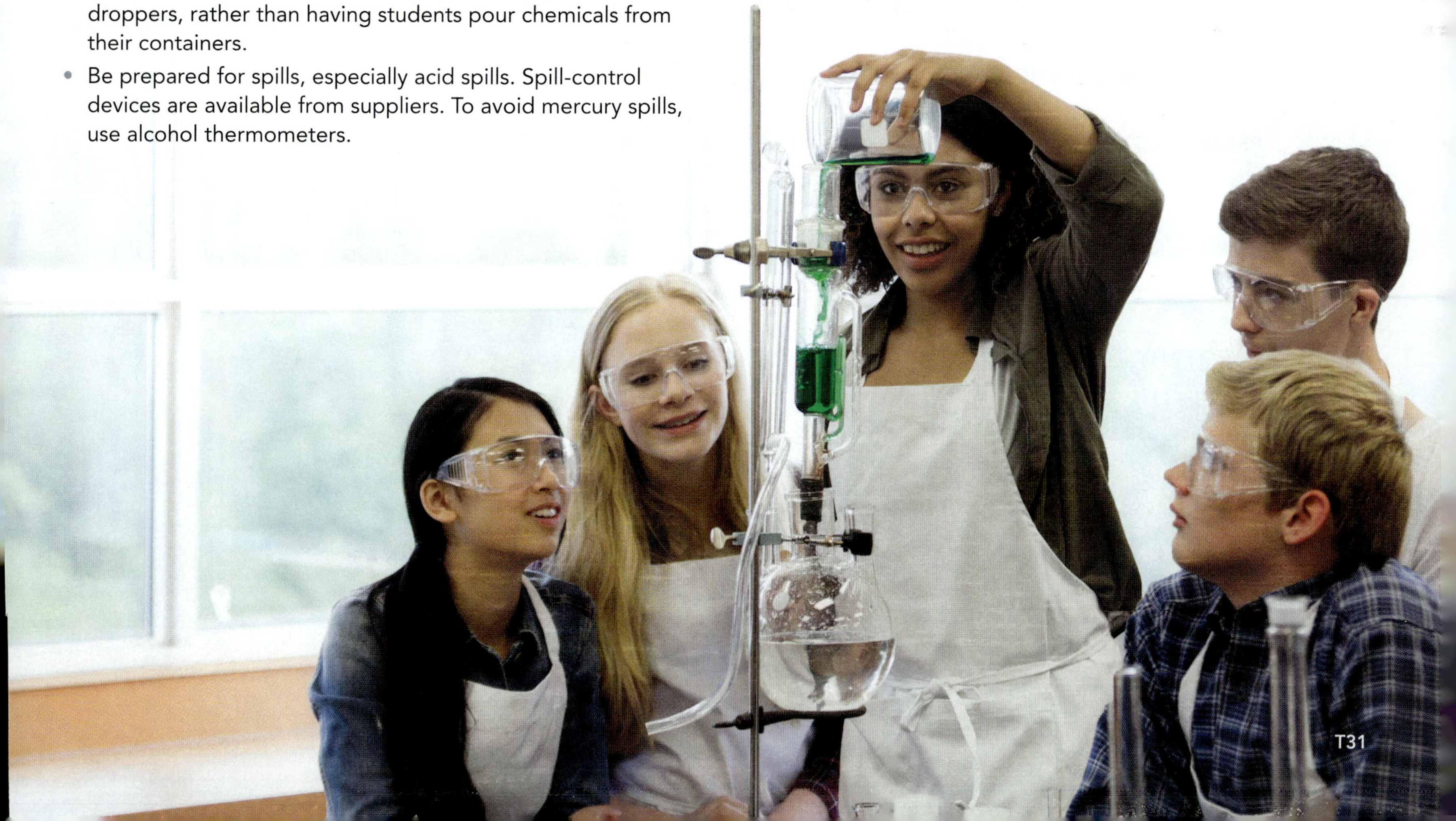

LEARNING PROGRESSION

Matter and Its Interactions

HS-PS1-1, HS-PS1-2, HS-PS1-3, HS-PS1-4, HS-PS1-5, HS-PS1-6, HS-PS1-7, HS-PS1-8

Use these grade-band endpoints to help you prioritize instruction and integrate the dimensions.

SCIENCE AND ENGINEERING PRACTICES	**Grades 9–12 Students should be capable of...**
SEP-2 DEVELOPING AND USING MODELS	...developing a model to support explanations of matter and predict phenomena.
SEP-3 PLANNING AND CARRYING OUT INVESTIGATIONS	...identifying variables and controls, tools, measurements, and the amount of data needed to support a claim.
SEP-5 USING MATHEMATICS AND COMPUTATIONAL THINKING	...using mathematical representations to describe and/or support scientific conclusions.
SEP-6 CONSTRUCTING EXPLANTIONS AND DESIGNING SOLUTIONS	...applying scientific reasoning to demonstrate why the evidence is adequate for the conclusion.

DISCIPLINARY CORE IDEAS	
PS1.A STRUCTURE AND PROPERTIES OF MATTER	...understanding that differences in composition and structure cause differences in properties.
PS1.B CHEMICAL REACTIONS	...recognizing that when a chemical change takes place, the atoms of the original substances are regrouped to form different molecules.
PS1.C NUCLEAR PROCESSES	...understanding how energy relates to nuclear fusion.
PS2.B TYPES OF INTERACTIONS	...explaining the forces between material objects and recognizing that forces act at a distance.
ETS1.C OPTIMIZING THE DESIGN SOLUTION	...understanding that there are systematic processes for evaluating solutions in regard to how well they meet criteria and constraints.

CROSSCUTTING CONCEPTS	
CCC-1 PATTERNS	...understanding how trends in the periodic table correlate to chemical properties.
CCC-5 ENERGY AND MATTER	...recognizing that matter is conserved and that energy transfer drives the cycling of matter.
CCC-7 STABILITY AND CHANGE	...realizing that changes in one part of a system may cause changes in another part of the system.

Experience Chemistry
Students are working toward...

...developing complex models of matter to explain changes that occur during chemical processes.

...identifying data needed to produce reliable measurements; considering limitations of the data, and refining designs accordingly.

...reinforcing conclusions by using calculations and measurements.

...building a scientific argument and applying sufficient evidence to provide an explanation of phenomena.

College & Careers
As adults, students can apply these skills by...

...applying mathematical modeling and other optimizing methods to interpret information as a research analyst.

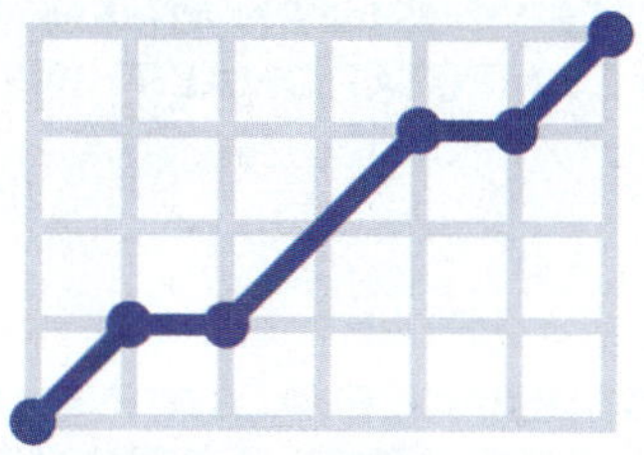

...realizing that different types of matter are composed of different types and numbers of atoms that are connected in different ways.

...recognizing and proving that matter cannot be created nor destroyed via chemical reactions, only converted.

...recognizing the connection between nuclear processes and energy.

....understanding that forces between electric charges explain the structure, properties, and transformations of matter.

...realizing that designs need to be tested and may need to be optimized to prioritize certain criteria.

...pursuing a career in civil engineering utilizing knowledge of the properties of matter.

...relating extensive and intensive properties of matter to patterns among elements.

...describing energy and matter flows into, out of, and within a system and how energy flows from warmer to colder objects.

...recognizing how a system changes or stays the same with changes in matter.

...designing systems to make buildings more energy-efficient.

Motion and Stability: Forces and Interactions

HS-PS2-4, HS-PS2-6

Use these grade-band endpoints to help you prioritize instruction and integrate the dimensions.

SCIENCE AND ENGINEERING PRACTICES	**Grades 9–12** **Students should be capable of...**
SEP-5 USING MATHEMATICS AND COMPUTATIONAL THINKING	...using calculations to support conclusions of forces and interactions. ...using computational thinking to describe and support explanations.
SEP-8 OBTAINING, EVALUATING, AND COMMUNICATING INFORMATION	...evaluating and summarizing information from a variety of sources.

DISCIPLINARY CORE IDEAS	
PS1.A STRUCTURE AND PROPERTIES OF MATTER	...understanding that differences in composition and structure cause differences in properties.
PS2.B TYPES OF INTERACTIONS	...discovering the connection between bonding interactions and properties of compounds. ...recognizing how ionic compounds conduct electricity.

CROSSCUTTING CONCEPTS	
CCC-1 PATTERNS	...describing patterns in data and relating that to differentiating between various types of matter. ...recognizing patterns between the measurable properties of a substance, such as melting point, boiling point, vapor pressure, and surface tension, and the strength of the attractive forces between the particles of the substance.
CCC-6 STRUCTURE AND FUNCTION	...analyzing different parts of systems to determine how they function.

Experience Chemistry
Students are working toward...

College & Careers
As adults, students can apply these skills by...

...using mathematical representations of phenomena to support claims.

...using mathematical thinking to interpret graphs and construct explanations to describe relationships among different factors.

...communicating scientific and technical information in multiple formats.

...organizing and analyzing medical data.

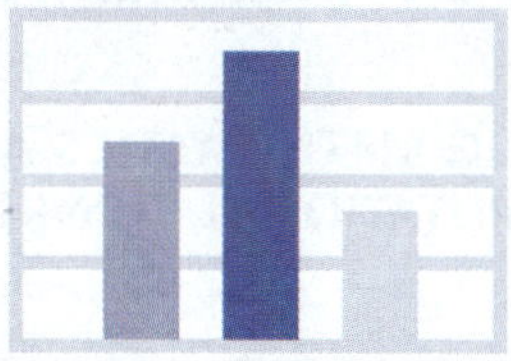

...explaining how electrical forces within and between atoms relates to the structure and interactions of matter.

...understanding how the presence or absence of substances affects interactions such as surface tension and cohesion.

...explaining why ionic compounds have the ability to conduct electricity only when they are melted or dissolved in water.

...testing the electrostatic attraction between ions.

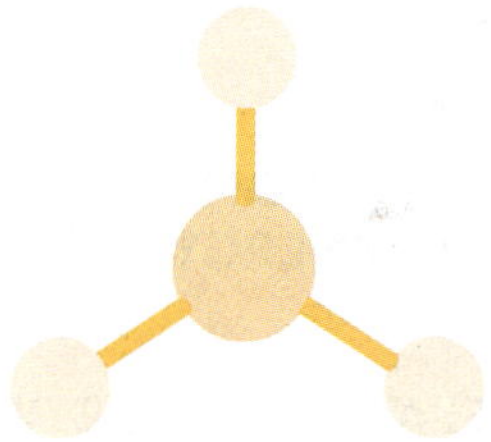

...categorizing compounds based on patterns from observations.

...understanding that the patterns of interactions between particles at the molecular scale are reflected in the patterns of behavior at the macroscopic scale.

...understanding how new systems or structures can be designed to solve a problem.

......discovering patterns in the solar system.

Energy

HS-PS3-1, HS-PS3-3, HS-PS3-4, HS-PS3-5

Use these grade-band endpoints to help you prioritize instruction and integrate the dimensions.

SCIENCE AND ENGINEERING PRACTICES	Grades 9–12 Students should be capable of...
SEP-2 DEVELOPING AND USING MODELS	...developing a model to support explanations of energy transfers and transformations and predict phenomena.
SEP-3 PLANNING AND CARRYING OUT INVESTIGATIONS	...identifying variables and controls, tools, measurements, and the amount of data needed to support a claim.
SEP-5 USING MATHEMATICS AND COMPUTATIONAL THINKING	...using mathematical representations to describe and/or support scientific conclusions.
SEP-6 CONSTRUCTING EXPLANATIONS AND DESIGNING SOLUTIONS	...identifying the problem in which they are designing a solution.

DISCIPLINARY CORE IDEAS	
PS3.A DEFINITIONS OF ENERGY	...defining how energy is the capacity for doing work or producing heat.
PS3.B CONSERVATION OF ENERGY AND ENERGY TRANSFER	...explaining the law of conservation of energy and how energy is converted into forms that are useful for human needs.
PS3.C RELATIONSHIP BETWEEN ENERGY AND FORCES	...relating how energy can be described as the result of forces acting over a distance.
PS3.D ENERGY IN CHEMICAL PROCESSES	...deciding whether energy is stored or released in chemical processes.
ETS1.A DEFINING AND DELIMITING ENGINEERING PROBLEMS	...identifying the criteria and constraints of a problem.

CROSSCUTTING CONCEPTS	
CCC-2 CAUSE AND EFFECT	...examining cause-and-effect relationships.
CCC-4 SYSTEMS AND SYSTEM MODELS	...exploring the flow of heat and energy within and among systems.
CCC-5 ENERGY AND MATTER	...understanding that energy moves between places, objects, and/or fields.

Experience Chemistry
Students are working toward...

...developing models of the different types of energy released and absorbed during reactions.

...carrying out investigations about thermal equilibrium and heat transfer.

...reinforcing conclusions by using calculations and computational thinking.

...designing solutions based on multiple considerations.

College & Careers
As adults, students can apply these skills by...

...investigating energy transfer in wind turbines.

...identifying and defining the different forms of energy.

...reinforcing that energy is conserved as chemical bonds are broken and formed.

...investigating repulsion and attraction and how energy stored in a field changes when objects interact in combination with forces.

...understanding energy in exothermic and endothermic chemical reactions.

...evaluating a device that can convert forms of energy.

...applying energy relationships as a nuclear physicist.

...recognizing factors that cause changes in forces and their effects.

...analyzing system models of how energy and matter cycle in and out.

...describing energy transfer in compounds and systems.

...pursuing a career as a systems specialist.

From Molecules to Organisms: Structures and Processes

HS-LS1-7

Use these grade-band endpoints to help you prioritize instruction and integrate the dimensions.

SCIENCE AND ENGINEERING PRACTICES	**Grades 9–12** **Students should be capable of...**
SEP-2 DEVELOPING AND USING MODELS	...developing a model to support explanations of matter and predict phenomena.

DISCIPLINARY CORE IDEAS	
LS1.C ORGANIZATION FOR MATTER AND ENERGY FLOW IN ORGANISMS	...understanding that within individual organisms, food is broken down and rearranged to form new molecules, to support growth, or to release energy.

CROSSCUTTING CONCEPTS	
CCC-5 ENERGY AND MATTER	...recognizing that matter is conserved and that energy transfer drives the cycling of matter.

Experience Chemistry
Students are working toward...

...developing complex models of matter to explain changes that occur during chemical processes.

...using models to illustrate the chemical process in which the bonds of food molecules and oxygen molecules are broken and new compounds are formed that can transport energy.

...describing energy and matter flows into, out of, and within a system and how energy flows within the body.

College & Careers
As adults, students can apply these skills by...

....studying the connection between cellular respiration and DNA.

...investigating cellular processes as a molecular biologist.

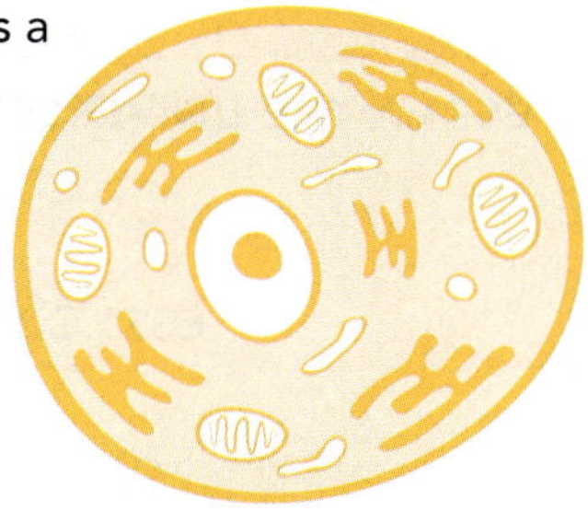

......developing new kinds of medicine.

LEARNING PROGRESSION

Earth's Place in the Universe

HS-ESS1-1, HS-ESS1-2, HS-ESS1-3, HS-ESS1-6

Use these grade-band endpoints to help you prioritize instruction and integrate the dimensions.

SCIENCE AND ENGINEERING PRACTICES	Grades 9–12 Students should be capable of...
SEP-2 DEVELOPING AND USING MODELS	...developing models to describe and support unobservable mechanisms.
SEP-6 CONSTRUCTING EXPLANATIONS AND DESIGNING SOLUTIONS	...applying scientific reasoning to demonstrate why the evidence is adequate for the conclusion.
SEP-8 OBTAINING, EVALUATING, AND COMMUNICATING INFORMATION	...evaluating and summarizing information from a variety of sources.

DISCIPLINARY CORE IDEAS	
ESS1.A THE UNIVERSE AND ITS STARS	...describing how models are used to explain patterns related to the sun, stars, and universe.
ESS1.C THE HISTORY OF PLANET EARTH	...recognizing that Earth formed a very long time ago.
PS1.C NUCLEAR PROCESSES	...understanding how energy relates to nuclear fusion.
PS3.D ENERGY IN CHEMICAL PROCESSES AND EVERYDAY LIFE	...explain the connection between nuclear fusion processes and stars.
PS4.B ELECTROMAGNETIC RADIATION	...identifying that electromagnetic radiation can be modeled as a wave.

CROSSCUTTING CONCEPTS	
CCC-3 SCALE, PROPORTION, AND QUANTITY	...describing how scale, proportion, and quantity are related.
CCC-5 ENERGY AND MATTER	...identifying that energy moves between places, objects, and/or fields.
CCC-7 STABILITY AND CHANGE	...explaining that changes in one part of a system may cause changes in another part.

Experience Chemistry
Students are working toward...

College & Careers
As adults, students can apply these skills by...

...developing models to explain the connections between nuclear processes and energy.

...building a scientific argument and applying sufficient evidence to provide an explanation of phenomena.

...communicating scientific and technical information in multiple formats.

...conducting research, writing a report, and publishing results in a scientific journal.

...recognizing the relationships among the movements of stars, their movements, and their distances from Earth.

...explaining how radiometric dating can be used to construct a timeline of Earth's early history.

...understanding how radiometric dating can be used to determine the ages of rocks and other materials.

...using models to explain how energy from the sun impacts Earth.

...using models to explain the atomic emission spectrum.

...pursuing a career as an astrogeologist.

...predicting the effect of a change in variable on another.

...describing energy transfer in compounds and systems.

...recognizing factors that contribute to stability and change in Earth's systems.

...designing tools to collect and analyze data about how the universe is changing.

LEARNING PROGRESSION

Earth's Systems

HS-ESS2-2, HS-ESS2-4, HS-ESS2-6

Use these grade-band endpoints to help you prioritize instruction and integrate the dimensions.

SCIENCE AND ENGINEERING PRACTICES	**Grades 9–12** **Students should be capable of...**
SEP-2 DEVELOPING AND USING MODELS	...developing models to describe and support unobservable mechanisms.
SEP-4 ANALYZING AND INTERPRETING DATA	...analyzing and interpreting data in order to make valid claims.

DISCIPLINARY CORE IDEAS	
ESS1.B EARTH AND THE SOLAR SYSTEM	...recognizing the interactions among Earth and the Solar System.
ESS2.A EARTH MATERIALS AND SYSTEMS	...understanding that Earth's systems are dynamic and always interacting.
ESS2.D WEATHER AND CLIMATE	...realizing that reflection, absorption, storage, and redistribution from the sun among Earth's systems drives global climate.

CROSSCUTTING CONCEPTS	
CCC-2 CAUSE AND EFFECT	...producing claims about specific causes and effects in Earth's systems.
CCC-5 ENERGY AND MATTER	...realizing that matter is conserved and that energy transfer drives the cycling of matter.
CCC-7 STABILITY AND CHANGE	...understanding that changes in one part of a system may cause changes in another part.

Experience Chemistry
Students are working toward...

College & Careers
As adults, students can apply these skills by...

...developing models to illustrate relationships between Earth's systems.

...analyzing and interpreting data from graphs and charts of Earth's systems.

...predicting weather forecasts.

...describing how Earth's systems are impacted by changes within the Solar System over very long periods of time.

...explaining how changes to Earth's systems cause feedback effects that impact other Earth systems.

...explaining factors that contribute to and alter weather and climate on Earth.

...mapping Earth's surface and explaining variations discovered.

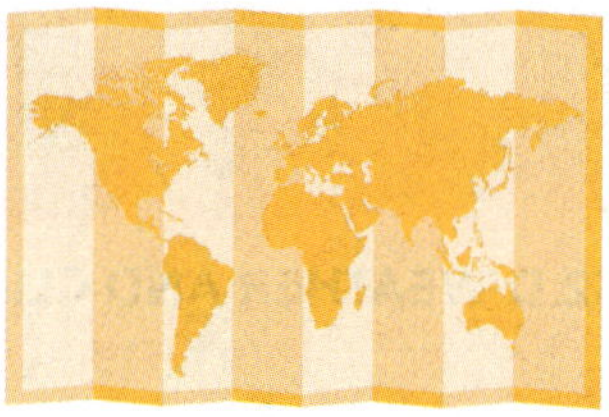

...explaining how a change to Earth can cause a feedback loop that changes other cycles.

...understanding how matter is cycled and the movement of matter between Earth's layers.

...recognizing factors that contribute to stability and change in Earth's systems.

...analyzing how water-related problems affect society and cities.

LEARNING PROGRESSION

Earth and Human Activity

HS-ESS3-2, HS-ESS3-3, HS-ESS3-4, HS-ESS3-5, HS-ESS3-6

Use these grade-band endpoints to help you prioritize instruction and integrate the dimensions.

SCIENCE AND ENGINEERING PRACTICES	**Grades 9–12** **Students should be capable of...**
SEP-4 ANALYZING AND INTERPRETING DATA	...analyzing and interpreting data in order to make and support valid claims.
SEP-5 USING MATHEMATICS AND COMPUTATIONAL THINKING	...using computational thinking to describe and support explanations.
SEP-6 CONSTRUCTING EXPLANATIONS AND DESIGNING SOLUTIONS	...identifying the problem in which they are designing a solution.
SEP-7 ENGAGING IN ARGUMENT FROM EVIDENCE	...citing evidence to support a claim and provide reasoning.

DISCIPLINARY CORE IDEAS	
ESS2.D WEATHER AND CLIMATE	...understanding climate models and how greenhouse gases affect weather and climate.
ESS3.A NATURAL RESOURCES	...understanding the cost and benefits of resource extraction.
ESS3.C HUMAN IMPACTS ON EARTH SYSTEMS	...identifying different impacts for different living things based on changes to Earth systems.
ESS3.D GLOBAL CLIMATE CHANGE	...recognizing human impacts to climate change and the ability for humans to model, predict, and manage impacts.
ETS1.B DEVELOPING POSSIBLE SOLUTIONS	...evaluating solutions by taking into account different constraints.

CROSSCUTTING CONCEPTS	
CCC-4 SYSTEMS AND SYSTEM MODELS	...defining boundaries of a system, describing it, and analyzing inputs and outputs.
CCC-7 STABILITY AND CHANGE	...realizing that change and rates of change can be modeled over different periods of time.

Experience Chemistry
Students are working toward...

College & Careers
As adults, students can apply these skills by...

...analyzing and interpreting data that describe the relationships between humans and Earth.

...using mathematical thinking to calculate Earth's changes.

...designing solutions based on multiple considerations.

...engaging in argument from evidence by analyzing the past and predicting future changes.

...advising farmers about how crops and agricultural practices impact Earth.

...realizing how changes to the climate might affect Earth.

...recognizing how natural resources are extracted, how they are used, and what risks and benefits they represent.

...explaining how human activities can be changed to lessen global impacts.

...understanding different types of evidence of climate change.

...developing solutions to climate change and negative impacts on Earth.

...becoming a global advocate for environmental policies.

...describing inputs and outputs of Earth systems and viewing this as a model.

...understanding actions of humans and the effect of those actions on the stability of Earth cycles.

...improving recycling systems.

Engineering Design

HS-ETS1-1, HS-ETS1-2, HS-ETS1-3, HS-ETS1-4

Use these grade-band endpoints to help you prioritize instruction and integrate the dimensions.

SCIENCE AND ENGINEERING PRACTICES	**Grades 9–12** **Students should be capable of...**
SEP-1 ASKING QUESTIONS AND DEFINING PROBLEMS	...asking questions that seek additional information to solve a problem.
SEP-5 USING MATHEMATICS AND COMPUTATIONAL THINKING	...using mathematical models to determine interactions between systems.
SEP-6 CONSTRUCTING EXPLANATIONS AND DESIGNING SOLUTIONS	...applying knowledge to determine a successful solution that includes meeting the criteria and constraints of the problem.

DISCIPLINARY CORE IDEAS	
ETS1.A DEFINING AND DELIMITING ENGINEERING PROBLEMS	...identifying the criteria and constraints of a problem that is impacting society.
ETS1.B DEVELOPING POSSIBLE SOLUTIONS	...testing ways of solving a problem and seeing which is the most efficient and economical.
ETS1.C OPTIMIZING THE DESIGN SOLUTION	...identifying whether a solution can be refined to be more successful.

CROSSCUTTING CONCEPTS	
CCC-4 SYSTEMS AND SYSTEM MODELS	...utilizing models to simulate systems and interactions.
INFLUENCE OF ENGINEERING, TECHNOLOGY, AND SCIENCE ON SOCIETY AND THE NATURAL WORLD	...realizing that people make decisions that ultimately guide the work of scientists and engineers.

Experience Chemistry
Students are working toward...

College & Careers
As adults, students can apply these skills by...

...evaluating whether questions are testable and relevant.

...using mathematics and computational thinking to aid in solving problems that impact Earth.

...evaluating and refining solutions based on scientific knowledge and evidence.

...pursing a career as a computer scientist.

...determining how engineering can address issues related to major global challenges.

...developing possible solutions for reducing impacts on Earth.

...using systematic processes to test and refine solutions that can be used to improve issues that impact society and the environment.

...developing new solutions for illnesses.

...understanding energy and matter flows within and between systems at different scales.

...understanding how advances in science, engineering, and technology have impacted the environment and people.

...developing new software.

NGSS CORRELATION

The *Experience Chemistry* program provides comprehensive coverage and assessment of the Next Generation Science Standards. Use this chart to track where the standards are covered in the Student Edition, Labs, and the Digital Course. (Connections to Nature of Science and Science, Technology, and Society are listed, where applicable, with Science and Engineering Practices and Crosscutting Concepts.)

Matter and Its Interactions HS-PS1

Students who demonstrate understanding can:

PERFORMANCE EXPECTATION HS-PS1-1	WHERE TO FIND IT...
Use the periodic table as a model to predict the relative properties of elements based on the patterns of electrons in the outermost energy level of atoms.	**SE, Vol. 1:** 13–14, 36–38, 39, 40 **Inquiry Labs:** Develop a Periodic Table; Periodic Trends and Properties; Elemental Metals, Nonmetals, and Metalloids **Digital Activities:** Periodic Properties, Predict Reactivity Using Periodic Trends **Performance-Based Assessments:** Evaluate Atomic Structure with Flame Tests, Gravimetric Analysis of Periodic Trends
DISCIPLINARY CORE IDEAS	
PS1.A: Structure and Properties of Matter Each atom has a charged substructure consisting of a nucleus, which is made of protons and neutrons, surrounded by electrons.	**SE, Vol. 1:** 12, 13, 21, 28
The periodic table orders elements horizontally by the number of protons in the atom's nucleus and places those with similar chemical properties in columns. The repeating patterns of this table reflect patterns of outer electron states.	**SE, Vol. 1:** 13–14, 36–38, 39, 46–48, 49, 50–51
PS2.B: Types of Interactions Attraction and repulsion between electric charges at the atomic scale explain the structure, properties, and transformations of matter, as well as the contact forces between material objects.	**SE, Vol. 1:** 73–76, 77–80, 81–90, 91–95
SCIENCE AND ENGINEERING PRACTICES	
Developing and Using Models	**SE, Vol. 1:** 55, 57, 58, 61 **Inquiry Labs:** Bean Bag Isotopes; Evaluate the Bohr Model of the Atom; Model Electron Configuration; Develop a Periodic Table; Elemental Metals, Nonmetals, and Metalloids; Periodic Trends and Properties **Digital Activity:** The Quantum Mechanical Model and Atomic Orbitals
CROSSCUTTING CONCEPTS	
Patterns	**SE, Vol. 1:** 26, 36, 39, 43, 45, 49, 59, 62, 63, 67, 69, 82, 86, 93 **Inquiry Labs:** Evaluate Atomic Spectra, Evaluate the Bohr Model of the Atom, Develop a Periodic Table, Periodic Trends and Properties **Digital Activities:** Periodic Properties, Predict Reactivity Using Periodic Trends **Performance-Based Assessments:** Evaluate Atomic Structure with Flame Tests, Gravimetric Analysis of Periodic Trends

PERFORMANCE EXPECTATION HS-PS1-2	WHERE TO FIND IT...
Construct and revise an explanation for the outcome of a simple chemical reaction based on the outermost electron states of atoms, trends in the periodic table, and knowledge of the patterns of chemical properties.	**SE, Vol. 1:** 43, 63, 232, 238–239, 240 **SE, Vol. 2:** 284 **Inquiry Labs:** Evaluate Chemical Reactions, Predict Chemical Reactions, Explore Iron Corrosion, Metal Activity **Engineering Design Challenge:** Water Purification **Digital Activities:** Reactivity of Metals, Cation Meets Anion **Performance-Based Assessments:** Identify Evidence of Chemical Reactions, Battery Challenge
DISCIPLINARY CORE IDEAS	
PS1.A: Structure and Properties of Matter The periodic table orders elements horizontally by the number of protons in the atom's nucleus and places those with similar chemical properties in columns. The repeating patterns of this table reflect patterns of outer electron states.	**SE, Vol. 1:** 13–14, 36–38, 39, 46–48, 50–51, 55, 82–87, 137–140, 232
PS1.B: Chemical Reactions The fact that atoms are conserved, together with knowledge of the chemical properties of the elements involved, can be used to describe and predict chemical reactions.	**SE, Vol. 1:** 220–221, 227, 232, 233, 238–239, 240, 241–242, 245, 246
SCIENCE AND ENGINEERING PRACTICES	
Constructing Explanations	**SE, Vol. 1:** 221, 224, 244, 246 **Inquiry Labs:** Chemical Names and Formulas, Evaluate Chemical Reactions, Predict Chemical Reactions **Digital Activities:** Ions and Electroplating, Analyzing Chemical Reactions, Predict Whether a Precipitate Will Form
CROSSCUTTING CONCEPTS	
Patterns	**SE, Vol. 1:** 227, 228, 229 **Inquiry Labs:** Evaluate Chemical Reactions, Types of Chemical Reactions, Predict Chemical Reactions **Performance-Based Assessment:** Identify Evidence of Chemical Reactions

PERFORMANCE EXPECTATION HS-PS1-3	WHERE TO FIND IT...
Plan and conduct an investigation to gather evidence to compare the structure of substances at the bulk scale to infer the strength of electrical forces between particles.	**SE, Vol. 1:** 142 **Inquiry Labs:** Correlate Material Properties and Bond Type, Melt Ionic and Covalent Compounds, Compressibility, Relationships Between Gas Variables, The Ideal Gas Law, Gas Diffusion **Digital Activities:** Intermolecular Forces in Liquids, Tough Tools, Gas Behavior in Popping Candy **Performance-Based Assessments:** Qualitative Analysis and Chemical Bonding, Identify Evidence of Chemical Reactions, Cartesian Divers

NGSS CORRELATION

DISCIPLINARY CORE IDEAS	
PS1.A: Structure and Properties of Matter The structure and interactions of matter at the bulk scale are determined by electrical forces within and between atoms.	**SE, Vol. 1:** 52–55, 59–60, 72–76, 77–80, 81–90, 91–95, 118–123, 125–134, 136–140, 141–147, 148–157 **SE, Vol. 2:** 27–28
PS2.B: Types of Interactions Attraction and repulsion between electric charges at the atomic scale explain the structure, properties, and transformations of matter, as well as the contact forces between material objects.	**SE, Vol. 1:** 52–55, 59–60, 72–76, 77–80, 81–90, 91–95, 118–123, 125–134, 136–140, 141–147, 148–157 **SE, Vol. 2:** 27–28
SCIENCE AND ENGINEERING PRACTICES	
Planning and Carrying Out Investigations	**Inquiry Labs:** Characteristics of Ionic Bonds; Investigate Metallic Bonds; Investigate Covalent Bonds, Intermolecular Forces; Correlate Material Properties and Bond Type; Measure the Energy of a Phase Change; Melt Ionic and Covalent Compounds; Modeling Metals, Ceramics, and Polymers; Investigate Surface Tension; Aqueous Solutions; The Thermodynamics of Hand Warmers, Compressibility, Relationships Between Gas Variables, The Ideal Gas Law, Gas Diffusion **Engineering Design Challenges:** Evaluate Metals for a Commercial Application, Abrasive Compounds, Building a Better Bike **Digital Activities:** Intermolecular Forces in Liquids, States of Matter, Tough Tools, Gas Behavior in Popping Candy **Performance-Based Assessments:** Measure Energy in Combustion Reactions, Qualitative Analysis and Chemical Bonding, Road Deicers, Identify Evidence of Chemical Reactions, Cartesian Divers
CROSSCUTTING CONCEPTS	
Patterns	**SE, Vol. 1:** 59, 62, 63, 67, 69, 82, 86, 93, 98, 104, 113, 162 **Inquiry Labs:** Correlate Material Properties and Bond Type, Melt Ionic and Covalent Compounds, Relationships Between Gas Variables, The Ideal Gas Law, Gas Diffusion **Performance-Based Assessments:** Qualitative Analysis and Chemical Bonding, Identify Evidence of Chemical Reactions

PERFORMANCE EXPECTATION HS-PS1-4	WHERE TO FIND IT...
Develop a model to illustrate that the release or absorption of energy from a chemical reaction system depends upon the changes in total bond energy.	**SE, Vol. 1:** 223–226, 228–229, 285–288, 291–294, 296 **Inquiry Labs:** Measure Energy Flow in Chemical Reactions, The Thermodynamics of Hand Warmers, Hess's Law and the Combustion of a Metal **Performance-Based Assessment:** Enthalpy of a Neutralization Reaction

DISCIPLINARY CORE IDEAS	
PS1.A: Structure and Properties of Matter A stable molecule has less energy than the same set of atoms separated; one must provide at least this energy in order to take the molecule apart.	**SE, Vol. 1:** 285–287 **SE, Vol. 2:** 169
PS1.B: Chemical Reactions Chemical processes, their rates, and whether or not energy is stored or released can be understood in terms of the collisions of molecules and the rearrangements of atoms into new molecules, with consequent changes in the sum of all bond energies in the set of molecules that are matched by changes in kinetic energy.	**SE, Vol. 1:** 223–225, 282, 373–375, 291–297 **SE, Vol. 2:** 163–165, 169–171
SCIENCE AND ENGINEERING PRACTICES	
Developing and Using Models	**SE, Vol. 1:** 226, 282, 286 **Inquiry Labs:** Measure Energy Flow in Chemical Reactions, Evaluate Chemical Reactions, Types of Chemical Reactions, The Thermodynamics of Hand Warmers, Hess's Law and the Combustion of a Metal
CROSSCUTTING CONCEPTS	
Energy and Matter	**SE, Vol. 1:** 215, 281, 290, 307 **Digital Activities:** Temperature Changes in Chemical Reactions, Heat of Fusion **Engineering Design Challenge:** Flameless Heating Systems **Performance-Based Assessments:** Measure Energy in Combustion Reactions, Enthalpy of a Neutralization Reaction

PERFORMANCE EXPECTATION HS-PS1-5	WHERE TO FIND IT...
Apply scientific principles and evidence to provide an explanation about the effects of changing the temperature or concentration of the reacting particles on the rate at which a reaction occurs.	**Inquiry Lab:** Reaction Rates: Iodine Clock **Digital Activity:** Reaction Rates and Activation Energy **Performance-Based Assessments:** Rates of Reaction and Dissolution, Calcium Carbonate and Shell Production
DISCIPLINARY CORE IDEAS	
PS1.B: Chemical Reactions Chemical processes, their rates, and whether or not energy is stored or released can be understood in terms of the collisions of molecules and the rearrangements of atoms into new molecules, with consequent changes in the sum of all bond energies in the set of molecules that are matched by changes in kinetic energy.	**SE, Vol. 1:** 223–225 **SE, Vol. 2:** 161–167, 168–169
SCIENCE AND ENGINEERING PRACTICES	
Constructing Explanations	**SE, Vol. 2:** 165, 167, 170, 191

NGSS CORRELATION

CROSSCUTTING CONCEPTS	
Patterns	**SE, Vol. 2:** 163, 169 **Inquiry Labs:** Evaluate Chemical Reactions, Types of Chemical Reactions, Reaction Rates: Iodine Clock, Collision Theory, Explore Chemical Equilibrium, Ocean Currents **Digital Activities:** Reactivity of Metals, Reaction Rates and Activation Energy **Performance-Based Assessments:** Rates of Reaction and Dissolution, Calcium Carbonate and Shell Production

PERFORMANCE EXPECTATION HS-PS1-6	WHERE TO FIND IT...
Refine the design of a chemical system by specifying a change in conditions that would produce increased amounts of products at equilibrium.	**Inquiry Lab:** Explore Chemical Equilibrium **Digital Activity:** Equilibrium Shifting **Performance-Based Assessments:** Rates of Reaction and Dissolution, Calcium Carbonate and Shell Production
DISCIPLINARY CORE IDEAS	
PS1.B: Chemical Reactions In many situations, a dynamic and condition-dependent balance between a reaction and the reverse reaction determines the numbers of all types of molecules present.	**SE, Vol. 2:** 174–179, 198–201, 203–207, 230–231, 236–237, 240–243, 260–263
ETS1.C: Optimizing the Design Solution Criteria may need to be broken down into simpler ones that can be approached systematically, and decisions about the priority of certain criteria over others (trade-offs) may be needed.	**Engineering Design Challenge:** Use Equilibrium for a Commercial Application
SCIENCE AND ENGINEERING PRACTICES	
Designing Solutions	**SE, Vol. 2:** 177, 225, 265 **Engineering Design Challenge:** Use Equilibrium for a Commercial Application
CROSSCUTTING CONCEPTS	
Stability and Change	**SE, Vol. 2:** 159, 175, 179, 231, 237, 241 **Inquiry Labs:** Explore Chemical Equilibrium, Measure Acid Strength, Titrations–The Study of Acid-Base Chemistry, Analysis of Buffer Solutions and Ranges, The pH of Seawater **Digital Activities:** Equilibrium Shifting, Explore Buffer Systems, Ocean pH, The Effect of Ocean Acidification on Shells

PERFORMANCE EXPECTATION HS-PS1-7	WHERE TO FIND IT...
Use mathematical representations to support the claim that atoms, and therefore mass, are conserved during a chemical reaction.	**Inquiry Labs:** Identify Unknowns Through Stoichiometry, Determination of Reaction Output, Formation of Barium Iodate **Digital Activities:** Understanding Stoichiometry, Limiting Reagent **Engineering Design Challenge:** Build a Film Canister Rocket **Performance-Based Assessments:** Analysis of Basic Copper Carbonate, The Stoichiometry of Filling a Balloon
DISCIPLINARY CORE IDEAS	
PS1.B: Chemical Reactions The fact that atoms are conserved, together with knowledge of the chemical properties of the elements involved, can be used to describe and predict chemical reactions.	**SE, Vol. 1:** 220–221, 232, 233, 238–239, 240, 252–257, 270–271, 274–275
SCIENCE AND ENGINEERING PRACTICES	
Using Mathematics and Computational Thinking	**SE, Vol. 1:** 177, 181, 185, 186, 189, 193, 194, 195, 197, 199, 201, 205, 206, 223, 252, 257, 260, 268, 279, 285, 292, 298 **Inquiry Labs:** Describe Small-scale Matter Using the Mole, Mole Ratios, Determine an Empirical Formula, Preparation of Solutions, Evaluate Chemical Reactions, Identify Unknowns Through Stoichiometry, Determination of Reaction Output, Formation of Barium Iodate, Hess's Law and the Combustion of a Metal **Digital Activities:** Mole Road Map, Making Dilutions **Performance-Based Assessments:** Analysis of Basic Copper Carbonate, Identify Evidence of Chemical Reactions, Quantitative Analysis of Acid Rain
CROSSCUTTING CONCEPTS	
Energy and Matter	**SE, Vol. 1:** 215, 255, 256, 281, 284, 290, 307 **Engineering Design Challenges:** An Empirical Formula Challenge, Build a Film Canister Rocket **Performance-Based Assessments:** The Stoichiometry of Filling a Balloon, Enthalpy of a Neutralization Reaction
Connections to Nature of Science Scientific Knowledge Assumes an Order and Consistency in Natural Systems	**SE, Vol. 1:** 220–221, 223–224, 256, 283

PERFORMANCE EXPECTATION HS-PS1-8	WHERE TO FIND IT...
Develop models to illustrate the changes in the composition of the nucleus of the atom and the energy released during the processes of fission, fusion, and radioactive decay.	**Inquiry Labs:** Radioactive Decay, Nuclear Energy **Performance-Based Assessment:** Natural Radiation
DISCIPLINARY CORE IDEAS	
PS1.C: Nuclear Processes Nuclear processes, including fusion, fission, and radioactive decays of unstable nuclei, involve release or absorption of energy. The total number of neutrons plus protons does not change in any nuclear process.	**SE, Vol. 2:** 361–364, 372, 379, 380, 381, 382 **Digital Activities:** Comparing Nuclear and Chemical Reactions, Geologic Variation and Radon Levels

SCIENCE AND ENGINEERING PRACTICES	
Developing and Using Models	**SE, Vol. 2:** 363, 379, 381, 382 **Inquiry Labs:** Radioactive Decay, Nuclear Energy **Performance-Based Assessment:** Natural Radiation
CROSSCUTTING CONCEPTS	
Energy and Matter	**SE, Vol. 2:** 373–374, 380 **Digital Activities:** Comparing Nuclear and Chemical Reactions, Geologic Variation and Radon Levels

Motion and Stability: Forces and Interactions HS-PS2

Students who demonstrate understanding can:

PERFORMANCE EXPECTATION HS-PS2-4	WHERE TO FIND IT...
Use mathematical representations of Newton's Law of Gravitation and Coulomb's Law to describe and predict the gravitational and electrostatic forces between objects.	**Inquiry Labs:** Characteristics of Ionic Bonds, Characteristics of Covalent Bonds, Intermolecular Forces **Digital Activities:** Formation of Ionic Compounds, Intermolecular Forces in Liquids **Performance-Based Assessment:** Qualitative Analysis and Chemical Bonding
DISCIPLINARY CORE IDEAS	
PS2.B: Types of Interactions Newton's law of universal gravitation and Coulomb's law provide the mathematical models to describe and predict the effects of gravitational and electrostatic forces between distant objects.	**SE, Vol. 1:** 52, 59, 68–76, 81, 88–90, 91–95, 148–149 **SE, Vol. 2:** 297, 361–364
Forces at a distance are explained by fields (gravitational, electric, and magnetic) permeating space that can transfer energy through space. Magnets or electric currents cause magnetic fields; electric charges or changing magnetic fields cause electric fields.	**SE, Vol. 1:** 52, 72–73 **SE, Vol. 2:** 361–364
SCIENCE AND ENGINEERING PRACTICES	
Using Mathematics and Computational Thinking	**SE, Vol. 1:** 76, 87 **Inquiry Labs:** Characteristics of Ionic Bonds, Investigate Covalent Bonds
CROSSCUTTING CONCEPTS	
Patterns	**SE, Vol. 1:** 59, 86 **Digital Activities:** Ions and Electroplating, Formation of Ionic Compounds, Intermolecular Forces in Liquids **Performance-Based Assessment:** Qualitative Analysis and Chemical Bonding

PERFORMANCE EXPECTATION HS-PS2-6	WHERE TO FIND IT...
Communicate scientific and technical information about why the molecular-level structure is important in the functioning of designed materials.*	**Inquiry Labs:** Investigate Different Hydrocarbons, Protein and Amino Acid Tests **Digital Activity:** Protein Structure and Food Design **Engineering Design Challenge:** Polymers: Bouncy Balls **Performance-Based Assessment:** Prepare and Characterize Biodiesel
DISCIPLINARY CORE IDEAS	
PS1.A: Structure and Properties of Matter The structure and interactions of matter at the bulk scale are determined by electrical forces within and between atoms.	**SE, Vol. 1:** 72–73, 78–79, 80, 141–143 **SE, Vol. 2:** 314–315, 320, 328–331, 347–348, 351
PS2.B: Types of Interactions Attraction and repulsion between electric charges at the atomic scale explain the structure, properties, and transformations of matter, as well as the contact forces between material objects.	**SE, Vol. 1:** 73–76, 77–80, 81–90, 91–95, 141–143 **SE, Vol. 2:** 314–315, 320, 328–331, 347–348, 351
SCIENCE AND ENGINEERING PRACTICES	
Obtaining, Evaluating, and Communicating Information	**SE, Vol. 2:** 339 **Digital Activity:** Protein Structure and Food Design **Engineering Design Challenge:** Polymers: Bouncy Balls
CROSSCUTTING CONCEPTS	
Structure and Function	**SE, Vol. 1:** 78, 79 **SE, Vol. 2:** 336 **Digital Activity:** Protein Structure and Food Design **Engineering Design Challenge:** Polymers: Bouncy Balls **Performance-Based Assessment:** Prepare and Characterize Biodiesel

Energy HS-PS3

Students who demonstrate understanding can:

PERFORMANCE EXPECTATION HS-PS3-1	WHERE TO FIND IT...
Create a computational model to calculate the change in the energy of one component in a system when the change in energy of the other component(s) and energy flows in and out of the system are known.	**Inquiry Labs:** The Thermodynamics of Hand Warmers, The Heat of Melting Ice **Performance-Based Assessment:** Enthalpy of a Neutralization Reaction
DISCIPLINARY CORE IDEAS	
PS3.A: Definitions of Energy Energy is a quantitative property of a system that depends on the motion and interactions of matter and radiation within that system. That there is a single quantity called energy is due to the fact that a system's total energy is conserved, even as, within the system, energy is continually transferred from one object to another and between its various possible forms.	**SE, Vol. 1:** 10, 215, 223–224, 281, 284 **SE, Vol. 2:** 186, 297–299

NGSS CORRELATION

PS3.B: Conservation of Energy and Energy Transfer Conservation of energy means that the total change of energy in any system is always equal to the total energy transferred into or out of the system.	**SE, Vol. 1:** 223–224, 283, 284
Energy cannot be created or destroyed, but it can be transported from one place to another and transferred between systems.	**SE, Vol. 1:** 223–224, 283, 284
Mathematical expressions, which quantify how the stored energy in a system depends on its configuration (e.g. relative positions of charged particles, compression of a spring) and how kinetic energy depends on mass and speed, allow the concept of conservation of energy to be used to predict and describe system behavior.	**SE, Vol. 1:** 284–289, 292–298, 300–303
The availability of energy limits what can occur in any system.	**SE, Vol. 1:** 125–129, 225, 287 **SE, Vol. 2:** 163, 168–170, 181
SCIENCE AND ENGINEERING PRACTICES	
Using Mathematics and Computational Thinking	**SE, Vol. 1:** 285, 286, 292, 293 **Inquiry Lab:** The Heat of Melting Ice **Performance-Based Assessment:** Enthalpy of a Neutralization Reaction
CROSSCUTTING CONCEPTS	
Systems and System Models	**SE, Vol. 1:** 10 **Inquiry Lab:** The Heat of Melting Ice **Performance-Based Assessment:** Enthalpy of a Neutralization Reaction
Connections to Nature of Science: Scientific Knowledge Assumes an Order and Consistency in Natural Systems	**SE, Vol. 1:** 10, 223

PERFORMANCE EXPECTATION HS-PS3-3	WHERE TO FIND IT...
Design, build, and refine a device that works within given constraints to convert one form of energy into another form of energy.*	**Inquiry Labs:** The Thermodynamics of Hand Warmers, Solar Cell Technology, Build a Micro Battery **Engineering Design Challenge:** Flameless Heating Systems **Performance-Based Assessment:** Battery Challenge
DISCIPLINARY CORE IDEAS	
PS3.A: Definitions of Energy At the macroscopic scale, energy manifests itself in multiple ways, such as in motion, sound, light, and thermal energy.	**SE, Vol. 1:** 9, 281, 283 **SE, Vol. 2:** 44, 55, 102, 145–146
PS3.D: Energy in Chemical Processes and Everyday Life Although energy cannot be destroyed, it can be converted to less useful forms—for example, to thermal energy in the surrounding environment.	**SE, Vol. 1:** 284
ETS1.A Defining and Delimiting Engineering Problems Criteria and constraints also include satisfying any requirements set by society, such as taking issues of risk mitigation into account, and they should be quantified to the extent possible and stated in such a way that one can tell if a given design meets them.	**SE, Vol. 1:** 415

SCIENCE AND ENGINEERING PRACTICES	
Designing Solutions	**SE, Vol. 2:** 309 **Inquiry Labs:** The Thermodynamics of Hand Warmers, Solar Cell Technology, Build a Micro Battery **Engineering Design Challenge:** Flameless Heating Systems **Performance-Based Assessment:** Battery Challenge
CROSSCUTTING CONCEPTS	
Energy and Matter	**SE, Vol. 2:** 309 **Performance-Based Assessment:** Battery Challenge
Connections to Engineering, Technology, and Applications of Science: Influence of Science, Engineering, and Technology on Society and the Natural World	**SE, Vol. 2:** 405, 410 **Inquiry Labs:** The Thermodynamics of Hand Warmers, Solar Cell Technology, Build a Micro Battery **Engineering Design Challenge:** Flameless Heating Systems **Performance-Based Assessment:** Battery Challenge

PERFORMANCE EXPECTATION HS-PS3-4	WHERE TO FIND IT...
Plan and conduct an investigation to provide evidence that the transfer of thermal energy when two components of different temperature are combined within a closed system results in a more uniform energy distribution among the components in the system (second law of thermodynamics).	**Inquiry Labs:** The Thermodynamics of Hand Warmers, The Heat of Melting Ice, Supersaturation and Thermodynamics
DISCIPLINARY CORE IDEAS	
PS3.B: Conservation of Energy and Energy Transfer Energy cannot be created or destroyed, but it can be transported from one place to another and transferred between systems.	**SE, Vol. 1:** 10, 223–224, 283 **SE, Vol. 2:** 44–46
Uncontrolled systems always evolve toward more stable states—that is, toward more uniform energy distribution (e.g., water flows downhill, objects hotter than their surrounding environment cool down).	**SE, Vol. 1:** 10, 223–224, 283 **SE, Vol. 2:** 44–46
PS3.D: Energy in Chemical Processes and Everyday Life Although energy cannot be destroyed, it can be converted to less useful forms—for example, to thermal energy in the surrounding environment.	**SE, Vol. 1:** 284
SCIENCE AND ENGINEERING PRACTICES	
Planning and Carrying Out Investigations	**SE, Vol. 1:** 300 **Inquiry Labs:** Measure the Energy of a Phase Change, The Thermodynamics of Hand Warmers, The Heat of Melting Ice, Supersaturation and Thermodynamics **Performance Based Assessment:** Enthalpy of a Neutralization Reaction
CROSSCUTTING CONCEPTS	
Systems and System Models	**SE, Vol. 1:** 283 **SE, Vol. 2:** 178, 183–184

PERFORMANCE EXPECTATION HS-PS3-5	WHERE TO FIND IT...
Develop and use a model of two objects interacting through electric or magnetic fields to illustrate the forces between objects and the changes in energy of the objects due to the interaction.	**Inquiry Labs:** Melt Ionic and Covalent Compounds; Modeling Metals, Ceramics, and Polymers; Investigate Surface Tension **Digital Activity:** Intermolecular Forces in Liquids **Performance-Based Assessment:** Qualitative Analysis and Chemical Bonding
DISCIPLINARY CORE IDEAS	
PS3.C: Relationship Between Energy and Forces When two objects interacting through a field change relative position, the energy stored in the field is changed.	**SE, Vol. 1:** 73–75, 78–79, 81–82, 88–90, 91–93
SCIENCE AND ENGINEERING PRACTICES	
Developing and Using Models	**SE, Vol. 1:** 52, 77, 89, 154 **Inquiry Labs:** Modeling Metals, Ceramics, and Polymers; Investigate Surface Tension
CROSSCUTTING CONCEPTS	
Cause and Effect	**SE, Vol. 1:** 71, 88

From Molecules to Organisms: Structures and Processes HS-LS1

Students who demonstrate understanding can:

PERFORMANCE EXPECTATION HS-LS1-7	WHERE TO FIND IT...
Use a model to illustrate that cellular respiration is a chemical process whereby the bonds of food molecules and oxygen molecules are broken and the bonds in new compounds are formed resulting in a net transfer of energy.	**SE, Vol. 2:** 344, 354 **Digital Activities:** Sugar, Starch, and Glycogen; Energy Densities of Foods
DISCIPLINARY CORE IDEAS	
LS1.C: Organization for Matter and Energy Flow in Organisms As matter and energy flow through different organizational levels of living systems, chemical elements are recombined in different ways to form different products.	**SE, Vol. 2:** 344, 354 **Digital Activities:** Sugar, Starch, and Glycogen; Energy Densities of Foods
As a result of these chemical reactions, energy is transferred from one system of interacting molecules to another. Cellular respiration is a chemical process in which the bonds of food molecules and oxygen molecules are broken and new compounds are formed that can transport energy to muscles. Cellular respiration also releases the energy needed to maintain body temperature despite ongoing energy transfer to the surrounding environment.	**SE, Vol. 2:** 311, 344, 354 **Digital Activities:** Sugar, Starch, and Glycogen; Energy Densities of Foods **Performance-Based Assessment:** Prepare and Characterize Biodiesel
SCIENCE AND ENGINEERING PRACTICES	
Developing and Using Models	**SE, Vol. 2:** 311, 354
CROSSCUTTING CONCEPTS	
Energy and Matter	**SE, Vol. 2:** 354

Earth's Place in the Universe HS-ESS1

Students who demonstrate understanding can:

PERFORMANCE EXPECTATION HS- ESS1-1	WHERE TO FIND IT...
Develop a model based on evidence to illustrate the life span of the sun and the role of nuclear fusion in the sun's core to release energy in the form of radiation.	**SE, Vol. 2:** 77, 89–90 **Digital Activity:** Energy to Earth
DISCIPLINARY CORE IDEAS	
ESS1.A: The Universe and Its Stars The star called the sun is changing and will burn out over a lifespan of approximately 10 billion years.	**SE, Vol. 2:** 77
PS3.D: Energy in Chemical Processes and Everyday Life Nuclear fusion processes in the center of the sun release the energy that ultimately reaches Earth as radiation.	**SE, Vol. 2:** 44, 55–56, 77, 381, 382 **Digital Activity:** Energy to Earth
SCIENCE AND ENGINEERING PRACTICES	
Developing and Using Models	**SE, Vol. 2:** 363, 365, 379, 382 **Digital Activity:** Energy to Earth
CROSSCUTTING CONCEPTS	
Scale, Proportion, and Quantity	**SE, Vol. 2:** 374, 384

PERFORMANCE EXPECTATION HS- ESS1-2	WHERE TO FIND IT...
Construct an explanation of the Big Bang theory based on astronomical evidence of light spectra, motion of distant galaxies, and composition of matter in the universe.	**SE, Vol. 2:** 376-377, 381–384, 385–386 **Digital Worksheet:** The Composition of Stars
DISCIPLINARY CORE IDEAS	
ESS1.A: The Universe and Its Stars The study of stars' light spectra and brightness is used to identify compositional elements of stars, their movements, and their distances from Earth.	**SE, Vol. 1:** 22–23 **SE, Vol. 2:** 383–386 **Inquiry Lab:** Evaluate Atomic Spectra **Digital Worksheet:** The Composition of Stars
The Big Bang theory is supported by observations of distant galaxies receding from our own, of the measured composition of stars and non-stellar gases, and of the maps of spectra of the primordial radiation (cosmic microwave background) that still fills the universe.	**SE, Vol. 2:** 376–377, 382–384
Other than the hydrogen and helium formed at the time of the Big Bang, nuclear fusion within stars produces all atomic nuclei lighter than and including iron, and the process releases electromagnetic energy. Heavier elements are produced when certain massive stars achieve a supernova stage and explode.	**SE, Vol. 2:** 382–384
PS4.B: Electromagnetic Radiation Atoms of each element emit and absorb characteristic frequencies of light. These characteristics allow identification of the presence of an element, even in microscopic quantities.	**SE, Vol. 1:** 22–24, 27 **Engineering Design Challenge:** Design a Spectroscope from Household Materials

NGSS CORRELATION

SCIENCE AND ENGINEERING PRACTICES	
Constructing Explanations	**SE, Vol. 2:** 377, 386
Connections to Nature of Science: Science Models, Laws, Mechanisms, and Theories Explain Natural Phenomena	**SE, Vol. 2:** 376
CROSSCUTTING CONCEPTS	
Energy and Matter	**SE, Vol. 2:** 386 **Digital Activity:** Comparing Nuclear and Chemical Reactions
Connections to Engineering, Technology, and Applications of Science: Interdependence of Science, Engineering, and Technology	**SE, Vol. 2:** 378, 405
Connections to Nature of Science: Scientific Knowledge Assumes an Order and Consistency in Natural Systems	**SE, Vol. 2:** 376–377, 378

PERFORMANCE EXPECTATION HS-ESS1-3	WHERE TO FIND IT...
Communicate scientific ideas about the way stars, over their life cycle, produce elements.	**SE, Vol. 2:** 380–386 **Digital Worksheet:** The Composition of Stars
DISCIPLINARY CORE IDEAS	
ESS1.A: The Universe and Its Stars The study of stars' light spectra and brightness is used to identify compositional elements of stars, their movements, and their distances from Earth.	**SE, Vol. 1:** 22–23 **SE, Vol. 2:** 383–386 **Inquiry Lab:** Evaluate Atomic Spectra **Digital Worksheet:** The Composition of Stars
Other than the hydrogen and helium formed at the time of the Big Bang, nuclear fusion within stars produces all atomic nuclei lighter than and including iron, and the process releases electromagnetic energy. Heavier elements are produced when certain massive stars achieve a supernova stage and explode.	**SE, Vol. 2:** 382–384
SCIENCE AND ENGINEERING PRACTICES	
Obtaining, Evaluating, and Communicating Information	**SE, Vol. 2:** 386 **Digital Worksheet:** The Composition of Stars
CROSSCUTTING CONCEPTS	
Energy and Matter	**SE, Vol. 2:** 372, 383–384

PERFORMANCE EXPECTATION HS- ESS1-6	WHERE TO FIND IT...
Apply scientific reasoning and evidence from ancient Earth materials, meteorites, and other planetary surfaces to construct an account of Earth's formation and early history.	**Digital Activity:** Geologic Age and Half-Life
DISCIPLINARY CORE IDEAS	
ESS1.C: The History of Planet Earth Although active geologic processes, such as plate tectonics and erosion, have destroyed or altered most of the very early rock record on Earth, other objects in the solar system, such as lunar rocks, asteroids, and meteorites, have changed little over billions of years. Studying these objects can provide information about Earth's formation and early history.	**SE, Vol. 2:** 371–372

PS1.C: Nuclear Processes Spontaneous radioactive decays follow a characteristic exponential decay law. Nuclear lifetimes allow radiometric dating to be used to determine the ages of rocks and other materials.	**SE, Vol. 2:** 368–372
SCIENCE AND ENGINEERING PRACTICES	
Constructing Explanations	**SE, Vol. 2:** 386 **Digital Activity:** The Composition of Stars
Connections to Nature of Science: Science Models, Laws, Mechanisms, and Theories Explain Natural Phenomena	**SE, Vol. 2:** 371–372
CROSSCUTTING CONCEPTS	
Stability and Change	**SE, Vol. 2:** 110, 357, 364, 366, 367

Earth's Systems HS-ESS2

Students who demonstrate understanding can:

PERFORMANCE EXPECTATION HS-ESS2-2	WHERE TO FIND IT...
Analyze geoscience data to make the claim that one change to Earth's surface can create feedbacks that cause changes to other Earth systems.	**Inquiry Labs:** Feedback and Climate Change, Energy in the Atmosphere, Observe Air Pollution, How Nature Records Changes in Climate, The pH of Seawater, Carbon Dioxide Levels in Water, The Fate of Carbonate in Acidifying Oceans **Digital Activities:** Wetlands and the Carbon Cycle, Sampling the Past, Flow of Energy and Greenhouse Gases, Glaciers on Rainier, Ocean pH, The Effect of Ocean Acidification on Shells **Performance-Based Assessments:** Microhabitat in a Bottle, Calcium Carbonate and Shell Production
DISCIPLINARY CORE IDEAS	
ESS2.A: Earth Materials and Systems Earth's systems, being dynamic and interacting, cause feedback effects that can increase or decrease the original changes.	**SE, Vol. 2:** 44–54, 66–75, 76–84, 85–95, 107–114, 230–237, 238–245, 260–269
ESS2.D: Weather and Climate The foundation for Earth's global climate systems is the electromagnetic radiation from the sun, as well as its reflection, absorption, storage, and redistribution among the atmosphere, ocean, and land systems, and this energy's re-radiation into space.	**SE, Vol. 2:** 44, 66–75, 77, 85–87, 89–92
SCIENCE AND ENGINEERING PRACTICES	
Analyzing and Interpreting Data	**SE, Vol 2:** 51, 67, 71, 74, 78, 80, 88, 94, 239, 256, 257 **Inquiry Labs:** Feedback and Climate Change, Energy in the Atmosphere, Observe Air Pollution, How Nature Records Changes in Climate, The pH of Seawater, Carbon Dioxide Levels in Water, The Fate of Carbonate in Acidifying Oceans **Digital Activities:** Wetlands and the Carbon Cycle, Sampling the Past, Flow of Energy and Greenhouse Gases, Glaciers on Rainier, Ocean pH, The Effect of Ocean Acidification on Shells

NGSS CORRELATION

CROSSCUTTING CONCEPTS	
Stability and Change	**SE, Vol. 2:** 43, 75, 77 **Inquiry Lab:** How Melting Ice Affects Sea Level **Performance-Based Assessment:** Calcium Carbonate and Shell Production
Connections to Engineering, Technology, and Applications of Science: Influence of Engineering, Technology, and Science on Society and the Natural World	**SE, Vol. 2:** 145–148, 150 **Inquiry Lab:** Solar Cell Technology **Digital Activity:** Renewable Energy and Energy Storage **Engineering Design Challenge:** Design a Green Roof

PERFORMANCE EXPECTATION HS-ESS2-4	WHERE TO FIND IT...
Use a model to describe how variations in the flow of energy into and out of Earth's systems result in changes in climate.	**Inquiry Labs:** Albedo and Composition of Earth's Surface, How Melting Ice Affects Sea Level, Observe Air Pollution, How Nature Records Changes in Climate **Digital Activities:** Flow of Energy and Greenhouse Gases, Glaciers on Rainier **Performance-Based Assessment:** Microhabitat in a Bottle
DISCIPLINARY CORE IDEAS	
ESS1.B: Earth and the Solar System Cyclical changes in the shape of Earth's orbit around the sun, together with changes in the tilt of the planet's axis of rotation, both occurring over hundreds of thousands of years, have altered the intensity and distribution of sunlight falling on the earth. These phenomena cause a cycle of ice ages and other gradual climate changes.	**SE, Vol. 2:** 78, 85–87, 100–106, 107–113
ESS2.A: Earth Materials and Systems The geological record shows that changes to global and regional climate can be caused by interactions among changes in the sun's energy output or Earth's orbit, tectonic events, ocean circulation, volcanic activity, glaciers, vegetation, and human activities. These changes can occur on a variety of time scales from sudden (e.g., volcanic ash clouds) to intermediate (ice ages) to very long-term tectonic cycles.	**SE, Vol. 2:** 76–84, 85–95, 100–106, 107–114, 115–116
ESS2.D: Weather and Climate The foundation for Earth's global climate systems is the electromagnetic radiation from the sun, as well as its reflection, absorption, storage, and redistribution among the atmosphere, ocean, and land systems, and this energy's re-radiation into space.	**SE, Vol. 2:** 44, 45–46, 55–56, 66–75, 77, 85–87, 89–92
Changes in the atmosphere due to human activity have increased carbon dioxide concentrations and thus affect climate.	**SE, Vol. 2:** 93–95, 101, 103, 115–121

SCIENCE AND ENGINEERING PRACTICES	
Developing and Using Models	**SE, Vol. 2:** 43, 51, 56, 61, 65, 87, 116 **Performance-Based Assessment:** Microhabitat in a Bottle
Connections to Nature of Science: Scientific Knowledge is Based on Empirical Evidence	**SE, Vol. 2:** 106, 114, 122, 132, 142, 144, 147, 154
CROSSCUTTING CONCEPTS	
Cause and Effect	**SE, Vol. 2:** 82, 139 **Inquiry Labs:** Albedo and Composition of Earth's Surface, How Melting Ice Affects Sea Level, Observe Air Pollution, How Nature Records Changes in Climate **Digital Activities:** Flow of Energy and Greenhouse Gases, Glaciers on Rainier **Performance-Based Assessment:** Microhabitat in a Bottle

PERFORMANCE EXPECTATION HS-ESS2-6	WHERE TO FIND IT...
Develop a quantitative model to describe the cycling of carbon among the hydrosphere, atmosphere, geosphere, and biosphere.	**Inquiry Labs:** Carbon Dioxide and Its Role in Climate, Human Activity and Carbon Emissions, Carbon Dioxide Levels in Water, Ocean Currents, The Fate of Carbonate in Acidifying Oceans **Engineering Design Challenge:** Design a Model of Ocean Acidification **Performance-Based Assessment:** Climate Change and the Carbon Cycle
DISCIPLINARY CORE IDEAS	
ESS2.D: Weather and Climate Gradual atmospheric changes were due to plants and other organisms that captured carbon dioxide and released oxygen.	**SE, Vol. 2:** 47–48, 66–67, 70, 79–80, 240–241
Changes in the atmosphere due to human activity have increased carbon dioxide concentrations and thus affect climate.	**SE, Vol. 2:** 53–54, 93–96, 115–122, 238–243, 264–265
SCIENCE AND ENGINEERING PRACTICES	
Developing and Using Models	**SE, Vol. 2:** 116, 243, 268, 269 **Inquiry Labs:** Carbon Dioxide and Its Role in Climate, Human Activity and Carbon Emissions, Carbon Dioxide Levels in Water, Ocean Currents, The Fate of Carbonate in Acidifying Oceans
CROSSCUTTING CONCEPTS	
Energy and Matter	**SE, Vol. 2:** 118, 119, 247, 259 **Inquiry Lab:** Human Activity and Carbon Emissions **Engineering Design Challenge:** Design a Model of Ocean Acidification

NGSS CORRELATION

Earth and Human Activity HS-ESS3

Students who demonstrate understanding can:

PERFORMANCE EXPECTATION HS-ESS3-2	WHERE TO FIND IT...
Evaluate competing design solutions for developing, managing, and utilizing energy and mineral resources based on cost-benefit ratios.	**Inquiry Labs:** Carbon Dioxide and Its Role in Climate, Solar Cell Technology, Investigate the Toxicity of Road Deicers, Green Chemistry Analysis of a Reaction **Digital Activity:** Paper Mill Wastewater Treatment **Engineering Design Challenges:** Uses and Production of Ash Water, Plastic from Biowaste **Performance-Based Assessment:** Climate Change and the Carbon Cycle
DISCIPLINARY CORE IDEAS	
ESS3.A Natural Resources All forms of energy production and other resource extraction have associated economic, social, environmental, and geopolitical costs and risks as well as benefits. New technologies and social regulations can change the balance of these factors.	**SE, Vol. 2:** 120–121, 143–153, 154, 155
ETS1.B Developing Possible Solutions When evaluating solutions, it is important to take into account a range of constraints, including cost, safety, reliability, and aesthetics, and to consider social, cultural, and environmental impacts.	**SE, Vol. 2:** 143–152, 155 **Digital Activity:** Paper Mill Wastewater Treatment **Engineering Design Challenges:** Uses and Production of Ash Water, Plastic from Biowaste
SCIENCE AND ENGINEERING PRACTICES	
Engaging in Argument from Evidence	**SE, Vol. 2:** 122, 132, 142, 144, 147, 154, 409, 424
CROSSCUTTING CONCEPTS	
Connections to Engineering, Technology, and Applications of Science: Influence of Engineering, Technology, and Science on Society and the Natural World	**SE, Vol. 2:** 146, 148, 150, 152 **Performance-Based Assessment:** Climate Change and the Carbon Cycle
Connections to Nature of Science: Science Addresses Questions About the Natural and Material World	**SE, Vol. 2:** 149

PERFORMANCE EXPECTATION HS-ESS3-3	WHERE TO FIND IT...
Create a computational simulation to illustrate the relationships among management of natural resources, the sustainability of human populations, and biodiversity.	**Digital Activities & Worksheets:** Model Your Carbon Footprint, Paper Mill Wastewater Treatment, Plot Resource Management Scenarios and Outcomes
DISCIPLINARY CORE IDEAS	
ESS3.C: Human Impacts on Earth Systems The sustainability of human societies and the biodiversity that supports them requires responsible management of natural resources.	**SE, Vol. 2:** 151–152, 415–416, 433, 434, 435
SCIENCE AND ENGINEERING PRACTICES	
Using Mathematics and Computational Thinking	**SE, Vol. 2:** 143–144, 151–152, 415–416, 433, 434, 435 **Digital Worksheet:** Plot Resource Management Scenarios and Outcomes

CROSSCUTTING CONCEPTS	
Stability and Change	**SE, Vol. 2:** 416
Connections to Engineering, Technology, and Applications of Science: Influence of Science, Engineering, and Technology on Society and the Natural World	**SE, Vol. 2:** 148, 150, 404, 405–406, 410 **Digital Activities & Worksheets:** Paper Mill Wastewater Treatment, Plot Resource Management Scenarios and Outcomes
Connections to Nature of Science: Science is a Human Endeavor	**SE, Vol. 2:** 405

PERFORMANCE EXPECTATION HS-ESS3-4	WHERE TO FIND IT...
Evaluate or refine a technological solution that reduces impacts of human activities on natural systems.*	**Inquiry Labs:** Toxicity of Road Deicers, Uses and Production of Ash Water, How to Recycle Polylactic Acid Plastics **Digital Activities & Worksheets:** Energy-Efficient Ammonia Production, Paper Mill Wastewater Treatment, Revise an Industrial Process, Plot Resource Management Scenarios and Outcomes **Engineering Design Challenge:** Plastic from Biowaste **Performance Based Assessment:** Make the Chemistry Lab Cleaner
DISCIPLINARY CORE IDEAS	
ESS3.C Human Impacts on Earth Systems Scientists and engineers can make major contributions by developing technologies that produce less pollution and waste and that preclude ecosystem degradation.	**SE, Vol. 2:** 151–152, 415–416, 433, 434, 435
ETS1.B: Developing Possible Solutions When evaluating solutions, it is important to take into account a range of constraints, including cost, safety, reliability, and aesthetics, and to consider social, cultural, and environmental impacts.	**SE, Vol. 2:** 143–152, 155
SCIENCE AND ENGINEERING PRACTICES	
Designing Solutions	**SE, Vol. 2:** 152, 154, 155, 418 **Digital Activities & Worksheets:** Reduce the Car Industry's Footprint, Paper Mill Wastewater Treatment **Engineering Design Challenge:** Plastic from Biowaste
CROSSCUTTING CONCEPTS	
Stability and Change	**SE, Vol. 2:** 416
Connections to Engineering, Technology, and Applications of Science: Influence of Science, Engineering, and Technology on Society and the Natural World	**SE, Vol. 2:** 150, 431–435

NGSS CORRELATION

PERFORMANCE EXPECTATION HS-ESS3-5	WHERE TO FIND IT...
Analyze geoscience data and the results from global climate models to make an evidence-based forecast of the current rate of global or regional climate change and associated future impacts to Earth systems.	**Inquiry Lab:** Model Climate Change with Melting Ice **Digital Activities & Worksheets:** Glaciers on Rainier, Graph Climate Change, Climate Change and Drought, Climate Change and Fire
DISCIPLINARY CORE IDEAS	
ESS3.D Global Climate Change Though the magnitudes of human impacts are greater than they have ever been, so too are human abilities to model, predict, and manage current and future impacts.	**SE, Vol. 2:** 123–132, 143–144, 149, 151–152
SCIENCE AND ENGINEERING PRACTICES	
Analyzing and Interpreting Data	**SE, Vol. 2:** 126, 128, 129, 131, 135, 140 **Inquiry Lab:** Model Climate Change with Melting Ice **Digital Activities & Worksheets:** Climate Change and Drought, Climate Change and Fire
Connections to Nature of Science: Scientific Investigations Use a Variety of Methods	**SE, Vol. 2:** 54, 124, 125, 127, 129, 130–132
Connections to Nature of Science: Scientific Knowledge is Based on Empirical Evidence	**SE, Vol. 2:** 102, 107–114, 122, 132, 142, 144, 147, 154
CROSSCUTTING CONCEPTS	
Stability and Change	**SE, Vol. 2:** 127, 130, 136 **Digital Activities & Worksheets:** Glaciers on Rainier, Climate Change and the Biosphere

PERFORMANCE EXPECTATION HS-ESS3-6	WHERE TO FIND IT...
Use a computational representation to illustrate the relationships among Earth systems and how those relationships are being modified due to human activity.	**Inquiry Labs:** Human Activity and Carbon Emissions, Climate Change and Keeping Cool
DISCIPLINARY CORE IDEAS	
ESS2.D Weather and Climate Current models predict that, although future regional climate changes will be complex and varied, average global temperatures will continue to rise. The outcomes predicted by global climate models strongly depend on the amounts of human-generated greenhouse gases added to the atmosphere each year and by the ways in which these gases are absorbed by the ocean and biosphere.	**SE, Vol. 2:** 125–131, 133–142
ESS3.D Global Climate Change Through computer simulations and other studies, important discoveries are still being made about how the ocean, the atmosphere, and the biosphere interact and are modified in response to human activities.	**SE, Vol. 2:** 125–131, 133–142, 236
SCIENCE AND ENGINEERING PRACTICES	
Use Mathematics and Computational Thinking	**SE, Vol. 2:** 121, 138 **Inquiry Labs:** Human Activity and Carbon Emissions, Climate Change and Keeping Cool **Digital Worksheet:** Climate Change and the Biosphere
CROSSCUTTING CONCEPTS	
Systems and System Models	**SE, Vol. 2:** 124, 125, 127

Engineering Design HS-ETS1

Students who demonstrate understanding can:

PERFORMANCE EXPECTATION HS-ETS1-1	WHERE TO FIND IT...
Analyze a major global challenge to specify qualitative and quantitative criteria and constraints for solutions that account for societal needs and wants.	**Inquiry Labs:** Toxicity of Road Deicers, How to Recycle Polylactic Acid Plastics **Engineering Design Challenges:** Evaluate Metals for a Commercial Application, Building a Better Bike, Water Purification, Design a Model of Ocean Acidification, Plastic from Biowaste **Performance-Based Assessment:** Prepare and Characterize Biodiesel **Problem-Based Learning:** The Chemistry of Cooking, Water as a Greenhouse Gas, Reducing Carbon Footprints, Sustainable Off-Grid Energy
DISCIPLINARY CORE IDEAS	
ETS1.A Defining and Delimiting Engineering Problems Criteria and constraints also include satisfying any requirements set by society, such as taking issues of risk mitigation into account, and they should be quantified to the extent possible and stated in such a way that one can tell if a given design meets them.	**SE, Vol. 2:** 143–144, 151–152, 155, 407–415
Humanity faces major global challenges today, such as the need for supplies of clean water and food or for energy sources that minimize pollution, which can be addressed through engineering. These global challenges also may have manifestations in local communities.	**SE, Vol. 2:** 53–54, 93–95, 120–121, 139–142, 407–415, 431–432
SCIENCE AND ENGINEERING PRACTICES	
Defining Problems	**SE, Vol. 1:** 147, 171, 203, 248, 274 **SE, Vol. 2:** 155 **Problem-Based Learning:** Water as a Greenhouse Gas, Reducing Carbon Footprints, Sustainable Off-Grid Energy
CROSSCUTTING CONCEPTS	
Connections to Engineering, Technology, and Applications of Science: Influence of Engineering, Technology, and Science on Society and the Natural World	**SE, Vol. 2:** 146, 148, 150 **Problem-Based Learning:** Water as a Greenhouse Gas, Reducing Carbon Footprints, Sustainable Off-Grid Energy

NGSS CORRELATION

PERFORMANCE EXPECTATION HS-ETS1-2	WHERE TO FIND IT...
Design a solution to a complex real-world problem by breaking it down into smaller, more manageable problems that can be solved through engineering.	**Inquiry Lab:** How to Recycle Polylactic Acid Plastics **Engineering Design Challenges:** Growing Crystals in Gel, Abrasive Compounds, Building a Better Bike, An Empirical Formula Challenge, Water Purification, Flameless Heating Systems, Use Equilibrium for a Commercial Application, Design a Model of Ocean Acidification, Uses and Production of Ash Water, Plastic from Biowaste **Performance-Based Assessment:** Prepare and Characterize Biodiesel
DISCIPLINARY CORE IDEAS	
ETS1.C Optimizing the Design Solution Criteria may need to be broken down into simpler ones that can be approached systematically, and decisions about the priority of certain criteria over others (trade-offs) may be needed.	**SE, Vol. 2:** 145–152
SCIENCE AND ENGINEERING PRACTICES	
Designing Solutions	**SE, Vol. 1:** 147, 160, 170 **SE, Vol. 2:** 152, 155, 265 **Problem-Based Learning:** Sustainable Off-Grid Energy

PERFORMANCE EXPECTATION HS-ETS1-3	WHERE TO FIND IT...
Evaluate a solution to a complex real-world problem based on prioritized criteria and trade-offs that account for a range of constraints, including cost, safety, reliability, and aesthetics as well as possible social, cultural, and environmental impacts.	**Inquiry Lab:** How to Recycle Polylactic Acid Plastics **Engineering Design Challenges:** Evaluate Metals for a Commercial Application, Abrasive Compounds, Building a Better Bike, Flameless Heating Systems, Uses and Production of Ash Water, Plastic from Biowaste **Performance-Based Assessment:** Prepare and Characterize Biodiesel
DISCIPLINARY CORE IDEAS	
ETS1.B Developing Possible Solutions When evaluating solutions, it is important to take into account a range of constraints, including cost, safety, reliability, and aesthetics, and to consider social, cultural, and environmental impacts.	**SE, Vol. 2:** 53–54, 93–95, 120–121, 139–142, 143–153, 405–409, 424–425
SCIENCE AND ENGINEERING PRACTICES	
Designing Solutions	**SE, Vol. 1:** 147, 170, 203, 248, 274 **SE, Vol. 2:** 155, 409, 424 **Performance-Based Assessment:** Prepare and Characterize Biodiesel **Problem-Based Learning:** Sustainable Off-Grid Energy
CROSSCUTTING CONCEPTS	
Connections to Engineering, Technology, and Applications of Science: Influence of Engineering, Technology, and Science on Society and the Natural World	**SE, Vol. 2:** 146, 148, 150 **Engineering Design Challenges:** Uses and Production of Ash Water, Plastic from Biowaste

PERFORMANCE EXPECTATION HS-ETS1-4	WHERE TO FIND IT...
Use a computer simulation to model the impact of proposed solutions to a complex real-world problem with numerous criteria and constraints on interactions within and between systems relevant to the problem.	**Digital Activities & Worksheets:** Model Your Carbon Footprint, Paper Mill Wastewater Treatment, Plot Resource Management Scenarios and Outcomes **Problem-Based Learning:** Reducing Carbon Footprints, Sustainable Off-Grid Energy
DISCIPLINARY CORE IDEAS	
ETS1.B Developing Possible Solutions Both physical models and computers can be used in various ways to aid in the engineering design process. Computers are useful for a variety of purposes, such as running simulations to test different ways of solving a problem or to see which one is most efficient or economical; and in making a persuasive presentation to a client about how a given design will meet his or her needs.	**SE, Vol. 2:** 123–131, 132
SCIENCE AND ENGINEERING PRACTICES	
Using Mathematics and Computational Thinking	**SE, Vol. 2:** 110, 121, 123–131, 138 **Digital Activities & Worksheets:** Model Your Carbon Footprint, Paper Mill Wastewater Treatment, Plot Resource Management Scenarios and Outcomes
CROSSCUTTING CONCEPTS	
Systems and System Models	**SE, Vol. 2:** 124–128

Science and Engineering Practices

The *Experience Chemistry* program provides comprehensive coverage of the Science and Engineering Practices identified in the *Framework for K–12 Science Education*. Use this chart to track where the Grade 9–12 practices are covered in the Student Edition, Labs, and the Digital Course.

SCIENCE AND ENGINEERING PRACTICES	WHERE TO FIND IT...
SEP-1 Asking Questions (for Science)	**SE, Vol. 1:** 129 **SE, Vol. 2:** 275, 347, 353 **Inquiry Labs:** Evaluate Atomic Spectra, Reaction Rates: Iodine Clock, Collision Theory, Explore Chemical Equilibrium **Performance-Based Assessments:** Evaluate Atomic Structure with Flame Tests, Rates of Reaction and Dissolution
SEP-1 Defining Problems (for Engineering)	**SE, Vol. 1:** 147, 171, 203, 248, 274 **SE, Vol. 2:** 155 **Engineering Design Challenges:** Build a Spectroscope from Household Materials, Growing Crystals in Gel, Evaluate Metals for a Commercial Application, Abrasive Compounds, Building a Better Bike, An Empirical Formula Challenge, Water Purification, Build a Film Canister Rocket, Flameless Heating Systems, What's in a Container?, Design a Green Roof, Use Equilibrium for a Commercial Application, Design a Natural pH Indicator, Design a Model of Ocean Acidification, Polymers: Bouncy Balls, Uses and Production of Ash Water, Plastic from Biowaste

SCIENCE AND ENGINEERING PRACTICES	WHERE TO FIND IT...
SEP-2 Developing and Using Models	**SE, Vol. 1:** 6, 7, 11, 17, 21, 29, 31, 46, 48, 51, 52, 55, 57, 58, 60, 61, 77, 89, 99, 103, 106, 107, 112, 119, 124, 137, 143, 154, 166, 176, 207, 213, 217, 219, 220, 222, 226, 230, 231, 232, 233, 234, 235, 237, 239, 242, 243, 247, 259, 262, 264, 269, 281, 282, 283, 286, 293, 302 **SE, Vol 2:** 5, 8, 16, 27, 29, 30, 35, 43, 51, 56, 61, 65, 69, 73, 87, 97, 104, 116, 164, 171, 178, 197, 202, 226, 243, 248, 268, 269, 277, 282, 287, 299, 300, 308, 314, 316, 328, 332, 335, 339, 345, 348, 354, 360, 365, 379, 382, 393 **Inquiry Labs:** Elements: The Building Blocks of Matter; Bean Bag Isotopes; Evaluate Atomic Spectra; Evaluate the Bohr Model of the Atom; Model Electron Configuration; Develop a Periodic Table; Elemental Metals, Nonmetals, and Metalloids; Periodic Trends and Properties; Investigate Metallic Bonds; Chemical Names and Formulas; Correlate Material Properties and Bond Type; Modeling Metals, Ceramics, and Polymers; Investigate Surface Tension; Describe Small-scale Matter Using the Mole; Preparation of Solutions; Evaluate Chemical Reactions; Types of Chemical Reactions; The Thermodynamics of Hand Warmers; Hess's Law and the Combustion of a Metal; Carbon Dioxide and Its Role in Climate; Human Activity and Carbon Emissions; Solar Cell Technology; Collision Theory; Measure pH with Indicators; Measure Acid Strength; The pH of Seawater; Carbon Dioxide Levels in Water; Ocean Currents; The Fate of Carbonate in Acidifying Oceans; Explore Iron Corrosion; Investigate Different Hydrocarbons; Radioactive Decay; Nuclear Energy **Digital Activities:** Predict Reactivity Using Periodic Trends, Modeling Gemstone Color Formation, Redox and Non-Redox Reactions, Energy-Efficient Ammonia Production **Performance-Based Assessments:** Evaluate Atomic Structure with Flame Tests, Gravimetric Analysis of Periodic Trends, Enthalpy of a Neutralization Reaction, Microhabitat in a Bottle, Climate Change and the Carbon Cycle, Quantitative Analysis of Acid Rain, Battery Challenge, Prepare and Characterize Biodiesel, Natural Radiation

SCIENCE AND ENGINEERING PRACTICES	WHERE TO FIND IT...
SEP-3 Planning and Carrying Out Investigations	**SE, Vol. 1:** 75, 111, 142, 146, 165, 193, 196, 204, 212, 249, 300 **SE, Vol 2:** 6, 26, 54, 173, 324 **Inquiry Labs:** Elements: The Building Blocks of Matter; Bean Bag Isotopes; Evaluate the Bohr Model of the Atom; Model Electron Configuration; Develop a Periodic Table; Elemental Metals, Nonmetals, and Metalloids; Periodic Trends and Properties; Characteristics of Ionic Bonds; Investigate Metallic Bonds; Investigate Covalent Bonds; Intermolecular Forces; Chemical Names and Formulas; Correlate Material Properties and Bond Type; Measure the Energy of a Phase Change; Melt Ionic and Covalent Compounds; Modeling Metals, Ceramics, and Polymers; Investigate Surface Tension; Aqueous Solutions; Describe Small-scale Matter Using the Mole; Mole Ratios; Determine an Empirical Formula; Preparation of Solutions; Types of Chemical Reactions; Predict Chemical Reactions; Identify Unknowns Through Stoichiometry; Determination of Reaction Output; Formation of Barium Iodate; Hess's Law and the Combustion of a Metal; Feedback and Climate Change; Albedo and Composition of Earth's Surface; How Melting Ice Affects Sea Level; Observe Air Pollution; Carbon Dioxide and Its Role in Climate; How Nature Records Changes in Climate; Human Activity and Carbon Emissions; Climate Change and Keeping Cool; Solar Cell Technology; Reaction Rates: Iodine Clock; Collision Theory; Explore Chemical Equilibrium; Supersaturation and Thermodynamics; Measure pH with Indicators; Measure Acid Strength; Titrations–The Study of Acid-Base Chemistry; Analysis of Buffer Solutions and Ranges; The pH of Seawater; Carbon Dioxide Levels in Water; Ocean Currents; The Fate of Carbonate in Acidifying Oceans; Explore Iron Corrosion; Metal Activity; Build a Micro Battery; Investigate Different Hydrocarbons; Ester Synthesis; Protein and Amino Acid Tests; Nuclear Radiation and Shielding; Investigate the Toxicity of Road Deicers; Green Chemistry Analysis of a Mixture; How to Recycle Polylactic Acid Plastics **Engineering Design Challenges:** Build a Spectroscope from Household Materials, Growing Crystals in Gel, Evaluate Metals for a Commercial Application, Abrasive Compounds, Building a Better Bike, An Empirical Formula Challenge, Water Purification, Build a Film Canister Rocket, Flameless Heating Systems, What's in a Container?, Design a Green Roof, Use Equilibrium for a Commercial Application, Design a Natural pH Indicator, Design a Model of Ocean Acidification, Polymers: Bouncy Balls, Uses and Production of Ash Water, Plastic from Biowaste **Digital Activities:** Intermolecular Forces in Liquids, Tough Tools, Reactivity of Metals , Modeling Gemstone Color Formation, Energy-Efficient Ammonia Production **Performance-Based Assessments:** Evaluate Atomic Structure with Flame Tests, Gravimetric Analysis of Periodic Trends, Qualitative Analysis and Chemical Bonding, Road Deicers, Analysis of Basic Copper Carbonate, Identify Evidence of Chemical Reactions, The Stoichiometry of Filling a Balloon, Enthalpy of a Neutralization Reaction, Cartesian Divers, Microhabitat in a Bottle, Climate Change and the Carbon Cycle, Rates of Reaction and Dissolution, Quantitative Analysis of Acid Rain, Calcium Carbonate and Shell Production, Battery Challenge, Prepare and Characterize Biodiesel, Natural Radiation, Make the Chemistry Lab Greener

NGSS CORRELATION

SCIENCE AND ENGINEERING PRACTICES	WHERE TO FIND IT...
SEP-4 Analyzing and Interpreting Data	**SE, Vol. 1:** 18, 23, 41, 126, 127, 131, 132, 134, 140, 152, 163, 175, 188, 191, 200, 208, 225, 228, 229, 245, 270, 271, 278, 287 **SE, Vol. 2:** 9, 11, 13, 15, 17, 32, 67, 71, 74, 78, 80, 88, 94, 108, 109, 111, 112, 113, 126, 128, 129, 131, 135, 140, 190, 193, 216, 219, 239, 256, 257, 297, 305, 315, 319, 323, 325, 370, 429 **Inquiry Labs:** Bean Bag Isotopes; Evaluate Atomic Spectra; Evaluate the Bohr Model of the Atom; Develop a Periodic Table; Elemental Metals, Nonmetals, and Metalloids; Periodic Trends and Properties; Characteristics of Ionic Bonds; Investigate Metallic Bonds; Investigate Covalent Bonds; Intermolecular Forces; Correlate Material Properties and Bond Type; Measure the Energy of a Phase Change; Melt Ionic and Covalent Compounds; Aqueous Solutions; Describe Small-scale Matter Using the Mole; Mole Ratios; Determine an Empirical Formula; Preparation of Solutions; Evaluate Chemical Reactions; Types of Chemical Reactions; Predict Chemical Reactions; Identify Unknowns Through Stoichiometry; Determination of Reaction Output; Formation of Barium Iodate; The Thermodynamics of Hand Warmers; Relationships Between Gas Variables; The Ideal Gas Law; Gas Diffusion; The Heat of Melting Ice; Feedback and Climate Change; Energy in the Atmosphere; Albedo and Composition of Earth's Surface; Observe Air Pollution; Carbon Dioxide and Its Role in Climate; Human Activity and Carbon Emissions; Model Climate Change with Melting Ice; Climate Change and Keeping Cool; Solar Cell Technology; Reaction Rates: Iodine Clock; Collision Theory; Explore Chemical Equilibrium; Supersaturation and Thermodynamics; Measure Acid Strength; Titrations–The Study of Acid-Base Chemistry; Analysis of Buffer Solutions and Ranges; The pH of Seawater; Carbon Dioxide Levels in Water; Ocean Currents; The Fate of Carbonate in Acidifying Oceans; Investigate Different Hydrocarbons; Ester Synthesis; Protein and Amino Acid Tests; Radioactive Decay; Investigate the Toxicity of Road Deicers; Green Chemistry Analysis of a Mixture; How to Recycle Polylactic Acid Plastics **Engineering Design Challenge:** Build a Film Canister Rocket **Digital Activities:** Gas Behavior in Popping Candy, Wetlands and the Carbon Cycle, Sampling the Past, Flow of Energy and Greenhouse Gases, Glaciers on Rainier, Ocean pH, The Effect of Ocean Acidification on Shells, Modeling Gemstone Color Formation, Protein Structure and Food Design, Geologic Variation and Radon Levels , Energy-Efficient Ammonia Production **Performance-Based Assessments:** Gravimetric Analysis of Periodic Trends, Qualitative Analysis and Chemical Bonding, Road Deicers, Analysis of Basic Copper Carbonate, Identify Evidence of Chemical Reactions, The Stoichiometry of Filling a Balloon, Enthalpy of a Neutralization Reaction, Climate Change and the Carbon Cycle, Rates of Reaction and Dissolution, Quantitative Analysis of Acid Rain, Calcium Carbonate and Shell Production, Prepare and Characterize Biodiesel

SCIENCE AND ENGINEERING PRACTICES	WHERE TO FIND IT...
SEP-5 Using Mathematical and Computational Thinking	**SE, Vol. 1:** 15, 18, 87, 175, 177, 181, 185, 186, 189, 193, 194, 195, 197, 199, 201, 205, 206, 223, 252, 257, 260, 266, 268, 279, 285, 292, 298 **SE, Vol. 2:** 2, 19, 22, 25, 90, 93, 110, 121, 138, 185, 198, 200, 205, 207, 218, 267, 344, 366, 413, 419 **Inquiry Labs:** Bean Bag Isotopes, Characteristics of Ionic Bonds, Investigate Covalent Bonds, Intermolecular Forces, Measure the Energy of a Phase Change, Describe Small-scale Matter Using the Mole, Mole Ratios, Determine an Empirical Formula, Preparation of Solutions, Evaluate Chemical Reactions, Types of Chemical Reactions, Predict Chemical Reactions, Identify Unknowns Through Stoichiometry, Determination of Reaction Output, Formation of Barium Iodate, Hess's Law and the Combustion of a Metal, The Heat of Melting Ice, Albedo and Composition of Earth's Surface, Climate Change and Keeping Cool, Measure Acid Strength, Titrations–The Study of Acid-Base Chemistry, Analysis of Buffer Solutions and Ranges, Explore Iron Corrosion, Metal Activity, Green Chemistry Analysis of a Mixture **Engineering Design Challenge:** Build a Film Canister Rocket **Digital Activities:** Understanding Stoichiometry, Limiting Reagent, Modeling Gemstone Color Formation

	Performance-Based Assessments: Gravimetric Analysis of Periodic Trends, Road Deicers, Analysis of Basic Copper Carbonate, Identify Evidence of Chemical Reactions, Enthalpy of a Neutralization Reaction, Cartesian Divers, Quantitative Analysis of Acid Rain, Battery Challenge, Prepare and Characterize Biodiesel, Natural Radiation
SCIENCE AND ENGINEERING PRACTICES	**WHERE TO FIND IT...**
SEP-6 Constructing Explanations (for Science)	**SE, Vol. 1:** 5, 8, 27, 40, 41, 43, 46, 47, 67, 72, 76, 80, 100, 114, 121, 135, 138, 148, 150, 151, 169, 182, 221, 224, 240, 244, 246, 251, 275, 294, 305, 306 **SE, Vol. 2:** 40, 52, 72, 79, 81, 92, 117, 161, 165, 170, 182, 187, 191, 197, 217, 221, 227, 234, 252, 270, 271, 280, 291, 296, 318, 326, 329, 330, 331, 343, 346, 350, 368, 372, 377, 386, 389, 397, 398, 406, 414, 420, 423, 426, 430, 433 **Inquiry Labs:** Investigate Metallic Bonds, Investigate Covalent Bonds, Intermolecular Forces, Chemical Names and Formulas, Investigate Surface Tension, Aqueous Solutions, Determine an Empirical Formula, Identify Unknowns Through Stoichiometry, Formation of Barium Iodate, The Heat of Melting Ice, Compressibility, Relationships Between Gas Variables, The Ideal Gas Law, Gas Diffusion, Feedback and Climate Change, Energy in the Atmosphere, How Melting Ice Affects Sea Level, Carbon Dioxide and Its Role in Climate, How Nature Records Changes in Climate, Solar Cell Technology, Supersaturation and Thermodynamics, Measure Acid Strength, Titrations–The Study of Acid-Base Chemistry, Analysis of Buffer Solutions and Ranges, The pH of Seawater, The Fate of Carbonate in Acidifying Oceans, Ester Synthesis, Protein and Amino Acid Tests, Radioactive Decay, Nuclear Radiation and Shielding, Investigate the Toxicity of Road Deicers, Green Chemistry Analysis of a Mixture, How to Recycle Polylactic Acid Plastics **Digital Activities:** Reactivity of Metals, Cation Meets Anion, Going for a Hike, Climate Change and Fire, Reaction Rates and Activation Energy, Exploring Acid Strength and Concentration, Redox and Non-Redox Reactions, Modeling Gemstone Color Formation, Identifying Types of Organic Compounds, Protein Structure and Food Design, Geologic Variation and Radon Levels, Paper Mill Wastewater Treatment **Performance-Based Assessments:** Qualitative Analysis and Chemical Bonding, Analysis of Basic Copper Carbonate, The Stoichiometry of Filling a Balloon, Microhabitat in a Bottle, Climate Change and the Carbon Cycle, Calcium Carbonate and Shell Production, Prepare and Characterize Biodiesel, Natural Radiation, Make the Chemistry Lab Greener
SEP-6 Designing Solutions (for Engineering)	**SE, Vol. 1:** 16, 140, 157, 202, 218, 288 **SE, Vol. 2:** 10, 18, 38, 47, 193, 290, 311, 339 **Inquiry Labs:** Determination of Reaction Output, Feedback and Climate Change, How Melting Ice Affects Sea Level, Observe Air Pollution, How Nature Records Changes in Climate, Model Climate Change with Melting Ice, The Fate of Carbonate in Acidifying Oceans, Investigate Different Hydrocarbons, Ester Synthesis, Protein and Amino Acid Tests, Radioactive Decay **Performance-Based Assessment:** Microhabitat in a Bottle **Engineering Design Challenges:** Build a Spectroscope from Household Materials, Growing Crystals in Gel, Evaluate Metals for a Commercial Application, Abrasive Compounds, Building a Better Bike, An Empirical Formula Challenge, Water Purification, Flameless Heating Systems, Design a Green Roof, Use Equilibrium for a Commercial Application, Design a Model of Ocean Acidification, Polymers: Bouncy Balls, Uses and Production of Ash Water

NGSS CORRELATION

SCIENCE AND ENGINEERING PRACTICES	WHERE TO FIND IT...
SEP-7 Engaging in Argument from Evidence	**SE, Vol. 1:** 16, 140, 157, 202, 218, 288 **SE, Vol. 2:** 10, 18, 38, 47, 193, 290, 311, 339 **Inquiry Labs:** Determination of Reaction Output, Feedback and Climate Change, How Melting Ice Affects Sea Level, Observe Air Pollution, How Nature Records Changes in Climate, Model Climate Change with Melting Ice, The Fate of Carbonate in Acidifying Oceans, Investigate Different Hydrocarbons, Ester Synthesis, Protein and Amino Acid Tests, Radioactive Decay **Performance-Based Assessment:** Microhabitat in a Bottle **Engineering Design Challenges:** Build a Spectroscope from Household Materials, Growing Crystals in Gel, Evaluate Metals for a Commercial Application, Abrasive Compounds, Building a Better Bike, An Empirical Formula Challenge, Water Purification, Flameless Heating Systems, Design a Green Roof, Use Equilibrium for a Commercial Application, Design a Model of Ocean Acidification, Polymers: Bouncy Balls, Uses and Production of Ash Water

SCIENCE AND ENGINEERING PRACTICES	WHERE TO FIND IT...
SEP-8 Obtaining, Communicating, and Evaluating Information	**SE, Vol. 1:** 16, 140, 157, 202, 218, 288 **SE, Vol. 2:** 10, 18, 38, 47, 193, 290, 311, 339 **Inquiry Labs:** Determination of Reaction Output, Feedback and Climate Change, How Melting Ice Affects Sea Level, Observe Air Pollution, How Nature Records Changes in Climate, Model Climate Change with Melting Ice, The Fate of Carbonate in Acidifying Oceans, Investigate Different Hydrocarbons, Ester Synthesis, Protein and Amino Acid Tests, Radioactive Decay **Performance-Based Assessment:** Microhabitat in a Bottle **Engineering Design Challenges:** Build a Spectroscope from Household Materials, Growing Crystals in Gel, Evaluate Metals for a Commercial Application, Abrasive Compounds, Building a Better Bike, An Empirical Formula Challenge, Water Purification, Flameless Heating Systems, Design a Green Roof, Use Equilibrium for a Commercial Application, Design a Model of Ocean Acidification, Polymers: Bouncy Balls, Uses and Production of Ash Water

Common Core State Standards for English Language Arts and Literacy in Science

The *Experience Chemistry* program engages students in reading, writing, speaking, and listening practices that connect to the Next Generation Science Standards.

READING STANDARDS	WHERE TO FIND IT...
RST.9-10.7 Translate quantitative or technical information expressed in words in a text into visual form (e.g., a table or chart) and translate information expressed visually or mathematically (e.g., in an equation) into words.	**SE, Vol. 1:** 14, 16, 17, 18, 21, 23, 48, 52, 57, 59 **Inquiry Labs:** Bean Bag Isotopes (Open and Advanced versions), Evaluate Atomic Spectra, Evaluate the Bohr Model of the Atom, Model Electron Configuration, Develop a Periodic Table, Elemental Metals, Nonmetals, and Metalloids, Periodic Trends and Properties **Digital Worksheets:** Physical Properties of Gaseous Elements, Reflect on Periodic Trends
RST.11-12.1 Cite specific textual evidence to support analysis of science and technical texts, attending to important distinctions the author makes and to any gaps or inconsistencies in the account.	**Authentic Readings:** Firework Colors Chemistry; Meet 115, the Newest Element on the Periodic Table; Charging Ahead: The Future of Batteries; Antarctica's Blood Red Waterfall; An Unexpected Side Effect of Drought: Higher Carbon Emissions; Is Geoengineering the Answer to Climate Change?; Fishless Lake in Adirondacks Shows Signs of Recovery; Boring Sponges; Fusion Start-ups; Androscoggin River Restoration
RST.11-12.2 Determine the central ideas or conclusions of a text; summarize complex concepts, processes, or information presented in a text by paraphrasing them in simpler but still accurate terms.	**SE, Vol. 2:** 97, 237, 245 **Authentic Readings:** Firework Colors Chemistry; Meet 115, the Newest Element on the Periodic Table; Charging Ahead: The Future of Batteries; Antarctica's Blood Red Waterfall; An Unexpected Side Effect of Drought: Higher Carbon Emissions; Is Geoengineering the Answer to Climate Change?; Fishless Lake in Adirondacks Shows Signs of Recovery; Boring Sponges; Fusion Start-ups; Androscoggin River Restoration
RST.11-12.7 Integrate and evaluate multiple sources of information presented in diverse formats and media (e.g., quantitative data, video, multimedia) in order to address a question or solve a problem.	**Engineering Design Challenges:** Build a Spectroscope from Household Materials, Growing Crystals in Gel, Evaluate Metals for a Commercial Application, Abrasive Compounds, Building a Better Bike, An Empirical Formula Challenge, Water Purification, Build a Film Canister Rocket, Flameless Heating Systems, What's in a Container?, Design a Green Roof, Use Equilibrium for a Commercial Application, Design a Natural pH Indicator, Design a Model of Ocean Acidification, Polymers: Bouncy Balls, Uses and Production of Ash Water, Plastic from Biowaste **Problem-Based Learning:** Minerals, Crystals, and Gemstones; The Chemistry of Cooking and the Properties of Baked Goods; Water as a Greenhouse Gas; Reducing Carbon Footprints; Sustainable Off-Grid Energy
RST.11-12.8 Evaluate the hypotheses, data, analysis, and conclusions in a science or technical text, verifying the data when possible and corroborating or challenging conclusions with other sources of information.	**Authentic Readings:** Meet 115, the Newest Element on the Periodic Table; Charging Ahead: The Future of Batteries; Antarctica's Blood Red Waterfall; An Unexpected Side Effect of Drought: Higher Carbon Emissions; Is Geoengineering the Answer to Climate Change?; Fishless Lake in Adirondacks Shows Signs of Recovery; Boring Sponges; Fusion Start-ups; Androscoggin River Restoration
RST.11-12.9 Synthesize information from a range of sources (e.g., texts, experiments, simulations) into a coherent understanding of a process, phenomenon, or concept, resolving conflicting information when possible.	**Problem-Based Learning:** Minerals, Crystals, and Gemstones; The Chemistry of Cooking and the Properties of Baked Goods; Water as a Greenhouse Gas; Reducing Carbon Footprints; Sustainable Off-Grid Energy **Digital Worksheet:** The Cost of Fighting Corrosion

NGSS CORRELATION

WRITING STANDARDS	WHERE TO FIND IT...
WHST.9-12.2 Write informative/explanatory texts, including the narration of historical events, scientific procedures/ experiments, or technical processes. **a.** Introduce a topic and organize complex ideas, concepts, and information so that each new element builds on that which precedes it to create a unified whole; include formatting (e.g., headings), graphics (e.g., figures, tables), and multimedia when useful to aiding comprehension. **b.** Develop the topic thoroughly by selecting the most significant and relevant facts, extended definitions, concrete details, quotations, or other information and examples appropriate to the audience's knowledge of the topic. **c.** Use varied transitions and sentence structures to link the major sections of the text, create cohesion, and clarify the relationships among complex ideas and concepts. **d.** Use precise language, domain-specific vocabulary and techniques such as metaphor, simile, and analogy to manage the complexity of the topic; convey a knowledgeable stance in a style that responds to the discipline and context as well as to the expertise of likely readers. **e.** Provide a concluding statement or section that follows from and supports the information or explanation provided (e.g., articulating implications or the significance of the topic).	**SE, Vol. 1:** 43, 49, 55, 58, 59, 63, 64, 65, 71, 72, 73, 75, 76, 77, 78, 79, 80, 88, 90, 96, 103, 107, 215, 224, 236, 248, 249 **SE, Vol. 2:** 161, 165, 167, 170, 173, 180, 229, 234, 237, 241, 243, 248, 249, 250, 252, 263, 266 **Inquiry Labs:** Elemental Metals, Nonmetals, and Metalloids; Periodic Trends and Properties; Characteristics of Ionic Bonds; Investigate Metallic Compounds; Investigate Covalent Bonds; Intermolecular Forces, Chemical Names and Formulas; Evaluate Chemical Reactions; Types of Chemical Reactions, Predict Chemical Reactions; Reaction Rates: Iodine Clock (Open and Advanced versions); Collision Theory, Explore Chemical Equilibrium; Calcium Carbonate and Shell Production; Carbon Dioxide Levels in Water, Ocean Currents; The Fate of Carbonate in Acidifying Oceans; Investigate Different Hydrocarbons; Protein and Amino Acid Tests **Digital Worksheets:** Thermodynamic Favorability of Combustion, Energy Density of Foods, A Bushel of Radiation Units
WHST.9-12.5 Develop and strengthen writing as needed by planning, revising, editing, rewriting, or trying a new approach, focusing on addressing what is most significant for a specific purpose and audience.	**SE, Vol. 1:** 71, 76, 224, 240, 246, 248 **SE, Vol. 2:** 213, 216, 217, 219, 221, 224, 225
WHST.9-12.7 Conduct short as well as more sustained research projects to answer a question (including a self-generated question) or solve a problem; narrow or broaden the inquiry when appropriate; synthesize multiple sources on the subject, demonstrating understanding of the subject under investigation.	**SE, Vol. 1:** 111, 165, 218, 300 **SE, Vol. 2:** 25, 193, 227 **Engineering Design Challenges:** Build a Spectroscope from Household Materials; Growing Crystals in Gel, Evaluate Metals for a Commercial Application, Abrasive Compounds, Building a Better Bike, An Empirical Formula Challenge, Water Purification, Build a Film Canister Rocket, Flameless Heating Systems, What's in a Container?, Design a Green Roof, Use Equilibrium for a Commercial Application, Design a Natural pH Indicator, Design a Model of Ocean Acidification, Polymers: Bouncy Balls, Uses and Production of Ash Water, Plastic from Biowaste **Problem-Based Learning:** Minerals, Crystals, and Gemstones; The Chemistry of Cooking and the Properties of Baked Goods; Water as a Greenhouse Gas; Reducing Carbon Footprints; Sustainable Off-Grid Energy **Digital Worksheets:** Nature of Science in Gas Laws, Energy Storage Technologies, Getting the Lead Out, Research Recycling Rates
WHST.9-12.9 Draw evidence from informational texts to support analysis, reflection, and research.	**SE, Vol. 1:** 73, 75, 76, 77, 78, 79, 80, 86, 88, 90, 95, 96, 98, 103, 114, 117, 119, 121, 123, 129, 131, 135, 138, 148, 155, 159, 162, 164, 169, 170, 171, 218, 236, 240, 244, 246, 248, 287 **SE, Vol. 2:** 38, 197, 213, 219, 224, 225 **Authentic Readings:** Meet 115, the Newest Element on the Periodic Table; Charging Ahead: The Future of Batteries; Antarctica's Blood Red Waterfall; An Unexpected Side Effect of Drought: Higher Carbon Emissions; Is Geoengineering the Answer to Climate Change?; Fishless Lake in Adirondacks Shows Signs of Recovery; Boring Sponges; Fusion Start-ups; Androscoggin River Restoration **Digital Worksheets:** Gas Volume and Temperature, Limnic Eruptions and CO_2

WRITING STANDARDS	WHERE TO FIND IT...
WHST.11-12.8 Gather relevant information from multiple authoritative print and digital sources, using advanced searches effectively; assess the strengths and limitations of each source in terms of the specific task, purpose, and audience; integrate information into the text selectively to maintain the flow of ideas, avoiding plagiarism and overreliance on any one source and following a standard format for citation.	**Engineering Design Challenges:** Build a Spectroscope from Household Materials, Growing Crystals in Gel, Evaluate Metals for a Commercial Application, Abrasive Compounds, Building a Better Bike, An Empirical Formula Challenge, Water Purification, Build a Film Canister Rocket, Flameless Heating Systems, What's in a Container?, Design a Green Roof, Use Equilibrium for a Commercial Application, Design a Natural pH Indicator, Design a Model of Ocean Acidification, Polymers: Bouncy Balls, Uses and Production of Ash Water, Plastic from Biowaste **Problem-Based Learning:** Minerals, Crystals, and Gemstones; The Chemistry of Cooking and the Properties of Baked Goods; Water as a Greenhouse Gas; Reducing Carbon Footprints; Sustainable Off-Grid Energy

SPEAKING AND LISTENING STANDARDS	WHERE TO FIND IT...
SL.11-12.5 Make strategic use of digital media (e.g., textual, graphical, audio, visual, and interactive elements) in presentations to enhance understanding of findings, reasoning, and evidence and to add interest.	**Problem-Based Learning:** Minerals, Crystals, and Gemstones; Water as a Greenhouse Gas; Reducing Carbon Footprints; Sustainable Off-Grid Energy

Common Core State Standards for Mathematics

The *Experience Chemistry* program engages students in mathematical practices that connect to the Next Generation Science Standards.

MATH STANDARDS	WHERE TO FIND IT...
MP.2 Reason abstractly and quantitatively.	**SE, Vol. 1:** 126, 127, 134, 163, 164, 187, 191, 194, 204, 252, 253, 255, 257, 266, 270, 271, 273, 279, 292, 293, 294, 301, 303, 304 **SE, Vol. 2:** 62, 71, 73, 74, 80, 87, 90, 93, 94, 101, 105, 109, 113, 121, 128, 137, 138, 146, 147, 153, 200, 213, 219, 234, 239, 253, 261, 267 **Inquiry Labs:** Characteristics of Ionic Bonds, Intermolecular Forces, Material Properties and Bond Type, Measure the Energy of a Phase Change, Melt Ionic and Covalent Compounds, Modeling Metals, Ceramics, and Polymers, Investigate Surface Tension, Aqueous Solutions, Describe Small-scale Matter Using the Mole, Mole Ratios, Determine an Empirical Formula, Preparation of Solutions, Evaluate Chemical Reactions, Types of Chemical Reactions, Predict Chemical Reactions, Identify Unknowns Through Stoichiometry, Determination of Reaction Output, Formation of Barium Iodate, The Thermodynamics of Hand Warmers, Hess's Law and the Combustion of a Metal, The Heat of Melting Ice, Feedback and Climate Change, Energy in the Atmosphere, Albedo and Composition of Earth's Surface, How Melting Ice Affects Sea Level, Observe Air Pollution, Carbon Dioxide and Its Role in Climate, How Nature Records Changes in Climate, Human Activity and Carbon Emissions, Model Climate Change with Melting Ice, Climate Change and Keeping Cool, Solar Cell Technology, Reaction Rates: Iodine Clock, Collision Theory, Explore Chemical Equilibrium, Measure Acid Strength, Titrations–The Study of Acid-Base Chemistry, Analysis of Buffer Solutions and Ranges, Calcium Carbonate and Shell Production, Carbon Dioxide Levels in Water, Ocean Currents, The Fate of Carbonate in Acidifying Oceans, Build a Micro Battery, Investigate the Toxicity of Road Deicers, Green Chemistry Analysis of a Mixture, How to Recycle Polylactic Acid Plastics
MP.4 Model with mathematics.	**SE, Vol. 1:** 87, 89, 100, 116, 117, 126, 127, 152, 225, 288, 290, 293, 304 **SE, Vol. 2:** 62, 73, 74, 75, 78, 80, 87, 90, 105, 108, 109, 110, 111, 112, 113, 116, 119, 121, 126, 128, 134, 135, 138, 146, 147, 153, 233, 239, 250, 253, 256, 259, 261, 267, 364, 365, 366, 367, 370, 374, 388, 394 **Inquiry Labs:** Investigate Metallic Compounds, Investigate Covalent Bonds, Chemical Names and Formulas, Measure the Energy of a Phase Change, Melt Ionic and Covalent Compounds, Evaluate Chemical Reactions, Types of Chemical Reactions, Predict Chemical Reactions, The Thermodynamics of Hand Warmers, Hess's Law and the Combustion of a Metal, The Heat of Melting Ice, Feedback and Climate Change, Energy in the Atmosphere, Albedo and Composition of Earth's Surface, Observe Air Pollution, Carbon Dioxide and Its Role in Climate, How Nature Records Changes in Climate, Human Activity and Carbon Emissions, Model Climate Change with Melting Ice, Climate Change and Keeping Cool, Solar Cell Technology, Calcium Carbonate and Shell Production, Carbon Dioxide Levels in Water, Ocean Currents, The Fate of Carbonate in Acidifying Oceans, Build a Micro Battery, Radioactive Decay, Nuclear Energy, Nuclear Radiation and Shielding

MATH STANDARDS	WHERE TO FIND IT...
HSN-Q.A.1 Use units as a way to understand problems and to guide the solution of multi-step problems; choose and interpret units consistently in formulas; choose and interpret the scale and the origin in graphs and data displays.	**SE, Vol. 1:** 57, 116, 125, 126, 127, 128, 131, 134, 152, 153, 163, 167, 175, 177, 179, 180, 181, 182, 185, 186, 187, 188, 189, 191, 193, 195, 197, 199, 204, 205, 206, 208, 209, 211, 223, 225, 226, 253, 255, 257, 258, 259, 260, 261, 263, 264, 265, 267, 268, 271, 272, 273, 276, 277, 278, 279, 281, 285, 286, 287, 288, 289, 290, 291, 292, 293, 294, 295, 296, 297, 298, 299, 300, 301, 302, 303, 304, 305 **SE, Vol. 2:** 11, 12, 13, 14, 15, 17, 20, 21, 24, 25, 28, 90, 93, 99, 108, 121, 146, 147, 153, 161, 162, 169, 170, 171, 200, 201, 214, 218, 219, 220, 223, 230, 233, 236, 239, 240, 241, 251, 252, 253, 256, 259, 261, 269, 297, 301, 375, 389, 405, 411, 419 **Inquiry Labs:** Describe Small-scale Matter Using the Mole, Mole Ratios, Determine an Empirical Formula, Preparation of Solutions, Identify Unknowns Through Stoichiometry, Determination of Reaction Output, Formation of Barium Iodate, Hess's Law and the Combustion of a Metal, The Heat of Melting Ice, Relationships Between Gas Variables, The Ideal Gas Law, Feedback and Climate Change, Energy in the Atmosphere, Titrations–The Study of Acid-Base Chemistry, Analysis of Buffer Solutions and Ranges, Calcium Carbonate and Shell Production, Carbon Dioxide Levels in Water, The Fate of Carbonate in Acidifying Oceans, Build a Micro Battery, Radioactive Decay, Nuclear Energy, Nuclear Radiation and Shielding
HSN-Q.A.2 Define appropriate quantities for the purpose of descriptive modeling.	**SE, Vol. 1:** 112, 143, 166, 175, 207, 220, 231, 269, 281, 286, 293 **SE, Vol. 2:** 164, 178, 277, 282, 287, 300, 316 **Inquiry Labs:** The Heat of Melting Ice, Titrations–The Study of Acid-Base Chemistry
HSN-Q.A.3 Choose a level of accuracy appropriate to limitations on measurement when reporting quantities.	**SE, Vol. 1:** 87, 116, 132, 167, 175, 177, 179, 180, 181, 185, 186, 189, 191, 193, 195, 197, 199, 206, 211, 223, 226, 255, 263, 265, 267, 268, 273, 276, 277, 285, 286, 288, 289, 292, 293, 295, 297, 298, 301, 303 **SE, Vol. 2:** 12, 14, 20, 24, 25, 33, 121, 146, 147, 162, 198, 200, 201, 214, 218, 220, 369, 375, 411 **Inquiry Labs:** Characteristics of Ionic Bonds, Describe Small-scale Matter Using the Mole, Mole Ratios, Determine an Empirical Formula, Preparation of Solutions, Identify Unknowns Through Stoichiometry, Determination of Reaction Output, Formation of Barium Iodate, The Thermodynamics of Hand Warmers, Hess's Law and the Combustion of a Metal, The Heat of Melting Ice, Relationships Between Gas Variables, The Ideal Gas Law, Feedback and Climate Change, Energy in the Atmosphere, Albedo and Composition of Earth's Surface, Observe Air Pollution, How Nature Records Changes in Climate, Model Climate Change with Melting Ice, Climate Change and Keeping Cool, Solar Cell Technology, Titrations–The Study of Acid-Base Chemistry, Analysis of Buffer Solutions and Ranges, Calcium Carbonate and Shell Production, Build a Micro Battery, Ester Synthesis, Radioactive Decay, Nuclear Energy, Nuclear Radiation and Shielding
HSA-SSE.A.1 Interpret expressions that represent a quantity in terms of its context.	**SE, Vol. 1:** 73, 76 **SE, Vol. 2:** 375, 419 **Digital Worksheet:** Interpret Emission Spectra
HSA-SSE.B.3 Choose and produce an equivalent form of an expression to reveal and explain properties of the quantity represented by the expression.	**SE, Vol. 1:** 167 **Digital Worksheet:** Interpret Emission Spectra

Atoms, Elements, and Molecules

In this storyline, students explore electron energy levels, atomic orbitals, and electron configurations. They discover patterns [CCC-1] in the periodic table and connect that to properties [PS1.A] of the elements in the table. Students investigate different types of chemical bonds. They explore intermolecular forces and attractions between molecules.

ANCHORING PHENOMENON

What distinguishes the minerals in this mountain?

Explaining Phenomena Students apply what they learn about atoms and their properties, and the bonds within and between molecules, to explain what distinguishes one mineral from another.

	INVESTIGATION 1	INVESTIGATION 2
OVERVIEW	**Atomic Structure** **11.5 days** Students investigate the structure and properties of atoms and the atomic emission spectra of elements. They gain knowledge of the electron configurations of atoms.	**The Periodic Table** **7.5 days** Students explore how the trends in the periodic table are used to identify the atomic structure of elements and how the trends are related.
INVESTIGATIVE PHENOMENON†	What causes the colors in a fireworks display?	Why are elements in pure form so rare?
CONNECTION TO THE ANCHORING PHENOMENON	Students relate the properties of atoms to the differences in mineral properties, and the atomic emission spectra of elements to light emitted by fireworks.	Students explain periodic trends of elements in relation to the differences in minerals.
EXPERIENCES‡	1 **The Particle Nature of Matter** (2 days), pp. 6–11 2 **Modeling Atoms** (2 days), pp. 13–21 3 **Atomic Emission Spectra and the Bohr Model** (2 days), pp. 22–27 4 **Modern Atomic Theory** (2 days), pp. 28–32 5 **Electrons in Atoms** (2 days), pp. 33–40	1 **The Periodic Table: An Overview** (2 days), pp. 44–49 2 **The Periodic Table and Atomic Structure** (2 days), pp. 50–55 3 **Periodic Trends** (2 days), pp. 56–64
INVESTIGATION EVALUATION§	**Performance-Based Assessment** Evaluate Atomic Structure with Flame Tests **3-D Assessment** Atomic Structure **Experience Notebook** Performance-Based Assessment, p. 41; **Appendix C** Problem Bank, pp. R10–R11	**Performance-Based Assessment** Gravimetric Analysis of Periodic Trends **3-D Assessment** The Periodic Table **Experience Notebook** Performance-Based Assessment, p. 65; **Appendix C** Problem Bank, pp. R11–R12
NEXT GENERATION SCIENCE STANDARDS	HS-PS1-1	HS-PS1-1, HS-PS1-2

*Pacing for Encounter Anchoring Phenomenon core instruction is a half-day.

†Pacing for Encounter Investigative Phenomenon core instruction is a half-day per Investigation.

‡Pacing for each Experience includes the Experience Notebook and core instructional activities.

§Pacing for core Investigation Assessment is approximately 1 day per Investigation.

GOT MORE TIME? Personalize and enhance your instructional plan by assigning the activities with the got-more-time icon, as time allows.

Anchoring Phenomenon Video Crystal Formations*

Experience Notebook Inquiry Launch, p. 2*

Problem-Based Learning Experience Minerals, Crystals, and Gemstones

INVESTIGATION 3

Chemical Bonding

11.5 days

Students explore different types of compounds and their properties. They investigate types of bonds and the intermolecular forces of bonds.

Why do gems have different properties than metals?

Students explain how differences in bonding produce differences in properties of gems and metals and apply the knowledge to explain how minerals are distinguished from one another.

Performance-Based Assessment Qualitative Analysis and Chemical Bonding

3-D Assessment Chemical Bonding

Experience Notebook Performance-Based Assessment, p. 107; Revisit Anchoring Phenomenon, p. 107; **Appendix C** Problem Bank, pp. R12–R13

HS-PS1-2, HS-PS1-3, HS-PS1-7, HS-PS2-4, HS-PS3-5

STORYLINE ASSESSMENT

Problem-Based Learning Experience Minerals, Crystals, and Gemstones

Benchmark 3-D Assessment Storylines 1 and 2

Notes:

STORYLINE 1

Atoms, Elements, and Molecules

Teacher Background

Understanding matter requires knowledge of the types of atoms in matter and the interactions between and within the atoms. Atoms are too small to be seen with the unaided eye, but they have even smaller substructures of their own—protons, neutrons, and electrons. Each element is defined by the number of protons in its nucleus. All matter is made up of only slightly more than 100 different elements, which combine in different ways to form molecules.

The periodic table includes all the elements arranged horizontally by increasing atomic number and vertically by families of elements with related chemical properties. The table's pattern is also related to the outermost electron patterns, which are important in understanding chemical reactivity and bond formation.

Points of Integration

In this Storyline, links are made across the domains of physical science, Earth and space science; and science, technology, and society.

Earth and Space Science As you teach the structure of atoms in Investigation 1, make connections with how stars produce elements over their lifetimes [ESS1.A].

Science, Technology, and Society As students learn about atoms, elements, and molecules, introduce them to how materials scientists are engineering at the atomic and molecular levels. Ask them to determine how these processes are useful in technology and society [ETS1.B]. Students can research metal organic frameworks, a new discovery that offers an inexpensive and fast way to engineer materials.

ENCOUNTER

ANCHORING PHENOMENON

What distinguishes the minerals in this mountain?

The Rainbow Mountains of Peru formed when that Nazca plate subducted under the South American plate and caused the mountains to uplift. Tectonic activity caused these mountains to tilt, exposing the unique striping patterns. The colorful stripes are caused by the distinctive mineralogy in the area. The red stripes indicate that iron oxide is present as a trace mineral; the yellow strips are from iron sulfide present as a trace mineral.

The Rainbow Mountains are an example of how slight elemental changes in minerals can yield dramatic visual changes. As students progress through the storyline, they will connect how atoms, elements, and molecules relate to the structure of minerals, crystals, and gems.

RELATED PHENOMENA

In addition to the Rainbow Mountains of Peru, consider using other phenomena as anchoring events for this storyline.

China's Rainbow Mountains Find photos of Zhangye National Geopark in Gansu, China. Compare the minerals in these rainbow mountains with those in the Rainbow Mountains of Peru.

Why Are They Different? Display some examples of pure elements, such as copper, magnesium, and carbon. Discuss with students why they think these samples have such different properties.

Crystal Formations

Anchoring Phenomenon Video Sodium chloride has a cubic crystal system, which is one of the most common types of crystal systems. Many metallic elements also have cubic structures. In the video, the cubic nature of the NaCl crystals is shown in the center of the water droplet.

- **Ask** Why are some of the crystals square shaped? (NaCl crystals are face-centered cubic systems. Their sides grow at right angles to each other.)
- **Ask** What happens when two crystals touch? (The crystals grow together irregularly.)
- **Ask** What would happen if you removed a crystal from the solution? (The crystal would not change unless the air was very damp. If the air was humid enough it could dissolve the crystal.)

Students will revisit this phenomenon at the end of the storyline to demonstrate their understanding of it.

Anchoring Phenomenon Video: Crystal Formations

Inquiry Launch

Experience Notebook Ask students what they know about the structure of rocks. Lead them to understand that most rocks are made up of minerals that have a crystalline structure. Discuss different kinds of minerals that students are familiar with, and compare and contrast their properties. (You may wish to show students some photos of very colorful minerals.) Then ask student pairs to answer these questions in their science notebooks.

- **Ask** What do you think causes the differences in the colors of the minerals in the Rainbow Mountains? (The color differences in the minerals are due to differences in the atoms and molecules making up the minerals.)
- Point out that the different layers in the mountains in the picture were laid down at different times during Earth's history. **Ask** What do you think caused the rock layers to have so many different colors at different periods on Earth? (The environment of the area changed over time, and as a result the materials that were available to form the minerals differed.)

Allow time for students to present their ideas. Then as a class brainstorm ideas for an experiment that would yield evidence that helps explain the phenomenon. Tell students that they will learn more about this phenomenon as they complete the PBL activity.

Experience Notebook, pp. 2–3

eTEXT

Minerals, Crystals, and Gemstones

Problem-Based Learning Experience Students research chromium, magnesium, and vanadium to determine what color each element produces in an aqueous solution. They also research the different colors of quartz and gemstones and what trace elements make the different colors. Students explore different crystal structures and then grow their own crystals. They identify which conditions produced the largest crystals and the crystal in the shortest amount of time.

- Before students start the activity, have them explain how they think minerals, crystals, and gemstones are similar and different. After the activity, have students revise their explanations based on their research and observations. Have students share their revised explanations with the class.
- Encourage students to include drawings, photos, and other images in their notes as they complete the activity.
- Consider having each group follow a different protocol for making their crystals; for example, using chenille stems versus string as the growing medium.
- For struggling or special needs students, guide them through each part of the activity. You may want to provide reliable Web sites for students to conduct research. You may also want to provide tables and graphic organizers for students to collect data and take notes.

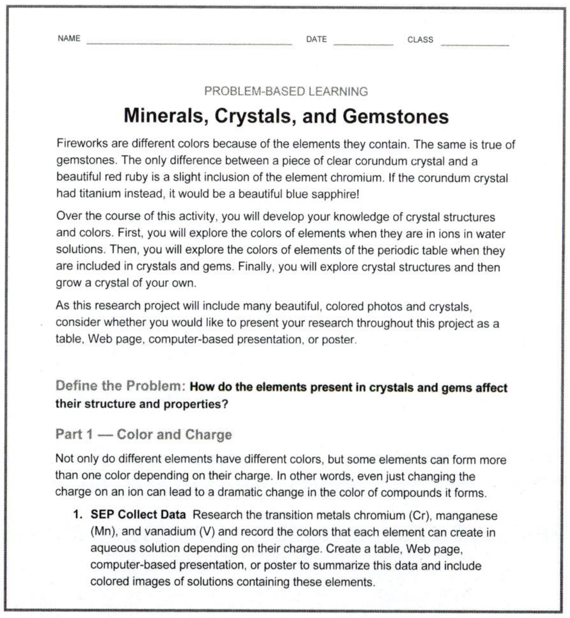
NAME ______ DATE ______ CLASS ______

PROBLEM-BASED LEARNING

Minerals, Crystals, and Gemstones

Fireworks are different colors because of the elements they contain. The same is true of gemstones. The only difference between a piece of clear corundum crystal and a beautiful red ruby is a slight inclusion of the element chromium. If the corundum crystal had titanium instead, it would be a beautiful blue sapphire!

Over the course of this activity, you will develop your knowledge of crystal structures and colors. First, you will explore the colors of elements when they are in ions in water solutions. Then, you will explore the colors of elements of the periodic table when they are included in crystals and gems. Finally, you will explore crystal structures and then grow a crystal of your own.

As this research project will include many beautiful, colored photos and crystals, consider whether you would like to present your research throughout this project as a table, Web page, computer-based presentation, or poster.

Define the Problem: **How do the elements present in crystals and gems affect their structure and properties?**

Part 1 — Color and Charge

Not only do different elements have different colors, but some elements can form more than one color depending on their charge. In other words, even just changing the charge on an ion can lead to a dramatic change in the color of compounds it forms.

1. **SEP Collect Data** Research the transition metals chromium (Cr), manganese (Mn), and vanadium (V) and record the colors that each element can create in aqueous solution depending on their charge. Create a table, Web page, computer-based presentation, or poster to summarize this data and include colored images of solutions containing these elements.

PBL Experience Interactive Worksheet

Atomic Structure

In this investigation, students deepen their understanding of energy and matter [CCC-5] through a study of atomic structure [PS1.A]. Students apply the laws of conservation of energy and matter as they investigate and develop system models of the types of atoms and isotopes and other related phenomena.

INVESTIGATIVE PHENOMENON

What causes the colors in a fireworks display?

Explaining Phenomena Students explore atomic structure, including atomic numbers, mass number, atomic mass, and atomic theory. They explore the Bohr model and the quantum mechanical model and apply those to understanding energy and the stability in electron configurations and atomic emission spectra. Students use what they learn to explain how the colors in fireworks and differences in minerals are a result of a difference in atoms and elements.

	EXPERIENCE 1	EXPERIENCE 2
	The Particle Nature of Matter **2 days** Students build upon what they already know about atoms, elements, molecules, and the three states of matter. They investigate the flow of energy in a system.	**Modeling Atoms** **2 days** Students use mathematics to identify the mass number and atomic number of atoms. They sketch models of helium atoms with differing protons and use models to compare isotopes.
CONNECTION TO THE INVESTIGATIVE PHENOMENON	Students learn about the main types of energy and relate that information to the phenomenon of what causes the colors in a fireworks display.	Students model different types of atoms and relate them to the phenomenon of colors in a fireworks display.
ENGAGE	**Teacher's Guide** Everyday Phenomenon What's in My Sugar?, p. 10	**Teacher's Guide** Everyday Phenomenon Seeing Without Looking, p. 16
EXPLORE	**Inquiry Lab** Elements: The Building Blocks of Matter **Analyzing Data** Physical Properties of Gaseous Elements +	**Inquiry Lab** Bean Bag Isotopes **Analyzing Data** Explore Atomic Particles +
EXPLAIN	**Claim-Evidence-Reasoning** Phase Change as a Physical Change **Experience Notebook,** pp. 6–10	**Modeling** Model Isotopes **Animation** A Quick Look at the Parts of an Atom + **Experience Notebook,** pp. 12–21
ELABORATE	**Discussion Rubric** Physical vs. Chemical Change **Analyzing Data** Intensive and Extensive Properties +	**Discussion Rubric** Dissect Atom Composition **Analyzing Data** Determine Atomic Mass +
EVALUATE	**Quiz** The Particle Nature of Matter **Experience Notebook** Revisit Investigative Phenomenon, p. 11	**Quiz** Modeling Atoms **Experience Notebook** Revisit Investigative Phenomenon, p. 21

*Pacing for Encounter Investigative Phenomenon core instruction is a half-day.

†Pacing for core Investigation Assessment is approximately 1 day.

GOT MORE TIME? Personalize and enhance your instructional plan by assigning the activities with the got-more-time icon, as time allows.

Investigative Phenomenon Video Designed Explosions*

Modeling Model the Investigative Phenomenon*

Experience Notebook, p. 5*

Authentic Reading Firework Colors Chemistry ⊕

Virtual Reality Experience ⊕

EXPERIENCE 3	EXPERIENCE 4	EXPERIENCE 5
Atomic Emission Spectra and the Bohr Model **2 days** Students identify an element that produces an unknown emission spectrum. They reference Bohr's atomic model.	**Modern Atomic Theory** **2 days** Students relate the quantum mechanical model to the Bohr model. They explore the atomic orbitals and the relative energies of subshells.	**Electrons in Atoms** **2 days** Students practice writing electron configurations and identify the patterns in the electron configurations. They explore electron dot structures.
Students compare and contrast wavelengths of light emitted from different colors and relate this to the phenomenon of colors in a fireworks display.	Students use the concepts from quantum mechanical models and orbital energies to refine explanations of colors in a fireworks display.	Students write an electron configuration for the element responsible for one color of firework and use this to refine explanations of colors in a fireworks display.
Teacher's Guide Everyday Phenomenon The Colors of Water, p. 22	**Teacher's Guide** Everyday Phenomenon Quantized Energy, p. 29	**Teacher's Guide** Everyday Phenomenon Electron Hotel, p. 35
Inquiry Lab Evaluate Atomic Spectra **Analyzing Data** Interpret Emission Spectra ⊕	**Inquiry Lab** Evaluate the Bohr Model of the Atom **Interactivity** The Quantum Mechanical Model and Atomic Orbitals ⊕	**Inquiry Lab** Model Electron Configuration **Analyzing Data** Patterns in Electron Configurations ⊕
Claim-Evidence-Reasoning Emission Spectra of Elements **Experience Notebook,** pp. 22–26	**Claim-Evidence-Reasoning** Evaluate Atomic Models **Experience Notebook,** pp. 28–31	**Modeling** Model Electron Configurations **Animation** How to Write Electron Configurations ⊕ **Experience Notebook,** pp. 33–39
Discussion Rubric Critique Explanations of the Emission Spectra **Engineering Design Challenge** Build a Spectroscope from Household Materials ⊕	**Discussion Rubric** Evaluate Atomic Models **Writing About Science** The History of Atomic Models ⊕	**Peer Review Rubric** Evaluate Electron Configuration Models **Writing About Science** Properties of Atoms: Size vs. Mass ⊕
Quiz Atomic Emission Spectra and the Bohr Model **Experience Notebook** Revisit Investigative Phenomenon, p. 27	**Quiz** Modern Atomic Theory **Experience Notebook** Revisit Investigative Phenomenon, p. 32	**Quiz** Electrons in Atoms **Experience Notebook** Revisit Investigative Phenomenon, p. 40

INVESTIGATION ASSESSMENT

Performance-Based Assessment Evaluate Atomic Structure with Flame Tests†

3-D Assessment Atomic Structure†

Experience Notebook Performance-Based Assessment, p. 41; Revisit Anchoring Phenomenon, p. 41†; **Appendix C** Problem Bank, pp. R10–R11

INVESTIGATION 1

Atomic Structure

Teacher Background

Students should already have some background knowledge of atoms, protons, and electrons before beginning this investigation. In the first experience, students learn about the particle nature of matter, the physical properties of matter, and phase changes. The second experience introduces the concepts of isotopes, atomic mass, and average atomic mass. The remainder of this investigation covers the behavior and distribution of electrons inside the atom. Atomic emission spectra provided the experimental evidence for the existence of electron energy levels. Later experiments refined this model to include the *s*, *p*, *d*, and *f* atomic orbitals within energy levels. Finally, the locations and energies of electrons within these orbitals were described concisely using electron configurations.

This investigation helps students to make the connection between the number of protons in the nucleus and the arrangement of valence electrons available for chemical reactions. In order to do this, students must understand electron energy levels, atomic orbitals, and electron configurations.

Learning Progression

In this investigation, students explore models [SEP-2] of the interior of atoms and the protons, neutrons, and electrons that they are made of. Next, students investigate atomic emission spectra and the experimental evidence for the electron energy levels shown in the Bohr model. Students explore the quantum mechanical model of the atom and atomic orbitals. They investigate how to add electrons to atomic orbitals and how to describe the location of each electron in an atom using electron configurations.

During this investigation, students develop several models of the atom, discover patterns [CCC-1] in the periodic table that correspond to electron configurations, and learn how the structure of atoms leads to many observable properties [PS1.A]. Students learn to compute [SEP-5] an average atomic mass, analyze and interpret [SEP-4] atomic emission spectrum data, learn to use the atomic orbital model, and explain the layout of the periodic table.

RELATED PHENOMENA

In addition to fireworks, consider using other phenomena to launch this investigation.

- **Auroras** Display a few pictures of auroras from the Internet. Tell students that charged particles from the sun cause auroras. Ask students how they think the charged particles might react with the atmosphere to produce the colors of the auroras.
- **What Stars Are Made Of** Show students the Hubble Telescope's famous "Deep Field" image and lead a class discussion to examine how scientists can know what elements are found within distant stars, planets, and galaxies.
- **Colored-Flame Candles** Light a set of candles that burns in different colors. As students watch the candles burn with red, green, blue, and purple flames, ask them to write what they think is occurring during this phenomenon.

TAKE IT LOCAL

Ask students what colors of light they have observed in a fireworks display. Do they think the fireworks would be as popular if they displayed only one color? Discuss what they think causes the different colors of fireworks.

ENCOUNTER

INVESTIGATIVE PHENOMENON

What causes the colors in a fireworks display?

Start this investigation by asking students why they think fireworks produce different colors of light when they are set off. Students may first assume that different colors are produced by different types of matter. This question leads to an investigation into the particle nature of matter (Experience 1). Students then investigate what makes atoms of different elements unique (Experience 2).

Learning more about atomic structure causes students to wonder what specific part of the atom could produce the multicolor display (Experience 3). This leads to an investigation of electron transitions (Experience 4) and the spectrum of colors that each element can emit (Experience 5).

Designed Explosions

Investigative Phenomenon Video Have students watch the video of a fireworks show and ask them to record their observations. Remind students that their observations must be things that they actually saw in the video, not things they assume are happening. Tell students they might also rely upon personal experience/recollection that they can add to the record of evidence. Have students share their observations with a partner. While they are sharing, have each pair come up with one question from the video that their observations prompted. Call on each pair to share their questions and the observation(s) that prompted them.

Firework Colors Chemistry

Investigative Phenomenon Authentic Reading Students read about how luminescence and incandescence produce the colors of fireworks. They construct an explanation [SEP-6] about how different elements and compounds produce the colors of fireworks and about what happens if the firework mixture is not pure. Have students individually complete the worksheet, either in class or as homework. Then as a class discuss the answers.

Model the Phenomenon

Modeling Have students review the video and Authentic Reading activity to develop a model of the phenomenon they observed. Remind students that a model does not have to look like the object or process it represents, but students should be able to use it to explain and/or predict. Have students complete Question 1 of the Modeling worksheet.

Remind students that their understanding of the phenomenon will be incomplete at this stage, but that they will revisit this activity as they learn more. Make sure to provide students with an opportunity to revisit their models throughout the investigation as well as at the end of the investigation for further revision and peer review.

Reflect on the Phenomenon

Experience Notebook Transition to the opener pages for Investigation 1 in the Experience Notebook and discuss the question on the photo, "What causes the colors in a fireworks display?"

If students struggle, then guide them to use what they've learned in the video and the Modeling activity to answer the driving question. Additionally, at the end of each experience, direct students to complete the writing prompt to Reflect on the Investigative Phenomenon.

Investigative Phenomenon Video

Authentic Reading

Authentic Reading Interactive Worksheet

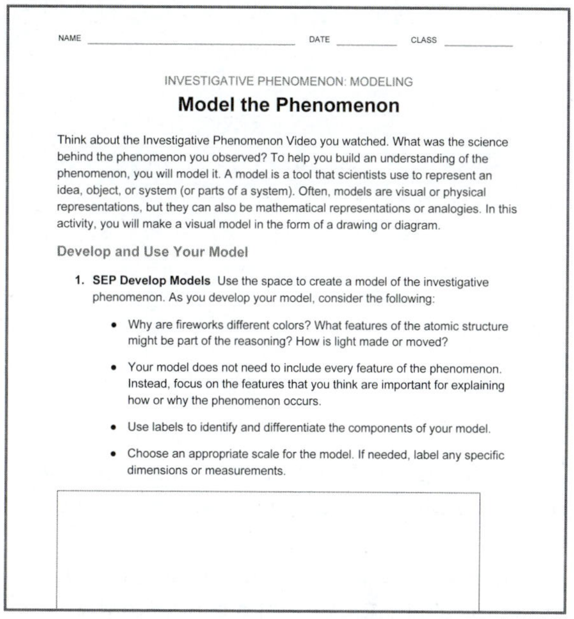

NAME ____________ DATE ________ CLASS ________

INVESTIGATIVE PHENOMENON: MODELING

Model the Phenomenon

Think about the Investigative Phenomenon Video you watched. What was the science behind the phenomenon you observed? To help you build an understanding of the phenomenon, you will model it. A model is a tool that scientists use to represent an idea, object, or system (or parts of a system). Often, models are visual or physical representations, but they can also be mathematical representations or analogies. In this activity, you will make a visual model in the form of a drawing or diagram.

Develop and Use Your Model

1. **SEP Develop Models** Use the space to create a model of the investigative phenomenon. As you develop your model, consider the following:
   - Why are fireworks different colors? What features of the atomic structure might be part of the reasoning? How is light made or moved?
   - Your model does not need to include every feature of the phenomenon. Instead, focus on the features that you think are important for explaining how or why the phenomenon occurs.
   - Use labels to identify and differentiate the components of your model.
   - Choose an appropriate scale for the model. If needed, label any specific dimensions or measurements.

Modeling Interactive Worksheet

Experience Notebook, pp. 4–5

eTEXT

EXPERIENCE 1

The Particle Nature of Matter

Teacher Background

Students will have been introduced to most of the content in this experience in their physical science classes, but these ideas will be reinforced through lab inquiries and the processes of analyzing data and constructing arguments using evidence and scientific reasoning. The content includes a brief discussion of the building blocks of matter, such as atoms and molecules, and how these particles are comprised of elements. Atomic and molecular models and descriptions of the three states of matter are presented. Students read about the main types of energy, including how oppositely charged particles have potential energy and will be attracted to each other when they are near each other. They relate the flow of energy to a system and its surroundings.

Objectives

- **Investigate and compare various properties of elements.**
- **Develop models to describe the atomic composition of simple molecules.**
- **Use particle-level models to explain interactions of energy and matter within a system.**
- **Use evidence to determine whether a physical or chemical change has occurred.**

ENGAGE

EVERYDAY PHENOMENON

What is sugar made of?

Use the teacher demo to prompt student discussion about how some matter is made of different kinds of atoms.

What's in My Sugar? (5)

Engage students with this demonstration of an everyday phenomenon to introduce the concept of atoms and molecules.

Materials Clear plastic cup with piece(s) of charcoal, labeled *Charcoal*; clear plastic cup with granulated sugar, labeled *Sugar*; capped test tube or jar, labeled *Hydrogen*; capped test tube or jar, labeled *Oxygen*

1. Display the four substances where students can see them. Give students 1 minute to discuss with a partner how the sugar is related to the other three substances. Then call on students to share their ideas.
2. Lead a discussion about how most matter is made of more than one kind of matter. Explain that sugar is made from carbon (the charcoal), oxygen, and hydrogen.
3. **Ask** If I mixed this oxygen, hydrogen, and charcoal, would sugar form? (no) Why or why not? Call on students to explain their thinking. Tell students that they will learn more about the substances that make up matter in this investigation. Remind them to apply what they learn in this demonstration to other activities in this investigation. Use the discussion to lead into the Inquiry Lab.

RELATED PHENOMENA

In addition to the What's in My Sugar? teacher demo, consider using other phenomena to launch this experience.

- **Changes in Wax** Introduce physical and chemical changes. Light a candle (not a dripless one). Have students observe the melting wax. Discuss that not all the wax forms drips of on the side of the candle. Point out that both mass and energy change during this process. **Ask** What happens to the rest of the wax? Why does some of the wax drip and the rest does not? Where does the energy come from to keep the candle burning?
- **Cola vs. Diet Cola** Show students a can of cola and a can of diet cola and note that their volumes are the same. Drop the cans into a plastic storage bin filled with water and tell students to observe what happens. Have students look at the labels on the cans and note that their masses are different. **Ask** Why is the mass of the regular cola so much larger than the mass of the diet cola? Relate this information to density.

EXPLORE

Elements: The Building Blocks of Matter

Inquiry Lab Students carry out an investigation [SEP-3] designed to familiarize themselves with different elements and the signs of a reaction while practicing their observational and measurement skills.

Lab Demo Video Watch the Lab Demo Video for advice on materials and preparation.

Choose Your Version Open-ended (O), Guided (G), Shortened (S), Advanced (A)

Materials aluminum strip, carbon rod, copper strip, 5 mL 1*M* copper(II) chloride solution, 5 mL 1*M* hydrochloric acid, 5 mL 3% hydrogen peroxide, iron strip, balance, 150-mL beaker, conductivity meter, Beral-type pipet, ruler, Vernier calipers, wash bottle, water

Safety A fume hood is required to safely conduct this experiment. Copper(II) chloride solution is a skin and eye irritant and is slightly toxic by ingestion. Hydrochloric acid solution is a corrosive liquid and is an eye and skin irritant. Hydrogen peroxide solution is an oxidizer and a skin and eye irritant. Make sure students wear chemical splash goggles, chemical-resistant gloves, and a lab coat or chemical-resistant apron. Tell students to wash their hands thoroughly with soap and warm water before leaving the laboratory.

Expected Outcome Students learn that different elements have different physical and chemical properties.

Lab Summary Video Watch the Lab Summary Video for support on connecting the lab investigation to the Investigative Phenomenon.

NAME ______ DATE ______ CLASS ______

INQUIRY LABS – OPEN

Elements: The Building Blocks of Matter

Matter is composed of atoms. Each atom corresponds to a specific element. If all the atoms within a specific material are the same then that material is also referred to as an element.

Focus on Science Practices

SEP 2 Developing and Using Models
SEP 3 Planning and Carrying Out Investigations
SEP 4 Analyzing and Interpreting Data

Materials Per Group

- Aluminum strip
- Carbon rod
- Copper strip
- Copper(II) chloride solution, $CuCl_2$, 1 M, 5 mL
- Hydrochloric acid, HCl, 1 M, 5 mL
- Hydrogen peroxide, H_2O_2, 3%, 5 mL
- Iron strip
- Balance, 0.1 g precision
- Beaker, 150 mL
- Conductivity meter
- Pipet, beral-type
- Ruler
- Vernier calipers
- Wash bottle
- Water

Safety

Copper(II) chloride solution is a skin and eye irritant and is slightly toxic by ingestion. Hydrochloric acid solution is a corrosive liquid and is an eye and skin irritant. Hydrogen peroxide solution is an oxidizer and a skin and eye irritant. Wear chemical splash goggles, chemical-resistant gloves, and a lab coat or chemical-resistant apron. Please follow all normal laboratory safety guidelines and wash hands thoroughly with soap and

O/G/S/A Lab Interactive Worksheets

INTEGRATE THE THREE DIMENSIONS

In the Inquiry Lab, students analyze data [SEP-4] to identify patterns [CCC-1] between atomic mass and density. They plan and carry out an investigation [SEP-3] to examine the reaction [PS1.B] of elemental samples and various solutions. They identify the most reactive elements.

Physical Properties of Gaseous Elements

Analyzing Data Students analyze and interpret data [SEP-4] related to elemental substances in their gas phase. They identify patterns [CCC-1] between atomic mass and the physical properties of density, melting point, and boiling point.

- Have students read the introductory paragraphs and review the two tables. If necessary, explain the meanings of *monatomic* and *diatomic*.
- Draw simple diagrams of the three isotopes of hydrogen without naming or labeling them. Ask students to identify the difference in the three diagrams. Call on students to tell whether the diagrams represent the same element and why. (They are the same element because they have the same number of protons.) Tell students that the diagrams represent isotopes of hydrogen. **Ask** How are isotopes related to the atomic mass of an element? (The atomic mass is the weighted average of the masses of the isotopes.) Make sure that students understand what *weighted* means in this case.
- Discuss density. **Ask** How is density related to matter? (Density is the ratio of the mass of a substance to the volume of the substance.) Why must density be reported at STP? (Pressure and temperature affect the distance between the particles of a substance, so at higher temperatures or lower pressures, fewer particles of a substance will be in a given area than at lower temperatures or higher pressures.)
- Discuss boiling point and melting point. Check that students do not use the terms *boiling* and *evaporation* interchangeably. Clarify that evaporation can occur at any temperature, but boiling occurs at specific temperatures and pressures.

NAME ______ DATE ______ CLASS ______

ANALYZING DATA

Physical Properties of Gaseous Elements

A student tests samples of six different gases. He records the density of each gas at standard temperature and pressure, or STP, which is defined as 273.15 K and 100 kPa. Next, he cools each gas until it becomes a solid. Then, he allows each gas to warm up and records the temperature at which it melts and forms a liquid, and then the temperature at which it boils to become a gas.

Three of the gases are monatomic (each molecule consists of just one atom). The other three gases are diatomic (each molecule consists of two atoms joined together).

Table 1 shows the results for the three monatomic gases. **Table 2** shows the results for the three diatomic gases. All measurements were taken at standard pressure.

Table 1

Experimental Results for Monatomic Gases			
Monatomic gas	**helium, He**	**neon, Ne**	**argon, Ar**
Approximate atomic mass	4	20	40
Density (g/L)	0.17	0.9	1.8
Melting point (K)	1	25	84
Boiling point (K)	4	27	87

Table 2

Experimental Results for Diatomic Gases			
Diatomic gas	**hydrogen, H_2**	**nitrogen, N_2**	**oxygen, O_2**

Analyzing Data Interactive Worksheet

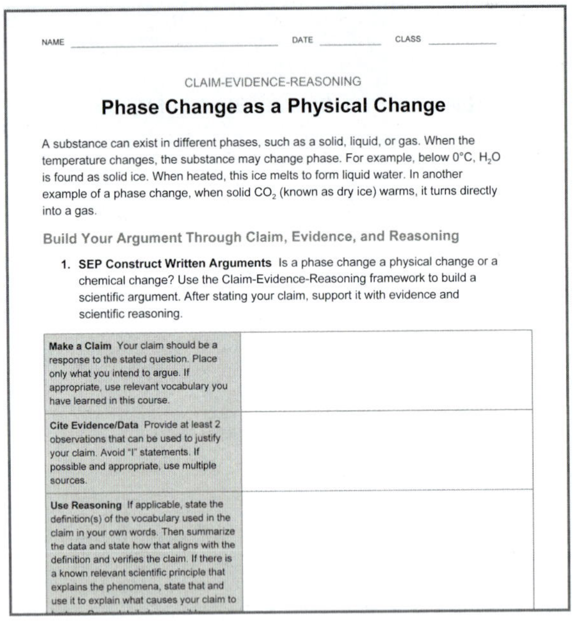

NAME ______________ DATE ________ CLASS ________

CLAIM-EVIDENCE-REASONING

Phase Change as a Physical Change

A substance can exist in different phases, such as a solid, liquid, or gas. When the temperature changes, the substance may change phase. For example, below 0°C, H_2O is found as solid ice. When heated, this ice melts to form liquid water. In another example of a phase change, when solid CO_2 (known as dry ice) warms, it turns directly into a gas.

Build Your Argument Through Claim, Evidence, and Reasoning

1. **SEP Construct Written Arguments** Is a phase change a physical change or a chemical change? Use the Claim-Evidence-Reasoning framework to build a scientific argument. After stating your claim, support it with evidence and scientific reasoning.

Make a Claim Your claim should be a response to the stated question. Place only what you intend to argue. If appropriate, use relevant vocabulary you have learned in this course.	
Cite Evidence/Data Provide at least 2 observations that can be used to justify your claim. Avoid "I" statements. If possible and appropriate, use multiple sources.	
Use Reasoning If applicable, state the definition(s) of the vocabulary used in the claim in your own words. Then summarize the data and state how that aligns with the definition and verifies the claim. If there is a known relevant scientific principle that explains the phenomena, state that and use it to explain what causes your claim to	

CER Interactive Worksheet

ADDRESS PRECONCEPTIONS

Some students may think that liquids only change to solids at low temperatures. Place a piece of plastic wrap on your hand and then add some gallium. Show the gallium to students. It will be liquid. Then transfer the gallium to a desktop or tabletop. It will solidify. Make sure that students understand that changing to a solid at a higher temperature is the same process as freezing at a lower temperature.

ELD SUPPORT

Speaking Students will persuade others in conversations about whether a phase change is a physical change or a chemical change in the CER Worksheet.

- **Entering/Beginning** Help students discuss their arguments with others, using these examples:
  I see your point, but ________.
  I understand what you are saying. I think my idea is better because _____.
- **Developing/Expanding** Help students use oral counterarguments that use a growing number of learned phrases, such as, I see your point but I think that _____; I heard what you said, but did you think about _____?; I would also like you to think about _____.
- **Bridging** Help students acknowledge new information but then politely offer a counterpoint by first restating the new information the critique offered and then identifying at least one reason why they agree or disagree with the critique.

ASSESS ON THE SPOT

Give students 1 minute to answer this question in their science notebooks: In general, what trend exists in the relationship among the atomic mass, density, melting point, and boiling point of monatomic and diatomic gases? Call on students to write their answers on the board. As a class, discuss each answer and any revisions that should be made. Then have students revise their own answers in their student notebooks, if necessary.

INTEGRATE MATH

Students may not be familiar with the meaning of *amu* in Question 5 of the Analyzing Data activity. Explain that amu is a unit of mass. It is short for *atomic mass unit* and is equal to the mass of one-twelfth of the mass of a C-12 atom (the mass of an isotope of carbon with six protons and six neutrons in its nucleus). One amu is equal to approximately 1.66×10^{-24} grams. Tell students that oxygen has an atomic mass of 15.9994 amu. Call on students to explain what that means.

Point out the K in the first paragraph of the Analyzing Data worksheet. Explain that K stands for kelvin. A kelvin is the base unit of temperature in the Kelvin scale. A degree on the Kelvin scale is the same amount as on the Celsius scale except that in the Kelvin scale, absolute zero is 0 K, a temperature below which temperature does not exist. It corresponds to −273°C.

EXPLAIN

Phase Change as a Physical Change (15)

Claim-Evidence-Reasoning Students construct a written argument [SEP-6] about whether a phase change is a physical change or a chemical change. They support their claim with evidence and scientific reasoning. Students trade their arguments with classmates and critique each others' arguments. Then students evaluate [SEP-8] their classmates' feedback and revise their arguments.

- You may wish to provide some guidelines for critiquing the work of others, such as critique the work not the writer, be polite and avoid harmful and rude language, give specific suggestions for improvement, and point out the positive aspects of the work as well as the places where improvement is needed.
- Have students complete Step 1 independently. For Step 2, they can work in groups of three or four. Each student should share their argument, evidence, and reasoning with the group. The group should then identify two things that they particularly liked about the argument and two areas where they think it could be improved. Students should then individually complete Step 3.

DIFFERENTIATED INSTRUCTION

- **Support Struggling Students** Lead a discussion about the difference between water, ice, and water vapor. Ask a few volunteers to draw on the board a group of molecules that make up each of the three phases of water. Review the drawings. **Ask** How are the molecules alike? What is different about the molecules at these three stages?
- **Support Special Needs Students** Some students may have difficulty writing the answers on their worksheets. Allow these students to use a word processing program, or have them dictate their answers to a partner.

The Particle Nature of Matter

Experience Notebook Ideally, assign the Experience Notebook or Realize Reader for this experience the day before, and then follow up with any of the following suggested instructional strategies to fill knowledge gaps and deepen understanding.

Use these strategies to help students make sense of the images and text on the indicated pages, as well as to engage science skills.

- **Atoms and Molecules** (pp. 6–8) Display the Models of Molecules diagrams on page 7. **Ask** What does each ball represent in these models? (an atom) How are atoms and elements related? (Atoms are the basic particles that make up elements.) What do the atoms that are connected represent? (a molecule) What elements make up a methane molecule? (carbon and hydrogen) Point to the model of the nitrogen gas. **Ask** How can nitrogen be both an element and a molecule? (Atoms of nitrogen form a molecule of nitrogen gas.)
- Display the molecular model of carbon dioxide on page 7. **Ask** How many atoms of oxygen (red balls) are in a molecule of carbon dioxide? (two) How many atoms of carbon (blue ball)? (one) Point to the chemical formula for carbon dioxide, CO_2, and make sure students understand what the formula represents. Then **ask** What holds these atoms together? (chemical bonds)
- **Energy** (p. 9) Write the word *energy* on the board, and call on students to tell what it means. Explain that in science, *energy* has a different meaning than in its common use. For example, someone might say that he or she doesn't have any energy, meaning that the person is tired. But in science, *energy* refers to the ability to move or change matter.
- Remind students that the particles of matter are always in motion. Ask students to consider whether those particles cause other matter to move or change. Give pairs of students two marbles. Tell students that the marbles represent particles of a gas. Direct students to roll the marbles toward each other and observe what happens. Point out that particles of matter have energy.
- **Interaction of Matter and Energy** (p. 10) Lead a discussion about systems. Ask students to identify which of these examples are systems: the universe, a chemical reaction, an atom, a classroom. (All can be systems.) **Ask** If a system is described as the solution in a beaker, what are some components of the surroundings? (Example answers: the walls of the beaker, the air above the solution) In what ways can energy enter or exit this system? (Sample answers: Heat from the walls of the beaker or air can enter or exit the system, depending on the temperature differences between the system and the surroundings; energy can also enter as electrical energy if a current passes through it; energy enters if someone stirs the solution.)

ASSESS ON THE SPOT

One the board, write the titles of the sections in this experience. Call on students to go to the board and add one fact from any of the sections until all the content from the sections has been recorded. Then ask students about what facts they need additional explanations for.

PROFESSIONAL DEVELOPMENT

Inspire Your Students Help students understand the relationship between atoms and molecules. Organize students in groups of three. Provide each group with 10 each of: short bolts, long bolts, hex nuts, and square nuts. Tell students that each item represents an atom. Challenge groups to make as many different combinations (molecules) of nuts and bolts as possible in 3 minutes. Then ask groups to tell how many combinations they have made. Have all groups compare their combinations with those of other groups.

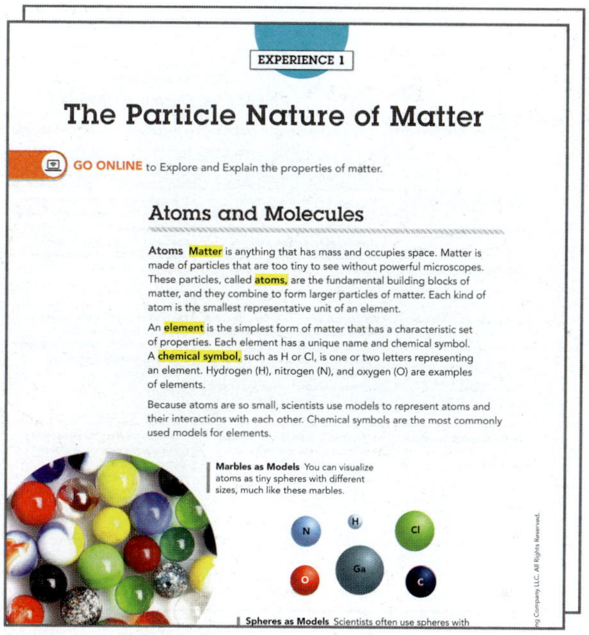
EXPERIENCE 1

The Particle Nature of Matter

GO ONLINE to Explore and Explain the properties of matter.

Atoms and Molecules

Atoms Matter is anything that has mass and occupies space. Matter is made of particles that are too tiny to see without powerful microscopes. These particles, called atoms, are the fundamental building blocks of matter, and they combine to form larger particles of matter. Each kind of atom is the smallest representative unit of an element.

An element is the simplest form of matter that has a characteristic set of properties. Each element has a unique name and chemical symbol. A chemical symbol, such as H or Cl, is one or two letters representing an element. Hydrogen (H), nitrogen (N), and oxygen (O) are examples of elements.

Because atoms are so small, scientists use models to represent atoms and their interactions with each other. Chemical symbols are the most commonly used models for elements.

Marbles as Models You can visualize atoms as tiny spheres with different sizes, much like these marbles.

Spheres as Models Scientists often use spheres with

Experience Notebook, pp. 6–10

eTEXT

ADDRESS PRECONCEPTIONS

Students sometimes think that elements are composed of a single atom. Point out the diatomic molecules of nitrogen on page 7 of the Experience Notebook. Explain that another common element that exists as a diatomic molecule is oxygen. However, helium, the gas often used to blow up some balloons, exists as individual atoms.

Students also sometimes think that very common substances, such as water, are elements because they are so common. Remind students that an element cannot be broken down into other substances.

NAME ______________ DATE ________ CLASS ________

DISCUSSION RUBRIC

Physical vs. Chemical Change

Use this rubric to help you assess your explanation of the differences between physical

	EXEMPLARY Score the work 3 if:	ACCOMPLISHED Score the work 2 if:
Claims and Evidence Student Score: ______ Teacher Score: ______	The claim clearly explains that in chemical changes, chemical reactions occur that form new products, and in physical changes, the substances involved change in form but do not change in their chemical composition.	The claim explains either that chemical changes involve chemical reactions that form new products or that in physical changes, the substances involved change in form but do not change in their chemical composition.
Evaluation and Critique Student Score: ______ Teacher Score: ______	Alternate descriptions of the differences between physical and chemical changes are acknowledged and refuted in an attempt to strengthen the claim. For example, reversibility is not good evidence as both chemical and physical changes may be reversible.	The evaluation or critique makes an attempt to discuss alternate explanations for the differences between physical and chemical changes.
Reasoning and Synthesis Student Score: ______ Teacher Score: ______	The explanation accurately describes how the presence or absence of a chemical reaction that forms new substances differentiates between physical and chemical changes.	The explanation accurately describes physical and chemical changes and attempts to relate the presence or absence of a chemical reaction that forms new substances to the type of change that occurs.

Discussion Rubric Interactive Worksheet

NAME ______________ DATE ________ CLASS ________

ANALYZING DATA

Intensive and Extensive Properties

Scientists have identified over 100 elements. Each element has its own unique set of physical and chemical properties. However, differences may also exist between samples of the same element. For example, a sample of iron may have a mass of 1 milligram, 1 gram, or 1 kilogram. The shape of the sample may be a cube, an irregular shape, or many tiny filings.

The table shows the observed properties of several samples of three elements: hydrogen, sodium, and iron.

Properties of Element Samples

Sample	Element	State	Mass	Volume	Density	Appearance	Reactivity
1	hydrogen	gas	8.2 mg	100 cm^3		colorless	reacts explosively with oxygen
2	hydrogen	gas	4.1 mg	50 cm^3		colorless	reacts explosively with oxygen
3	hydrogen	gas	1.2 mg	15 cm^3		colorless	reacts explosively with oxygen
4	sodium	solid	9.7 g	10 cm^3		silvery-white cube	reacts vigorously at surface with water and oxygen
5	sodium	solid	2.4 g	2.5 cm^3		silvery-white pieces	reacts vigorously with water and oxygen
6	sodium	solid	5.2 g	5.4 cm^3		silvery-white flakes	reacts quickly and vigorously with water and oxygen
7	iron	solid	7.9 g	1.0 cm^3		shiny,	surface rusts

Analyzing Data Interactive Worksheet

CLASSROOM MODIFICATIONS

Based on your students' abilities and your schedule, you may wish to edit the Analyzing Data worksheet to make the activity more open ended or more guided.

- **More Open Ended** Have students write a question of their own similar to the ones in Steps 4 and 5. They can then exchange questions with a partner to answer the questions. Then combine all questions into a single document that all students can use for extra support.
- **More Guided** You may wish to calculate the densities in Step 1 as a class. Or, as a class, calculate three of the four densities for each element and have students individually or in pairs calculate the remaining density for each.

ELABORATE

Physical vs. Chemical Change

Discussion Rubric With a group, students discuss the differences between physical and chemical changes.

- Each student in a group will give his or her explanation of what the differences between physical and chemical changes are. As each student speaks, another group member will record the ideas. After all students in the group have provided explanations, the group should summarize what students identified as the differences. Then students should individually revise their argument for the CER activity.
- Collect all the arguments, and review for any confusing or incorrect arguments. If necessary, address any incorrect understandings before continuing on to the next activity in the experience.

Intensive and Extensive Properties

Analyzing Data Students use computational thinking [SEP-5] to calculate density and then identify patterns [CCC-1] in data. They analyze data [SEP-4] to identify examples of extensive and intensive properties. They engage in written argument [SEP-7] about a stated claim.

- Point out that intensive properties can often be used to identify substances. Density, for example, is often used to identify solids because it does not change in value no matter how much of the sample is present.
- Use the following questions to ensure students understand that atomic mass, while sounding extensive, is actually intensive. **Ask** Is the mass of a sample extensive or intensive? Why? (extensive; It changes based on the amount present.) Is atomic mass extensive or intensive? Why? (intensive; It doesn't change with amount.)
- Review with the class how to calculate density by working a problem on the board. For example, a 10-cm^3 sample of a substance has a mass of 166 g. What is its density?

$$D = m/V = 166\ g/10\ cm^3 = 16.6\ g/cm^3$$

Then provide another density problem and ask volunteers to go to the board to calculate the answer: mass = 3.1 g; volume = 0.35 cm^3 (8.9 g/cm^3)

ASSESS ON THE SPOT

Call on four pairs of students to go to the board. Allow 1 minute for pairs to list on the board all the extensive properties they can think of. Then as a class review what students have listed and add any other properties that the class suggests. Repeat the process with different student pairs and intensive properties.

EVALUATE

The Particle Nature of Matter

Quiz Assign the quiz in online technology-enhanced, auto-graded format or as an editable quiz worksheet. Use the scoring notes and remediation strategies found online to assess students' responses and to provide targeted feedback for each item to remediate well before assigning the summative 3-D Assessment.

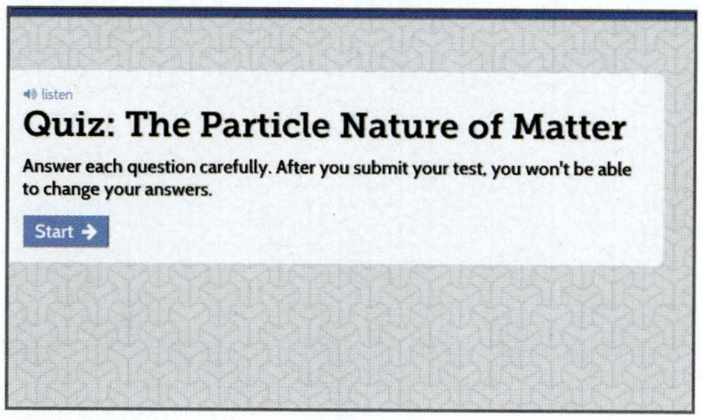

Interactive Online Quiz

Quiz Interactive Worksheet

REMEDIATION SUGGESTIONS

- **If** students have difficulty understanding how atoms make up molecules, **then** have them review page 7 of the Experience Notebook.
- **If** students struggle to understand how solids, liquids, and gases are alike and different, **then** tell them to study the diagram on page 8 of the Experience Notebook and the Analyzing Data activity, Physical Properties of Gaseous Elements.
- **If** students do not understand how energy affects the state of matter, **then** suggest that they review pages 8 and 9 in their Experience Notebook and their worksheet for the CER activity, Phase Change as a Physical Change.
- **If** students are confused by what a system and its surroundings are, **then** have them reread page 10 of the Experience Notebook.
- **If** students have difficulty identifying extensive and intensive properties, **then** tell them to review their worksheet for the Analyzing Data activity, Intensive and Extensive Properties.

Revisit
INVESTIGATIVE PHENOMENON

Support Reflection Students can complete the reflection prompt, where they will unpack and make sense of the Investigative Phenomenon, based on practices and understandings that have been reinforced over the course of the experience.

- Call on students to go to the board and make drawings of these molecules, identifying each atom: NH_4, H_2O, CH_4, and N_2.
- Display the investigation opener image of the fireworks. Ask students to identify any forms of energy they see in the photo.

Refine Your Model Have students answer Question 2 in the Modeling worksheet, relating their model to the Investigative Phenomenon. Have students add any evidence they have collected from the activities so far in this investigation. Evidence may include that molecules have stored chemical energy and that energy can flow into a system from the surroundings and can also flow out of a system into the surroundings.

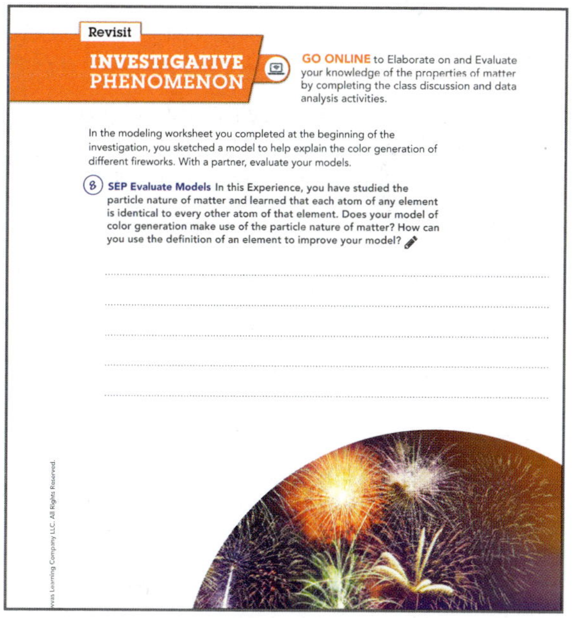
Revisit
INVESTIGATIVE PHENOMENON

GO ONLINE to Elaborate on and Evaluate your knowledge of the properties of matter by completing the class discussion and data analysis activities.

In the modeling worksheet you completed at the beginning of the investigation, you sketched a model to help explain the color generation of different fireworks. With a partner, evaluate your models.

8 **SEP Evaluate Models** In this Experience, you have studied the particle nature of matter and learned that each atom of any element is identical to every other atom of that element. Does your model of color generation make use of the particle nature of matter? How can you use the definition of an element to improve your model?

Experience Notebook, p. 11

eTEXT

EXPERIENCE 2

Modeling Atoms

Teacher Background

Experience 2 provides a discussion of atomic structure (protons, neutrons, and electrons), chemical symbols, atomic number, and mass number. These concepts were most likely encountered in earlier grades, but in this experience, students apply these concepts to explore isotopes and atomic mass units through modeling, data analysis, and lab activities.

This experience focuses mostly on the nucleus of atoms; electrons will come later. As you teach this material, be sure that students have a good understanding of balanced atomic charge due to the equal number of protons and electrons and the difference between atomic mass and atomic number. It is extremely important that students have a solid understanding of these foundational concepts before moving forward, so don't be afraid to spend a little extra time on remediation here, if necessary.

Objectives

- **Describe atomic structure using a model of the atom that includes protons, neutrons, and electrons.**
- **Compare and contrast atoms of different elements and isotopes of the same element.**
- **Calculate the atomic mass of an element given isotope data.**

ENGAGE

EVERYDAY PHENOMENON

What's inside the box?

Use this teacher demo to help students understand how scientists are able to probe the interior of atoms to determine subatomic structure.

Seeing Without Looking

Engage students with this demonstration of an everyday phenomenon to introduce the concept of Rutherford scattering and to teach students how the interior of atoms was discovered [NoS-8].

Materials 2 or 3 polygons cut out of wood (math teachers usually have these; shapes with fewer sides work best), 2 pieces of clear plastic, metal ball bearings or BBs (no thicker than the wooden polygons). Before class begins, sandwich one of the wooden polygons between the two pieces of plastic. Secure the polygon in place with some poster tack or tape. Cover the plastic with paper so the students can't see inside.

1. Explain to students that you want to figure out how many sides the polygon between the sheets of plastic has without looking at it. Ask for suggestions of how to solve this problem.
2. Prop the plastic "sandwich" up at a slight angle and slowly roll ball bearings in from one side of the sandwich. As the bearings hit the shape inside, they will either continue straight or change their course. Performing this step on a document camera can make it much easier for students to see.
3. Rotate the "sandwich" and continue rolling ball bearings through until you have completed a full revolution.

RELATED PHENOMENA

In addition to the Seeing Without Looking demonstration, consider using other phenomena to launch this experience.

- **Model Atoms** Place a strong magnet on the screen of an old CRT (cathode ray tube) monitor or television to produce interference patterns. Explain how J. J. Thomson's experiment used a similar apparatus to discover the electron and prove that there were particles lighter than atoms. If your science department does not have a CRT, use a video to demonstrate how the electron was found. Focus on the evidence and how the scientific model of the atom changed over time.

4. Ask students if they can determine when the bearings hit a flat spot in the shape, and then ask them to estimate how many sides the shape has. Remove the paper from the plastic to show students how the ball bearings are deflected.
5. Connect this demonstration to the way Rutherford used alpha particles to detect the atomic nucleus, even though he couldn't observe it directly. Remind students that we were able to see the shape directly in this demonstration, but scientists must rely on indirect observation to "see" things as small as atomic nuclei.
6. Remind students that in the fireworks video, they observed different colors of light. The colors originate from something that is too small to see with our eyes. **Ask** How might the structure of atoms influence the colors you see in a fireworks display?

EXPLORE

Bean Bag Isotopes

Inquiry Lab In this lab, students investigate the mass and relative abundance of isotopes for the "bean bag" element (symbol Bg) and calculate **[SEP-5]** the atomic mass of this element. Reinforce that all of these "atoms" are from the same element (beans), but that each different size of bean represents a different isotope of that element. It is important that students don't think of each type of bean as a different type of atom.

Lab Demo Video Watch the Lab Demo Video for advice on materials and preparation.

Choose Your Version Open-ended (O), Guided (G), Shortened (S), Advanced (A)

Materials centigram balance, 100 g navy beans, 280 g kidney beans, 500 g lima beans, 100 g peas, 20 large zipper-lock bags, labeling marker, 4 weighing dishes

Advanced Preparation See the online Teacher Support for guidance in preparing the "bean bag" elements in advance.

Expected Outcome Students identify that the different bean samples represent isotopes of element Bg. Students separate, count, and calculate abundance of each. Ultimately, students calculate the atomic mass of element Bg.

Lab Summary Video Watch the Lab Summary Video for support on connecting the lab investigation to the Investigative Phenomenon.

NAME ________ DATE ________ CLASS ________

MODELING ATOMS INQUIRY LABS – OPEN

Bean Bag Isotopes

What is an isotope? Are all atoms of an element the exact same? An element has multiple isotopes among which atoms of the same element can have different numbers of neutrons and the same number of protons. In this lab, you will model isotopes using dried beans.

Focus on Science Practices

SEP 3 Planning and Carrying Out Investigations
SEP 4 Analyzing and Interpreting Data
SEP 5 Using Mathematics and Computational Thinking

Materials Per Group

- Balance, centigram (0.01-g precision)
- "Bean bag" element, symbol Bg, approximately 50 g
- Labeling marker
- Weighing dishes, 4

Safety

Although the materials used in this activity are considered non hazardous, please observe all normal laboratory safety guidelines. The food-grade items that have been brought into the lab are considered laboratory chemicals and are for lab use only. Do not taste or ingest any materials in the chemistry laboratory. Wash hands thoroughly with soap and water before leaving the laboratory.

Procedure

O/G/S/A Lab Interactive Worksheets

CLASSROOM MODIFICATIONS

Based on your students' abilities and your schedule, you might want to utilize another version of the Inquiry Lab to be more advanced or more guided.

- **Advanced Inquiry Lab** In the Advanced Lab, students delve deeper into isotopes and their detection in the widely used instrumental analysis of mass spectrometry. The lab begins with a small activity with dried beans, and the analysis solidifies the concepts.
- **Guided Inquiry Lab** In the Guided Lab, students are provided with a structured procedure to follow to complete the Isotopes Data Table. Questions in the Analyze and Interpret Data section also provide more direction on how to calculate the percent abundance and relative abundance of each isotope.

ASSESS ON THE SPOT

As students finish working on the lab, have them fill out a quick exit card to assess whether they understand the key points of the lab. Ask students to define *isotope* in their own words and to briefly describe the steps for calculating the average atomic mass of a sample.

Explore Atomic Particles

Analyzing Data In this activity, students analyze a dataset **[SEP-4]** to discover how the number of protons, not the number of neutrons or electrons, determines the identity of each element **[PS1.A]**. They also investigate how ionic charge is determined from the relative number of protons and electrons.

- Allow students to complete this activity before they complete the reading in the Experience Notebook. Discovering patterns **[CCC-1]** in atomic number for themselves will allow students to retain this information much better. The reading will then reinforce these concepts.
- Challenge students to name subatomic particles that seem to have an impact on the overall charge of the atom. **Ask** If the proton always has a positive charge and the electron always has a negative charge, how can the overall charge of the atom be zero? (The positive and negative charges cancel each other.)

NAME ________ DATE ________ CLASS ________

ANALYZING DATA

Explore Atomic Particles

An atom is the smallest unit of an element that retains the chemical properties of that element. When scientists first proposed the concept of the atom, they thought that atoms were indivisible, like tiny marbles or pellets. Over time, however, scientists discovered the tiny particles that make up an atom. Every atom includes a nucleus, generally containing both positively charged particles called protons and uncharged particles called neutrons. In the space surrounding the nucleus are negatively charged particles called electrons. The table shows the particle compositions of atoms or ions of five elements.

Particles in the Atoms or Ions of Five Elements

Element identity	Atomic number	Number of protons	Number of neutrons	Number of electrons	Charge
boron atom	5	5	5	5	0
boron atom	5	5	6	5	0
carbon atom	6	6	6	6	0
carbon atom	6	6	7	6	0
nitrogen atom	7	7	7	7	0
nitrogen ion	7	7	7	10	3–
nitrogen ion	7	7	8	4	3+
oxygen atom	8	8	8	8	0
oxygen atom	8	8	10	8	0
oxygen ion	8	8	8	10	2–

Analyzing Data Interactive Worksheet

PhET Simulation: Build an Atom

PhET Simulation: Isotopes and Atomic Mass

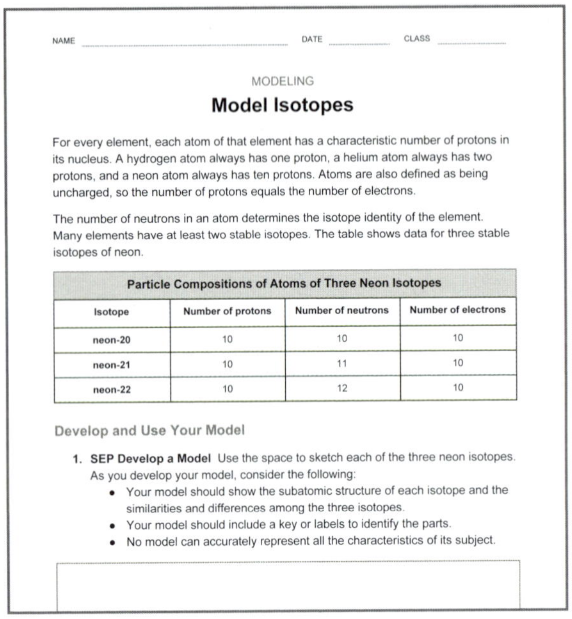
NAME ______ DATE ______ CLASS ______

MODELING

Model Isotopes

For every element, each atom of that element has a characteristic number of protons in its nucleus. A hydrogen atom always has one proton, a helium atom always has two protons, and a neon atom always has ten protons. Atoms are also defined as being uncharged, so the number of protons equals the number of electrons.

The number of neutrons in an atom determines the isotope identity of the element. Many elements have at least two stable isotopes. The table shows data for three stable isotopes of neon.

Particle Compositions of Atoms of Three Neon Isotopes

Isotope	Number of protons	Number of neutrons	Number of electrons
neon-20	10	10	10
neon-21	10	11	10
neon-22	10	12	10

Develop and Use Your Model

1. **SEP Develop a Model** Use the space to sketch each of the three neon isotopes. As you develop your model, consider the following:
   - Your model should show the subatomic structure of each isotope and the similarities and differences among the three isotopes.
   - Your model should include a key or labels to identify the parts.
   - No model can accurately represent all the characteristics of its subject.

Modeling Interactive Worksheet

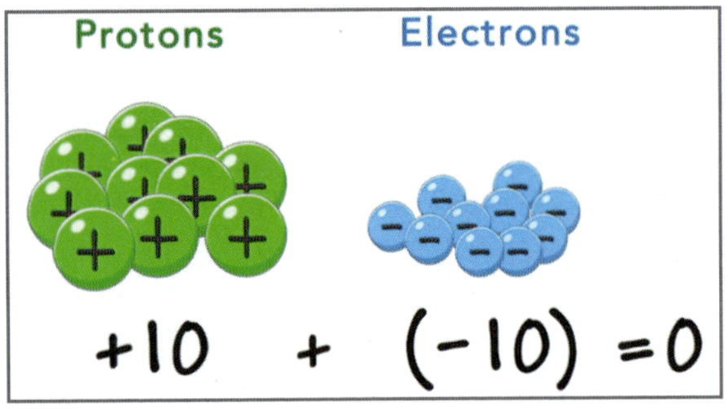

Animation: A Quick Look at the Parts of an Atom

ELD SUPPORT

Speaking Have students work in pairs or small groups to exchange information and ideas about relationships among protons, neutrons, and electrons while they watch the animation.

- **Emerging/Beginning** Have students ask and answer simple, yes/no questions while discussing their atomic models. For example, **ask** Do each of the neon atoms have the same number of protons?
- **Developing/Expanding** Provide students with a list of more detailed questions as an example of the exchanges they should have while working on this assignment. Students should paraphrase these questions instead of reading them verbatim.
- **Bridging** Have students ask and answer detailed, on-topic questions of their own design using the academic vocabulary introduced in this experience.

Build an Atom

PhET Simulation Use this simulation to reinforce the different parts of an atom.

Isotopes and Atomic Mass

PhET Simulation Use this interactive game to help reinforce the concept of isotopes and how abundance relates to the average atomic mass of an element.

EXPLAIN

Model Isotopes

Modeling Students draw models [SEP-2] of three different isotopes of neon to clarify their understanding of what parts of all atoms of a given element are the same and what parts of the atoms make isotopes of that element different.

- Have students label the charges on protons, neutrons, and electrons in their models to reinforce these concepts.
- Students may not know exactly how to draw the electrons yet (electron shells and configurations will be covered in a future experience). Instead, simply be sure that the electrons are shown surrounding the nucleus. You may also encourage students to draw the electrons smaller than the protons and neutrons, to help reinforce the relatively small electron mass.

ASSESS ON THE SPOT

Make a set of cards with each card showing one element model. Vary the number of protons, neutrons, and electrons in each model such that they can be grouped as isotopes of the same element, ions of the same element, different elements, and ions with the same charge. On the back of each card, add matching symbols for the cards in a given group so students can check their own work. As students complete the Modeling activity, give them a set of cards and ask them to sort them into the groups described above.

A Quick Look at the Parts of an Atom

Animation This animation uses diagram models [SEP-2] to show the locations and relationships among protons, neutrons, and electrons [PS1.A]. Choose among these strategies as you use the animation:

- Pause the animation at key spots and ask volunteers to summarize the important information presented. If students have difficulty with the concepts presented in any segment, play that part of the animation again.
- Encourage students to use what they learn in the animation to refine their models of isotopes in the Modeling activity.

Modeling Atoms

Experience Notebook This section of the Experience Notebook works best when assigned alongside the other activities described here, as opposed to reading the whole experience at one time. Have students read the relevant sections of the notebook after completing the assignments and activities that support those sections.

Use the strategies shown below to help students better understand the content found on the indicated pages.

- **Visualizing the Atom** (p. 12) Call on volunteers to go to the board and draw an atom, based on what they already know. Then discuss the parts of the atom shown in the image on the page. Afterward, ask students which models that students drew on the board should be revised and how.

- **Types of Atoms** (pp. 13–14) Students may require additional reinforcement to get a good grasp on identifying atoms based on their structure [CCC-6]. **Ask** What element is shown in the diagram on the previous page? What evidence [SEP-7] is there that it is an atom of carbon? How many electrons should be present in the electron cloud, assuming the overall charge of the atom is zero?
- **Mass Number** (p. 15) If students need more guidance filling out the table at the bottom of the page, work through a few more examples using different notation methods (i.e., $^{14}_{6}C$ and carbon-13).
- **Isotopes** (p. 16) Discuss how to identify isotopes and why isotopes can have different mass numbers. Reinforce that isotopes are atoms that have the same number of protons but different numbers of neutrons. They also have different mass numbers.
- Be sure to emphasize how the use of subscripts and superscripts in chemical symbols differs from their use in mathematics class. When representing isotopes with a symbol, as shown on the page, the superscripts and subscripts are located to the left of the chemical symbol. Emphasize that these superscripts and subscripts indicate important information about an element. Help students relate the superscripts and subscripts shown for the isotope symbols of oxygen with the information directly below each symbol.
- **Atomic Mass** (p. 17) Connecting abstract concepts like average atomic mass to the real world as much as possible is important. Remind students that calculations like this are used to better understand and describe the world around us. **Ask** Why do we put an average on your report card instead of listing the grade for every individual assignment? (It takes up less space and is easier to understand.) Why is finding the average atomic mass for an element important for scientists? (Real samples of elements contain a mixture of different isotopes. An average is much easier to understand than listing every individual isotope mass.)
- **Understanding Atomic Mass Figure** (p. 17) Some students may struggle to understand the electron to proton or neutron mass relationship expressed in scientific notation. To help students understand the differences in mass, provide them with an example of a direct comparison between protons and electrons. For example, 1 proton is approximately 1840 electrons.
- **Calculating Atomic Mass** (p. 19) Remind students that when they are multiplying or dividing by percentage, they need to change the number to a decimal first.
- **Sample Problem** (p. 20) Provide extra Sample Problem practice, while you circulate and help out as needed.

  Note that the following problem requires students to calculate the percent abundance first. If students have a hard time with that, you can provide the percentages (75.2% for postassium-39, 16.3% for potassium-40, and 8.5% for potassium-41).

  A group of scientists produces a sample of potassium by extracting it from a giant truckload of bananas. 97.00 kg of the potassium is $^{39}_{19}K$ (38.897 amu), 21.00 kg of the potassium is $^{40}_{19}K$ (39.955 amu), and 11.00 kg of the potassium is $^{41}_{19}K$ (40.965 amu). What is the average atomic mass of the potassium in this sample? (39.246 amu)

DIFFERENTIATED INSTRUCTION

- **Support Struggling Students** Review the Sample Problem as a class. Guide students through the steps to accurately estimate atomic masses. Use data from hydrogen, helium, or nitrogen to model this process so that students can check their answers. Have students restate the steps they used for practice before estimating the atomic mass for carbon and bromine.
- **Support Advanced Students** Scientists use mass spectroscopy data to determine the isotopic composition of element samples. Teach advanced students to use a mass spectrograph to obtain percent composition data by using the relative abundance percentage (y-axis). Each isotope can be assigned to a peak by realizing that the lighter atoms will have a lower mass-to-charge ratio (putting them further left on the x-axis).

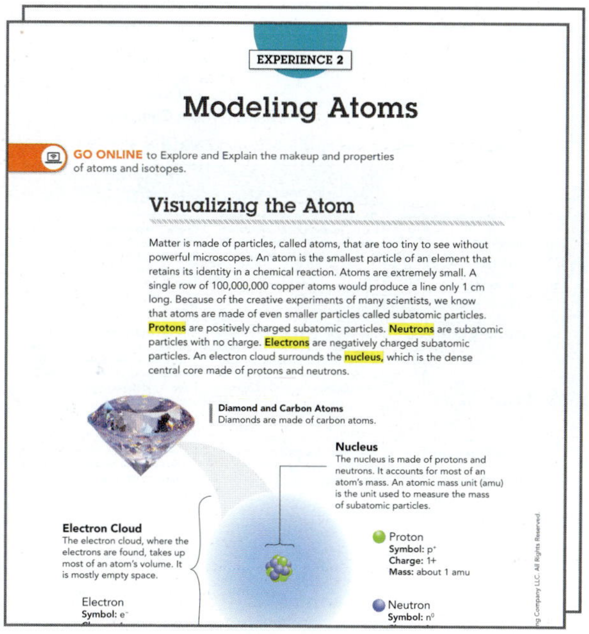
EXPERIENCE 2

Modeling Atoms

GO ONLINE to Explore and Explain the makeup and properties of atoms and isotopes.

Visualizing the Atom

Matter is made of particles, called atoms, that are too tiny to see without powerful microscopes. An atom is the smallest particle of an element that retains its identity in a chemical reaction. Atoms are extremely small. A single row of 100,000,000 copper atoms would produce a line only 1 cm long. Because of the creative experiments of many scientists, we know that atoms are made of even smaller particles called subatomic particles. **Protons** are positively charged subatomic particles. **Neutrons** are subatomic particles with no charge. **Electrons** are negatively charged subatomic particles. An electron cloud surrounds the **nucleus,** which is the dense central core made of protons and neutrons.

Experience Notebook, pp. 12–21

eTEXT

SAMPLE PROBLEM SUPPORT

Students can get caught up in the details of a problem and forget to ask themselves if their answer makes sense. When performing average atomic mass calculations, remind students that their answer must lie somewhere between the highest and lowest atomic mass. (After all, if you get a 95 and a 83 on two assignments, could your course average be a 70?) Also, the average should end up closest to the isotope that has the highest abundance (just like your course average should be closest to the grade you get the most often).

ADDRESS PRECONCEPTIONS

Many students may think that the number of protons and neutrons is always equal. Stress that this is not always the case and provide examples of isotopes that reinforce this claim. Contrast this with the number of protons and electrons for a neutral atom, which are always equal to each other. Remind students that the charge of the positive protons must be cancelled by the charge of the negative electrons, but neutrons have no charge so they don't need to be balanced.

NAME ______________ DATE ________ CLASS ________

DISCUSSION RUBRIC

Dissect Atom Composition

Use this rubric to help you assess your explanation of the effect of varying numbers of subatom

	EXEMPLARY Score the work 3 if:	ACCOMPLISHED Score the work 2 if:
Articulating the Explanation Student Score: ______ Teacher Score: ______	The explanation is clearly articulated and the relationship between the element's identity and the number of each subatomic particle is described.	The explanation correctly correlates element identity with the numbers of subatomic particles, but the relationships are only vaguely described, or one type of subatomic particle was not included in the explanation.
Evidence and Reasoning Student Score: ______ Teacher Score: ______	The evidence presented supports the explanation. The reasoning incorporates all three types of subatomic particles and shows a clear understanding of their relationship to element identity.	The evidence presented somewhat supports the explanation but may be tangential or not directly related. The reasoning incorporates more than one type of subatomic particle.
Revising the Explanation Student Score: ______ Teacher Score: ______	When new evidence is presented, it is seamlessly incorporated into the explanation.	When new evidence is presented, it is considered, and an attempt is made to incorporate it into the explanation.

Discussion Rubric Interactive Worksheet

INTEGRATE THE THREE DIMENSIONS

In the Discussion Rubric, students construct an explanation [SEP-6] of the effect [CCC-6] of varying numbers of subatomic particles on element identity. Students support their explanation with evidence and reasoning that incorporates all three types of subatomic particles [PS1.A]. Students use specific evidence from their models to justify claims [SEP-7] to show a clear understanding of their relationship to element identity.

NAME ______________ DATE ________ CLASS ________

ANALYZING DATA

Determine Atomic Mass

Suppose you measured the mass of a collection of 400 pennies and then divided that mass by 400. Would your result equal the mass of one penny? The answer is yes, but only if all 400 pennies are identical. In fact, some pennies in circulation are slightly more massive than others. For this reason, your calculation would show the average mass of a penny and not the mass of one specific penny.

Calculating atomic mass is similar to calculating the average mass of a penny. The masses of atoms of a particular element differ among isotopes.

Table 1 shows the isotopes of carbon and their masses in atomic mass units (amu). **Table 2** shows the isotopes for several more elements. Atomic mass is calculated by multiplying the percent abundance of each isotope by its mass and then adding the products for all the isotopes together, as shown with this equation for carbon.

$$\text{Atomic mass of carbon} = (98.89\% \times 12.000 \text{ amu}) + (1.11\% \times 13.003 \text{ amu})$$
$$= (0.9889 \times 12.000 \text{ amu}) + (0.0111 \times 13.003 \text{ amu})$$
$$= 11.8668 \text{ amu} + 0.1443 \text{ amu}$$
$$= 12.011 \text{ amu}$$

Table 1

Natural Percent Abundance of Stable Isotopes of Carbon				
Name	**Isotope**	**Natural percent abundance**	**Mass (amu)**	**Atomic mass**
carbon	carbon-12 carbon-13	98.89 1.11	12.000 13.003	12.011

Analyzing Data Interactive Worksheet

Virtual Nerd Video: How Do You Use an Equation to Find a Part of a Whole?

PhET Simulation: Rutherford Scattering

ELABORATE

Dissect Atom Composition

Discussion Rubric Refer students to the Model Isotopes worksheet, in which they modeled isotopes of neon. Encourage students to review this worksheet as you discuss these questions as a class.

- How many protons and neutrons were in each of the neon isotopes?
- What did the isotopes have in common? How were they different?
- How does varying the number of protons or electrons affect an element's identity?

Allow a few minutes for students to revise their models. Tell students to make sure that they are using specific evidence from their models to justify claims [SEP-7]. Then have students complete the rubric to assess their explanations of the effect of varying numbers of subatomic particles on element identity.

Determine Atomic Mass

Analyzing Data In this activity, students use computational thinking [SEP-5] to determine the atomic mass for six elements by multiplying percent abundance of each element's isotope by its mass and then adding the products for all its isotopes. They also use data about the number of protons and neutrons in an isotope to determine the atomic mass of the isotope.

- If necessary, go over the sample calculation as a class. Make sure students know how to convert a percentage to a decimal.
- After students complete Table 2, have them compare the atomic mass to the atomic number of each element and note the close correlation. **Ask** Why isn't the atomic mass exactly equal to the atomic number?

ASSESS ON THE SPOT

As students complete the Analyzing Data worksheet, circulate among them to assess their calculations. If any students are having difficulty, call on other students who have correctly calculated to write their calculations on the board and to explain their thinking.

PROFESSIONAL DEVELOPMENT

Inspire Your Students In 2018, David Nadlinger captured a photograph of a single atom for the first time. A single atom of strontium was held in place by strong magnetic fields and bombarded with energy from a laser. The atom absorbed the energy and then re-emitted it, giving off tiny amounts of light. The scientist used a camera to gather all the light until the atom could be seen with the unaided eye. If possible, obtain and display the photograph.

How Do You Use an Equation to Find a Part of a Whole?

Virtual Nerd Video Use this video tutorial to reinforce decimals, percentages, and multiplication.

Rutherford Scattering

PhET Simulation Students can use this simulation to perform Rutherford's experiment.

EVALUATE

Modeling Atoms

Quiz Assign the quiz in online technology-enhanced, auto-graded format or as an editable quiz worksheet. Use the scoring notes and remediation strategies found online to assess students' responses and to provide targeted feedback for each item to remediate well before assigning the summative 3-D Assessment.

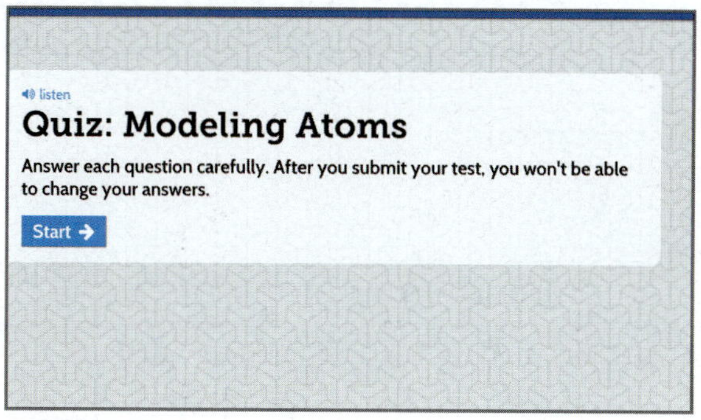

Interactive Online Quiz

Quiz Interactive Worksheet

REMEDIATION SUGGESTIONS

- **If** students have trouble describing the structure of atoms, **then** have them review their Model Isotopes worksheet. Provide additional isotope groups for other elements, including number of protons, neutrons, and electrons, and have students draw models of these as well. Finally, have students review the atomic models on page 16 of the Experience Notebook.
- **If** students cannot distinguish between different elements and isotopes of the same element, **then** have them review the Bean Bag Isotopes Inquiry Lab activity.
- **If** students do not understand that an atom is only a different element if it has a different number of protons, **then** have them review the Explore Atomic Particles worksheet for more clarification, as necessary.
- **If** students are having a hard time calculating the average atomic mass of an element, **then** have them review the Sample Problem on page 20 of the Experience Notebook and complete the other Sample Problems in the table at the bottom of the page.

Revisit INVESTIGATIVE PHENOMENON

Support Reflection Students can complete the reflection prompt, where they will unpack and make sense of the Investigative Phenomenon, based on practices and understandings that have been reinforced over the course of the experience.

- Call on students to list the three subatomic particles discussed in this experience and to provide their charges and relative masses. Also, ask students to name the number of protons, neutrons, and electrons in a specific element if they are given atomic number, atomic mass, and/or atomic charge.
- Prompt students to explain how they think the differences in the number of protons, neutrons, and electrons, in the atoms of different elements relates to the colors in a fireworks display.
- Ask students to define what an isotope is and to provide an example of two atoms that are isotopes of a given element.
- Have students work through one more average atomic mass calculation and ask them how comfortable they are with solving this type of problem. Go back and review the steps for solving these problems as needed before assigning the quiz.

Refine Your Model Have students answer Question 2 in the Modeling worksheet relating their model to the Investigative Phenomenon. Have students add any evidence they have collected from the activities so far in this investigation. Evidence may include that the number of protons determines the identity of an element, atoms of the same element have the same number of protons but may have different numbers of protons, and isotopes of an element share some characteristics but also have differences.

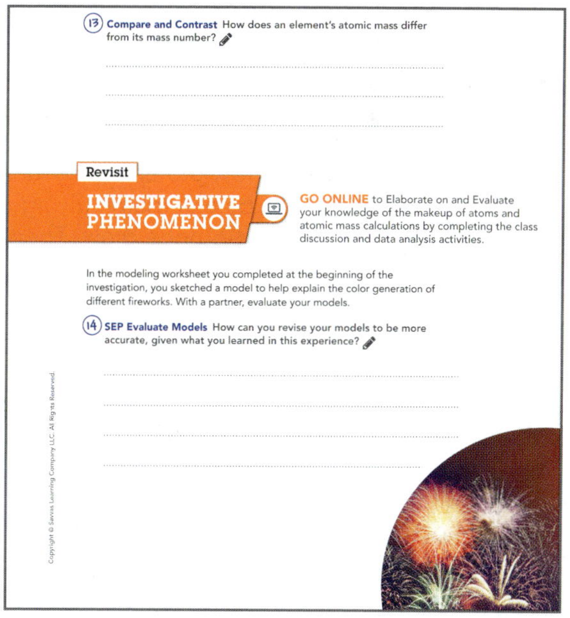

Experience Notebook, p. 21

eTEXT

EXPERIENCE 3

Atomic Emission Spectra and the Bohr Model

Teacher Background

Experience 3 introduces the periodic table as a model that can be used to predict properties of elements based on patterns of electrons. Students explore how electrons, when excited by an outside energy source, produce characteristic emission spectra. These ideas are introduced as students relate atomic emission spectra to the energy of electrons in atoms and investigate the quantization of energy. While the Bohr model is no longer considered a completely accurate representation of the atom, it does provide a framework for understanding electron behavior. The main take-aways for students are that electrons exist in energy levels in atoms, atomic emission spectra provide data about the existence of these energy levels, and the Bohr model of the atom can be used to explain these concepts.

Objectives

- **Develop and use Bohr models for atoms, illustrating electron energy levels and the placement of electrons within those levels.**
- **Use the Bohr model to explain why elements have unique atomic emission spectra.**
- **Relate the spectra of elements to the structure of their atoms, particularly the patterns of electrons and changes in their energy.**

ENGAGE

EVERYDAY PHENOMENON

How do we know that water is present on Mars?

Use this teacher demo to prompt discussion of how scientists can identify the elements present on other planets even though humans have never set foot on the planet.

The Colors of Water

Engage students with this demonstration of an everyday phenomenon to introduce the concept of using atomic emission spectra to identify elements.

Materials atomic emission discharge tube power supply, hydrogen discharge tube, oxygen discharge tube, water vapor discharge tube, class set of diffraction gratings or diffraction grating glasses. (If you don't have these materials, check with your physics teachers.)

1. Hand out the diffraction gratings. Help students look through them properly by pointing them at some fluorescent lights.
2. Turn off the classroom lights and show students the discharge tube with hydrogen. Make note of the intense purple color and then have students look at the tube through their diffraction gratings. They should observe one bright purple line and another bright red line. The blue-violet and blue-green lines may be somewhat harder to see.
3. Have students look at the discharge tube of oxygen. They should observe many more lines in this spectrum due to the greater number of electrons in the oxygen atom.

RELATED PHENOMENA

In addition to the demo The Colors of Water, consider using other phenomena to launch this experience.

- **Neon Signs** Show a video or photo featuring neon signs and explain how the electrons in neon atoms are excited by electricity, giving off their characteristic red-orange glow. Then show signs with different colors that are made using different gases, such as xenon and argon. Discuss how the color of a flame could be used to identify substances.
- **Observe Different Sources of Light** Observe light from various sources, such as sunlight, fluorescent light tubes, and LED light sources. Spectra will differ from one another. Ask students what they know about why the emitted light differs among sources.

4. Ask what the chemical formula for water is. Write it on the board. Ask the class what they expect the spectrum of water vapor to look like.
5. Show the discharge tube of water vapor. Students should analyze the spectrum and recognize the bright purple hydrogen spectrum line and the bright blue and red spectral lines from the oxygen.
6. Explain how scientists use atomic emission spectroscopy to determine the elements present in many objects.
7. Lead a discussion about how the differences in spectra among elements might lead to the various colors in fireworks.

EXPLORE

Evaluate Atomic Spectra

Inquiry Lab In this lab, students observe light passing through a diffraction grating and analyze the observed spectrum of colors.

Lab Demo Video Watch the Lab Demo Video for advice on materials and preparation.

Choose Your Version Open-ended (O), Guided (G), Shortened (S), Advanced (A)

Materials light sources (flashlight, light bulb, street lamp, novelty neon lamps), C-spectra square, gas discharge tubes (hydrogen, helium, mercury, or neon), spectroscope, power supply

Safety Power supplies and spectrum tubes operate at very high voltages and can produce a large electric shock. Tell students not to touch the ends of the tube, a spectrum tube, or the contacts on the transformer when the power supply is on. Students should always turn off the power supply before inserting, removing, or adjusting the position of the spectrum tube.

Spectrum tubes typically emit ultraviolet radiation, which is damaging to the eyes. Students should wear safety glasses or goggles that offer UV protection by filtering UV radiation. Spectrum tubes may get very hot. After turning off the power, allow the tube to cool before removing it from the power supply.

Expected Outcome Students observe the emission spectra of different light sources using a diffraction grating and spectroscope. They discover the various colors and determine that the colors are due to emission of photons by the electrons.

Lab Summary Video Watch the Lab Summary Video for support on connecting the lab investigation to the Investigative Phenomenon.

ASSESS ON THE SPOT

As students finish the lab, have them write a brief description of the energies of different colors of light that they observed in the lab. Tell them that they are not allowed to use any jargon or technical vocabulary in this description. This will help ensure they actually understand what they observed in the lab.

Interpret Emission Spectra

Analyzing Data In this activity, students calculate [CCC-5] the speed of light waves of different frequencies. They analyze their data [CCC-4] to draw a conclusion about the speed of light. They explain why it is helpful to study the emission spectra of elements.

- Have students read the first introductory paragraph, and then call on several students to explain what an emission spectrum is. If students have difficulty understanding the concept, have them read pages 22 and 23 in the Experience Notebook before they begin the activity.
- Some students may need help working with exponents. If necessary, demonstrate one or two of the calculations in Question 1, focusing on how to use the exponents.

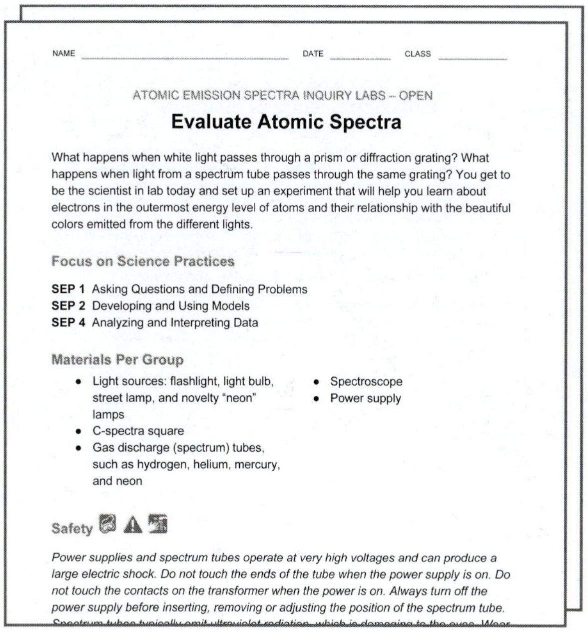

NAME ________ DATE ________ CLASS ________

ATOMIC EMISSION SPECTRA INQUIRY LABS – OPEN

Evaluate Atomic Spectra

What happens when white light passes through a prism or diffraction grating? What happens when light from a spectrum tube passes through the same grating? You get to be the scientist in lab today and set up an experiment that will help you learn about electrons in the outermost energy level of atoms and their relationship with the beautiful colors emitted from the different lights.

Focus on Science Practices

SEP 1 Asking Questions and Defining Problems
SEP 2 Developing and Using Models
SEP 4 Analyzing and Interpreting Data

Materials Per Group

- Light sources: flashlight, light bulb, street lamp, and novelty "neon" lamps
- C-spectra square
- Gas discharge (spectrum) tubes, such as hydrogen, helium, mercury, and neon
- Spectroscope
- Power supply

Safety

Power supplies and spectrum tubes operate at very high voltages and can produce a large electric shock. Do not touch the ends of the tube when the power supply is on. Do not touch the contacts on the transformer when the power is on. Always turn off the power supply before inserting, removing or adjusting the position of the spectrum tube.

O/G/S/A Lab Interactive Worksheets

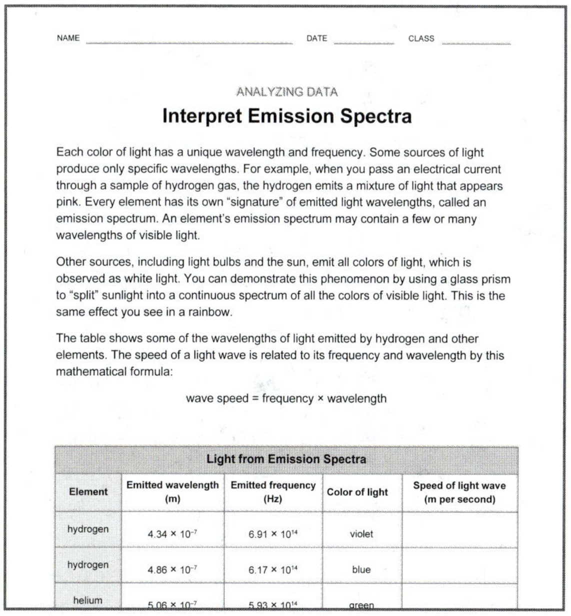

NAME ________ DATE ________ CLASS ________

ANALYZING DATA

Interpret Emission Spectra

Each color of light has a unique wavelength and frequency. Some sources of light produce only specific wavelengths. For example, when you pass an electrical current through a sample of hydrogen gas, the hydrogen emits a mixture of light that appears pink. Every element has its own "signature" of emitted light wavelengths, called an emission spectrum. An element's emission spectrum may contain a few or many wavelengths of visible light.

Other sources, including light bulbs and the sun, emit all colors of light, which is observed as white light. You can demonstrate this phenomenon by using a glass prism to "split" sunlight into a continuous spectrum of all the colors of visible light. This is the same effect you see in a rainbow.

The table shows some of the wavelengths of light emitted by hydrogen and other elements. The speed of a light wave is related to its frequency and wavelength by this mathematical formula:

wave speed = frequency × wavelength

Light from Emission Spectra				
Element	Emitted wavelength (m)	Emitted frequency (Hz)	Color of light	Speed of light wave (m per second)
hydrogen	4.34×10^{-7}	6.91×10^{14}	violet	
hydrogen	4.86×10^{-7}	6.17×10^{14}	blue	
helium	5.06×10^{-7}	5.93×10^{14}	green	

Analyzing Data Interactive Worksheet

CLASSROOM MODIFICATIONS

Based on your students' abilities and your schedule, you can edit the Interpret Emission Spectra worksheet to be more open ended or more guided.

- **More Open Ended** Provide students with the information in the opening paragraphs and in the table. Then ask students to complete Steps 3, 4, and 7.
- **More Guided** Complete the Steps 1 to 4 as a class. Then have students complete the remaining steps individually or with a partner.

NAME ______ DATE ______ CLASS ______

CLAIM-EVIDENCE-REASONING

Emission Spectra of Elements

In the Bohr model of an atom, negatively charged electrons are located in specific orbits around a positively-charged nucleus. If an electron gains a specific amount of energy, it can jump to a higher-energy orbit. An electron can subsequently lose a specific amount of energy and fall to a lower-energy orbit. Electrons falling to lower-energy orbits emit light of specific wavelengths, which generates each element's unique emission spectrum. An emission spectrum is the light of specific wavelengths that an element emits when electrons in the atoms go from higher-energy orbits to lower-energy ones.

Build Your Argument Through Claim, Evidence, and Reasoning

1. **SEP Construct Written Arguments** Why do elements have unique emission spectra? Use the Claim-Evidence-Reasoning framework to build a scientific argument. After stating your claim, support it with evidence and scientific reasoning.

Make a Claim Your claim should be a response to the question stated above.	
Cite Evidence Identify data or knowledge that support your claim.	
Use Reasoning Justify how the data and knowledge count as evidence toward supporting	

CER Interactive Worksheet

ELD SUPPORT

Speaking Students work with a partner to discuss how to present clear explanations for the CER activity, Emission Spectra of Elements.

- **Emerging/Beginning** Provide simple statements that students can use to tell a partner about a weakness they identified in the partner's claim or evidence. For example, you might provide this sentence for students to complete: I think you could make your explanation clearer if you _____.
- **Developing/Expanding** Make statements about problems students might find with a partner's work, such as: The claim is not clear. Ask students to say a sentence that they could use to politely convey that message to a partner.
- **Bridging** Have students write a sentence or two that they could use to convince a partner that their own argument is well supported.

CONNECT TO CAREERS

Physicist Tell students that the Bohr model of an atom is named after Niels Bohr, a Danish physicist. Explain that physicists are scientists who deal with all aspects of matter and energy. Point out that because the study of physics includes many categories, many physicists tend to specialize in one of those categories, such as atomic physics. Have students research three different categories of the career that interest them. Have them organize their findings in a table that summarizes the nature of the work, educational and training requirements, employment outlook, and what they find interesting about these careers.

EXPLAIN

Emission Spectra of Elements (15)

Claim-Evidence-Reasoning In this activity, students construct explanations [SEP-6] that connect electron energy levels with the unique emission spectrum produced by each element.

- **Ask** What parts of the atom do you think cause [CCC-2] every element's emission spectrum to be unique? Why? (The protons affect the spectra because different numbers of protons make each element unique. The electrons affect the spectra because they gain energy and move within the atom.)
- Students should notice that, for some elements, emission lines seem to form in clusters of similar frequencies. Prompt students to investigate whether there is a pattern [CCC-1] related to the clustering and the number of electrons of the atom.
- If students struggle with the concept of characteristic emission lines for each element, have them think about the energy levels like rungs on a ladder (or a staircase, as shown on page 24 of the Experience Notebook) with the lowest energy level at the bottom. As electrons "climb" from lower energy levels to higher levels, they require the input of energy (similar to the energy input required to move up rungs on a ladder). When electrons then "fall" back to a lower state, they give off light energy, with the color of the light proportional to the "distance" the electron "falls." Electrons always return to a lower energy state, so the same colors of light are always produced by a given element.
- Point out that, although a ladder is a good model for electron levels, it does have limitations. Unlike rungs of a ladder, electron energy levels are not evenly spaced, so the spacing among emission lines does not show a regular pattern.
- Expand on the explanation that different elements produce unique spectra because of their atomic structure. Nuclei have stronger or weaker attractions to the electrons, depending on the number of protons and interactions among electrons themselves. Because of these interactions, each element has a unique "ladder" of energy levels.

Atomic Emission Spectra and the Bohr Model (20)

Experience Notebook Ideally, assign the Experience Notebook or Realize Reader for this experience the day before, and then follow up with any of the following suggested instructional strategies to fill knowledge gaps and deepen understanding. Alternatively, assign it alongside the Claim-Evidence-Reasoning activity as support for the activity.

Use these strategies to help students make sense of the images and text on the indicated pages, as well as to engage science skills:

- **Atomic Emission Spectra** (pp. 22–23) Ask students if they think it is possible to tell which isotope of strontium is represented by the atomic emission spectrum on this page. **Ask** If every sample of the unknown element produces the exact same spectrum, what does that tell you about the involvement of neutrons in emission spectra? (Because isotopes don't matter, neutrons are not involved.)
- **The Bohr Model** (pp. 24–25) If students are struggling with connecting atomic emission spectra with electron energy levels, then take students to a staircase and use a ball to represent an electron. Use a staircase with steps that are not of equal size, such as a hillside staircase, to reinforce that not all quantum have the same amount of energy.

  1. Have one student stand at the bottom of the stairs (at the lowest energy level) while a few other students stand on the steps above them.

2. Have the student at the bottom of the stairs throw the "electron" ball to the student on the next step above them. Have that student roll the ball back down to the first student.
3. Repeat this, but this time throw the ball to the student on the highest step and let the student roll it back down.
4. **Ask** Did the electron gain or lose energy when it transitioned from the lowest energy level to the highest? (gained energy) Did the electron gain or lose energy when it transitioned from the highest energy level back to the lowest? (lost energy) Which transition required the greatest input of energy? (from the lowest energy level to the highest energy level) Which transition released the most energy? (from the highest energy level to the lowest energy level) Can the ball transition to any points between students? (no, it cannot, just like the electron cannot transition to a point in between energy levels)
5. Finally, connect the different transitions and energy levels to the different spectral lines in a emission spectrum.

- **Bohr Model Representations of Atoms** (p. 26) Emphasize that the Bohr model (like other models) is one way of showing some of the characteristics of an atom, but it is not a completely accurate representation. The usefulness of the model is that it correctly represents certain observable features and allows for predictions about the behavior and properties of elements. Have students discuss why we don't use a model that is an exact replica of an atom. (We don't observe the structure of atoms directly but infer the structure from data about how atoms interact.)

DIFFERENTIATED INSTRUCTION

- **Support Struggling Students** Students may be confused about the concepts of orbits and energy levels and why energy must be added to move an electron to a higher orbit. Have them consider the attraction between an electron and the nucleus. In a low orbit, the attraction is very strong, while in a higher orbit it is less strong because the distance is greater. So, energy must be added to make the electron and the nucleus move away from one another.
- **Support Advanced Students** Some advanced students may notice that certain atoms produce several groups of emission lines. Have students research the energy levels and how the difference between them decreases as the level increases, and then use this information to explain how hydrogen with one electron can have several emission lines. Relate that explanation to atoms with electrons in several different ground states.

ASSESS ON THE SPOT

Have students examine the illustration about emission of specific wavelengths of light on page 23 of the Experience Notebook. **Ask** Based on the diagram, what can you conclude about absorption of light by an atom? (Atoms can only absorb certain wavelengths of light that correspond to the movement of an electron to a higher energy level.)

PROFESSIONAL DEVELOPMENT

Explaining Phenomena Direct students' attention to the diagram on page 22 of the Experience Notebook. **Ask** What is the difference between the spectrum of light from an ordinary light bulb and the spectrum from a hydrogen lamp? (The light bulb spectrum shows a continuous display of all the colors of visible light. The hydrogen lamp shows discrete bands of only certain frequencies of light.) Explain that the frequencies correspond to transitions of electrons in the hydrogen atom. **Ask** Why is hydrogen a good model for studying the correlation between emission spectrum and atomic structure? (Hydrogen, with only one electron, has the simplest electron configuration and thus the simplest emission spectrum.)

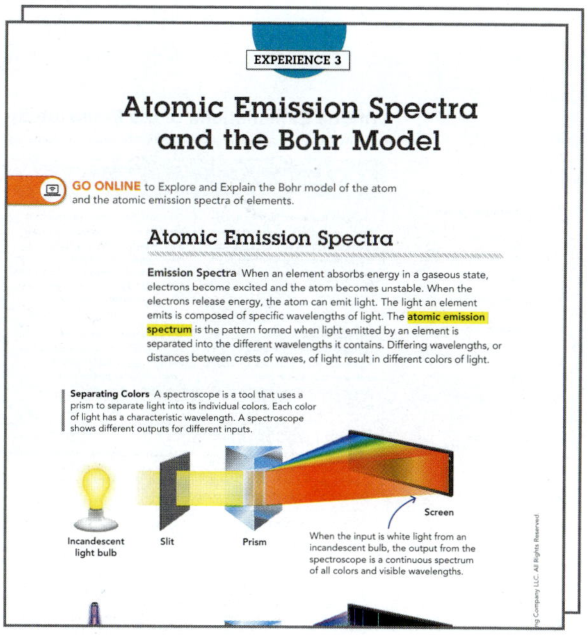
EXPERIENCE 3

Atomic Emission Spectra and the Bohr Model

GO ONLINE to Explore and Explain the Bohr model of the atom and the atomic emission spectra of elements.

Atomic Emission Spectra

Emission Spectra When an element absorbs energy in a gaseous state, electrons become excited and the atom becomes unstable. When the electrons release energy, the atom can emit light. The light an element emits is composed of specific wavelengths of light. The **atomic emission spectrum** is the pattern formed when light emitted by an element is separated into the different wavelengths it contains. Differing wavelengths, or distances between crests of waves, of light result in different colors of light.

Separating Colors A spectroscope is a tool that uses a prism to separate light into its individual colors. Each color of light has a characteristic wavelength. A spectroscope shows different outputs for different inputs.

Experience Notebook, pp. 22–27

eTEXT

ELD SUPPORT

Reading Students work with a partner to explain the meaning of *quantum* after reading about the Bohr Model in the Experience Notebook.

- **Emerging/Beginning** Have students draw a diagram that explains the meaning of *quantum* as it is use on page 24 of the Experience Notebook.
- **Developing/Expanding** Ask student pairs to explain to each other the meaning of *quantum*, using the images on page 24 of the Experience Notebook.
- **Bridging** Have student pairs explain how climbing stairs relates to the meaning of *quantum*.

ADDRESS PRECONCEPTIONS

Students may have a preconception that the light emitted by an atom corresponds to a *change* in energy level of the electron, not to an energy level itself. Ask these questions to clarify the preconceptions about the Bohr model: When is a photon emitted from an atom? (when an electron moves from a higher energy level to a lower energy level) How can the addition of heat energy cause an element to appear to glow? (Adding heat energy allows electrons to move to a higher energy level. Light is emitted when electrons move to a lower level, causing the material to glow). Explain that energy is only absorbed or emitted during a change in energy level and that energy level is not the same thing as distance from the nucleus, even though the Bohr model represents it as distance.

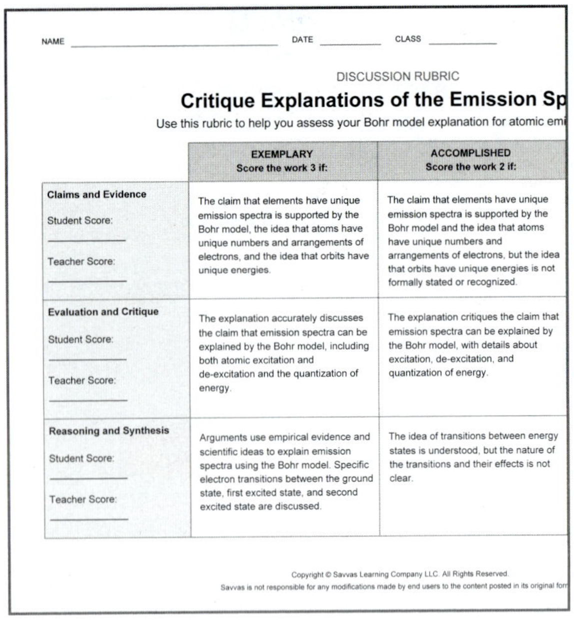

NAME ______________ DATE ________ CLASS ________

DISCUSSION RUBRIC

Critique Explanations of the Emission Sp

Use this rubric to help you assess your Bohr model explanation for atomic emi

	EXEMPLARY Score the work 3 if:	ACCOMPLISHED Score the work 2 if:
Claims and Evidence Student Score: ______ Teacher Score: ______	The claim that elements have unique emission spectra is supported by the Bohr model, the idea that atoms have unique numbers and arrangements of electrons, and the idea that orbits have unique energies.	The claim that elements have unique emission spectra is supported by the Bohr model and the idea that atoms have unique numbers and arrangements of electrons, but the idea that orbits have unique energies is not formally stated or recognized.
Evaluation and Critique Student Score: ______ Teacher Score: ______	The explanation accurately discusses the claim that emission spectra can be explained by the Bohr model, including both atomic excitation and de-excitation and the quantization of energy.	The explanation critiques the claim that emission spectra can be explained by the Bohr model, with details about excitation, de-excitation, and quantization of energy.
Reasoning and Synthesis Student Score: ______ Teacher Score: ______	Arguments use empirical evidence and scientific ideas to explain emission spectra using the Bohr model. Specific electron transitions between the ground state, first excited state, and second excited state are discussed.	The idea of transitions between energy states is understood, but the nature of the transitions and their effects is not clear.

Discussion Rubric Interactive Worksheet

ELABORATE

Critique Explanations of the Emission Spectra

Discussion Rubric Lead a discussion with the class on how the use of the Bohr model can be used as a tool to connect electrons in an atom to its atomic emission spectrum and how the model can be used to predict the relationship between electrons and energy emission. Show the hydrogen emission spectrum and draw on the board a Bohr model of hydrogen showing at least five energy levels. Ask the following questions during the discussion:

- How do the lines in an atomic emission spectrum provide evidence that electrons can only exist in specific energy levels within the atom? (Each line corresponds to a specific change in energy. No other emissions of light occur.)
- Which transition in a hydrogen atom corresponds to the purple (410 nm) line in the hydrogen emission spectrum? (Remind students that a shorter wavelength corresponds to higher energy.) (transition from the ground state, level 1, to the fifth energy level)
- Why do the spectral lines for a transition in another element not occur at the same wavelength as the hydrogen lines? (Each element has unique characteristic orbits, or energy levels, based on the atomic structure of the element.)
- Have the class decide how to modify the Bohr model to illustrate these concepts: excitation (process), excited state and de-excitation (process), ground state and quantization of energy. (excitation–arrow showing movement to higher energy level; excited state–electron in higher energy level; de-excitation–arrow showing movement to a lower energy level; ground state–electron in lowest energy level; quantization of energy–discrete gaps between energy levels)

Instruct students to use the rubric to evaluate their own explanations for the link between the model and the data [SEP-8].

ASSESS ON THE SPOT

Give students 3 minutes to write about one piece of evidence to support the idea that atoms have unique numbers and arrangements of electrons.

PROFESSIONAL DEVELOPMENT

Background Notes Spectroscopy is one of the basic tools that scientists use to study the universe, including objects such as stars, black holes, neutron stars, and galaxies. That is because spectra are not just produced for visible light; they can be produced for any light energy, from low-energy radio waves to very high-energy gamma rays. Astronomers study the emission spectra of objects to understand how the objects produce light. Objects produce light by many different mechanisms, and each mechanism has a characteristic spectrum.

Astronomers can look at the width of the spectral line of an object, such as a star, to figure out how fast it is moving and to find out about its winds. They can not only determine what elements the star is composed of, but they can also determine the temperature and density of an element in the star. Spectral lines also indicate any magnetic field of the star. If the spectral lines shift back and forth, scientists learn that the star may be orbiting another star. They can study spectral lines to determine the mass and size of a star and about materials around a star. Light from matter between stars informs scientists what type of matter fills the space between stars.

Build a Spectroscope from Household Materials

Engineering Design Challenge In this Engineering Design Challenge, students investigate [SEP-3] spectroscopes and then build a functioning spectroscope. They test [SEP-6] their spectroscopes and evaluate whether the tool was successful.

Materials 1.5 cm square holographic diffraction grafting, cardboard tube, clear tape, colored pencils, $4\frac{1}{2}$ in. × 2 in. black construction paper, black electrical tape, hole punch, pencil, ruler, scissors

Expected Outcome Students successfully build a functioning spectroscope.

Use the following strategies to guide students as they complete indicated steps in the Engineering Design Challenge.

- **Step 1** If students have difficulty identifying the problem, read aloud the introductory paragraph on the worksheet. **Ask** Which sentence identifies the problem [SEP-1]? (last sentence)
- **Step 5 Ask** Why might a group of students want to build their own spectroscopes rather than buy them? (Common spectroscopes can be costly.) What kinds of materials would you use to make an inexpensive spectroscope? (everyday common objects such as cardboard paper-towel tubes) Relate these answers to criteria for the spectroscope.
- **Step 5** Remind students to consider the criteria and constraints of the problem as they determine a rough idea of how to build the spectroscope. Model the method to build a functioning spectroscope if students are struggling to follow the procedure.
- **Step 7** Remind students that their test results should be evaluated against the criteria to determine whether the spectroscope was successful. If results do not meet criteria, ask students to explain how they think they could have improved their model. Point out that designs sometimes cannot meet all criteria. In those cases, designers must decide which criteria are most important.

DIFFERENTIATED INSTRUCTION

- **Support Special Needs Students** To help students with hearing impairments, provide the student and at least one other group member with a computer or tablet that can be used to exchange ideas.
- Students with auditory processing disorders often work best in a quiet environment. Have these students complete the activity with partners, rather than in a group, in a quiet area of the classroom.
- **Support Less Proficient Readers** Help less proficient readers by providing a diagram or series of diagrams of the procedure in Step 5. For the other steps, read through the text and have the students underline key words that relate to the task, such as *problem* in Step 1, *criteria* and *constraints* in Step 2, and *research* in Step 3.

NAME ______________ DATE ________ CLASS ________

ENGINEERING DESIGN CHALLENGE

Build a Spectroscope from Household Materials

A spectroscope is a device for observing the color spectrum of visible light. A spectrum is produced when light from any source is bent or dispersed. Does every type of light show the same spectrum? Common spectroscopes can be costly and are usually made of nonreusable parts. Find out by using common household materials and a holographic diffraction grating to build a simple, working spectroscope.

Focus on Engineering Practices

SEP 1 Defining Problem
SEP 3 Planning and Carrying Out Investigations
SEP 6 Designing Solutions

Materials Per Group

- Holographic diffraction grating, 1.5-cm square
- Cardboard tube
- Tape, clear
- Colored pencils
- Construction paper, black, 4½" × 2"
- Electrical tape, black
- Hole punch
- Pencil
- Ruler, 1-mm precision
- Scissors

Safety

The materials used in this activity are considered safe. Caution students against looking directly at the sun, even through the spectroscope. Students should follow all normal classroom safety guidelines.

Engineering Design Challenge Interactive Worksheet

INTEGRATE THE THREE DIMENSIONS

In the Engineering Design Challenge, students build functioning spectroscopes to explore how spectroscopes can be utilized for observing the color spectrum of visible light. Students test and evaluate [SEP-8] the success of the spectroscopes by considering the criteria and constraints of the design solution [ETS1.B]. Students should support their claims with evidence that describes the patterns [CCC-1] they observe about each spectrum.

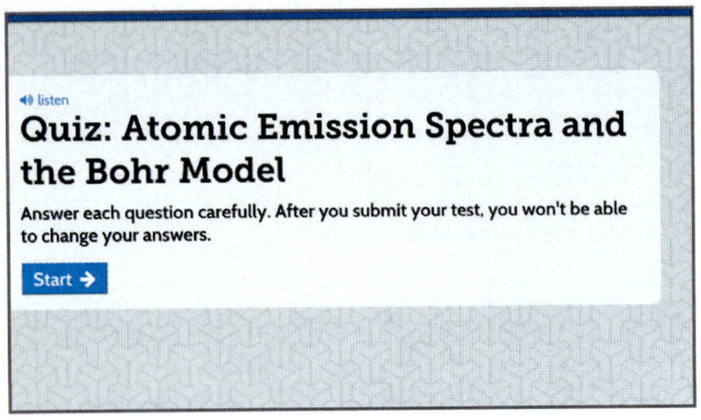
listen

Quiz: Atomic Emission Spectra and the Bohr Model

Answer each question carefully. After you submit your test, you won't be able to change your answers.

Start →

Interactive Online Quiz

Quiz Interactive Worksheet

EVALUATE

Atomic Emission Spectra and the Bohr Model

Quiz Assign the quiz in online technology-enhanced, auto-graded format or as an editable quiz worksheet. Use the scoring notes and remediation strategies found online to assess students' responses and to provide targeted feedback for each item to remediate well before assigning the summative 3-D Assessment.

REMEDIATION SUGGESTIONS

- **If** students have trouble correctly placing electrons in the proper energy levels in a Bohr model, **then** have them review the Explore Bohr Model Patterns worksheet. They can study the visual in the worksheet and work with a more proficient partner to better understand the concept.
- **If** students have difficulty relating why hydrogen atoms produce specific emission spectra, **then** have them look at the hydrogen lamp diagram on page 22. **Ask** What does a prism do? (separates light according to different wavelengths, or colors) What colors are produced when the light from a hydrogen light passes through a prism? (purple, blue, green, red) What are the colors of the spectral lines for hydrogen? (same as the colors of light produced when the light from the hydrogen lamp passes through the prism)
- **If** students are struggling to describe the atomic emission spectrum, **then** have them review the spectroscopes they built and tested in the Engineering Design Challenge.

Revisit

INVESTIGATIVE PHENOMENON

GO ONLINE to Elaborate on and Evaluate your knowledge of atomic emission spectra by completing the class discussion and engineering design activities.

In the modeling worksheet you completed at the beginning of the investigation, you sketched a model to help explain the color generation of different fireworks. With a partner, evaluate your models.

24 **SEP Construct an Explanation** Compare and contrast the colors and wavelengths of the light emitted from two different colors of fireworks, based on the elements they contain. Explain why these elements have different atomic emission spectra.

Experience Notebook, p. 27

eTEXT

Revisit

INVESTIGATIVE PHENOMENON

Support Reflection Students can complete the reflection prompt, where they will unpack and make sense of the Investigative Phenomenon, based on practices and understandings that have been reinforced over the course of the experience.

- Ask students to use the Bohr model to explain how atoms can absorb energy and emit light of different colors. Next, prompt the class to identify the energy source in the fireworks scenario that excites the electrons in the atoms and allows them to then relax back to the ground state, emitting energy that we perceive as light. (heat from the explosion)
- To help students answer Question 18, have them revisit the different emission spectra on page 23 of the Experience Notebook. **Ask** What colors are present in the emission spectrum of sodium? (purple and yellow) What color of light would be given off if a firework were made of sodium? (purple and yellow)

Further Develop Your Model Have students add any evidence they have collected in this experience. Allow time for them to make any additional changes based on information they have collected from the activities in this learning experience. Evidence might include that each element produces a specific emission spectrum because atoms absorb or release light with an energy exactly equal to the energy difference between energy levels in the atom.

EXPERIENCE 4

Modern Atomic Theory

Teacher Background

As scientists learned more about the behavior of electrons in atoms, a new, more complete, and more complex model was developed. Instead of finding electrons in neat orbits around the nucleus (as in the Bohr model), modern atomic theory predicted areas in which the electron was most probably found at any given moment in time (an orbital). This new probabilistic picture of electrons was based on integrating the observed wavelike properties of electrons into existing models of the atom.

This experience focuses on how the modern atomic model adds new subshells to each energy level that the electrons can occupy. These subshells are described by the abbreviations *s*, *p*, *d*, and *f* (in order of increasing energy). Note that the way electrons fill these orbitals will be covered in the next experience, so focus on the orbitals themselves while teaching this content.

Objectives

- **Investigate how the quantum mechanical nature of the electron gave rise to modern atomic orbital theory.**
- **Evaluate how the quantum mechanical nature of the electron can be used to refine models of the atom.**

ENGAGE

EVERYDAY PHENOMENON

Does the same change always produce the same amount of energy?

Use this teacher demo to help students understand the concept of quantized energy.

Quantized Energy

Engage students with this demonstration to introduce the concept of electrons and quantum energy. The energy changes relating to a bouncing ball provide a macroscopic model in which the conversions of potential and kinetic energies represent the changes between electron energy and light.

Materials small rubber ball that bounces easily, bookshelf, meter stick

1. Place the ball on the bottom shelf of the bookshelf. (If a bookshelf beside a hard floor is not available, arrange several different surfaces, such as table and chairs, to provide various heights.) Ask students to describe what they think will happen when the ball rolls off the shelf.
2. Gently start the ball rolling so that it falls to the floor. Measure the height that the ball bounces. Repeat several times and record the results on the board.
3. Repeat, using a higher shelf or surface, so that the ball falls farther.
4. Repeat, using an even higher drop.
5. Ask students to identify patterns [CCC-1] in the data and relate the height of the bounce to the shelf from which the ball fell. Explain that the ball has a given amount of potential energy that is converted to kinetic energy. Because the shelves have discrete heights, the amount of potential energy had only one of three possible values.

RELATED PHENOMENA

In addition to the teacher demo, Quantized Energy, consider using other phenomena to launch this experience.

- **Compare Observations and Models** Demonstrate a simple flame test using salts of several alkali metals: lithium, sodium, and potassium. Have students relate variations of energy in light frequency emitted to differences in the Bohr models of atoms.
- **Model an Electron Cloud** Use a tabletop electric fan to model the concept of an electron cloud. Have students observe the number and position of the blades with the fan off and compare to observations with the fan on. **Ask** Can you locate an individual blade with the fan turned on? Can you describe a general area in which the blades are located?

6. Call on students to explain how this model [SEP-2] might relate to the energy released by electrons in an atom. Then ask how energy released by electrons might help to explain why fireworks produce light of different colors. Explain that they will find out whether their explanations are correct as they complete Experience 4.

EXPLORE

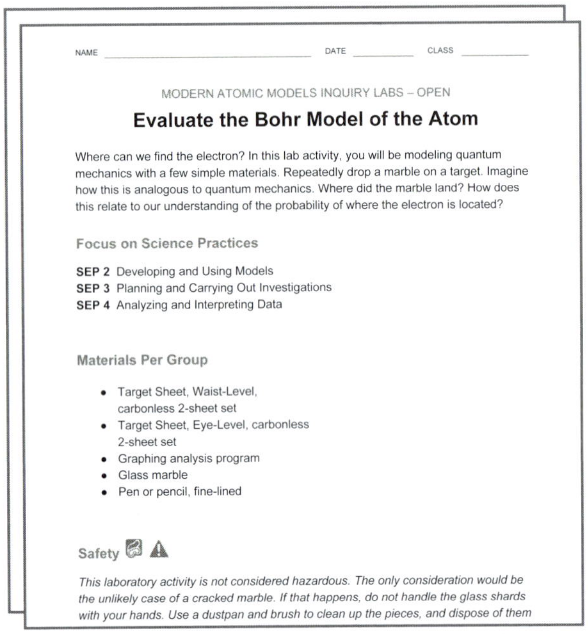

NAME ______ DATE ______ CLASS ______

MODERN ATOMIC MODELS INQUIRY LABS – OPEN

Evaluate the Bohr Model of the Atom

Where can we find the electron? In this lab activity, you will be modeling quantum mechanics with a few simple materials. Repeatedly drop a marble on a target. Imagine how this is analogous to quantum mechanics. Where did the marble land? How does this relate to our understanding of the probability of where the electron is located?

Focus on Science Practices

SEP 2 Developing and Using Models
SEP 3 Planning and Carrying Out Investigations
SEP 4 Analyzing and Interpreting Data

Materials Per Group

- Target Sheet, Waist-Level, carbonless 2-sheet set
- Target Sheet, Eye-Level, carbonless 2-sheet set
- Graphing analysis program
- Glass marble
- Pen or pencil, fine-lined

Safety

This laboratory activity is not considered hazardous. The only consideration would be the unlikely case of a cracked marble. If that happens, do not handle the glass shards with your hands. Use a dustpan and brush to clean up the pieces, and dispose of them

O/G/S/A Lab Interactive Worksheets

Evaluate the Bohr Model of the Atom

Inquiry Lab In this lab, students carry out an investigation [SEP-3] to model quantum mechanics. Students explore whether it is possible to know the precise location of an electron around the nucleus of an atom at any given time.

Lab Demo Video Watch the Lab Demo Video for advice on materials and preparation.

Choose Your Version Open-ended (O), Guided (G), Shortened (S), Advanced (A)

Materials carbonless target sheet, glass marble, fine-lined pen or pencil, graphing analysis program

Expected Outcome This activity will help students gain an understanding of the concept of probability and visualize the shapes and relative positions of the orbitals in a hydrogen atom.

Lab Summary Video Watch the Lab Summary Video for support on connecting the lab investigation to the Investigative Phenomenon.

The Quantum Mechanical Model and Atomic Orbitals

Interactivity In this activity, students explore the different atomic orbitals and see how the electrons in each element fill the orbitals from lowest energy to highest. They build models [SEP-2] of different atoms using *s*, *p*, *d*, and *f* orbital shapes. This activity works best when each student can manipulate the interactivity on their own, so have students work individually for this assignment.

- As students complete this activity, ensure they understand that all of the orbitals actually overlap somewhat. For example, the 1*s* and 2*s* orbitals have the same general spherical shape, and both are centered on the nucleus. The 1*s* orbital is smaller and lies mostly inside the area occupied by the 2*s* orbital. This is why atoms are often portrayed as tiny spheres—the overlapping orbitals take on an overall spherical shape.
- Students can use the subshell energies diagram on page 31 of the Experience Notebook to help them place the correct orbitals into their atomic models. Remind students that electrons will always fill the lowest-energy orbitals first—just like a ball will roll to the bottom of a hill on its own.

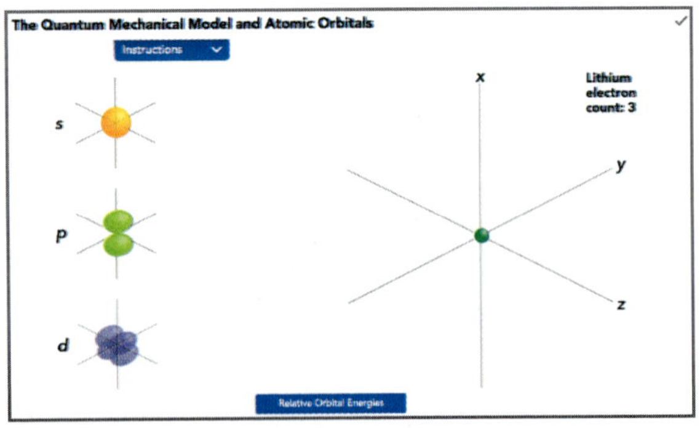

Interactivity: The Quantum Mechanical Model and Atomic Orbitals

ASSESS ON THE SPOT

As a quick check that students are assigning the proper atomic orbitals to different elements, have them tell you what the highest energy-occupied orbital is for different elements. This will also set the groundwork for identifying the different orbital blocks in the periodic table in the next experience.

EXPLAIN

Evaluate Atomic Models

Claim-Evidence-Reasoning Students develop an evidence-based argument [SEP-7] explaining whether we should continue to use the Bohr model of the atom even though the quantum mechanical model is more accurate. Students should write their initial CER statements by themselves but then work in groups of three or four to critique and refine their statements.

- **Using Models** Ask students to give another example of a model that we continue to use even though we know it has flaws. For example, the continents shown on a flat map are extremely skewed in size, but these projections are still used because they are sometimes easier to handle than a globe. Remind students that a model does not have to be an exact replicate of the object or system being studied. It only needs to be useful for explaining phenomenon and making predictions.
- **Compare and Contrast Models** Remind students that the subshells shown in the quantum mechanical model exist within energy levels, or shells, just as predicted in the Bohr model. The main difference is in the position and wavelike nature of the electrons (existing spread out within 3-D space rather than a point moving in a circle).

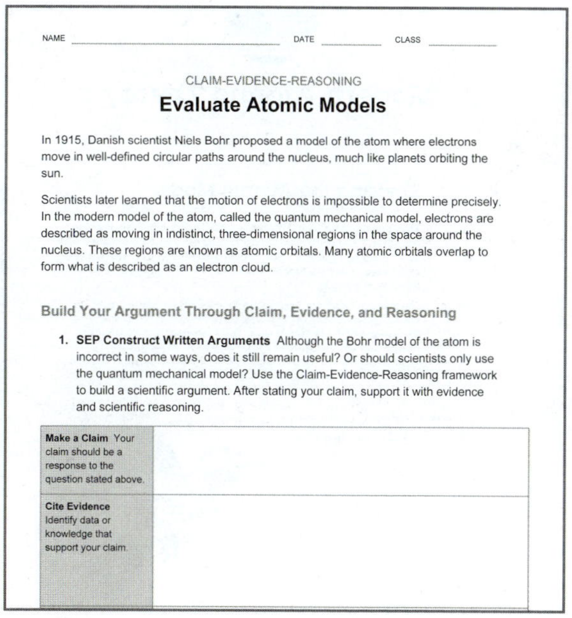

NAME ______ DATE ______ CLASS ______

CLAIM-EVIDENCE-REASONING

Evaluate Atomic Models

In 1915, Danish scientist Niels Bohr proposed a model of the atom where electrons move in well-defined circular paths around the nucleus, much like planets orbiting the sun.

Scientists later learned that the motion of electrons is impossible to determine precisely. In the modern model of the atom, called the quantum mechanical model, electrons are described as moving in indistinct, three-dimensional regions in the space around the nucleus. These regions are known as atomic orbitals. Many atomic orbitals overlap to form what is described as an electron cloud.

Build Your Argument Through Claim, Evidence, and Reasoning

1. **SEP Construct Written Arguments** Although the Bohr model of the atom is incorrect in some ways, does it still remain useful? Or should scientists only use the quantum mechanical model? Use the Claim-Evidence-Reasoning framework to build a scientific argument. After stating your claim, support it with evidence and scientific reasoning.

Make a Claim Your claim should be a response to the question stated above.	
Cite Evidence Identify data or knowledge that support your claim.	

CER Interactive Worksheet

DIFFERENTIATED INSTRUCTION

- **Support Special Needs Students** Have students work with a partner to research the history of atomic models. Provide students with a specific atomic model and scientist to research. As students are researching, help them identify experimental evidence and reasoning that supported the model. Have students record and summarize their findings for the class. After each pair shares, discuss why they think earlier models of the atom were replaced and how each model was important for the development of the next model.
- **Support Advanced Students** Many interesting thought experiments were proposed as a result of the discovery of the quantum mechanical model of matter. These thought experiments helped scientists understand the strange behavior of particles at the quantum level due to their wavelike properties. Have students select one of these thought experiments and describe its meaning to the class as part of their research. Examples include Schrödinger's cat, Heisenberg's microscope, and Einstein's EPR paradox.

CLASSROOM MODIFICATIONS

Based on your students' abilities and your schedule, you can modify the Evaluate Atomic Models activity to be more open ended or more guided.

- **More Open Ended** Instead of having students go through the structured CER activity, they can explain why we still use the Bohr model if we now know that it is technically not as correct as the quantum mechanical model of the atom. Encourage students to use evidence to back up their claims, as outlined in the activity.
- **More Guided** Organize the class into two groups and instruct one half to develop arguments for continued use of the Bohr model while the other half argues for sole use of the quantum mechanical model. This can help stimulate class discussion later during the teacher-led discussion.

PROFESSIONAL DEVELOPMENT

Background Notes Experimental evidence for the atomic orbitals was first seen in the atomic emission spectra of alkali metals. The spectral lines were described as being "sharp, principal, diffuse, and fundamental." When theorists connected this experimental evidence with the orbitals they predicted from the Schrödinger equation, the names were shortened to *s*, *p*, *d*, and *f*. These letters each represent a different angular momentum value for the electrons.

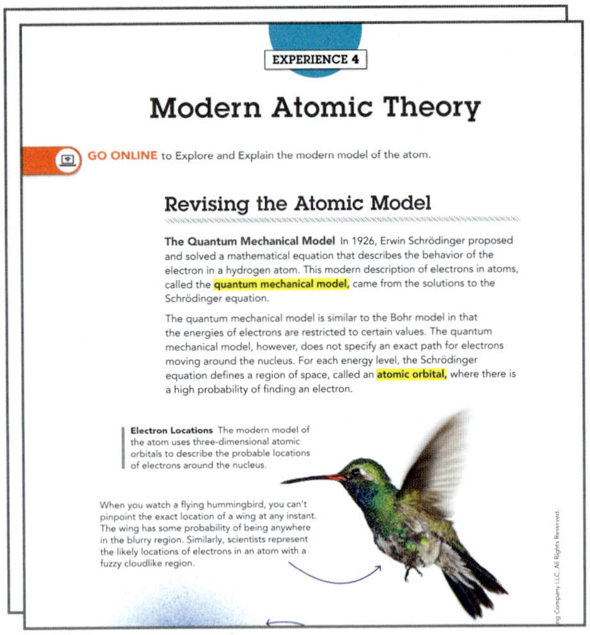
EXPERIENCE 4

Modern Atomic Theory

GO ONLINE to Explore and Explain the modern model of the atom.

Revising the Atomic Model

The Quantum Mechanical Model In 1926, Erwin Schrödinger proposed and solved a mathematical equation that describes the behavior of the electron in a hydrogen atom. This modern description of electrons in atoms, called the **quantum mechanical model,** came from the solutions to the Schrödinger equation.

The quantum mechanical model is similar to the Bohr model in that the energies of electrons are restricted to certain values. The quantum mechanical model, however, does not specify an exact path for electrons moving around the nucleus. For each energy level, the Schrödinger equation defines a region of space, called an **atomic orbital,** where there is a high probability of finding an electron.

Electron Locations The modern model of the atom uses three-dimensional atomic orbitals to describe the probable locations of electrons around the nucleus.

When you watch a flying hummingbird, you can't pinpoint the exact location of a wing at any instant. The wing has some probability of being anywhere in the blurry region. Similarly, scientists represent the likely locations of electrons in an atom with a fuzzy cloudlike region.

Experience Notebook, pp. 28–32

eTEXT

ELD SUPPORT

Speaking Students work with a partner to discuss various aspects of the Bohr model and atomic orbital model after reading the Experience Notebook.

- **Emerging/Beginning** Ask students to participate in a group discussion describing the similarities and differences between the Bohr model and atomic orbital model by asking yes/no questions.
- **Developing/Expanding** Have students describe in their own words the main differences between the Bohr model and the atomic orbital model.
- **Bridging** Have students debate the relative merits of the Bohr and atomic orbital models using domain-specific language and evidence from the text.

ADDRESS PRECONCEPTIONS

Most students will understand that electrons are found in an electron cloud, but be sure they do not think that the electron cloud is made of some other material. Remind them that the electron cloud is a model that shows the area where the probability of finding electrons is likely. Direct students to look at the diagram of the electron cloud on page 28 of the Experience Notebook. **Ask** Why is the cloud darker in some places than in other places? (The darker the area, the greater the probability of finding an electron is.)

Modern Atomic Theory

20

Experience Notebook This section of the Experience Notebook or Realize Reader works best when used as a reference and reinforcement for the activities covered in this lesson. Avoid assigning this section as reading until students have the proper context around the significance of atomic orbitals, which they should gain by completing the interactivity and the CER activity.

Use these strategies to help students make sense of the images and text on the indicated pages, as well as to engage science skills.

- **Revising the Atomic Model** (pp. 28–29) Call on a volunteer to draw a Bohr model of neon on the board. Ask students if they could easily draw a Bohr model of radon, which has an atomic number of 86. (Students should realize that showing 86 electrons in the atom's orbits would be difficult and ineffective.) Then direct students' attention to the shell model on page 29. Explain that this model makes representing atoms with larger numbers of electrons much easier. Review the diagram with the class.
- **Atomic Orbitals** (pp. 30–31) Remind students that another difficulty for using the Bohr model for some situations is that the model shows the electrons in specific locations, which is not correct because electrons are constantly moving. Tell students to think of a beehive. All the bees associated with the hive visit it sometimes, but they also can be other places. Draw a beehive on the board, and tell students that the area around the hive is a very large field. **Ask** Where would you most likely see a bee? (near the hive) How would the probability of seeing a bee change as you move farther from the hive? (It would decrease.)
- To help students understand the shapes of the *s* and *p* orbitals, push three skewers through a foam ball at right angles to each other and as close to the ball's center as possible. **Ask** What type of orbital does this represent? (s) Identify the *x*-, *y*-, and *z*-axes. Then push a skewer through two balls to represent a *p* orbital. Tell students that the skewer can represent any one of the three axes. **Ask** Where along the axis is the atomic nucleus? (at the point between the two balls)
- Students may have trouble remembering the relative energies of the different types of subshells. In that case, have them create a sentence using *s*, *p*, *d*, and *f* as the first letters in each word as a mnemonic device to help them remember. Encourage students to make these silly so they are easier to remember. For example: Sticky paint dries fast.
- **Subshell Energies Diagram** (p. 31) Don't spend any time getting students to remember this diagram at this point. Once they can recognize the orbital-filling pattern in the layout of the periodic table in a future experience, they won't have to memorize this. Allow students to use this diagram in any activities and exercises in this experience.

ASSESS ON THE SPOT

Generate at least five true or false questions about the shell model and how it relates to atomic orbitals. Divide the class into two groups. State one of the true or false questions and allow groups time to deliberate. Tell groups to have a designated person state the answer and the reasoning for the answer. Assign one point for each correct answer and reason. The group with the most points wins.

ELABORATE

Evaluate Atomic Models

Discussion Rubric Students use the rubric as a scoring guide to evaluate their claim about whether the Bohr model is still useful.

- After students complete their rubrics, lead a class discussion to compare and contrast the value of the Bohr and quantum mechanical models [SEP-2] of the atom. When students offer conflicting answers, especially to the question about the value of the Bohr model, have them offer critiques of each other's answers, and encourage the class to engage in constructive argument [SEP-7].
- Use the following questions to prompt discussion:
  a. Describe how each model represents electrons in the second energy level. Sketch a picture or diagram to show this.
  b. The quantum mechanical model is the more recent model. How is it more accurate than the Bohr model?

The History of Atomic Models

Writing About Science Students conduct research about the history of atomic models and the scientists who developed the models. They identify experimental evidence and reasoning that supported each model. Then they explain why earlier models of the atom were replaced and how each model was important for the development of the next model [NoS-3].

- Remind students to use only reputable sources and have them generate a bibliography of texts, articles, and Web sites used in their research.
- Consider having students share their findings in a presentation. Instead of having every group present the same material to the class, have students record their presentations in a video before submitting them for evaluation. Provide a rubric for the presentation if the assignment will be graded.

ASSESS ON THE SPOT

On the board, draw a dartboard with concentric circles. Draw about 20 small solid dots on the dartboard, so that the concentration of dots decreases as you move away from the bull's-eye. Tell students that the dots represent dart holes made by a dart player. Call on students to describe the distribution of dots. **Ask** How is the distribution of holes analogous to the distribution of electrons in an atom? (In an atom, the probability of finding an electron at a particular place diminishes with distance from the nucleus.) Discuss the disadvantages of using this as a model for an atom, such as an atom is three-dimensional and the diagram is two-dimensional.

Atomic Structure

Virtual Reality Experience Students explore how atoms interact with each other based on their atomic structure.

NAME ______ DATE ______ CLASS ______

DISCUSSION RUBRIC

Evaluate Atomic Models

Use this rubric to help you assess your evaluations of the modern model and Bohr

	EXEMPLARY Score the work 3 if:	ACCOMPLISHED Score the work 2 if:
Components of the Model Student Score: ____ Teacher Score: ____	The greater accuracy of the QM model is acknowledged and described, as is the usefulness of the Bohr model for predicting chemical properties and behavior in chemical reactions. The value of both models is acknowledged.	The greater accuracy of the QM model or the usefulness of the Bohr model is discussed, but the model discounts or dismisses one of these properties. A claim may exaggerate a strength or weakness of one model in support of another.
Limitations of the Model Student Score: ____ Teacher Score: ____	Limitations include the inaccuracy of the planetary orbits in the Bohr model or the difficulty of identifying electrons in the QM model. Claims are strengthened when the limitations are acknowledged and addressed fully.	Limitations in the value of one or both atomic models are acknowledged but addressed minimally or superficially. Claims are not strengthened by acknowledging the limitations.
Relationships and Connections Student Score: ____ Teacher Score: ____	Both models are discussed in the context of how they would be used by chemists and chemistry students in various situations. The observation that all models are inaccurate in some respects is acknowledged.	Both models are discussed but are evaluated independently of how they might be used in different situations by different people. Accuracy may be presented as the most important or significant criteria for a model.

Discussion Rubric Interactive Worksheet

NAME ______ DATE ______ CLASS ______

WRITING ABOUT SCIENCE

The History of Atomic Models

Use the information provided and information gathered from authoritative sources on your own to answer Questions 1 and 2.

The idea of atoms may have first been proposed by Democritus, a philosopher of ancient Greece. In modern times, scientists identified the particles that make up the atom and how these particles relate to one another. The diagrams of historical atomic models (the Dalton, Thomson, Rutherford, Bohr, and quantum mechanical models) over time show our changing knowledge and ideas about atoms and subatomic particles as a result of new observations and advanced technologies. Although the most recent model is now almost 100 years old, scientists continue to test and revise their ideas about atomic structure.

Dalton Model (1803) Thomson Plum Pudding Model (1897) Rutherford Model (1911)

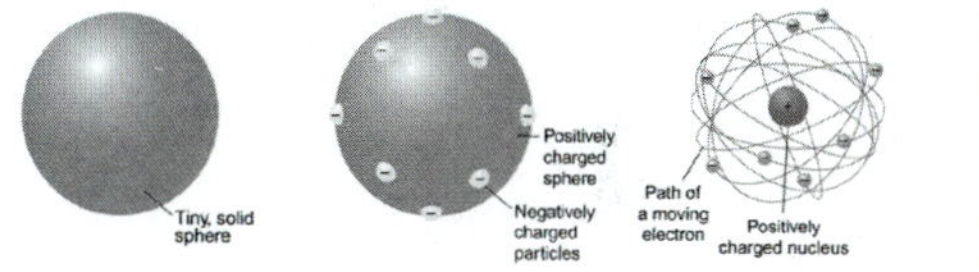

Bohr Model (1913) Quantum Mechanical Model (1926)

Writing About Science Interactive Worksheet

INTEGRATE THE THREE DIMENSIONS

In the Writing About Science activity, students research [SEP-8] how over time historical atomic models [NoS-3] have shown the changing knowledge and ideas [NoS-4] about atoms and subatomic particles [PS1.A] as a result of new observations and advanced technologies [NoS-7].

Virtual Reality Experience: Atomic Structure

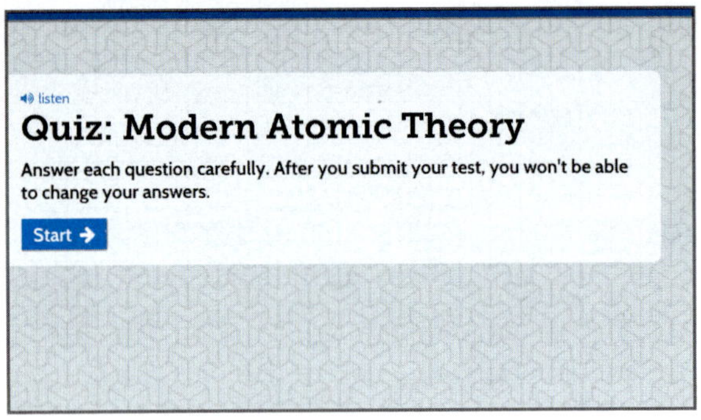

Interactive Online Quiz

Quiz Interactive Worksheet

EVALUATE

Modern Atomic Theory

Quiz Assign the quiz in online technology-enhanced, auto-graded format or as an editable quiz worksheet. Use the scoring notes and remediation strategies found online to assess students' responses and to provide targeted feedback for each item to remediate well before assigning the summative 3-D Assessment.

REMEDIATION SUGGESTIONS

- **If** students are having trouble adding the *s*, *p*, *d*, and *f* subshells to atomic models, **then** have them revisit the interactivity The Quantum Mechanical Model and Atomic Orbitals. Assign additional elements for them to model in the interactivity, and ensure they are following the subshell energies order shown on page 31 of the Experience Notebook.
- **If** students are unable to describe the strengths and weaknesses of both the Bohr model and the modern, quantum mechanical model of the atom, **then** encourage students to go back and read the Evaluate Atomic Models CER activity they completed. Have students make two T-charts showing pros and cons of using each model. Reinforce that imperfect models aren't always useless.

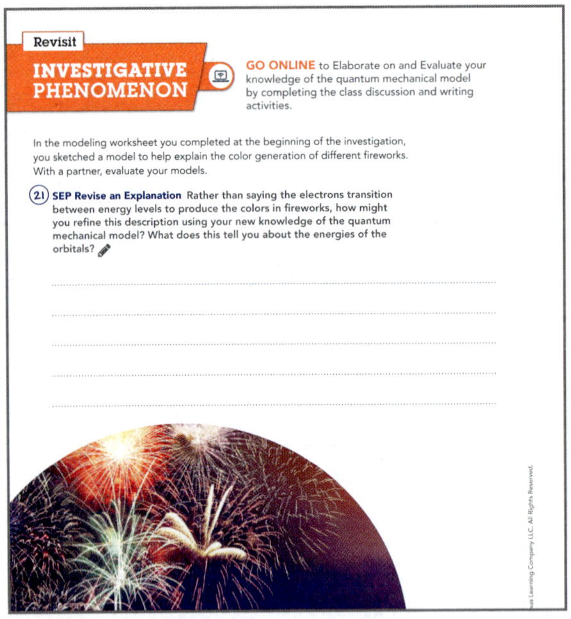
Revisit

INVESTIGATIVE PHENOMENON

GO ONLINE to Elaborate on and Evaluate your knowledge of the quantum mechanical model by completing the class discussion and writing activities.

In the modeling worksheet you completed at the beginning of the investigation, you sketched a model to help explain the color generation of different fireworks. With a partner, evaluate your models.

21 **SEP Revise an Explanation** Rather than saying the electrons transition between energy levels to produce the colors in fireworks, how might you refine this description using your new knowledge of the quantum mechanical model? What does this tell you about the energies of the orbitals?

Experience Notebook, p. 32

eTEXT

Revisit INVESTIGATIVE PHENOMENON

Support Reflection Students can complete the reflection prompt, where they will unpack and make sense of the Investigative Phenomenon, based on practices and understandings that have been reinforced over the course of the experience.

- Call on students to explain the relationship between energy and orbits in an atom. Ask students to describe how this relationship causes the colors in a fireworks display.
- As a group, list the electron subshells in order from lowest energy to highest energy. Remind students that this order only applies within a shell. **Ask** Is a *p* subshell ever higher in energy than a *d* subshell? (Yes, 4*p* is higher in energy than 3*d*.)

Further Develop Your Model Have students add any evidence they have collected in this experience. Allow time for them to make any additional changes based on information they have collected from the activities in this learning experience. Evidence may include that different orbitals contain electrons of different energies, similar to the way that different colors of light have different amounts of energy.

EXPERIENCE 5

Electrons in Atoms

Teacher Background

In the previous experience, students learned how to assign subshells to atoms based on the number of electrons. In this experience, students learn how to fill those subshells and to describe the configuration of electrons in each element, using both standard and noble gas notation. They discover that the pattern of orbital filling matches the layout of elements in the periodic table. Finally, students identify how noble gas notation can be used to quickly determine the number of valence (outermost shell) electrons in an atom and draw its electron dot structure.

Most electron models used in chemistry only deal with the valence electrons because they are the most reactive and therefore the most important in chemical reactions. Electron configurations are the only commonly used electron model that describes the energy and location of every electron in an atom.

Objectives

- **Predict the electron configuration of atoms using the periodic table as a model.**
- **Use electron dot structures to represent an atom's valence electrons.**

ENGAGE

EVERYDAY PHENOMENON

How do guests decide where to stay in a hotel?

Use this teacher demo to help students understand how electrons follow specific rules when filling atomic orbitals. Go through the discussion without mentioning electrons first, and then go back and explain how the analogy applies to electron behavior.

Electron Hotel

Engage students with this discussion of an everyday phenomenon to introduce the concept of atomic orbitals and electron-filling rules.

1. Draw on the board a picture of a hotel with three floors. There should be one room on the first floor (the 1*s* orbital), two rooms on the second floor (the 2*s* and 2*p* orbitals), and three rooms on the third floor (the 3*s*, 3*p*, and 3*d* orbitals). Draw one bunk bed in each room for every two electrons the orbital holds (so, one in the "s" rooms, three in the "p" rooms, and five in the "d" room).
2. Explain that the guests of this hotel are relatively lazy (electrons seek the lowest energy state) and not fond of each other (electrons repel each other). Their laziness takes precedence over their dislike for each other (being close to the nucleus is overall lower in potential energy than being separate, until too many electron repulsions force additional electrons further out).
3. Ask where the first hotel guest would stay, assuming that the guest is both lazy and wants to be alone. Students should assign the first guest to the first-floor room on the bottom bunk. Draw a dot in this position, representing the $1s^1$ electron.

RELATED PHENOMENA

In addition to the Electron Hotel demo, consider using other phenomena to launch this experience.

- **Blocks and Atomic Orbitals** Show students an image of the periodic table with the *s*, *p*, *d*, and *f* blocks colored in. Lead a class discussion to discover why these blocks have the same label as the atomic orbitals.
- **Patterns in Properties** Display a periodic table. Point out that within a period of the table, elements in the *s*-block and *p*-block are very different from one another. Elements in the *d*-block have similar properties, and in the *f*-block are very similar. Discuss why that pattern might exist.

CONNECT TO CAREERS

Particle Physicist Particle physicists work to investigate subatomic particles and the forces that govern their behavior. Many of these scientists work at facilities such as the Large Hadron Collider at CERN near Geneva, Switzerland. This giant facility accelerates subatomic particles to a velocity very near the speed of light before smashing them into one another. The huge amounts of energy released in these collisions have allowed scientists to discover particles inside protons and neutrons (quarks) and have expanded our model of the atom beyond protons, neutrons, and electrons.

NAME ______ DATE ______ CLASS ______

ELECTRONS IN ATOMS INQUIRY LAB – OPEN

Model Electron Configuration

How do we know where the electrons are located around the nucleus of the atom? You and your partners have a task. A concert is happening tonight and your help is needed to seat all of the guests. This activity will help you understand how to assign an element's electron configuration with a concert seating chart analogy. Get ready to have some fun and stay engaged!

Focus on Science Practices

SEP 2 Developing and Using Models
SEP 3 Planning and Carrying Out Investigations

Materials Per Group

- Seating chart
- Concert floor plan
- Pencil

Safety

All of the materials used in this activity are considered non hazardous. Practice all normal lab safety rules.

Procedure

1. Obtain a copy of the seating chart and a concert floor plan.
2. Notice the diagonal arrows on the seating chart. What do the diagonal arrows indicate?

O/G/S/A Lab Interactive Worksheets

NAME ______ DATE ______ CLASS ______

ANALYZING DATA

Patterns in Electron Configurations

As described by the quantum mechanical model of the atom, every electron has a precise amount of energy and occupies a specific atomic orbital. An electron configuration is the way that the electrons of an atom are arranged in the atomic orbitals. Scientists have identified three rules that explain the most stable electron configuration for atoms. In this activity, you will use observed patterns to infer these three rules.

The table shows the patterns in electron configurations, but the table is incomplete. When complete, the table will show the ground state electron configurations for the first 12 elements. The middle section of the table uses boxes to represent atomic orbitals. Each arrow (pointing up or down) represents an electron that occupies the orbital. The column at the far right represents electron configurations using numbers, letters, and superscripts.

Electron Configurations of the First 12 Elements

Atomic number	Element	1s	2s	$2p_x$	$2p_y$	$2p_z$	3s	Electron configuration
1	H	↑						$1s^1$
2	He							
3	Li	↑↓	↑					$1s^22s^1$
4	Be							
5	B							
6	C	↑↓	↑↓	↑	↑			$1s^22s^22p^2$
7	N	↑↓	↑↓	↑	↑	↑		$1s^22s^22p^3$
8	O	↑↓	↑↓	↑↓	↑	↑		$1s^22s^22p^4$

Analyzing Data Interactive Worksheet

CLASSROOM MODIFICATIONS

Based on your students' abilities and your schedule, you can modify the Patterns in Electron Configurations activity to be more open ended or more guided.

- **More Open Ended** Have students use the Electron Configuration Examples table on page 33 of the Experience Notebook to develop three rules for adding electrons to atomic orbitals. Next, have them find these elements on the periodic table and ask them to describe the relationship between electron configurations and placement of elements on the periodic table.
- **More Guided** Have students identify patterns in specific parts of the electron configurations. For example, have them describe which orbitals are filled first, how many total arrows (electrons) are shown in each row, and when electrons are allowed to pair up within a single orbital.

4. Next, have the class assign the second guest to a room. This time, they should assign the guests to the top bunk in the first-floor room. Remind students that the guests consider being closer to the ground floor more important than being alone, as long as there is space for them.
5. Continue assigning guests to the hotel rooms, asking students to assign them following the two simple rules outlined above.
6. Lead a class discussion to explain how this example relates to electron behavior in atoms. Students should take away that electrons fill from lowest energy to highest energy and, due to their mutual repulsion, fill empty spaces in orbitals one at a time.
7. Ask students to explain how they think electron behavior in atoms might cause the colors in a fireworks display.

EXPLORE

Model Electron Configuration

Inquiry Lab In this activity, students use a concert seating chart analogy to discover how electrons are arranged in atomic orbitals and to practice writing electron configurations. Students should work in small groups of two to three on this assignment.

Lab Demo Video Watch the Lab Demo Video for advice on materials and preparation.

Choose Your Version Open-ended (O), Guided (G), Shortened (S), Advanced (A)

Materials seating chart, concert floor plan, worksheet, periodic table, pencil

Expected Outcome Students will master the electron-filling order of the elements on the periodic table.

Lab Summary Video Watch the Lab Summary Video for support on connecting the lab investigation to the Investigative Phenomenon.

ASSESS ON THE SPOT

As students finish the lab, have them write a one-sentence summary that describes the link between this lab and the atomic orbitals that were discussed in the previous experience. Read through these responses to confirm that students made the connection that concert seats represent atomic orbitals and that attendees represent the electrons filling those orbitals.

Patterns in Electron Configurations

Analyzing Data Students use patterns [CCC-1] in a set of electron configurations to deduce the rules for adding electrons to atomic orbitals. They then analyze [SEP-4] the patterns they observed in filling-electron orbitals with the pattern of element placement in the periodic table.

- Students should start to notice that the lowest-energy orbitals are always filled before higher energy orbitals gain electrons. **Ask** Why do you think more electrons don't go into the lower energy levels? (There isn't as much space close to the nucleus and electrons would repel each other if there were too many.)
- Encourage students to mark a copy of the periodic table with the different atomic orbital blocks that they discover during this activity.

EXPLAIN

Model Electron Configurations

Modeling In this activity, students use existing models of electron configurations as a basis for creating their own electron configuration models [SEP-2]. This exercise will help students understand the information conveyed by the standard model of electron configurations and the limitations of using models.

- Encourage students to use different colors and shapes in their models to represent information. Color is not often used in models like these because it limits the formats in which the models can be used, but this may inspire some students to generate creative solutions.
- As students complete this activity, **ask** Why is it important to use one standard model for communicating information such as this? (so different people all over the world can understand what is being shown)
- Encourage advanced students to analyze the provided electron configuration model and list all of the information it contains before designing their own models. Next, have them list any information about the atom that the model may be missing (3-D shape of orbitals, number of neutrons, exact energy values for each electron, etc.). Finally, have students write a short critique either defending or rejecting the choices made in designing this model. They should explain why each piece of information should or should not appear in an electron configuration model.

NAME ______ DATE ______ CLASS ______

MODELING

Model Electron Configurations

Electron configurations can be represented in a variety of ways. Scientists often use boxes containing arrows to represent electrons in atomic orbitals, as shown in the table. The same information can be represented by a notation consisting of numbers, letters, and superscripts.

Element	1*s*	2*s*	2p_x	2p_y	2p_z	Electron configuration
N	↑↓	↑↓	↑	↑	↑	$1s^2 2s^2 2p^3$
O	↑↓	↑↓	↑↓	↑	↑	$1s^2 2s^2 2p^4$

Develop and Use Your Model

1. **SEP Develop a Model** Use the space to develop your ideas for a new model, that is different from the table that is shown, for the electron configuration of either nitrogen (N) or oxygen (O). Be sure to consider the following criteria:
   - Show each electron and identify its atomic orbital.
   - Clearly distinguish the outermost, or valence, electrons.
   - Include labels and/or captions to make your meaning clear.

Modeling Interactive Worksheet

DIFFERENTIATED INSTRUCTION

- **Support Struggling Students** Students may have a difficult time generating complete electron configuration models from scratch in the Modeling activity. In that case, suggest that they start by taking an existing model (such as the energy shell model on page 29 of the Experience Notebook) and modifying it to include all of the required information. Explain that this is often how scientists develop new models.
- **Support Special Needs Students** As a class, complete Steps 1 and 2 of the activity, Model Electron Configurations. Provide a sample diagram if students are struggling to develop an idea for a new model. Then discuss how the electrons in an oxygen or nitrogen atom are arranged. Call on students to explain how the model, combined with an explanation, enhanced their understanding of the concepts. Have students work with a partner to complete Steps 3 and 4. Have pairs share their revised models and responses with the class.

INTEGRATE THE THREE DIMENSIONS

In the activity, Model Electron Configurations, students demonstrate their knowledge of electrons of an atom and their atomic orbitals [PS1.A] by developing and then revising a new model [SEP-2] for the electron configuration of nitrogen or oxygen. They then construct explanations [SEP-6] of the patterns [CCC-1] in how the electrons are arranged.

How To Write Electron Configurations

Animation This animation connects the Bohr model of the atom with the quantum mechanical model by moving electrons from their Bohr orbits into their proper atomic orbitals. Students see how standard electron configuration notation corresponds to electron placement within these orbitals.

- Have students write an explanation of how electrons can fit in overlapping orbitals even though they repel each other. Students should understand that the orbitals are just places where the electrons can be found. The electrons actually are free to move around within this space and tend to avoid each other.
- Ask students to point out which of the electrons in the electron configuration match with the electrons in the outermost orbital, according to the animation. Reinforce that these valence electrons determine many of an element's chemical properties.

model of arsenic atom

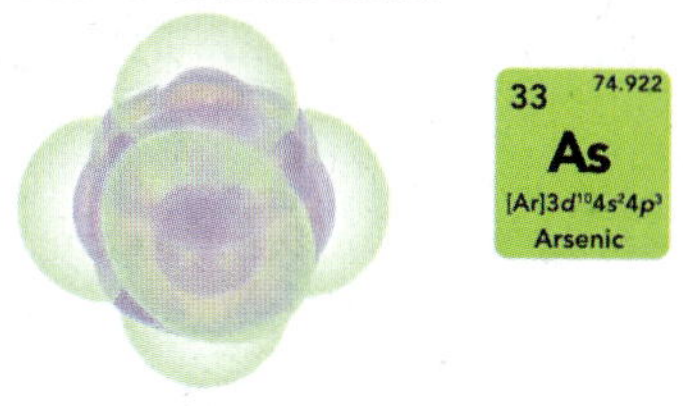

$1s^2 2s^2 2p^6 3s^2 3p^6 3d^{10} 4s^2 4p^3$

Animation: How to Write Electron Configurations

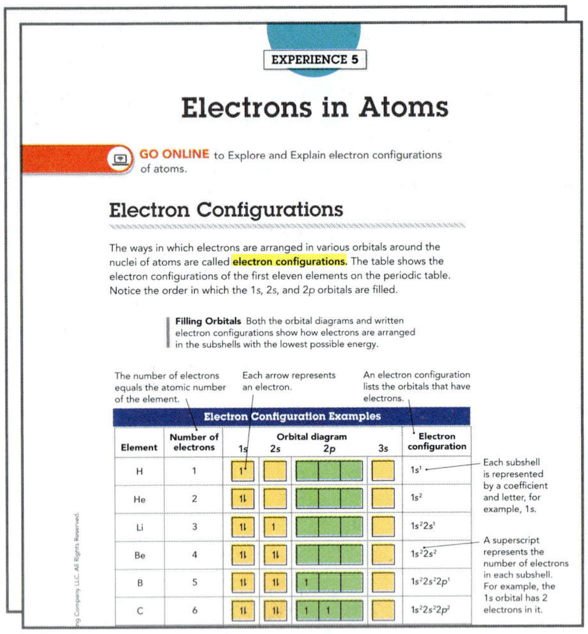
EXPERIENCE 5

Electrons in Atoms

GO ONLINE to Explore and Explain electron configurations of atoms.

Electron Configurations

The ways in which electrons are arranged in various orbitals around the nuclei of atoms are called **electron configurations.** The table shows the electron configurations of the first eleven elements on the periodic table. Notice the order in which the 1*s*, 2*s*, and 2*p* orbitals are filled.

Filling Orbitals Both the orbital diagrams and written electron configurations show how electrons are arranged in the subshells with the lowest possible energy.

The number of electrons equals the atomic number of the element.

Each arrow represents an electron.

An electron configuration lists the orbitals that have electrons.

Electron Configuration Examples

Element	Number of electrons	Orbital diagram 1s	2s	2p			3s	Electron configuration
H	1	↑						$1s^1$
He	2	↑↓						$1s^2$
Li	3	↑↓	↑					$1s^2 2s^1$
Be	4	↑↓	↑↓					$1s^2 2s^2$
B	5	↑↓	↑↓	↑				$1s^2 2s^2 2p^1$
C	6	↑↓	↑↓	↑	↑			$1s^2 2s^2 2p^2$

Each subshell is represented by a coefficient and letter, for example, 1s.

A superscript represents the number of electrons in each subshell. For example, the 1s orbital has 2 electrons in it.

Experience Notebook, pp.33–40

eTEXT

ELD SUPPORT

Writing Students provide written responses affirming their understanding about the trend of radius and mass within periods and groups on the periodic table after reading the Experience Notebook.

- **Emerging/Beginning** Have students identify key words from the Experience Notebook and tell a partner the meaning of each word.
- **Developing/Expanding** Have students write explanations to the questions in the assignment using complete sentences, vocabulary words, and more formal language.
- **Bridging** Students should write more detailed responses to the prompts using proper organization, more complex sentence structure, and concise summaries of the information they gathered in their research.

SAMPLE PROBLEM SUPPORT

One easy way that students can check their work when completing electron configurations is to add all of the superscripts in their answer. This total should match the total number of electrons for that atom (which, in turn, matches that atom's atomic number). Students can also use this check for noble gas notation configurations by adding the superscripts in their configuration to the total number of electrons in the noble gas.

ASSESS ON THE SPOT

As students complete the animation activity, have them draw Bohr models for neon and then sketch the atomic orbital model as well. Have students draw arrows to show where each electron from the Bohr model is located in the atomic orbitals. Finally, have students write the full electron configuration for neon below their drawings and draw arrows to show where each electron from the configuration is located in the atomic orbital model. This will help reinforce the connection between the familiar energy levels in the Bohr model and the numbers in the standard electron configuration notation.

Electrons in Atoms (20)

Experience Notebook Students should read through these pages in the Experience Notebook or Realize Reader the day before you plan to cover this material in class. Use these strategies to help students make sense of the images and text on the indicated pages, as well as to engage in science practices.

- **Electron Configurations** (p. 33) Be sure that students reference the Subshell Energies diagram from page 31 in the Experience Notebook when initially working on this section. If necessary, have them come back and complete a few more examples of electron configurations after they have identified the pattern [CCC-1] in the periodic table to practice using the table instead of the Subshell Energies diagram.
- **Patterns in Electron Configurations** (p. 36) Students may forget that the *d*-block elements are actually adding electrons to a *d*-subshell that is one energy level lower than the current row. Help them to remember this by picturing themselves walking across the top of the periodic table. As they reach the *d* block, they have to step down, indicating that these *d* electrons are one energy shell lower than the *s* electrons that came before. When they get to the *p* block, they have to step back up again, indicating the *p* electrons are added back to the highest energy shell. *F* block elements require an even lower step down, indicating that the *f*-subshell electrons are added to an energy shell that is two lower than the current row.
- **Sample Problem** (p. 37) Provide extra Sample Problem practice, while you circulate and help out as needed:
  a. What is the full electron configuration of calcium (Ca)? ($1s^2 2s^2 2p^6 3s^2 3p^6 4s^2$)
  b. What is the noble gas electron configuration for the potassium +1 ion (K^+)? (Ar)
  c. How many valence electrons does phosphorous (P) have? (five)
- **Writing Noble Gas Configurations** (p. 38) As students get more comfortable writing these configurations, encourage them to use the periodic table to make the task easier. Students should find their element on the periodic table and then move up one row. They should follow that row to the right, and then write that noble gas to start their noble gas notation. From that point, they should go back to the start of the row that contains their element and add the orbitals as they move across the different blocks of the periodic table.
- **Valence Electrons** (p. 39) Walk students through how to draw electron dot structures and what direction to start with. Tell students to imagine that there is a box around the chemical symbol. Explain that they should put a dot on each side of the box, one at a time, clockwise around the box. Point out that if there are four valence electrons, there should be one dot on each side of the box. If there are more than four valence electrons, students should go around the box again until there are none left. Explain that students should never have more than 8 dots for electron dot structures.

PROFESSIONAL DEVELOPMENT

Background Notes When assigning electron configurations for student practice, avoid assigning elements from the block before first checking the actual electron configurations for these elements. The *s* and *d* orbitals of these elements are very close in energy, causing some of the configurations to follow nonstandard filling orders to minimize electron repulsions. For example, the actual electron configuration of chromium is $[Ar]4s^1 3d^5$ instead of the expected $[Ar]4s^2 3d^4$.

ELABORATE

Evaluate Electron Configuration Models

Peer Review Rubric Use the Peer Review Rubric to help students analyze and evaluate [SEP-4] the electron configuration models [SEP-2] their classmates completed in the Modeling activity.

- As students critique and evaluate each other's electron configuration models, have them describe how the standard electron configuration model conveys the information described in the rubric.
- After students have completed their rubrics, lead a class discussion to brainstorm the benefits of using the standard and noble gas electron configuration models. Students should describe how these models, while not perfect, do communicate a large amount of data in a small space.

PROFESSIONAL DEVELOPMENT

Develop Classroom Collaboration Have students discuss their evaluations of the Evaluate Electron Configuration Models. Model some techniques students can use to engage in a productive discussion with their classmates. Have students practice asking and answering questions such as:

- Can you say more about that?
- So, I think you're saying ___________. Is that right?
- What evidence led you to that idea?
- Why do you think that?

Note that these questions are neutral and open-ended and that asking these types of questions is a skill that is developed with practice. Remind students that they should give their partner a few moments to form an answer, and not to interrupt them.

Properties of Atoms: Size vs. Mass

Writing About Science In this writing activity, students conduct research [SEP-8] to explain [SEP-6] the seemingly contradictory fact that atoms within a period actually get smaller in radius as they gain mass [PS1.A]. Remind students to only use appropriate sources in their research.

- Help students to understand the decreasing atomic radius trend by referring back to the Everyday Phenomenon at the beginning of this experience. Electrons being added to existing shells (or rooms from the demo) are the same distance from the nucleus (or they are all on the same floor). The nucleus is gaining protons and therefore pulls more strongly on the electrons.
- Demonstrate the increasing pull of the nucleus by using a few magnets. Have the students hold two magnets at a fixed distance from each other, close enough to feel their mutual attraction. Add a third magnet on top of one of the magnets and have students feel the increased pull that results.

ASSESS ON THE SPOT

Ask students to summarize the most important point from their Writing About Science research into a single, concise sentence. This will help them to pull out the most important parts of their findings and distill the radius versus mass trend in a way that will help them remember it in the future.

NAME ______________ DATE ________ CLASS ________

PEER REVIEW RUBRIC

Evaluate Electron Configuration Models

Use this rubric to help you assess a classmate's model for the electron configura

	EXEMPLARY Score the work 3 if:	ACCOMPLISHED Score the work 2 if:	DEVELOPING Score the work 1 if:
Components of the Model Score: ______	The model shows all electrons of the atom and identifies their atomic orbitals, accurately showing at most two electrons in each orbital. The model also has labels or captions that help explain the components of the model.	The model shows all electrons of the atom and identifies their atomic orbitals, accurately showing at most two electrons in each orbital. However, the model is missing labels or caption(s).	The model shows electrons without details about their atomic orbitals, or some details may be described inaccurately or lack clear labels.
Relationships Score: ______	The model clearly distinguishes the valence electrons and inner-shell electrons.	A label or caption identifies valence electrons, but the distinction is not clear in the model.	The model represents valence electrons and inner-shell electrons identically or inaccurately.
Limitations of the Model Score: ______	Limitations of this model are described, including that it does not accurately represent the cloudlike nature of atomic orbitals.	The explanation acknowledges that this model has limitations, though they are not clearly and specifically identified or described.	The student attempts to define a limitation but does not identify a rational one.

Peer Review Rubric Interactive Worksheet

ADDRESS PRECONCEPTIONS

All of the electron configurations discussed in this experience are describing ground-state atoms because the atoms that participate in chemical reactions are almost always in their ground-state configuration. Students may begin to think that electrons can never disobey the electron-filling "rules" they discovered in this activity. Remind students that, in the excited state, electrons can break these rules and occupy any orbital, not just the lowest-energy one.

NAME ______________ DATE ________ CLASS ________

WRITING ABOUT SCIENCE

Properties of Atoms: Size vs. Mass

Use the information provided and information gathered from authoritative sources on your own to answer Questions 1 and 2. Think about the task of modeling an atom of each element, beginning with hydrogen (atomic number 1) and ending with the elements of atomic number 110 and higher. To revise each model in the series to produce a model for the next element, you would need to add 1 proton, 1 electron, and generally, at least 1 neutron. You might expect that the mass of each atom would become greater, and typically this is true.

However, you might also expect that the size of each atom would also become greater, and this is often false. In fact, atomic size generally decreases as you move across a row of the periodic table. How do you explain this phenomenon?

Obtain and Evaluate Information

1. **SEP Obtain and Evaluate Information** Conduct research to learn more about the relative sizes, or atomic radii, of atoms. Find out how scientists define this property, and identify specific examples. Verify the claim that atomic size tends to decrease across a row of the periodic table.

2. **SEP Construct an Explanation** How can you explain the observation that atomic size tends to decrease across a row of the periodic table? (Hint: Electrons

Writing About Science Interactive Worksheet

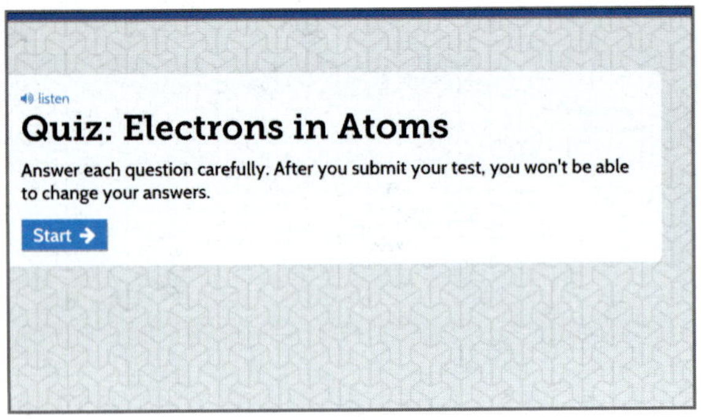

Interactive Online Quiz

Quiz Interactive Worksheet

EVALUATE

Electrons in Atoms

Quiz Assign the quiz in online technology-enhanced, auto-graded format or as an editable quiz worksheet. Use the scoring notes and remediation strategies found online to assess students' responses and to provide targeted feedback for each item to remediate well before assigning the summative 3-D Assessment.

REMEDIATION SUGGESTIONS

- **If** students are struggling with identifying the rules for adding electrons to atomic orbitals, **then** have them review the Patterns in Electron Configurations worksheet and/or review the Electron Configuration Examples table on page 33 of the Experience Notebook.
- **If** students can't write the full electron configuration for an element in standard notation, **then** have them review the How to Write Electron Configurations animation and their electron configuration model. These assets should help students understand what information is required in the electron configuration and how the notation connects to the atomic orbital model.
- **If** students don't understand how an atom with more mass can have a smaller atomic radius, **then** have them re-write their questions to the writing assignment Properties of Atoms: Size vs. Mass. You may also ask student volunteers to share their answers with struggling students so the struggling students can see the reason for this phenomenon in another student's words.

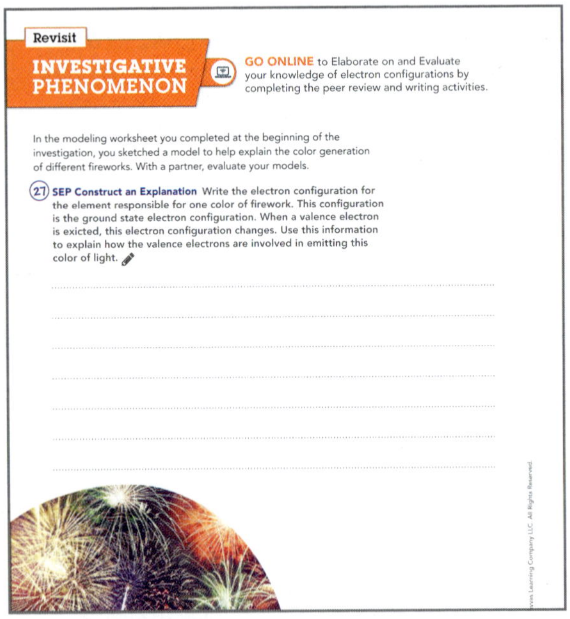
Revisit
INVESTIGATIVE PHENOMENON

GO ONLINE to Elaborate on and Evaluate your knowledge of electron configurations by completing the peer review and writing activities.

In the modeling worksheet you completed at the beginning of the investigation, you sketched a model to help explain the color generation of different fireworks. With a partner, evaluate your models.

(27) **SEP Construct an Explanation** Write the electron configuration for the element responsible for one color of firework. This configuration is the ground state electron configuration. When a valence electron is exicted, this electron configuration changes. Use this information to explain how the valence electrons are involved in emitting this color of light.

Experience Notebook, p. 40

eTEXT

Revisit
INVESTIGATIVE PHENOMENON

Support Reflection Students can complete the reflection prompt, where they will unpack and make sense of the Investigative Phenomenon, based on practices and understandings that have been reinforced over the course of the experience.

- Have students demonstrate how to write the electron configurations of a few elements in both standard and noble gas notation. **Ask** Can any two elements can have the same electron configuration? (No, each element has a different number of electrons, therefore producing a unique electron configuration.)
- Have students draw the electron dot structures for a few elements, using the noble gas electron configuration to determine the number of valence electrons.
- Call on students to explain how electron configurations relate to the colors that are observed in a fireworks display.

Evaluate and Revise Your Model Have students answer Questions 3, 4, and 5 in the Modeling activity and reevaluate their model based on peer feedback. Students should add any additional evidence they have collected in this Investigation. Evidence may include that each element has a unique electron configuration. This may be the reason that different materials create different colors of light in the fireworks display.

EVALUATE

Atomic Structure

3-D Assessment For a summative assessment of Investigation 1, assign the 3-D Assessment, which is available online, as an ExamView bank, or as an editable worksheet.

Evaluate Atomic Structure with Flame Tests

Performance-Based Assessment Use this Performance-Based Assessment to assess students' mastery of the standards. In this activity, students carry out a small-scale investigation [SEP-3] to select the chemicals used in a big fireworks display. When students predict the number of electrons in various energy diagrams using bingo chips, they will have a visual model [SEP-2] of the probability of where the electrons reside in the atomic structure of the atom [PS1.A].

Expected Outcome Flame tests prove that all chemicals can be scaled up for the scenario of a Homecoming fireworks display. Open discussions of electrons in energy level diagrams enhances student understanding of atomic structure.

Safety Make sure students fully extinguish the wooden splints by immersing them in a beaker of water before discarding them in the trash to avoid trash can fires. All students should wear chemical splash goggles, chemical-resistant gloves, and a chemical-resistant apron while perming this lab. Students should wash their hands with soap and warm water before leaving the lab.

Experience Notebook (p. 41) After students complete the Performance-Based Assessment, have them complete the reflection prompt in the Experience Notebook.

DIFFERENTIATED INSTRUCTION

- **Support Special Needs Students** Provide students with an opportunity to review their notes and activities from this investigation to use as evidence to support their explanations for the assessment. Some students may benefit from observing the flame test as part of a class demonstration before analyzing and interpreting data to reduce the total number of steps they must work through to complete the assessment.
- **Support Less Proficient Readers** To support less proficient readers, provide an opportunity for the assessment to be read aloud as students follow along. Some students may also benefit from the opportunity to respond orally to assessment questions.

What distinguishes the minerals in this mountain?

Revisit Anchoring Phenomenon At the end of Investigation 1, have students revisit the Anchoring Phenomenon question about what distinguishes the minerals in the Rainbow Mountains in Peru. Then, with a partner, have students discuss what role they think atomic structure has in distinguishing the minerals in the Rainbow Mountains and causing the colors in a fireworks display. Have pairs share their explanations with the class.

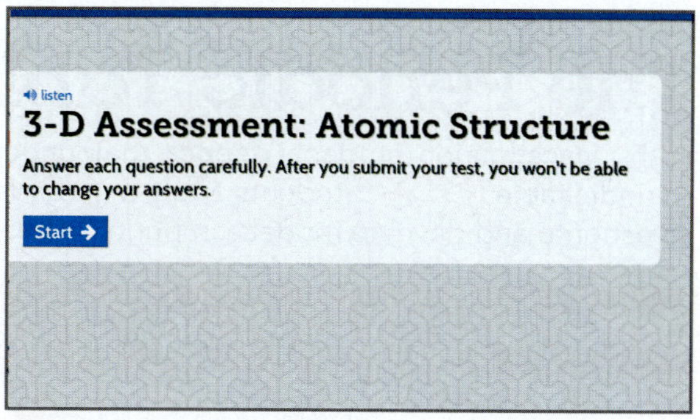

listen

3-D Assessment: Atomic Structure

Answer each question carefully. After you submit your test, you won't be able to change your answers.

Start →

Interactive Online 3-D Assessment

Interactive ExamView 3-D Assessment

3-D Assessment Interactive Worksheet

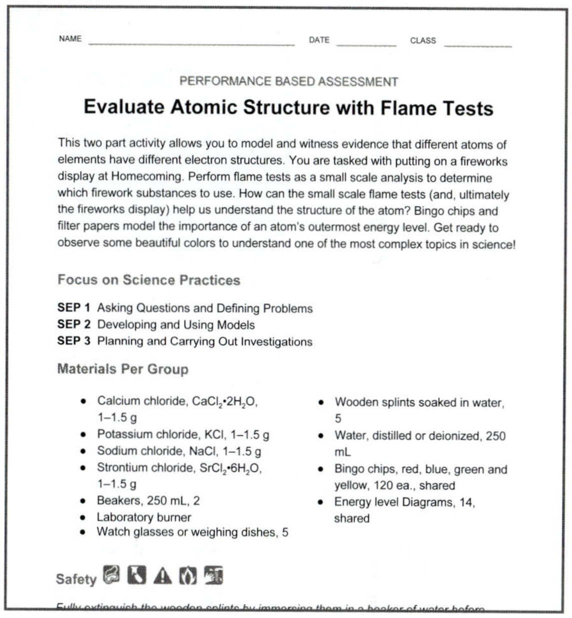

NAME ______ DATE ______ CLASS ______

PERFORMANCE BASED ASSESSMENT

Evaluate Atomic Structure with Flame Tests

This two part activity allows you to model and witness evidence that different atoms of elements have different electron structures. You are tasked with putting on a fireworks display at Homecoming. Perform flame tests as a small scale analysis to determine which firework substances to use. How can the small scale flame tests (and, ultimately the fireworks display) help us understand the structure of the atom? Bingo chips and filter papers model the importance of an atom's outermost energy level. Get ready to observe some beautiful colors to understand one of the most complex topics in science!

Focus on Science Practices

SEP 1 Asking Questions and Defining Problems
SEP 2 Developing and Using Models
SEP 3 Planning and Carrying Out Investigations

Materials Per Group

- Calcium chloride, $CaCl_2 \cdot 2H_2O$, 1–1.5 g
- Potassium chloride, KCl, 1–1.5 g
- Sodium chloride, NaCl, 1–1.5 g
- Strontium chloride, $SrCl_2 \cdot 6H_2O$, 1–1.5 g
- Beakers, 250 mL, 2
- Laboratory burner
- Watch glasses or weighing dishes, 5
- Wooden splints soaked in water, 5
- Water, distilled or deionized, 250 mL
- Bingo chips, red, blue, green and yellow, 120 ea., shared
- Energy level Diagrams, 14, shared

Safety

Performance-Based Assessment Interactive Worksheet

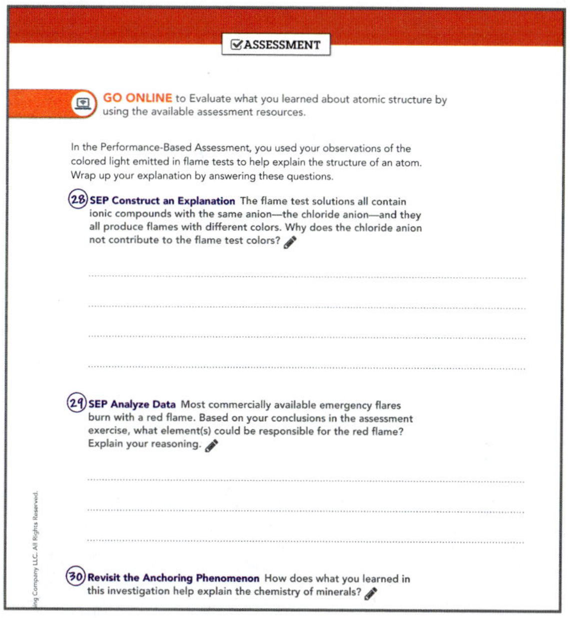

ASSESSMENT

GO ONLINE to Evaluate what you learned about atomic structure by using the available assessment resources.

In the Performance-Based Assessment, you used your observations of the colored light emitted in flame tests to help explain the structure of an atom. Wrap up your explanation by answering these questions.

28 **SEP Construct an Explanation** The flame test solutions all contain ionic compounds with the same anion—the chloride anion—and they all produce flames with different colors. Why does the chloride anion not contribute to the flame test colors?

29 **SEP Analyze Data** Most commercially available emergency flares burn with a red flame. Based on your conclusions in the assessment exercise, what element(s) could be responsible for the red flame? Explain your reasoning.

30 **Revisit the Anchoring Phenomenon** How does what you learned in this investigation help explain the chemistry of minerals?

Experience Notebook, p. 41

eTEXT

The Periodic Table

In this investigation, students deepen their understanding of patterns [CCC-1] through a study of the periodic table [PS1.A]. Students apply their understanding of the observed patterns of nature as they investigate and develop models on periodic trends as well as other related phenomena.

INVESTIGATIVE PHENOMENON

Why are elements in pure form so rare?

Explaining Phenomena Students explore how the periodic table relates to atomic structure and how trends in the periodic table can be explained by forces between subatomic particles that give each element its unique properties. Students use their knowledge of the periodic table to explain what distinguishes minerals in a mountain.

	EXPERIENCE 1	EXPERIENCE 2
	The Periodic Table: An Overview **2 days** Students model and construct explanations of the periodicity of the periodic table, note patterns in the table, and make connections between the characteristics of atoms in the columns and rows of the table.	**The Periodic Table and Atomic Structure** **2 days** Students construct explanations of the pattern of electron configuration and effective nuclear charge across a period of main group elements of the periodic table. They use Coulomb's law to explain effective nuclear charge of atomic particles.
CONNECTION TO THE INVESTIGATIVE PHENOMENON	Students use patterns in the periodic table to explain why elements in pure form are so rare.	Students apply what they learn about atomic structure and effective nuclear charge to explain why elements in pure form are so rare.
ENGAGE	**Teacher's Guide** Everyday Phenomenon Coin Categories, p. 46	**Teacher's Guide** Everyday Phenomenon What makes an element valuable?, p. 52
EXPLORE	**Inquiry Lab** Develop a Periodic Table **Analyzing Data** Graphing Periodic Properties	**Inquiry Lab** Elemental Metals, Nonmetals, and Metalloids **Interactivity** Periodic Properties
EXPLAIN	**Claim-Evidence-Reasoning** Periodic Trends **Animation** The Design of the Periodic Table **Experience Notebook,** pp. 44–48	**Claim-Evidence-Reasoning** Electron Configuration and Element Properties **Experience Notebook,** pp. 50–55
ELABORATE	**Discussion Rubric** Make a Claim About Periodic Trends **Writing About Science** Reflect on Periodic Trends	**Peer Review Rubric** Evaluate a Claim About Electron Configurations **Analyzing Data** Size Trends and Shielding Effect
EVALUATE	**Quiz** The Periodic Table: An Overview **Experience Notebook** Revisit Investigative Phenomenon, p. 49	**Quiz** The Periodic Table and Atomic Structure **Experience Notebook** Revisit Investigative Phenomenon, p. 55

*Pacing for Encounter Investigative Phenomenon core instruction is a half-day.

†Pacing for core Investigation Assessment is approximately 1 day.

GOT MORE TIME? Personalize and enhance your instructional plan by assigning the activities with the got-more-time icon, as time allows.

Notes:

Investigative Phenomenon Video Diving for Precious Metal*

Claim-Evidence-Reasoning Discuss the Investigative Phenomenon*

Authentic Reading Meet 115, The Newest Element on the Periodic Table

Virtual Reality Experience

Experience Notebook, p. 42*

EXPERIENCE 3

Periodic Trends

2 days

Students use periodic trends to explain some chemical properties of elements. They use the concepts of ionization energy, net effective charge, and atomic radius to explain reactivity patterns in the periodic table.

Students use the concepts from periodic trend models to refine their explanations of why elements in pure form are so rare.

Teacher's Guide **Everyday Phenomenon** Salt Bubbles, p. 58

Inquiry Lab Periodic Trends and Properties

Virtual Lab Predict Reactivity Using Periodic Trends

Claim-Evidence-Reasoning Effective Nuclear Charge and Electron Shielding

Animation Ionization Energy

Experience Notebook, pp. 56–63

Discussion Rubric Make a Claim About Effective Nuclear Charge and Shielding

Engineering Design Challenge Growing Crystals in Gels

Quiz Periodic Trends

Experience Notebook **Revisit Investigative Phenomenon,** p. 64

INVESTIGATION ASSESSMENT

Performance-Based Assessment Gravimetric Analysis of Periodic Trends†

3-D Assessment The Periodic Table†

Experience Notebook Performance-Based Assessment, p. 65; **Revisit Anchoring Phenomenon,** p. 153†; **Appendix C** Problem Bank, pp. R11–R12

INVESTIGATION 2

The Periodic Table

Teacher Background

The periodic table is much more than a chart that students can use to determine the number of protons in an element. The reasoning that led to the table's structure incorporates trends in the properties of all matter in the universe. These trends can be explained by forces between subatomic particles that give each element unique physical properties and ranges of reactivity. As you prepare to teach Investigation 2, keep in mind the various trends within the table so that you are able to speak to how each relates to the properties and behavior of an element. By guiding students through the history of claims and evidence that revealed these trends and how they intersect, you will help students see the periodic table as a complex and highly useful model of matter.

Learning Progression

In this investigation, students gain a historical perspective on the periodic table and a sense of the scientific process as one in which claims are open to revision in light of new evidence [NoS-3]. Students also begin to explore the arrangement of the periodic table and the reasoning behind its rows and columns [PS1.A]. Students begin to see the table as a model [SEP-2] that reveals patterns [CCC-1] in the properties of elements. They observe and pose questions [SEP-1] about trends in the periodic table, make a claim about what underlies those trends, and argue their claim from evidence [SEP-7].

Note that this investigation lays the foundation for achieving several Performance Expectations (PEs). The investigation is anchored in a variety of phenomena that students will investigate through laboratory experiments [SEP-3], application of models [SEP-2], data analysis [SEP-4], and explanations based on evidence [SEP-6].

ENCOUNTER

INVESTIGATIVE PHENOMENON

Why are elements in pure form so rare?

Introduce this investigation with a discussion of precious metals (such as gold, silver, and platinum) and their rarity on Earth. The lack of reactivity of these precious metals prompts students to investigate their properties through the periodic table. They begin by thinking about how objects (and elements) might be arranged in meaningful categories (Experience 1). Then they explore grouping elements based on shared characteristics (Experience 2) and begin to see patterns in the periodic table. Finally, they are able to identify trends in the periodic table and explain why they occur (Experience 3).

RELATED PHENOMENA

In addition to precious metals, consider using other phenomena to launch this investigation.

- **Smartphones** Search online for an infographic that breaks down the component elements in a smartphone. Then challenge students to identify the design criteria for why these materials were selected.
- **Elements in the Atmosphere** Display a pie chart that shows the gases in Earth's atmosphere and their formulas. With students, make a list of all the elements that are found in the atmosphere.

TAKE IT LOCAL

If there are mines in your county, tell your students what is being mined and ask if they think workers are mining the pure element or a mineral containing its compounds, and why. Ask them to think of elements they have seen for sale at a home store or on the vitamin shelf. Are these being sold as pure elements or as compounds, mixed with other elements?

Diving for Precious Metal

Investigative Phenomenon Video Pair students and tell them to write answers to the following questions:

a. What are these coins made of? Why do you think they are so valuable? Why does society put so much value on these kinds of metals?

b. What properties do these kinds of metals share? Why is nonreactivity considered such a "precious" property?

c. What are some other ways that metals such as gold and silver are used in the modern world? How do designers make use of their properties?

Ask students to share what objects with pure elements they have seen and where they have seen them. Be prepared for preconceptions. For example, students may think that milk or vitamins contain calcium metal. If you provide a vitamin label as evidence, students will quickly find calcium listed as calcium citrate or calcium carbonate. Point out that calcium is typically found as the calcium ion in compounds. As a follow-up, place a small piece of calcium metal in a test tube of water. Use the surprisingly reactive outcome as evidence that calcium is not typically found in the elemental state.

Meet 115, the Newest Element on the Periodic Table

Investigative Phenomenon Authentic Reading This reading introduces students to element 115, which was made in Russia. Through a question-and-answer format, with answers provided by Paul Hooker, a chemistry professor, students discover how the element was made and why scientists make new elements. Students also find out why an element is not officially named as soon as it is discovered.

- After students complete their worksheets, discuss what they think the benefit is in making such short lived-elements. Discuss how these elements give scientists new insight into natural laws. Point out that isotopes of some of these short-lived elements have distinct properties that make them important in medical and industrial applications. For example, an isotope of the first artificially made element, technetium, is the most frequently used isotope of medical imaging.

Discuss the Phenomenon

Claim-Evidence-Reasoning Have students review the video and Authentic Reading activity to explain their understanding of the phenomenon they observed. To help build understanding of the phenomenon, brainstorm a list of questions about the observed phenomenon. Have students complete Question 1 of the CER worksheet and start thinking about the evidence they need to answer their question.

Remind students that their understanding of the phenomenon will be incomplete at this stage, but that they will revisit this activity as they learn more. Make sure to provide students with an opportunity to revisit their CER arguments throughout the investigation as well as at the end of the investigation for further revision and peer review.

Reflect on the Phenomenon

Experience Notebook Transition to the questions on the opener page for Investigation 2 in the Experience Notebook. With students working in pairs, guide them through discussion of the question. Remind them they should reference the video, Authentic Reading activity, and CER activity to answer the question. Invite student pairs to share their thoughts. Then, as a class, discuss how the reflection questions relate to the Investigative Phenomenon. **Ask** How can the periodic table help us explain why elements in pure form are so rare?

Investigative Phenomenon Video

Authentic Reading

Authentic Reading Interactive Worksheet

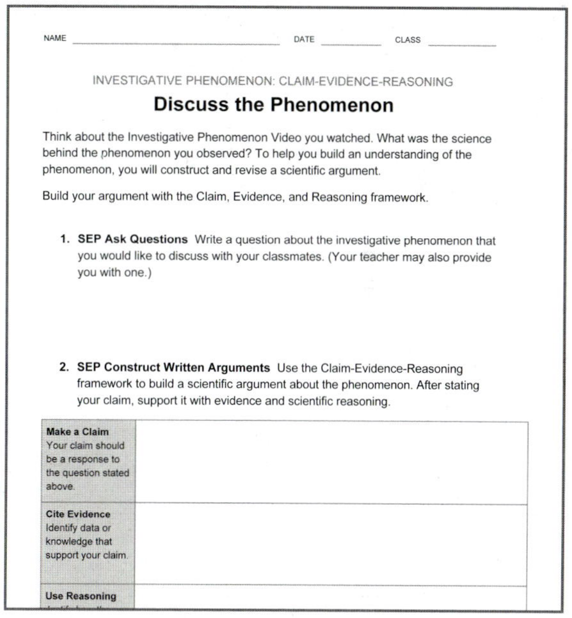

NAME ______ DATE ______ CLASS ______

INVESTIGATIVE PHENOMENON: CLAIM-EVIDENCE-REASONING

Discuss the Phenomenon

Think about the Investigative Phenomenon Video you watched. What was the science behind the phenomenon you observed? To help you build an understanding of the phenomenon, you will construct and revise a scientific argument.

Build your argument with the Claim, Evidence, and Reasoning framework.

1. **SEP Ask Questions** Write a question about the investigative phenomenon that you would like to discuss with your classmates. (Your teacher may also provide you with one.)

2. **SEP Construct Written Arguments** Use the Claim-Evidence-Reasoning framework to build a scientific argument about the phenomenon. After stating your claim, support it with evidence and scientific reasoning.

Make a Claim Your claim should be a response to the question stated above.	
Cite Evidence Identify data or knowledge that support your claim.	
Use Reasoning	

CER Interactive Worksheet

Experience Notebook, pp. 42–43

eTEXT

EXPERIENCE 1

The Periodic Table: An Overview

Teacher Background

Experience 1 is an overview of the development of the periodic table and the groups and trends represented by the table's structure. Students model and explain the periodicity of the table, noting patterns and making connections between characteristics of atoms in the columns and rows of the table. They also draw conclusions and make predictions about the chemical nature of an element based on its place in the table. This investigation requires students to generate graphs, for which they should have the necessary mathematics background.

Objectives

- **Describe how elements in the periodic table are arranged by the numbers of protons in atoms.**
- **Identify how the arrangement of the main groups of the periodic table reflects the patterns of outermost electrons.**
- **Explain how the position of an element in the table can be used to predict some of its chemical properties.**

RELATED PHENOMENA

In addition to the Coin Categories demo, consider using other phenomena to launch this experience.

- **Location Prediction** Prompt students to describe how things are arranged in a grocery store and how that helps them predict where to find specific items. **Ask** What do items in a particular aisle have in common? At a particular location in that aisle? On a particular shelf within that location? What is the reasoning behind the way items are arranged? How do you think that idea relates to the periodic table?
- **Classroom Item Organization** Gather a selection of items from around the classroom and work with students to organize them into categories. **Ask** What characteristics seem most important when making categories? Guide students in making a grid to categorize the items.

ENGAGE

EVERYDAY PHENOMENON

How can categorizing and arranging objects help us make predictions about their properties?

Use this teacher demo to prompt student discussion about categorizing objects. Encourage students to articulate their reasoning of how they fill in the blanks on the grid and of how being able to categorize can help them predict something about the objects being categorized.

Coin Categories 10

Engage students with this demonstration of an everyday phenomenon to introduce the concept of categorization as a way to make predictions.

Materials 4 of each: penny, nickel, dime, quarter. Each of the four should have a different mint date (i.e., one penny each minted in 2013, 2014, 2015, and 2016). If possible, make mint dates the same across ascending coin types.

1. Set up a projector to show students what you are doing. Draw a 16-square grid on a sheet of paper.
2. Begin to fill in the grid with coins, leaving about half of the squares blank. Coins should go in ascending value from left to right, and descending mint year from top to bottom.
3. Ask students to make predictions about which coins will go in the blank squares on the grid. Make sure they explain their reasoning.
4. Work with the group to develop rules that would apply to the grid. Use the rules to fill in the grid with the rest of the coins.
5. Guide a class discussion about how this exercise could relate to the process that occurred during the development of the periodic table. Use this discussion to transition to the Inquiry Lab.

EXPLORE

Develop a Periodic Table

Inquiry Lab In this lab, students carry out investigations [SEP-3] in which they experiment with organizing sets of items—a set of plastic animals and a set of element cards. Students arrange the items by following patterns [CCC-1] in the characteristics of the items. They evaluate the limitations of each model [SEP-2].

Lab Demo Video Watch the Lab Demo Video for advice on materials and preparation.

Choose Your Version Open-ended (O), Guided (G), Shortened (S), Advanced (A)

Materials 15 plastic animals, deck of element cards

Expected Outcome Students will come to understand that while elements can be arranged in different ways on a periodic table, depending on the arrangement, predictions can be made regarding undiscovered elements.

Lab Summary Video Watch the Lab Summary Video for support on connecting the lab investigation to the Investigative Phenomenon.

NAME ______ DATE ______ CLASS ______

THE PERIODIC TABLE: AN OVERVIEW INQUIRY LABS – OPEN

Develop a Periodic Table

How did the periodic table get its shape? Looking for patterns and developing models can help us to make sense of the world. In this activity you will make your own "periodic table of the animals" by applying scientific thinking and looking for patterns. Afterward you will play "periodic table solitaire" by arranging cards with real elemental data.

Focus on Science Practices

SEP 2 Developing and Using Models
SEP 3 Planning and Carrying Out Investigations
SEP 4 Analyzing and Interpreting Data

Materials Per Group

- Plastic farm animals, 15
- Deck of element cards

Procedure

1. Assuming that the 15 plastic animals you have been given represent all the elements that exist, attempt to arrange them in an order that makes sense in a 3 x 5 grid on your desk. Make a record of your suggested model.

O/G/S/A Lab Interactive Worksheets

ASSESS ON THE SPOT

Circulate as students work to arrange their items in the Inquiry Lab, and ask questions such as: Why did you place these two items together in a row/column? Based on the placement of this item, what characteristic of the item(s) can you predict?

Graphing Periodic Properties

Analyzing Data In this activity, students make graphs [SEP-2] using data about element numbers, melting points, and boiling points. They use these graphs to note patterns [CCC-1] in the relationship between atomic number and melting/boiling point. They then make predictions about the characteristics of hypothetical elements given their atomic numbers or melting and boiling points.

- Encourage students to get a sense for the scale their graphs will need to accommodate before they begin to draw the graph. Tell them to look at the range of atomic numbers and the range of boiling and melting point values. (Atomic numbers range from 2 to 88. Melting points range from –272°C to 3500°C. Boiling points range from –269°C to 4827°C.) Model for students the process of scaling a graph by drawing a demonstration graph on the board. Let the *x*-axis be *Minutes/day spent watching streaming video*, and range from 50 to 225. Let the *y*-axis be *Minutes/day spent studying*, and range from 75 to 268. Take suggestions from the class on how to divide the space on the axes, being sure to allow for some suggestions that will need to be modified once students see how they turn out.

NAME ______ DATE ______ CLASS ______

ANALYZING DATA

Graphing Periodic Properties

The periodic table relies on patterns and similarities of the electron configuration and chemical properties of elements. The data table lists some melting points and boiling points of elements in Groups 18, 17, 14, and 2. Look where the elements in the table are located on the periodic table as you complete the activity, to help you understand their periodicity.

Element	Atomic Number	Melting Point (°Celsius)	Boiling Point (°Celsius)
	Group 18		
He	2	–272	–269
Ne	10	–249	–246
Ar	18	–189	–186
Kr	36	–157	–153
Xe	54	–112	–108
Rn	86	–71	–62
	Group 17		
F	9	–220	–188
Cl	17	–101	–35
Br	35	–7	59
I	53	114	184
At	85	302	337
	Group 14		

Analyzing Data Interactive Worksheet

DIFFERENTIATED INSTRUCTION

- **Support Special Needs Students** Students with visual disabilities may not be able to complete the graph on the Analyzing Data worksheet. Provide larger graphs that students can use, and have them work with a partner who can read aloud the text.
- **Support Advanced Students** Invite students to review the elements they have data for and locate them on the periodic table. Challenge them to craft a sentence describing relationships they have learned about among groups of those elements.

CLASSROOM MODIFICATIONS

Based on your students' abilities and your schedule, you may wish to edit the Graphing Periodic Properties worksheet to make it more open ended or more guided.

- **More Open Ended** Have students develop their own data table of elements from different groups and conduct research to identify atomic number, melting point, and boiling point for each element. Students should use this data to complete the activity.
- **More Guided** Students may need help determining the scale for their graphs. You might want to provide a template for them.

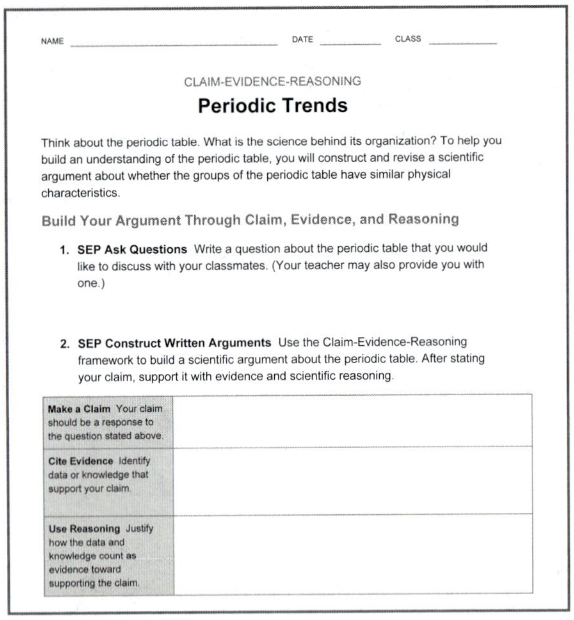
NAME ______________ DATE ________ CLASS ________

CLAIM-EVIDENCE-REASONING

Periodic Trends

Think about the periodic table. What is the science behind its organization? To help you build an understanding of the periodic table, you will construct and revise a scientific argument about whether the groups of the periodic table have similar physical characteristics.

Build Your Argument Through Claim, Evidence, and Reasoning

1. **SEP Ask Questions** Write a question about the periodic table that you would like to discuss with your classmates. (Your teacher may also provide you with one.)

2. **SEP Construct Written Arguments** Use the Claim-Evidence-Reasoning framework to build a scientific argument about the periodic table. After stating your claim, support it with evidence and scientific reasoning.

Make a Claim Your claim should be a response to the question stated above.	
Cite Evidence Identify data or knowledge that support your claim.	
Use Reasoning Justify how the data and knowledge count as evidence toward supporting the claim.	

CER Interactive Worksheet

INTEGRATE THE THREE DIMENSIONS

In the CER activity, students demonstrate their knowledge of the periodic table by describing its arrangement into columns and periods based on observable patterns [CCC-1], with periods arranged by number of protons and columns arranged by shared chemical properties [PS1.A]. They should be able to construct explanations [SEP-6] of why elements in a column have similar properties. This understanding creates the foundation for progressive mastery of the PE.

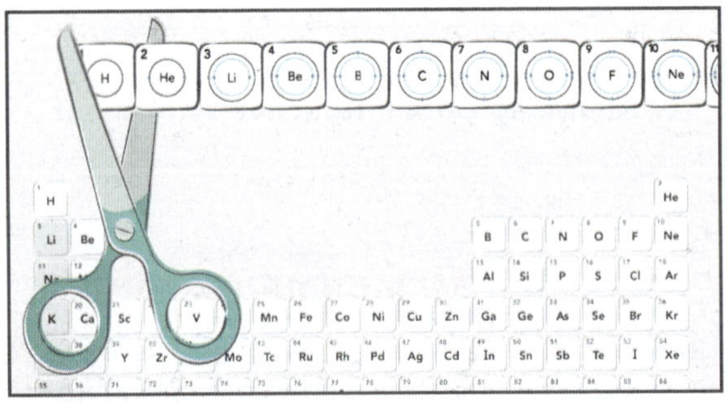

Animation: The Design of the Periodic Table

EXPLAIN

Periodic Trends

Claim-Evidence-Reasoning In this activity, students look for patterns [CCC-1] in the modern periodic table. Then students write an argument [SEP-7] about whether groups have similar physical characteristics [PS1.A]. Students support their arguments with observed evidence and scientific reasoning.

- Encourage students to think about what they learned in the Coin Categories demonstration and the Inquiry Lab. Discuss how this information can be applied to the periodic table.
- With the class, make a list on the board about what they already know about the periodic table. Then have students make a list of questions [SEP-1] about the periodic table that come to mind when they look at these facts.
- Instruct students to individually choose one of the questions, or a different one, to complete Step 1 of the worksheet. Follow this with Step 2 of the worksheet. Later, after students view the animation and review the information in the Experience Notebook, follow up with a round of revision, which can be assigned as homework. Then have students complete Steps 3 and 4 in class.

The Design of the Periodic Table

Animation This animation provides an explanation for the arrangement of elements in the periodic table [PS1.A]. It demonstrates that the atomic number of an element relates to the number of protons and that the position of an element in the table relates to its number of valence electrons. Students may use this information to revise their claims about periodic trends. Choose among these strategies as you use the animation:

- Before the animation, tell students to find a partner and identify a periodic trend in an elemental property. Tell them to look for an explanation of that trend in the animation, and discuss it after watching the animation.
- Tell students to take notes on information in the animation that they want to use to revise their claims, evidence, or reasoning from the CER exercise. After the animation, give students a few minutes to incorporate revisions.

ASSESS ON THE SPOT

Challenge students to write a 12-word summary of their claim and the evidence for it. Pair students and tell them to share their summaries. Invite students to share their summaries with the class.

The Periodic Table: An Overview

Experience Notebook Ideally, assign the Experience Notebook or Realize Reader first, and then follow up with any of the following suggested instructional strategies to fill knowledge gaps and deepen understanding.

Use these strategies to help students make sense of the images and text on the indicated pages, as well as to engage in science practices.

- **Development of the Periodic Table** (pp. 44–45) Group students into triads. Tell groups to choose one student to take notes on Dobereiner's triads, one to take notes on Newland's octaves, and the other to take notes on Mendeleev's periodic table. Together, the triad should evaluate each model [SEP-2], and discuss:
  a. What are the strengths of this model?
  b. What is this model missing or incorrectly demonstrating?
  c. What knowledge is needed to improve the model? [NoS-3]

Then tell students who are taking notes on Dobereiner's triads to move to a new group, and students taking notes on Mendeleev's table to move to a different group. Instruct students to present to their new groups the notes they took in the previous one.

- **The Modern Periodic Table** (pp. 46–48) **Ask** What does an element's position in the table indicate about its properties? (The properties of an element are similar to those of other elements in the same group.) Display the periodic table on page 48. To emphasize the concept that elements in the same group, or column, of the periodic table have similar properties, isolate one group with two sheets of paper. Describe some physical and chemical properties of the elements in that group. Then point to the group on the far right, and explain that all of these elements are gases that do not normally form compounds. Have students compare these elements to those in other groups.
- As a class, discuss what properties might have given Mendeleev clues about how to group the elements vertically. Discuss how Mendeleev's table and explanation for groups might have been different if he had known about the structure of atoms.
- Explain the color key of the periodic table, and use the color coding to help identify the sections of the table that correspond to metals, nonmetals, and metalloids. Emphasize the periodic trend across each period from metals to nonmetals. **Ask** Which class of elements do most of the elements belong to? (metals) What do the three numbers at the top of each column represent? (different systems for numbering the groups)
- Challenge students to think of examples of metals, nonmetals, and metalloids. Discuss how specific elements appear in everyday life and how that might relate to their categorization in the periodic table.

DIFFERENTIATED INSTRUCTION

- **Support Struggling Students** If students are more visual learners, then assist them in developing a graphic organizer that illustrates how the periodic trends intersect for each element.
- **Support Less Proficient Readers** Using a large poster-size display of the periodic table, trace one period across the table. On the display, note some physical and chemical properties of each element in that period. Then have students research the properties of each element in the period below the one you just highlighted. Tell them to write a statement comparing the properties of both periods.
- **Support Special Needs Students** Provide a large periodic table mat and colored chips or blocks to use as markers. Have students place a marker(s) on the element(s) that is being discussed. Allow students to use these tactile objects during assessments.
- **Support Advanced Students** Invite students to make drawings or models of Group 1 or Group 2 elements, showing how valence electrons give rise to chemical similarities in the group. Students could also research semiconductors; students should define the term and note where the elements that are used for the application are located in the periodic table.

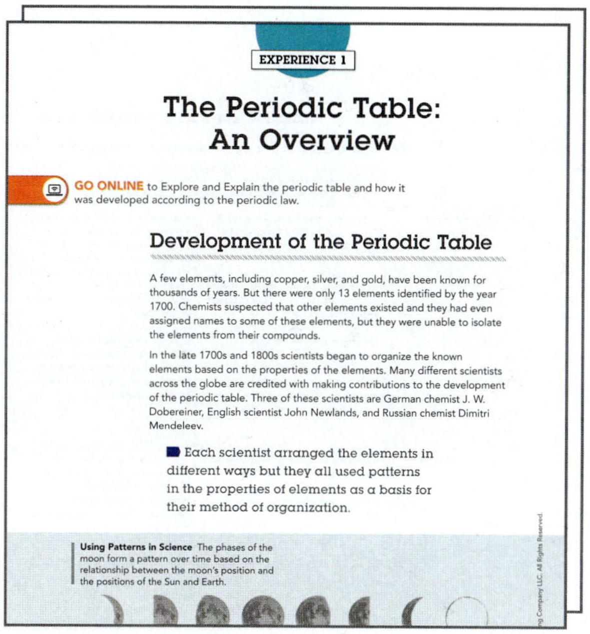

EXPERIENCE 1

The Periodic Table: An Overview

GO ONLINE to Explore and Explain the periodic table and how it was developed according to the periodic law.

Development of the Periodic Table

A few elements, including copper, silver, and gold, have been known for thousands of years. But there were only 13 elements identified by the year 1700. Chemists suspected that other elements existed and they had even assigned names to some of these elements, but they were unable to isolate the elements from their compounds.

In the late 1700s and 1800s scientists began to organize the known elements based on the properties of the elements. Many different scientists across the globe are credited with making contributions to the development of the periodic table. Three of these scientists are German chemist J. W. Dobereiner, English scientist John Newlands, and Russian chemist Dimitri Mendeleev.

Each scientist arranged the elements in different ways but they all used patterns in the properties of elements as a basis for their method of organization.

Using Patterns in Science The phases of the moon form a pattern over time based on the relationship between the moon's position and the positions of the Sun and Earth.

Experience Notebook, pp. 44–48

eTEXT

ADDRESS PRECONCEPTIONS

While students are learning about periodic trends, they may assume that the elements are also arranged by increasing atomic mass. To address this preconception, remind students that the atomic number is equal to the number of protons and is constant for each element, but the number of neutrons can vary. Send students on an "elemental scavenger hunt," to find instances where elements are not arranged by increasing atomic mass.

ELD SUPPORT

Speaking/Listening Students pairs use the content on The Periodic Table: An Overview pages of the Experience Notebook to adapt the language choices they use in communicating ideas.

- **Emerging/Beginning** Have student pairs identify one or more text features (heads, captions, illustrations). Have students take turns explaining how text features help or hinder understanding.
- **Developing/Expanding** Have student pairs choose one periodic table and corresponding text in the section and evaluate whether the author's word choice helped or hindered the students' understanding of the text. Then have student pairs list ways to adapt the language to a younger audience.
- **Bridging** Have student pairs choose a component of the periodic table, such as how to identify metals, nonmetals, and metalloids, and develop their own report or slide presentation for an audience of younger students or for an audience of English Language Learners. Have student pairs explain how they adapted their use of language to their audience.

NAME ______________ DATE ________ CLASS ________

DISCUSSION RUBRIC

Make a Claim About Periodic Trends

Use this rubric to help you assess your discussion of the trends found in the p

	EXEMPLARY Score the work 3 if:	ACCOMPLISHED Score the work 2 if:
Claims and Evidence Student Score: ______ Teacher Score: ______	The periodic table and its organization are accurately and clearly described. The difference between groups and periods are accurately explained. Trends in the periodic table are accurately described. The claim reveals that the periodic table is organized such that it reveals trends.	The periodic table and its organization are accurately and clearly described. The difference between groups and periods are accurately explained. Trends in the periodic table are partially described. The claim reveals a connection between the periodic table and trends.
Evaluation and Critique Student Score: ______ Teacher Score: ______	Critiques reveal that there are exceptions to trends and that elements in a group have similar properties, but not the same properties. Claims are strengthened when the critique is acknowledged and addressed fully.	Critiques about exceptions and properties are acknowledged, but addressed minimally or superficially. Claims are not strengthened after the critique is addressed.
Reasoning and Synthesis Student Score: ______ Teacher Score: ______	Reasoning for elements' similarities and periodic trends should involve a discussion of groups and periods. Attempts should be made to explain exceptions.	The argument for choosing one proposal over another is based on evidence and logical reasoning. However, more evidence and more detail could have been used to support the argument.

Discussion Rubric Interactive Worksheet

NAME ______________ DATE ________ CLASS ________

WRITING ABOUT SCIENCE

Reflect on Periodic Trends

Use the information provided and information gathered from authoritative sources on your own to answer Questions 1 and 2.

Chemist Dmitri Mendeleev is credited with being the first person to note that patterns emerge when elements are arranged according to their properties. He organized elements based on properties and atomic mass. After parts of an atom and isotopes were discovered, the current periodic table was constructed using atomic number, electron configurations, and chemical and physical properties.

Obtain and Evaluate Information

1. **CCC Patterns** Mendeleev was not the only person who attempted to organize the elements. For example, Alexandre Béguyer de Chancourtois tried to organize the elements using atomic weights. A portion of his "table" is shown. Describe the pattern in his table. How is Chancourtois's table similar to the modern periodic table? Why is the modern periodic table more useful?

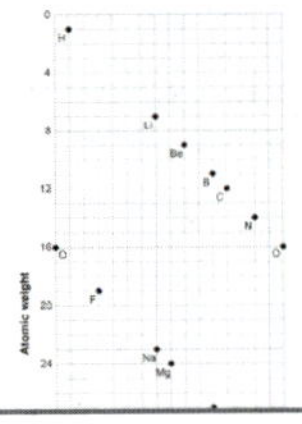

Writing About Science Interactive Worksheet

CLASSROOM MODIFICATIONS

Based on your students' abilities and your schedule, you may wish to edit the Reflect on Periodic Trends writing activity to make it more open ended or more guided.

- **More Open Ended** Offer Chancourtois's table as an example of an earlier periodic table, and offer the option that students can research and reflect on a different historical verion of the periodic table.
- **More Guided** Include an image of the modern periodic table along with brief suggestions of features that might be compared.

ELABORATE

Make a Claim About Periodic Trends

Discussion Rubric Students discuss the trends they observed and the claims they made about the periodic table in the CER activity, Periodic Trends.

Group students into pairs to discuss the following questions:

- Describe the periodic table and its organization [PS1.A]. What patterns [CCC-1] did Mendeleev and others see when putting it together?
- Why are elements in a group similar but elements in a period are not similar?
- Describe some trends in the table. Construct explanations [SEP-6] for these trends.

Give students several minutes to discuss each question. When they are done discussing, tell students to look at the rubric and evaluate themselves based on how confident they feel about meeting the goals of the rubric.

PROFESSIONAL DEVELOPMENT

Develop Classroom Collaboration Before students begin conversing about the discussion questions, have the class brainstorm a list of questions that partners can ask each other. Model some techniques students can use to help partners articulate their ideas. Use prompts such as:

- Would you please state that in another way?
- What evidence led you to that idea?

Note that asking these types of questions is a skill that we develop with practice. Remind students that they should give their partner a few moments to form an answer, and not to interrupt them.

Reflect on Periodic Trends

Writing About Science In this writing activity, students observe patterns [CCC-1] in older versions of the periodic table and compare their organization to the modern periodic table. Then students describe why organizing the elements into a periodic table was useful during the days of Mendeleev and Chancourtois and why the organization is useful now.

- Have students individually read the introduction and the first question. Then have students reflect on the following questions: What patterns [CCC-1] do you observe in the modern periodic table? What patterns occur in Chancourtois's system?
- To prompt thoughts that can help students in their writing, discuss any or all of the following questions as a class. Encourage students to take notes.
  a. Are there other shapes or organizations you can imagine the periodic table having, such as spirals or a diagonal arrangement? What would be advantages and disadvantages of different shapes for the periodic table?
  b. How is the periodic table useful to us?
  c. Why were so many scientists driven to develop a table of the elements? In what ways did they hope it would be helpful to them?

ASSESS ON THE SPOT

When students are finished writing, tell them to list three ideas they described in their responses to the questions in the Reflect on Periodic Trends activity. Then ask them to turn to their neighbor, who will share the three ideas they wrote. Circulate through the room to get a sense of students' thinking.

EVALUATE

The Periodic Table: An Overview

Quiz Assign the quiz in online technology-enhanced, auto-graded format or as an editable quiz worksheet. Use the scoring notes and remediation strategies found online to assess students' responses and to provide targeted feedback for each item to remediate well before assigning the summative 3-D Assessment.

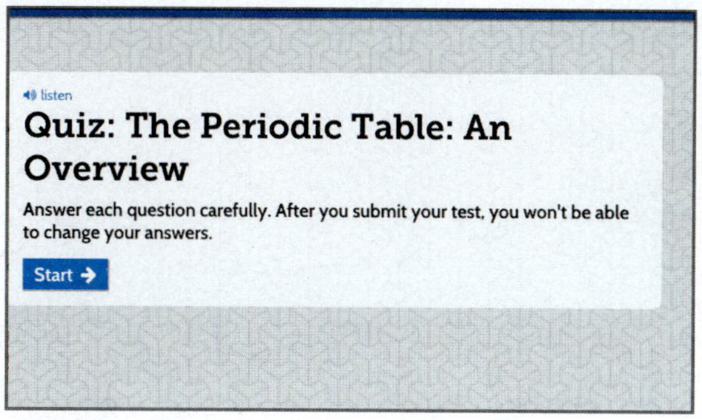

Interactive Online Quiz

Quiz Interactive Worksheet

REMEDIATION SUGGESTIONS

- **If** students are struggling with the story of the development of the periodic table, **then** ask them to storyboard the history with a set of sketches that include the scientists' ideas and unanswered questions.
- **If** students are struggling to connect the text to the graphic on page 45, **then** guide them in reading through the text and stopping to locate related sections of the graphic.
- **If** students are struggling to integrate the concepts of groups and periods, **then** give them a periodic table and let them highlight groups and periods. Tell them to annotate the table with reasoning for groups and periods, citing information from the text.
- **If** students are struggling to understand how elements are grouped, **then** review the animation and guide students through arranging the element cards in the Inquiry Lab, with visual representation of valence electrons in mind.
- **If** students are struggling to understand why organization in the periodic table is important, **then** have them review the CER activity, Periodic Trends, and the writing activity, Reflect on Periodic Trends.

Revisit INVESTIGATIVE PHENOMENON

Support Reflection Students can complete the reflection prompt, where they will unpack and make sense of the Investigative Phenomenon, based on practices and understandings that have been reinforced over the course of the experience.

- Tell students to count off in 1s and 2s. Ask students with the number 1 to write a few sentences in response to the first prompt in Question 7. Students with number 2 should respond to the second. Place students in pairs for discussion and encourage them to add to each other's responses.
- As a class, make a visual time line for the development of the periodic table. The time line should focus on noting scientists' observations of patterns, how those patterns inspired or contributed to the organization of the table, and what patterns are now used to organize the periodic table.
- Discuss how the periodic table can be used as a model to identify properties that make elements in pure form so rare.

Develop a Draft CER Argument Have students answer Question 2 in the CER worksheet and develop a draft of a CER argument to address the Investigative Phenomenon. Have students add any evidence they have collected from the activities so far in this investigation. Evidence may include properties of elements in a group, data about melting and boiling points, and the positions of elements relative to each other in the table.

Revisit
INVESTIGATIVE PHENOMENON
GO ONLINE to Elaborate and Evaluate your understanding of the design of the periodic table by completing the class discussion and writing activities.

7 CCC Patterns What patterns did you observe in the development of the periodic table? How were the patterns related to the timeline?

Experience Notebook, p. 49

eTEXT

EXPERIENCE 2

The Periodic Table and Atomic Structure

Teacher Background

Experience 2 introduces students to how two atomic phenomena—electron configuration and effective nuclear charge—are reflected in the structure of the periodic table. Students make predictions about electron configuration and effective nuclear charge across periods of the table. Depending on the existing knowledge level of your students, you may want to briefly review atomic structure and the configurations of electrons, neutrons, and protons in each element. Students are also introduced to the equation for electrical force, Coulomb's law. They are not required to perform calculations but must understand the proportional effect of distance on force between charges.

Objectives

- **Describe how electron configuration gives rise to trends in the periodic table.**
- **Explain how the periodic table can be used to predict electron configuration of an element.**
- **Use Coulomb's law to explain effective nuclear charge and why the positive charge exerted by an atomic nucleus is not equal to the charge of its protons.**
- **Explain patterns of effective nuclear charge across a period of main group elements.**

ENGAGE

EVERYDAY PHENOMENON

What's so special about silicon?

Use this teacher demo to prompt student discussion about one property of some elements—electrical conductivity. As students ask new questions about the phenomenon, challenge them to find answers as they complete the Inquiry Lab.

What makes an element valuable?

Engage students with this demonstration of an everyday phenomenon to introduce the concept of metals, nonmetals, and metalloids.

Materials silicon lump or chip, silicon crystal, conductivity meter

1. Guide a brief discussion about silicon. **Ask** What do we use silicon for? What makes it good for that? Where is it in the periodic table?
2. Ask students to name some metal elements and guide a discussion about what characteristics they share. Do the same for nonmetals. Then ask students what characteristics they think silicon, a metalloid, has.
3. Show them the silicon chip/lump and the crystal. Explain that they are both solid forms of silicon.
4. Test each bit of silicon with the conductivity meter, asking students to note the results. If time allows, do the demonstration by building a circuit with a light bulb rather than using a conductivity meter.
5. Explain that conductors of electricity are usually good conductors of heat as well. Ask students to describe what types of elements are used in pots and pans to heat foods quickly on a stove. **Ask** Do you observe any patterns? (Metals are good conductors.)

RELATED PHENOMENA

In addition to the What makes an element valuable? demo, consider using other phenomena to launch this experience.

- **Model Electron Configurations** Use everyday objects, such as coins or beads, to model the atomic structures and electron configurations of sodium and chlorine for students. Note the electrons in the outer energy level, and ask students how they think those electron configurations might affect how the two elements interact.
- **Observe Trends** Have students test a variety of elements with $CuCl_2$ (including a few metals, one or two nonmetals, and a metalloid. For example, you could test calcium, aluminum, magnesium, zinc, carbon, sulfur, and silicon). Have students make a data table to write their observations. Students should look for overall trends. (The metals react with $CuCl_2$; the nonmetals and metalloid do not react with $CuCl_2$.)

6. Ask students to explain if they think cotton string would be a good conductor of electricity. Prompt them to support their explanation with evidence.
7. Prompt students to consider how we value elements based on their characteristic properties, such as whether they can conduct electricity. Have students recall the video about coins they viewed at the beginning of the investigation. Prompt students to identify the properties that they think make the metals of the coins valuable.

EXPLORE

Elemental Metals, Nonmetals, and Metalloids

Inquiry Lab In this lab, students carry out an investigation [SEP-3] to classify different elemental samples as either metal, nonmetal, or metalloid. They use the elements' positions on the periodic table [PS1.A] to identify patterns [CCC-1] associated with metallic character.

Lab Demo Video Watch the Lab Demo Video for advice on materials and preparation.

Choose Your Version Open-ended (O), Guided (G), Shortened (S), Advanced (A)

Materials aluminum strip, carbon rod, iron nail, silicon lump, sulfur lump, mossy tin, conductivity meter, bar magnet, paper

Safety Stress to students that they are not to heat the elements nor are they to try and carry out reactions with them. Also tell students that silicon is slightly toxic by ingestion and can cause eye damage or irritation. Carbon and silicon are both flammable when powdered. Make sure students wear gloves and eye protection.

Expected Outcome Students will conclude that moving down a group on the periodic table correlates with an increase in metallic character and that moving across a period correlates to a decrease in metallic character.

Lab Summary Video Watch the Lab Summary Video for support on connecting the lab investigation to the Investigative Phenomenon.

ASSESS ON THE SPOT

As students complete the lab, have them write a description of the part of the lab that they struggled with the most. Collect responses and review the most common problems with the entire class the following day.

Periodic Properties

Interactivity This online Interactivity allows students to explore the reactivity of different elements with water and to compare electron configurations among elements. Students should note patterns [CCC-1] that allow them to explain the existence of groups in the periodic table.

Choose among these strategies to engage students with the interactivity:

- Pair students and have them work together with the interactivity to respond to the following prompts.
  a. Elements that react with water are in group(s) …
  b. Elements in the group(s) are alike in …
  c. Electrons in the atoms of the groups(s) are configured …
- Go through the Interactivity as a class, allowing students to direct the exploration by calling on individuals and asking them what step to take next. After each step, discuss what students observe and how that might connect with the structure of the periodic table and observations in the Inquiry Lab. Guide the class to a conclusion about the relationship between electron configuration and groups in the table.

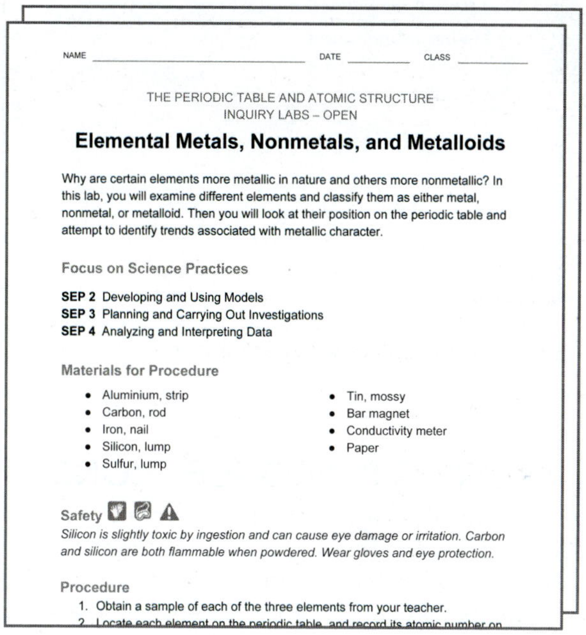
NAME ______ DATE ______ CLASS ______

THE PERIODIC TABLE AND ATOMIC STRUCTURE
INQUIRY LABS – OPEN

Elemental Metals, Nonmetals, and Metalloids

Why are certain elements more metallic in nature and others more nonmetallic? In this lab, you will examine different elements and classify them as either metal, nonmetal, or metalloid. Then you will look at their position on the periodic table and attempt to identify trends associated with metallic character.

Focus on Science Practices

SEP 2 Developing and Using Models
SEP 3 Planning and Carrying Out Investigations
SEP 4 Analyzing and Interpreting Data

Materials for Procedure

- Aluminium, strip
- Carbon, rod
- Iron, nail
- Silicon, lump
- Sulfur, lump
- Tin, mossy
- Bar magnet
- Conductivity meter
- Paper

Safety

Silicon is slightly toxic by ingestion and can cause eye damage or irritation. Carbon and silicon are both flammable when powdered. Wear gloves and eye protection.

Procedure

1. Obtain a sample of each of the three elements from your teacher.

O/G/S/A Lab Interactive Worksheets

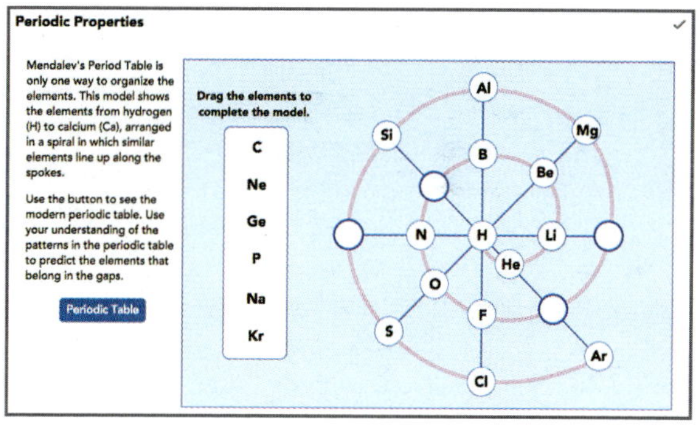

Interactivity: Periodic Properties

CONNECT TO CAREERS

Analytical Chemist Some scientists who study and use methods and instruments to obtain information about the composition and structure of matter are analytical chemists. Some analytical chemists separate materials, identify the components, and determine how much there is of each component. The services they provide have applications in areas such as environmental protection, medicine, product development, and forensics. Encourage students to investigate some of the specialties of analytical chemistry and what the focus of each specialty is.

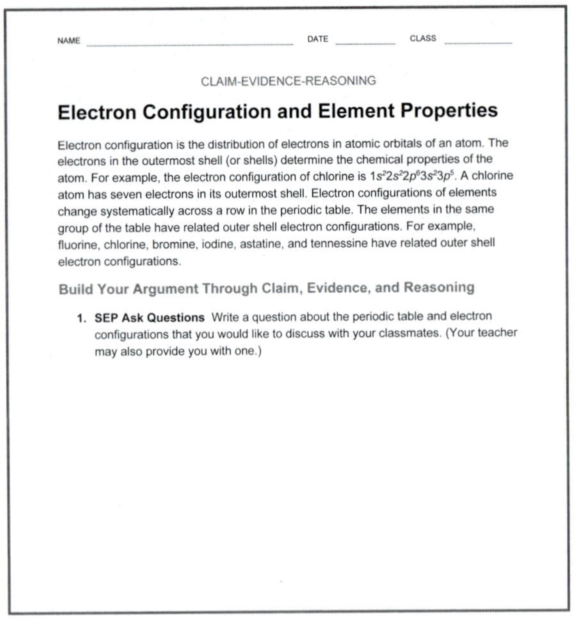

NAME ____________ DATE ______ CLASS ______

CLAIM-EVIDENCE-REASONING

Electron Configuration and Element Properties

Electron configuration is the distribution of electrons in atomic orbitals of an atom. The electrons in the outermost shell (or shells) determine the chemical properties of the atom. For example, the electron configuration of chlorine is $1s^22s^22p^63s^23p^5$. A chlorine atom has seven electrons in its outermost shell. Electron configurations of elements change systematically across a row in the periodic table. The elements in the same group of the table have related outer shell electron configurations. For example, fluorine, chlorine, bromine, iodine, astatine, and tennessine have related outer shell electron configurations.

Build Your Argument Through Claim, Evidence, and Reasoning

1. **SEP Ask Questions** Write a question about the periodic table and electron configurations that you would like to discuss with your classmates. (Your teacher may also provide you with one.)

CER Interactive Worksheet

ADDRESS PRECONCEPTIONS

Students often form the preconception that electrons orbit atomic nuclei in circles or similar to the way Earth orbits the sun. Explain to students that we use circles to represent energy levels of electrons, which orbit the nucleus in three-dimensional, cloudlike shapes. Bring the class into a discussion of the strengths and weaknesses of the visual models.

DIFFERENTIATED INSTRUCTION

- **Support Struggling Students** For students having difficulty connecting the interactivity, lab results, and periodic patterns, help them make a chart to compare elements in terms of lab observations, electron configuration, and position in the periodic table.
- **Support Advanced Students** Invite students to do class or small-group demonstrations similar to those in the Inquiry Lab. Tell students to help their peers make connections between what is happening in the reaction and groupings in the periodic table.

EXPLAIN

Electron Configuration and Element Properties (15)

Claim-Evidence-Reasoning Students ask a question [SEP-1] and write an argument in which they make a claim about the relationship between the periodic table and electron configurations [PS1.A]. They support their argument with observed evidence and scientific reasoning.

To help define each stage of the CER framework, you may find it helpful to work through a simple example as a class before students begin. For example:

- **Claim** Atoms in the same column as fluorine will have similar chemical properties.
- **Evidence** This is true for other columns of the table. Group 1 elements only bond with one other atom, Group 2 elements will make two bonds. Atoms in each of these groups have the same electron configuration.
- **Reasoning** Because atoms in the same column as fluorine all have the same electron configuration, they will all have similar properties.

Consider having students revisit their claims and evidence after the class completes the reading and discussion of the information in the Experience Notebook. They can make any revisions to their writing as homework before the class completes the Peer Review Rubric.

ASSESS ON THE SPOT

Ask students to write something they feel unclear about in the relationship between electron configuration and chemical properties of an element. Invite students to partner with their neighbors for help clarifying the material.

PROFESSIONAL DEVELOPMENT

Use Outside Resources Collaborate with your school's physics teacher to discuss the importance of electron configurations in the physics of Group 4 elements, particularly carbon, silicon, and germanium. Ask the teacher to bring and discuss models to demonstrate how electron configuration contributes to the conductivity of these elements, while maintaining other chemical and physical properties that make them well suited for use in semiconductor chips and nanotechnology.

The Periodic Table and Atomic Structure

Experience Notebook Ideally, assign the Experience Notebook or Realize Reader first, and then follow up with any of the following suggested instructional strategies to fill knowledge gaps and deepen understanding.

Use these strategies to help students make sense of the images and text on the indicated pages, as well as to engage in science practices.

- **The Periodic Table as a Predictive Model** (pp. 50–51) Pair students to paraphrase the descriptions of each of the groups and blocks in the illustration. Each student should paraphrase two descriptions, and then take turns presenting their wording to one another. The two students then write a statement together describing how the information in the graphic allows us to make predictions about elements in the table [PS1.A].
- **Coulomb's Law** (p. 52) Ask students to reflect on their experiences with magnets and the forces observed when bringing like and opposite poles together, as well as the force exerted by stronger or weaker magnets. Discuss how this models [SEP-2] Coulomb's law and atomic particles.
- **The Shielding Effect and Effective Nuclear Charge** (pp. 53–55) Group students and invite them to think of everyday analogies to the shielding effect. For example, a car may drive through a puddle and splash more water on the person closer to the puddle. Ask groups to share their analogies and evaluate them for strengths, weaknesses, and accuracy. You may wish to have the class select or vote on their favorite analogy.
- **Effective Nuclear Charge as a Periodic Trend** (p. 54) To help students see the relationship between element group, valence electrons, and effective charge, students can prepare a four-column chart with these heads: *Element*, *Valence electrons*, *Group number*, and *Effective nuclear charge*. Students should fill in the chart with Group 1 and 2 elements. Students can discuss in small groups what pattern they see and why the pattern [CCC-1] exists.

INTEGRATE MATH

Proportions To help students grasp the main idea behind the equation for Coulomb's law, give them this example to demonstrate proportional relationships: Suppose you have a job where you get paid \$100 for 5 hours of work. The proportion is $\frac{100}{5}$. How does the pay rate change if you increase the numerator versus increasing the denominator? How does this relate to Coulomb's law?

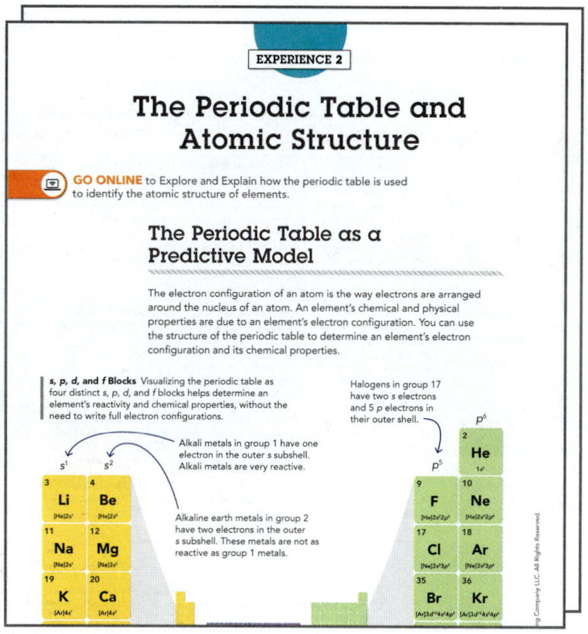
EXPERIENCE 2

The Periodic Table and Atomic Structure

GO ONLINE to Explore and Explain how the periodic table is used to identify the atomic structure of elements.

The Periodic Table as a Predictive Model

The electron configuration of an atom is the way electrons are arranged around the nucleus of an atom. An element's chemical and physical properties are due to an element's electron configuration. You can use the structure of the periodic table to determine an element's electron configuration and its chemical properties.

Experience Notebook, pp. 50–55

eTEXT

INTEGRATE THE THREE DIMENSIONS

The material in the Experience Notebook builds on students' understanding of the periodic table as a model [SEP-2] reflecting similar chemical properties [PS1.A] and repeating patterns in outer electron states. After students have completed the reading in their Experience Notebook, they should be able to use models [SEP-2] of atoms to explain [SEP-6] the source of effective nuclear charge. By recognizing the pattern [CCC-1] of effective nuclear charge among columns in the table, they are able to use the table as a model to predict effective nuclear charge of other atoms.

ELD SUPPORT

Speaking/Listening Students develop questions about electron configuration and element properties to aid in identifying questions to ask about information in the Experience Notebook.

- **Emerging/Beginning** Have student pairs develop and ask each other yes/no questions about electron configurations and element properties described in this experience.
- **Developing/Expanding** Have students work in small groups to develop multiple-choice questions about the following sections: Coulomb's Law and The Shielding Effect and Effective Nuclear Charge.
- **Bridging** As a class, have students develop and ask each other questions that require a detailed answer that would force students to draw upon information outside of the direct question.

NAME ______________ DATE ______ CLASS ______

PEER REVIEW RUBRIC

Evaluate a Claim About Electron Configurations

Use this rubric to help you assess your classmates' claims about electron configurations a

	EXEMPLARY Score the work 3 if:	ACCOMPLISHED Score the work 2 if:	DEVELOPING Score the work 1 if:
Components of the Claim Score: ______	The claim states that atoms with the same outer shell electron configurations have similar chemical and physical properties and distinguishes between the types of properties.	The claim states that atoms with the same outer shell electron configurations have similar properties, but does not distinguish between chemical and physical properties.	The claim does not state that atoms with the same outer shell electron configurations have similar properties.
Relationships Score: ______	Atoms react with other atoms so that they all have filled outer shells, so atoms with the same number of electrons in their partially empty outer shells will bond the same way.	The reasoning explains bonding using electrons from their outer shells but does not state that an atom bonds with another atom or atoms such that the atoms all have filled outer shells.	The model attempts to describe how atoms bond.
Connections Score: ______	The claim makes sense and fully connects electron configurations to elemental properties.	The claim makes sense, but does not fully connect electron configurations to elemental properties.	The claim is unclear and does not connect electron configurations and elemental properties.
Limitations of the Claim Score: ______	Limitations of this claim are described: properties of elements are based on more than electron configurations.	The explanation acknowledges that this claim has limitations, though they are not clearly and specifically identified or described.	The claim attempts to acknowledge limitations.

Peer Review Interactive Worksheet

NAME ______________ DATE ______ CLASS ______

ANALYZING DATA

Size Trends and Shielding Effect

The shielding effect is when an atom's electrons in the inner electron shells shield the outer electrons from the nuclear charge and the attraction between the atom's nucleus and its outer electrons is weakened. The table shows the radii of atoms in the first three periods and the estimated effective nuclear charge for atoms in the first two periods.

Atomic No.	Element Name	Atomic Radius (pm)	Effective Nuclear Charge	Atomic No.	Element Name	Atomic Radius (pm)
1	Hydrogen	53	1+	**19**	Potassium	243
2	Helium	31	2+	**20**	Calcium	194
3	Lithium	167	1+	**21**	Scandium	184
4	Beryllium	112	2+	**22**	Titanium	176
5	Boron	87	3+	**23**	Vanadium	171
6	Carbon	67	4+	**24**	Chromium	166
7	Nitrogen	56	5+	**25**	Manganese	161
8	Oxygen	48	6+	**26**	Iron	156
9	Fluorine	42	7+	**27**	Cobalt	152
10	Neon	38	8+	**28**	Nickel	149
11	Sodium	190	1+	**29**	Copper	145
12	Magnesium	145	2+	**30**	Zinc	142
13	Aluminum	118	3+	**31**	Gallium	136
14	Silicon	111	4+	**32**	Germanium	125

Analyzing Data Interactive Worksheet

CLASSROOM MODIFICATIONS

Based on your students' abilities and your schedule, you may wish to edit the Size Trends and Shielding Effect worksheet to make it more open ended or more guided.

- **More Open Ended** Allow students to draw their own comparisons about which atoms in the table would be larger and smaller than others and to provide reasoning for comparisons using both periodic trends and shielding.
- **More Guided** As students study their graphs, prompt them to consider the effect of shielding and to compare net nuclear charge of atoms at the peaks and valleys of the graph.

ELABORATE

Evaluate a Claim About Electron Configurations

Peer Review Rubric Students use the rubric as a scoring guide to evaluate claims made by their peers in the CER activity, Electron Configuration and Element Properties.

- Arrange students in groups of three. Tell each person to pass the claim he or she has written to the student on the right. In turn, each student will evaluate on a separate rubric the claim written by the person to the left and include the person's name and the name of the claim's author. After 4 minutes, tell students to pass the claim they were evaluating, along with their evaluation, to their right. Give students 4 minutes to write the second evaluation and then pass claims and evaluations to the right again.
- Once students have their evaluations back, have them look for consistencies among the critiques and revise their original claims, evidence, and reasoning. If necessary, students can make their revisions as homework.

ASSESS ON THE SPOT

Have students reflect on their claims by making a brief presentation about what they learned from both writing their claims and reviewing those of their peers.

Size Trends and Shielding Effect

Analyzing Data In this activity, students develop a model [SEP-2] of the relationship between atomic number and atomic radius by graphing a set of data. They then connect patterns [CCC-1] revealed by the data to related patterns in the periodic table and use them to predict the radius of other atoms. While the most obvious pattern that emerges is the alternating peaks and valleys of atomic radius, encourage students to note periodic patterns in their data. **Ask:**

- What pattern do you see when comparing the smallest atoms in each period? (The radius of the smallest atom in each period gets a little bigger with each row.)
- What pattern of smaller peaks and valleys emerges as you move to atoms with more and more electrons? (Rather than just going up and down, small peaks emerge and large peaks get farther apart as the periods in the table get longer.)
- What pattern do you see in the difference in radius between the biggest and smallest atoms in a period? (It remains largely the same.)

DIFFERENTIATED INSTRUCTION

- **Support Struggling Students** For students who are challenged to connect data in the graph in the Analyzing Data worksheet with patterns in the periodic table, give them a printed periodic table and tell them to mark the elements with the largest atomic radius on the table in one color and then mark those with the smallest radius with a different color.
- **Support Advanced Students** Invite students to write a short paragraph explaining why the graph takes the shape it does. Why does atomic radius jump suddenly when going from fluorine to sodium and chlorine to potassium? What properties might we expect to find related to atomic radius?

EVALUATE

The Periodic Table and Atomic Structure

Quiz Assign the quiz in online technology-enhanced, auto-graded format or as an editable quiz worksheet. Use the scoring notes and remediation strategies found online to assess students' responses and to provide targeted feedback for each item to remediate well before assigning the summative 3-D Assessment.

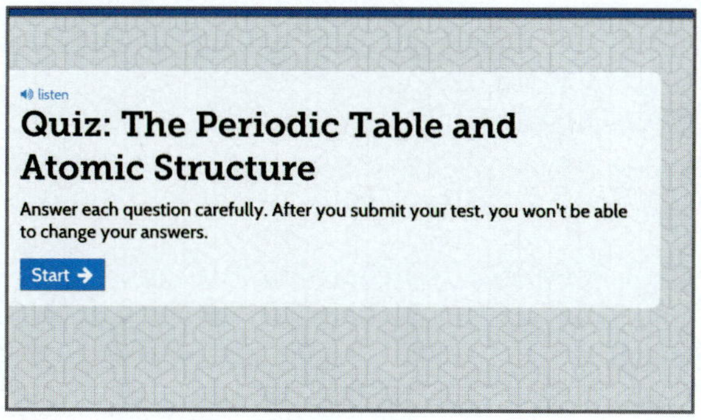

Interactive Online Quiz

Quiz Interactive Worksheet

REMEDIATION SUGGESTIONS

- **If** students are struggling with connecting electron configuration and element group, **then** suggest that students review the CER activity, Electron Configuration and Element Properties, and their Peer Review Rubric. Students can also review the graphic on page 50 and label a periodic table with the number of valence electrons in the elements of each group.
- **If** students are struggling to grasp the concept of effective nuclear charge, **then** guide them through the illustrations on pages 53 and 54 and the Analyzing Data worksheet, Size Trends and Shielding Effect, to draw out protons and electrons in the atoms and canceling them out until there are only electrons let.
- **If** students are struggling to grasp why atomic radius decreases going right in a period, **then** suggest they reread page 53, underlining phrases that connect net nuclear charge to the attraction between electrons and nucleus.
- **If** students are struggling to connect the data in their graph with the periodic table, **then** give them a periodic table and tell them to label the data points with the corresponding element and then choose several elements from one period of the table and compare their sizes with data from the graph.

Revisit
INVESTIGATIVE PHENOMENON

Support Reflection Students can complete the reflection prompt, where they will unpack and make sense of the Investigative Phenomenon, based on practices and understandings that have been reinforced over the course of the experience.

- Tell students to read the Revisit question carefully and write a script or an outline of their answers as if they were going to present them to an audience. When students are done writing, tell them to pair with another student and take turns presenting their answers to each other, using a periodic table to highlight key points. Remind students to take notes on any additional information that they learn from their partners.
- Suggest that students review the illustration of effective nuclear charge across a period of elements on page 54 of the Experience Notebook. Ask students to raise their hands if they feel confident that they could explain the concept of effective nuclear charge and its role in the periodic table. Invite those students to be peer tutors and informally address questions from other students one-on-one or in small groups throughout the room.
- Lead a discussion about how knowing about patterns in the periodic table can help students explain the Investigative Phenomenon, Why are elements in pure form so rare?

Further Develop Your CER Argument Have students add any additional evidence they have collected in this experience. Evidence may include properties of various elements and their locations on the periodic table, data about atomic nuclei, and the patterns of effective nuclear charge across groups in the periodic table.

Revisit
INVESTIGATIVE PHENOMENON

GO ONLINE to Elaborate and Evaluate your knowledge of the periodic table and atomic structure by completing the peer review and data analysis activities.

In the CER worksheet, you drafted a scientific argument for how electrons and the nucleus determine atomic structure and how this is reflected in the periodic table. You also defended your argument with evidence. With a partner, reevaluate the evidence cited in your arguments.

11 SEP Support Your Explanation with Evidence Explain why the periodic table is organized by atomic number. Provide evidence about atomic nuclei to support your explanation.

Experience Notebook, p. 55

eTEXT

EXPERIENCE 3

Periodic Trends

Teacher Background

Experience 3 takes students deeper into concepts that relate to chemical reactivity. Students test reactivity of elements and reflect on their findings as they learn about ionization energy, electron affinity, and the formation of ions. By integrating this knowledge, students arrive at detailed explanations for trends in the periodic table. It is important to note that electronegativity is defined and described as a periodic trend in Experience 3 of Investigation 3.

Some of the ideas in this investigation will be new to students, and some students may need extra support to grasp subtle differences between concepts such as ionization energy and electron affinity. Some students may struggle with the abstract nature of the material, and alternative approaches such as hands-on models and graphic organizers might be useful.

Objectives

- **Investigate and explain reactivity patterns in the periodic table using concepts of ionization energy, net effective charge, and atomic radius.**
- **Use models of elements to explain the formation of ions.**
- **Use periodic trends to explain some chemical properties of elements.**

ENGAGE

EVERYDAY PHENOMENON

What can periodic trends tell us about how reactive an element is?

Use this teacher demo to prompt discussion about why two elements react differently with baking soda. Encourage students to take notes and add them to their observations during the Inquiry Lab.

Salt Bubbles

Engage students in this demonstration of baking soda chemistry to introduce the idea that different elements show different chemical behavior and that behavior is governed by relationships between particles that make up the atom.

Materials calcium chloride powder, potassium chloride powder, 2 200-mL flasks or beakers (or everyday clear glasses), baking soda, water

Arrange materials so all students can see what is happening, or use a projector.

1. Tell students what your chemical ingredients are.
   a. First, discuss the calcium and potassium salts. Ask students to locate calcium and potassium on the periodic table, and invite them to describe what they know about those two elements based on their positions in the table.
   b. Then ask students to describe what baking soda is and does. (It is sodium bicarbonate, and it acts as a leavening agent.) When the right compounds are added to it, the bicarbonate atoms will react to produce CO_2 gas.
2. Place about a half-teaspoon of calcium chloride in one flask and a half-teaspoon of potassium chloride in the other. Label the flasks so that students can see the labels.

RELATED PHENOMENA

In addition to the Salt Bubbles demo, consider using other phenomena to launch this experience.

- **Silver Polish** Put together a collection of oxidized metals: silver, copper, zinc, magnesium or calcium turnings. Explain that all these metals react with oxygen in the air, and that silver polish reacts with the silver oxide to remove it. Use a silver polishing cloth with the different metals, and ask students to come up with an explanation for why silver polish cannot be used on some metals.
- **Electron Configurations of Metals** Provide an article on precious metals and information that states that alkali metals and alkali earth metals are never found in the elemental state. Have students compare the electron configurations of transition metals to the alkali/alkali earth metals.

3. Add a half-teaspoon of baking soda to each flask. Ask students what they think might happen when you add water to each of the salts, and ask them to explain their reasoning.
4. Add about 100 mL of water to the potassium chloride. Ask students to make observations.
5. Add about 100 mL of water to the calcium chloride, and ask students to make observations again.
6. After the bubbling dies down, guide students in a discussion about what they observed. **Ask** Why did calcium react to form bubbles while potassium did not? (The electron configurations of the two ions are the same, but the calcium ion has greater charge so the calcium ion is more reactive than the sodium ion in this experiment.)
7. Prompt students to begin thinking about patterns [CCC-1] of reactivity they might observe as they put different elements into contact with baking soda. Encourage them to share thoughts about how they might plan an investigation [SEP-3] to test for those patterns.

EXPLORE

Periodic Trends and Properties

Inquiry Lab In this lab, students carry out an investigation [SEP-3] to qualitatively determine the activity and solubility of various Group 2 metals and their salts.

Lab Demo Video Watch the Lab Demo Video for advice on materials and preparation.

Choose Your Version Open-ended (O), Guided (G), Shortened (S), Advanced (A)

Materials aluminum foil, barium chloride, calcium turnings, calcium chloride, hydrochloric acid, magnesium ribbon, magnesium chloride, potassium iodate, sodium carbonate, sodium sulfate, strontium chloride, distilled or deionized water, 24-well reaction plate, Beral pipets, forceps, black and white sheets of paper, red litmus paper, small beaker or weighing dish, thermometer. (For the advanced inquiry, you will also need to prepare the four unknown solutions according to the Teacher Support document.)

Expected Outcome Students will identify that, for the metals and salts provided, moving down the group increases activity and decreases solubility. They will also identify that moving across a period decreases activity.

Lab Summary Video Watch the Lab Summary Video for support on connecting the lab investigation to the Investigative Phenomenon

DIFFERENTIATED INSTRUCTION

- **Support Special Needs Students** For students who have difficulty working with a group, invite them to do the investigation on their own or with a peer who can guide them through it. Engage with the student as necessary to help sustain curiosity.
- **Support Advanced Students** Invite students to test transition metals and salts in the same ways they tested the Groups 1, 2, and 3 metals. Suggest that they choose two or three metals from different columns of the table. Tell them to compare their results with their earlier trials and write a possible explanation for their findings.

Periodic Trends

Virtual Reality Experience Students identify periodic trends by observing the placement of the elements in the periodic table.

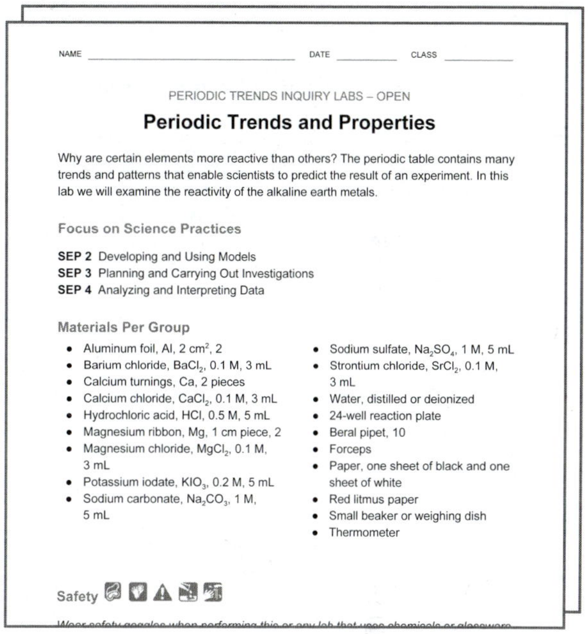

NAME ______ DATE ______ CLASS ______

PERIODIC TRENDS INQUIRY LABS – OPEN

Periodic Trends and Properties

Why are certain elements more reactive than others? The periodic table contains many trends and patterns that enable scientists to predict the result of an experiment. In this lab we will examine the reactivity of the alkaline earth metals.

Focus on Science Practices

SEP 2 Developing and Using Models
SEP 3 Planning and Carrying Out Investigations
SEP 4 Analyzing and Interpreting Data

Materials Per Group

- Aluminum foil, Al, 2 cm^2, 2
- Barium chloride, $BaCl_2$, 0.1 M, 3 mL
- Calcium turnings, Ca, 2 pieces
- Calcium chloride, $CaCl_2$, 0.1 M, 3 mL
- Hydrochloric acid, HCl, 0.5 M, 5 mL
- Magnesium ribbon, Mg, 1 cm piece, 2
- Magnesium chloride, $MgCl_2$, 0.1 M, 3 mL
- Potassium iodate, KIO_3, 0.2 M, 5 mL
- Sodium carbonate, Na_2CO_3, 1 M, 5 mL
- Sodium sulfate, Na_2SO_4, 1 M, 5 mL
- Strontium chloride, $SrCl_2$, 0.1 M, 3 mL
- Water, distilled or deionized
- 24-well reaction plate
- Beral pipet, 10
- Forceps
- Paper, one sheet of black and one sheet of white
- Red litmus paper
- Small beaker or weighing dish
- Thermometer

Safety

O/G/S/A Lab Interactive Worksheets

ADDRESS PRECONCEPTIONS

Some students develop the preconception that ionization energy is a quantity an atom has that allows it to remove an electron. Thus, an atom with low ionization energy would be one from which it is harder to remove an electron. Address this preconception by explaining that ionization energy is energy from outside the atom and is used to remove the electron. In other words, electrons are most easily removed from elements that require the least energy from outside to do so.

You can reinforce this concept by letting a student compare the difficulty in removing an iron object from a strong magnet versus a weak magnet. Removing the object from the strong magnet requires more energy from their muscles than does removing the object from the weak magnet.

Virtual Reality Experience: Periodic Trends

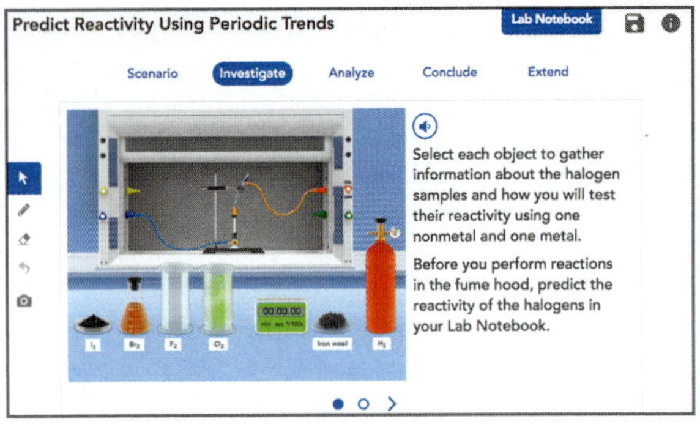

Virtual Lab: Predict Reactivity Using Periodic Trends

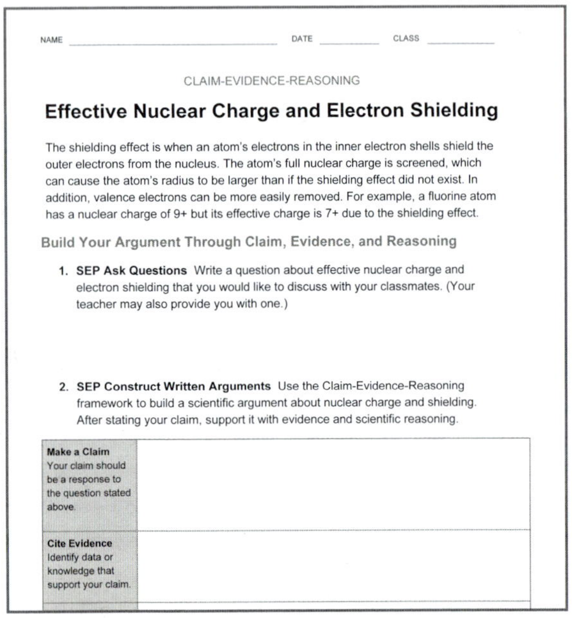

NAME ______ DATE ______ CLASS ______

CLAIM-EVIDENCE-REASONING

Effective Nuclear Charge and Electron Shielding

The shielding effect is when an atom's electrons in the inner electron shells shield the outer electrons from the nucleus. The atom's full nuclear charge is screened, which can cause the atom's radius to be larger than if the shielding effect did not exist. In addition, valence electrons can be more easily removed. For example, a fluorine atom has a nuclear charge of 9+ but its effective charge is 7+ due to the shielding effect.

Build Your Argument Through Claim, Evidence, and Reasoning

1. **SEP Ask Questions** Write a question about effective nuclear charge and electron shielding that you would like to discuss with your classmates. (Your teacher may also provide you with one.)

2. **SEP Construct Written Arguments** Use the Claim-Evidence-Reasoning framework to build a scientific argument about nuclear charge and shielding. After stating your claim, support it with evidence and scientific reasoning.

Make a Claim Your claim should be a response to the question stated above.	
Cite Evidence Identify data or knowledge that support your claim.	

CER Interactive Worksheet

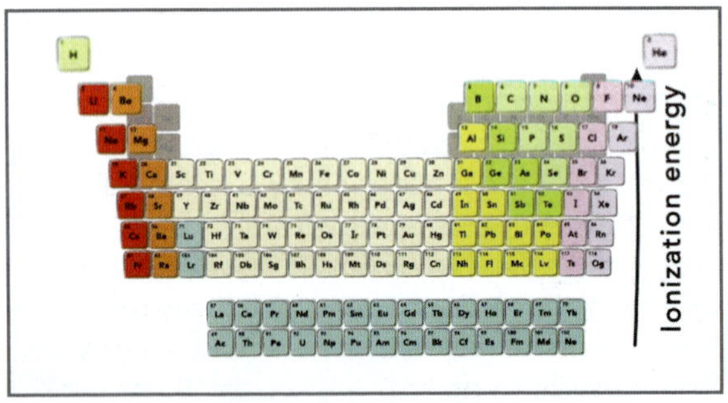

Animation: Ionization Energy

Predict Reactivity Using Periodic Trends

Virtual Lab In this Virtual Lab, students investigate the reactivity of halogens. They learn how to use atomic size and electron affinity to help identify patterns [CCC-1] in order to predict reactivity. They will then carry out an investigation [SEP-3] to test their hypotheses.

- Before students begin, review with them what they will be doing in the lab and be sure they are clear on what they are trying to achieve. You may wish to write the goals of the lab in a place that is visible to students.
- Advise students to make notes in their science notebooks about their lab data and look for patterns that can help them draw conclusions. Students will confirm that atomic radius increases down through the group. They identify that reactivity decreases as ionization energy increases.
- After the lab, discuss findings as a class.

ASSESS ON THE SPOT

After students complete the Virtual Lab, have them complete an exit card and respond to the question: How are the patterns of atomic radius and reactivity related to the number of electrons in a halogen atom? Review responses to assess students' understanding.

EXPLAIN

Effective Nuclear Charge and Electron Shielding

Claim-Evidence-Reasoning Students write an argument [SEP-7] in which they make a claim about the relationship between the effective nuclear charge and electron shielding. They then support their argument with observed evidence and scientific reasoning.

- For Question 1, you may wish to give students tables which show trends of effective nuclear charge and shielding effects. They might also benefit by reviewing the information on page 53 of the Experience Notebook.
- If students have difficulty identifying appropriate questions, discuss as a group some possibilities, such as: Which atom experiences a greater shielding effect—beryllium or fluorine?
- If students are unable to identify appropriate evidence in Question 2, suggest that they review the information in Experiences 1 and 2 and underline the information that applies to their claim.

Allow students to revisit their claims and evidence after they read and discuss page 59 in the Experience Notebook and before they complete the rubric.

Ionization Energy

Animation This animation describes the factors within an atom that affect ionization energy, electronegativity, and electron affinity and explains how these factors give rise to other periodic trends.

Explain that copper appears to be different from the other metals shown in the animation because the energies of its 4*s* and 3*d* electrons are very similar. The double ring in the copper illustration indicates this similarity. Because of this, all of the 3*d* and 4*s* electrons can be treated as outer shell electrons in terms of nuclear shielding, increasing the effective nuclear charge compared to an atom in which all of the *d* electrons are in the inner shells. Copper, therefore, has a much higher ionization energy and smaller radius than potassium.

ASSESS ON THE SPOT

Give students notecards and tell them to write a response to the following prompt: How are ionization energy and electronegativity related? Students can then exchange notecards and evaluate each other's answers.

Periodic Trends

Experience Notebook Ideally, assign the Experience Notebook or Realize Reader first, and then follow up with any of the following suggested instructional strategies to fill knowledge gaps and deepen understanding.

Use these strategies to help students make sense of the images and text on the indicated pages, as well as to engage in science practices.

- **Atomic Radius** (pp. 56–58) Choose two elements from the same group or the same period of the periodic table. **Ask** The atoms of which element are bigger? Students should explain their reasoning. If students need a hint, they can look at the graphic on page 57. Repeat questioning as needed, using different elements.
- Before students draw their graphs in response to Question 12, pair them and ask them to discuss how each partner would make the graph. They should address:
  - What elements they would include
  - How they would label the axes
  - What they predict their graph will look like

  Note that students' graphs don't all have to look the same, but they will look similar and indicate similar patterns [CCC-1].
- Give each student a notecard and tell them to draw an atomic model [SEP-2] for the formation of one cation from Group 1A, 2A, or 3A, and one anion from Group 5A, 6A, or 7A. They should include information about protons and electrons in each atom and indicate whether the neutral or ionic atom is larger. Ask volunteers to show their cards to the class (via projector) and explain their reasoning.
- **Ionization Energy** (p. 59) As a class, compare and contrast the pattern [CCC-1] of ionization energy in the periodic table to other periodic trends. Discuss why ionization energy and atomic radius have opposite trends.
- **Successive Ionization Energies** (p. 60) Review the ionization energy chart with students. **Ask:**
  a. Which electron on the chart is the most difficult to remove? Which is the easiest?
  b. Why does it take so much more energy to remove an electron from chlorine than from sodium?
  c. Why is does it take more energy to remove the second electron from magnesium than it takes to remove the first electron?
  d. Why does it take almost ten times more energy to remove a second electron from sodium?
- **Electron Affinity** (p. 61) Pair students and let them compose a short explanation [SEP-6] of why atoms with a high effective nuclear charge readily attract electrons. Gather explanations and discuss them as a class.
- **Common Charges in Representative Elements** (p. 62) Review as a class the pattern [CCC-1] of electron gain or loss represented by columns 1A–5A. Encourage students to remind themselves of the reasoning for this pattern, as they will rely on understanding it as their knowledge of chemistry progresses.
- **Connecting the Trends** (p. 63) Divide students into groups of three or four. Task each group with devising a model [SEP-2] showing all of the periodic trends they know about and explanations for them. Invite groups to study and critique each others' models in terms of how well each one conveys the underlying patterns and connections between them.

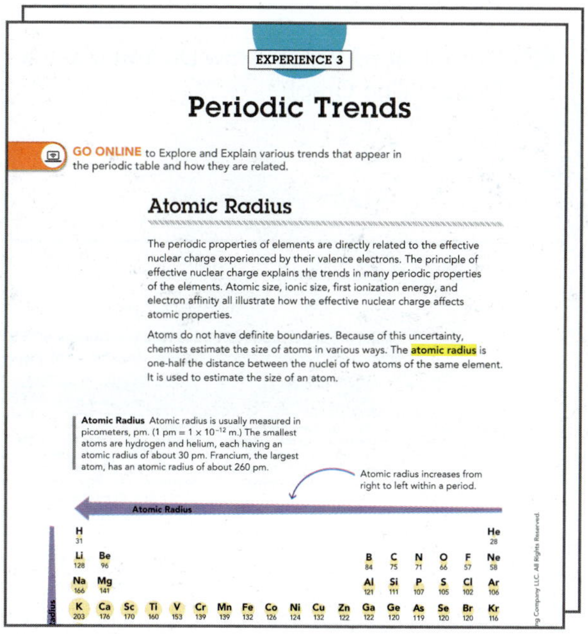
EXPERIENCE 3

Periodic Trends

GO ONLINE to Explore and Explain various trends that appear in the periodic table and how they are related.

Atomic Radius

The periodic properties of elements are directly related to the effective nuclear charge experienced by their valence electrons. The principle of effective nuclear charge explains the trends in many periodic properties of the elements. Atomic size, ionic size, first ionization energy, and electron affinity all illustrate how the effective nuclear charge affects atomic properties.

Atoms do not have definite boundaries. Because of this uncertainty, chemists estimate the size of atoms in various ways. The atomic radius is one-half the distance between the nuclei of two atoms of the same element. It is used to estimate the size of an atom.

Experience Notebook, pp. 56–63

eTEXT

INTEGRATE THE THREE DIMENSIONS

The Experience Notebook weaves together the various patterns [CCC-1] in the periodic table to present it as a complex and predictive model [SEP-2] of how matter in the universe is organized [PS1.A]. Students gain the knowledge to explain [SEP-6] the phenomena of atomic size, ionization energy, and electron affinity and the patterns each follows in the periodic table.

ELD SUPPORT

Speaking After students read pages 56–58 in the Experience Notebook, they work in pairs or small groups to plan and deliver brief oral presentations about atomic radius and atomic size, using appropriate technology.

- **Emerging/Beginning** Students explain atomic radius and atomic size using their own words.
- **Developing/Expanding** Students describe atomic radius and atomic size using the vocabulary and models from the text.
- **Bridging** Students describe atomic radius and atomic size using the vocabulary and models from the text. Their presentations should be organized to describe how atomic radius and atomic size are related, as well as how these properties can be identified in the periodic table.

Virtual Nerd Video: How Do You Make a Double Line Graph?

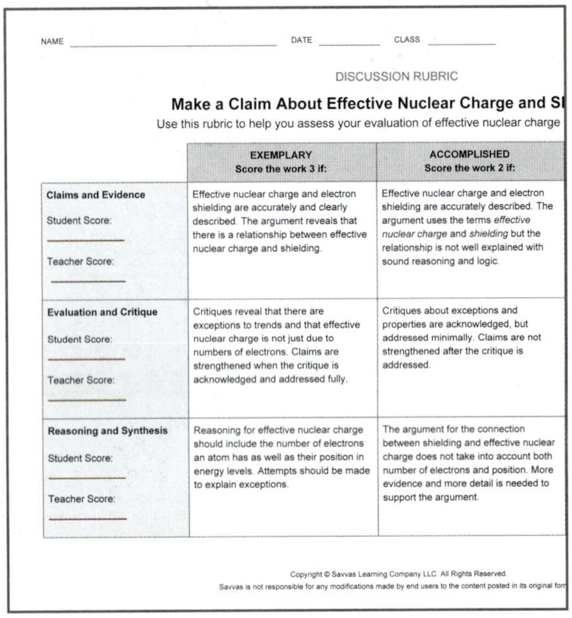

NAME ______ DATE ______ CLASS ______

DISCUSSION RUBRIC

Make a Claim About Effective Nuclear Charge and Sl

Use this rubric to help you assess your evaluation of effective nuclear charge

	EXEMPLARY Score the work 3 if:	**ACCOMPLISHED** Score the work 2 if:
Claims and Evidence Student Score: ______ Teacher Score: ______	Effective nuclear charge and electron shielding are accurately and clearly described. The argument reveals that there is a relationship between effective nuclear charge and shielding.	Effective nuclear charge and electron shielding are accurately described. The argument uses the terms *effective nuclear charge* and *shielding* but the relationship is not well explained with sound reasoning and logic.
Evaluation and Critique Student Score: ______ Teacher Score: ______	Critiques reveal that there are exceptions to trends and that effective nuclear charge is not just due to numbers of electrons. Claims are strengthened when the critique is acknowledged and addressed fully.	Critiques about exceptions and properties are acknowledged, but addressed minimally. Claims are not strengthened after the critique is addressed.
Reasoning and Synthesis Student Score: ______ Teacher Score: ______	Reasoning for effective nuclear charge should include the number of electrons an atom has as well as their position in energy levels. Attempts should be made to explain exceptions.	The argument for the connection between shielding and effective nuclear charge does not take into account both number of electrons and position. More evidence and more detail is needed to support the argument.

Discussion Rubric Interactive Worksheet

CONNECT TO CAREERS

Materials Scientist Materials scientists research and study the structures and chemical properties of various materials. They investigate ways to strengthen or combine materials to develop new materials with specific properties and purposes. Suggest students research this career, write a paragraph about the nature of the work, and make a list of educational requirements and employment opportunities. They may also wish to describe what they would find interesting about this career.

How Do You Make a Double Line Graph?

Virtual Nerd Video Use this video tutorial to reinforce how to make a double line graph.

ELABORATE

Make a Claim About Effective Nuclear Charge and Shielding

Discussion Rubric Students discuss the patterns [CCC-1] they observed and the claims they made about effective nuclear charge and electron shielding and assess their performance.

Lead a class discussion and **Ask:**

- What is effective nuclear charge? (Effective nuclear charge is the net positive nuclear charge experienced by an electron in an atom.)
- What is electron shielding? (Electron shielding is the reduction of the full nuclear charge experienced by an electron as a result of shielding by inner electrons.)
- How does electron shielding affect the effective nuclear charge of an atom? (The amount of shielding an electron experiences depends on which orbital the electron is in. Electrons closer to the nucleus shield, or cancel, part of the positive nuclear charge, but valence electrons do not shield one another.)

Then organize students into groups of three and tell them to take turns presenting their claim, evidence, and reasoning to group members. Remind students that they should devise a concrete, answerable question, as well as identify evidence and refer to it while clearly stating the reasoning behind their claim and revisions. When students have finished their discussion, tell them to use the rubric to evaluate their understanding and communication, keeping in mind that they will be assessed on the accuracy of their self-evaluation.

PROFESSIONAL DEVELOPMENT

Support Language Demands in Science Before students present their CERs to other group members during the activity, Make a Claim About Effective Nuclear Charge and Shielding, explain that scientists presenting their work to colleagues use the same format. In order to succinctly communicate their ideas, scientists present to colleagues using scientific and academic language. Invite students to write a short script of how they can present their CERs to members of the scientific community, stressing that they should use the appropriate and concise terms. Have them role play, presenting their ideas at a scientific conference as they share their CERs with their group.

Growing Crystals in Gels

Engineering Design Challenge In this activity, students define the problem of impurities in crystals and identify the criteria [ETS1.A] of the pure crystal they would like to grow. They then propose a formula for their crystal [ETS1.B], produce their crystal, and evaluate and refine their approach.

Materials and Advance Preparation 1 *M* copper(II) chloride solution, 1 *M* cobalt(II) chloride solution, 1 *M* zinc(II) chloride solution, 1 *M* iron(III) nitrate solution, 1 *M* sodium phosphate monobasic solution, 15% sodium silicate solution, 25-mL graduated cylinder, test-tube rack, test-tube, test-tube stopper, safety goggles, gloves

Expected Outcome Students discover that their success or failure is linked to periodicity.

Safety Discuss safety precautions, including safe handling of the compounds—this is a chance to familiarize students with Material Safety Data Sheets (MSDS). Be sure students wear safety goggles and gloves while testing their mixtures and making their gels. Remind student to be careful when handling glass and to alert you should any glass break.

Use the following strategies to guide students as they complete indicated steps in the Engineering Design Challenge:

- **Step 3** Remind students as they research that they should keep in mind criteria for reliable Web sites. Students can search for pigments in the OSHA handbook or other documents that list toxicities.
- **Step 5** Remind students that their test results should be evaluated against the criteria. If results do not meet criteria, consider how solubility rules apply to their proposed mixture and suggest an alternative.

DIFFERENTIATED INSTRUCTION

- **Support Less Proficient Readers** Pair less proficient readers with partners who are more proficient. Before partners begin each part of the Engineering Design Challenge, have the proficient reader slowly read aloud the text as the less proficient reader follows along. Instruct partners to ask each other questions after they read each section. Provide assistance to each pair of students as needed.
- **Support Struggling Students** Some students may have difficulty identifying criteria and constraints. Have these students make a two-column chart. In the first column, have them list some qualities that they think would make the crystal the best it can be. In the other column tell them to write some problems that someone might have making the crystal or using it. Then tell students that they just identified the criteria and constraints.
- **Support Special Needs Students** Pair visually-impaired students with a sighted partner. The partner can read the text on the worksheet, if necessary, and aid in the research in Step 3. The pair can discuss possible formulas in Step 4 and then work together to complete Step 5. The sighted partner can describe what he or she is doing in Step 5. If possible, provide tools to magnify the growing crystals in Step 5 for students who can see an enlarged image. In Step 7, allow visually impaired students feel the crystals if groups grow crystals that are large enough.

ASSESS ON THE SPOT

Have students write two or three sentences that summarize what they learned in the Engineering Design Challenge and cite an example of how they applied the periodic table to predict an element's properties. Collect the writing samples and critique them for understanding. Return them to students and guide a class discussion on any points that were confusing or challenging.

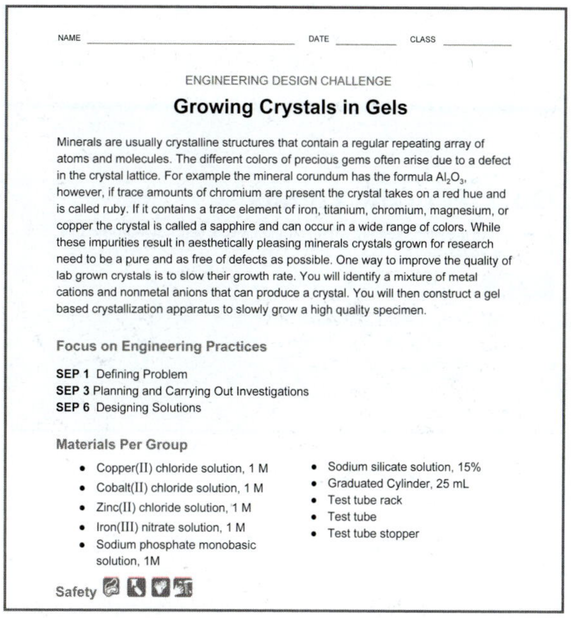

NAME ______ DATE ______ CLASS ______

ENGINEERING DESIGN CHALLENGE

Growing Crystals in Gels

Minerals are usually crystalline structures that contain a regular repeating array of atoms and molecules. The different colors of precious gems often arise due to a defect in the crystal lattice. For example the mineral corundum has the formula Al_2O_3, however, if trace amounts of chromium are present the crystal takes on a red hue and is called ruby. If it contains a trace element of iron, titanium, chromium, magnesium, or copper the crystal is called a sapphire and can occur in a wide range of colors. While these impurities result in aesthetically pleasing minerals crystals grown for research need to be a pure and as free of defects as possible. One way to improve the quality of lab grown crystals is to slow their growth rate. You will identify a mixture of metal cations and nonmetal anions that can produce a crystal. You will then construct a gel based crystallization apparatus to slowly grow a high quality specimen.

Focus on Engineering Practices

SEP 1 Defining Problem
SEP 3 Planning and Carrying Out Investigations
SEP 6 Designing Solutions

Materials Per Group

- Copper(II) chloride solution, 1 M
- Cobalt(II) chloride solution, 1 M
- Zinc(II) chloride solution, 1 M
- Iron(III) nitrate solution, 1 M
- Sodium phosphate monobasic solution, 1M
- Sodium silicate solution, 15%
- Graduated Cylinder, 25 mL
- Test tube rack
- Test tube
- Test tube stopper

Safety

Engineering Design Challenge Interactive Worksheet

CLASSROOM MODIFICATIONS

Based on your students' abilities and your schedule, you may wish to edit Growing Crystals in Gels to make it more open ended or more guided.

- **More Open Ended** Allow students to get a greater sense of the range of possibilities for crystals they can grow by letting them research a range of crystals and then decide on criteria. They may then also need to research their constraints.
- **More Guided** Rather than having students devise the formula for their crystal, offer them a list of alternatives to choose from. You may also list some properties of the metal nitrates as example criteria.

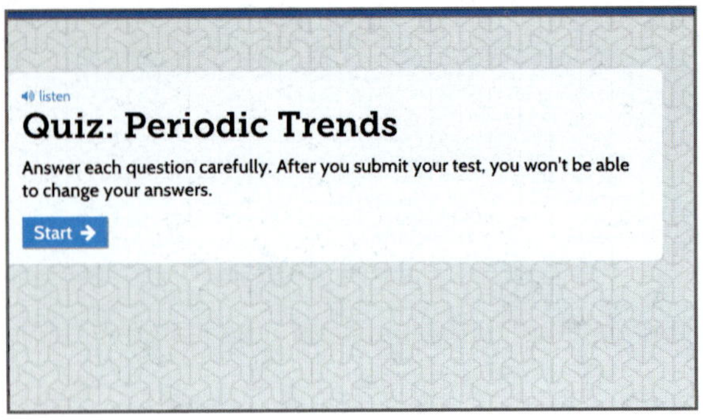

Interactive Online Quiz

Quiz Interactive Worksheet

EVALUATE

Periodic Trends

Quiz Assign the quiz in online technology-enhanced, auto-graded format or as an editable quiz worksheet. Use the scoring notes and remediation strategies found online to assess students' responses and to provide targeted feedback for each item to remediate well before assigning the summative 3-D Assessment.

REMEDIATION SUGGESTIONS

- **If** students are struggling to connect reactivity with the periodic table, **then** suggest they return to the Inquiry Lab and try to explain the results in terms of periodic trends.
- **If** students are struggling to define the differences between ionization energy and electron affinity, **then** review the animation with them, asking them to explain in their own words what is happening.
- **If** students are struggling to grasp how ionic charge arises, **then** suggest they review the graphic on page 58 and then choose elements from Groups 1, 2, and 17 and practice determining how their numbers of electrons will change when they become ions.
- **If** students are struggling to connect the various periodic trends, **then** suggest they reread the Experience Notebook, underlining key points about each trend, and then annotate a periodic table with those points.

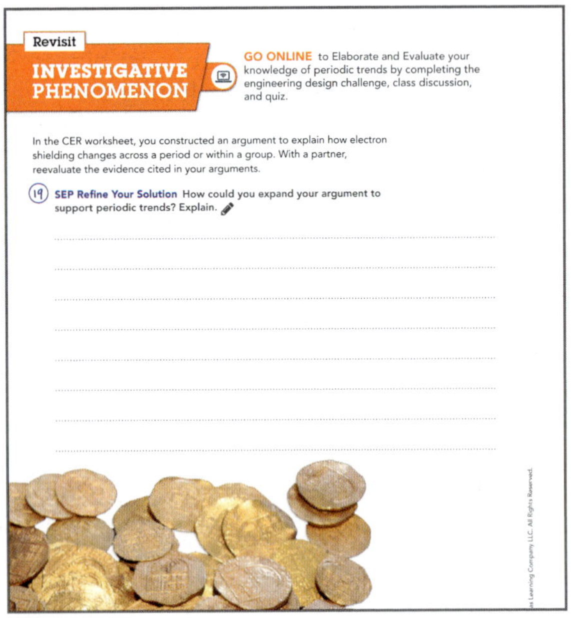

Revisit

INVESTIGATIVE PHENOMENON

GO ONLINE to Elaborate and Evaluate your knowledge of periodic trends by completing the engineering design challenge, class discussion, and quiz.

In the CER worksheet, you constructed an argument to explain how electron shielding changes across a period or within a group. With a partner, reevaluate the evidence cited in your arguments.

19 SEP Refine Your Solution How could you expand your argument to support periodic trends? Explain.

Experience Notebook, p. 64

eTEXT

Revisit

INVESTIGATIVE PHENOMENON

Support Reflection Students can complete the reflection prompt, where they will unpack and make sense of the Investigative Phenomenon, based on practices and understandings that have been reinforced over the course of the experience.

- Tell students to look over their results from the Inquiry Lab and work in pairs to explain them, reflecting on what they now know and can explain about those results. Invite some pairs to share their thoughts with the class.
- Ask students to raise their hands if they feel confident in explaining why:
  a. sulfur has a high ionization energy
  b. oxygen has a relatively small atomic radius
  c. magnesium has effective nuclear charge of +2
  d. a chloride ion has a larger radius than a chlorine atom
- Discuss with students how they can use their understanding of ionization energy and electron affinity to explain why elements in pure form as so rare.

Evaluate and Revise Your CER Argument Have students answer Questions 3 and 4 in the CER activity and re-evaluate the claims they made. Students should add any additional evidence they have collected in this investigation and revise their CERs. Evidence may include that elements with low ionization energy tend to be reactive, the atomic radius of an atom affects its reactivity, or main group elements with a higher ionization energy also have higher electron affinity and release more energy when taking on an additional electron.

EVALUATE

The Periodic Table

3-D Assessment For a summative assessment of Investigation 2, assign the 3-D Assessment, which is available online, as an ExamView bank, or as an editable worksheet.

Gravimetric Analysis of Periodic Trends

Performance-Based Assessment Use this Performance-Based Assessment to assess students' mastery of the standards. In this activity, students carry out an investigation **[SEP-3]** to quantitatively determine the solubility of sodium halide salts in methanol. They use their results to make a prediction about the solubility of sodium fluoride.

Safety Do not dry the students' filter paper in an oven as the methanol vapors could ignite.

Expected Outcome The sodium halide salts that are further down the periodic table have higher solubility.

Experience Notebook (p. 65) After students complete the Performance-Based Assessment, have them complete the reflection prompts in the Experience Notebook.

DIFFERENTIATED INSTRUCTION

- **Support Special Needs Students** Set up a model of vacuum filtration as shown in Figure 1 for the class to view. To help students with visual disabilities, ask a partner to explain the parts in vacuum filtration and the information in the figure using the vacuum filtration setup you placed in front of the class. Have the partner read aloud the text as the students who are visually impaired touch the appropriate parts of the experimental setup. Then the partner can read aloud the remaining information beginning with the start of the procedure.
- **Support Advanced Students** Have advanced students research the history of gravimetric analysis. They should explore early experiments that used gravimetric analysis and write a one-page summary of their findings.

What distinguishes the minerals in this mountain?

Revisit Anchoring Phenomenon At the end of Investigation 2, have students revisit the Anchoring Phenomenon question about what distinguishes the minerals in the Rainbow Mountains in Peru. Lead a class discussion about how an element's electron configuration relates to an element's chemical and physical properties. Then, in small groups, have students write an explanation that describes how they think different elements' chemical and physical properties impact the Rainbow Mountains. Students should also include a prediction about how the mountains might change if the elements' properties changed. Have groups share their explanations with the class.

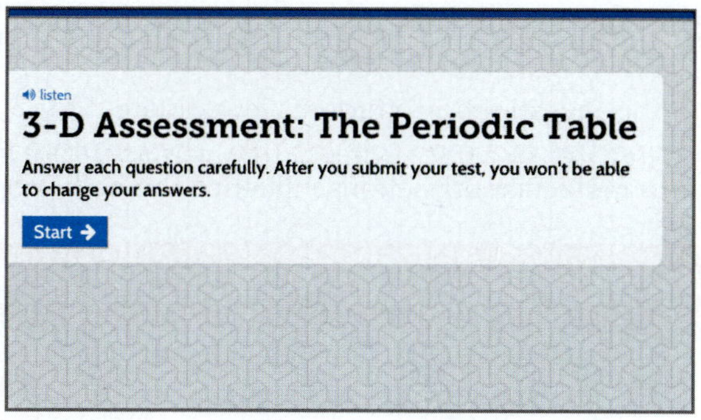

Interactive Online 3-D Assessment

Interactive ExamView 3-D Assessment

3-D Assessment Interactive Worksheet

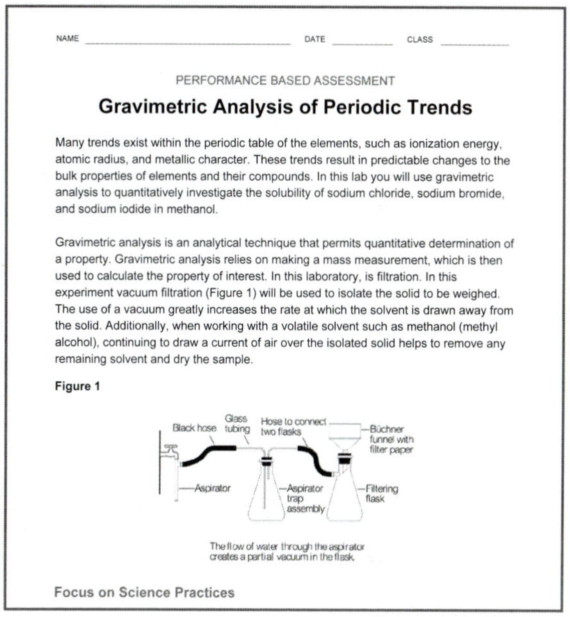

NAME ______ DATE ______ CLASS ______

PERFORMANCE BASED ASSESSMENT

Gravimetric Analysis of Periodic Trends

Many trends exist within the periodic table of the elements, such as ionization energy, atomic radius, and metallic character. These trends result in predictable changes to the bulk properties of elements and their compounds. In this lab you will use gravimetric analysis to quantitatively investigate the solubility of sodium chloride, sodium bromide, and sodium iodide in methanol.

Gravimetric analysis is an analytical technique that permits quantitative determination of a property. Gravimetric analysis relies on making a mass measurement, which is then used to calculate the property of interest. In this laboratory, is filtration. In this experiment vacuum filtration (Figure 1) will be used to isolate the solid to be weighed. The use of a vacuum greatly increases the rate at which the solvent is drawn away from the solid. Additionally, when working with a volatile solvent such as methanol (methyl alcohol), continuing to draw a current of air over the isolated solid helps to remove any remaining solvent and dry the sample.

Figure 1

The flow of water through the aspirator creates a partial vacuum in the flask.

Focus on Science Practices

Performance-Based Assessment Interactive Worksheet

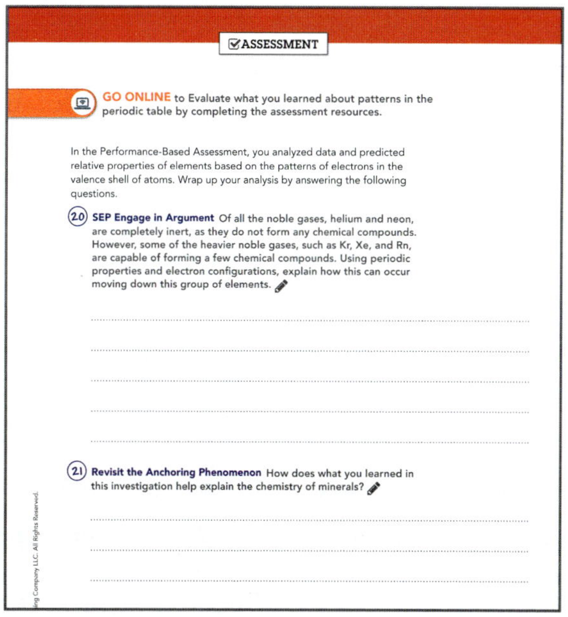

ASSESSMENT

GO ONLINE to Evaluate what you learned about patterns in the periodic table by completing the assessment resources.

In the Performance-Based Assessment, you analyzed data and predicted relative properties of elements based on the patterns of electrons in the valence shell of atoms. Wrap up your analysis by answering the following questions.

20 **SEP Engage in Argument** Of all the noble gases, helium and neon, are completely inert, as they do not form any chemical compounds. However, some of the heavier noble gases, such as Kr, Xe, and Rn, are capable of forming a few chemical compounds. Using periodic properties and electron configurations, explain how this can occur moving down this group of elements.

21 **Revisit the Anchoring Phenomenon** How does what you learned in this investigation help explain the chemistry of minerals?

Experience Notebook, p. 65

eTEXT

INVESTIGATION 3 PLANNER

Chemical Bonding

In this investigation, students investigate [SEP-3] the types of chemical bonds and how they affect the properties of a molecule [PS1.A]. They explore the types of attractions between molecules and how intermolecular attractions influence the bulk properties of a material.

INVESTIGATIVE PHENOMENON

Why do gems have different properties than metals?

Explaining Phenomena Students explore covalent bonds, polar molecules, and dipole interactions. As students develop the ability to compare and contrast the types of intermolecular forces in materials and their resulting properties, they are able to construct explanations of what distinguishes one mineral from another.

	EXPERIENCE 1	EXPERIENCE 2
	Ionic Bonds **2 days** Students explore the octet rule and how the electrostatic attractions between cations and anions form ions bonds. They describe how the structure of ionic compounds affect their properties.	**Metallic Bonds** **2 days** Students explain how the bonding in metals and alloys affects their properties. They describe the sea of electrons model, and they compare ionic and metallic bonds.
CONNECTION TO THE INVESTIGATIVE PHENOMENON	Students write about bonding and the properties of the mineral corundum and relate that information to why gems have different properties than metals.	Students construct an explanation for how bonding in gold makes it possible to make gold leaf and relate that to why gems have different properties than metals.
ENGAGE	**Teacher's Guide** Everyday Phenomenon Surprisingly Stable Salt, p. 70	**Teacher's Guide** Everyday Phenomenon Modeling Metals with Magnets, p. 77
EXPLORE	**Inquiry Lab** Characteristics of Ionic Bonds **Interactivity** Ions and Electroplating ⊕	**Inquiry Lab** Investigate Metallic Bonds **Analyzing Data** Patterns in Melting Points of Metals ⊕
EXPLAIN	**Modeling** Electron Dot Structures for Ionic Compounds **Animation** Formation of Ionic Compounds ⊕ **Experience Notebook,** pp. 68–75	**Claim-Evidence-Reasoning** Compare Metallic and Ionic Substances **Experience Notebook,** pp. 77–79
ELABORATE	**Peer Review Rubric** Evaluate Electron Dot Structures **Writing About Science** Describe Ionic Bonding and Properties ⊕	**Discussion Rubric** Compare Metallic and Ionic Substances **Engineering Design Challenge** Evaluate Metals for a Commercial Application ⊕
EVALUATE	**Quiz** Ionic Bonds **Experience Notebook** Revisit Investigative Phenomenon, p. 76	**Quiz** Metallic Bonds **Experience Notebook** Revisit Investigative Phenomenon, p. 80

*Pacing for Encounter Investigative Phenomenon core instruction is a half-day.

†Pacing for core Investigation Assessment is approximately 1 day.

GOT MORE TIME? Personalize and enhance your instructional plan by assigning the activities with the got-more-time icon, as time allows.

Investigative Phenomenon Video Tools of the Trade*

Claim-Evidence-Reasoning Discuss the Investigative Phenomenon*

Virtual Reality Experience (+)

Experience Notebook, p. 66*

EXPERIENCE 3	EXPERIENCE 4	EXPERIENCE 5
Covalent Bonds **2 days** Students investigate molecular geometry and polarity. They estimate the difference in electronegativities between two elements to determine polarity.	**Intermolecular Attractions** **2 days** Students explore hydrogen bonds and draw models showing dispersion forces. They explain how intermolecular attractions between molecules affect the properties of a material.	**Names and Formulas of Compounds** **2 days** Students explain the rules for naming compounds and acids, including how to name a compound when given its formula. The predict bond types in a compound based on its name or formula.
Students compare molecules in beads to the bonding in gemstones to refine explanations on why gems have properties that are different from those of metals.	Students compare rock candy and the bonding in ionic and molecular compounds to the bonding in gemstones to refine explanations on why gems have different properties than metals.	Students explore that gemstones are silicate minerals, and use this information to refine explanations on why gems have properties that are different from those of metals.
Teacher's Guide Everyday Phenomenon Covalent Conductors, p. 84	**Teacher's Guide** Everyday Phenomenon Evaporating Liquids, p. 90	**Teacher's Guide** Everyday Phenomenon Why do roads have different names?, p. 96
Inquiry Lab Characteristics of Covalent Bonds **Analyzing Data** Calculate Bond Polarity (+)	**Inquiry Lab** Intermolecular Forces **Virtual Lab** Intermolecular Forces in Liquids (+)	**Inquiry Lab** Chemical Names and Formulas **Analyzing Data** Infer Rules for Naming Compounds (+)
Modeling Electron Dot Structures for Molecular Substances **Animation** Formation of Covalent Bonds (+) **Experience Notebook,** pp. 81–90	**Claim-Evidence-Reasoning** Compare Molecular Compound Properties **Experience Notebook,** pp. 91–95	**Claim-Evidence-Reasoning** Comparing Compound Nomenclatures **Animation** Predicting Bond Type (+) **Experience Notebook,** pp. 97–105
Discussion Rubric Compare Covalent and Ionic Bonds and Their Substances **Analyzing Data** Investigate Molecule Polarity (+)	**Peer Review Rubric** Review Molecular Compound Properties **Writing About Science** Water's Behavior on Earth (+)	**Discussion Rubric** Compare Element Combinations and Nomenclature **Analyzing Data** Infer Rules for Naming Acids (+)
Quiz Covalent Bonds **Experience Notebook** Revisit Investigative Phenomenon, p. 90	**Quiz** Intermolecular Attractions **Experience Notebook** Revisit Investigative Phenomenon, p. 96	**Quiz** Names and Formulas of Compounds **Experience Notebook** Revisit Investigative Phenomenon, p. 106

INVESTIGATION ASSESSMENT

Performance-Based Assessment Qualitative Analysis and Chemical Bonding†

3-D Assessment Chemical Bonding†

Experience Notebook Performance-Based Assessment, p. 107; Revisit Anchoring Phenomenon, p 107†; **Appendix C** Problem Bank, pp. R12–R13

INVESTIGATION 3

Chemical Bonding

Teacher Background

Chemical bonding is the foundation of chemistry. The breaking of existing bonds and the making of new ones define a chemical reaction. To make this rather abstract topic more concrete, emphasize to students that every facet of their lives—cooking a meal, digesting food, washing dishes, and trying to get a spaghetti stain out of a shirt—involves changes in chemical bonding.

Throughout the investigation, keep a list of examples of everyday phenomena that arise from chemical bonding—ionic, metallic, and covalent bonds, as well as intermolecular forces. Use these examples whenever possible to engage students' interest. In addition, create hands-on models of atoms and bonding, allowing students to understand the concepts in a tactile way.

Learning Progression

In this investigation, students explore the types of chemical bonds and how they influence the properties of matter [PS1.A]. They investigate the cause-and-effect relationship [CCC-2] between the locations of electrons and the formation of bonds. They explain [SEP-6] how the electron configuration and electronegativity within a molecule determine the nature of its bonding. By looking at patterns [CCC-1] in the names and formulas of compounds, students devise naming rules. Throughout the investigation, they pose questions [SEP-1] about the nature of chemical bonds, answer those questions using an argument based on evidence and reasoning [SEP-7], and communicate [SEP-8] their ideas to peers.

RELATED PHENOMENA

In addition to exploring why gems have properties that differ from those of metals, consider using other phenomena to launch this investigation.

- **Brittle or Not?** Use a hammer to strike a variety of common materials, such as salt, gold or silver, water, or a fatty substance. Discuss the effect of the strike on the different kinds of materials and the cause of those differences. Everyone in the classroom should wear safety goggles for this activity.
- **Dissolving of Ionic vs. Covalent Compounds** Demonstrate that sodium chloride dissolves to create a conductive solution, but sugar does not. **Ask** Why does salt make a conductive solution but sugar does not? Guide students in a discussion that this difference arises from ionic versus covalent bonding.
- **Images of Bonds** Find interesting images of ionic, metallic, and covalent bonds that reveal electron clouds around atoms. Have students predict which type of bond is represented by each image. As a class, discuss the images, describing how the bonds differ and how that might relate to the differing properties of the materials in the images.

TAKE IT LOCAL

Find a local jewelry maker and show the jeweler's work to students. Ask students how they think the jeweler gets the gemstones into the shapes he or she wants, and how they think the jeweler works with metal. Ask students why they think a jeweler cannot just make a gem stick to jewelry, rather than use a bezel to secure it. You may even wish to invite the jeweler to talk with the class about the differences between working with metals and gemstones.

ENCOUNTER

INVESTIGATIVE PHENOMENON

Why do gems have different properties than metals?

Lead into this investigation with a discussion of jewelry making. The properties and shapes of gemstones lead students to ionic bonds (Experience 1), while the working of metal settings for the gems brings them to metallic bonds (Experience 2). Students consider how compounds that are neither gems nor metals behave due to covalent bonds (Experience 3) and how the bonds between molecules give rise to some of a substance's properties (Experience 4). Finally, they name the compounds that make up gems, using chemical nomenclature (Experience 5).

Tools of the Trade

Investigative Phenomenon Video Pair students to watch the video. Tell them to take notes on what they observe. Afterward, **ask** How do the gems in the bowl differ from each other? (They are different shapes, sizes, and colors.) Which properties are determined by the kinds of atoms in the gems' molecules? (The color is determined by the kinds of atoms in the molecules of the gems. Shape could also depend on the crystalline structure of its atoms.) Display examples of metals, such as aluminum foil or jewelry, and examples of minerals, such as quartz or materials in rocks. As a class, make a list of how minerals and metals differ from each other in terms of properties and how we use them.

Discuss the Phenomenon

Claim-Evidence-Reasoning To help build student's understanding of the video, brainstorm a list of questions about the observed phenomenon. Have students complete Question 1 of the CER worksheet and start thinking about the evidence they need to answer their question.

Remind students that their understanding of the phenomenon will be incomplete at this stage, but that they will revisit this activity as they learn more. Make sure to provide students with an opportunity to revisit their CER arguments throughout the investigation, as well as at the end of the investigation, for further revision and peer review.

Reflect on the Phenomenon

Experience Notebook Transition to the opener pages for Investigation 3 in the Experience Notebook and discuss the question on the photo: Why do gems have different properties than metals?

If students struggle, then guide them through the information in the video and material they wrote in the CER activity to craft answers to the driving question. Additionally, at the end of each experience, direct students to complete the writing prompt to reflect on the Investigative Phenomenon.

Investigative Phenomenon Video: Tools of the Trade

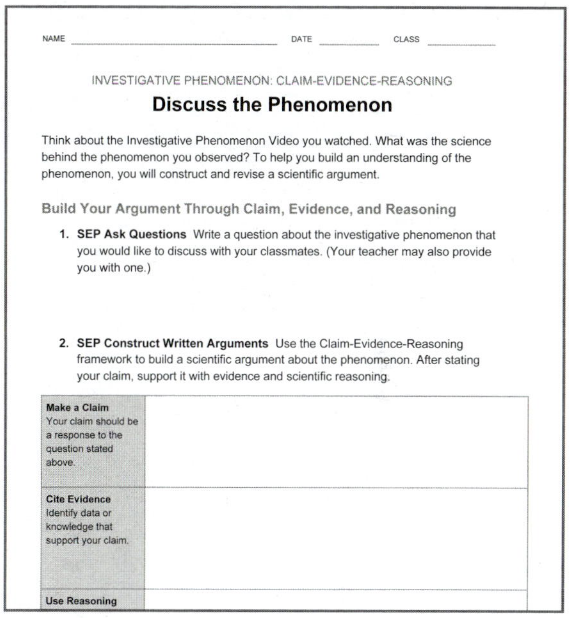

NAME ______________ DATE ________ CLASS ________

INVESTIGATIVE PHENOMENON: CLAIM-EVIDENCE-REASONING

Discuss the Phenomenon

Think about the Investigative Phenomenon Video you watched. What was the science behind the phenomenon you observed? To help you build an understanding of the phenomenon, you will construct and revise a scientific argument.

Build Your Argument Through Claim, Evidence, and Reasoning

1. **SEP Ask Questions** Write a question about the investigative phenomenon that you would like to discuss with your classmates. (Your teacher may also provide you with one.)

2. **SEP Construct Written Arguments** Use the Claim-Evidence-Reasoning framework to build a scientific argument about the phenomenon. After stating your claim, support it with evidence and scientific reasoning.

Make a Claim Your claim should be a response to the question stated above.	
Cite Evidence Identify data or knowledge that support your claim.	
Use Reasoning	

CER Interactive Worksheet

Experience Notebook, pp. 66–67

eTEXT

EXPERIENCE 1

Ionic Bonds

Teacher Background

Experience 1 introduces the process in which metals and nonmetals form ionic bonds by exchanging electrons. This exchange forms positive and negative ions that attract each other. Metals tend to lose electrons in these reactions to achieve a stable octet valence electron configuration, whereas nonmetals gain electrons to fill their valence shells. The strength of an ionic bond is determined by the distance between the charges and the overall charges of the individual ions (Coulomb's law).

Students learn how ionic compounds form crystals made of regular, repeating patterns of positive and negative ions. They discover that ionic compounds have relatively high melting points due to the strength of the electrostatic attraction between ions. They also investigate how ionic compounds conduct electricity when either dissolved in an appropriate solvent or melted, due to the presence of mobile electron carriers (ions).

Objectives

- **Explain that atoms gain or lose electrons to form ions so that they have a full valence shell, which makes them more stable.**
- **Explain that ionic bonds are electrostatic attractions between cations and anions.**
- **Describe how the structures of ionic compounds affect their properties.**

ENGAGE

EVERYDAY PHENOMENON

What happens when you mix an explosive metal with a poisonous gas?

Use the teacher demo to help students understand how elements form ionic bonds to reach a more stable electron configuration.

Surprisingly Stable Salt

Engage students with this discussion of an everyday phenomenon to introduce the concept that ionic compounds have properties that are different from the elements they are made of.

Materials water, potassium metal (or a video of potassium reacting with water), potassium chloride (available as sodium-free salt at the supermarket), safety goggles, gloves, lab coat

Safety If demonstrating the reaction of potassium and water, both teacher and students should wear safety goggles. Conduct the demo in a fume hood.

1. Show students the reaction of potassium metal with water. Emphasize how violent the reaction is and how much energy is released.
2. Explain how dangerous chlorine gas is and how it was used as a chemical warfare agent in World War I. You may also want to show a video of chlorine reacting with another substance to reinforce how reactive the element is.
3. Ask students to predict the properties of a compound made of potassium and chlorine. Encourage students to assume that the dangerous properties of both potassium and chlorine will be present in the potassium chloride.

RELATED PHENOMENA

In addition to the Surprisingly Stable Salt demonstration, consider using other phenomena to launch this experience.

- **Microscopic Solids** Provide several samples of ionic solids and have students look at them under a microscope to observe their regular crystal structures. Discuss the crystal lattice, which contains an alternating array of positive and negative ions. Take a large crystal of copper sulfate and whack it with a hammer. (It breaks in clean lines.) Ask students why it breaks in this manner. Draw a picture of the crystal lattice with charged ions. Ask students what happens on a molecular level when a force is applied to the array of positive and negative ions. (The force pushes ions of similar charge too close to each other and the electrostatic repulsion can cleave the lattice, lending to brittle character.)
- **Electric Sodium Chloride** Using a Meeker burner and a ceramic crucible, melt a sample of sodium chloride (this usually takes more than an hour, so start it before class) and demonstrate how it conducts electricity. **Ask** What happens on a molecular level to allow the melted salt to conduct electricity?

4. Put on all of your personal protective equipment. Goggles, gloves, a splash apron, and even a face shield—all will add to the surprise for the class.
5. Very carefully—for dramatic effect—take a small amount of potassium chloride and add it to a beaker of water. When nothing dramatic happens, lead a class discussion about why this salt is so stable, based on what students have learned about electron configurations and properties of matter. Use this demo to further discuss differences in properties related to gems and metals.

EXPLORE

Characteristics of Ionic Bonds

Inquiry Lab In this lab, students carry out an investigation [SEP-3] to identify the compounds with the strongest interparticle forces in a group of four compounds, based on observations of physical properties [PS1.A].

Lab Demo Video Watch the Lab Demo Video for advice on materials and preparation.

Choose Your Version Open-ended (O), Guided (G), Shortened (S), Advanced (A)

Materials 2 g dextrose, 2 g potassium chloride, 2 g sodium chloride, 2 g sucrose, 50 mL distilled or tap water, balance, butane safety lighter, metal ring with clamp, glass stirring rod

Safety Advise students to be careful when working with an open flame. See the Teacher Support document for additional safety concerns.

Expected Outcome Potassium chloride and sodium chloride have high experimental melting points and will conduct electricity in aqueous solutions, whereas dextrose and sucrose have relatively low melting points and relatively low or no conductivity in aqueous solutions.

Lab Summary Video Watch the Lab Summary Video for support on connecting the lab investigation to the Investigative Phenomenon.

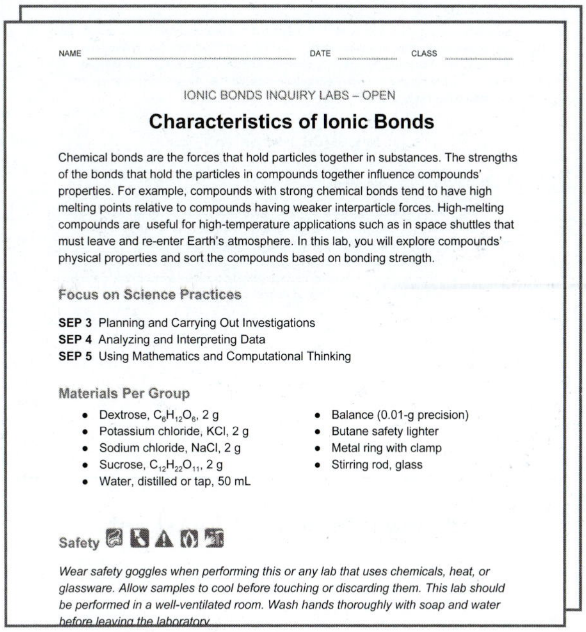
NAME ______ DATE ______ CLASS ______

IONIC BONDS INQUIRY LABS – OPEN

Characteristics of Ionic Bonds

Chemical bonds are the forces that hold particles together in substances. The strengths of the bonds that hold the particles in compounds together influence compounds' properties. For example, compounds with strong chemical bonds tend to have high melting points relative to compounds having weaker interparticle forces. High-melting compounds are useful for high-temperature applications such as in space shuttles that must leave and re-enter Earth's atmosphere. In this lab, you will explore compounds' physical properties and sort the compounds based on bonding strength.

Focus on Science Practices

SEP 3 Planning and Carrying Out Investigations
SEP 4 Analyzing and Interpreting Data
SEP 5 Using Mathematics and Computational Thinking

Materials Per Group

- Dextrose, $C_6H_{12}O_6$, 2 g
- Potassium chloride, KCl, 2 g
- Sodium chloride, NaCl, 2 g
- Sucrose, $C_{12}H_{22}O_{11}$, 2 g
- Water, distilled or tap, 50 mL
- Balance (0.01-g precision)
- Butane safety lighter
- Metal ring with clamp
- Stirring rod, glass

Safety

Wear safety goggles when performing this or any lab that uses chemicals, heat, or glassware. Allow samples to cool before touching or discarding them. This lab should be performed in a well-ventilated room. Wash hands thoroughly with soap and water before leaving the laboratory.

O/G/S/A Lab Interactive Worksheets

Ions and Electroplating

Interactivity In this interactivity, students face the scenario of helping an artist choose a zinc salt that will help protect her decorative spoons from rusting. They test and research different types of zinc salts to see which can conduct electricity. Students determine which salt dissolved the most completely and the relationship between conductivity and how easily the salts dissolved.

- Have students describe how the water molecules are oriented around the dissolved ions. They should notice that the water molecule has both partially positive and partially negative sides and that these sides are attracted to their opposite ions.
- Have students use Coulomb's law to explain [SEP-6] the solubility of different compounds. Challenge students to use observations from the interactivity to describe what bonds are broken and formed when an ionic compound dissolves. (The ionic bonds between atoms are broken, and weak "bonds" between ions and water molecules are formed.)
- Have students explain why zinc oxide and zinc sulfide are not good options for electroplating iron spoons. (These two do not fully dissolve in water and cannot conduct electricity.)

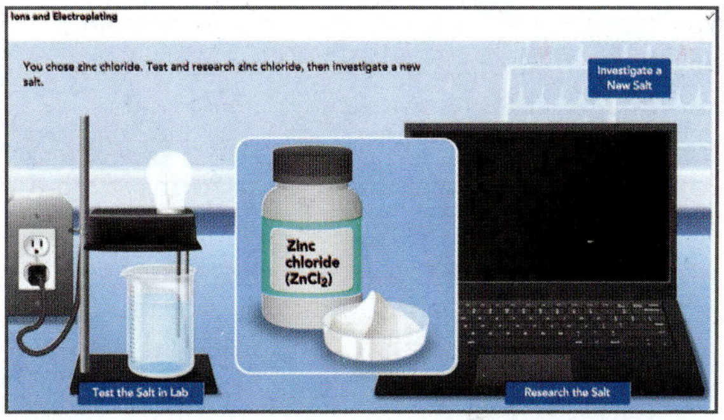

Interactivity: Ions and Electroplating

ASSESS ON THE SPOT

Ask students to draw how one molecule of zinc chloride would look after it is dissolved in water and to orient the water molecules correctly, showing their positive dipoles pointing toward the negative ion and their negative dipoles pointing toward the positive ion.

ELD SUPPORT

Writing Students write about how ionic compounds dissolve in water after completing the Ions and Electroplating interactivity.

- **Emerging/Beginning** Have students write sentences describing what happened to the atoms in the compound when it dissolved in the water.
- **Developing/Expanding** Have students complete the Emerging activity and then use more advanced sentence structures to write a paragraph that explains what happened to both the ions in the compound and the water molecules when the compound dissolved.
- **Bridging** Have students write a one-page summary that identifies the sequence of events for any ionic compound dissolving in water by generalizing the process they observed in this interactivity. Then ask students to exchange summaries with other students for editing.

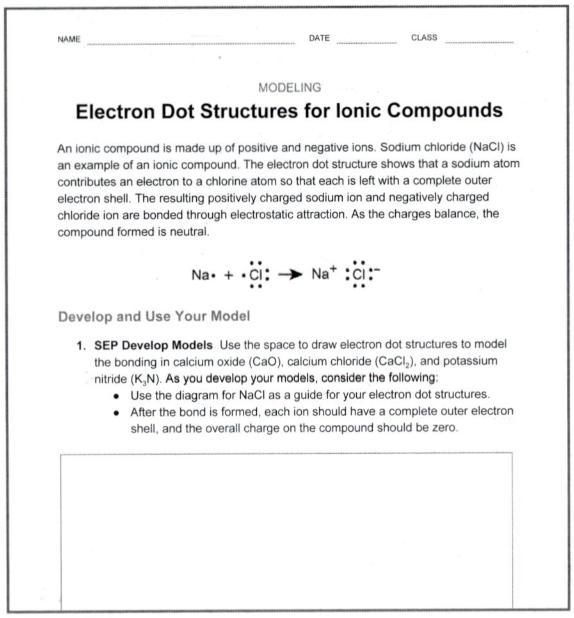
NAME ______ DATE ______ CLASS ______

MODELING

Electron Dot Structures for Ionic Compounds

An ionic compound is made up of positive and negative ions. Sodium chloride (NaCl) is an example of an ionic compound. The electron dot structure shows that a sodium atom contributes an electron to a chlorine atom so that each is left with a complete outer electron shell. The resulting positively charged sodium ion and negatively charged chloride ion are bonded through electrostatic attraction. As the charges balance, the compound formed is neutral.

Na• + •C̈l: → Na^+ :C̈l:$^-$

Develop and Use Your Model

1. **SEP Develop Models** Use the space to draw electron dot structures to model the bonding in calcium oxide (CaO), calcium chloride ($CaCl_2$), and potassium nitride (K_3N). As you develop your models, consider the following:
   - Use the diagram for NaCl as a guide for your electron dot structures.
   - After the bond is formed, each ion should have a complete outer electron shell, and the overall charge on the compound should be zero.

Modeling Interactive Worksheet

INTEGRATE THE THREE DIMENSIONS

In the Modeling activity, students model [SEP-2] the bonding in ionic compounds by drawing the electron dot structures. They use these models to identify patterns [CCC-1] that explain the ratio of chlorine ions to calcium ions is 2:1 when calcium chloride forms [PS1.A]. Students also use the models to construct an explanation [SEP-6] about why the overall charge of an ionic compound is zero. Students identify limitations of their models and then demonstrate improvements to their models by showing several ions bonded together in a three-dimensional lattice.

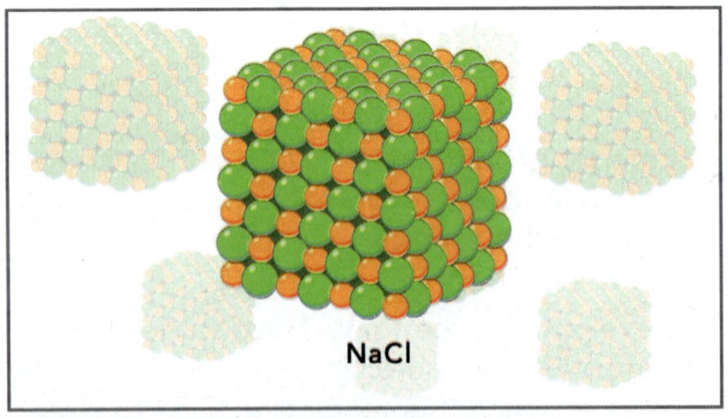

Animation: Formation of Ionic Compounds

EXPLAIN

Electron Dot Structures for Ionic Compounds

Modeling In this activity, students draw electron dot structures for several ionic compounds and use those models to explain [SEP-6] the properties [PS1.A] of ionic compounds. Begin this activity by drawing on the board the electron dot structure for sodium chloride while students follow along on their worksheets. Next, organize the class into pairs and have pairs complete Question 1 of the worksheet. After students complete the question, call on volunteers to write their models on the board. Discuss the models and with students help make any needed revisions.

- Have students review the Ionic Bond Formation in the Sodium Chloride diagram on page 70 of the Experience Notebook if they are struggling to understand how electrons are transferred between the atoms in this kind of bond.
- When students draw these models for the first time, make sure they draw the Lewis structures of the individual atoms first and then use arrows to show how the electrons move between atoms to form ions. This provides an opportunity for students to identify any errors in their thinking so that they can correct them early.

ASSESS ON THE SPOT

Have students write a sample quiz question that asks for the electron dot model of an ionic compound. Allow students to find or make an ionic compound that is different from those they modeled in the Modeling activity. Instruct students to write answer keys for their questions as well. Collect these quiz questions and review them to be sure students understand how to properly draw diagrams of ionic compounds.

Formation of Ionic Compounds

Animation This animation shows how electrons are transferred from one atom to another to form ionic compounds. Use this animation in a whole-class discussion of electron transfers in ionic bonding.

- Before showing this animation to the class, instruct students to focus on how the electrons move between atoms and what that movement does to the charges of the atoms.
- Encourage students to think of electron affinity (or electronegativity) as an atom's "strength" when taking electrons from other atoms. Extremely electronegative elements, such as fluorine, can take electrons from almost any other atom. Show students a video of fluorine reacting with various compounds to reinforce this concept.
- Have students discuss why ionic compounds are stable. (They are stable because the ions have filled valence shells.)

DIFFERENTIATED INSTRUCTION

- **Support Struggling Students** Help struggling students understand the Formation of Ionic Compounds animation by explaining that ionic bonds always involve a metal (elements on the left side of the periodic table) and a nonmetal (elements on the right side of the periodic table). Most periodic tables have a bolded "staircase" line separating the metals and nonmetals. Using a periodic table can make it much easier to identify which atom will lose electrons and which will gain electrons during ionic bond formation.
- **Support Advanced Students** Coulomb's law can be used to explain electron affinity as well as ionic bond strength. Show students a periodic table with electron affinity and atomic radius data. Ask students to describe the pattern [CCC-1] of electron affinity and then use Coulomb's law to explain why that pattern exists. (Students should describe that electron affinity decreases as atomic radius increases because the distance between nucleus and valence shell increases, leading to a weaker nuclear attraction. Students should explain that electron affinity increases across a period as valence electrons are roughly the same distance from the nucleus but the nuclear charge increases, leading to a stronger nuclear attraction.)

Ionic Bonds

Experience Notebook Have students read this section of the Experience Notebook or Realize Reader before you start the various activities in this experience. Use these strategies to help students make sense of the images and text on the indicated pages, as well as to engage science skills.

- **Ions and the Octet Rule** (pp. 68–69) Remind students that it may be easy to focus only on valence electrons in this section, but be sure students draw at least a few full Bohr models [SEP-2] for atoms so they can see how the inner shell electrons form a full octet when the valence electrons are removed.
- Explain that the octet rule is helpful for predicting ionic charges of most representative elements. Caution students that this rule does not apply to all elements, as some elements have several different ionic charges. Point out examples of stable ions formed by the transition elements, such as Mn^{2+} and Mn^{3+}.
- **Ionic Bonds** (pp. 70–71) Remind students that the total number of electrons in the unbound atoms must be the same as those found in the final ionic compound. Students can use this fact to check their work when drawing dot diagrams of ionic compounds.
- **Ionic Compounds** (pp. 72–73) Find additional examples of ionic crystals to share with the class, and have students describe the patterns [CCC-1] they observe. Students should note that, no matter the crystal lattice pattern, positive ions are surrounded by negative ions, and negative ions are surrounded by positive ions.
- **Properties of Ionic Compounds** (pp. 74–75) Use the sodium chloride model on page 75 to explain why ionic compounds have the property [PS1.A] of brittleness. Have students draw a two-dimensional NaCl crystal with alternating positive and negative ions. Next, have them model [SEP-2] what would happen if the crystal were struck by an outside force, shifting one row of ions over by one atom. The model should show that the ions are now surrounded by other ions with the same charge. The resulting repulsion interaction [PS2.B] of the atoms causes a crack to form in the crystal.
- Explain that the formation of positive ions and negative ions are simultaneous and interdependent processes that occur when electrons transfer from one set of atoms to another set of atoms. Emphasize that an ionic compound consists entirely of ions.

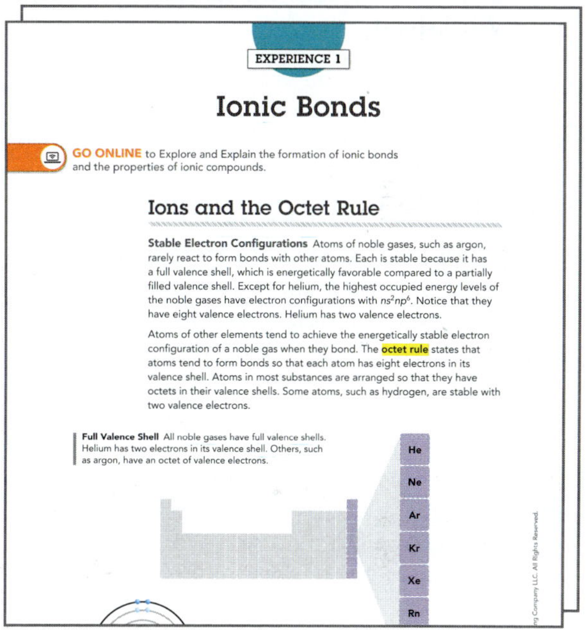
EXPERIENCE 1

Ionic Bonds

GO ONLINE to Explore and Explain the formation of ionic bonds and the properties of ionic compounds.

Ions and the Octet Rule

Stable Electron Configurations Atoms of noble gases, such as argon, rarely react to form bonds with other atoms. Each is stable because it has a full valence shell, which is energetically favorable compared to a partially filled valence shell. Except for helium, the highest occupied energy levels of the noble gases have electron configurations with ns^2np^6. Notice that they have eight valence electrons. Helium has two valence electrons.

Atoms of other elements tend to achieve the energetically stable electron configuration of a noble gas when they bond. The **octet rule** states that atoms tend to form bonds so that each atom has eight electrons in its valence shell. Atoms in most substances are arranged so that they have octets in their valence shells. Some atoms, such as hydrogen, are stable with two valence electrons.

Full Valence Shell All noble gases have full valence shells. Helium has two electrons in its valence shell. Others, such as argon, have an octet of valence electrons.

Experience Notebook, pp. 68–75

eTEXT

SAMPLE PROBLEM SUPPORT

Students may find it useful to color-code the electrons from each atom involved in the ionic bond when drawing the models on page 71. This color-coding can make it easier to identify which atoms gained electrons, which lost electrons, and where the electrons came from. Encourage students to use color in these problems until they are more comfortable with the moving electrons.

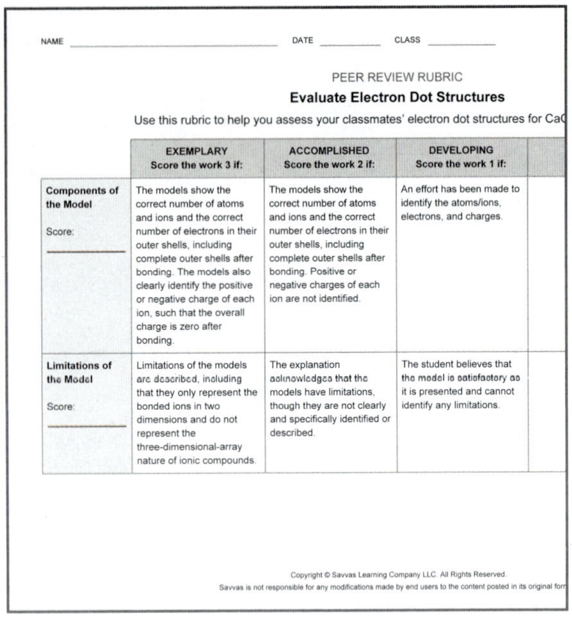

NAME ______________ DATE ________ CLASS ________

PEER REVIEW RUBRIC

Evaluate Electron Dot Structures

Use this rubric to help you assess your classmates' electron dot structures for CaC

	EXEMPLARY Score the work 3 if:	ACCOMPLISHED Score the work 2 if:	DEVELOPING Score the work 1 if:
Components of the Model Score: ______	The models show the correct number of atoms and ions and the correct number of electrons in their outer shells, including complete outer shells after bonding. The models also clearly identify the positive or negative charge of each ion, such that the overall charge is zero after bonding.	The models show the correct number of atoms and ions and the correct number of electrons in their outer shells, including complete outer shells after bonding. Positive or negative charges of each ion are not identified.	An effort has been made to identify the atoms/ions, electrons, and charges.
Limitations of the Model Score: ______	Limitations of the models are described, including that they only represent the bonded ions in two dimensions and do not represent the three-dimensional-array nature of ionic compounds.	The explanation acknowledges that the models have limitations, though they are not clearly and specifically identified or described.	The student believes that the model is satisfactory as it is presented and cannot identify any limitations.

Peer Review Rubric Interactive Worksheet

ADDRESS PRECONCEPTIONS

Clarify and emphasize to students that an ionic solid is a collection of independent ions. Explain that no individual particles join to form molecules. State that each ion "belongs" as much to one of its nearest neighbors as it belongs to any other. Point out that the arrangement in an ionic crystal is such that each ion is surrounded by ions of opposite charge, which produces a strong bonding force. Help students by walking through several examples to be sure students understand this point.

ELABORATE

Evaluate Electron Dot Structures

Peer Review Rubric In this activity, students use the rubric as a scoring guide to evaluate [SEP-8] classmates' electron-dot structures for calcium oxide, calcium chloride, and aluminum fluoride and to discuss their methods when drawing the electron dot structures. Students also evaluate the limitations of the models that their peers identify. Encourage students to refer to the rubric as they evaluate their classmates' models.

- If students find an error in the structures they review, have them correct it but also write a short summary of why the structure was wrong. For example, they may find that the overall charge of the compound wasn't balanced because some extra electrons were added by mistake.
- After completing their review, assign another two or three compounds for students to model as additional practice. Struggling students can use their peers' models as scaffolding to help them draw the structures correctly.

DIFFERENTIATED INSTRUCTION

- **Support Less Proficient Readers** For less proficient readers, read aloud the rubric as they follow along. Clarify and/or restate the expectations of the models at the Exemplary, Accomplished, and Developing stages after each of the two components are read.
- **Support Special Needs Students** Some students may benefit from completing this activity over multiple days or with a partner. Alternatively, providing struggling and special needs students with a structured amount of time to complete each step could help keep students focus on the task at hand.
- **Support Advanced Students** Have advanced students model an additional molecule of their choosing. Encourage students to choose a molecule that is substantially different from the ones they have already modeled. Then they should evaluate their model using the rubric.

PROFESSIONAL DEVELOPMENT

Background Notes One property of ionic solids is that they are brittle. In the layers of their lattice structure, each cation is surrounded by anions. The cations and ions are held together by a specific three-dimensional array of relatively strong attractive forces, which is accompanied by minimal repulsion of like ions. The crystal structure is brittle because the attractive interactions are specifically arranged within the crystal structure. The layers of the lattice structure can shift slightly when enough stress is applied to it. When this happens, ions with the same charge will be moved closer together, and they will repel each other. As a result, the lattice structure breaks into smaller pieces.

Describe Ionic Bonding and Properties

Writing About Science In this writing activity, students conduct research to determine the connection between the bonding and the properties [PS1.A] of ionic compounds. They use the research to construct and support explanations [SEP-6] about how the bonding in ionic compounds contributes to their high melting points and brittle crystalline structure and why ionic compounds only have the ability to conduct electricity when they are melted or dissolved in water. Have students work in small groups to conduct their research, but have them construct their own explanations [SEP-8] to these questions.

- Consider having student groups present their findings in a short, narrated video. Instruct students to write their explanation in a script and then find some appropriate images to show while they discuss the properties of ionic compounds.
- Ensure that students connect these properties to the structure [CCC-6] of the ionic bond in their explanations. They should connect all of these visible physical properties to the underlying concept of electron transfer and electrostatic attraction [PS2.B] between ions.

ASSESS ON THE SPOT

Tell students that you have discovered a new compound and want to test it to find out what kinds of bonds are within its molecules. Ask students to identify and describe three tests you could perform on the sample and what the results of the tests should be if the compound is ionic. For example, students may say that you could test the melting point of the sample. If it has a high melting point, it may be ionic.

PROFESSIONAL DEVELOPMENT

Explaining Phenomena Many solar power facilities use molten salt to store energy gathered during the day in order to keep electricity production going at night or during the day when other sources of electricity are not sufficient. At standard temperature and pressure, salt is a solid. In a molten-salt, energy-storage system, sunlight is used to heat salt to its melting point (~550°C) as it circulates through specialized piping during the day. Afterward, the molten salt is pumped into storage tanks until electricity is needed. At this point, the molten salt is pumped from the storage tank through heat exchangers to generate super-heated steam, which then powers a generator turbine.

Salt, an ionic compound, is used for this purpose because the extremely high energy required to melt this type of substance, results in a molten substance that stores a large amount of energy. The molten salt never needs replacing because it travels through a closed system. Allow students to conduct further research on the advantages and disadvantages of molten salt energy storage.

NAME ______ DATE ______ CLASS ______

WRITING ABOUT SCIENCE

Describe Ionic Bonding and Properties

Use the information provided and information gathered from authoritative sources on your own to answer questions 1 and 2. Most ionic compounds exist as solids with crystal lattice structures and have high melting points. For example, NaCl melts at about 800°C. Ionic compounds also conduct an electric current when they are melted or dissolved in water.

Obtain and Evaluate Information

1. **SEP Construct an Explanation** How does the nature of the bonding in ionic compounds contribute to their high melting points and brittle crystalline structure?

2. **SEP Construct an Explanation** Use what you know about how ionic compounds conduct electricity to explain why they only have this ability when they are melted or dissolved in water.

Writing About Science Interactive Worksheet

CLASSROOM MODIFICATIONS

Based on your students' abilities and your schedule, you can modify the Writing About Science activity to be more open ended or more guided.

- **More Open Ended** Have students write a short paper that describes how the nature of ionic bonds determines the observable physical properties of ionic compounds. Allow students to research what these properties are and how they are explained by the nature of ionic bonds.
- **More Guided** Provide students with a list of approved sources for the research portion of this assignment. You may also ask students to explain how the bond strength of ionic compounds leads to high melting points after asking them why ionic compounds have high melting points.

EVALUATE

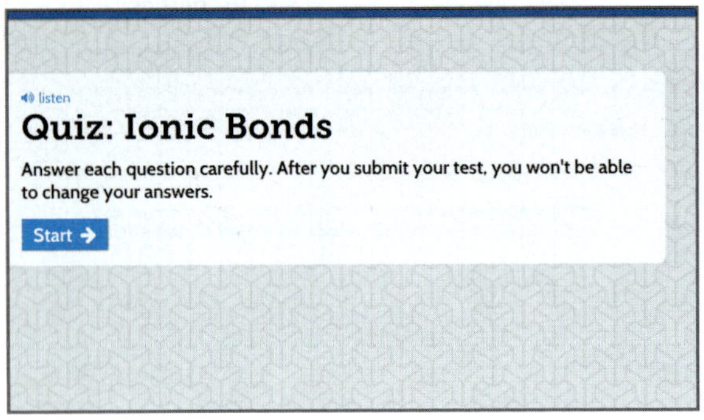

Interactive Online Quiz

Quiz Interactive Worksheet

Ionic Bonds

Quiz Assign the quiz in online technology-enhanced, auto-graded format or as an editable quiz worksheet. Use the scoring notes and remediation strategies found online to assess students' responses and to provide targeted feedback for each item to remediate well before assigning the summative 3-D Assessment.

REMEDIATION SUGGESTIONS

- **If** students have trouble drawing structures for ionic compounds and describing how electrons are transferred during ionic bonding, **then** have them review the Formation of Ionic Compounds animation and model a few extra ionic compound structures as additional practice.
- **If** students struggle with the concept that ionic bonds are electrostatic attractions between charged particles, **then** have them review the Coulomb's Law and Ionic Bonds graphic on page 73 of the Experience Notebook. Have them write a short description of Coulomb's law in their own words.
- **If** students struggle to link the nature of ionic bonds to the physical properties of ionic compounds, **then** have them review their answers to the Describe Ionic Bonding and Properties writing assignment and review the Properties of Ionic Compounds section of the Experience Notebook on pages 74 and 75.

Revisit
INVESTIGATIVE PHENOMENON

GO ONLINE to Elaborate on and Evaluate your knowledge of ionic bonds by completing the peer review and writing activities.

In the CER worksheet you completed at the beginning of the investigation, you drafted an explanation for the differences in properties of gems and metals. With a partner, reevaluate your arguments.

9 SEP Construct an Explanation Sapphires and rubies are forms of the mineral corundum, Al_2O_3. Corundum is one of the hardest known natural materials. The hardness of ionic compounds depends on the structure of the crystal and the strength of the ionic bonds. The distance between the aluminum ions (Al^{3+}) and oxide ions (O^{2-}) is 191 pm. Use Coulomb's law to explain how the bonding in Al_2O_3 influences its properties.

Experience Notebook, p. 76

eTEXT

Revisit

INVESTIGATIVE PHENOMENON

Support Reflection Students can complete the reflection prompt, where they will unpack and make sense of the Investigative Phenomenon, based on practices and understandings that have been reinforced over the course of the experience.

- Ask students if they are comfortable drawing the dot structure for an ionic compound. Have students model a few more of these problems with the class as a review.
- Call on students to describe the properties of ionic compounds and explain why they have these properties, based on the nature of ionic bonds. Have students relate properties of ionic compounds to gems and metals. Ask them to discuss with other students how the properties are similar and different.
- Discuss with students how knowing the properties of ionic compounds can help them explain why gems have different properties than metals.

Develop a Draft CER Argument Have students answer Question 2 in the CER worksheet and develop a draft of a CER argument to address the Investigative Phenomenon. Have students add any evidence they have collected from the activities so far in this investigation. Evidence may include the fact that ionically bonded solids are brittle due to their crystal lattice structures.

EXPERIENCE 2

Metallic Bonds

Teacher Background

Metals bond with each other by sharing loosely bound valence electrons between many positively charged nuclei, forming a sea of electrons. This sea of electrons model explains the physical properties of metals, including their malleability, ductility, electrical conductivity, thermal conductivity, and high melting points.

In Experience 2, students investigate the properties of metals and compare them with the properties of ionic compounds that they learned about in the previous experience. Students interpret and use the electron sea model to explain these properties.

Objectives

- **Describe the electron sea model of metallic bonds.**
- **Explain how the bonding in metals and alloys affects their properties.**

ENGAGE

EVERYDAY PHENOMENON

Why can metals be formed into different shapes?

Use this teacher demo to help students understand how positive nuclei in a sea of delocalized electrons allow metals to be formed into various shapes.

Modeling Metals with Magnets

Engage students with this demonstration of an everyday phenomenon to introduce the idea that metals are malleable and ductile due to their type of bonds.

Materials short video showing metals being hammered, drawn, and bent; set of magnetic spheres

1. Show students a short video of metals being hammered, drawn, and bent into various shapes. **Ask** What property of metals is being highlighted in the video? (Metals are malleable, or you can shape metals.) Compare this characteristic to ionic compounds that you learned about in the last experience. What happens when you apply force to ionic compounds? (They break. They are brittle.) Why do they behave this way? (The ions have opposite charges and can't be pushed too close to one another.) Think about metals on a molecular level. When force is applied, the atoms slide into new positions rather than push away from one another. What conclusion can you draw about the atoms in a metallic substance? (They do not have opposite charges, or they do not repel each other.)
2. Show students the set of magnetic spheres. Call on volunteers to mold the spheres into a sheet, a long string, a cube, and various other shapes.
3. **Ask** How is the behavior of the spheres different from the behavior of the ions in an ionic compound? (The spheres all attract each other; none repel.)
4. Explain how the metal nuclei in a metallic bond and the magnetic spheres shown here act in a similar way. (The delocalized valence electrons of metals travel freely between the positive nuclei, allowing metals to bond in any orientation, not in a single crystal lattice as with ionic compounds.)

RELATED PHENOMENA

In addition to the Modeling Metals with Magnets demo, consider using other phenomena to launch this experience.

- **Malleability** Have students twist a piece of copper wire around a pencil a few times to observe how malleable it is and how it work-hardens (changing crystal structure). **Ask** How do you think the atoms in the copper are arranged to allow this property?
- **Hearing and Feeling Changes to Crystal Lattices** Allow students to bend a thin bar of tin to observe how metals can be shaped. Students can also hear and feel the tin "crackle" as crystal lattices rearrange.

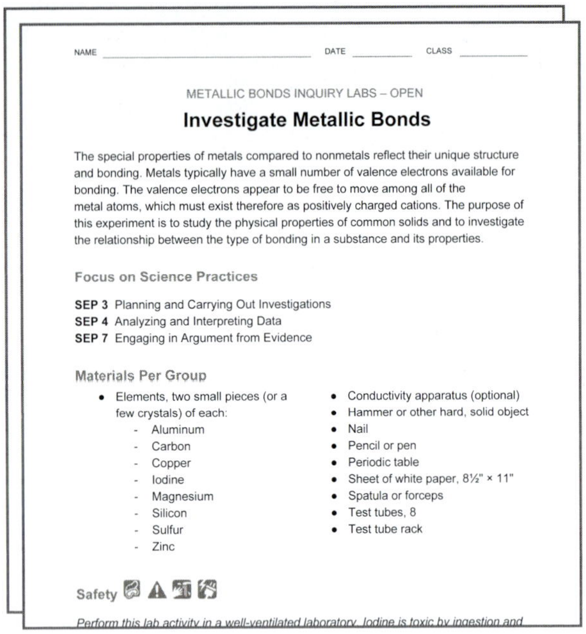

NAME ______ DATE ______ CLASS ______

METALLIC BONDS INQUIRY LABS – OPEN

Investigate Metallic Bonds

The special properties of metals compared to nonmetals reflect their unique structure and bonding. Metals typically have a small number of valence electrons available for bonding. The valence electrons appear to be free to move among all of the metal atoms, which must exist therefore as positively charged cations. The purpose of this experiment is to study the physical properties of common solids and to investigate the relationship between the type of bonding in a substance and its properties.

Focus on Science Practices

SEP 3 Planning and Carrying Out Investigations
SEP 4 Analyzing and Interpreting Data
SEP 7 Engaging in Argument from Evidence

Materials Per Group

- Elements, two small pieces (or a few crystals) of each:
  - Aluminum
  - Carbon
  - Copper
  - Iodine
  - Magnesium
  - Silicon
  - Sulfur
  - Zinc
- Conductivity apparatus (optional)
- Hammer or other hard, solid object
- Nail
- Pencil or pen
- Periodic table
- Sheet of white paper, 8½" × 11"
- Spatula or forceps
- Test tubes, 8
- Test tube rack

Safety

Perform this lab activity in a well-ventilated laboratory. Iodine is toxic by ingestion and

O/G/S/A Lab Interactive Worksheets

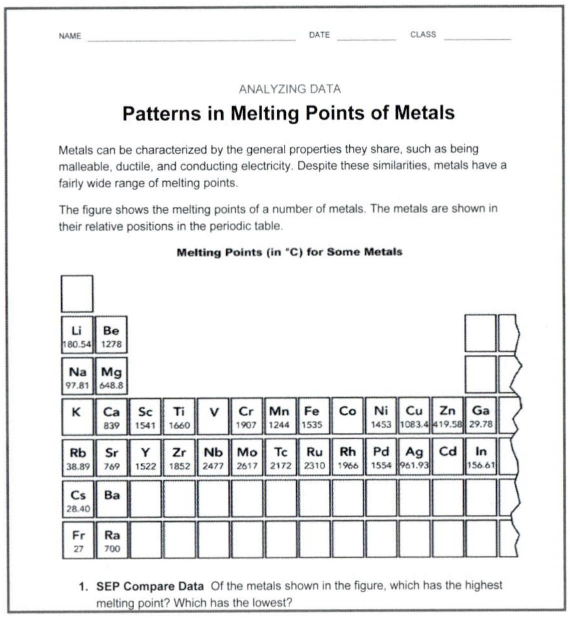

NAME ______ DATE ______ CLASS ______

ANALYZING DATA

Patterns in Melting Points of Metals

Metals can be characterized by the general properties they share, such as being malleable, ductile, and conducting electricity. Despite these similarities, metals have a fairly wide range of melting points.

The figure shows the melting points of a number of metals. The metals are shown in their relative positions in the periodic table.

Melting Points (in °C) for Some Metals

Li 180.54	Be 1278											
Na 97.81	Mg 648.8											
K	Ca 839	Sc 1541	Ti 1660	V	Cr 1907	Mn 1244	Fe 1535	Co	Ni 1453	Cu 1083.4	Zn 419.58	Ga 29.78
Rb 38.89	Sr 769	Y 1522	Zr 1852	Nb 2477	Mo 2617	Tc 2172	Ru 2310	Rh 1966	Pd 1554	Ag 961.93	Cd	In 156.61
Cs 28.40	Ba											
Fr 27	Ra 700											

1. **SEP Compare Data** Of the metals shown in the figure, which has the highest melting point? Which has the lowest?

Analyzing Data Interactive Worksheet

CONNECT TO CAREERS

Metallurgical Engineer Metallurgical engineers use their knowledge of the properties of various metals and alloys to solve engineering problems. These professionals often work with mines and smelting facilities to ensure that the materials produced in these places meet the specifications required by their customers. Metallurgical engineers are critical for the construction of buildings, bridges, and all kinds of vehicles.

5. Brainstorm with the class ways in which metals are used by consumers. In the kitchen? In sports? For transportation? What characteristics make them useful to us? From this discussion, let students come to the realization that metals have physical properties such as thermal and electrical conductivity, malleability, and a range of medium to high melting points.

EXPLORE

Investigate Metallic Bonds

35

Inquiry Lab In this lab, students develop a procedure [SEP-3] to classify samples as metals, nonmetals, or metalloids, based on their physical properties [PS1.A].

Lab Demo Video Watch the Lab Demo Video for advice on materials and preparation.

Choose Your Version Open-ended (O), Guided (G), Shortened (S), Advanced (A)

Materials 2 small pieces or a few crystals of each of these elements: aluminum, carbon, copper, iodine, magnesium, silicon, sulfur, zinc; conductivity apparatus (optional); hammer or other hard solid object; nail; periodic table; white paper ($8\frac{1}{2}$ in × 11 in); spatula or forceps; 8 test tubes; test tube rack

Safety Perform this lab activity in a well-ventilated laboratory. Tell students that iodine is toxic by ingestion and inhalation; it is corrosive to the skin, eyes, and the respiratory tract. Students should avoid inhalation of iodine vapors by keeping the iodine bottle covered throughout the lab. Tell them to avoid contact of all chemicals with eyes and all body tissues. Students should wear chemical splash goggles, chemical-resistant gloves, and a chemical-resistant apron. Make sure students wash their hands thoroughly with soap and warm water before leaving the laboratory.

Expected Outcome Metals and metalloids will present as malleable and shiny and will conduct electricity. Nonmetals will present as brittle and dull and will not conduct electricity.

Lab Summary Video Watch the Lab Summary Video for support on connecting the lab investigation to the Investigative Phenomenon.

Patterns in Melting Points of Metals

15

Analyzing Data In this activity, students analyze [SEP-4] melting point data for various metals to find patterns [CCC-1] in this property and use those patterns to predict the melting point of another element.

- You may want to have students graph the melting point data from this assignment to more easily see the pattern and predict the melting point of the unknowns. Have students graph the elements within Groups 1 and 2 and within Period 4 on separate charts, or use different colors on the same chart.
- Hardness and electrical conductivity are both trends that can be explained by metallic bonding. Have students graph the trend in hardness and/or electrical conductivity for the Group 1 and Group 2 metals and explain the trend using the electron sea model of metallic bonds.

ASSESS ON THE SPOT

As students are working through the Analyzing Data activity, ask them which two metals have the smallest and largest atomic radius. (smallest—chromium; largest—cesium) Remind students of the relationship between melting point and atomic radius—that as you descend a group in the periodic table, atomic radii increase.

PROFESSIONAL DEVELOPMENT

Discrepant Event Mercury is the only metal that is liquid at standard temperature and pressure. This unusual property is due to the fact that mercury's valence electrons are relatively tightly bound to the nucleus, unlike most other metals. Mercury's electrons are in stable, full subshells and are traveling so fast (due to mercury's high nuclear mass) that they are actually more massive than most electrons (due to relativistic effects), causing them to orbit closer to the nucleus. As a result, groups of mercury atoms do not share electrons as well, weakening the metallic bond between atoms. This weak bond is easy to break at low temperatures, causing mercury to melt at −38°C.

EXPLAIN

Compare Metallic and Ionic Substances

Claim-Evidence-Reasoning In this activity, students ask a question [SEP-1] about the difference between metals and ionic compounds and then investigate that question using the claim-evidence-reasoning framework.

- Before this assignment begins, brainstorm with the class some of the properties [PS1.A] of metals and ionic compounds. List these properties on the board to help students develop a question about the differences in these properties.
- Tell students that differences between metallic and ionic compounds could include properties other than heat conductivity, such as melting and boiling points or ductility.
- Remind students that their claims and evidence do not have to be perfect. As long as they come up with something that is logical and well written, it does not have to be the "right" answer. Students will have a chance to go back and revise their claims after getting feedback from other students.

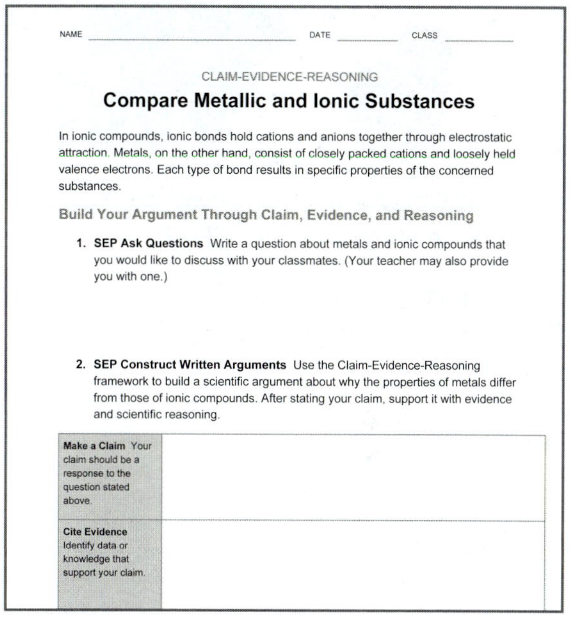

NAME ______ DATE ______ CLASS ______

CLAIM-EVIDENCE-REASONING

Compare Metallic and Ionic Substances

In ionic compounds, ionic bonds hold cations and anions together through electrostatic attraction. Metals, on the other hand, consist of closely packed cations and loosely held valence electrons. Each type of bond results in specific properties of the concerned substances.

Build Your Argument Through Claim, Evidence, and Reasoning

1. **SEP Ask Questions** Write a question about metals and ionic compounds that you would like to discuss with your classmates. (Your teacher may also provide you with one.)

2. **SEP Construct Written Arguments** Use the Claim-Evidence-Reasoning framework to build a scientific argument about why the properties of metals differ from those of ionic compounds. After stating your claim, support it with evidence and scientific reasoning.

Make a Claim Your claim should be a response to the question stated above.	
Cite Evidence Identify data or knowledge that support your claim.	

CER Interactive Worksheet

ASSESS ON THE SPOT

Have students construct a quick Venn diagram that shows the similarities and differences between metals and ionic compounds. Collect the diagrams and review them to ensure students understand that both substances contain positive nuclei, have high melting points, and can conduct electricity (only when dissolved or melted in the case of ionic compounds), but metals have delocalized electrons and make excellent conductors of heat and electricity (even when in solid form).

DIFFERENTIATED INSTRUCTION

- **Support Special Needs Students** Students with visual disabilities may benefit from working on the Claim-Evidence-Reasoning activity with a partner who can read aloud the text. The partners can discuss each section of the framework and then record the answers on an audio recording device.
- **Support Less Proficient Readers** Less proficient readers might have difficulty understanding the meaning of and using the terms *cations, anions,* and *electrostatic attraction.* Explain the meaning of the terms and then have student pairs act out the meaning of each term.

CLASSROOM MODIFICATIONS

Based on your students' abilities and your schedule, you can modify the Compare Metallic and Ionic Substances activity to be more open ended or more guided.

- **More Open Ended** Instead of using the CER worksheet, ask student pairs to research the reason that metals make better thermal conductors than ionic compounds do. Have student pairs work with another student pair or two to compile their findings in a short presentation.
- **More Guided** Provide each group with a prewritten question about the difference between metals and ionic compounds. Make a rubric that students can use to critique their peers' arguments (Question 3 on the assignment worksheet).

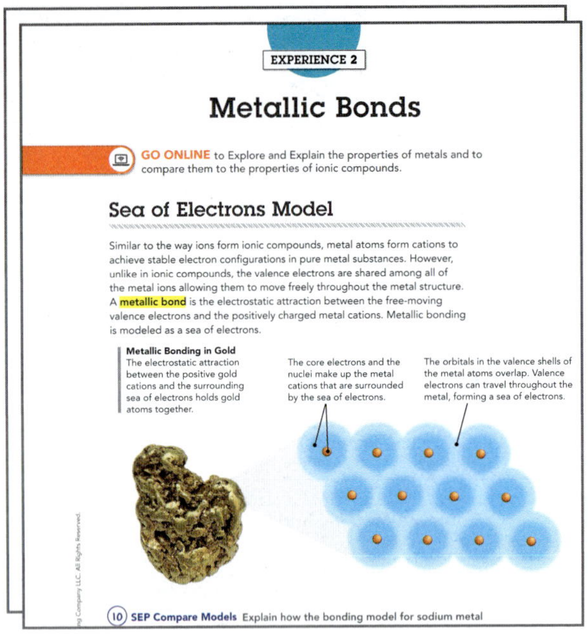

EXPERIENCE 2

Metallic Bonds

GO ONLINE to Explore and Explain the properties of metals and to compare them to the properties of ionic compounds.

Sea of Electrons Model

Similar to the way ions form ionic compounds, metal atoms form cations to achieve stable electron configurations in pure metal substances. However, unlike in ionic compounds, the valence electrons are shared among all of the metal ions allowing them to move freely throughout the metal structure. A metallic bond is the electrostatic attraction between the free-moving valence electrons and the positively charged metal cations. Metallic bonding is modeled as a sea of electrons.

(10) SEP Compare Models Explain how the bonding model for sodium metal

Experience Notebook, pp. 77–79

eTEXT

ELD SUPPORT

Reading Have student pairs summarize information about the properties of metals after they read pages 78 and 79 in the Experience Notebook.

- **Emerging/Beginning** Have students find important sentences in the text about metallic properties. Tell them to rewrite the sentences in their own words.
- **Developing/Expanding** Ask student pairs to use information in the text to write two short sentences about malleability and ductility of metals and two sentences on melting point and boiling point of metals.
- **Bridging** Have students use the diagrams and text on pages 78 and 79 to explain the properties of metals to their partners.

Virtual Reality Experience: Chemical Bonding

Metallic Bonds

(20)

Experience Notebook Have students read this section of the Experience Notebook or Realize Reader after completing the activities in this section to reinforce the concepts presented here. Use these strategies to help students make sense of the images and text on the indicated pages, as well as to engage science skills.

- **Sea of Electrons Model** (p. 77) Have student pairs model **[SEP-2]** the difference between metallic and ionic bonds by using a few inflated balloons to represent electrons. Give each student pair a balloon. One partner can be a metal and the other a nonmetal. Ask students to demonstrate ionic bonding by having the nonmetal take the electron (balloon) from the metal. Next, demonstrate metallic bonding by having the class as a group throw the balloons into the air and to try to keep them airborne as long as possible. Explain how the electrons (balloons) in a metallic bond are free to move between nuclei (students), keeping them bound together but still free to move. You can even model electrical conduction by pointing a fan (voltage) at the balloons to push them from one side of the room to the other.
- Emphasize that metals and ionic compounds are held together by strong attractive forces. In ionic solids, the attractions are between ions with opposite charges. In metals, the attractions are between metal ions and mobile valence electrons.
- **Properties of Metals** (pp. 78–79) Show students a small sample of elemental copper, or a copper alloy, and a sample of a copper-containing, crystalline, ionic mineral such as chalcocite (Cu_2S).Wear safety goggles and stand far from students. Smash both samples with a hammer. Allow time for students to observe the samples. Then discuss why the two substances respond differently to the stress of the hammer blow. Be sure students contrast the metallic bond properties [PS1.A] shown here with the properties of ionic bonds covered in the previous experience. **Ask** If ionic compounds also have crystal structures, why are they brittle but metals are malleable? (Ionic compounds rely on a specific arrangement of positive and negative ions to stay bonded. Metals have a sea of electrons that can bind them in many different orientations.)

Chemical Bonding

(30)

Virtual Reality Experience Students discover how the interaction between atoms results in different types of chemical bonds.

PROFESSIONAL DEVELOPMENT

Use Outside Resources The ASM (American Society of Metals) Education Foundation runs free Materials Camps all over the country every summer. These camps provide teachers with a huge variety of metal and material science lessons, labs, and activities that can be incorporated into the curriculum. They are also a great way to get in touch with materials scientists and engineers close to your school. During the camp, you will perform many hands-on experiments and learn how to create material science demonstrations for your class.

ELABORATE

Compare Metallic and Ionic Substances

Discussion Rubric Lead a class discussion to answer the question: Why are metals better than ionic compounds at conducting heat? After discussing the question with the class, have students explain [SEP-6] the answers to their partners. Then partners use the rubric to score their partner's explanation.

- Use a Newton's cradle to help students visualize how free electrons transfer thermal energy [PS3.B] in the electron sea surrounding metal nuclei. Explain that when thermal energy is applied to one side of a metal, energy is transferred through electron collisions to the far side, thus conducting heat. When electrons are locked in place (as in ionic and covalent bonds), this transfer can only happen with colliding atoms.
- Ask students to extend this discussion by explaining why metals also make good conductors of electricity. They should realize that the free electrons in a metallic bond also allow electricity to flow through metals freely.

ASSESS ON THE SPOT

Give students 3 minutes to write an explanation or make a diagram to describe why metals conduct heat better than ionic compounds. Collect students' responses and review for understanding. If necessary, revisit the topic before continuing to the next activity in this experience.

DIFFERENTIATED INSTRUCTION

- **Support Struggling Students** Instead of having students summarize the Discussion Rubric discussion on their own, write several versions of the explanation for metals being good thermal conductors. Include errors in some of the explanations and have students use the rubric to critique them.
- **Support Special Needs Students** Students with auditory processing disorders may benefit from a guided discussion. Provide students with prompts to help them organize their responses.
- **Support Advanced Students** Ask advanced students to outline an experimental procedure for measuring the thermal conductivity of different metals. Remind them that they need some way to measure the rate of thermal conduction and that they must identify how they will control other variables that are not being measured, such as the thickness of the materials and the temperature of heat source. If time permits, allow these students to carry out their investigation.

NAME ____________ DATE ________ CLASS ________

DISCUSSION RUBRIC

Compare Metallic and Ionic Substances

Use this rubric to help you assess explanations for why metals conduct heat better th

	EXEMPLARY Score the work 3 if:	ACCOMPLISHED Score the work 2 if:
Articulating the Explanation Student Score: ______ Teacher Score: ______	The explanation is clearly articulated and the means of heat transfer in ionic compounds and metals is described, including the movement of free electrons in metals.	The explanation correctly describes heat conduction in ionic compounds and metals, but the method of heat transfer via free electrons in metals is only vaguely described.
Evaluation and Critique Student Score: ______ Teacher Score: ______	Alternate explanations for the differences in heat conductivity are proposed and refuted, when appropriate. For example, the difference might be explained as being due to the strong bonds between the atoms, but this does not adequately explain the high speed of heat transfer in metals.	The critique mentions different explanations, such as the density of the packing of the particles, but these explanations are not refuted or addressed in an attempt to strengthen the claim.
Revising the Explanation Student Score: ______ Teacher Score: ______	When new evidence or reasoning is presented, it is incorporated into the explanation.	When new evidence or reasoning is presented, it is considered, and an attempt is made to incorporate it into the explanation.

Discussion Rubric Interactive Worksheet

INTEGRATE THE THREE DIMENSIONS

In the Discussion Rubric, students develop an explanation [SEP-6] of why metals conduct heat better than ionic compounds. By clearly describing the transfer of thermal energy [CCC-5] in ionic compounds and metals, including the movement of free electrons, students demonstrate their ability to clearly communicate information [SEP-8]. They propose and refute alternate explanations for differences in properties [PS1.A] of heat conductivity and incorporate this into their explanation.

NAME ______ DATE ______ CLASS ______

ENGINEERING DESIGN CHALLENGE

Evaluate Metals for a Commercial Application

The bus company that your school uses is thinking about changing the material that makes their current fleet of buses because the buses are running into problems with corrosion, the reaction of metals with oxygen present in air to form metal oxides that are not structurally sound and are visually unappealing. In addition, the current construction material is difficult to shape and is not visually attractive. The bus company has asked your teacher to recommend an alternative material that could be used to manufacture the next round of buses needed for your school and other schools in the district. In addition to meeting certain chemical and physical requirements, the material recommended must also be affordable.

Focus on Engineering Practices

SEP 1 Defining Problems
SEP 3 Planning and Carrying Out Investigations
SEP 6 Designing Solutions

Materials Per Group

- Aluminum foil
- Aluminum nitrate solution, $Al(NO_3)_3$, 0.1 M, 20 mL
- Copper strip, Cu, 1.2 × 15 cm
- Copper(II) sulfate solution, $CuSO_4$, 0.1 M, 20 mL
- Iron strips, Fe, 1.2 × 15 cm, 10
- Iron(II) sulfate heptahydrate, $FeSO_4 \cdot 7H_2O$, 8 g
- Magnesium nitrate solution, $Mg(NO_3)_2$, 0.1 M, 20 mL
- Zinc foil, Zn, 7 cm × 7 cm, 20 squares
- Forceps or tweezers, to remove metals from solutions
- Pipets, Beral-type, 75
- Reaction plate, 24-well, or test tubes
- Sandpaper, to sand metals (optional)
- Scissors, to cut metal foil
- Toothpicks, to submerge metals

Engineering Design Challenge Interactive Worksheet

Evaluate Metals for a Commercial Application

Engineering Design Challenge In this Engineering Design Challenge, students choose the best metal to use as a construction material [PS1.A] for a new fleet of school buses. The material must resist corrosion, or reaction with atmospheric oxygen, and it must be malleable and visually appealing. Moreover, the material must be cost effective for use in school buses.

Students will collaborate in groups as they go through the engineering design process, including setting criteria [ETS1.A], researching [SEP-8] metal costs and availabilities, choosing and testing [SEP-3] several metals and the relationship of energy and force [PS3.C] on the metals, interpreting the results of their investigation, and making suggestions for improvements to their solution [SEP-6].

Materials aluminum foil; 20 mL 0.1*M* aluminum nitrate solution; copper strip, 1.2 cm × 15 cm; 20 mL 0.1*M* copper(II) sulfate solution; 10 iron strips, 1.2 cm × 15 cm; 8 g iron(II) sulfate heptahydrate; 20 mL 0.1*M* magnesium nitrate solution; 90 cm magnesium ribbon; distilled water; 20 mL 0.1*M* zinc sulfate solution; 20 squares zinc foil, 7 cm × 7 cm; forceps or tweezers; 75 Beral pipettes; 24-well reaction plate or test tubes; sandpaper to sand metals (optional); scissors to cut metal foil; toothpicks (optional); wash bottle

Safety Tell students that silver nitrate is slightly toxic by ingestion and will stain skin and clothing. Copper(II) sulfate and iron(II) sulfate solutions are toxic by ingestion. Magnesium nitrate solution is a skin and eye irritant. Remind students that metal pieces may have sharp edges and should be handled with care. Students should avoid contact of all chemicals with eyes and skin. Students should wear chemical splash goggles, chemical-resistant gloves, and a chemical-resistant apron. Before leaving the lab, make sure students wash their hands thoroughly with soap and warm water.

Expected Outcome Students find that copper can be a recommended material for building a fleet of buses because it has a low relative reactivity, is inexpensive, and is easily available. Students may also note that aluminum is the most inexpensive and is less dense than copper, but is less resistant to corrosion.

Use the following strategies to guide students as they complete indicated steps in the Engineering Design Challenge.

- **Step 2** You may wish to decide as a class what criteria should be met. See the teacher notes on the lab sheet for some ideas. Make sure students understand the terms *corrosion* and *malleable*.
- **Step 3** Consider providing students with links to Web sites that they can use to research the information, such as the United States Geological Survey and the Bureau of Labor Statistics of the United States Department of Labor.
- **Step 4** Remind students to consider their criteria [ETS1.A] as they choose which metals to test.

EVALUATE

Metallic Bonds

Quiz Assign the quiz in online technology-enhanced, auto-graded format or as an editable quiz worksheet. Use the scoring notes and remediation strategies found online to assess students' responses and to provide targeted feedback for each item to remediate well before assigning the summative 3-D Assessment.

REMEDIATION SUGGESTIONS

- **If** students have a hard time understanding the sea of electrons model of metallic bonding, **then** have them review page 77 of the Experience Notebook and write a short summary, in their own words, explaining why metals can so easily share valence electrons in this manner.
- **If** students cannot connect the physical properties of metals to the nature of metallic bonding, **then** have them review pages 78 and 79 of the Experience Notebook and their answers to the questions at the bottom of each page.
- **If** students do not remember the differences between ionic bonds and metallic bonds, **then** have them review their response to the Compare Metallic and Ionic Substances CER activity they completed earlier.

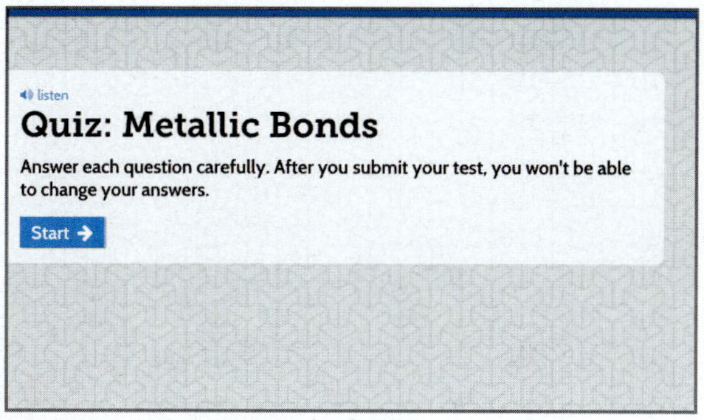

Interactive Online Quiz

Quiz Interactive Worksheet

Revisit
INVESTIGATIVE PHENOMENON

Support Reflection Students can complete the reflection prompt, where they will unpack and make sense of the Investigative Phenomenon, based on practices and understandings that have been reinforced over the course of the experience.

- Ask students to describe the sea of electrons model. Make sure they understand that metallic bonds form through the delocalization of valence electrons and the attraction of those electrons to the positively charged nuclei of metal atoms.
- Be sure that students can use this model of metallic bonding to explain the physical properties of metals, including malleability, ductility, and high melting points. Have students explain how these specific properties differ from the properties of most gems.

Further Develop Your CER Argument Have students add any evidence they have collected in this experience. Evidence may include that metallic bonds are omnidirectional and the electrons within these bonds are free to move between nuclei.

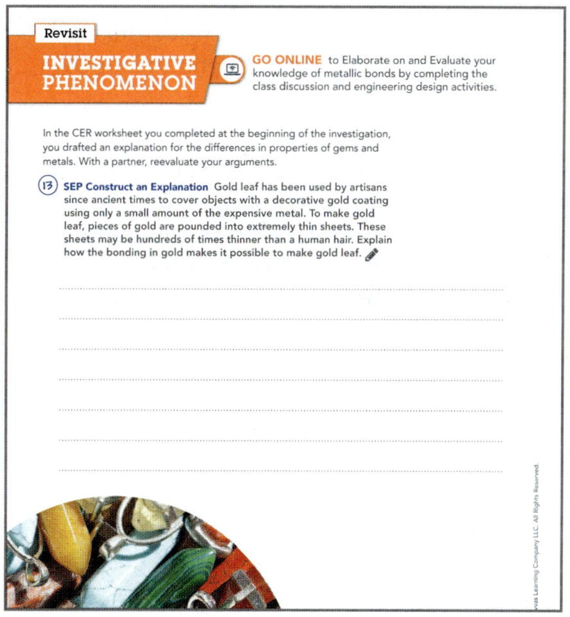

Revisit

INVESTIGATIVE PHENOMENON

GO ONLINE to Elaborate on and Evaluate your knowledge of metallic bonds by completing the class discussion and engineering design activities.

In the CER worksheet you completed at the beginning of the investigation, you drafted an explanation for the differences in properties of gems and metals. With a partner, reevaluate your arguments.

13 **SEP Construct an Explanation** Gold leaf has been used by artisans since ancient times to cover objects with a decorative gold coating using only a small amount of the expensive metal. To make gold leaf, pieces of gold are pounded into extremely thin sheets. These sheets may be hundreds of times thinner than a human hair. Explain how the bonding in gold makes it possible to make gold leaf.

Experience Notebook, p. 80

eTEXT

EXPERIENCE 3

Covalent Bonds

Teacher Background

In this experience, students learn how groups of nonmetals can share electrons to fill their valence shells and form covalent bonds between the atoms. Students learn how to draw electron dot structures to represent these molecular compounds. Remind students as they work through the experience that in forming compounds, atoms tend to achieve the electron configuration of the noble gases. Before beginning the experience, you may wish to review noble gases and why their electron configuration makes them such stable elements.

Objectives

- **Explain how nonmetals share electrons to complete their valence shell octet, resulting in the formation of a covalent bond.**
- **Identify single, double, and triple covalent bonds and draw electron dot diagrams for each.**
- **Describe how elements of different electronegativities can share electrons unequally, leading to the formation of a polar covalent bond.**

RELATED PHENOMENA

In addition to the Covalent Conductors demo, consider using other phenomena to launch this experience.

- **Compare Sugar and Salt** Using a projecting microscope, show students some salt crystals and some sugar crystals. Put a little of each compound in separate test tubes. Gently heat each test tube. Discuss what might cause only one of the compounds (sugar) to melt.

ENGAGE

EVERYDAY PHENOMENON

How are covalent compounds different from ionic compounds?

Use this teacher demo to help students understand how the shared electrons in covalent compounds give them properties that are different from the properties of ionic and metallic compounds.

Covalent Conductors

Engage students with this demonstration of an everyday phenomenon to introduce the idea that covalent compounds have properties that are different from the properties of ionic or metallic substances.

Materials conductivity probe, deionized water, salt, sugar, 2 beakers (any size)

1. Write the chemical formulas of salt ($NaCl$) and sugar ($C_6H_{12}O_6$) on the board.
2. Fill both beakers about halfway with deionized water. Note that if you use tap water for this demonstration, it will not work correctly.
3. Add 5–10 g of salt to one beaker and the same amount of sugar to the other beaker. Clearly label each beaker.
4. Ask the class to predict what will happen when you place the conductivity probe in the solution containing the salt. (It will conduct electricity.) Take a moment to review why dissolved ionic compounds can conduct electricity—they have mobile electron carriers in the form of ions.
5. Test the conductivity of the salt solution and write the results on the board under the chemical formula of salt.
6. Rinse the conductivity probe with deionized water. Test the conductivity of the sugar solution and write the results on the board.
7. Lead a class discussion about why the salt solution was able to conduct electricity but the sugar solution was unable to conduct electricity. Tell students that the Inquiry Lab will help them answer this question.

EXPLORE

Characteristics of Covalent Bonds

Inquiry Lab In this lab, students carry out an investigation [SEP-3] to identify the covalent compounds in a group of four compounds, based on the compounds' physical properties [PS1.A].

Lab Demo Video Watch the Lab Demo Video for advice on materials and preparation.

Choose Your Version Open-ended (O), Guided (G), Shortened (S), Advanced (A)

Materials 2 g dextrose; 2 g potassium chloride, 2 g sodium chloride, 2 g sucrose, 50 mL distilled or tap water, balance, butane safety lighter, metal ring with clamp, glass stirring rod, support stand, 4 glass test tubes, test tube clamp, test tube stand, 4 aluminum evaporating dishes, Bunsen burner

Safety Remind students to take care when conducting melting point tests as these require the use of an open flame. Good ventilation is required because burning samples can generate smoke. Students should wear chemical splash goggles and heat-resistant gloves throughout the experiment.

Expected Outcome Potassium chloride and sodium chloride have high experimental melting points and will conduct electricity in aqueous solutions, whereas dextrose and sucrose have relatively low melting points and relatively low or no conductivity in aqueous solutions. These results indicate dextrose and sucrose are covalent compounds.

Lab Summary Video Watch the Lab Summary Video for support on connecting the lab investigation to the Investigative Phenomenon.

Calculate Bond Polarity

Analyzing Data In this activity, students analyze [SEP-4] electronegativity data for several elements to identify the polarity of different covalent bonds. Then they identify patterns [CCC-1] in the electron configuration of elements and their electronegativities.

- Be sure to reinforce that ionic bonds are not simply extremely polar covalent bonds. **Ask** What makes a polar covalent bond different from an ionic bond? (In an ionic bond, the electron is actually taken by the more electronegative element, not shared.) What evidence do we have that ionic bonds are fundamentally different? (Ionic compounds conduct electricity when dissolved in water or melted; covalent compounds do not.)
- Have students visually model [SEP-2] bond polarity by drawing a number line with zero in the middle and the two atoms in the bond at each end of the line (mark these +2 and –2, respectively). Place the more electronegative element on the right (positive) and the less electronegative element on the left (negative). Next, have students calculate the absolute value of the difference in electronegativity between the elements. Use that number to place the electrons on the number line. (The more polar the bond, the closer the electrons will be to the more electronegative element.)

ASSESS ON THE SPOT

Give students a stack of cards with a covalent bond on each. Have them sort the cards into two piles—one for polar bonds and the other for nonpolar bonds. As students finish sorting, check their piles to be sure they properly identified the polarity of each bond.

NAME ______ DATE ______ CLASS ______

COVALENT BONDS INQUIRY LABS – OPEN

Characteristics of Covalent Bonds

Covalent bonds are defined as the net attractive forces resulting from pairs of electrons that are shared between atoms (the shared electrons are attracted to the nuclei of both atoms in the bond). A group of atoms held together by covalent bonds is called a molecule. Covalent compounds have different physical properties than non-covalent compounds because the strength of the interactions between molecules are weaker than the strengths of the interactions between the particles that make up ionic compounds, for example. Also, when covalent compounds dissolve in water they do not break up into ions, or atoms. They maintain their molecular structures. In this lab you are going to compare the strengths of the chemical bonds or interparticle forces present in two different types of compounds by observing some of their physical properties.

Focus on Science Practices

SEP 3 Planning and Carrying Out Investigations
SEP 4 Analyzing and Interpreting Data
SEP 5 Using Mathematics and Computational Thinking

Materials Per Group

- Dextrose, $C_6H_{12}O_6$, 2 g
- Potassium chloride, KCl, 2 g
- Sodium chloride, NaCl, 2 g
- Sucrose, $C_{12}H_{22}O_{11}$, 2 g
- Water, distilled or tap, 50 mL
- Aluminum evaporating dishes, 4
- Balance (0.01-g precision)
- Bunsen burner
- Butane safety lighter
- Metal ring with clamp
- Stirring rod, glass
- Support stand
- Test tubes, glass, 4
- Test tube clamp
- Test tube stand

O/G/S/A Lab Interactive Worksheets

NAME ______ DATE ______ CLASS ______

ANALYZING DATA

Calculate Bond Polarity

Electronegativity is the ability of an atom of an element to attract electrons when the atom is in a compound. A covalent bond is formed by sharing one or more pairs of electrons between two atoms. The bond is polar if the electrons are shared unequally between the two atoms. Atoms with higher electronegativity values attract electrons more strongly and gain a slightly negative charge. The less electronegative atom in a bond gains a slightly positive charge, as its electrons are pulled toward the other atom.

Figure 1 lists the electronegativity values for a few main-group elements. **Figure 2** shows how the electronegativity difference between two atoms is related to the type of bond that is likely to form.

Figure 1

Electronegativity Values and Other Data for Selected Elements							
Element	Na	H	C	Cl	N	O	F
Electronegativity (Pauling units)	0.9	2.1	2.5	3.0	3.0	3.5	4.0
Atomic number							
Number of valence electrons							

Figure 2

Electronegativity Differences and Bond Types

Analyzing Data Inveractive Worksheet

CLASSROOM MODIFICATIONS

Based on your students' abilities and your schedule, you can modify the Calculate Bond Polarity activity to be more open ended or more guided.

- **More Open Ended** Provide students with a list of covalent compounds, their bond types, and a periodic table with electronegativity values. Ask students to determine what makes a bond polar or nonpolar by analyzing this data and looking for patterns. Have students summarize their discovery in a short statement.
- **More Guided** You may want to rephrase the questions asking students to identify the relationship to provide more structure. For example, **ask** As the atomic number of an element increases, its electronegativity __________. (decreases)

PhET Simulation: Coulomb's Law

PhET Simulation: Molecular Polarity

PhET Simulation: Molecule Shapes

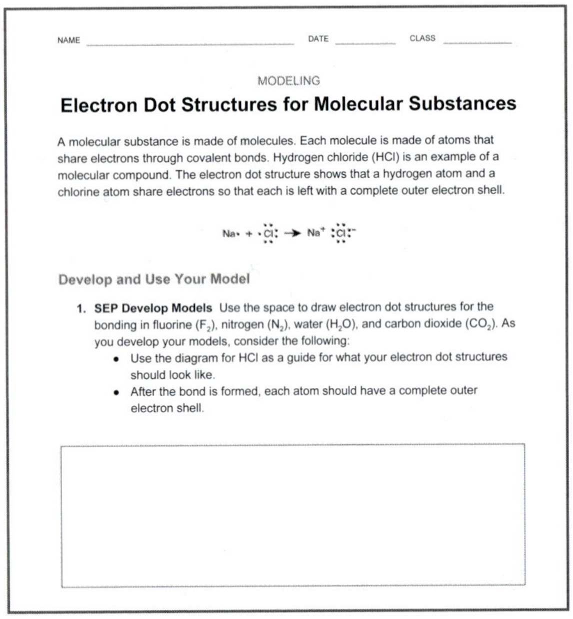

NAME ____________ DATE ________ CLASS ________

MODELING

Electron Dot Structures for Molecular Substances

A molecular substance is made of molecules. Each molecule is made of atoms that share electrons through covalent bonds. Hydrogen chloride (HCl) is an example of a molecular compound. The electron dot structure shows that a hydrogen atom and a chlorine atom share electrons so that each is left with a complete outer electron shell.

$Na\cdot + \cdot\ddot{Cl}: \rightarrow Na^+ :\ddot{Cl}:^-$

Develop and Use Your Model

1. **SEP Develop Models** Use the space to draw electron dot structures for the bonding in fluorine (F_2), nitrogen (N_2), water (H_2O), and carbon dioxide (CO_2). As you develop your models, consider the following:
   - Use the diagram for HCl as a guide for what your electron dot structures should look like.
   - After the bond is formed, each atom should have a complete outer electron shell.

Modeling Interactive Worksheet

INTEGRATE THE THREE DIMENSIONS

In the Modeling activity, students develop and use models [SEP-2] of electron dot structures to show the structure [PS1.A] and interaction of atoms in the bonding in fluorine, nitrogen, water, and carbon dioxide. They construct an explanation [SEP-6] about why each oxygen atom bonds to two hydrogen atoms when water forms. By using these models, students explore patterns [CCC-1] of attraction and describe the cause-and-effect relationship [CCC-2] between forces and the change of energy amongst molecules.

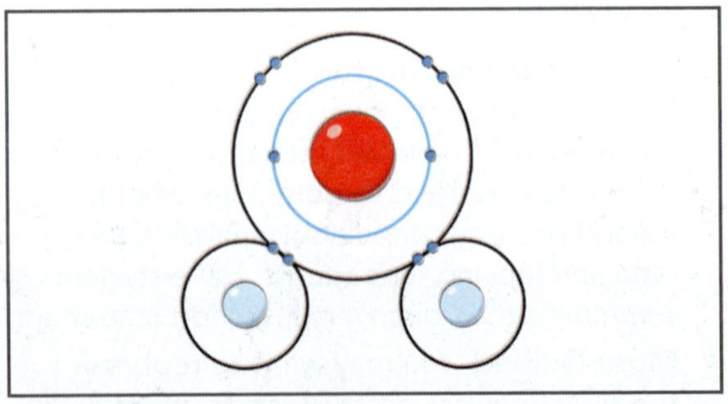

Animation: Formation of Covalent Bonds

Virtual Nerd Video: How Do You Subtract Decimals?

Coulomb's Law

PhET Simulation Students can observe Coulomb's Law in action in this interactivity.

Molecule Polarity

PhET Simulation Use this interactivity to reinforce concepts of what makes a molecule polar.

Molecule Shapes

PhET Simulation Students can build 3-D molecules in this simulation.

EXPLAIN

Electron Dot Structures for Molecular Substances

Modeling Students draw electron dot structures for several compounds and identify the geometry of each molecule, as predicted by VSEPR theory. They use their models [SEP-2] to explain why covalent molecules form these bonds.

- It may help students to draw each electron in their diagrams for a while instead of drawing the "sticks" to represent a pair of shared electrons. They can color-code the electrons from each atom to keep track of them more easily and ensure their final models have the correct number of electrons.
- Some students may forget to add lone pairs to their models. Remind them that these lone pairs have a drastic impact on the geometry of the molecules and should always be included.

ASSESS ON THE SPOT

As students complete this Modeling activity, give them the names of some compounds and have them draw electron dot diagrams for covalent compounds. Be sure the compounds you choose cover a variety of bond types and molecular geometries. After reviewing the diagrams, invite volunteers to draw their diagrams on the board.

Formation of Covalent Bonds

Animation This animation shows how atoms form covalent bonds to achieve more stable, full-valence-shell electron configurations. The animation uses Bohr representations (instead of the more accurate molecular orbital model) to help students focus on how valence shell electrons achieve a full octet.

- After students view the animation, show the Formation of Ionic Bonds animation from Experience 1. Ask students to compare and contrast the two animations.
- Ask students to write a short explanation [SEP-6] of how each of the atoms in the animation changed as a result of the covalent bond formation. (Every atom paired with an unpaired valence electron; all atoms, except hydrogen, had a total of eight valence electrons after bonding.)

PROFESSIONAL DEVELOPMENT

Discrepant Event Covalent compounds do not generally conduct electricity very well. Graphene, an isomer of carbon, is formed by a single layer of of very tightly bonded carbon atoms organized into a hexagonal lattice. It is an excellent conductor of both heat and electricity because the aromatic rings that form graphene are all joined, allowing electrons to move freely between carbon atoms in a fashion similar to the delocalized electrons in a metal. These highly mobile electrons allow electricity and heat to flow through graphene with very low resistance.

How Do You Subtract Decimals?

Virtual Nerd Video Use this video to reinforce how to subtract numbers including decimals.

Covalent Bonds

Experience Notebook This section is somewhat longer than most, so it works best when split into two reading assignments. Have students read about covalent bonds and dot diagrams (pages 81–85) first. The following day, assign bond polarity and molecular geometry (pages 86–90). Use these strategies to help students make sense of the images and text on the indicated pages, as well as to practice science skills.

- **Molecular Compounds** (p. 81) If students have trouble with the orbital hybridization information in this section, have them come back to it after reviewing molecular geometry on page 88. The number of electron pairs around the central atom indicates the number of hybrid orbitals that molecule has. Central atoms with two electron pairs have two hybrid orbitals (*sp* hybridization). Central atoms with three electron pairs have three hybrid orbitals (*s*, *p*, and *p* or sp^2 hybridization) and those with four electron pairs have four hybrid orbitals (*s*, *p*, *p*, and *p* or sp^3 hybridization).
- **The Octet Rule in Molecules** (pp. 82–83) Have students make traditional ball-and-stick molecule models [SEP-2] of the compounds they draw in this section. These models allow students to see the three-dimensional shape of the molecules more accurately and may help them gain a better understanding of molecular geometry and polarity.
- **Types of Covalent Bonds** (p. 84) Remind students that in a covalent bond, all of the bonding electrons are shared by both atoms. It can help to draw a different colored circle around each atom and their full octet of electrons in these types of diagrams to double-check that every atom has a full valence shell.
- **Electronegativity and Bonding** (pp. 86–87) Students can estimate the difference in electronegativity between two elements by looking at their relative positions on the periodic table. In general, the farther apart two nonmetals are, the greater the difference in electronegativity will be. Ask students to explain [SEP-6] why this is true.
- Stress to students that bond character lies on a spectrum. It is not black or white, or ionic or covalent.
- **Geometry and Polar Molecules** (pp. 88–90) Students might have trouble visualizing the common molecular shapes shown on page 88. Provide 3-D models [SEP-2] and allow students to hold the models and pass them around the class to get a better idea of the shapes.

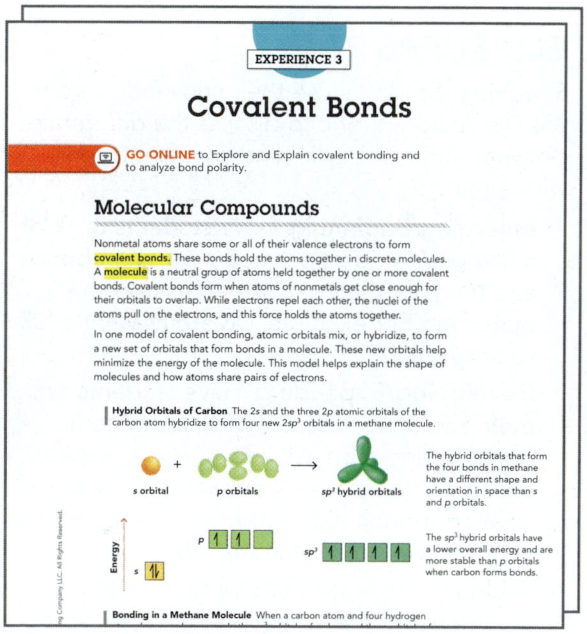
EXPERIENCE 3

Covalent Bonds

GO ONLINE to Explore and Explain covalent bonding and to analyze bond polarity.

Molecular Compounds

Nonmetal atoms share some or all of their valence electrons to form **covalent bonds.** These bonds hold the atoms together in discrete molecules. A **molecule** is a neutral group of atoms held together by one or more covalent bonds. Covalent bonds form when atoms of nonmetals get close enough for their orbitals to overlap. While electrons repel each other, the nuclei of the atoms pull on the electrons, and this force holds the atoms together.

In one model of covalent bonding, atomic orbitals mix, or hybridize, to form a new set of orbitals that form bonds in a molecule. These new orbitals help minimize the energy of the molecule. This model helps explain the shape of molecules and how atoms share pairs of electrons.

Hybrid Orbitals of Carbon The 2*s* and the three 2*p* atomic orbitals of the carbon atom hybridize to form four new $2sp^3$ orbitals in a methane molecule.

Bonding in a Methane Molecule When a carbon atom and four hydrogen

Experience Notebook, pp. 81–90

eTEXT

SAMPLE PROBLEM SUPPORT

Two rules can help students avoid common mistakes when drawing electron dot structures for molecular substances. (1) Carbon has the maximum number of unpaired electrons in its valence shell and is almost always in the center of these structures. If a compound has more than one carbon, the carbons should be linked together in the center of the structure. (2) Hydrogen is often a "filler" element and can only form one bond. Always place hydrogens last when drawing these structures.

ELABORATE

Compare Covalent and Ionic Bonds and Their Substances

Discussion Rubric Lead a discussion on the similarities and differences between ionic and covalent bonds and the substances that contain these bonds. Then ask students to summarize and explain [SEP-6] these differences in writing. Finally, have students exchange their summaries with each other for critique and review [SEP-8], using the provided rubric.

- Have students organize their thoughts using a table or chart before writing their summary of the discussion. Venn diagrams for ionic bonds versus covalent bonds and ionic compounds versus covalent compounds work well for this.

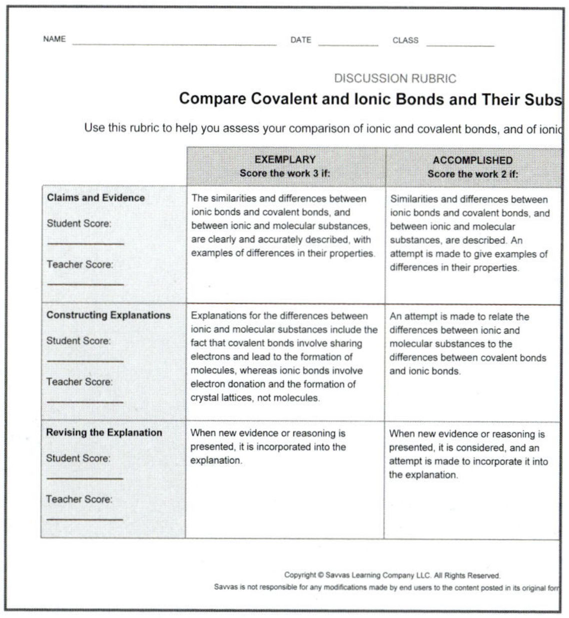
NAME ______ DATE ______ CLASS ______

DISCUSSION RUBRIC

Compare Covalent and Ionic Bonds and Their Subs

Use this rubric to help you assess your comparison of ionic and covalent bonds, and of ionic

	EXEMPLARY Score the work 3 if:	ACCOMPLISHED Score the work 2 if:
Claims and Evidence Student Score: ____ Teacher Score: ____	The similarities and differences between ionic bonds and covalent bonds, and between ionic and molecular substances, are clearly and accurately described, with examples of differences in their properties.	Similarities and differences between ionic bonds and covalent bonds, and between ionic and molecular substances, are described. An attempt is made to give examples of differences in their properties.
Constructing Explanations Student Score: ____ Teacher Score: ____	Explanations for the differences between ionic and molecular substances include the fact that covalent bonds involve sharing electrons and lead to the formation of molecules, whereas ionic bonds involve electron donation and the formation of crystal lattices, not molecules.	An attempt is made to relate the differences between ionic and molecular substances to the differences between covalent bonds and ionic bonds.
Revising the Explanation Student Score: ____ Teacher Score: ____	When new evidence or reasoning is presented, it is incorporated into the explanation.	When new evidence or reasoning is presented, it is considered, and an attempt is made to incorporate it into the explanation.

Discussion Rubric Interactive Worksheet

ELD SUPPORT

Speaking Students use their knowledge from the Discussion Rubric to discuss the differences between ionic, metallic, and covalent bonds with a partner.

- **Emerging/Beginning** Have students think of a few yes/no questions about covalent bonds and then ask their partners to answer the questions. For example, Do atoms want a full valence shell?
- **Developing/Expanding** Have students ask their partners a question about covalent bonding and then ask a follow-up question based on the answer. For example, How are covalent bonds different from ionic bonds? How can we see that in the lab?
- **Bridging** Have students write a summary of the difference between ionic and covalent bonds and read it to their partners. Ask the student who is listening to write three questions as they listen and ask them at the end. Have students switch roles and repeat, this time focusing on the similarities between ionic and covalent bonds.

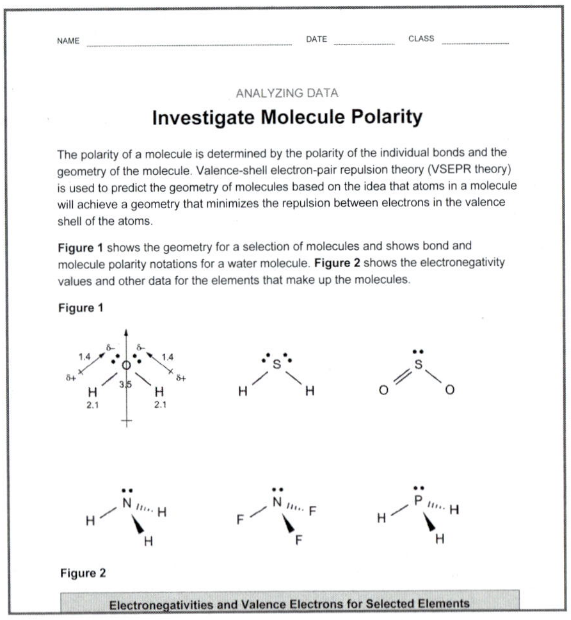
NAME ______ DATE ______ CLASS ______

ANALYZING DATA

Investigate Molecule Polarity

The polarity of a molecule is determined by the polarity of the individual bonds and the geometry of the molecule. Valence-shell electron-pair repulsion theory (VSEPR theory) is used to predict the geometry of molecules based on the idea that atoms in a molecule will achieve a geometry that minimizes the repulsion between electrons in the valence shell of the atoms.

Figure 1 shows the geometry for a selection of molecules and shows bond and molecule polarity notations for a water molecule. **Figure 2** shows the electronegativity values and other data for the elements that make up the molecules.

Figure 1

Figure 2

Electronegativities and Valence Electrons for Selected Elements

Analyzing Data Interactive Worksheet

ASSESS ON THE SPOT

Collect the table or chart that students made for the Discussion Rubric to organize their thoughts and review them while students use their rubrics to review their classmates' written summaries. Quickly look through the diagrams to be sure students understand that covalent bonds involve the sharing of electrons and that covalent compounds have lower melting points and do not generally conduct electricity.

Investigate Molecule Polarity

Analyzing Data In this assignment, students use a combination of VSEPR diagrams of a selection of molecules and a table of electronegativity values and other data to determine the polarity of several molecules. They complete diagrams for two compounds by adding several properties [PS1.A] to the diagrams. They then compare diagrams to determine which molecules are most and least polar.

- Find an online, three-dimensional simulation of models of molecular compounds that shows electron density and overall molecular polarity. Allow students to manipulate one of these simulations to get a better understanding of the way geometry can influence polarity.
- Students often get confused that a molecule containing polar bonds can be nonpolar. Remind students that a molecule must have some asymmetry to be polar. Explain that if they imagine themselves standing on the central atom and the molecule looks the same in every direction, the molecule is symmetrical and, therefore, must be nonpolar even if the bonds between atoms are polar.

DIFFERENTIATED INSTRUCTION

- **Support Struggling Students** Help struggling students understand molecular polarity by using two pieces of string tied together in the middle so a t-shape is formed when the string is laid out flat. Tell students that each of the four ends of the strings represent each bond around the central atom in their molecule. Have students work in pairs so that each student can hold two ends of the string. Ask them to model [SEP-2] different molecules by pulling on their string harder or softer, depending on the polarity of the bond. They should notice that, when all of the pulls are balanced, no net force acts on the string and the string stays in place, even when the individual forces are strong. When any of the pulls are stronger than the others, however, the string moves (indicating the molecule is polar).
- **Support Advanced Students** Ask students to explain why molecular compounds always have dipoles instead of isolated positive and negative charges (as found in ionic compounds). They should realize that electrons are simply being pushed from one place on the molecule to another. There is no gain or loss of charged particles and, therefore, the overall charge of the molecule remains neutral. When one side of the molecule gains electron density and becomes more negative, the other side must lose that density and become more positive.

EVALUATE

Covalent Bonds

Quiz Assign the quiz in online technology-enhanced, auto-graded format or as an editable quiz worksheet. Use the scoring notes and remediation strategies found online to assess students' responses and to provide targeted feedback for each item to remediate well before assigning the summative 3-D Assessment.

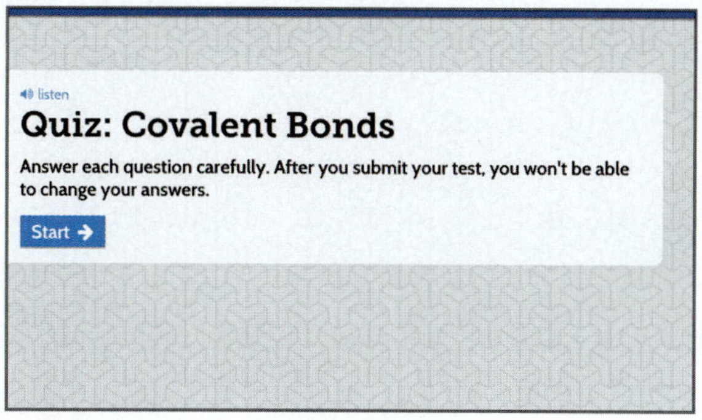

Interactive Online Quiz

Quiz Interactive Worksheet

REMEDIATION SUGGESTIONS

- **If** students have a hard time determining whether a covalent bond is polar or nonpolar, **then** have them review the Calculate Bond Polarity activity and write in their own words a short description of how to find bond polarity.
- **If** students cannot determine the geometry for a molecule, **then** have them review page 88 of the Experience Notebook. Provide students with a few electron dot diagrams for molecules and ask them to identify the geometry. Then provide them with a few molecular formulas and have them draw the dot diagrams themselves before identifying the geometry of the molecule.
- **If** students struggle with determining whether a molecule is polar or nonpolar, **then** ask them to review the Investigate Molecule Polarity activity. Use a model kit to build example molecules from the assignment and ask students to identify the polarity of each bond and the overall polarity of the molecule.

Revisit INVESTIGATIVE PHENOMENON

Support Reflection Students can complete the reflection prompt, where they will unpack and make sense of the Investigative Phenomenon, based on practices and understandings that have been reinforced over the course of the experience.

- Ask students how comfortable they are drawing electron dot diagrams for covalent compounds. On the board, work through a few more examples with single, double, and triple bonds. Ask students to tie in how differences in bonding produce differences in properties of metals and nonmetals. Have students relate this to differences between gems and metals.
- Have students determine the polarity of a few example covalent bonds using the relative positions of the elements on the periodic table as a guide.
- Ask students if they can identify the polarity of a molecule given its electron dot diagram. Provide two or three more examples of polar and nonpolar molecules to the class as a review.

Further Develop Your CER Argument Have students add any evidence they have collected in this experience. Evidence may include that covalently bonded substances generally have much lower melting points than metallic and ionic substances.

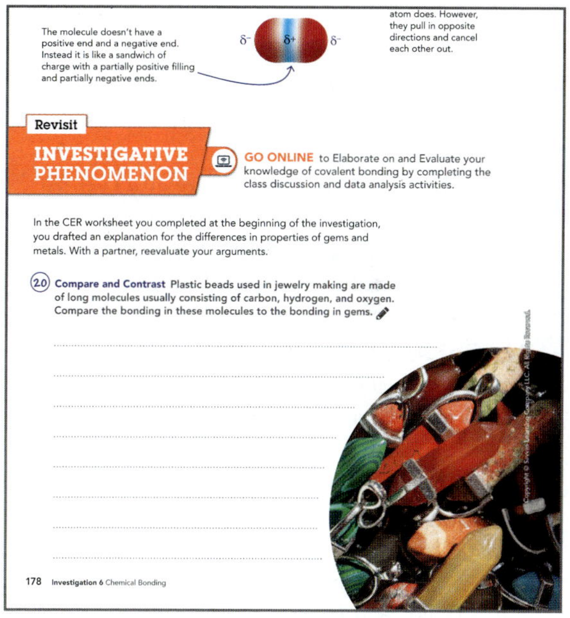
atom does. However, they pull in opposite directions and cancel each other out.

The molecule doesn't have a positive end and a negative end. Instead it is like a sandwich of charge with a partially positive filling and partially negative ends.

δ- δ+ δ-

Revisit
INVESTIGATIVE PHENOMENON

GO ONLINE to Elaborate on and Evaluate your knowledge of covalent bonding by completing the class discussion and data analysis activities.

In the CER worksheet you completed at the beginning of the investigation, you drafted an explanation for the differences in properties of gems and metals. With a partner, reevaluate your arguments.

(20) Compare and Contrast Plastic beads used in jewelry making are made of long molecules usually consisting of carbon, hydrogen, and oxygen. Compare the bonding in these molecules to the bonding in gems.

178 Investigation 6 Chemical Bonding

Experience Notebook, p. 90

eTEXT

EXPERIENCE 4

Intermolecular Attractions

Teacher Background

In this experience, students explore the different types of intermolecular forces between covalently bonded molecules and how those forces determine many observable physical properties of those substances, including volatility, melting point, and boiling point. Students learn to predict the relative values of these properties based on the structures of these compounds.

You may wish to begin this experience by asking students what they know about other topics that involve polarity, such as magnetism and electricity. Remind students that in cases of electrical polarity, the polarity occurs due to the distribution of positive and negative charges. Discuss how students think this might relate to molecular compounds.

Objectives

- **Describe the types of attractions between molecules.**
- **Explain how intermolecular attractions between molecules influence the bulk properties of a material.**

ENGAGE

EVERYDAY PHENOMENON

Why does hand sanitizer evaporate much more quickly than water?

Use this teacher demo to help students understand how intermolecular forces can affect observable physical properties.

Evaporating Liquids (10)

Engage students with this demonstration of an everyday phenomenon to introduce the idea that different intermolecular forces can influence surface tension and evaporation rates.

Materials water, hand sanitizer, isopropyl alcohol, plastic pipette

Safety Isopropyl alcohol is flammable.

1. Ask for two student volunteers. Give one volunteer a few drops of water and the other an equal amount of hand sanitizer. Tell them both to clean their hands with the material. Tell them to raise their hands when they feel dry.
2. Ask the class why the hand sanitizer dried so much faster than the water.
3. Gather the class around a desk or lab bench. Explain that isopropyl alcohol is the primary ingredient in most hand sanitizers.
4. Place 5 drops of water and 5 drops of isopropyl alcohol on the lab bench. **Ask** What do you notice is different about these? (The water drops bead up the most and isopropyl alcohol is a little flatter.)
5. Gently fan the pools of liquid to help them evaporate a little faster. Students should see that the isopropyl alcohol evaporates first and the water does not evaporate much at all.
6. Show the chemical structures of water and isopropyl alcohol to the class and ask students how they think the chemical structures of these compounds caused the differences they just observed. Tell students that they will learn more about this phenomenon as they complete this experience.

RELATED PHENOMENA

In addition to the Evaporating Liquids demo, consider using other phenomena to launch this experience.

- **Viscosity Tests** Perform a viscosity test for several different liquids of various molecular weights. Then discuss with students how intermolecular force strength impacts cohesion.
- **Alcohol As a Solvent** Ask students why perfumes and colognes use alcohol as a solvent instead of water. Lead this into a discussion of volatility based on intermolecular force strength.
- **Charged Balloon** Place a charged balloon next to burets of water and then hexane. (Use caution with hexane because it is flammable. A thin stream of liquid is needed to see the repulsion versus lake of repulsion.) The polar water is attracted to the charged balloon and the nonpolar hexane is not. Discuss why water and hexane behave differently with the charged balloon.
- **The Old Spoon Trick** Rub your nose with a tissue to remove any oils. Breathe on the curved part of the spoon so that moisture (water molecules) collects on the spoon. Put the curve of the spoon against your nose and slowly let go. Ask students why the spoon stuck to your nose even though your skin is mostly water.

EXPLORE

Intermolecular Forces

Inquiry Lab In this lab, students plan a series of procedures to determine which liquid—water or ethyl alcohol—has the stronger intermolecular forces [PS3.C].

Lab Demo Video Watch the Lab Demo Video for advice on materials and preparation.

Choose Your Version Open-ended (O), Guided (G), Shortened (S), Advanced (A)

Materials 30 mL anhydrous ethyl alcohol, 30 mL distilled or deionized water, 50-mL buret, 2 100-mm capillary tubes, 2 glass slides, 2 microspatulas, disposable Petri dish, 2 microtip Beral-type pipets, 2 polyethylene slides, ruler

Safety Remind students that ethyl alcohol is a dangerous fire risk; it is flammable, and the addition of denaturants makes ethyl alcohol poisonous. Students should wear chemical splash goggles, chemical-resistant gloves, and a chemical-resistant apron. Students should wash hands thoroughly with soap and warm water before leaving the laboratory.

Expected Outcome Students study the drop widths and heights of water and ethyl alcohol on glass and polyethylene slides, the height achieved by each liquid by capillary action, and the number of drops of each liquid needed to fill a microspatula tip. Their results indicate that water has stronger intermolecular forces, in particular stronger hydrogen bonding, than ethyl alcohol.

Lab Summary Video Watch the Lab Summary Video for support on connecting the lab investigation to the Investigative Phenomenon.

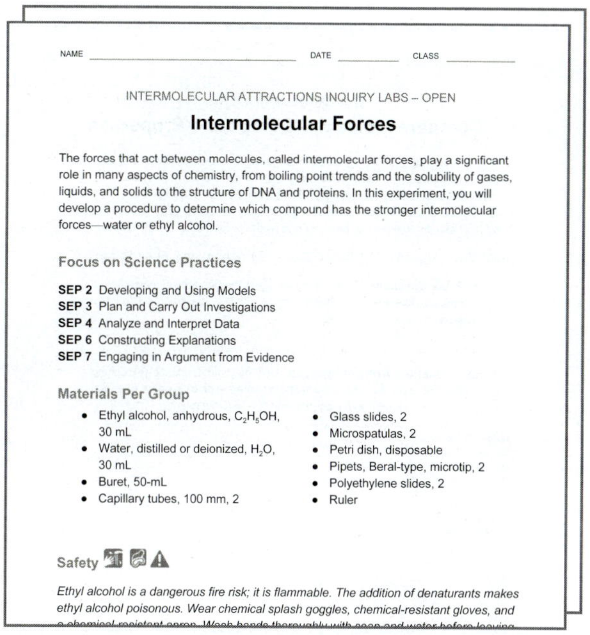
NAME ______ DATE ______ CLASS ______

INTERMOLECULAR ATTRACTIONS INQUIRY LABS – OPEN

Intermolecular Forces

The forces that act between molecules, called intermolecular forces, play a significant role in many aspects of chemistry, from boiling point trends and the solubility of gases, liquids, and solids to the structure of DNA and proteins. In this experiment, you will develop a procedure to determine which compound has the stronger intermolecular forces—water or ethyl alcohol.

Focus on Science Practices

SEP 2 Developing and Using Models
SEP 3 Plan and Carry Out Investigations
SEP 4 Analyze and Interpret Data
SEP 6 Constructing Explanations
SEP 7 Engaging in Argument from Evidence

Materials Per Group

- Ethyl alcohol, anhydrous, C_2H_5OH, 30 mL
- Water, distilled or deionized, H_2O, 30 mL
- Buret, 50-mL
- Capillary tubes, 100 mm, 2
- Glass slides, 2
- Microspatulas, 2
- Petri dish, disposable
- Pipets, Beral-type, microtip, 2
- Polyethylene slides, 2
- Ruler

Safety

Ethyl alcohol is a dangerous fire risk; it is flammable. The addition of denaturants makes ethyl alcohol poisonous. Wear chemical splash goggles, chemical-resistant gloves, and

O/G/S/A Lab Interactive Worksheets

ASSESS ON THE SPOT

After the Inquiry Lab, have students make a Venn diagram comparing and contrasting water and ethyl alcohol. They should include molecule size, drop size, ion–dipole attraction, and intermolecular attraction.

Intermolecular Forces in Liquids

Virtual Lab In this Virtual Lab, students investigate the importance of the properties of water to living things. They explore the boiling point and surface tension of several substances with different predominant intermolecular forces. They observe how intermolecular forces impact these physical properties [PS1.A] by performing various experiments and analyzing the resulting data [SEP-4].

- After students complete the Virtual Lab, ask them to rank the boiling points of water, glycerol, isopropyl alcohol, and hexane based on the observations they made in the lab. Be sure students can explain why water has the highest boiling point based on its intermolecular forces.
- Glass capillary tubes are most often used in adhesion experiments, like those simulated in this lab. Tell students that the surface of glass is polar. **Ask** Do you think the samples in the capillary tubes would rise to the same height if they were made of a nonpolar substance like plastic? (No, the plastic can only exhibit weak dispersion forces so the adhesive force would be weaker.)

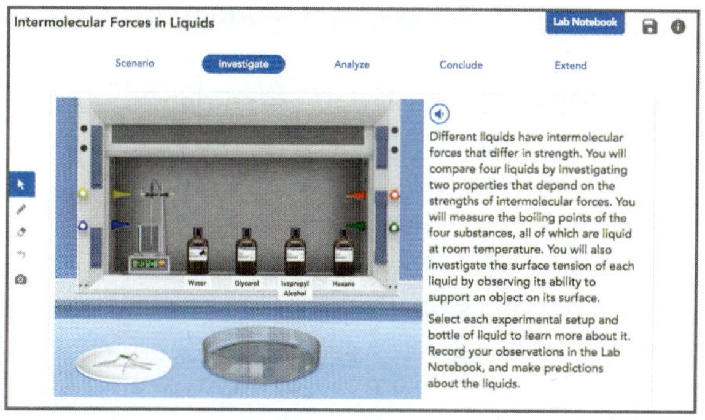

Virtual Lab: Intermolecular Forces in Liquids

PROFESSIONAL DEVELOPMENT

Explaining Phenomena Kevlar® is a material that is used in bulletproof vests because it is so strong that it can stop a bullet. The reason that Kevlar is so amazingly strong is that each Kevlar molecule is very long, leading to very strong dispersion forces, and the Kevlar monomer has nitrogen and oxygen atoms located within it in perfect position to form hydrogen bonds. This combination of hydrogen bonding and dispersion forces is what makes Kevlar strong enough to stop bullets.

CLASSROOM MODIFICATIONS

Based on on your students' abilities and your schedule, you may wish to modify the Intermolecular Forces in Liquids Virtual Lab to be more open ended or more guided.

- **More Open Ended** Ask students to rank water, glycerol, isopropyl alcohol, and hexane in order of increasing surface tension and provide evidence from the lab to support their claim. Allow them to perform the experiments in the Virtual Lab in any order as long as they obtain the proper data to justify their answer.
- **More Guided** Provide a set of questions to ask as students progress through the experiment to ensure they are gaining necessary learning from each property measurement.

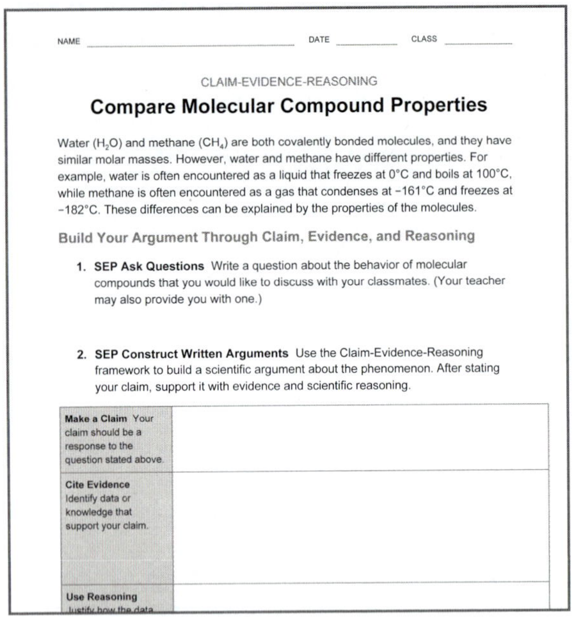

NAME ________ DATE ________ CLASS ________

CLAIM-EVIDENCE-REASONING

Compare Molecular Compound Properties

Water (H_2O) and methane (CH_4) are both covalently bonded molecules, and they have similar molar masses. However, water and methane have different properties. For example, water is often encountered as a liquid that freezes at 0°C and boils at 100°C, while methane is often encountered as a gas that condenses at −161°C and freezes at −182°C. These differences can be explained by the properties of the molecules.

Build Your Argument Through Claim, Evidence, and Reasoning

1. **SEP Ask Questions** Write a question about the behavior of molecular compounds that you would like to discuss with your classmates. (Your teacher may also provide you with one.)

2. **SEP Construct Written Arguments** Use the Claim-Evidence-Reasoning framework to build a scientific argument about the phenomenon. After stating your claim, support it with evidence and scientific reasoning.

Make a Claim Your claim should be a response to the question stated above.	
Cite Evidence Identify data or knowledge that support your claim.	
Use Reasoning Justify how the data	

CER Interactive Worksheet

ELD SUPPORT

Writing Students work in pairs or small groups to use what they have learned in the Claim-Evidence-Reasoning activity to write a persuasive argument that links the intermolecular forces in water and methane to their physical properties.

- **Emerging/Beginning** Have students use teacher-created sentence stems to outline their argument. For example, have them complete the sentence, *Methane shows weaker intermolecular forces because* ________.
- **Developing/Expanding** Have students respond to example questions about their argument. For example, **ask** Why would the boiling point of water be higher than the boiling point of methane?
- **Bridging** Have students construct their own questions and then have a partner answer them based on the background knowledge on intermolecular forces they have gained so far in this lesson.

EXPLAIN

Compare Molecular Compound Properties

Claim-Evidence-Reasoning In this activity, students ask a question [SEP-1] about the behavior of molecular compounds and their properties [PS1.A]. They use the claim-evidence-reasoning framework to construct an argument [SEP-6] about the phenomenon. Students then work in pairs or small groups to complete the rest of the assignment.

- Before beginning this assignment, walk students through an example claim-evidence-reasoning argument to remind them how to use the table in the activity.
- If necessary, review with students the Inquiry Lab and the Virtual Lab. Tell students to use what they learned in those activities to construct their questions and arguments.
- You may wish to brainstorm a list of different questions as a class and then have the class vote on the best question for everyone to use in the CER activity.

DIFFERENTIATED INSTRUCTION

- **Support Less Proficient Readers** Give students as many opportunities as possible to see three-dimensional models of molecules. When you talk about molecules or write formulas on the board, try to display a three-dimensional model or to pass one around the class. This will help students interpret two-dimensional drawings of the three-dimensional figures.
- **Support Advanced Students** After students complete their CER revisions, have them share their revisions in groups of three or four students. Assign advanced students to be group leaders as the groups develop lists of some common features they find in their evidence and reasoning. Then group leaders can meet to make and post a list of the features for all students to see.
- **Support Special Needs Students** Offer students materials such as modeling clay and straws to mimic models of covalently bonded molecules. Display the models in the classroom and use them as you discuss these molecules. Be sure to give credit to the models' creators when referencing one.

Intermolecular Attractions

Experience Notebook Have students read this section of the Experience Notebook or Realize Reader before you start the various activities in this experience. Use these strategies to help students make sense of the images and text on the indicated pages, as well as to engage science skills.

- **Intermolecular Attractions** (pp. 91–96) Discuss how the sharing of electrons binds atoms into molecules. Point out that if no other forces [PS3.C] were present at the molecular level, all covalently bonded molecules would be gases at any temperature because no attractive force would tend to pull them together to form a liquid or a solid. Tell students that forces do exist between covalently bonded molecules.
- **Van der Waals Forces** (pp. 91–92) One good way to demonstrate dispersion forces is with hook-and-loop fastening material. Provide student pairs each with two strips of hook and fastener material. Tell students to make a connection between the strips using the smallest surface area possible. Afterward, tell them to pull apart the strips and note how much force [PS3.C] was needed. Point out that each individual hook–loop connection is very weak. Then have students increase the surface area that they connect and then pull apart the two strips. Discuss how the force needed to do that compares with the force needed to pull apart a smaller surface area. Point out how adding more surface area (by using a bigger piece of material) can increase the total dispersion force strength.

- **Dipole Interactions in ICl Diagram** (p. 92) Provide student pairs with two bar magnets. Have them explore how different parts of the magnets interact and then relate the interactions to the discussion of dipole interactions.
- **Hydrogen Bonds** (p. 93) Students may need help remembering which elements can participate in hydrogen bonds. Give them a mnemonic device to remember: FON (pronounced "phone") elements can produce hydrogen bonds. These elements are neighbors on the periodic table.
- Work through a Lewis structure view of hydrogen bonding so that students can see the lone pairs of electrons interacting with hydrogen.
- Help students understand the strength of hydrogen bonding. Place 300 mL of each of these substances in different stoppered flasks: glycerol, ethylene glycol, water, ethanol. Gently rotate one flask so that its contents begin to swirl. Have students time the interval between your ceasing to rotate the flask and the disappearance of the vortex. Record the time on the board. Repeat the procedure for each flask. Be sure to rotate the flask the same number of times. The longest to shortest time should be: ethanol, water, ethylene glycol, and glycerol. Ask students what caused the differences. (Hydrogen bonding increases a liquid's surface tension and viscosity. Thus, liquids with a relatively high degree of hydrogen bonding generally stop swirling more quickly.)
- **Properties of Molecular Substances** (pp. 94–95) Help students practice identifying the type and strength of intermolecular force in a substance by making a set of flash cards with a molecule or element on one side and the dominant type of intermolecular force on the other. This type of low-risk, high-volume practice can really help students retain this information better.
- Tell students that a covalent network solid is made of many atoms that are held together in large lattices by covalent bonds, which extend throughout the crystalline structure. A network solid does not have discrete molecules; the entire crystal is the molecule. Because the units of covalent network solids contain a continuous network of covalent bonds, these substances are extremely strong. Breaking them is difficult because doing so requires breaking many covalent bonds. They have high melting points and are poor conductors. Daimond, graphite, and quartz are network solids.

ASSESS ON THE SPOT

On the board, write: NH_3 and CH_4. Tell students that the two molecules have different intermolecular forces and ask them to determine which would have the higher boiling point and why. (Ammonia (NH_3) has a higher boiling point due to hydrogen bonding between hydrogen atoms and the unbonded electron pair.) Collect these responses and review them to be sure students understand the link between molecular structure and physical properties.

PROFESSIONAL DEVELOPMENT

Background Notes The Dutch physicist Johannes van der Waals (1837–1923) surmised that gas behavior could not be described exactly by the ideal gas law because the law assumes that gas molecules have no volume and that no attractive forces exist between gas molecules. Van der Waals adjusted the ideal gas equation by introducing two factors: one to take cognizance of the real volume of gas molecules; the other to account for intermolecular forces between molecules. For his work in developing an understanding of intermolecular attractions, he was awarded the Nobel Prize in Physics in 1910.

Atomic Interactions

PhET Simulation Students can explore the interactions between various combinations of atoms to see how changing the atomic diameter and interaction strength affects the interaction.

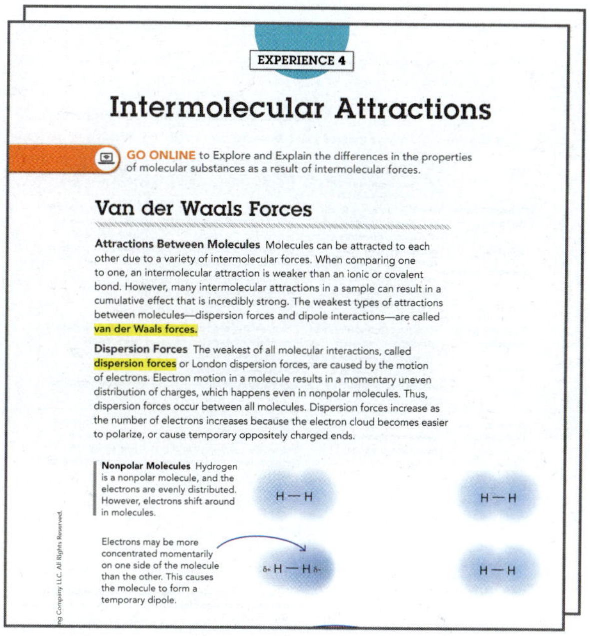

EXPERIENCE 4

Intermolecular Attractions

GO ONLINE to Explore and Explain the differences in the properties of molecular substances as a result of intermolecular forces.

Van der Waals Forces

Attractions Between Molecules Molecules can be attracted to each other due to a variety of intermolecular forces. When comparing one to one, an intermolecular attraction is weaker than an ionic or covalent bond. However, many intermolecular attractions in a sample can result in a cumulative effect that is incredibly strong. The weakest types of attractions between molecules—dispersion forces and dipole interactions—are called van der Waals forces.

Dispersion Forces The weakest of all molecular interactions, called dispersion forces or London dispersion forces, are caused by the motion of electrons. Electron motion in a molecule results in a momentary uneven distribution of charges, which happens even in nonpolar molecules. Thus, dispersion forces occur between all molecules. Dispersion forces increase as the number of electrons increases because the electron cloud becomes easier to polarize, or cause temporary oppositely charged ends.

Nonpolar Molecules Hydrogen is a nonpolar molecule, and the electrons are evenly distributed. However, electrons shift around in molecules.

Electrons may be more concentrated momentarily on one side of the molecule than the other. This causes the molecule to form a temporary dipole.

Experience Notebook, pp. 91–95

eTEXT

ADDRESS PRECONCEPTIONS

Students may think that intermolecular forces are related to bonds being broken. Make sure that they understand that intermolecular forces do not result from bonds being broken nor from reactions occurring. The forces and their strength depend on molecular size, shape, and electronegativity.

PhET Simulation: Atomic Interactions

ELABORATE

Review Molecular Compound Properties (15)

Peer Review Rubric In this activity, students review and evaluate each other's claims about the connection between molecular structure and physical properties [PS1.A]. Have students complete this activity after finishing the CER exercise and after reading through this experience of the Experience Notebook.

- Have students give their CER argument to another student for evaluation. Tell students to use the Peer Review Rubric to make the evaluation.
- Give students about 5 minutes to complete their review. Point out that the explanations that students record for the scores should contain only constructive comments.

NAME ______________ DATE ________ CLASS ________

PEER REVIEW RUBRIC

Review Molecular Compound Properties

Use this rubric to help you assess your classmates' claims about the differences in the proper

	EXEMPLARY Score the work 3 if:	ACCOMPLISHED Score the work 2 if:	DEVELOPING Score the work 1 if:
Components of the Claim Score: ______	Molecular polarity is clearly described as being the result of the relative positions of atoms, having different electronegativities, within the molecule. The effect of polarity on intermolecular forces is identified.	An attempt is made to describe how the polarity of molecules results from the relative positions of atoms, having different electronegativities, within the molecule. An attempt is made to relate polarity to intermolecular forces.	An attempt is made to show that different molecules have different polarities.
Reasoning and Synthesis Score: ______	Reasoning for the differences in molecular compounds' properties involves the effect of polarity on the relative strengths of intermolecular forces.	An attempt is made to identify the effect of intermolecular forces on the differing properties, though the reasoning is not clear.	An attempt is made to relate the polarity of molecules to the properties of a molecular compound.
Revising the Explanation Score: ______	When new evidence or reasoning is presented, it is incorporated into the explanation.	When new evidence or reasoning is presented, it is considered, and an attempt is made to incorporate it into the explanation.	When new evidence is presented, it is rejected without enough consideration.

Peer Review Rubric Interactive Worksheet

INTEGRATE THE THREE DIMENSIONS

In the Review Molecular Compound Properties activity, students apply their knowledge of differences in the properties [PS1.A] and structure [CCC-6] of molecular compounds to evaluate [SEP-8] their classmates' claims. They incorporate new evidence [SEP-7] into their own explanations.

Water's Behavior on Earth (20)

Writing About Science In this writing activity, students use what they know about the intermolecular forces [PS3.C] between water molecules and the geometry of the water molecule to write an explanation [SEP-6] about why snowflakes always have six sides and why ice is less dense than water. They also explain why it is advantageous that water does not evaporate quickly on Earth.

- Students can work in small groups to conduct research, but each student should write his or her own explanation.
- You may wish to provide students with a list of approved Web sites for their research to help focus them in the right direction.
- As an extension, have students explain why it is so important that frozen water floats instead of sinking. Ask students to explain what the impact to life on Earth would be if solid ice sank in water.
- Connect the shape of crystalline water to the crystal shapes of ionic compounds discussed in Experience 1. Have students compare and contrast the properties of ionic compound crystals with those of water crystals.

NAME ______________ DATE ________ CLASS ________

WRITING ABOUT SCIENCE

Water's Behavior on Earth

Because water has an unusual combination of polarity and strong intermolecular forces, it is a liquid at normal temperatures on Earth. Unlike most other substances, when water solidifies, it becomes less dense and thus floats on its own liquid. This phenomenon is related to the fact that snowflakes always have six sides. This consistent six-sided shape fascinated scientists as early as 135 BC, when a Chinese scientist wrote about six-pointed "snow flowers." Scientists are still fascinated by ice today.

Obtain and Evaluate Information

1. **Apply Concepts** Use what you know about the intermolecular forces between water molecules and the geometry of the water molecule to explain why snowflakes always have six sides and why ice is less dense than water. Perform additional research as needed.

2. **CCC Cause and Effect** Explain why it is advantageous that water does not evaporate quickly on Earth.

Writing About Science Interactive Worksheet

DIFFERENTIATED INSTRUCTION

- **Support Struggling Students** Struggling students may require more scaffolding in the questions for the Writing About Science activity. Break each question into parts and have students tell in their own words what they are being asked to do.
- **Support Advanced Students** Scientists are excited by the prospect of finding water on Mars and other planets because water's unique properties are considered essential for life as we know it. Ask advanced students to determine the properties of water that make it so important for life and to research whether there are other substances that may have similar properties.

ASSESS ON THE SPOT

Give students 3 minutes to write an explanation of how polarity helps to determine why different compounds have different properties.

EVALUATE

Intermolecular Attractions

Quiz Assign the quiz in online technology-enhanced, auto-graded format or as an editable quiz worksheet. Use the scoring notes and remediation strategies found online to assess students' responses and to provide targeted feedback for each item to remediate well before assigning the summative 3-D Assessment.

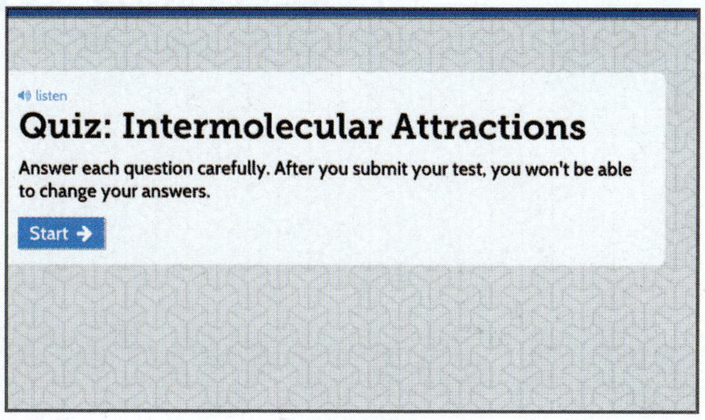

Interactive Online Quiz

Quiz Interactive Worksheet

REMEDIATION SUGGESTIONS

- **If** students have difficulty understanding the behavior of molecular compounds, **then** have them return to the CER activity, Compare Molecular Compound Properties.
- **If** students have trouble identifying the different types of intermolecular forces in molecular compounds, **then** have them review pages 91–92 in the Experience Notebook and work with a partner to summarize each type of intermolecular force in their own words.
- **If** students struggle with the connection between different types of intermolecular forces and the physical properties of substances, **then** have them review pages 94–95 in the Experience Notebook.
- **If** students have difficulty with the concept of different liquids having intermolecular forces that differ in strength, **then** have them return to the Virtual Lab, Intermolecular Forces in Liquids.

Revisit INVESTIGATIVE PHENOMENON

Support Reflection Students can complete the reflection prompt, where they will unpack and make sense of the Investigative Phenomenon, based on practices and understandings that have been reinforced over the course of the experience.

- Ask students to explain the differences between dispersion forces, dipole interactions, and hydrogen bonds. Show a few example molecules and ask students to predict what type of intermolecular forces would be dominant in a sample of that substance.
- Have students name some properties of substances that are influenced by the strength of their intermolecular forces. Melting point, boiling point, surface tension, and viscosity are all examples of properties that are determined by the type of intermolecular forces present in a sample. Have students relate this back to why gems have different properties than metals.

Further Develop Your CER Argument Have students add any evidence they have collected in this experience. Evidence may include that the intermolecular forces of attraction between molecular compounds are generally much weaker than ionic and metallic bonds.

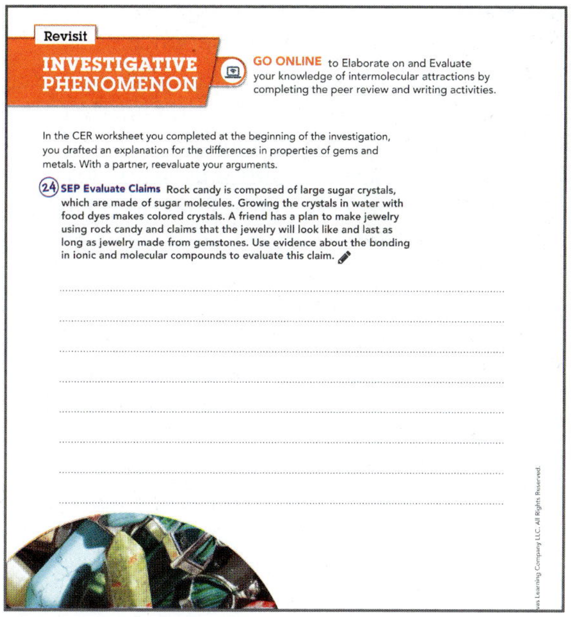

Revisit INVESTIGATIVE PHENOMENON

GO ONLINE to Elaborate on and Evaluate your knowledge of intermolecular attractions by completing the peer review and writing activities.

In the CER worksheet you completed at the beginning of the investigation, you drafted an explanation for the differences in properties of gems and metals. With a partner, reevaluate your arguments.

(24) **SEP Evaluate Claims** Rock candy is composed of large sugar crystals, which are made of sugar molecules. Growing the crystals in water with food dyes makes colored crystals. A friend has a plan to make jewelry using rock candy and claims that the jewelry will look like and last as long as jewelry made from gemstones. Use evidence about the bonding in ionic and molecular compounds to evaluate this claim.

Experience Notebook, p. 96

eTEXT

EXPERIENCE 5

Names and Formulas of Compounds

Teacher Background

In Experience 5, students utilize what they have learned about different types of chemical bonds to investigate the logic underlying how compounds are named and how their formulas are written. They will infer their own sets of rules from looking at examples of names and formulas, and consider how the name of a compound allows them to predict the type of bonds within it. They practice writing formulas from compound names and vice versa.

Objectives

- **Explain the rules for naming molecular compounds, ionic compounds, and acids.**
- **Demonstrate how to determine a neutral compound's chemical formula using its name and the periodic table.**
- **Explain how to name a chemical compound when given its formula.**
- **Predict bond types in a compound based on its name or formula.**

RELATED PHENOMENA

In addition to the demo Why do roads have different names?, consider using other phenomena to launch this experience.

- **Clothing Item Names** Give students examples of articles of clothing with modifiers that relate to the garment's function, such as *waterproof jacket* or *buttonfly jeans*. Ask students what the names of the products tell about their properties, and discuss what type of prior knowledge a person must have to understand the meaning.
- **Computer File Names** Ask students how they organize their files on their computer. Let them know that many companies adopt naming conventions for their computer files. Make a class list of types of information that would be useful to include in a file name. Discuss how working on complex projects is simplified by having such information contained in the file name.

ENGAGE

EVERYDAY PHENOMENON

What can the name of something tell us about its structure and properties?

Use this teacher demo to prompt discussion about information contained in the names of objects and compounds.

Why do roads have different names? (5)

Engage students with this demonstration of street-naming conventions to introduce the concept of naming conventions that convey information.

Materials projector, digital presentation slide with naming convention rules, map of your local area

Advance Preparation Locate a map of your area with street names clearly marked. Be sure the map includes a variety of street types, such as avenue, street, drive, boulevard, lane, court, place, and terrace.

Then prepare a slide with the following naming rules:

- road—a throughway that connects two nonspecific points
- street—a road with buildings on one or both sides of it
- avenue—a road with buildings on one or both sides, perpendicular to, and often longer than, a street
- boulevard—a wider road, often with two lanes and a divider
- court—a narrow street that ends in a circle or cul-de-sac
- drive—a curving road that follows contours of the natural landscape

1. As a class, make a list of words used to describe roads. Ask students to describe how they think a street differs from a boulevard or how an avenue is different than a drive. Point out that the designation of the road tells us something about its physical characteristics.

2. Project the prepared slide and explain to students that there is a system for how roads are named. Point out that these conventions are not always followed, but students should be able to identify some patterns [CCC-1] of these conventions in their own town.
3. Project the map of your area, and point out a few roads with varying names. Ask students to describe what they think they can identify about the road from the name. For example, Lakeview Drive is probably a curving road that runs near a lake; 34th St. SW would likely be in the southwest area of the city, 34 blocks from a dividing boundary, and run perpendicular to the town's avenues.
4. Ask students to explain why having such naming conventions is important. (because it allows people to have knowledge about the roadway and make predictions about its location and traffic conditions)
5. Tell students that chemical substances also have naming conventions. Ask students to describe what information a chemical name might provide. (what atoms it is made of, how many of each, what the charges are on the ions that make up an ionic compound, what type of bond holds the compound together)
6. Guide a discussion of the benefits of naming conventions as a transition into the Inquiry Lab. Further discuss how metals and gems are named and how this reflects their unique differences.

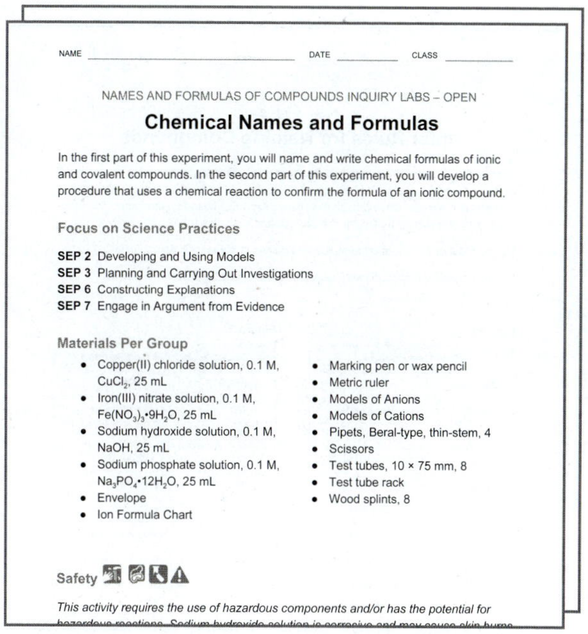
NAME ______ DATE ______ CLASS ______

NAMES AND FORMULAS OF COMPOUNDS INQUIRY LABS – OPEN

Chemical Names and Formulas

In the first part of this experiment, you will name and write chemical formulas of ionic and covalent compounds. In the second part of this experiment, you will develop a procedure that uses a chemical reaction to confirm the formula of an ionic compound.

Focus on Science Practices

SEP 2 Developing and Using Models
SEP 3 Planning and Carrying Out Investigations
SEP 6 Constructing Explanations
SEP 7 Engage in Argument from Evidence

Materials Per Group

- Copper(II) chloride solution, 0.1 M, $CuCl_2$, 25 mL
- Iron(III) nitrate solution, 0.1 M, $Fe(NO_3)_3 \cdot 9H_2O$, 25 mL
- Sodium hydroxide solution, 0.1 M, NaOH, 25 mL
- Sodium phosphate solution, 0.1 M, $Na_3PO_4 \cdot 12H_2O$, 25 mL
- Envelope
- Ion Formula Chart
- Marking pen or wax pencil
- Metric ruler
- Models of Anions
- Models of Cations
- Pipets, Beral-type, thin-stem, 4
- Scissors
- Test tubes, 10 × 75 mm, 8
- Test tube rack
- Wood splints, 8

Safety

This activity requires the use of hazardous components and/or has the potential for

O/G/S/A Lab Interactive Worksheets

EXPLORE

Chemical Names and Formulas

Inquiry Lab In this lab, students name and write chemical formulas of ionic and covalent compounds. Then they develop a procedure [SEP-3] that uses a chemical reaction [PS1.B] to confirm the formula of an ionic compound.

Lab Demo Video Watch the Lab Demo Video for advice on materials and preparation.

Choose Your Version Open-ended (O), Guided (G), Shortened (S), Advanced (A)

Materials 25 mL 0.1*M* copper(II) chloride solution, 25 mL 0.1*M* iron(III) nitrate solution, 25 mL 0.1*M* sodium hydroxide solution, 25 mL 0.1*M* sodium phosphate solution, envelope, ion formula chart, marking pen or wax pencil, metric ruler, models of anions, models of cations, 4 thin-stem Beral-type pipets, scissors, 8 10 mm × 75 mm test tubes, test tube rack, 8 wood splints

Safety This activity requires the use of hazardous components and/or has the potential for hazardous reactions. Advise students to avoid all body tissue contact when working with these chemicals and to wear chemical splash goggles, chemical-resistant gloves, and a chemical-resistant apron. Students should wash their hands with soap and warm water before leaving the lab.

Expected Outcome Students gain a high level of comfort with naming and writing chemical formulas for ionic and covalent compounds. Moreover, students recognize the need to use Roman numerals to name compounds that have cations with more than one charge. They recognize and avoid mistakes common to naming covalent compounds, including the "ao" rule. Finally, students determine how to experimentally confirm the formulas of ionic compounds.

Lab Summary Video Watch the Lab Summary Video for support on connecting the lab investigation and the Investigative Phenomenon.

ASSESS ON THE SPOT

As students complete the lab, have them write a description of the part of the lab that they struggled with the most. Collect responses and review the most common problems with the entire class the following day.

CLASSROOM MODIFICATIONS

Based on on your students' abilities and your schedule, you may wish to have students use the more guided version of the lab or the more advanced version of the lab.

- **Guided Inquiry Lab** Students are given more practice with naming and writing formulas of ionic and covalent compounds. They do not develop a procedure to confirm the formula of an ionic compound.
- **Advanced Inquiry Lab** Students develop a procedure to confirm the formula of an ionic compound.

CONNECT TO CAREERS

Chemical Safety Specialist Tell students that understanding names and formulas of chemicals is especially important in safely using and disposing of chemicals. Employees in many fields, such as first responders, construction site supervisors, and stockroom staff at hospitals, are trained by experts in chemical safety.

Have students research the Occupational Safety and Health Administration (OSHA) Web site for types of chemical safety training. Then tell them to make a short list of requirements for certification, as well as types of places that need chemical safety specialists.

NAME ______________________ DATE __________ CLASS __________

ANALYZING DATA

Infer Rules for Naming Compounds

Compounds are named according to standard rules. By following the rules, you can work out the name of a compound simply by looking at its chemical formula. You can also go the other way and work out the chemical formula based on the name. The rules are slightly different for molecular compounds and ionic compounds.

Figure 1 shows the chemical formulas and names of some ionic compounds.

Figure 2 shows the formulas and names of some binary molecular compounds.

Figure 1

Ionic Compounds	
Formula	**Name**
NaCl	sodium chloride
CdS	cadmium sulfide
CaI_2	calcium iodide
LiCl	lithium chloride
Na_2O	sodium oxide
Al_3C_4	aluminum carbide
BaF_2	barium fluoride
Mg_3N_2	magnesium nitride

Figure 2

Binary Molecular Compounds	
Formula	**Name**
CO	carbon monoxide
CO_2	carbon dioxide
SO_2	sulfur dioxide
NO	nitrogen monoxide
S_2Cl_2	disulfur dichloride
N_2O	dinitrogen monoxide
CCl_4	carbon tetrachloride
PCl_5	phosphorus pentachloride

Analyzing Data Inveractive Worksheet

NAME ______________________ DATE __________ CLASS __________

CLAIM-EVIDENCE-REASONING

Comparing Compound Nomenclatures

The naming of ionic and molecular compounds relates to the electronegativities of the atoms that make up the compounds. There are different rules for naming ionic compounds and molecular compounds. For example, molecular compound names contain number prefixes such as *mono-*, *di-*, and *tri-*, which are absent from ionic compound names.

Build Your Argument Through Claim, Evidence, and Reasoning

1. **SEP Ask Questions** Write a question about the naming of ionic and molecular compounds that you would like to discuss with your classmates. (Your teacher may also provide you with one.)

2. **SEP Construct Written Arguments** Use the Claim-Evidence-Reasoning framework to build a scientific argument about the phenomenon. After stating your claim, support it with evidence and scientific reasoning.

Make a Claim Your claim should be a response to the question stated above.	
Cite Evidence Identify data or knowledge that support your claim.	

CER Interactive Worksheet

ELD SUPPORT

Speaking Students work in pairs to articulate evidence and reasoning for their claims about naming rules in the CER activity.

- **Emerging/Beginning** Tell each student to read his or her claim to a partner, either in English or home language. Partners review each other's claims and help find supportive evidence in the lab or data analysis activity.
- **Developing/Expanding** Tell pairs to complete the Emerging activity, and then use the evidence to craft reasoning for the argument.
- **Developing/Bridging** Group student pairs into fours, and tell each student to present to the group their argument, citing evidence and explaining reasoning. Individuals in the group can then provide constructive comments.

Infer Rules for Naming Compounds

Analyzing Data In this activity, students identify patterns [CCC-1] in the names and formulas of molecular and ionic compounds. They construct explanations [SEP-6] for these patterns and devise their own rules for naming compounds, based on the analysis of data [SEP-4] provided.

- Before students write a set of rules for naming a binary molecular compound, have them make two lists that identify the similarities and differences between the two charts in the worksheet to determine how the compounds should be named.
- Be sure all students have a periodic table or that one is posted where everyone can see it. Remind students that the periodic table can be helpful in revealing patterns to the naming conventions.

DIFFERENTIATED INSTRUCTION

- **Support Struggling Students** Pair struggling students with others in the class who may be able to guide them in discerning patterns. Encourage pairs to ask each other questions as they work and support each other in answering.
- **Support Special Needs Students** Students with attention issues may welcome more structure for the project. Prepare a list of steps to guide them to responses for the questions that accompany the charts. For example: Look at the atom listed first in ionic and molecular compounds. Where are these atoms located in the periodic table?

EXPLAIN

Comparing Compound Nomenclatures

Claim-Evidence-Reasoning Students ask a question [SEP-1] and write an argument in which they make a claim about the naming of ionic and molecular compounds [PS1.A]. They support their argument with observed evidence [SEP-7] and scientific reasoning.

- You may wish to provide students with several questions and allow them to choose one on which to base their claim.
- If students have difficulty with writing a question, have them revisit what they learned in the Inquiry Lab and Analyzing Data activity. Tell them to write questions they had after completing the activities.
- After students finish their written arguments, have them share their writing with one or more classmates. Remind students that a claim must be backed with facts and scientific reasoning. The claim should be clearly stated. Evidence should be communicated [SEP-8] in an organized manner.

Consider having students revisit their claims and evidence after the class completes the reading and discussion of the information in the Experience Notebook. They can make any revisions to their writing as homework before the class completes the Discussion Rubric.

Predicting Bond Type

Animation This animation shows students how to use the periodic table to predict whether the bonds in a molecule are covalent or ionic. Using examples with main-group elements, students observe how differences in electronegativity, which follow a pattern [CCC-1] in the periodic table, influence what type of bond forms.

- Watch the animation together as a class, stopping occasionally to tell students to make notes of important points. Remind them also to write questions they have about the video.
- Pair students to discuss the questions they have and compare any differences in the notes they took.
- As a class, discuss any unanswered questions and do a review summary of the important points of the animation.

ASSESS ON THE SPOT

On the board, write the question: Why don't we need to use number prefixes in the names of ionic compounds? Hand out notecards. Ask students to write a response to the question and hand it in to you as they leave class.

Names and Formulas of Compounds (20)

Experience Notebook This section of the Experience Notebook or Realize Reader works best when assigned alongside the other activities described here, as opposed to reading the whole experience at one time. Have students read the relevant sections of the notebook after completing the assignments and activities that support those sections.

Use the strategies shown below to help students better understand the content found on the indicated pages.

- **Naming Ions** (pp. 97–98) Review with students the meanings of the terms *ion*, *anion*, and *cation*. Have students work with a partner and construct an explanation [SEP-6] that describes the ionic charges that form from main group metal and nonmetal ions in terms of valence electrons. Invite pairs to share their explanations.
- Direct students' attention to the table of common polyatomic ions on page 98. Note that the table is divided into sections according to charge. Then invite students to write the formulas on the board for all of the *-ate* and *-ite* pairs. **Ask** What do you notice about each of these pairs? (They have the same charge.) Emphasize that it is not the charge but rather the number of oxygen atoms in the members of these pairs that determines the endings of the names.
- **Formulas for Ionic Compounds** (p. 100) Ask students to identify which ion—cation or anion—comes first in the examples given in the Experience Notebook: $CaCl_2$ and MnO_2. (cation) Give students a selection of ions of transition metals (for example, Cr^{2+}, Cr^{3+}, Sn^{2+}, Sn^{4+}, Cu^{1+}, Cu^{2+}). Tell them to work individually and to use the sample problems on page 190 to guide them in writing names and formulas for the compounds that form [PS1.B] when each of these ions bonds with chlorine, oxygen, and phosphate. Then pair students to compare their answers. Discuss the correct answers as a class.
- **Names of Molecular Compounds** (p. 103) To help students remember the prefixes, go through the list and come up with familiar words containing each prefix. For example, *monotonous* means "one tone," and *tricycle* is "something that has three wheels." Ask students to describe how each prefix applies to specific names of compounds you provide.
- **Identifying Molecular Compounds Sample Problem** (p. 105) Prepare a list of 10 to 15 ionic and molecular compounds, some by name and others by formula. Pair students and present the compounds one by one, telling pairs to write the name or formula and state whether it is ionic or molecular and how they know. After each compound, call on pairs to share their responses.

ASSESS ON THE SPOT

Give students 5 minutes to summarize the naming rules for molecular and ionic compounds as they understand them. Then call on students to read aloud their summaries.

INTEGRATE MATH

When a formula contains parentheses, students may be confused by standard rules of exponents that they have learned in math. For example, $(2x)^3$ in math means 2^3x^3—that is, the exponent is applied to both the 2 and the *x* inside the parentheses. Stress that this is not the case when a charge has been assigned to a polyatomic ion. The charge is the total charge for the entire ion and is not distributed to the element in the parentheses.

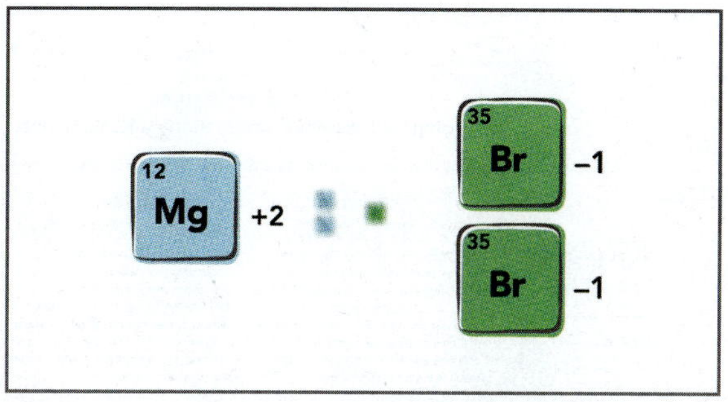

Animation: Predicting Bond Type

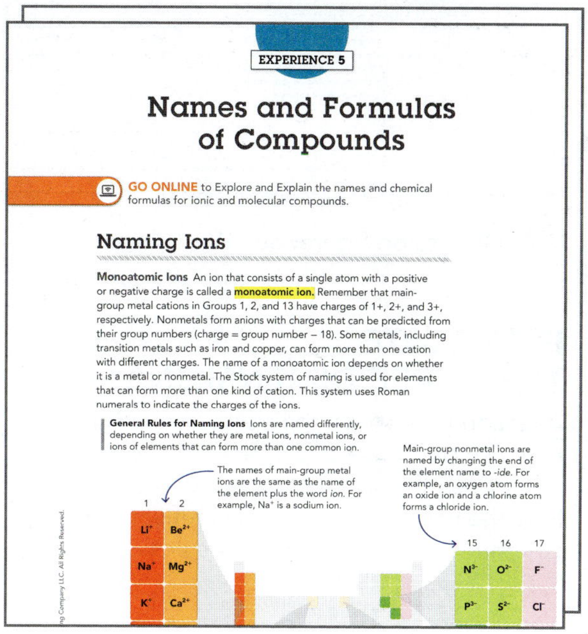

EXPERIENCE 5

Names and Formulas of Compounds

GO ONLINE to Explore and Explain the names and chemical formulas for ionic and molecular compounds.

Naming Ions

Monoatomic Ions An ion that consists of a single atom with a positive or negative charge is called a **monoatomic ion.** Remember that main-group metal cations in Groups 1, 2, and 13 have charges of 1+, 2+, and 3+, respectively. Nonmetals form anions with charges that can be predicted from their group numbers (charge = group number – 18). Some metals, including transition metals such as iron and copper, can form more than one cation with different charges. The name of a monoatomic ion depends on whether it is a metal or nonmetal. The Stock system of naming is used for elements that can form more than one kind of cation. This system uses Roman numerals to indicate the charges of the ions.

General Rules for Naming Ions Ions are named differently, depending on whether they are metal ions, nonmetal ions, or ions of elements that can form more than one common ion.

Experience Notebook, pp. 97–105

eTEXT

ADDRESS PRECONCEPTIONS

Students often confuse empirical (simplest) formulas and molecular formulas. Explain that the subscripts in a molecular formula are not necessarily written in the smallest whole-number ratio of the atoms. For example, ethane is correctly represented by the formula C_2H_6 because the molecule actually contains two carbon atoms and six hydrogen atoms. It would be incorrect to represent ethane by its empirical formula, which is CH_3.

SAMPLE PROBLEM SUPPORT

While working through sample problems on identifying ionic and molecular compounds, point out that the first step is to determine whether the compound is ionic or molecular. Using a periodic table, ask students to explain how to make that determination. Next, review similarities in determining a formula from a name for both types of compounds, and then highlight differences, making sure students understand why those differences exist. Finally, do the same for determining a name from a chemical formula.

NAME ______________ DATE ________ CLASS ________

DISCUSSION RUBRIC

Compare Element Combinations and Nomenclat

Use this rubric to help you assess explanations of the difference in nomenclatures for mole

	EXEMPLARY Score the work 3 if:	ACCOMPLISHED Score the work 2 if:
Articulating the Explanation Student Score: ______ Teacher Score: ______	The differences in nomenclatures for molecular and ionic compounds are accurately and clearly described. The claim reveals that while the same elements can form different combinations of atoms in molecular compounds, there is only one way for ions to combine and result in a neutral compound.	The differences in nomenclatures are accurately and clearly described. An att is made to relate the nomenclatures to t fact that the same elements can form different molecular compounds through different covalent bonding, but there is c one way for ions to bond in order to resu a neutral compound.
Reasoning and Synthesis Student Score: ______ Teacher Score: ______	Reasoning includes the need to identify the number of atoms of each element in a molecule, while in ionic compounds it is only necessary to identify the charge of the cation and anion and make sure the ratio results in a net zero charge.	An attempt is made to explain why nomenclatures differ for molecular compounds and ionic compounds but is incomplete or incorrect, for example, by trying to use charges to explain how to r molecular compounds.
Extend the Knowledge Student Score: ______ Teacher Score: ______	The student is able to use the basic principles of ionic and molecular compounds to explain the nomenclatures of a wide variety of binary compounds, including expanding the rules to compounds not yet seen.	When new compounds are encountered student may have difficulty deciding on correct nomenclature rules to apply.

Discussion Interactive Worksheet

INTEGRATE THE THREE DIMENSIONS

As students work on their Discussion Rubrics, they use patterns [CCC-1] and the periodic table to construct an explanation [SEP-6] of how the names of compounds reflect to the structure [PS1.A] of their molecules.

NAME ______________ DATE ________ CLASS ________

ANALYZING DATA

Infer Rules for Naming Acids

Acids are a group of ionic compounds with unique properties. You can consider an acid to consist of an anion combined with as many hydrogen ions as needed to make the compound electrically neutral. Instead of following the normal conventions for naming ionic compounds, there are specific rules for the naming of acids.

Figure 1 shows the names and formulas for some common acids. **Figure 2** shows the names and formulas for some common anions.

Figure 1

Common Acids	
Formula	**Name**
HCl	hydrochloric acid
HBr	hydrobromic acid
HI	hydroiodic acid
H_2SO_4	sulfuric acid
H_2SO_3	sulfurous acid
HNO_3	nitric acid
HNO_2	nitrous acid
H_3PO_4	phosphoric acid
H_2CO_3	carbonic acid

Figure 2

Common Anions	
Formula	**Name**
Cl^-	chloride ion
Br^-	bromide ion
I^-	iodide ion
SO_4^{2-}	sulfate ion
SO_3^{2-}	sulfite ion
NO_3^-	nitrate ion
NO_2^-	nitrite ion
PO_4^{3-}	phosphate ion
CO_3^{2-}	carbonate ion

Analyzing Data Interactive Worksheet

PBL CONNECTION

In the Problem-Based Learning Experience, Minerals, Crystals, and Gems, students will explore minerals and their structures. Remind students to apply what they have learned about the names and formulas of compounds as they research minerals.

ELABORATE

Compare Element Combinations and Nomenclature

Discussion Rubric Students revisit the claims they made in the CER activity about differences in nomenclatures for molecular and ionic compounds. They revise their claims after discussing them with peers.

- Place students in groups of four. Give students 5 minutes to look over their CERs and make any revisions they would like to make.
- Tell students to take turns presenting their CER statements to their group members.
- After hearing their group's presentations, give students 5 minutes to critique their own CERs, using the rubric as a scoring guide to evaluate their claims about the naming of molecular and ionic compounds.

Remind students that they should aim to devise a concrete, answerable question [SEP-1], as well as identify evidence and refer to it while clearly stating the reasoning behind their claim and revisions [SEP-7]. Also, remind students that they will be assessed on the accuracy of their self-evaluation.

Infer Rules for Naming Acids

Analyzing Data In this activity, students identify patterns [CCC-1] in the names and formulas of acids. They construct explanations [SEP-6] for these patterns and devise their own rules for naming compounds, based on the analysis of data [SEP-4] provided.

- Have students identify relationships between the ion and the acid name (i.e., hydrochloric acid and chloride ion).
- Prepare a short list of other acids and ions. Pair students and tell them to name and/or give the formula for the acids.
- Allow students to work independently to draft rules for naming acids. Invite several students to share one part of their rules with the class.

ASSESS ON THE SPOT

Call on students to finish these sentences:

- If an acid is diatomic, its name begins with _____.
- If the acid is formed from an ion with a name that ends with *-ate*, its name is formed by _____.
- If the acid is formed from an ion with a name that ends with *-ite*, the acid name is formed by _____.

PROFESSIONAL DEVELOPMENT

Science and Engineering Notebooks Have your students contribute to their science notebooks by recording at least one thought or question about naming and formulas of compounds each day for a week. Provide students an opportunity each day to share thoughts or ask questions from their notebooks. At the end of the designated period, lead a discussion about how recording thoughts and questions in the notebook enhanced their science learning and allowed them to better see differences in naming ionic and molecular compounds.

EVALUATE

Names and Formulas of Compounds

Quiz Assign the quiz in online technology-enhanced, auto-graded format or as an editable quiz worksheet. Use the scoring notes and remediation strategies found online to assess students' responses and to provide targeted feedback for each item to remediate well before assigning the summative 3-D Assessment.

REMEDIATION SUGGESTIONS

- **If** students are struggling to articulate patterns in the naming of ionic and molecular compounds, **then** ask them to return to the charts in the Analyzing Data activity Infer Rules for Naming Compounds and list shared characteristics they see.
- **If** students find it difficult to explain why names of molecular compounds need number prefixes but those of ionic compounds do not, **then** tell them to review the animation, Predicting Bond Type.
- **If** students are having difficulty with naming rules for acids, **then** tell them to sketch a flowchart that reflects patterns they see in the naming examples given in the Infer Rules for Naming Acids activity.

Revisit INVESTIGATIVE PHENOMENON

Support Reflection Students can complete the reflection prompt, where they will apply what they learned to the Investigative Phenomenon, based on practices and understandings that have been reinforced over the course of the experience.

- Give students a few minutes to work on their own to answer the reflection prompt. Then, as a class, discuss their responses. Review why Roman numerals are used in the formula for fayalite, but they are not used in the formula for fosterite.
- Lead a discussion on how having knowledge about how to name compounds allows you to gain additional knowledge about the properties of different compounds. Extend the discussion to naming and properties of metals and gems.

Evaluate and Revise Your CER Argument Have students answer Questions 3 and 4 in the CER activity and reevaluate the claim they made. Students should add any additional evidence they have collected in this investigation and revise their CER. Evidence may include that metal and nonmetal ions are named based on the property of charges.

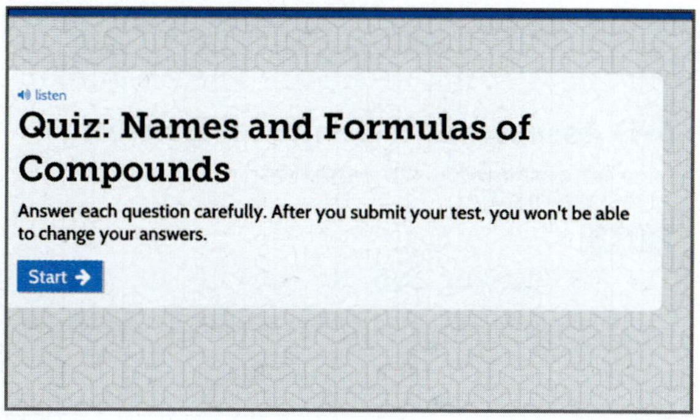

Interactive Online Quiz

Quiz Interactive Worksheet

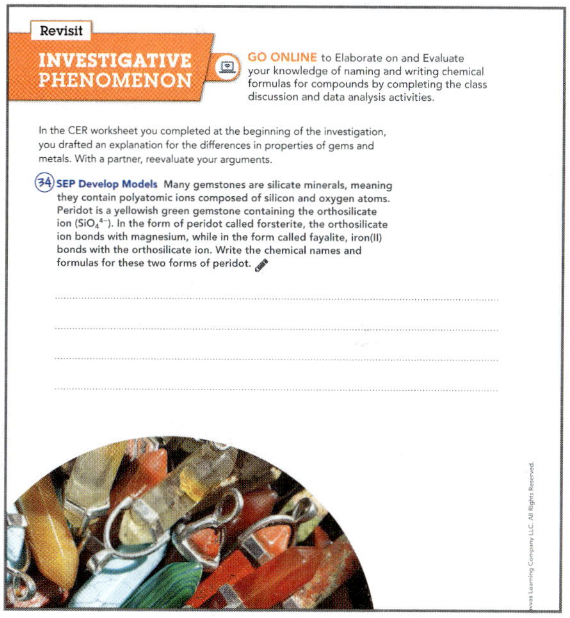
Revisit
INVESTIGATIVE PHENOMENON

GO ONLINE to Elaborate on and Evaluate your knowledge of naming and writing chemical formulas for compounds by completing the class discussion and data analysis activities.

In the CER worksheet you completed at the beginning of the investigation, you drafted an explanation for the differences in properties of gems and metals. With a partner, reevaluate your arguments.

34 **SEP Develop Models** Many gemstones are silicate minerals, meaning they contain polyatomic ions composed of silicon and oxygen atoms. Peridot is a yellowish green gemstone containing the orthosilicate ion (SiO_4^{4-}). In the form of peridot called forsterite, the orthosilicate ion bonds with magnesium, while in the form called fayalite, iron(II) bonds with the orthosilicate ion. Write the chemical names and formulas for these two forms of peridot.

Experience Notebook, p. 106

eTEXT

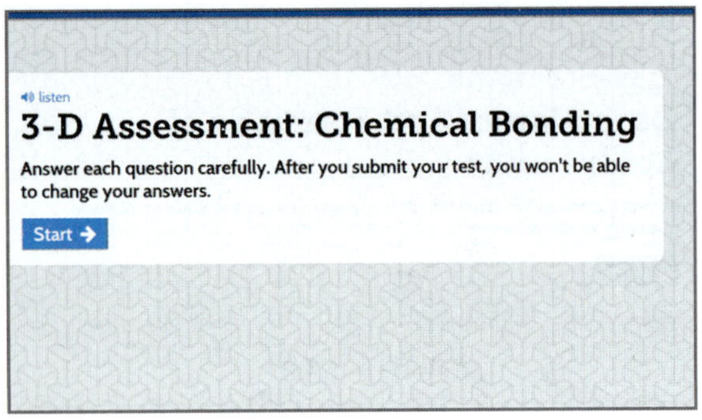

listen

3-D Assessment: Chemical Bonding

Answer each question carefully. After you submit your test, you won't be able to change your answers.

Start →

Interactive Online 3-D Assessment

Interactive ExamView 3-D Assessment

3-D Assessment Interactive Worksheet

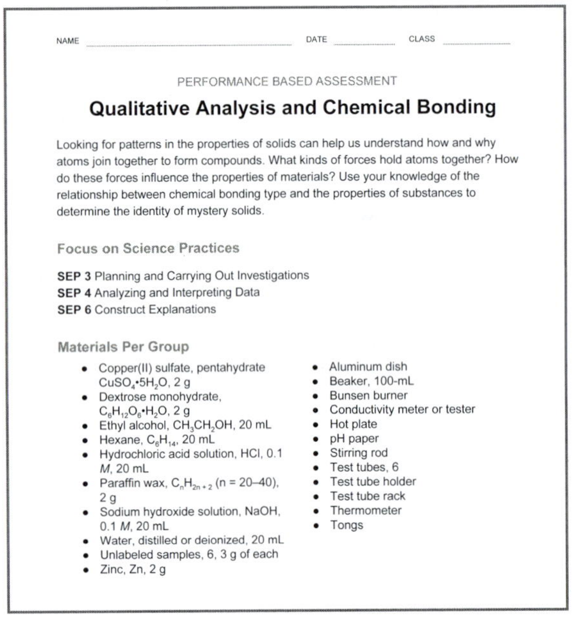

NAME ______ DATE ______ CLASS ______

PERFORMANCE BASED ASSESSMENT

Qualitative Analysis and Chemical Bonding

Looking for patterns in the properties of solids can help us understand how and why atoms join together to form compounds. What kinds of forces hold atoms together? How do these forces influence the properties of materials? Use your knowledge of the relationship between chemical bonding type and the properties of substances to determine the identity of mystery solids.

Focus on Science Practices

SEP 3 Planning and Carrying Out Investigations
SEP 4 Analyzing and Interpreting Data
SEP 6 Construct Explanations

Materials Per Group

- Copper(II) sulfate, pentahydrate $CuSO_4 \cdot 5H_2O$, 2 g
- Dextrose monohydrate, $C_6H_{12}O_6 \cdot H_2O$, 2 g
- Ethyl alcohol, CH_3CH_2OH, 20 mL
- Hexane, C_6H_{14}, 20 mL
- Hydrochloric acid solution, HCl, 0.1 *M*, 20 mL
- Paraffin wax, C_nH_{2n+2} (n = 20–40), 2 g
- Sodium hydroxide solution, NaOH, 0.1 *M*, 20 mL
- Water, distilled or deionized, 20 mL
- Unlabeled samples, 6, 3 g of each
- Zinc, Zn, 2 g
- Aluminum dish
- Beaker, 100-mL
- Bunsen burner
- Conductivity meter or tester
- Hot plate
- pH paper
- Stirring rod
- Test tubes, 6
- Test tube holder
- Test tube rack
- Thermometer
- Tongs

Performance-Based Assessment Interactive Worksheet

EVALUATE

Chemical Bonding

3-D Assessment For a summative assessment of Investigation 3, assign the 3-D Assessment, which is available online, as an ExamView bank, or as an editable worksheet.

Qualitative Analysis and Chemical Bonding

Performance-Based Assessment Use this Performance-Based Assessment to assess students' mastery of the standards. In this activity, students identify a group of unknown solids based on systematic testing of their physical and chemical properties [PS1.A]. The lab begins with an introductory activity to select measurable properties that will help identify the type of bonding in a solid. Given four solids that represent the four types of chemical bonds—ionic, polar covalent, nonpolar covalent, and metallic—students review the properties of each solid with a minimum of four tests. The results provide a basis for the design of a flow chart procedure to distinguish and identify a set of unknown solids and the types of chemical bonds that hold their atoms or constituent particles together in the solid state. They construct explanations [SEP-6] about trends [CCC-1] in melting point data and explain why some compounds have higher melting points than others. They conclude and evaluate [SEP-8] whether the compounds can conduct electricity. You may elect to have students skip the introductory activity if they have been sufficiently exposed to covalent, ionic and metallic bonding in previous exercises.

Expected Outcome Students understand how the type of chemical bonds in a compound affects that compound's physical and chemical properties. For example, students learn through experiment that ionic compounds are high-melting and conduct electricity in aqueous solution; that covalent compounds are low melting and do not conduct electricity; and that metallic compounds are high-melting and conductors of electricity in the solid state.

Safety Hexane and ethyl alcohol are flammable organic solvents and dangerous fire risks. Make sure students keep these away from flames, heat, and other sources of ignition. Remind students to cap the solvent bottles and work with hexane and ethyl alcohol in a fume hood or designated work area. Addition of a denaturant makes ethyl alcohol poisonous; it cannot be made nonpoisonous. Copper(II) sulfate is a skin and respiratory tract irritant and is toxic by ingestion. Graphite powder is a fire and inhalation risk. Dilute sodium hydroxide and acid solutions are irritating to skin and eyes. Remind students to avoid contact of all chemicals with their eyes and skin. Students should wear chemical splash goggles, chemical resistant gloves, and a chemical-resistant apron. Make sure students wash their hands thoroughly with soap and warm water before leaving the lab.

Experience Notebook (p. 107) After students complete the Performance-Based Assessment, have them complete the reflection prompt in the Experience Notebook.

DIFFERENTIATED INSTRUCTION

- **Support Less Proficient Readers** Some students might have difficulty writing and then reading their flowcharts in Part B of the procedure. Pair less proficient readers with a more advanced student to complete the Performance-Based Assessment.
- **Support Advanced Students** Have advanced students research the everyday usage and application of the four representative chemicals: copper(II) sulfate, dextrose, paraffin wax, and zinc. Students should relate how the bonding and physical properties of these chemicals make sense for the specific uses.

Revisit

ANCHORING PHENOMENON

What distinguishes the minerals in this mountain? (5)

Experience Notebook At the completion of Investigation 3, revisit the Anchoring Phenomenon question and have students think about how distinguishing minerals from one another is a problem that engineers seek to solve. Have them use the graphic organizer to define criteria and constraints of possible solutions.

Students should now have a better understanding of what distinguishes one mineral from another. Discuss with students why it is important to specifically distinguish minerals and not generally group them. Ask students to consider the properties and bonding of minerals. Ideas from this class discussion will be further explored in the Problem-Based Learning Experience.

PROFESSIONAL DEVELOPMENT

Develop Classroom Collaboration Organize students into small groups of three to four. Have students bring to class some rocks they have collected. If students do not have any rocks, then you can provide some to the groups. Ask groups to describe the physical properties of the rocks. Have groups use those properties to research the bonding and suspected naming of the rocks. Allow groups to present how they were able to use their observations and research to distinguish the different rocks from each other.

Minerals, Crystals, and Gemstones (40)

Problem-Based Learning Experience At the completion of Investigation 3, students develop their knowledge of crystal structures and colors. First, they explore the colors of elements when they are in ions in water solutions. Then they explore the colors of elements of the periodic table when they are included in crystals and gems. Finally, students explore crystal structures and then grow crystals of their own. They observe the growth of their crystals, compare their crystals with a pure crystal, and explain why the crystals formed.

As this research project will include many beautiful colored photos and crystals, students are asked to consider whether they would like to present their research throughout this project as a Web page, computer-based presentation, or poster.

- Some students may have difficulty completing all four parts in a timely manner. Assist them in completing one of the parts, or have them work with a partner to complete one or more parts.
- As an extension to this PBL, consider taking students on a field trip to a crystal museum or a museum of natural history with a display of minerals. Some museums and universities also have digital images of minerals.

Storylines 1 and 2 (90)

Benchmark 3-D Assessment For a summative assessment of Storylines 1 and 2, assign the Benchmark 3-D Assessment, which is available online, as an ExamView bank, or as an editable worksheet.

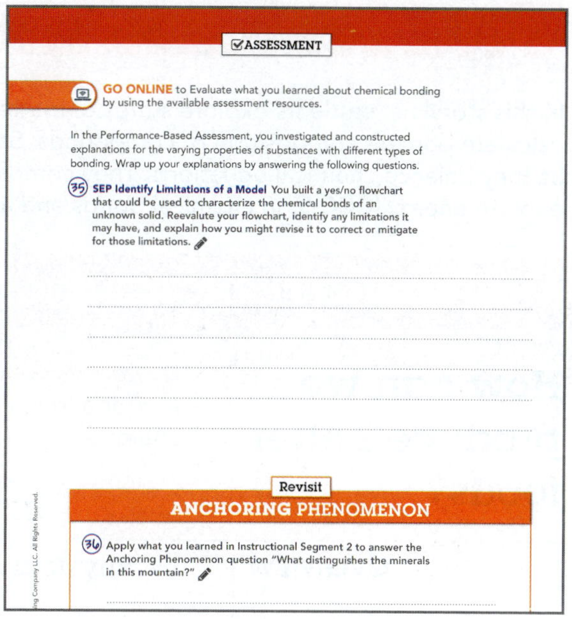
ASSESSMENT

GO ONLINE to Evaluate what you learned about chemical bonding by using the available assessment resources.

In the Performance-Based Assessment, you investigated and constructed explanations for the varying properties of substances with different types of bonding. Wrap up your explanations by answering the following questions.

35 SEP Identify Limitations of a Model You built a yes/no flowchart that could be used to characterize the chemical bonds of an unknown solid. Reevaluate your flowchart, identify any limitations it may have, and explain how you might revise it to correct or mitigate for those limitations.

Revisit

ANCHORING PHENOMENON

36 Apply what you learned in Instructional Segment 2 to answer the Anchoring Phenomenon question "What distinguishes the minerals in this mountain?"

Experience Notebook, p. 107

eTEXT

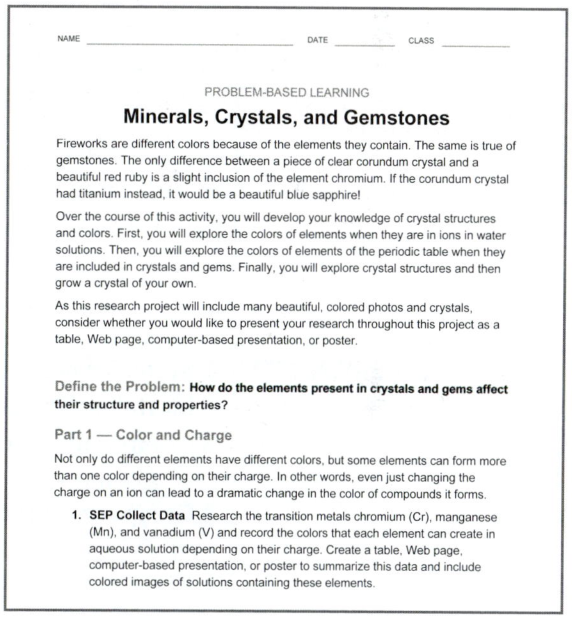
NAME ______ DATE ______ CLASS ______

PROBLEM-BASED LEARNING

Minerals, Crystals, and Gemstones

Fireworks are different colors because of the elements they contain. The same is true of gemstones. The only difference between a piece of clear corundum crystal and a beautiful red ruby is a slight inclusion of the element chromium. If the corundum crystal had titanium instead, it would be a beautiful blue sapphire!

Over the course of this activity, you will develop your knowledge of crystal structures and colors. First, you will explore the colors of elements when they are in ions in water solutions. Then, you will explore the colors of elements of the periodic table when they are included in crystals and gems. Finally, you will explore crystal structures and then grow a crystal of your own.

As this research project will include many beautiful, colored photos and crystals, consider whether you would like to present your research throughout this project as a table, Web page, computer-based presentation, or poster.

Define the Problem: **How do the elements present in crystals and gems affect their structure and properties?**

Part 1 — Color and Charge

Not only do different elements have different colors, but some elements can form more than one color depending on their charge. In other words, even just changing the charge on an ion can lead to a dramatic change in the color of compounds it forms.

1. **SEP Collect Data** Research the transition metals chromium (Cr), manganese (Mn), and vanadium (V) and record the colors that each element can create in aqueous solution depending on their charge. Create a table, Web page, computer-based presentation, or poster to summarize this data and include colored images of solutions containing these elements.

Problem-Based Learning Experience Interactive Worksheet

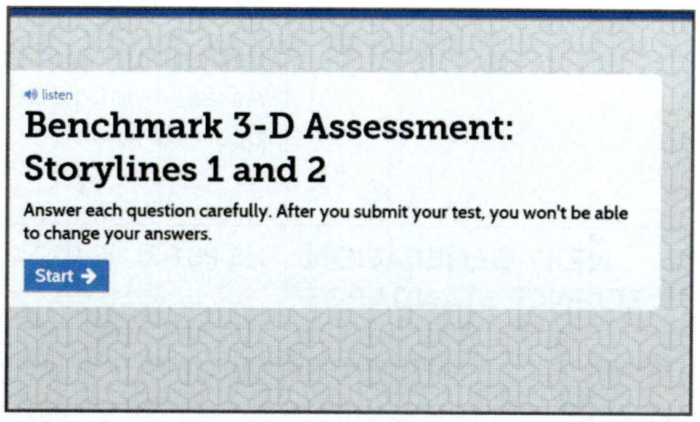

Interactive Benchmark 3-D Assessment

Understanding Chemical Reactions

In this storyline, students explore states of matter and phase changes. They investigate molar relationships and calculate percent composition of compounds. Students analyze different types of chemical reactions [PS1.B] as they balance chemical equations. They complete chemical calculations on moles, mass, and volume. They explore energy [CCC-5] in chemical bonds and analyze enthalpy in changes of state.

ANCHORING PHENOMENON

How can we produce better foods?

Designing Solutions Students design solutions to make better foods. As students investigate matter and energy and apply it toward designing food, they develop understandings about chemical reactions, how to quantify matter, and various properties of materials.

	INVESTIGATION 4	INVESTIGATION 5
OVERVIEW	**Physical Properties of Materials** **13.4 days** Students discover the structure and attractive forces of solids, liquids, and gases. They compare ionic and molecular compounds and metals and nonmetals. They investigate bonding and surface tension of water in aqueous systems.	**Chemical Quantities** **9.5 days** Students measure and count matter and moles and investigate the relationship between moles, mass, and volume. Students calculate percent composition and determine empirical and molecular formulas of compounds. They practice calculating molarity.
INVESTIGATIVE PHENOMENON†	How do we design materials for a specific function?	Why do we quantify matter in different ways?
CONNECTION TO THE ANCHORING PHENOMENON	Students identify properties of different states of matter and use this to better produce materials and foods.	Students use their knowledge of molar and mass relationships to explain how to quantify different types of matter and to apply these calculations to producing better foods.
EXPERIENCES‡	1 **States of Matter** (2 days), pp. 112–124 2 **Modeling Phase Changes** (2 days), pp. 125–135 3 **Comparing Ionic and Molecular Compounds** (2 days), pp. 136–140 4 **Comparing Metals and Nonmetals** (2 days), pp. 141–147 5 **Water and Aqueous Systems** (2 days), pp. 148–160 6 **Properties of Solutions** (2 days), pp. 161–170	1 **The Mole Concept** (2 days), pp. 174–182 2 **Molar Relationships** (2 days), pp. 183–191 3 **Percent Composition and Empirical Formulas** (2 days), pp. 192–202 4 **Concentrations of Solutions** (2 days), pp. 203–212
INVESTIGATION EVALUATION§	**Performance-Based Assessment** Road Deicers **3-D Assessment** Physical Properties of Materials **Experience Notebook** Performance-Based Assessment, p. 171; **Appendix C** Problem Bank, pp. R13–R14	**Performance-Based Assessment** Analysis of Basic Copper Carbonate **3-D Assessment** Chemical Quantities **Experience Notebook** Performance-Based Assessment, p. 213; **Appendix C** Problem Bank, pp. R14–R15
NEXT GENERATION SCIENCE STANDARDS	HS-PS1-3, HS-PS2-4, HS-PS3-5	HS-PS1-7

*Pacing for Encounter Anchoring Phenomenon core instruction is a half-day.
†Pacing for Encounter Investigative Phenomenon core instruction is a half-day per Investigation.
‡Pacing for each Experience includes the Experience Notebook and core instructional activities.
§Pacing for core Investigation Assessment is approximately 1 day per Investigation.

GOT MORE TIME? Personalize and enhance your instructional plan by assigning the activities with the got-more-time icon, as time allows.

Anchoring Phenomenon Video Food as Fuel*

Experience Notebook Inquiry Launch, p. 108*

Problem-Based Learning Experience The Chemistry of Cooking and the Properties of Baked Goods

INVESTIGATION 6	INVESTIGATION 7	INVESTIGATION 8
Chemical Reactions **7.5 days** Students explore types of chemical reactions and balance their equations. They predict the products of reactions.	**Stoichiometry** **8 days** Students quantify and interpret balanced equations. They complete molar calculations. They explore limiting and excess reagents and determine percent and theoretical yields.	**Thermochemistry** **8 days** Students explore enthalpy of a system and the need for activation energy. They apply Hess's law while calculating enthalpy of fusion, solidification, vaporization, and condensation.
How is energy obtained from chemical reactions?	What can make a recipe fail?	Why do you get hot when you exercise?
Students explain how energy is obtained from chemical reactions using knowledge of the different types of reactions. They apply this knowledge while explaining chemical reactions in food and how to produce better foods.	Students apply knowledge of limiting and excess reagents to explain why a recipe fails. They also explain limiting and excess ingredients in foods.	Students use knowledge of system enthalpy to explain why we get hot when we exercise. They further apply this to enthalpy of foods and how to change it.
1 **Modeling Chemical Reactions** (2 days), pp. 216–226 2 **Predicting Outcomes of Chemical Reactions** (2 days), pp. 227–240 3 **Reactions in Aqueous Solution** (2 days), pp. 241–248	1 **Quantifying Reactants and Products** (2 days), pp. 252–258 2 **Chemical Calculations** (2.5 days), pp. 259–268 3 **Limiting Reagent and Percent Yield** (2 days), pp. 269–278	1 **Energy in Chemical Bonds** (2.5 days), pp. 282–290 2 **Enthalpies of Formation and Reaction** (2 days), pp. 291–298 3 **Enthalpy in Changes of State** (2 days), pp. 299–306
Performance-Based Assessment Identify Evidence of Chemical Reactions **3-D Assessment** Chemical Reactions **Experience Notebook** Performance-Based Assessment, p. 249; **Appendix C** Problem Bank, pp. R15–R16	**Performance-Based Assessment** The Stoichiometry of Filling a Balloon **3-D Assessment** Stoichiometry **Experience Notebook** Performance-Based Assessment, p. 279; **Appendix C** Problem Bank, pp. R17–R19	**Performance-Based Assessment** Enthalpy of a Neutralization Reaction **3-D Assessment** Thermochemistry **Experience Notebook** Performance-Based Assessment, p. 307; **Revisit Anchoring Phenomenon**, p. 307; **Appendix C** Problem Bank, pp. R19–R21
HS-PS1-2, HS-PS1-4, HS-PS1-5, HS-PS1-7	HS-PS1-7	HS-PS1-4, HS-PS1-5, HS-PS1-7

STORYLINE ASSESSMENT

Problem-Based Learning Experience The Chemistry of Cooking and the Properties of Baked Goods

Benchmark 3-D Assessment Storylines 1 and 2

STORYLINE 2

Understanding Chemical Reactions

Teacher Background

The properties of any kind of matter, including the food we eat, can be explained in terms of its atoms and molecules and the attractions and repulsions of electric charges within and between them. Atoms are constantly in motion, and the motion varies depending on the substance they form and its state (solid, liquid, or gas). The motion of atoms and how they interact is affected by temperature and pressure.

Many substances react chemically with other substances to form new substances with different properties. All chemical reactions involve changes in bond energies. Some chemical reactions release energy and others require an energy input. Chemical reactions and energy transfers can be explained by the collision of molecules and the rearrangement of atoms. The conservation of mass and the chemical properties of the elements involved can be used to predict chemical reactions. Chemical processes and the properties of materials are the foundation of many biological and geophysical phenomena.

Points of Integration

In this Storyline, links are made across the domains of physical science, Earth and space science, and engineering design.

Earth and Space Science As you discuss modeling phase changes in Investigation 4, use the real-world example of the phases of water on Earth [ESS2.C]. Water can be found in the atmosphere as vapor, ice crystals, or precipitation; on land as liquid; and on mountains as snow and ice. Earth and the Earth's atmosphere act as a closed system where the energy and matter [CCC-5] are conserved. Remind students that this means that the same atoms that are in the atmosphere as water vapor will someday fall to the Earth as precipitation, freeze at the top of a mountain, melt, and flow down a river to the ocean.

Engineering Design As you are discussing alloys, students take part in the engineering design process when they are asked to think about designing a bicycle frame [ETS1.A] and to evaluate rope materials to determine which material will function best [ETS1.B] at the top of mountains.

ENCOUNTER

ANCHORING PHENOMENON

How can we produce better foods?

Every food we eat is a product of chemical reactions. Chemical reactions cause seeds to germinate, all plant parts to form, animals to grow and reproduce, and eggs to form. They determine how long foods remain fresh and how safe they are. The chemical reactions that take place in our foods determine what nutrients are in different foods and how long nutrients remain available in the foods. They are responsible for how our foods taste.

Food chemistry deals with how foods change when they are cooked or preserved and how we can enhance or prevent the changes from happening. Good chefs understand the chemistry behind the techniques they use to produce their own recipes. Make chemistry more relative to students by incorporating examples from foods or cooking techniques when discussing chemical reactions.

RELATED PHENOMENA

In addition to preparing food, consider using other phenomena as anchoring events for this storyline.

- **Space Food** Search on the Internet to find videos about how foods are prepared and preserved for astronauts. Discuss which of the techniques involve chemical changes.
- **Maillard Reaction** Display several different kinds of foods, such as fresh and canned fruits and vegetables, a slice of bread, some cooked meat, and cheese. Ask students which foods are the result of chemical reactions.

Food as Fuel

Anchoring Phenomenon Video As students watch the Anchoring Phenomenon Video, ask them to record any questions they may have. Have them turn to a partner and discuss the video.

- **Ask** What is happening to the properties of the marshmallow? (The properties are changing; the marshmallow changes from white to black.)
- **Ask** Do you think the white marshmallow and the black marshmallow are the same material with the same chemical composition? (No, they are different materials with different chemical compositions.)
- **Ask** What happened to cause this change? (A chemical reaction [combustion] is producing a new substance.)

Students will revisit this phenomenon at the end of the storyline to demonstrate their understanding of it.

Inquiry Launch

Experience Notebook Use the classroom discussion from the Anchoring Phenomenon Video activity to discuss the photo on pages 108 and 109. Have student pairs make a two-column chart with these titles for the two column heads: *Chemical Change* and *Physical Change*. Instruct students to list in each column as many examples of food changes taking place in the photo as they can. Have student pairs share their completed lists with the class. Then lead a discussion about the advantage for a chef of having knowledge of food chemistry.

- **Ask** Do you think an understanding of chemistry would help these chefs? Why or why not?
- **Ask** What types of information might a chef need to prepare a perfect meal?
- **Ask** What questions do you think a chef would need and want answered to properly prepare a meal?

The Chemistry of Cooking and the Properties of Baked Goods

Problem-Based Learning Experience Students prepare a leaflet on baking with substitutions for people with allergies or health concerns. They choose a common ingredient found in baked goods, identify the chemical composition of the ingredient and the role the ingredient plays in the final product, and then research a possible substitute for the ingredient. In Part 2, They design and test a recipe using the substituted ingredient. In Part 3, students find the amount of kilocalories in each ingredient they used and calculate the number of kilocalories in a serving of the original recipe and their new recipe.

- **Safety** Before any food is brought into the classroom, check whether any students have allergies to any of the ingredients. Students that have food allergies should be excused from class that day. Prompt students to wear safety goggles and heat-resistant gloves when cooking food. Monitor students closely while handling objects that are hot. Remind students that they cannot eat or drink anything in the lab.
- You may wish to assign a specific ingredient to each group in Part 1 so that all ingredients are analyzed.
- Guide struggling students through the conversions and calculations in Parts 2 and 3.
- Provide students an alternative option to make their leaflet after they complete the other questions in Parts 1–3.
- After the activity, have groups present their leaflets to the class.

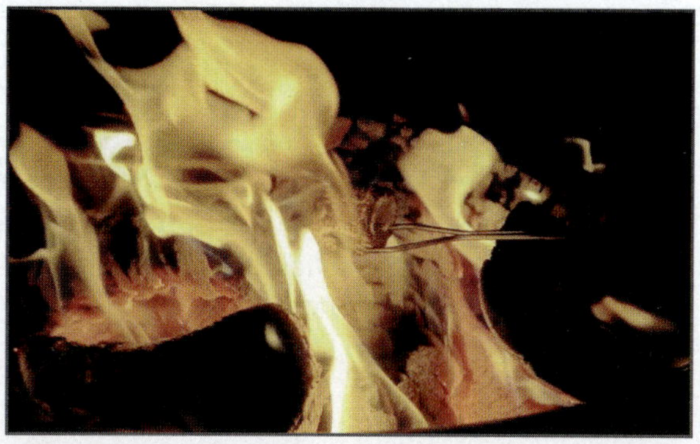

Anchoring Phenomenon Video: Food as Fuel

Experience Notebook, pp. 108–109

eTEXT

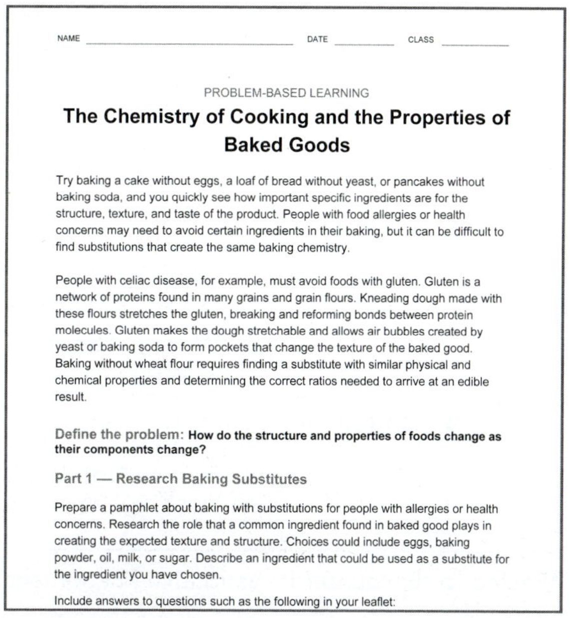

NAME ______ DATE ______ CLASS ______

PROBLEM-BASED LEARNING

The Chemistry of Cooking and the Properties of Baked Goods

Try baking a cake without eggs, a loaf of bread without yeast, or pancakes without baking soda, and you quickly see how important specific ingredients are for the structure, texture, and taste of the product. People with food allergies or health concerns may need to avoid certain ingredients in their baking, but it can be difficult to find substitutions that create the same baking chemistry.

People with celiac disease, for example, must avoid foods with gluten. Gluten is a network of proteins found in many grains and grain flours. Kneading dough made with these flours stretches the gluten, breaking and reforming bonds between protein molecules. Gluten makes the dough stretchable and allows air bubbles created by yeast or baking soda to form pockets that change the texture of the baked good. Baking without wheat flour requires finding a substitute with similar physical and chemical properties and determining the correct ratios needed to arrive at an edible result.

Define the problem: **How do the structure and properties of foods change as their components change?**

Part 1 — Research Baking Substitutes

Prepare a pamphlet about baking with substitutions for people with allergies or health concerns. Research the role that a common ingredient found in baked good plays in creating the expected texture and structure. Choices could include eggs, baking powder, oil, milk, or sugar. Describe an ingredient that could be used as a substitute for the ingredient you have chosen.

Include answers to questions such as the following in your leaflet:

PBL Experience Interactive Worksheet

Physical Properties of Materials

In this investigation, students deepen their understanding of structures and functions [CCC-6] of matter through a study of physical properties of materials [PS1.A]. Students investigate and develop system models [CCC-4] of intermolecular forces, bond energies and melting points, solubility and pressure, as well as other related phenomena.

INVESTIGATIVE PHENOMENON

How do we design materials for a specific function?

Explaining Phenomena In order to fully understand the phenomenon of designing materials for a specific function, students must explore the specifics of states of matter, phase changes, metals and nonmetals, aqueous systems, and solution properties. As students develop the ability to analyze and model phase changes, conductivity, and surface tension and polarity they determine the functions of materials.

	EXPERIENCE 1	EXPERIENCE 2	EXPERIENCE 3
	States of Matter **2 days** Students describe three states of matter—gases, liquids, and solids. They explain behaviors of gases with changes in temperature, pressure, and volume. They relate intermolecular forces and the states of matter.	**Modeling Phase Changes** **2 days** Students investigate the behavior of particles in the different states of matter. They relate variations in kinetic energy among particles to constant evaporation and condensation. They interpret phase diagrams.	**Comparing Ionic and Molecular Compounds** **2 days** Students differentiate between the representative units of ionic and molecular compounds. They relate the properties of molecular and ionic compounds to the internolecular forces and bonds between their particles.
CONNECTION TO THE INVESTIGATIVE PHENOMENON	Students draw a model for the energy of gases at different altitudes and relate that to the phenomenon of designing materials for a specific function.	Students explain why boiling point changes as altitude changes and relate that to the phenomenon of designing materials for a specific function.	Students investigate using ionic or molecular compounds when designing a hand warmer and relate what they learn to designing materials for a specific function.
ENGAGE	**Teacher Guide** Everyday Phenomenon Frozen Solid, p. 112	**Teacher Guide** Everyday Phenomenon Melting Ice, p. 119	**Teacher Guide** Everyday Phenomenon Sweet and Salty, p. 125
EXPLORE	**Inquiry Lab** Correlate Material Properties and Bond Type **Virtual Lab** States of Matter +	**Inquiry Lab** Measure the Energy of a Phase Change **Analyzing Data** Analyze Phase Diagrams +	**Inquiry Lab** Melt Ionic and Covalent Compounds **Virtual Lab** Tough Tools +
EXPLAIN	**Claim-Evidence-Reasoning** Relate Intermolecular Forces to States of Matter **Experience Notebook,** pp. 112–123	**Modeling** Phase Changes and Intermolecular Forces **Animation** Phase Transitions and Particle Motion + **Experience Notebook,** pp. 125–134	**Claim-Evidence-Reasoning** Discuss Melting Materials **Experience Notebook,** pp. 136–140
ELABORATE	**Discussion Rubric** Relate Intermolecular Forces and States of Matter **Writing About Science** States of Water +	**Peer Review Rubric** Phase Change and Intermolecular Forces Model Review **Analyzing Data** Phase Change Graphs +	**Discussion Rubric** Melting Materials **Engineering Design Challenge** Abrasive Compounds +
EVALUATE	**Quiz** States of Matter **Experience Notebook** Revisit Investigative Phenomenon, p. 124	**Quiz** Modeling Phase Changes **Experience Notebook** Revisit Investigative Phenomenon, p. 135	**Quiz** Comparing Ionic and Molecular Compounds **Experience Notebook** Revisit Investigative Phenomenon, p. 140

*Pacing for Encounter Investigative Phenomenon core instruction is a half-day.

†Pacing for core Investigation Assessment is approximately 1 day.

GOT MORE TIME? Personalize and enhance your instructional plan by assigning the activities with the got-more-time icon, as time allows.

Investigative Phenomenon Video Subzero Properties*

Claim-Evidence-Reasoning Discuss the Investigative Phenomenon*

Experience Notebook, p. 110*

Authentic Reading Charging Ahead: The Future of Batteries

Virtual Reality Experience

EXPERIENCE 4	EXPERIENCE 5	EXPERIENCE 6
Comparing Metals and Nonmetals **2 days** Students explore delocalized electrons and their relationship to metallic properties. They identify the defining properties of metals and compare metals and nonmetals and explain their differences.	**Water and Aqueous Systems** **2 days** Students investigate polarity in hydrogen bonding between water molecules and how this bonding affects surface tension, boiling point, and the formation of ice. They model solvation within an aquous solution.	**Properties of Solutions** **2 days** Students investigate the role of temperature and surface area in the formation of solutions. They interpret solubility curves and factors that affect the solubility of a substance.
Students design a rope system using knowledge of metal strength and malleability and use this to refine explanations on designing materials for a specific function.	Students describe how fabric could be designed to keep water out and let air circulate and use this to refine explanations on designing materials for a specific function.	Students design a solution for emergency treatment of AMS at high altitude and use what they learn to refine explanations on designing materials for a specific function.
Teacher Guide Everyday Phenomenon Wrapping It Up, p. 132	**Teacher Guide** Everyday Phenomenon Hydrophobic Water Drops, p. 138	**Teacher Guide** Everyday Phenomenon Fun With Salt, p. 145
Inquiry Lab Modeling Metals, Ceramics, and Polymers **Analyzing Data** Metals and Nonmetals: Data About Their Properties	**Inquiry Lab** Investigate Surface Tension **Analyzing Data** The Density of Freezing Salt Water	**Inquiry Lab** Aqueous Solutions **Interactivity** Dissolution Rate
Claim-Evidence-Reasoning Make a Claim About Extruded Materials **Animation** Metallic Solids and Covalent Network Solids **Experience Notebook,** pp. 141–147	**Modeling** Model Surface Tension and Polarity **Animation** Intermolecular Forces and Surface Tension in Water **Experience Notebook,** pp. 148–159	**Modeling** Model Concentration's Effect on Conductivity **Experience Notebook,** pp. 161–169
Discussion Rubric Differences Between Metals and Nonmetals **Engineering Design Challenge** Building a Better Bike	**Peer Review Rubric** Evaluate Surface Tension–Polarity Models **Analyzing Data** Compare Intermolecular Forces in Fresh and Salt Water	**Peer Review Rubric** Ionic Concentration and Conductivity Modeling Rubric **Writing About Science** Solubility and Temperature
Quiz Comparing Metals and Nonmetals **Experience Notebook** Revisit Investigative Phenomenon, p. 147	**Quiz** Water and Aqueous Systems **Experience Notebook** Revisit Investigative Phenomenon, p. 160	**Quiz** Properties of Solutions **Experience Notebook** Revisit Investigative Phenomenon, p. 170

INVESTIGATION ASSESSMENT

Performance-Based Assessment Road Deicers†

3-D Assessment Physical Properties of Materials†

Experience Notebook Performance-Based Assessment, p. 171; Revisit Anchoring Phenomenon, p. 171†; **Appendix C** Problem Bank, pp. R13–R14

INVESTIGATION 4

Physical Properties of Materials

Teacher Background

Introduce this investigation with a discussion about how students think materials are designed for a specific purpose. Stress that the physical properties of materials are important factors in how materials can be used. A variety of factors affect the physical properties of materials, including melting point, boiling point, and surface tension. By comparing the structure of substances at the bulk scale, the strength of electrical forces between particles of the substances can be inferred. These particles include ions, atoms, molecules, and networked materials, such as graphite.

As you teach Investigation 4, provide opportunities for students to discuss how the concepts in the experiences are related. Encourage students to consider materials they use and the different ways in which they use them and how the properties of the materials are related to the concepts they investigate.

Learning Progression

In the beginning of this investigation, students explore how the structure of materials is related to the properties of materials [CCC-6] by first identifying how the arrangement of particles in solids, liquids, and gases are related to their properties [PS1.A]. As students investigate the relationship between the structure and properties of matter and how different types of interactions can impact these properties, students gain a deeper understanding about why molecular-level structure is important in the functioning of designed materials. They will have the opportunity to construct models [SEP-2] of phase changes and molecular bonds and of ions conducting electricity in water.

RELATED PHENOMENA

Consider using other materials-related phenomena to launch this investigation.

- **Why doesn't dry ice melt?** Have students observe some dry ice until a change in its size is obvious. **Ask** What happened to make this dry ice become smaller?
- **Glass Blowing** Show students a short video of a person blowing glass to form objects. Discuss how the properties of glass make it suitable for such a use.
- **Warm Solid Iodine** Place a few pieces of solid iodine in a 250-mL Erlenmeyer flask and add a rubber stopper. Gently warm the flask on a hot plate in a fume hood. A purple gas will form as the iodine sublimes. When the flask cools, solid iodine will deposit on the sides of the flask. **Ask:** Do you think the material that forms on the sides of the flask is the same as or different from the original material? Why?

TAKE IT LOCAL

Have students design materials that can be used to solve a local problem. Students should identify the specific problem and then describe the material they would use to solve it. They should include the criteria and restraints for the material and explain how their choices meet them.

ENCOUNTER

INVESTIGATIVE PHENOMENON

How do we design materials for a specific function?

Introduce this investigation with a discussion about how students think materials are designed for a specific purpose. Students explore the physical properties of solids, liquids, and gases (Experience 1) and the relationship between temperature and phase changes of materials (Experience 2). They determine compound types and the properties of ionic and molecular compounds (Experience 3). They explore specific properties of metal materials (Experience 4). They investigate hydrogen bonding and how structure affects properties of a solid (Experience 5). Finally, students explore properties of solutions, focusing on solubility and temperature (Experience 6).

Subzero Properties

Investigative Phenomenon Video Students can view the video as a class. Tell them to note any new facts they learn as they watch the video. Discuss how temperature influences the properties of materials, such as the banana was soft at room temp, but when it was placed in liquid nitrogen (−196°C), it became hard and brittle in the extreme cold. Transition to a discussion of how the conditions affecting material properties impact how we design material.

Charging Ahead: The Future of Batteries

Investigative Phenomenon Authentic Reading The Authentic Reading activity informs students about future improvements to lithium-ion batteries and the idea of engineering new types of batteries. Before students read the text, go over the diagram of the lithium-ion rechargeable battery. Lead them through the steps of charge and discharge, using the Professional Development notes. Assign the worksheet as an in-class assignment if time allows, or as homework. If desired, find an online video about battery improvements over time to help kick off the reading assignment.

PROFESSIONAL DEVELOPMENT

Explaining Phenomena The charging and discharge of a lithium-ion battery can be summarized in simple steps.

Charge Mechanism

- In the cathode, all lithium atoms are electrically neutral. An oxidation-reduction reaction at the cathode results in some negatively charged electrons.
- The resulting positively charged ions from the cathode are dissolved in the electrolyte. They travel to the anode.
- In the anode, the ions combine with electrons deposited by the connected wire and become electrically neutral.

Discharge Mechanism

- Lithium atoms in the anode are ionized and separated from their electrons. The released electrons flow through an external wire, providing electric current.
- The lithium ions pass through an electrolyte to the cathode.
- In the cathode, the ions combine with their electrons and again become electrically neutral.

Discuss the Phenomenon

Claim-Evidence-Reasoning Have students review the video and Authentic Reading activity to explain their understanding of the phenomenon they observed. To help build understanding of the phenomenon, brainstorm a list of questions about the observed phenomenon. Have students complete Question 1 of the CER worksheet and to start thinking about the evidence they need to answer their question.

Remind students that their understanding of the phenomenon will be incomplete at this stage, but that they will revisit this activity as they learn more. Make sure to provide students with an opportunity to revisit their CER arguments throughout the investigation as well as at the end of the investigation for further revision and peer review.

Reflect on the Phenomenon

Experience Notebook Transition to the questions on the opener page for Investigation 4 in the Experience Notebook. With students working in pairs, guide them through a discussion of the questions. Remind them they should reference the video, Authentic Reading activity, and CER activity to answer the questions. Invite student pairs to share their thoughts. Then, as a class, discuss how the reflection questions relate to the Investigative Phenomenon. **Ask** How do we design materials for a specific function?

Investigative Phenomenon Video: Subzero Properties

Authentic Reading

Authentic Reading Interactive Worksheet

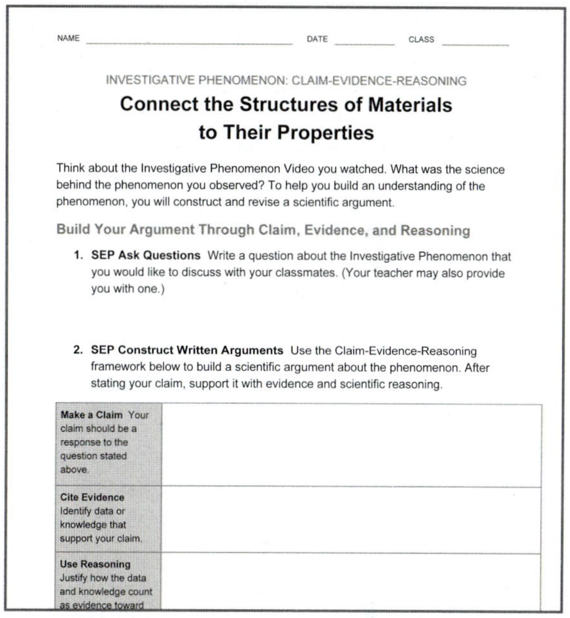

NAME ______ DATE ______ CLASS ______

INVESTIGATIVE PHENOMENON: CLAIM-EVIDENCE-REASONING

Connect the Structures of Materials to Their Properties

Think about the Investigative Phenomenon Video you watched. What was the science behind the phenomenon you observed? To help you build an understanding of the phenomenon, you will construct and revise a scientific argument.

Build Your Argument Through Claim, Evidence, and Reasoning

1. **SEP Ask Questions** Write a question about the Investigative Phenomenon that you would like to discuss with your classmates. (Your teacher may also provide you with one.)

2. **SEP Construct Written Arguments** Use the Claim-Evidence-Reasoning framework below to build a scientific argument about the phenomenon. After stating your claim, support it with evidence and scientific reasoning.

Make a Claim Your claim should be a response to the question stated above.	
Cite Evidence Identify data or knowledge that support your claim.	
Use Reasoning Justify how the data and knowledge count as evidence toward	

CER Interactive Worksheet

Experience Notebook, pp. 110–111

eTEXT

EXPERIENCE 1

States of Matter

Teacher Background

Experience 1 introduces students to the states of matter, focusing on solid, liquid, and gas. Students likely have been introduced to the concept of states of matter in earlier grades, and this experience builds on that knowledge. Students investigate the states of matter on both a physical and molecular level. They develop models for the kinetic theory of gases and for the influence of intermolecular forces on the state of a particular compound at room temperature.

Objectives

- **Investigate and describe three states of matter (solid, liquid, gas).**
- **Develop models to explain behaviors of gases with changes in temperature, pressure, and volume.**
- **Develop a model of intermolecular forces and use it to explain states of matter.**

RELATED PHENOMENA

In addition to the Frozen Solid teacher demo, consider using other phenomena to launch this experience.

- **Kettle Change** Place a tea kettle on a hot plate. When it begins to whistle, ask students to explain the phenomena in terms of state change.
- **Cooling Lava** Discuss the difference between hot flowing lava and the rocks that form when it cools. **Ask** What qualities change as the lava cools?

ENGAGE

EVERYDAY PHENOMENON

Why do solid water and solid carbon dioxide behave differently?

Use this teacher demo to prompt student discussion about the phase changes they observe. Note new ideas from students as they arise, and as students make their way through the Inquiry Lab, remind them of these ideas to help them answer questions.

Frozen Solid

Engage students with this demonstration of an everyday phenomenon to introduce the concept of phase change and its occurrence in everyday life.

Materials block of ice, block of dry ice, heat-resistant gloves to handle the dry ice, plates to rest each of the blocks on. If possible, let the block of ice melt a bit on its plate for 15 to 30 minutes before the presentation, depending on the size of the block.

1. Set out the plate with the block of ice on it. Ask students to note the appearance of the block. **Ask** Do you think it is the same size and shape as it was when it was first placed on the plate? If not, how and why has it changed? (No, the block of ice might be smaller and have a less defined shape because it's melting.)
2. Ask students to predict what will happen to the block of ice over time.
3. Using the heat-resistant gloves, place the block of dry ice on the other plate. **Ask** What do you observe? Is the shape of the block changing?
4. **Ask** What states of matter did you observe in this demo? (solid, liquid, gas)
5. Guide students through a discussion of why they think solid water and solid carbon dioxide might behave so differently at room temperature.
6. Ask students how they might plan an investigation to explore states of matter and state changes in everyday life. Use the ideas to transition to the Inquiry Lab.

EXPLORE

Correlate Material Properties and Bond Type

Inquiry Lab In this lab, students carry out an investigation [SEP-3] to determine if bulk properties [PS1.A] can be correlated to the types of bonds within a substance.

Lab Demo Video Watch the Lab Demo Video for advice on materials and preparation.

Choose Your Version Open-ended (O), Guided (G), Shortened (S), Advanced (A)

Materials 0.5 g aluminum granule, 2 mL ethanol, 5 mL hexane, 2 mL methanol, 5 mL canola oil, 0.2–0.3 g silicon dioxide, 0.2–0.3 g sodium chloride, 0.2–0.3 g stearic acid, 0.2–0.3 g sucrose, distilled or deionized water in a wash bottle, balance, 150-mL beaker, boiling stone, Bunsen burner, conductivity tester, hot plate, marking pen, 5 Beral-type pipettes, spatula, stirring rod, 7 small test tubes, test tube rack, test tube holder (clamp), 5 weighing dishes

Safety Tell students that hexane, methanol, and ethanol are flammable organic solvents and a dangerous fire risk. Keep away from flames, heat, and other sources of ignition. Make sure students cap the solvent bottles and work with them in a fume hood or designated work area. They should avoid contact of all chemicals with eyes and skin. Instruct students to wear chemical splash goggles and chemical-resistant gloves and apron. Remind students to wash their hands thoroughly with soap and warm water before leaving the lab.

Expected Outcome Students find that bonds can be broadly defined as ionic, metallic, covalent, and covalent-network. They also find that there are certain observable properties usually associated with each type of bonding.

Lab Summary Video Watch the Lab Summary Video for support on connecting the lab investigation to the Investigative Phenomenon.

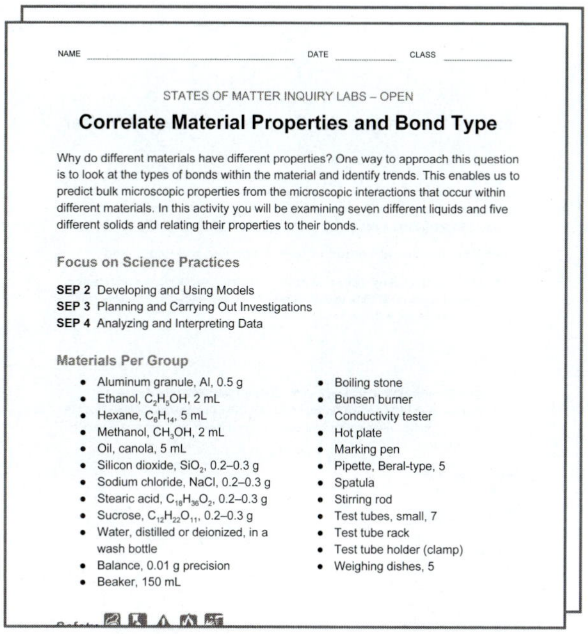

NAME ______ DATE ______ CLASS ______

STATES OF MATTER INQUIRY LABS – OPEN

Correlate Material Properties and Bond Type

Why do different materials have different properties? One way to approach this question is to look at the types of bonds within the material and identify trends. This enables us to predict bulk microscopic properties from the microscopic interactions that occur within different materials. In this activity you will be examining seven different liquids and five different solids and relating their properties to their bonds.

Focus on Science Practices

SEP 2 Developing and Using Models
SEP 3 Planning and Carrying Out Investigations
SEP 4 Analyzing and Interpreting Data

Materials Per Group

- Aluminum granule, Al, 0.5 g
- Ethanol, C_2H_5OH, 2 mL
- Hexane, C_6H_{14}, 5 mL
- Methanol, CH_3OH, 2 mL
- Oil, canola, 5 mL
- Silicon dioxide, SiO_2, 0.2–0.3 g
- Sodium chloride, NaCl, 0.2–0.3 g
- Stearic acid, $C_{18}H_{36}O_2$, 0.2–0.3 g
- Sucrose, $C_{12}H_{22}O_{11}$, 0.2–0.3 g
- Water, distilled or deionized, in a wash bottle
- Balance, 0.01 g precision
- Beaker, 150 mL
- Boiling stone
- Bunsen burner
- Conductivity tester
- Hot plate
- Marking pen
- Pipette, Beral-type, 5
- Spatula
- Stirring rod
- Test tubes, small, 7
- Test tube rack
- Test tube holder (clamp)
- Weighing dishes, 5

O/G/S/A Lab Interactive Worksheets

States of Matter

Virtual Lab In this lab, students carry out investigations [SEP-3] in a virtual heating chamber, noting and explaining how changes at the molecular level result in changes in structure [CCC-6] at the macroscopic level.

Expected Outcome Students identify three distinct states of matter—solid, liquid, and gas—and associate phase transitions with changes at the molecular level that lead to changes in physical properties.

- As a brief review, ask students to volunteer one new thing that they have learned so far about states of matter. Write student contributions on the board or other place where all students can see.
- Explain to students that they will be investigating changes in nitrogen, which in its natural state is a gas on Earth and a solid on the surface of Pluto. They will look at some properties of nitrogen in its various states.
- Before students begin the lab, go over the virtual interface and be sure that all students understand how the lab works.
- Advise students to make notes in their science notebooks about their observations during the lab. Encourage them to draw pictures with either captions or labels.

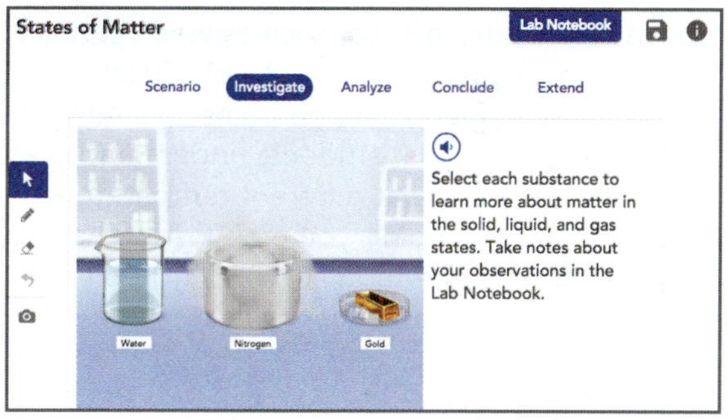

Virtual Lab: States of Matter

ASSESS ON THE SPOT

Assess students' understanding of the states of matter by having them consider a burning candle. **Ask** How are the three states of matter involved when a candle burns? (Solid wax has a definite shape and volume; the melted wax is shapeless and runs down the candle; the vapor that forms above the wick has no shape.)

INTEGRATE THE THREE DIMENSIONS

In this Virtual Lab students carry out an investigation to discover the relationship between the properties of the states of matter [PS1.A]. They build a scientific argument about the phenomena and support it with evidence [SEP-7]. They explain how a material's state is affected [CCC-2] by the structure of the material's particles.

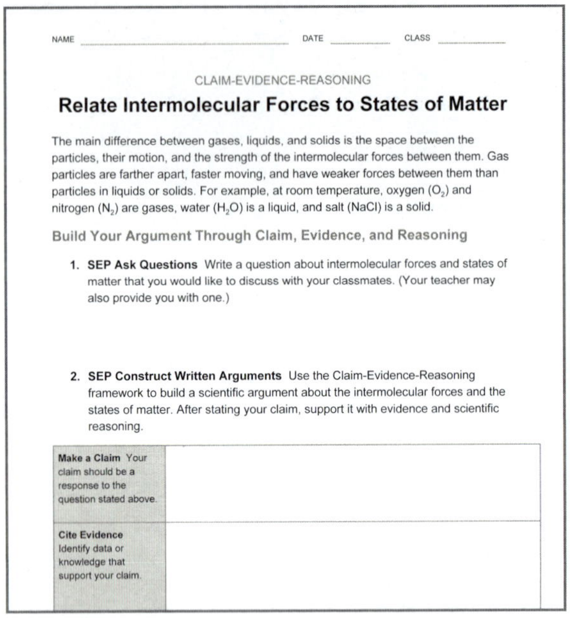

NAME ____________ DATE ________ CLASS ________

CLAIM-EVIDENCE-REASONING

Relate Intermolecular Forces to States of Matter

The main difference between gases, liquids, and solids is the space between the particles, their motion, and the strength of the intermolecular forces between them. Gas particles are farther apart, faster moving, and have weaker forces between them than particles in liquids or solids. For example, at room temperature, oxygen (O_2) and nitrogen (N_2) are gases, water (H_2O) is a liquid, and salt (NaCl) is a solid.

Build Your Argument Through Claim, Evidence, and Reasoning

1. **SEP Ask Questions** Write a question about intermolecular forces and states of matter that you would like to discuss with your classmates. (Your teacher may also provide you with one.)

2. **SEP Construct Written Arguments** Use the Claim-Evidence-Reasoning framework to build a scientific argument about the intermolecular forces and the states of matter. After stating your claim, support it with evidence and scientific reasoning.

Make a Claim Your claim should be a response to the question stated above.	
Cite Evidence Identify data or knowledge that support your claim.	

CER Interactive Worksheet

ADDRESS PRECONCEPTIONS

When discussing the kinetic theory and the states of matter, some students may incorrectly think that materials can have properties of only one state of matter. Address this preconception by showing students an ice cube and a container of water. Ask students how the properties of the two states of water differ. Point out that the state of matter of a material can be changed by changing the temperature. For example, gases can be frozen to produce a solid, such as when carbon dioxide gas is cooled enough to produce dry ice, which students observed in the teacher demo. Make sure that students understand that the materials solidify at different temperatures. To emphasize the point, you may wish to have students find the freezing and melting point of some common metals.

PhET Simulation: States of Matter: Basics

Virtual Nerd Video: What Is Dimensional, or Unit, Analysis?

Virtual Nerd Video: How Do You Use Dimensional Analysis to Convert Units on Both Parts of a Rate?

EXPLAIN

Relate Intermolecular Forces to States of Matter

Claim-Evidence-Reasoning Students write arguments in which they make a claim about the state of matter of a substance, its properties, and the bonds between molecules of the substance. Students should support their claims with observed evidence and scientific reasoning.

- For example, if students claim that the bonds between particles in a substance can be broken if enough heat is added, they can use evidence from the Virtual Lab as support for their claim.
- Another claim students can make is that solids have the strongest bonds based on molar enthalpies of vaporization. As evidence, students should list the energy needed to vaporize solids versus the energy needed to vaporize liquids and gases at standard temperature and pressure. For example, the molar enthalpy of vaporization for oxygen is 6.8 kJ/mol, and the molar enthalpy of vaporization of water is 40.7 kJ/mol. (Solids have larger enthalpies of vaporization because they have stronger intermolecular forces than liquids and solids.)

Provide students with an opportunity to revisit their CER arguments throughout the experience for further revision and peer review.

PROFESSIONAL DEVELOPMENT

Explaining Phenomena Changes of state are typically associated with changes in temperature. However, the state of matter can also be affected by other variables. Thixotropic materials are solidlike materials that liquefy when subjected to shearing forces. For example, many paints are thixotropic; they thin out when brushed on a surface and thicken when the brush stroke stops, thus keeping the paint from sliding off the wall. A shearing force has an opposite effect on quicksand. Quick movements "thicken" the quicksand and make it much more difficult for a person or animal trapped in it to move. (A shearing force causes two layers to move in opposite directions along a plane of contact.)

ASSESS ON THE SPOT

Ask students to write one or two sentences to answer this question: What can be used as evidence of the relationship between states of matter and the strengths of the intermolecular forces in substances? (patterns of interactions between particles observed at multiple scales)

States of Matter: Basics

PhET Simulation Use this interactive game to help reinforce the concept of changes of state.

What Is Dimensional, or Unit, Analysis?

Virtual Nerd Video Use this tutorial to review dimensional analysis.

How Do You Use Dimensional Analysis to Convert Units on Both Parts of a Rate?

Virtual Nerd Video Use this tutorial to reinforce the concept of conversion factors and rates.

States of Matter

Experience Notebook Ideally, assign the Experience Notebook or Realize Reader for this experience the day before, and then follow up with any of the following suggested instructional strategies to fill knowledge gaps and deepen understanding.

Use these strategies to help students make sense of the images and text on the indicated pages, as well as to engage in science practices.

- **Kinetic Theory and a Model for Gases** (p. 112) Pair students and let them develop their own model [CCC-4] for what is happening at the molecular level in a real-life situation involving a gas. Invite pairs to share their models with the class. Make sure that students understand that the space between the gas particles is not filled with air or any other substance.
- **Common Gases** (p. 113) Ask students what gases they think are in the air we breathe. Note that our air is mostly nitrogen gas, with oxygen, argon, and carbon dioxide. Ask students what patterns [CCC-1] they note when looking at which elements are in these gases and where those elements are located in the periodic table. (Nitrogen, oxygen, and carbon are all grouped together in the upper right-hand corner of the table, elements 6, 7, and 8. Argon is near them, one row below in the noble gas column).
- **Gas Pressure** (pp. 114–115) Ask students this question before they read the page: Given the information you have read so far, why do you think a balloon bursts if you keep blowing it up? After students read the page, help them understand that the pressure of a gas is caused [CCC-2] by collisions of the particles with the walls of the container. Point out that the magnitude of the pressure is related to how often and how hard the particles strike the walls.
- **Units of Pressure Diagram** (p. 115) Guide a class discussion of scenarios in which each of the units of gas pressure measurement might be useful. To help students understand conversions between units, model problem solving for them by showing how to convert familiar units. For example, how many cookies are in 3.7 dozen? Set up a conversion equation, explaining the logic behind it, and then show how the units cancel to provide an answer in units of number of cookies. Invite students to find the number of seconds in a month or the number of nickels in $37.
- **Kinetic Energy and Particle Motion in Solids, Liquids, and Gases** (p. 117) Ask five or six student volunteers to come to the front of the class and model [SEP-2] translational, rotational, and vibrational energy.
  a. Guide a discussion about vibrational energy. Ask volunteers to pretend they are particles in a substance and demonstrate how they would behave if they were in a solid. After the demonstration, ask volunteers to explain why they moved the way they did. Do the same for rotational energy and then translational energy.
  b. Encourage volunteers to tell other students how to move so that they are modeling particles in a gas. Prompt students to explain the reasoning [SEP-6] behind their directions.
- **Liquids and Intermolecular Forces** (pp. 118–119) Conduct a jigsaw activity to help students understand intermolecular forces. Organize the class into five groups (A–E), and assign each group one of the types of intermolecular forces described on page 119. Tell groups to become experts on their topics and make notes on what they want to say to explain the topic to others. Then reshuffle students into new groups of five, with each group having one student from the original groups A–E. Tell students to teach their new group members about their topic. Then instruct students to return to their original groups and share what they learned about each of the four topics they aren't "experts" in.

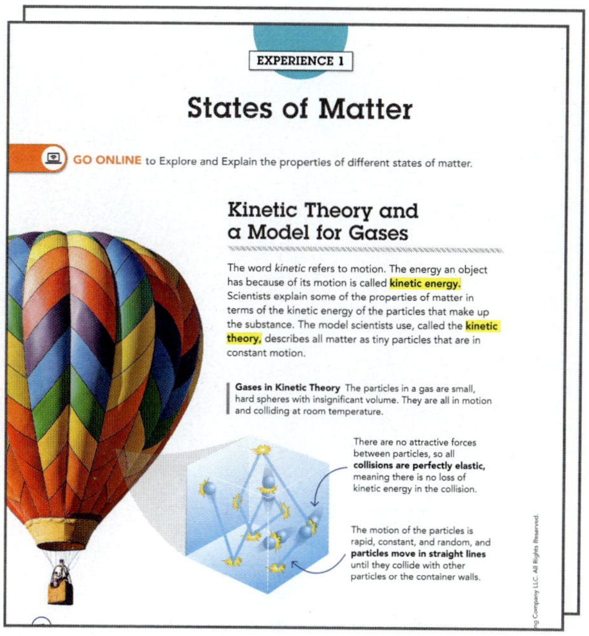
EXPERIENCE 1

States of Matter

GO ONLINE to Explore and Explain the properties of different states of matter.

Kinetic Theory and a Model for Gases

The word *kinetic* refers to motion. The energy an object has because of its motion is called **kinetic energy.** Scientists explain some of the properties of matter in terms of the kinetic energy of the particles that make up the substance. The model scientists use, called the **kinetic theory,** describes all matter as tiny particles that are in constant motion.

Gases in Kinetic Theory The particles in a gas are small, hard spheres with insignificant volume. They are all in motion and colliding at room temperature.

There are no attractive forces between particles, so all **collisions are perfectly elastic,** meaning there is no loss of kinetic energy in the collision.

The motion of the particles is rapid, constant, and random, and **particles move in straight lines** until they collide with other particles or the container walls.

Experience Notebook, pp. 112–123

eTEXT

ELD SUPPORT

Reading Students work in pairs to read and understand the text describing states of matter.

- **Emerging/Beginning** Have each pair read a subsection of the text, such as Gas Pressure or Units of Pressure. Then have them identify the main ideas together.
- **Developing/Expanding** Student pairs can read the section they chose and then identify relationships between the text and the images in the section. For example, students who read the section on gas pressure can discuss the figure on page 114, and students who read the section about units of pressure can discuss the figure on page 115.
- **Bridging** Have student pairs select a section of the text or project a figure and explain it to the class.

SAMPLE PROBLEM SUPPORT

If students are struggling to convert between units of pressure, guide them through the steps to convert units by using whole numbers and single letters to represent units. As students become more confident with the process, have them convert more complex units. Encourage students to write or talk through the conversions they are struggling with.

- **Solids and Attractive Force** (pp. 120–121) Have student pairs choose a substance, either solid, liquid, or gas, and make some predictions about what the molecular or particle structure of that substance is. Encourage them to cite evidence [SEP-7] based on properties of that substance at room temperature. Invite pairs to share their examples and discuss the examples as a class. (Sample answers: Sugar is a molecule, and it is solid at room temperature, so it would be a molecular solid held together by intermolecular forces. Because it is a solid, the particles would only have vibrational energy. Copper is a metal, held together by metallic bonds, and because it is solid, the atoms would only have vibrational energy. Fluorine is a gas at room temperature. Because of its electron structure, the gas will be diatomic. Gas particles will not be bonded to each other, and they will have vibrational, rotational, and translational energy.)
- **Crystal Structure** (pp. 122–123) Tell students to look at the particle structure [PS1.A] of the three types of crystals (simple cubic, body centered, face centered). As a class, use evidence and reasoning to rank the crystals in order of how much movement the constituent particles have. (The simple cubic crystal has the most empty space in each cell, so atoms within them have the most vibrational movement. Unit cells of body-centered crystals are more tightly packed than simple cubic cells, so atoms within them would have less movement. The unit cells of face-centered crystals are the most tightly packed, and atoms in those crystals have the least movement.)

Virtual Reality Experience: Physical Properties of Materials

Physical Properties of Materials

Virtual Reality Experience Students discover how the physical properties of matter are determined by electrical forces within and between atoms.

ELABORATE

Relate Intermolecular Forces and States of Matter

Discussion Rubric Students discuss the trends they observed and the claims they made in the CER activity, Relate Intermolecular Forces to States of Matter, and then assess their performance.

- Pair students and tell them to exchange their completed CER worksheets. Partner 1 should read partner 2's question and give partner 2 a chance to clearly communicate the answer [SEP-8] by providing evidence and reasoning for the claim [SEP-7]. Partners should then switch roles, with partner 2 reading partner 1's question, and partner 1 providing an answer. When students have finished, tell them to work individually, using the rubric to evaluate their understanding and communication, keeping in mind that they will be assessed on the accuracy of their self-evaluation.

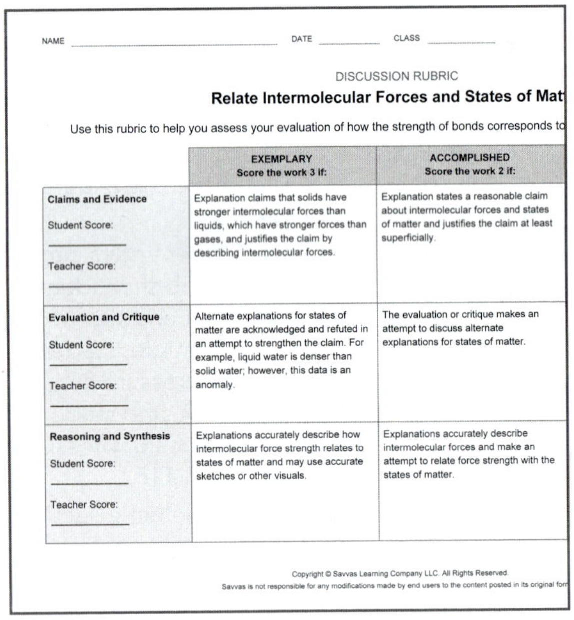

NAME ______ DATE ______ CLASS ______

DISCUSSION RUBRIC

Relate Intermolecular Forces and States of Mat

Use this rubric to help you assess your evaluation of how the strength of bonds corresponds to

	EXEMPLARY Score the work 3 if:	ACCOMPLISHED Score the work 2 if:
Claims and Evidence Student Score: ______ Teacher Score: ______	Explanation claims that solids have stronger intermolecular forces than liquids, which have stronger forces than gases, and justifies the claim by describing intermolecular forces.	Explanation states a reasonable claim about intermolecular forces and states of matter and justifies the claim at least superficially.
Evaluation and Critique Student Score: ______ Teacher Score: ______	Alternate explanations for states of matter are acknowledged and refuted in an attempt to strengthen the claim. For example, liquid water is denser than solid water; however, this data is an anomaly.	The evaluation or critique makes an attempt to discuss alternate explanations for states of matter.
Reasoning and Synthesis Student Score: ______ Teacher Score: ______	Explanations accurately describe how intermolecular force strength relates to states of matter and may use accurate sketches or other visuals.	Explanations accurately describe intermolecular forces and make an attempt to relate force strength with the states of matter.

Discussion Rubric Interactive Worksheet

DIFFERENTIATED INSTRUCTION

- **Support Struggling Students** Students struggling to grasp what is happening at the molecular level in the Relate Intermolecular Forces and States of Matter discussion can make a hands-on model [SEP-2]. Use small objects to represent molecules, and guide students through investigating how the molecules would behave as they begin to move faster. If you have small, weak magnets, you can demonstrate the waning force relative to distance between molecules.
- **Support Advanced Students** Have students conduct research on the crystalline structure [PS1.A] and formation of natural, synthetic, and simulated diamonds. They can write a paper or make a visual presentation to compare the three types of crystalline structure.

CONNECT TO CAREERS

Engineer Explain to students that many of the molecules we usually find in the gas phase have important medical uses when they are cooled to their liquid phase. For example, doctors often use liquid nitrogen to remove warts and moles, and oxygen that will help patients with respiratory problems is often transported and stored in its liquid form. Tell students to research how engineers produce "liquid gases" and make a list of skills and education that a person would need to design the production process. Invite students to make a list of industries that would require someone with those skills to produce their products.

States of Water

Writing About Science In this writing activity, students explain [SEP-6] how the molecules differ in different states of matter and relate their responses to a glass of ice water on a warm day. Students also explain how they would plan an investigation [SEP-3] to determine if a freezer has a temperature of −10°C by using a glass of water.

- To prompt thoughts that can help students in their writing, discuss any or all of the following questions as a class. Encourage students to take notes in their Science and Engineering Notebooks on ideas that stand out to them. **Ask:**
- How would you describe the appearance of a glass of ice cubes on a hot day? Which of the details that come to mind can be explained by phenomena at the particle level?
- How do intermolecular forces between water molecules relate to the appearance of these details?
- How does the energy of water molecules change as water goes from 0°C to −10°C?

If students are struggling to complete Step 2, remind them that the melting point of water is 0°C and the boiling point is 100°C. (They do not need the latter, but it is ok for students to have to figure out which information is relevant.)

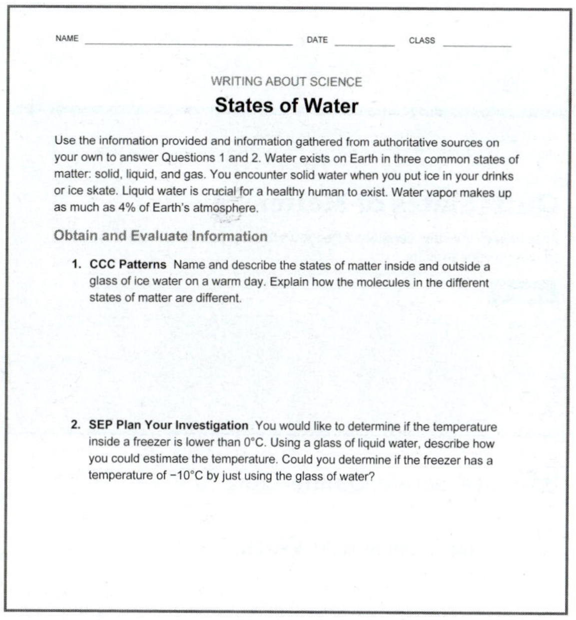

NAME ______ DATE ______ CLASS ______

WRITING ABOUT SCIENCE

States of Water

Use the information provided and information gathered from authoritative sources on your own to answer Questions 1 and 2. Water exists on Earth in three common states of matter: solid, liquid, and gas. You encounter solid water when you put ice in your drinks or ice skate. Liquid water is crucial for a healthy human to exist. Water vapor makes up as much as 4% of Earth's atmosphere.

Obtain and Evaluate Information

1. **CCC Patterns** Name and describe the states of matter inside and outside a glass of ice water on a warm day. Explain how the molecules in the different states of matter are different.

2. **SEP Plan Your Investigation** You would like to determine if the temperature inside a freezer is lower than 0°C. Using a glass of liquid water, describe how you could estimate the temperature. Could you determine if the freezer has a temperature of −10°C by just using the glass of water?

Writing About Science Interactive Worksheet

DIFFERENTIATED INSTRUCTION

- **Support Struggling Students** Students may need additional support to answer Question 2 of the Writing About Science activity. Use questions such as these to lead students to the final answer: At what temperature does water freeze? What is the warmest temperature that the freezer could be for the water to freeze? Would you be able to see any change in the water if it gets colder than the freezing point?
- **Support Special Needs Students** For students who have difficulty expressing themselves in writing, provide other options such as allowing them to audio record their answers or to tell their answers to a partner.

ASSESS ON THE SPOT

Give each student a notecard. Ask students to write something they found interesting about the Writing About Science activity and something they still feel like they do not clearly understand. Collect the notecards and use the information to help guide a class review before the experience assessment and as engagement strategies for the next experience.

PROFESSIONAL DEVELOPMENT

Science and Engineering Notebooks Before they start the writing activity, have students start a Notes entry by writing two facts they know about the states of water. If time permits, have students share their facts and then lead into a class discussion. Use the questions from the writing activity to guide the discussion. Remind students that they can use their notes from the discussion and any research they conduct while writing their explanations. For struggling students, guide the process of taking notes by first identifying relevant information that can be used as evidence for their explanations, and then modeling how the information should be noted in their notebooks.

CLASSROOM MODIFICATIONS

Based on your students' abilities and your schedule, you may wish to edit the Writing About Science document to make the activity more open ended or more guided.

- **More Open Ended** For Step 2, allow students to suggest materials and a procedure that they could use to determine the temperature of the freezer.
- **More Guided** If necessary, provide guidance for Step 1 by reviewing with students the diagrams on page 117 of the Experience Notebook. Help students relate each diagram to a state of water. Then ask what happens to a glass of water if it is left on a table outside for a while. Help students apply that information to Step 2.

ADDRESS PRECONCEPTIONS

While many students can explain the state change of melting ice, they may have preconceptions about how condensation forms. Explain that condensation does not come from within the container and move to the outside. Clarify that condensation does form from the air surrounding the glass, and review with students what gases are in the air. Be sure they understand that condensation forms when water vapor in the air loses kinetic energy when it is near the cooler container holding the ice.

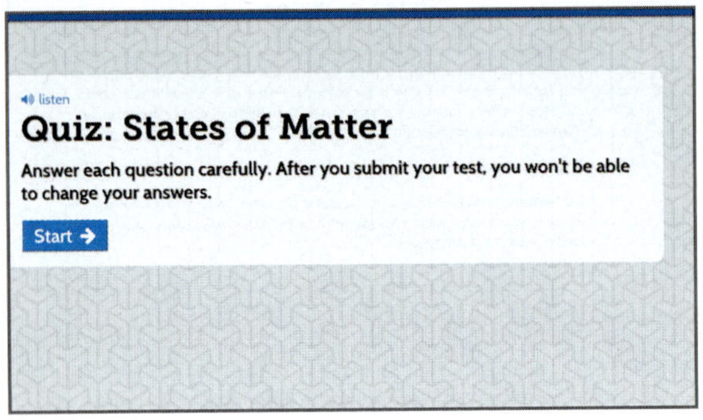

Interactive Online Quiz

Quiz Interactive Worksheet

EVALUATE

States of Matter

Quiz Assign the quiz in online technology-enhanced, auto-graded format or as an editable quiz worksheet. Use the scoring notes and remediation strategies found online to assess students' responses and to provide targeted feedback for each item to remediate well before assigning the summative 3-D Assessment.

REMEDIATION SUGGESTIONS

- **If** students are having trouble connecting the kinetic theory of gases to changes in pressure as a result of a change in volume or the number of particles, **then** work with them to review the Gas Pressure graphic on page 114 of the Experience Notebook.
- **If** students are struggling to grasp what happens on the particle level as heat is added to a substance, **then** invite them to review concepts of state change by using the Virtual Lab.
- **If** students have difficulty visualizing translational, rotational, and vibrational energy, **then** encourage them to make a model and help them demonstrate how a gas particle can move in the three different ways.
- **If** students are having difficulty differentiating the types of intermolecular forces, **then** direct them to the illustration Intermolecular Forces on page 119 and prompt them to verbalize what is happening in each example.

Revisit INVESTIGATIVE PHENOMENON

Support Reflection Students can complete the reflection prompt, where they will unpack and make sense of the Investigative Phenomenon, based on practices and understandings that have been reinforced over the course of the experience.

- Take students through a review of intermolecular forces. Prompt them to think of examples in which intermolecular forces play a role. Offer a few everyday examples, such as boiling water and heating oil in a pan. Discuss how intermolecular forces are taken into account when materials are engineered.
- Tell students to discuss with a partner the effect of changes in kinetic energy on the structure of water in its three different phases. Invite pairs to share their thoughts.

Develop a Draft CER Argument Have students answer Question 2 in the CER worksheet and develop a draft of a CER argument to address the Investigative Phenomenon. Have students add any evidence they have collected from the activities so far in this investigation. Evidence may include kinetic energy of particles, density of particles, or number of collisions between particles.

Revisit INVESTIGATIVE PHENOMENON

GO ONLINE to Elaborate and Evaluate your knowledge of states of matter by completing the class discussion and writing task activities.

In the CER worksheet, you drafted a scientific argument to explain how materials used on mountaintops are engineered. With a partner, reevaluate the evidence cited in your arguments.

13 **SEP Develop a Model** Mountain climbers need really warm clothing because it gets colder at higher altitudes. Sketch molecular models for equal-mass samples of air at different altitudes. Use your models to show why there might be less energy in the samples at higher altitudes.

Experience Notebook, p. 124

eTEXT

EXPERIENCE 2

Modeling Phase Changes

Teacher Background

Experience 2 brings students into an examination of what occurs during a phase change in terms of kinetic energy and intermolecular forces. Students develop and revise models of phase changes and analyze data in phase diagrams. It is likely that students will be familiar with phase changes generally, but not at the molecular level. This experience requires students to graph data and interpret graphs. Some students may need additional support creating and interpreting graphs.

Objectives

- **Describe how variations in kinetic energy among particles result in constant evaporation and condensation, even without heating or cooling.**
- **Summarize the mechanisms by which gas bubbles in a heated liquid exert enough pressure to break free of the surface, resulting in boiling.**
- **Relate the melting point of different solids to the strength of intermolecular forces or bonds between their particles, and apply that understanding to predict the bond energy of a compound with a known melting point.**
- **Relate the weakness of intermolecular forces between particles of a substance to the ability of that substance to sublimate at STP.**
- **Interpret phase diagrams to determine the state of water at various pressure and temperature points, and apply that understanding to predict the state of carbon dioxide at STP based on its phase diagram.**

ENGAGE

EVERYDAY PHENOMENON

What happens to temperature when ice melts?

Use this teacher demo to prompt student discussion about what happens when phase changes occur. Note ideas and questions from students as they arise, and refer to them while doing the Inquiry Lab.

Melting Ice

Engage students with this demonstration to prompt student discussion about observations that can be made when phase changes are modeled.

Materials large beaker, clock or stopwatch, crushed ice, thermometer, stirring rod

1. Place about 6 cm of crushed ice in the bottom of the beaker. Place a thermometer on the ice and then fill the beaker with additional crushed ice.
2. Record the temperature of the ice.
3. Place the beaker on a hot plate and heat the ice slowly. Stir the ice frequently. Record the temperature every 5 to 10 seconds until all the ice has melted.
4. Continue to heat the beaker and water. Record temperature readings until the water reaches room temperature.

RELATED PHENOMENA

In addition to the Melting Ice demo, consider using other phenomena to launch this experience.

- **Smash a Rose** Submerge a rose in a dewar of liquid nitrogen. Let students predict what is happening to the rose. Remove the rose, and smash it on the lab bench. Guide a discussion about how the demo modeled phase changes.
- **Shrinking Balloons** Place a balloon in a dewar of liquid nitrogen. As the balloon shrinks, ask students what is happening to the particles inside the balloon. **Ask** What causes the balloon to shrink? What will happen when I remove the balloon from the dewar and place it on the desk?

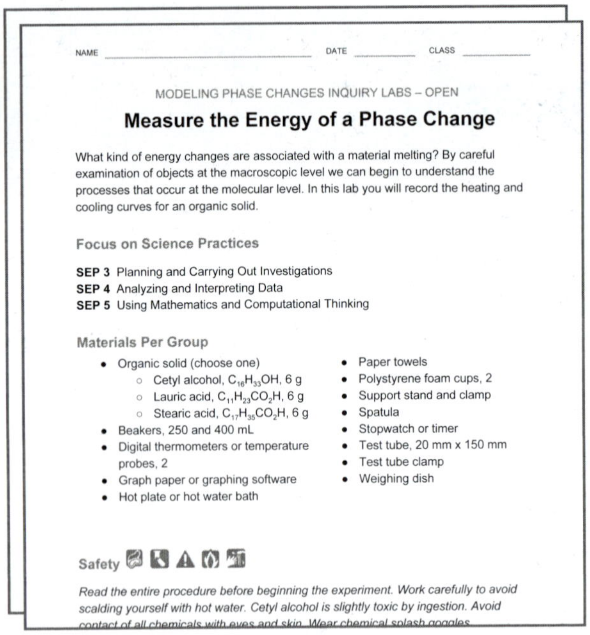
NAME ______________ DATE ________ CLASS ________

MODELING PHASE CHANGES INQUIRY LABS – OPEN

Measure the Energy of a Phase Change

What kind of energy changes are associated with a material melting? By careful examination of objects at the macroscopic level we can begin to understand the processes that occur at the molecular level. In this lab you will record the heating and cooling curves for an organic solid.

Focus on Science Practices

SEP 3 Planning and Carrying Out Investigations
SEP 4 Analyzing and Interpreting Data
SEP 5 Using Mathematics and Computational Thinking

Materials Per Group

- Organic solid (choose one)
  - Cetyl alcohol, $C_{16}H_{33}OH$, 6 g
  - Lauric acid, $C_{11}H_{23}CO_2H$, 6 g
  - Stearic acid, $C_{17}H_{35}CO_2H$, 6 g
- Beakers, 250 and 400 mL
- Digital thermometers or temperature probes, 2
- Graph paper or graphing software
- Hot plate or hot water bath
- Paper towels
- Polystyrene foam cups, 2
- Support stand and clamp
- Spatula
- Stopwatch or timer
- Test tube, 20 mm x 150 mm
- Test tube clamp
- Weighing dish

Safety

Read the entire procedure before beginning the experiment. Work carefully to avoid scalding yourself with hot water. Cetyl alcohol is slightly toxic by ingestion. Avoid contact of all chemicals with eyes and skin. Wear chemical splash goggles

O/G/S/A Lab Interactive Worksheets

CLASSROOM MODIFICATIONS

Based on your students' abilities and your schedule, you can choose either the Open-Ended Inquiry Lab or the Guided Inquiry Lab.

- **Open-Ended Inquiry Lab** Students plan and conduct an investigation to gather data about the change in temperature over time as an organic solid is heated and then cooled. They use the data to plot a cooling curve and a heating curve of the organic solid and to estimate its melting point.
- **Guided Inquiry Lab** Students are guided through the steps of the investigation to gather data about the change in temperature over time as an organic solid is heated and then cooled. They plot a cooling curve and a heating curve of the organic solid and estimate its melting point.

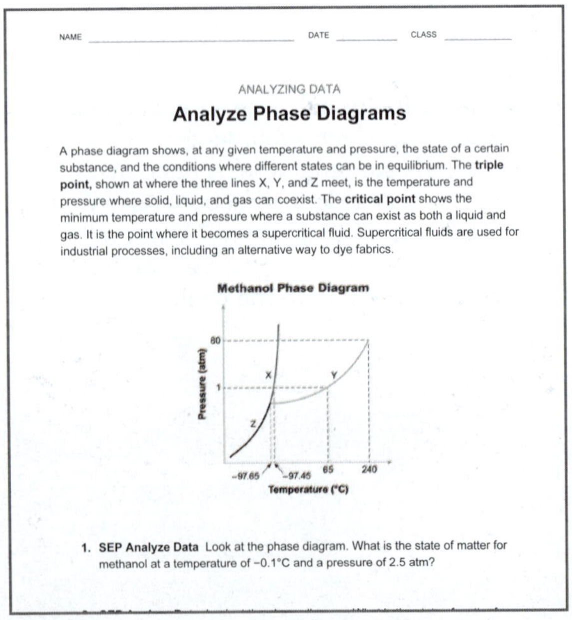
NAME ______________ DATE ________ CLASS ________

ANALYZING DATA

Analyze Phase Diagrams

A phase diagram shows, at any given temperature and pressure, the state of a certain substance, and the conditions where different states can be in equilibrium. The **triple point,** shown at where the three lines X, Y, and Z meet, is the temperature and pressure where solid, liquid, and gas can coexist. The **critical point** shows the minimum temperature and pressure where a substance can exist as both a liquid and gas. It is the point where it becomes a supercritical fluid. Supercritical fluids are used for industrial processes, including an alternative way to dye fabrics.

Methanol Phase Diagram

1. **SEP Analyze Data** Look at the phase diagram. What is the state of matter for methanol at a temperature of −0.1°C and a pressure of 2.5 atm?

Analyzing Data Interactive Worksheet

5. Point to the recorded temperatures. **Ask** What pattern [CCC-1] do you see in this data? (The temperature did not increase while the ice was melting.) Remind students that the heat energy from the burner was transferred to the beaker and ice. **Ask** What explanation can you give for the pattern you observed? (Accept reasonable answers at this point.) Tell students that they will revisit this question after they complete the Inquiry Lab and the Analyzing Data worksheet.

EXPLORE

Measure the Energy of a Phase Change

Inquiry Lab In this lab, students carry out an investigation [SEP-3] to develop heating and cooling curves of an organic solid.

Lab Demo Video Watch the Lab Demo Video for advice on materials and preparation.

Choose Your Version Open-ended (O), Guided (G), Shortened (S), Advanced (A)

Materials organic solid (choose one): 6 g cetyl alcohol, 6 g lauric acid, or 6 g stearic acid; 250- and 400-mL beakers; 2 digital thermometers or temperature probes; graph paper or graphing software; hot plate or hot water bath; paper towels; 2 polystyrene foam cups; support stand and clamp; spatula; stopwatch or timer; 20 mm × 150 mm test tube; test tube clamp; weighing dish

Safety Cetyl alcohol is slightly toxic by ingestion. Remind students to wear a protective apron, safety goggles, and safety gloves.

Expected Outcome Students observe a plateau in the curves when the material is either melting or freezing.

Lab Summary Video Watch the Lab Summary Video for support on connecting the lab investigation to the Investigative Phenomenon.

Analyze Phase Diagrams

Analyzing Data In this activity, students use phase diagrams as a model [SEP-2] to predict the state of a substance at varying temperature and pressure conditions. They analyze data in a phase diagram [SEP-4] for methanol and note the conditions that will produce change in the system [CCC-7].

- Students may initially find the phase diagrams confusing. Demonstrate how to interpret the data using the diagram. **Ask** At what temperature does methanol boil and freeze? Tell students to locate 1 atm on the *y*-axis, and then move along the *x*-axis to find the temperature where methanol is a solid and where it becomes a gas. (97.65°C)
- Explain that atmospheric pressure is lower at high elevations, such as on top of a tall mountain. Ask students what phase methanol is in at conditions of 1 atm and 78°C. (gas)

ASSESS ON THE SPOT

List a series of temperature–pressure values on the board. Have students state which phase of methanol is most stable at each set of conditions and explain why.

EXPLAIN

Phase Changes and Intermolecular Forces

Modeling In this activity, students develop models [SEP-2] to show the relationship between intermolecular forces and states of matter. They then use the models to explain how molecules change as they change phase and how the energy changes during the phase changes. Before engaging students in this activity, you may wish to review intermolecular forces from the previous investigation.

Choose from these suggested strategies to guide students in developing their model of phase change.

- **Use Different Media** Some students may prefer to work with pen and paper to make their models, whereas others may prefer to develop three-dimensional models using objects such as beans for particles. Allow students to choose the medium that inspires them the most.
- **List Features** Remind students that they do not need to include every feature of phase change in their models, only those features required to clearly communicate their explanations of how phase change occurs. Encourage students to make a list of features that relate to phase change and evaluate which features they want to include in their models. Tell them to use those features as they start making their models.

Let students know they will be returning to this activity later in the investigation.

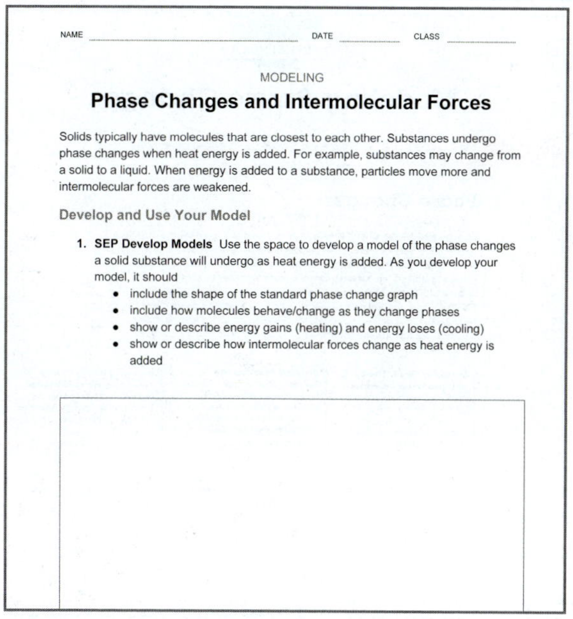
NAME ________________ DATE ________ CLASS ________

MODELING

Phase Changes and Intermolecular Forces

Solids typically have molecules that are closest to each other. Substances undergo phase changes when heat energy is added. For example, substances may change from a solid to a liquid. When energy is added to a substance, particles move more and intermolecular forces are weakened.

Develop and Use Your Model

1. **SEP Develop Models** Use the space to develop a model of the phase changes a solid substance will undergo as heat energy is added. As you develop your model, it should
   - include the shape of the standard phase change graph
   - include how molecules behave/change as they change phases
   - show or describe energy gains (heating) and energy loses (cooling)
   - show or describe how intermolecular forces change as heat energy is added

Modeling Interactive Worksheet

ASSESS ON THE SPOT

When students are done making their models, encourage them to reflect. **Ask:**

- What was challenging about making this model?
- What do you feel confident explaining about your model?
- What aspects of phase change do you think you could understand better?

Survey the class for responses, and keep them in mind as you move into the animation and Experience Notebook portions of the investigation.

Phase Transitions and Particle Motion

Animation This animation presents students with a model of what is happening at the molecular scale during phase transitions. They learn how changes in energy result in changes to the system [CCC-5] and, therefore, to the phase the substance is in. Encourage students to use what they learn in the animation to refine their models [SEP-2] from the Phase Changes and Intermolecular Forces Modeling activity. Choose one of these strategies as you use the animation:

- Pair students to watch the animation. Encourage them to pause the animation and take notes or make sketches of what they see in the animation, adding thoughts about how they might be able to use the ideas to improve their models.
- Watch the animation as a class. Pause it after an important concept is presented, and ask students how the concept applies to the models they made.

Ensure that students can describe what happens at the molecular level when a substance is heated first to its melting point and then to its boiling point. Students should also be able to explain what happens to added energy when the temperature remains constant while a substance is melting or boiling.

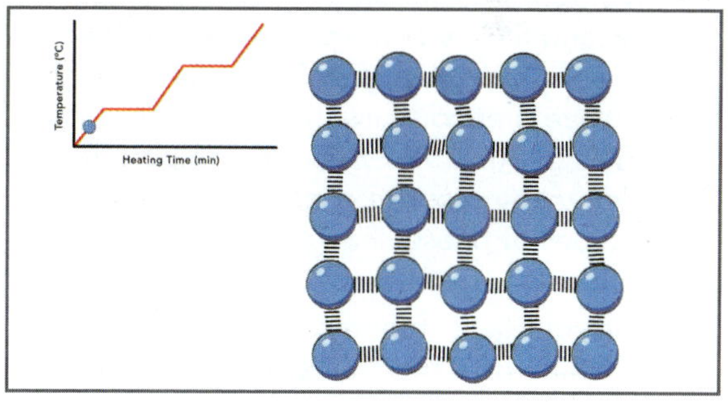

Animation: Phase Transitions and Particle Motion

How Do You Make a Scatter Plot?

Virtual Nerd Video This video tutorial allows students to take data from a table and plot it to create a scatter plot.

Virtual Nerd Video: How Do You Make a Scatter Plot?

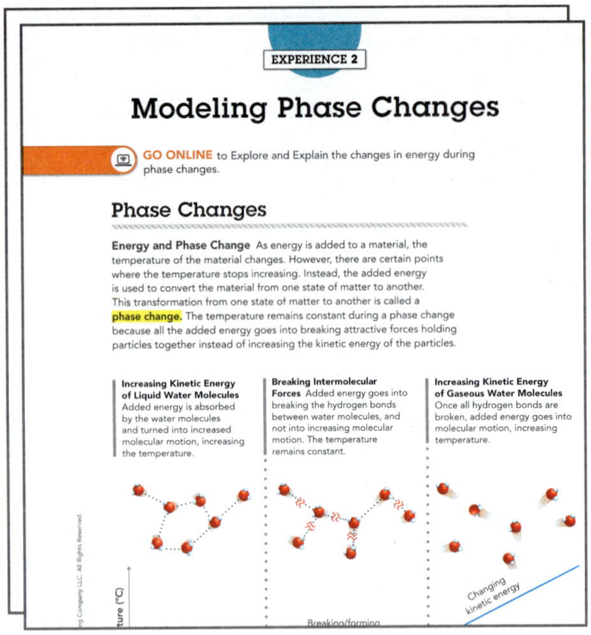

EXPERIENCE 2

Modeling Phase Changes

GO ONLINE to Explore and Explain the changes in energy during phase changes.

Phase Changes

Energy and Phase Change As energy is added to a material, the temperature of the material changes. However, there are certain points where the temperature stops increasing. Instead, the added energy is used to convert the material from one state of matter to another. This transformation from one state of matter to another is called a **phase change.** The temperature remains constant during a phase change because all the added energy goes into breaking attractive forces holding particles together instead of increasing the kinetic energy of the particles.

Increasing Kinetic Energy of Liquid Water Molecules Added energy is absorbed by the water molecules and turned into increased molecular motion, increasing the temperature.

Breaking Intermolecular Forces Added energy goes into breaking the hydrogen bonds between water molecules, and not into increasing molecular motion. The temperature remains constant.

Increasing Kinetic Energy of Gaseous Water Molecules Once all hydrogen bonds are broken, added energy goes into molecular motion, increasing temperature.

Experience Notebook, pp. 125–134

eTEXT

ELD SUPPORT

Writing Students provide written responses affirming understanding of the types of phase changes after they read page 126 in the Experience Notebook.

- **Emerging/Beginning** Have students match the phase change with its state of matter. Then ask students to complete a three-column KWL chart (What I Know/Want to Know/Learned).
- **Developing/Expanding** Have students draw and fill in a concept map about the types of phase changes. Then pair students and have them discuss their concept maps with each other. Ask them to compare their understanding of the connections between the types of phase changes and states of matter.
- **Bridging** Have students write paragraphs describing how the states of matter change phases. Then ask students to exchange paragraphs with other students for editing.

Modeling Phase Changes

20

Experience Notebook Ideally, assign the Experience Notebook or Realize Reader for this experience the day before, and then follow up with any of the following suggested instructional strategies to help students make sense of the images and text on the indicated pages, as well as to engage science skills.

- **Phase Changes** (pp. 125–126) Display the graph on page 125 and help students relate it to the graph they viewed in the animation. Call on students to point to specific parts of the graph as you describe them; for example, boiling point, particles are sliding past each other, etc.
- Place students in groups of three and ask them to think of an analogy to describe what happens during a phase change in terms of kinetic energy and intermolecular forces. Invite groups to share their analogies and discuss the analogies' strong points and limitations.
- **Heating a Liquid** (p. 127) Allow students to work in pairs or individually to graph the data in the chart. Tell them to write an explanation for the pattern [CCC-1] they see in the graphs. Then pair students with new partners to discuss their explanations [SEP-6]. Remind students to revise their written explanations if they get new information from their partners.
- **Evaporation and Condensation** (pp. 128–129) Guide a class discussion about what happens at the molecular level as a puddle on the sidewalk dries up on a sunny day and as water condenses on the side of a glass containing a cool drink.
- You may also wish to have students again view the Phase Transitions and Particle Motion animation to help them better visualize what is happening during evaporation. Then discuss how the diagram on page 128 explains why some molecules are able to escape the liquid when others cannot.
- **Vapor Pressure and Boiling** (pp. 130–131) On the board, write the definition of *vapor pressure* according to the Experience Notebook: "the pressure of the gas above the liquid." Group students in pairs or trios and tell them to write a definition for *vapor pressure* in their own words. Let them know they can use any of the information on the page as a resource. Invite groups to share their definitions and discuss them as a class.
- **Heating a Solid** (p. 132) You may wish to have students graph the data in Question 18 and then make their predictions about bond energy. Afterward, call on students to guide you through making and interpreting the graph [SEP-4]. Ask them to provide you with steps on how to draw the graph and then prompt you with questions that will help you understand how to predict the bond energy of calcium fluoride.
- **Sublimation** (p. 133) Make two columns on the board, one for compounds that sublime at STP and the other for those that don't. As a class, divide the compounds in the table in Question 19 among the two columns. Discuss similarities between substances in each column and how they affect whether that substance sublimes.
- **Phase Diagrams** (p. 134) Display the Phase Diagram for Water so that the whole class can see it. Point to the curve on the left side of the diagram. Make sure that students understand that it represents the freezing/melting curve for water. Note the point labeled as *Normal melting point.* **Ask** At 1.00 atm, in which state will water be at temperatures to the left of that point? (solid) In what state will water be at temperatues between that point and the one to the right of it? (liquid) What is the triple point of water? (0.0060 atm and 0.01°C)

PROFESSIONAL DEVELOPMENT

Background Notes A phase change diagram is a kind of fingerprint of a compound. Each compound has a unique phase diagram, affected by intermolecular forces, molecular weight, and other factors. The triple points represent the temperature and pressure at which all three phases exist in equilibrium. In other words, it isn't just that all phases exist but that particles are going into and out of each of the three phases at the same rate. The lines on the graph represent equilibrium between the two phases on either side of the line. For example, in water at 1 atm and 90°C, some nearby gas particles will join the liquid while some of the water particles are turning into gas. This explains why a pot of water will steam before it boils.

ELABORATE

Phase Change and Intermolecular Forces Model Review

Peer Review Rubric Students return to their models of phase changes and review them in light of new information they have learned. They then assess a partner's model and use their partner's assessment to revise their own model.

- Tell students to work individually, making changes and additions to their models [SEP-2] based on what they have learned since they made them. Then ask them to respond to Question 3 in the Modeling activity and describe approximations or assumptions of their models and their limitations.
- Next, pair students to review each other's models, using the rubric as a guide. Tell students to make notes explaining their reviews, and then present their notes to their partners. Remind them that reviews should assess the model as a way of not only representing a system but also as understanding and predicting the behavior of molecules.

DIFFERENTIATED INSTRUCTION

- **Support Less Proficient Readers** For less proficient readers, read aloud the rubric as they follow along. Clarify and/or restate the expectations of the models at the Exemplary, Accomplished, and Developing stages after all of each stage's components are read.
- **Support Special Needs Students** Some students may benefit from completing this activity over multiple days. Alternatively, providing struggling and special needs students with a structured amount of time to complete each step could help keep students focused on the task at hand.

Phase Change Graphs

Analyzing Data In this activity, students analyze a graph [SEP-4] that relates temperature to phase changes. They use the graph as a model [SEP-2] to predict events on the molecular level as temperature increases or decreases and to explain how changes in temperature affect [CCC-2] behavior of molecules.

- Tell students to answer the first four data analysis questions on their own. As a class, discuss the answers. Pair students and have them discuss any challenges or preconceptions they have in analyzing the graph.
- Tell students to continue to work in pairs to respond to the remaining four questions, making sure they support their claims with evidence and reasoning. Discuss their responses as a class.

INTEGRATE MATH

Slope of a Line As students study and analyze the graph of temperature versus heat energy, encourage them to consider what the slope of the line is telling them about changes in the average energy of particles in the substance. Ask what the horizontal parts of the graph reveal about changes in the average energy of particles as heat is being added. Ask students to predict the slope of a line for a substance that changes state very quickly, as well the slope for a substance that sublimes at room temperature.

How Do You Make Predictions Using a Line of Fit?

Virtual Nerd Video This tutorial shows students how to draw a line of fit on a scatter plot to make a prediction based on the data already given.

NAME ____________ DATE ________ CLASS ________

PEER REVIEW RUBRIC

Phase Change and Intermolecular Forces Model Revi

Use this rubric to help you assess your classmates' models and explanations of

	EXEMPLARY Score the work 3 if:	ACCOMPLISHED Score the work 2 if:	DEVELOPING Score the work 1 if:	
Components of the Model Score: ______	The model shows phase changes and clearly shows the different states of matter.	The model shows phase changes but does not clearly show the different states of matter.	The model does not fully show phase changes or clearly show the different states of matter.	
Relationships Score: ______	The model describes phase changes or changes from one state to another using intermolecular forces, molecular movement, and spaces between molecules.	The model describes phase changes but does not use intermolecular forces or spaces between molecules in the description.	The model makes an attempt to describe phase changes.	
Connections Score: ______	The model makes sense and can be applied to build understanding of other systems in which a substance undergoes phase changes.	The model makes sense but is more specific to one type of phase change and may not be applied to understand all phase changes.	The model could be more clearly explained and would not be effectively applied to understand phase changes.	
Limitations of the Model Score: ______	The explanation acknowledges that this model has limitations, and it is clearly described. (For example, the sketch could be more thorough.)	The explanation acknowledges that this model has limitations, though they are not clearly and specifically identified or described.	The model is presented as perfect without any room for improvement.	

Peer Review Rubric Interactive Worksheet

NAME ____________ DATE ________ CLASS ________

ANALYZING DATA

Phase Change Graphs

At a certain pressure, a substance may undergo phase changes as its temperature changes. The diagram shows how a change in temperature affects the phase for rock salt at a pressure of 1 atm as its heat energy changes.

The Melting Points and Boiling Points of Rock Salt, NaCl(s)

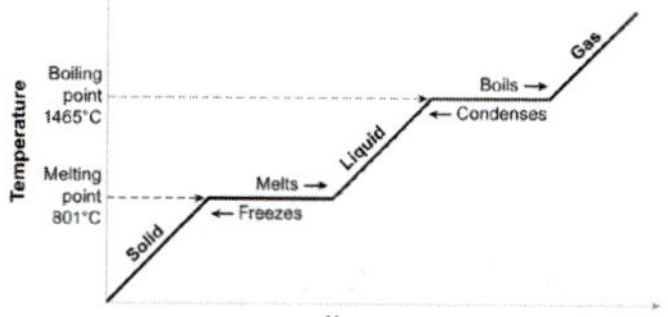

1. **SEP Analyze Data** Look at the diagram. At what temperature does rock salt (a) melt, (b) vaporize, (c) freeze, and (d) condense?

2. **Infer** What happens to the molecules in liquid rock salt as the temperature of the

Analyzing Data Interactive Worksheet

INTEGRATE THE THREE DIMENSIONS

Through the activities in this investigation, students get a three-dimensional picture of the relationship between kinetic energy, intermolecular forces, intramolecular forces, and phases of matter [PS1.A]. By making and using their own models [SEP-2] of phase change, students demonstrate that changing [CCC-7] conditions have an impact on the state of matter of a substance. They explain [SEP-6] these changes as evidence of forces between and within particles of a substance.

Virtual Nerd Video: How Do You Make Predictions Using a Line of Fit?

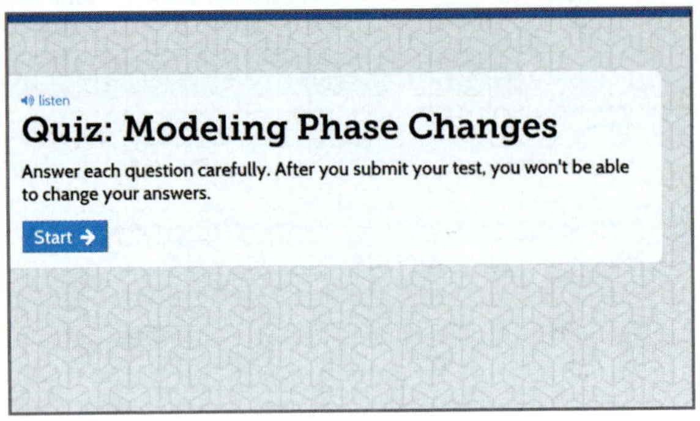

Interactive Online Quiz

Quiz Interactive Worksheet

EVALUATE

Modeling Phase Changes

Quiz Assign the quiz in online technology-enhanced, auto-graded format or as an editable quiz worksheet. Use the scoring notes and remediation strategies found online to assess students' responses and to provide targeted feedback for each item to remediate well before assigning the summative 3-D Assessment.

REMEDIATION SUGGESTIONS

- **If** students are having difficulty making their models in the Phase Changes and Intermolecular Forces activity, **then** suggest that they review the text and graphic for phase changes on pages 125 and 126 in the Experience Notebook.
- **If** students are challenged by the relationship between vapor pressure and boiling point, **then** encourage them to review the text and graphs in the section Vapor Pressure and Boiling in the Experience Notebook and write a sentence or two explaining why the curves of the graph appear as they do.
- **If** students are struggling to interpret phase diagrams, **then** tell them to review the Analyzing Data activity, Analyze Phase Diagrams. Students can also review the section in the Experience Notebook about reading phase diagrams, and compare the temperature and pressure conditions required for the substance to be a gas, a liquid, or a solid.
- **If** students are having trouble figuring out how to incorporate new ideas into their models in the Phase Changes and Intermolecular Forces activity, **then** tell them to make a sketch of the new concept and consider how they can add that sketch to their models.

Revisit
INVESTIGATIVE PHENOMENON

GO ONLINE to Elaborate and Evaluate your knowledge of phase changes by completing the peer review and data analysis activities.

In the CER worksheet, you drafted a scientific argument to explain how materials used on mountaintops are engineered. With a partner, reevaluate the evidence cited in your arguments.

21 SEP Construct an Explanation At high altitude, the boiling point of water changes. Does it go up or down? Why? How would this affect cooking on a mountain? Explain why the boiling point changes at higher altitude and design a solution to this cooking problem.

Experience Notebook, p. 135

eTEXT

Revisit INVESTIGATIVE PHENOMENON

Support Reflection Students can complete the reflection prompt, where they will unpack and make sense of the Investigative Phenomenon, based on practices and understandings that have been reinforced over the course of the experience.

- Ask students to define *boiling point* in terms of vapor pressure, and discuss how atmospheric pressure arises.
- To help students think through the questions, prompt them with these questions:
  a. How does the amount of atmospheric gas at the top of a mountain compare with that at sea level?
  b. How does the amount of gas relate to the atmospheric pressure?
  c. Would a climber need to take more or less fuel as he or she climbs up the mountain?

Further Develop Your CER Argument Have students add any additional evidence they have collected in this experience. Evidence might include how temperature and pressure affect the state of a material and how intermolecular bonds affect phase changes.

EXPERIENCE 3

Comparing Ionic and Molecular Compounds

Teacher Background

Experience 3 is an overview of the electrostatic forces of ionic compounds and the intermolecular forces of attraction in molecular compounds and how the strength of these forces affects the characteristic properties of matter. Students investigate the strength of intermolecular bonds in substances that contain metal and nonmetal elements to determine whether the substances are ionic or molecular compounds. They relate characteristic properties to chemical bonding and intermolecular forces.

Objectives

- **Differentiate between the representative units of molecular and ionic compounds.**
- **Identify patterns in the location of elements making up ionic and molecular compounds on the periodic table.**
- **Relate the properties of molecular and ionic compounds at the bulk scale to the intermolecular forces and bonds between their particles.**

ENGAGE

EVERYDAY PHENOMENON

What have you noticed about crystals?

Use this teacher demo to prompt student discussion about the differences in the physical properties of solid crystals.

Sweet and Salty

Engage students with this demonstration of an everyday phenomenon to introduce the concept of physical properties in ionic and molecular solids.

Materials table salt (sodium chloride), table sugar (sucrose), tape, glass microscope slide, microscope attached to document camera. Depending on equipment accessibility, you can substitute images of salt and sugar crystals for the microscope setup.

1. Begin by asking students if they ever have looked at small crystals in rocks or viewed crystals in museums. Encourage them to describe the crystals they have seen. Point out that both salt and sugar are made of crystals.
2. Place a few salt and sugar crystals on a piece of clean two-sided tape and tape the crystals to a glass microscope slide (can be done in advance).
3. Place the slide under the microscope and focus the image on the front board. **Ask** What differences do you see in the shape of the crystals? What do you think gives crystals their shape? (Sample answer: I see cube shapes and hexagonal shapes. I think crystals get their shape from their atomic structure.)
4. Explain to the students that crystals are a result of orderly arrangement of bonding atoms. The cube shapes that they see are salt crystals, and the hexagonal shapes are sugar crystals. **Ask** How might differences in crystal shape affect the properties of raw materials? Then transition this discussion to the discussion in the Inquiry Lab.

RELATED PHENOMENA

In addition to the Sweet and Salty demo, consider using other phenomena to launch this experience.

- **Crystal Properties** Grow borax, sugar, and alum crystals in class. Have students make observations and describe the similarities and differences in the physical properties of the crystals.
- **Shape Orientation** Use glass beads of several sizes, small cubes (such as dice), and other small regularly shaped objects. Place a number of objects of one type in a small container and shake gently. Have students observe how different shapes orient as they pack together. Discuss how orientation of atoms might affect the properties of a substance.

EXPLORE

Melt Ionic and Covalent Compounds

Inquiry Lab Students carry out an investigation [SEP-3] to determine the melting points of different compounds. They determine that the melting point is related to the degree of ionic character.

Lab Demo Video Watch the Lab Demo Video for advice on materials and preparation.

Choose Your Version Open-ended (O), Guided (G), Shortened (S), Advanced (A)

Materials 5 mL glacial acetic acid, 5 g ammonium acetate, 5 g anhydrous sodium acetate, 5 g sodium chloride, balance, 250-mL beaker, Bunsen burner, ice water, 3 test tubes, heavy-walled test tube holder, thermocouple, 3 weighing dishes

Safety Make sure students wear safety goggles when performing this or any lab that uses chemicals, heat, or glassware. Tell students that glacial acetic acid is corrosive and has a strong odor, so they should not open the sealed sample. Ammonium acetate can break down to produce acetamide (a suspected carcinogen) when heated; only heat in a fume hood or well ventilated area and avoid breathing any fumes released. Have students wash their hands thoroughly with soap and warm water before leaving the laboratory.

Expected Outcome Samples that are more ionic in nature will have higher melting points.

Lab Summary Video Watch the Lab Summary Video for support on connecting the lab investigation to the Investigative Phenomenon.

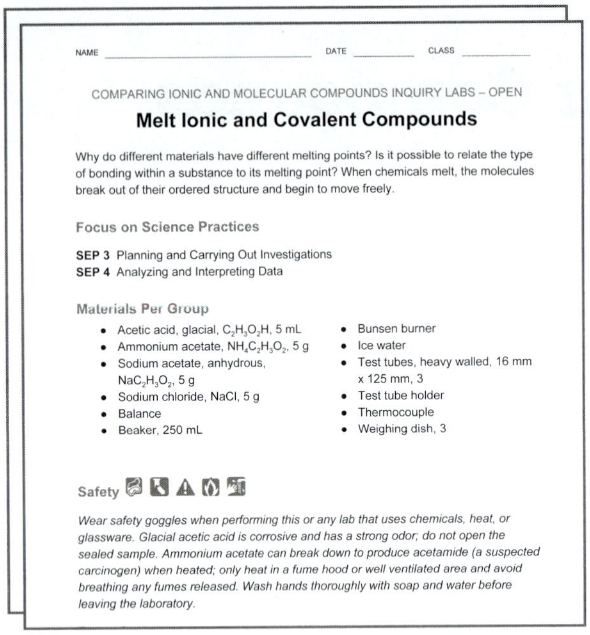

NAME ____________ DATE ________ CLASS ________

COMPARING IONIC AND MOLECULAR COMPOUNDS INQUIRY LABS – OPEN

Melt Ionic and Covalent Compounds

Why do different materials have different melting points? Is it possible to relate the type of bonding within a substance to its melting point? When chemicals melt, the molecules break out of their ordered structure and begin to move freely.

Focus on Science Practices

SEP 3 Planning and Carrying Out Investigations
SEP 4 Analyzing and Interpreting Data

Materials Per Group

- Acetic acid, glacial, $C_2H_3O_2H$, 5 mL
- Ammonium acetate, $NH_4C_2H_3O_2$, 5 g
- Sodium acetate, anhydrous, $NaC_2H_3O_2$, 5 g
- Sodium chloride, NaCl, 5 g
- Balance
- Beaker, 250 mL
- Bunsen burner
- Ice water
- Test tubes, heavy walled, 16 mm x 125 mm, 3
- Test tube holder
- Thermocouple
- Weighing dish, 3

Safety

Wear safety goggles when performing this or any lab that uses chemicals, heat, or glassware. Glacial acetic acid is corrosive and has a strong odor; do not open the sealed sample. Ammonium acetate can break down to produce acetamide (a suspected carcinogen) when heated; only heat in a fume hood or well ventilated area and avoid breathing any fumes released. Wash hands thoroughly with soap and water before leaving the laboratory.

O/G/S/A Lab Interactive Worksheets

Tough Tools

Virtual Lab In this Virtual Lab, students conduct an investigation [SEP-3] that allows them to determine the characteristics of ionic, covalent, and covalent network solids. Students analyze qualitative observations (luster, hardness) and quantitative observations (melting point, conductivity) of several different compounds. After analysis of the compounds, students categorize them [CCC-1] based on the data collected. Students use the results from this lab to determine which solid might be most useful for making a high-speed cutting tool. This lab should be assigned after students have a solid understanding of how molecular structure and intermolecular bonding forces in a substance affect the properties of a substance.

- Have students analyze the data and formulate an explanation. **Ask** How does the types of elements that make up a compound affect the properties of the compound? (Compounds with both metal and nonmetal elements tend to have high melting points and are hard. Compounds with only nonmetals tend to have lower melting points and are not as hard. Unlike metals, none of the compounds are conductive solids even if they have metal elements in their composition.)
- Students will need to make connections to understand that substances can share some physical properties (hardness, luster); however, melting points and conductivity are quantitative characteristic properties that can be used to help identify a substance. An example could be that two different metal compounds may share the same color in a flame test but will have different melting points.

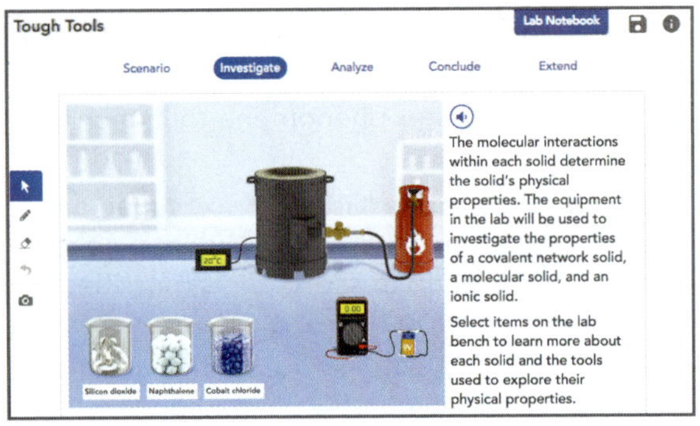

Virtual Lab: Tough Tools

ASSESS ON THE SPOT

Give students notecards and tell them to write a response to the following prompt: How can you identify an ionic solid, a molecular solid, and a covalent network solid? Students can then exchange notecards and evaluate each other's answers.

EXPLAIN

Discuss Melting Materials

Claim-Evidence-Reasoning Use this activity after students have an opportunity to investigate the relationship between the measurable properties of a substance, such as melting point, boiling point, vapor pressure, and surface tension, and the strength of the attractive forces between the particles of the substance. Students consider the melting points of diamond, gold, salt, and sugar. They make a claim about why materials melt at different temperatures. They build a scientific argument about the phenomenon using supportive evidence [SEP-7] and scientific reasoning.

Choose from these suggested strategies to guide students in deepening their understanding of how the properties [PS1.A] of ionic and molecular compounds differ.

- You may wish to provide students with several questions and allow them to choose one on which to base their claim.
- If students have difficulty with writing a question, have them revisit what they learned in the Inquiry Lab and the Virtual Lab.
- After students finish their written argument, have them share their writing with one or more classmates. Remind students that a claim must be backed with facts and scientific reasoning. It should also be clearly stated. Evidence should be presented in an organized and easy-to-understand manner.

DIFFERENTIATED INSTRUCTION

- **Support Struggling Students** Some students may have difficulty constructing a question at the beginning the CER activity. Instruct those students to work with a partner to make a concept map of the information that they gathered as they completed the Inquiry Lab and the Virtual Lab. Groups can analyze the concepts they identify and think about what more they need to know to understand the relationships in the map.
- **Support Advanced Students** After students complete their CER revisions, have them share their revisions in groups of three or four students. Assign advanced students to be group leaders as the groups develop a list of some common features they find in their evidence and reasoning. Then group leaders can meet to make and post a list of the features for all students to see.

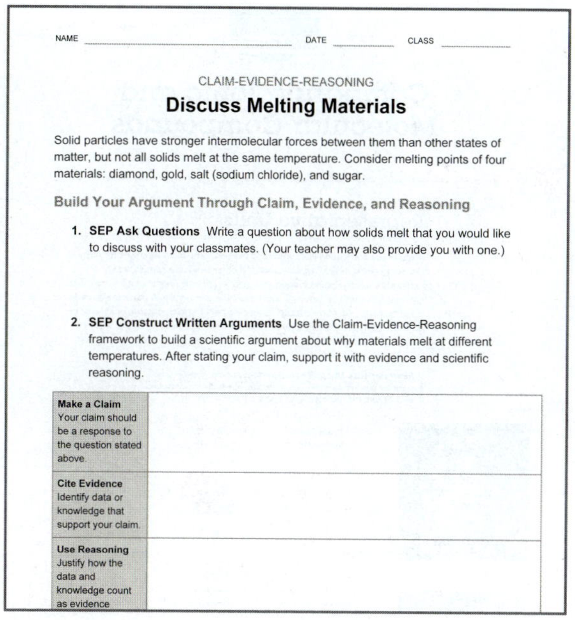
NAME ______ DATE ______ CLASS ______

CLAIM-EVIDENCE-REASONING

Discuss Melting Materials

Solid particles have stronger intermolecular forces between them than other states of matter, but not all solids melt at the same temperature. Consider melting points of four materials: diamond, gold, salt (sodium chloride), and sugar.

Build Your Argument Through Claim, Evidence, and Reasoning

1. **SEP Ask Questions** Write a question about how solids melt that you would like to discuss with your classmates. (Your teacher may also provide you with one.)

2. **SEP Construct Written Arguments** Use the Claim-Evidence-Reasoning framework to build a scientific argument about why materials melt at different temperatures. After stating your claim, support it with evidence and scientific reasoning.

Make a Claim Your claim should be a response to the question stated above.	
Cite Evidence Identify data or knowledge that support your claim.	
Use Reasoning Justify how the data and knowledge count as evidence	

CER Interactive Worksheet

INTEGRATE THE THREE DIMENSIONS

In the CER activity, students construct explanations [SEP-6] about a physical property (melting) of a material by relating it to the type of compound that the material is. They build understanding that the patterns [CCC-1] of interactions [PS2.B] between particles at the molecular scale are reflected in the patterns of behavior at the macroscopic scale.

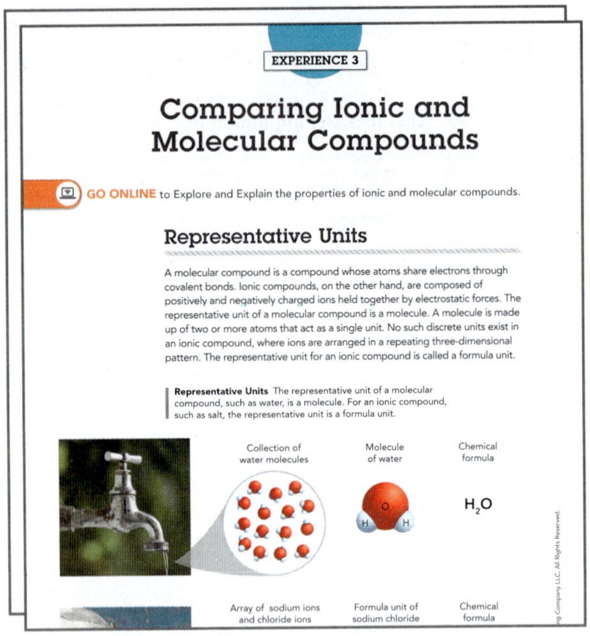
EXPERIENCE 3

Comparing Ionic and Molecular Compounds

GO ONLINE to Explore and Explain the properties of ionic and molecular compounds.

Representative Units

A molecular compound is a compound whose atoms share electrons through covalent bonds. Ionic compounds, on the other hand, are composed of positively and negatively charged ions held together by electrostatic forces. The representative unit of a molecular compound is a molecule. A molecule is made up of two or more atoms that act as a single unit. No such discrete units exist in an ionic compound, where ions are arranged in a repeating three-dimensional pattern. The representative unit for an ionic compound is called a formula unit.

Representative Units The representative unit of a molecular compound, such as water, is a molecule. For an ionic compound, such as salt, the representative unit is a formula unit.

Experience Notebook, pp. 136–140

eTEXT

ELD SUPPORT

Speaking Students will work in small groups to describe the diagrams about allotropes on page 139 of the Experience Notebook and explain how they are different.

- **Emerging/Beginning** Ask each group to define *allotropes* in their own words to share with their peers.
- **Developing/Expanding** Have each group summarize the diagram, Other Crystalline Forms of Carbon, and explain how it models allotropes. Students should prepare the presentation so that they could present it to another group.
- **Bridging** Ask each group to develop an oral presentation about allotropes that they could deliver to a middle school class. Remind them that their descriptions should be adapted for people who may not be familiar with chemistry terms.

ADDRESS PRECONCEPTIONS

Students tend to get the terms *intermolecular* and *intramolecular* confused because they sound familiar. Reinforce that intermolecular bonding is between molecules and intramolecular bonding is between atoms. Tell students that intramolecular has an *a* like in the word *atom*. So intramolecular forces are between atoms that create a molecule.

Comparing Ionic and Molecular Compounds

Experience Notebook Ideally, assign the Experience Notebook or Realize Reader for this experience the day before. Then follow up with any of the following strategies to fill students' knowledge gaps and deepen understanding. Alternatively, you may wish to assign the reading alongside the CER activity.

- **Representative Units** (p. 136) Organize the class into two groups. One half of the class can model [SEP-2] a group of water molecules, and the other group can model an array of sodium and chloride ions.
  1. Two students in the water-molecule group can represent hydrogen by holding hands with another student representing oxygen. Once the water molecule is made, these students should be an arm's length away from other "water molecules" in the group. Instruct this group to discuss how their model represents a molecular compound.
  2. In the array group, half the students raise one of their hands to represent sodium ions, and the other half holds both hands down to represent chloride ions. Students can clump together as tightly as possible. Instruct this group to discuss how their model represents an ionic compound. Have one person from each group explain their model to the other groups.
  3. Have students explain why we do not refer to molecules in an ionic compound but do in a molecular compound. **Ask** Which compound—water or salt—do you think has stronger bonding forces? Why do you think this is so? (I think water has stronger bonding forces because it is a molecular compound.)
- **Determining Compound Type** (p. 137) Reinforce that ionic compounds generally form between metals and nonmetals, whereas molecular compounds form between nonmetals.
  1. Make a set of notecards that have the element symbols for hydrogen (H), potassium (K), bromine (Br), and chlorine (Cl). Write the formulas for potassium bromide (KBr) and hydrochloric acid (HCl), and post them on opposite sides of the classroom. Also, post the terms *metal*, *nonmetal*, *molecular*, and *ionic* on the classroom walls.
  2. Give each student a different card and tell students, based on their cards, to move to the metal or nonmetal sign. Once settled, call on students to use a periodic table to explain why they chose to move to that area.
  3. Next, have students partner with another student to create potassium bromide or hydrochloric acid with their cards and move to the metal or nonmetal card. Again, call on students to tell why they chose the area.
  4. Ask students to explain how the periodic table can be used to determine whether a compound is ionic or covalent. Then have the student pairs (K-Br or H-Cl) move to the molecular or ionic compound side of the classroom. Allow students to discuss why they chose this area.
  5. Ask students what questions they have about the activity that was just completed. Then assign individual expectations for completion of the Ionic and Molecular Compound table on page 137.
- **Properties of Ionic and Molecular Compounds** (p. 138) As a class, discuss how the bond strength between molecules of a compound relates to its melting or boiling point. Make a card set containing covalent and ionic compounds with a picture of the compound at STP on one side and the molecular formula on the other side. Challenge students to order them from lowest to highest boiling point. Discuss the reason for their ordering.

ASSESS ON THE SPOT

Have pairs of students generate a set of questions and answers based on the Experience Notebook. One student asks a question and the partner answers, and then vice versa. Circulate and observe students as they work. Collect students' questions/answers at the end to check for learning. Students' questions should attempt to address:

- Distinguishing an ionic and molecular compound using the periodic table
- Relating properties of molecular and ionic compounds to the intermolecular forces and bonds between their atoms
- Relating these properties to melting and boiling point

How Do You Use a Scatter Plot to Find a Line of Fit?

Virtual Nerd Video In this tutorial, students will learn how to graph data on a coordinate plane and draw a line-of-fit for that data.

Virtual Nerd Video: How Do You Use a Scatter Plot to Find a Line of Fit?

ELABORATE

Melting Materials (15)

Discussion Rubric Before students complete the Discussion Rubric, begin a class discussion about factors that affect the melting point of ionic and molecular compounds. Encourage students to express their ideas and explanations using vocabulary from this experience.

- To help stimulate discussion, ask students to identify the compounds in the CER activity that had the lowest and highest melting points.
- Stress to students that claims should be justified [SEP-7] by citing the characteristics of the types of solids.
- Remind students that evidence should offer specific facts that help explain why the claim is supportable.
- Tell students that reasoning should provide facts about the melting points of materials.
- Give students about 5 minutes to complete the rubric.

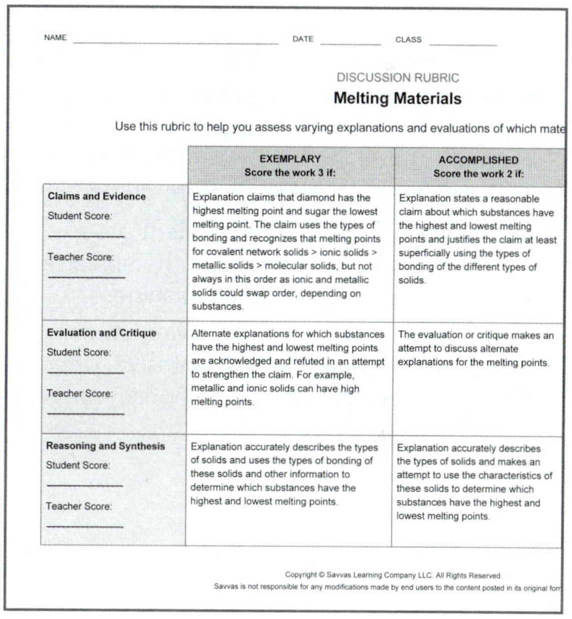

NAME ____________ DATE ________ CLASS ________

DISCUSSION RUBRIC

Melting Materials

Use this rubric to help you assess varying explanations and evaluations of which mate

	EXEMPLARY Score the work 3 if:	ACCOMPLISHED Score the work 2 if:
Claims and Evidence Student Score: ______ Teacher Score: ______	Explanation claims that diamond has the highest melting point and sugar the lowest melting point. The claim uses the types of bonding and recognizes that melting points for covalent network solids > ionic solids > metallic solids > molecular solids, but not always in this order as ionic and metallic solids could swap order, depending on substances.	Explanation states a reasonable claim about which substances have the highest and lowest melting points and justifies the claim at least superficially using the types of bonding of the different types of solids.
Evaluation and Critique Student Score: ______ Teacher Score: ______	Alternate explanations for which substances have the highest and lowest melting points are acknowledged and refuted in an attempt to strengthen the claim. For example, metallic and ionic solids can have high melting points.	The evaluation or critique makes an attempt to discuss alternate explanations for the melting points.
Reasoning and Synthesis Student Score: ______ Teacher Score: ______	Explanation accurately describes the types of solids and uses the types of bonding of these solids and other information to determine which substances have the highest and lowest melting points.	Explanation accurately describes the types of solids and makes an attempt to use the characteristics of these solids to determine which substances have the highest and lowest melting points.

Discussion Rubric Interactive Worksheet

ASSESS ON THE SPOT

After the discussion, challenge students to write a 12-word summary of how they will adjust their claim based on their evaluation from the rubric. Pair students and tell them to share their summaries with each other. Then invite students to share their summaries with the class.

PROFESSIONAL DEVELOPMENT

Background Notes A covalent network solid is made up of a network of the same or different atoms that are held together by covalent bonds. Localized electrons are shared between the atoms, and the atoms are in a fixed position. This network of covalent bonds extends throughout the solid, so the structure is similar to a very large molecule. The difference is that a network solid does not have distinct molecules, and the number of atoms is not fixed; it depends on the size of the structure. Some examples of network solids are diamond, graphite, and silicon dioxide (quartz).

Network solids tend to be hard and brittle with extremely high melting and boiling points because the covalent bonds holding them together are strong and not easily broken. They tend to be poor electrical conductors because all of their valence electrons are bound in covalent bonds. The strong covalent bonds in network solids also generally make them insoluble.

CONNECT TO CAREERS

Pharmacist When people get sick, they go to a pharmacist to get the medication their doctor prescribes. Pharmacists focus on the properties of different substances and making formulations to treat specific health problems. They dispense medications and tell people how to safely use the medications. Some pharmacists also provide health and wellness screening and provide immunizations. They often provide information about over-the-counter medications. The training to become a licensed pharmacist is rigorous, requiring a Doctor of Pharmacy degree.

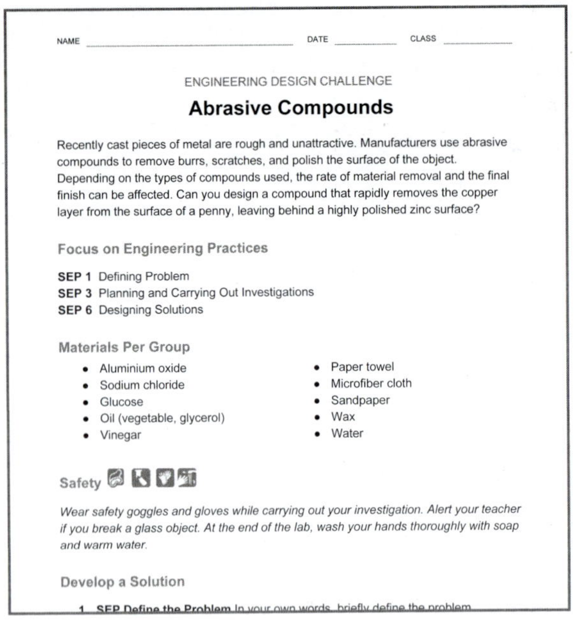
NAME ______ DATE ______ CLASS ______

ENGINEERING DESIGN CHALLENGE

Abrasive Compounds

Recently cast pieces of metal are rough and unattractive. Manufacturers use abrasive compounds to remove burrs, scratches, and polish the surface of the object. Depending on the types of compounds used, the rate of material removal and the final finish can be affected. Can you design a compound that rapidly removes the copper layer from the surface of a penny, leaving behind a highly polished zinc surface?

Focus on Engineering Practices

SEP 1 Defining Problem
SEP 3 Planning and Carrying Out Investigations
SEP 6 Designing Solutions

Materials Per Group

- Aluminium oxide
- Sodium chloride
- Glucose
- Oil (vegetable, glycerol)
- Vinegar
- Paper towel
- Microfiber cloth
- Sandpaper
- Wax
- Water

Safety

Wear safety goggles and gloves while carrying out your investigation. Alert your teacher if you break a glass object. At the end of the lab, wash your hands thoroughly with soap and warm water.

Develop a Solution

1. **SEP Define the Problem** In your own words, briefly define the problem.

Engineering Design Challenge Interactive Worksheet

CLASSROOM MODIFICATIONS

Based on your students' abilities and your schedule, you may wish to edit the Abrasive Compounds Engineering Design Challenge to make it more open ended or more guided.

- **More Open Ended** Have student groups challenge each other to make the abrasive that polishes with the greatest shine.
- **More Guided** Rather than having students devise the formula for their abrasive, offer them a list of alternatives to choose from.

Abrasive Compounds

Engineering Design Challenge In this Engineering Design Challenge, students design a compound that rapidly removes the copper layer from the surface of a penny and leaves behind a highly polished zinc surface. After identifying criteria and constraints of the problem [ETS1.A] and conducting research, students develop a formula for their abrasive compound and then test it. Groups evaluate their compounds and explain whether they think their abrasive compound was successful. Finally, groups describe how they might improve [ETS1.C] their compounds to better meet the criteria and constraints.

Materials and Advance Preparation aluminum oxide, sodium chloride, glucose, vegetable oil or glycerol, vinegar, paper towel, microfiber cloth, sandpaper, wax, water

Safety Remind students to wear safety goggles and gloves while carrying out the investigation. Students should be reminded to be careful when handling glass and to alert you should any glass break. At the end of the lab, make sure students wash their hands with soap and warm water.

Use the following strategies to guide students as they complete the indicated steps in the Engineering Design Challenge.

- **Step 2** Students may have difficulty determining the criteria and constraints of the engineering problem. Remind them that criteria are the goals that the design must accomplish and that they are derived from the defined problem. Constraints are the limits on materials or resources that affect how the problem can be addressed. If a significant number of students are struggling with these concepts, address the question as a class discussion.
- **Step 3** Remind students that as they research, they should use only reliable Web sites. You may wish to provide a list of pre-approved sites.
- **Step 8** Have each group describe to the class their solution to the problem and how well the solution worked. They should also describe their proposed refinements.

PROFESSIONAL DEVELOPMENT

Background Notes Abrasives tend to have crystalline structures that can be ionic, covalent, or molecular.

- Ionic crystals are hard and brittle, but they shatter easily under stress. Ions in crystals are held together by electrostatic attraction. Sodium chloride is an ionic crystal.
- Covalent crystals are hard and often brittle. The atoms in covalent crystals are covalently bonded with neighboring atoms, forming one large "molecule." Breaking these bonds requires a large amount of energy. Examples of covalent crystals are diamond and silicon dioxide.
- Molecular crystals tend to be soft, and they melt at relatively low temperatures. Their molecules are held together by relatively weak intermolecular forces. Examples of molecular crystals are ice and sugar.

EVALUATE

Comparing Ionic and Molecular Compounds

Quiz Assign the quiz in online technology-enhanced, auto-graded format or as an editable worksheet. Use the scoring notes and remediation strategies found online to assess students' responses and to provide targeted feedback for each item to remediate well before assigning the summative 3-D Assessment.

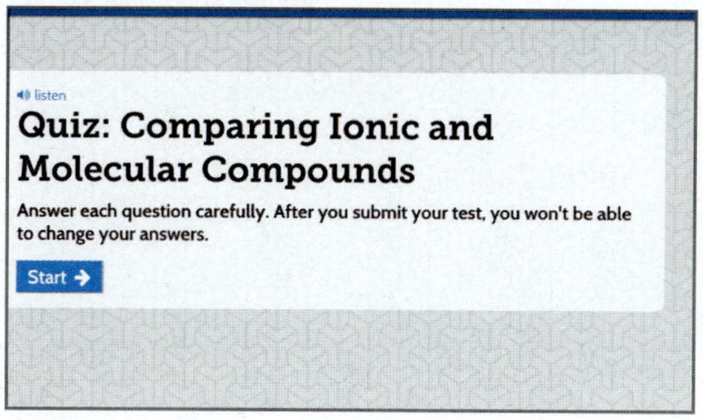

Interactive Online Quiz

Quiz Interactive Worksheet

REMEDIATION SUGGESTIONS

- **If** students are having trouble describing how the types of elements that make up a compound affect the properties of the compound, **then** have them review the Virtual Lab and their responses to the questions.
- **If** students are having difficulty identifying the representative units of an ionic and molecular compound, **then** have them look at the diagram on page 136 of the Experience Notebook and identify the respective representative units in each compound type.
- **If** students are not able to distinguish whether a compound is ionic or molecular based on its chemical formula, **then** have students write the names and chemical formulas of common ionic and molecular compounds on notecards. Then they can use a periodic table to sort them into ionic and molecular compound categories.
- **If** students struggle with verbalizing the concept of intermolecular forces of attraction, **then** have students revisit the information and diagrams on page 138 of the Experience Notebook.

Revisit

INVESTIGATIVE PHENOMENON

Support Reflection Students can complete the reflection prompt, where they will unpack and make sense of the Investigative Phenomenon, based on practices and understandings that have been reinforced over the course of the experience.

- Ask students to develop a connection between bond energy and heat energy.
- Have student pairs discuss the effects of high-bond-energy compounds versus low-bond-energy compounds on the temperature of a hand warmer. Have students form a consensus group by joining with another pair to discuss their ideas. Wrap up the discussion with a whole-class consensus.
- Allow students time to use evidence and reasoning to address how differences in strength between ionic and covalent bonds connect to the Investigative Phenomenon.

Further Develop Your CER Argument Have students add any additional evidence they have collected in this experience. Encourage students to expand their arguments to include other materials, such as molecular compounds, ionic compounds, and network solids.

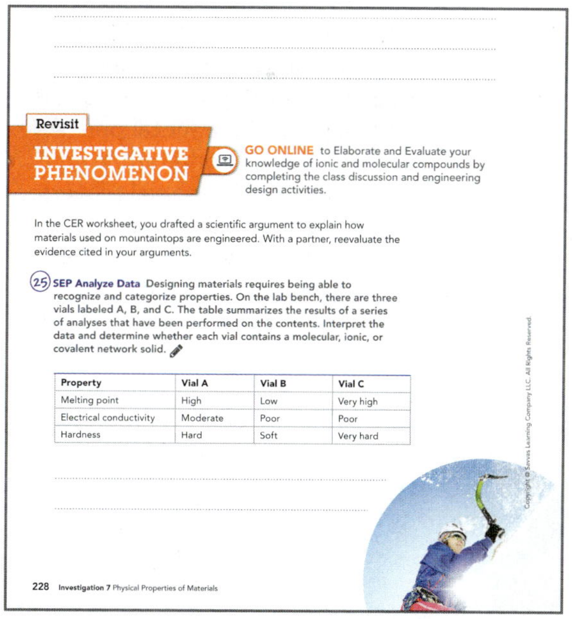
Revisit

INVESTIGATIVE PHENOMENON

GO ONLINE to Elaborate and Evaluate your knowledge of ionic and molecular compounds by completing the class discussion and engineering design activities.

In the CER worksheet, you drafted a scientific argument to explain how materials used on mountaintops are engineered. With a partner, reevaluate the evidence cited in your arguments.

(25) **SEP Analyze Data** Designing materials requires being able to recognize and categorize properties. On the lab bench, there are three vials labeled A, B, and C. The table summarizes the results of a series of analyses that have been performed on the contents. Interpret the data and determine whether each vial contains a molecular, ionic, or covalent network solid.

Property	Vial A	Vial B	Vial C
Melting point	High	Low	Very high
Electrical conductivity	Moderate	Poor	Poor
Hardness	Hard	Soft	Very hard

Copyright © Savvas Learning Company LLC. All Rights Reserved.

228 Investigation 7 Physical Properties of Materials

Experience Notebook, p. 140

eTEXT

EXPERIENCE 4

Comparing Metals and Nonmetals

Teacher Background

Experience 4 provides information about the differences between metals and nonmetals, focusing on the delocalized nature of electrons in metals and how this structure leads to metallic properties. Students learn what makes one metal more malleable or ductile than another. They engineer a bike frame suited to a specific use. Students plan and carry out investigations about the nature of metallic properties.

Objectives

- **Analyze data comparing metals and nonmetals and construct explanations for their differences.**
- **Summarize defining properties of metals.**
- **Describe how delocalized electrons give rise to metallic properties.**

RELATED PHENOMENA

In addition to the Wrapping It Up teacher demo, consider using other phenomena to launch this experience.

- **Metal Comparison** Heat a chunk of sulfur and compare it with heating a chunk of zinc or copper. Ask students to explain why the metal doesn't liquefy or give off a scent.
- **Wood or Metal?** Ask students to describe how playing with a wooden racket or bat is different from playing with a metal one. **Ask** How does a metal bat feel different from a wooden bat? Professional baseball players sometimes crack their wooden bats when they hit the ball. What property describes why a metal bat would never crack or splinter?
- **Similar and Different** Show students a chunk of iodine and a chunk of dark metal, such as lead. Discuss (or demonstrate) why even though iodine and the metal look similar, they have differences in electrical conductivity and malleability.

ENGAGE

EVERYDAY PHENOMENON

How does aluminum foil compare with plastic wrap?

Use this teacher demo to prompt student discussion about how metals differ from nonmetals. Address ideas and questions from students as they arise, and refer to them while doing the Inquiry Lab.

Wrapping It Up

Engage students with this demonstration of the differences between aluminum foil and plastic wrap to get them thinking about the properties of metals and nonmetals.

Materials roll of aluminum foil, roll of plastic wrap

1. Show students the rolls of foil and plastic wrap. Note that the plastic wrap has no metal in it, and the foil is aluminum. Point out that we use both materials to wrap food, but because they have different properties, we use them in different ways.
2. Tell students to observe as you tear off a sheet from each roll. **Ask** How do the sheets tear differently? (The aluminum foil tears off more easily.) How do those differences relate to the sheet being metal or nonmetal? (The foil is thicker and smoother, which helps it to tear in a cleaner way.)
3. Make each sheet into a ball. Roll each ball and have students observe. **Ask** How do the materials behave differently after being balled up? (The plastic wrap, unlike the foil, sticks slightly as it is rolled.) Prompt students to describe other differences they observe between the foil and plastic wrap. List the differences on the board. **Ask** Where have you seen metals bend, dent, or change shape? Compile a class list.
4. Ask students to discuss why they might choose one material instead of another for a specific function. **Ask** How can you use what you learned in this demonstration to change the properties of a pure metal? What property would you change?

EXPLORE

Modeling Metals, Ceramics, and Polymers

(35)

Inquiry Lab In this lab, students develop models [SEP-2] to examine properties [PS1.A] of metals, ceramics, and polymers.

Lab Demo Video Watch the Lab Demo Video for advice on materials and preparation.

Choose Your Version Open-ended (O), Guided (G), Shortened (S), Advanced (A)

Materials 10 bamboo skewers, 50-mL beaker, 30 chenille wires, 14 1-in. expanded-polystyrene balls, 50-mL graduated cylinder, 10 cm x 10 cm x 5 cm plastic tub, scissors, water

Expected Outcome Students observe that metals can conduct electricity, that ceramics are strong but rigid, and that adding branches and crosslinks to polymers results in a stronger, more rigid, plastic.

Lab Summary Video Watch the Lab Summary Video for support on connecting the lab investigation to the Investigative Phenomenon.

NAME ______ DATE ______ CLASS ______

COMPARING METALS AND NONMETALS INQUIRY LABS – OPEN

Modeling Metals, Ceramics, and Polymers

What gives different materials their properties? The modern materials that we encounter on a daily basis are tailored to their application. By constructing models we can start to rationalize why specific properties arise and how to more efficiently develop new materials. In this activity you will make models of metals as well as nonmetallic ceramics and polymers.

Focus on Science Practices

SEP 2 Developing and Using Models
SEP 3 Planning and Carrying Out Investigations

Materials Per Group

- Bamboo skewers, 10
- Beaker, 50 mL
- Chenille wires, 30
- Expanded polystyrene balls, 1 in., 14
- Graduated cylinder, 50 mL
- Plastic tub, approximately 10 cm x 10 cm x 5 cm
- Scissors
- Water

Procedure

Part 1. Metals

1. Place an expanded polystyrene ball into the beaker. This ball represents a metal atom.
2. Add 20 ml of water to beaker. This represents the metal atom's delocalized electrons.
3. Pour the contents of the beaker into the plastic tub.

O/G/S/A Lab Interactive Worksheets

PROFESSIONAL DEVELOPMENT

Background Notes Most ceramics are inorganic compounds that are held together by ionic and covalent bonds. General properties include:

- insulators of electricity and heat
- very hard and stiff
- abrasion resistant
- brittle; cannot be reshaped easily
- resistant to corrosive elements and high temperatures

Most polymers are organic substances and are composed of huge chains of hydrocarbons. They generally have these properties:

- insulator of electricity and heat
- flexible
- relatively soft; can be easily formed
- unstable at high temperatures
- lightweight

Metals and Nonmetals: Data About Their Properties

(15)

Analyzing Data In this activity, students compare data [SEP-4] about melting points, boiling points, and densities of a set of metals and nonmetals. They identify patterns [CCC-1] that can help them categorize metals and nonmetals. Then students construct an explanation [SEP-6] to describe what the data suggests about the strengths of the molecular bonds in the substances. Finally, students explain whether they agree with the claim [SEP-8] that silicon should be classified as a metal.

Pair students to discuss trends they observe in the data. **Ask:**

- What patterns do you see in terms of states of matter, boiling points, melting points, and densities? (The metals have higher melting points and boiling points. The nonmetals have lower densities.)
- What can you infer about physical properties of metals versus nonmetals? (Metals are stronger than nonmetals.)

As a class, discuss possible reasons for the difference in melting and boiling points between metals and nonmetals. Guide students through using reasoning to predict the melting and boiling points of sulfur and calcium.

NAME ______ DATE ______ CLASS ______

ANALYZING DATA

Metals and Nonmetals: Data About Their Properties

The elements in the periodic table can be divided into metals and nonmetals. Metals have characteristic properties, such as being good conductors of heat and electricity and generally being strong, malleable, and ductile. Nonmetals tend to be brittle and are relatively poor conductors of heat and electricity.

Figure 1 shows the melting and boiling points of some metals and nonmetals at standard pressure. **Figure 2** shows their densities at standard temperature and pressure.

Analyzing Data Interactive Worksheet

CLASSROOM MODIFICATIONS

Based on your students' abilities and your schedule, you may wish to edit the Analyzing Data worksheet to make it more open ended or more guided.

- **More Open Ended** Replace Questions 1 through 5 with directions to students to use the information in the figures to identify trends in the data.
- **More Guided** Read the temperature of the classroom from a thermometer, and write it on the board. Have students circle all elements that have melting points below room temperature. Have them draw a box around the elements that have boiling points below room temperature. Or you may wish to display the tables and mark them up as a class. Help students use their marked-up table to answer the questions.

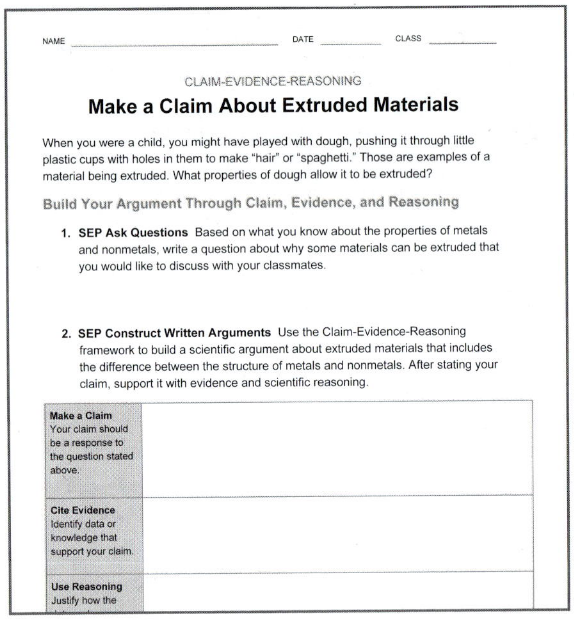
NAME ______________ DATE ________ CLASS ________

CLAIM-EVIDENCE-REASONING

Make a Claim About Extruded Materials

When you were a child, you might have played with dough, pushing it through little plastic cups with holes in them to make "hair" or "spaghetti." Those are examples of a material being extruded. What properties of dough allow it to be extruded?

Build Your Argument Through Claim, Evidence, and Reasoning

1. **SEP Ask Questions** Based on what you know about the properties of metals and nonmetals, write a question about why some materials can be extruded that you would like to discuss with your classmates.

2. **SEP Construct Written Arguments** Use the Claim-Evidence-Reasoning framework to build a scientific argument about extruded materials that includes the difference between the structure of metals and nonmetals. After stating your claim, support it with evidence and scientific reasoning.

Make a Claim Your claim should be a response to the question stated above.	
Cite Evidence Identify data or knowledge that support your claim.	
Use Reasoning Justify how the	

CER Interactive Worksheet

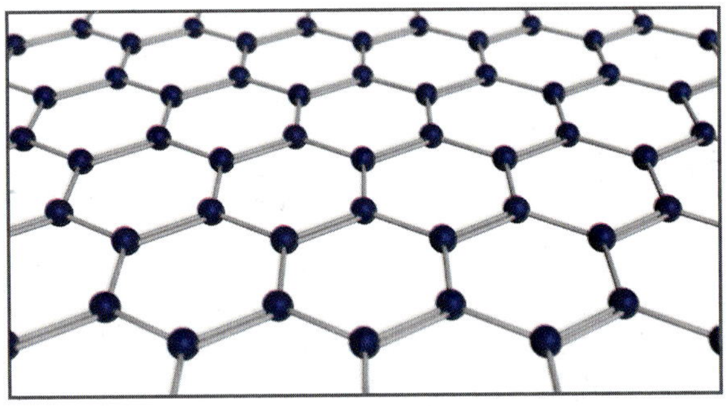

Animation: Metallic Solids and Covalent Network Solids

ELD SUPPORT

Listening Small groups of students use what they learn in the animation to relate how properties and molecular structures vary between materials.

- **Emerging/Beginning** Ask students to identify the concept being discussed in the animation and make one statement about it. Repeat the section of the animation if students need to hear it again.
- **Developing/Expanding** Have students verbally compare and contrast bonding in metals and nonmetals.
- **Bridging** Ask students to summarize verbally how the difference in bonding between metals and nonmetals gives rise to their properties.

ASSESS ON THE SPOT

As a class, make a concept map that describes how melting point, boiling point, density, and metals/nonmetals are related. Provide time for students to ask questions and have other students respond to the questions.

EXPLAIN

Make a Claim About Extruded Materials

Claim-Evidence-Reasoning Students make a claim about extruded materials that includes the difference between the structure of metals and nonmetals.

- Tell students to think about what they learned in the activity, Metals and Nonmetals: Data About Their Properties. Encourage them to discuss with a partner how this information can be used as evidence to support their claim in this activity.
- As a class, develop a list of properties that describe metals and nonmetals. Prompt students to identify as many of these properties in their explanation to support their claims.
- Provide students with an opportunity to revisit their CER arguments throughout this experience for further revision and peer review.

Metallic Solids and Covalent Network Solids

Animation This animation explores the differences in the bonding of metallic solids and covalent network solids. Through visual models [SEP-2], students see how structure on the atomic level of copper, graphite, and diamond gives rise to macroscopic structure and function [PS1.A].

- Before students view the animation, explain that the material we think of as pencil lead is actually carbon in its graphite form. Tell them that diamonds are also pure carbon. Encourage students to consider what might be happening on the atomic level to give these two materials such different properties. **Ask** How can two solids, both pure forms of carbon, have such different properties? (The carbon atoms are arranged in two different ways. They have different properties due to the different types of bonding in those solids.)
- Pair students to watch the animation. Tell them to pause the animation to take notes and to record any questions it raises for them. When pairs finish watching, ask students to share their questions and discuss the answers. Call on other students in the class to contribute explanations.

ASSESS ON THE SPOT

Have students use a Venn diagram to compare metallic solids and covalent network solids. Collect the completed diagram and assess understanding. If necessary, review the animation again as a class, stopping to ask questions to clarify information as needed.

Comparing Metals and Nonmetals

Experience Notebook Ideally, assign the Experience Notebook or Realize Reader first, and then follow up with any of the following suggested instructional strategies to fill knowledge gaps and deepen understanding.

Use these strategies to help students make sense of the images and text on the indicated pages, as well as to engage in science practices.

- **Delocalized Electrons** (p. 141) Call on students to tell what they think the word *delocalized* means and to give a sentence using *delocalized* with that meaning. Then point out that the word can have different meanings in different situations. Explain that in chemistry, *delocalized electrons* refer to electrons that are not associated with a single atom or covalent bond. Use the diagram on the page to further discuss delocalized electrons.
- **Ductility and Malleability** (p. 142) As a class, make a list of metal items that students are familiar with. Compare malleability among items and guide a class discussion of what the differences are at the atomic level between the more and less malleable metals.
- **Conductivity and Luster** (p. 143) Have student partners make a list of the five properties [PS1.A] of metals that arise from the presence of delocalized electrons (ductility, malleability, luster, thermal and electrical conductivity). Prompt them to share with the class at least one example of how we make use of these properties in objects that we design. Then identify any patterns [CCC-1] in the metals used for the types of examples students provide.
- **Crystalline Structure and Properties of Metals** (p. 144) Have partners build models [SEP-2] of a crystalline structure using spaghetti and mini-marshmallows or putty to help them better understand the slippage planes in FCC and BCC structures. Circulate among pairs to be sure they form the correct structures. Then guide a discussion about how these structures affect ductility.
- **Defects and the Properties of Metals** (pp. 145–146) Have groups review the figure and discuss the following prompts:
  a. Use the diagrams on page 146 to explain why moving dislocations in a metal would make it more brittle.
  b. What kind of dislocation does the network of atoms have?
  c. How do you think different types of dislocations affect the hardness of a metal? Explain your reasoning, and consider the alloy of iron and carbon to make steel.

Have groups share their responses and discuss as a class.

DIFFERENTIATED INSTRUCTION

- **Support Special Needs Students** Assess what environment students need to best complete the Experience Notebook, considering which students work best in pairs and which will benefit most from being able to work alone. Create both quiet and active spaces for students and assess which environment they will benefit most from.
- **Support Struggling Students** Suggest that students who are struggling with a concept underline passages or circle graphics they do not understand. Encourage them to look for words that explain the graphic or a graphic that illustrates the words and make connections between them.
- **Support Less Proficient Readers** Provide students with a vocabulary list that includes words from the Experience Notebook and appropriate scientific vocabulary that they may not have mastered yet. Have students underline unfamiliar words as they read. Then review the definitions of these words. Students may also write the definition in their own words.
- **Support Advanced Students** Challenge students to make a hands-on model that demonstrates how delocalized electrons contribute to malleability and ductility of metals. Invite them to share their models with classmates.

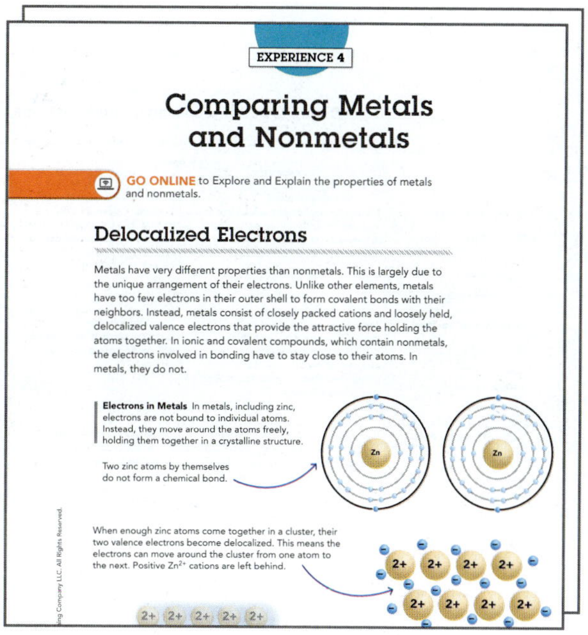
EXPERIENCE 4

Comparing Metals and Nonmetals

GO ONLINE to Explore and Explain the properties of metals and nonmetals.

Delocalized Electrons

Metals have very different properties than nonmetals. This is largely due to the unique arrangement of their electrons. Unlike other elements, metals have too few electrons in their outer shell to form covalent bonds with their neighbors. Instead, metals consist of closely packed cations and loosely held, delocalized valence electrons that provide the attractive force holding the atoms together. In ionic and covalent compounds, which contain nonmetals, the electrons involved in bonding have to stay close to their atoms. In metals, they do not.

Electrons in Metals In metals, including zinc, electrons are not bound to individual atoms. Instead, they move around the atoms freely, holding them together in a crystalline structure.

Two zinc atoms by themselves do not form a chemical bond.

When enough zinc atoms come together in a cluster, their two valence electrons become delocalized. This means the electrons can move around the cluster from one atom to the next. Positive Zn^{2+} cations are left behind.

Experience Notebook, pp. 141–147

eTEXT

CONNECT TO CAREERS

Metallurgist Many metal objects students use each day were designed by scientists or engineers who specialize in understanding the properties of metals. Metallurgists are engineers or materials scientists who determine how to extract a metal from an ore, investigate ways to leverage the properties of metals for different applications, or design processes for creating alloys with a desired set of characteristics. Invite students to choose an everyday metal object, such as silverware, buttons, or a trash can, and devise a list of properties the metal would require for the object to fulfill its purpose and last over time. Then tell students to research how a metallurgist would work with people in other fields, such as a product designer, to create the product.

NAME ________ DATE ______ CLASS ______

DISCUSSION RUBRIC

Differences Between Metals and Nonmetals

Use this rubric to help you assess your evaluation of which materials can b

	EXEMPLARY Score the work 3 if:	**ACCOMPLISHED** Score the work 2 if:
Claims and Evidence Student Score: ____ Teacher Score: ____	Explanation claims that materials that are malleable or ductile can be extruded and describes the delocalization of valence electrons that allow metals to be both.	Explanation states a reasonable claim about what materials can be extruded and justifies the claim at least superficially using the characteristics of metals.
Evaluation and Critique Student Score: ____ Teacher Score: ____	The explanation acknowledges that it is not the labels nonmetal and metal that determine whether a material can be extruded but the characteristics of the material and the type of bonding and/or intermolecular forces.	The explanation makes an attempt to discuss alternate explanations for why certain materials can be extruded.
Reasoning and Synthesis Student Score: ____ Teacher Score: ____	Explanation accurately describes the characteristics of metals and nonmetals and connects the characteristics of materials that can be extruded. Delocalized electrons in metals which allow atoms to slide past each other is discussed. Other attributes of pastes (which are mixtures) may be discussed.	Explanations accurately describe characteristics of metals and nonmetals and make an attempt to connect the characteristics and bonding/intermolecular forces of materials that can be extruded.

Discussion Rubric Interactive Worksheet

NAME ________ DATE ______ CLASS ______

ENGINEERING DESIGN CHALLENGE

Building a Better Bike

Every year between 15 and 20 million new bikes are sold in America. The two largest components of any bicycle are the frame and the wheels. The type of material used in the bicycle's frame has a major effect on its properties. An ideal frame needs to be lightweight, long lasting, inexpensive, and easy to assemble. Can you design a model bicycle frame that can stand up to the rigors of daily use?

Focus on Engineering Practices

SEP 1 Defining the Problem
SEP 3 Planning and Carrying Out Investigations
SEP 6 Designing Solutions

Materials Per Group (Suggested)

- Aluminum strips
- Aluminum wire, 16 gauge
- Bamboo skewer
- Cardstock, rolled
- Chenille wire
- Clay
- Tape

Develop a Solution

1. **SEP Define the Problem** In your own words, briefly define the problem.

Engineering Design Challenge Interactive Worksheet

INTEGRATE THE THREE DIMENSIONS

In the Engineering Design Challenge, students research to obtain information [SEP-8] about the structure and function [CCC-6] of bicycle frames. They plan and carry out an investigation [SEP-3] to test the materials they have chosen for the bicycle frame. Students should consider the contact forces [PS2.B] between material objects, such as how much weight the frame support, when identifying the criteria and constraints of their design prototype.

ELABORATE

Differences Between Metals and Nonmetals

Discussion Rubric Students revisit the claims they made in the CER activity, Make a Claim about Extruded Materials, and revise them after discussing with their peers.

- Form small groups of students that have similar claims. Have students work together to discuss their evidence and reasoning. Tell groups to compare their claims, evidence, and reasoning and revise their previous work.
- If any students have claims dissimilar to the claims of other classmates, group them together and have them present their claims, evidence, and reasoning to each other individually.
- After all students have reviewed and revised their claims, have them use the rubric to evaluate themselves. Remind them that for this activity, the accuracy of their self-evaluation is important.

Building a Better Bike

Engineering Design Challenge In this Engineering Design Challenge, student groups define the problem [ETS1.A] of how to develop a bicycle frame that is tough and inexpensive. They identify criteria and constraints and determine materials for their design prototype. Students test their bicycle frames and evaluate their solutions [ETS1.C].

Materials aluminum strips, 16-gauge aluminum wire, bamboo skewer, cardboard tubes, chenille wire, clay, tape

Safety Monitor students while they construct the bicycle frames.

Expected Outcome Students gain an appreciation for the properties of different types of materials and their applications.

Use the following strategies to guide students as they complete indicated steps in the Engineering Design Challenge.

- **Step 2** Copy the chart onto the board and fill it in as the whole class works together to identify the criteria and constraints. Encourage students to think about the type of environment their bicycle would be used in as they develop criteria.
- **Step 3** If possible, provide students with URLs for some Web sites that they could use for their research.
- **Step 6** Remind students that they should think of tests that challenge the entire frame and not just a portion of it. Dropping, rocking, and swaying the frame might all be options to see how the frame handles different types of impacts and stressors.

ASSESS ON THE SPOT

Have students write two or three sentences that summarize what they learned in the design challenge and cite an example of how it can be applied to designing products on a larger scale, such as trains or airplanes. Collect the writing samples and critique them for understanding. Return them to students and guide a class discussion on any points that were confusing or challenging.

EVALUATE

Comparing Metals and Nonmetals

Quiz Assign the quiz in online technology-enhanced, auto-graded format or as an editable quiz worksheet. Use the scoring notes and remediation strategies found online to assess students' responses and to provide targeted feedback for each item to remediate well before assigning the summative 3-D Assessment.

REMEDIATION SUGGESTIONS

- **If** students are struggling to understand the properties of metals and nonmetals, **then** direct them back to the Analyzing Data activity, Metals and Nonmetals: Data About Their Properties.
- **If** students are having difficulty grasping the differences between atomic bonding in pure nonmetals versus pure metals, **then** suggest they review the animation, writing clarification questions that they can discuss with you or another classmate.
- **If** students are struggling to understand how delocalized electrons make metals ductile and malleable, **then** direct them to study the graphic on page 142 and draw their own model that is labeled with explanations.
- **If** students are struggling to describe how dislocations affect the hardness of metal, **then** have them build a three-dimensional model of the graphic, Shear Force, on page 146 of the Experience Notebook to assess the strength of the structure, move the dislocation, and reassess.
- **If** students are having difficulty grasping the importance of understanding properties of materials when designing products, **then** have them revisit the Engineering Design Challenge, Building a Better Bike.

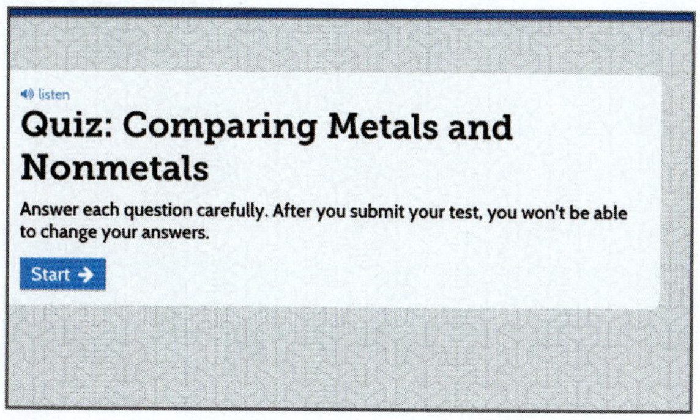
listen

Quiz: Comparing Metals and Nonmetals

Answer each question carefully. After you submit your test, you won't be able to change your answers.

Start

Interactive Online Quiz

Quiz Interactive Worksheet

Revisit

INVESTIGATIVE PHENOMENON

Support Reflection Students can complete the reflection prompt, where they will unpack and make sense of the Investigative Phenomenon, based on practices and understandings that have been reinforced over the course of this experience.

- Have students work in pairs to make a list of criteria a climbing rope needs to meet to be reliable and useful for a climber. Remind students that they can review the Inquiry Lab, Analyzing Data activity, and Experience Notebook for information on properties of metals and nonmetals. Suggest that pairs consider:

  a. Weather and climate elements the rope must withstand
  b. The path a rope may have to follow across a rock face
  c. How a climber can get a good grip on the rope
  d. Whether their design can reasonably be manufactured

Further Develop Your CER Argument Have students add any additional evidence they have collected in this experience. Evidence may include patterns of bonding in metals and nonmetals, the role of delocalized electrons in lending metals their ductility and malleability, and the effects of different metal crystalline structures of ductility.

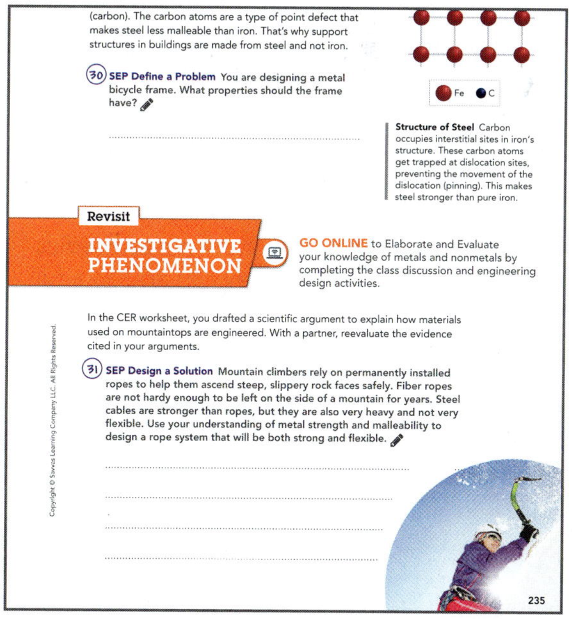
(carbon). The carbon atoms are a type of point defect that makes steel less malleable than iron. That's why support structures in buildings are made from steel and not iron.

30 **SEP Define a Problem** You are designing a metal bicycle frame. What properties should the frame have?

Fe C

Structure of Steel Carbon occupies interstitial sites in iron's structure. These carbon atoms get trapped at dislocation sites, preventing the movement of the dislocation (pinning). This makes steel stronger than pure iron.

Revisit INVESTIGATIVE PHENOMENON

GO ONLINE to Elaborate and Evaluate your knowledge of metals and nonmetals by completing the class discussion and engineering design activities.

In the CER worksheet, you drafted a scientific argument to explain how materials used on mountaintops are engineered. With a partner, reevaluate the evidence cited in your arguments.

31 **SEP Design a Solution** Mountain climbers rely on permanently installed ropes to help them ascend steep, slippery rock faces safely. Fiber ropes are not hardy enough to be left on the side of a mountain for years. Steel cables are stronger than ropes, but they are also very heavy and not very flexible. Use your understanding of metal strength and malleability to design a rope system that will be both strong and flexible.

Copyright © Savvas Learning Company LLC. All Rights Reserved.

235

Experience Notebook, p. 147

eTEXT

EXPERIENCE 5

Water and Aqueous Systems

Teacher Background

Experience 5 is a basic overview of hydrogen bonding, aqueous solutions, and hydrates. Students describe and model hydrogen bonding and then discover how it underlies many basic phenomena, such as surface tension, boiling point and the flotation of ice in water. Investigations will be carried out to discover the effect of polarity on the formation of solutions and a solution's ability to conduct electricity. Water can also be bonded tightly to solid structures, as students discover when they look at hydrates.

Objectives

- **Investigate the role of polarity in hydrogen bonding between water molecules.**
- **Discover how hydrogen bonding affects surface tension, boiling point, and the formation of ice.**
- **Develop a model that demonstrates the process of solvation within an aqueous solution.**
- **Diagram and explain why electrolytes conduct electricity and nonelectrolytes do not.**
- **Analyze the role of pressure in the efflorescence of hydrates.**

ENGAGE

EVERYDAY PHENOMENON

Can you make water "wetter"?

Use this teacher demo to prompt student discussion about why we use detergents to clean our dishes and clothes.

Hydrophobic Water Drops

Engage students with this demonstration of an everyday phenomenon to introduce the concept of surfactants and their role in our lives.

Materials pipettes, wax paper, dish detergent, water

1. Place a sheet of wax paper approximately 30 cm long on a tabletop.
2. Using the pipette, place several drops of water on the sheet of wax paper.
3. Ask students to observe the shape of the droplets and to formulate a hypothesis as to why they are shaped this way.
4. Ask students to predict what will happen if a drop of dish detergent is added to a water drop.
5. Using the pipette, add a drop of dish detergent to each of the water drops.
6. Ask students to diagram the shape of the drops before and after detergent was added. Encourage them to think about how this phenomenon enables water to clean more effectively. Use what students learn in this demo to introduce the Inquiry Lab.

RELATED PHENOMENA

In addition to the Hydrophobic Water Drops teacher demo, consider using other phenomena to launch this experience.

- **Sinking CD** Demonstrate that a compact disc (CD) will not sink if placed on the surface of a water in a container. Then add a few drops of liquid detergent to the water and note that the CD sinks. Ask students why they think this happens.
- **Paper Clip Frenzy** Ask students to predict how many paper clips they can add to a full cup of water before the water runs over the side of the cup. They will typically be able to add hundreds of paper clips! The water will not overflow due to surface tension.

EXPLORE

Investigate Surface Tension

Inquiry Lab In this lab, students work in small groups to carry out an investigation [SEP-3] examining surface tension. By analyzing their data [SEP-4] and identifying patterns [CCC-1], students determine how they can change the surface tension of water.

Lab Demo Video Watch the Lab Demo Video for advice on materials and preparation.

Choose Your Version Open-ended (O), Guided (G), Shortened (S), Advanced (A)

Materials paper clip, tap water, soap, 3 pennies, 1 beral pipet, Petri dish, cotton swab, paper towel, paraffin wax

Expected Outcome Students find that adding soap to water causes the paper clip to sink. They also find that the penny with wax on its face can hold more water droplets than the one with soap on its face.

Lab Summary Video Watch the Lab Summary Video for support on connecting the lab investigation to the Investigative Phenomenon.

NAME ______ DATE ______ CLASS ______

WATER AND AQUEOUS SYSTEMS INQUIRY LABS – OPEN

Investigate Surface Tension

How are water strider insects able to walk on water? In this lab you will investigate the way that water interacts with other objects.

Focus on Science Practices

SEP 2 Developing and Using Models
SEP 3 Planning and Carrying Out Investigations

Materials Per Group

- Paper clip
- Water, tap
- Soap
- Pennies, 3
- Pipet, beral, 1
- Petri dish
- Cotton swab
- Paper towel
- Paraffin wax

Procedure

Part 1. Floating a paperclip

1. Fill the petri dish ¾ full with tap water.
2. Hold the paper clip along its long axis, between the tips of your thumb and forefinger.
3. Carefully lower the paper clip so that it just contacts the surface of the water. (The body of the paper clip should be parallel to the surface of the water).
4. Release the paper clip. It should float on the surface of the water. If the paper clip sinks, remove it from the water and dry it with the paper towel before trying

O/G/S/A Lab Interactive Worksheets

The Density of Freezing Salt Water

Analyzing Data In this activity, students investigate density, the salinity of ocean water, and factors that affect [CCC-2] them. Students construct an explanation [SEP-6] about how changes in salinity affect aquatic organisms.

- Before students begin to answer the questions, review the two figures. Discuss the differences in the lagoon before and after freezing.
- Remind students that *brine* is another term for *salt water*.
- Tell students that a lagoon is a shallow body of water that is separated from a larger body of water by a natural barrier, such as a coral reef, a sandbar, or a barrier reef. Point out that the lagoon referred to in this activity is a body of water near the ocean shore where rivers empty fresh water.

NAME ______ DATE ______ CLASS ______

ANALYZING DATA

The Density of Freezing Salt Water

Ocean water contains over 40 elements, with sodium chloride being the greatest component. Seawater has an average salinity of about 3.5%, though it varies by location. The density of ocean water increases with increasing salinity. The density of ocean water decreases with increasing temperature. Ocean water and fresh water freeze at different temperatures. In near-shore lagoons, outflowing rivers may decrease salinity compared to ocean water, so near-shore lagoons can freeze over.

Figure 1 depicts a salt-water lagoon in the summertime. **Figure 2** depicts the same lagoon after the water has frozen in deep wintertime.

Figure 1

Salt-Water Lagoon Before Freezing

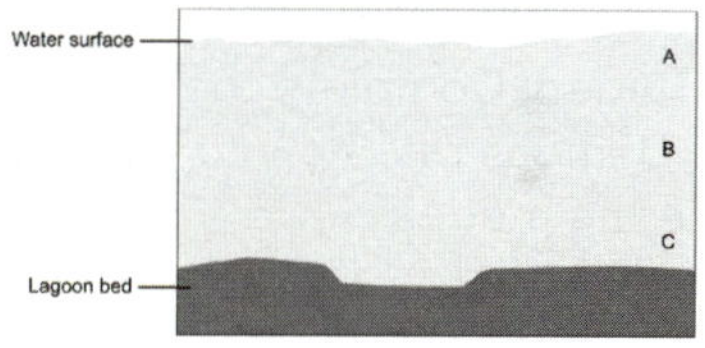

Analyzing Data Interactive Worksheet

ASSESS ON THE SPOT

As students are working through the Analyzing Data activity, ask them if an increase in temperature will make water more or less dense. If students are having trouble answering, remind them that as liquids are heated their molecules move farther apart, making them less dense.

CONNECT TO CAREERS

Oceanographer Oceanographers investigate many aspects of the ocean. Biological oceanographers study the living organisms in the ocean. Chemical oceanographers study the composition of ocean water and its processes and cycles, including the effects of pollutants. Geological oceanographers explore the ocean floor and the processes that make its features, such as volcanic processes and hydrothermal circulation. Physical oceanographers investigate the conditions and physical processes within the ocean, including waves, currents, and tides.

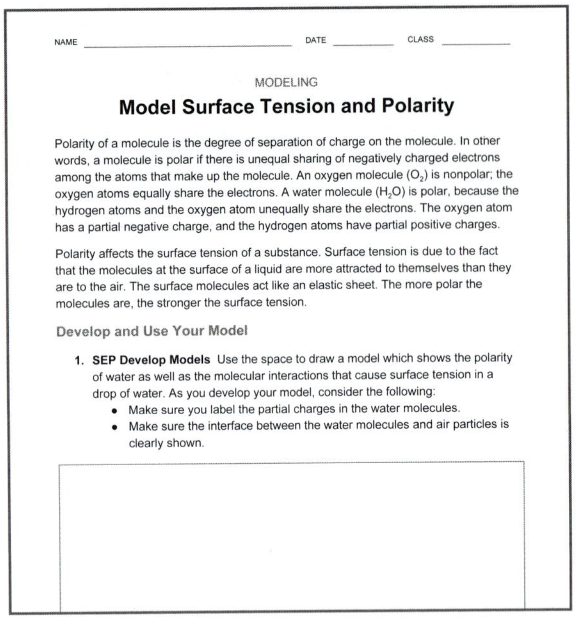

NAME ______ DATE ______ CLASS ______

MODELING

Model Surface Tension and Polarity

Polarity of a molecule is the degree of separation of charge on the molecule. In other words, a molecule is polar if there is unequal sharing of negatively charged electrons among the atoms that make up the molecule. An oxygen molecule (O_2) is nonpolar; the oxygen atoms equally share the electrons. A water molecule (H_2O) is polar, because the hydrogen atoms and the oxygen atom unequally share the electrons. The oxygen atom has a partial negative charge, and the hydrogen atoms have partial positive charges.

Polarity affects the surface tension of a substance. Surface tension is due to the fact that the molecules at the surface of a liquid are more attracted to themselves than they are to the air. The surface molecules act like an elastic sheet. The more polar the molecules are, the stronger the surface tension.

Develop and Use Your Model

1. **SEP Develop Models** Use the space to draw a model which shows the polarity of water as well as the molecular interactions that cause surface tension in a drop of water. As you develop your model, consider the following:
   - Make sure you label the partial charges in the water molecules.
   - Make sure the interface between the water molecules and air particles is clearly shown.

Modeling Interactive Worksheet

CLASSROOM MODIFICATIONS

Based on your students' abilities and your schedule, you may wish to edit the Modeling document to make Model Surface Tension and Polarity more open ended or more guided.

- **More Open Ended** Have students design a three-diensional model that illustrates the forces acting to cause surface tension on the surface of a body of water.
- **More Guided** Complete the activity as a class. Demonstrate how to make and evaluate the model.

ADDRESS PRECONCEPTIONS

When discussing phase changes, solvation, and other processes involving intermolecular bonds, students may sometimes assume that the molecules themselves are being disassembled or formed. Intermolecular bonds, like hydrogen bonds, are always indicated with dotted lines, as opposed to chemical bonds, which are indicated with solid lines. When an intermolecular bond has been broken or formed, only a physical change has occurred—the molecules themselves remain intact. When ice melts into liquid, only intermolecular bonds are broken, but if the H_2O molecule is broken down into its constituent atoms, then a chemical change has occurred, bcecause covalent bonds have been broken.

EXPLAIN

Model Surface Tension and Polarity

Modeling Use this activity after students have had the opportunity to observe and explore surface tension and polarity. Ideally, this would be after students perform the Inquiry Lab. In this activity, students develop and refine models [SEP-2] of a water droplet to demonstrate the relationship between polarity and surface tension.

Choose from these suggested strategies to guide students in deepening their understanding of polarity and surface tension.

- **Developing Models** Students may choose different formats to make their models. For example, they could construct a particle diagram where each molecule is represented by a sphere. Students could also make a model where each sphere represents an atom; a water molecule would, therefore, be comprised of two H atoms on one side and an O atom on the other. Alternatively, a ball-and-stick model could be drawn, with the sticks representing the H-bonds between water molecules.
- **Related Examples** If students are having trouble with modeling polarity and surface tension, then provide them with examples. An insect known as a water strider is able to move along the surface of water as a result of surface tension. (You may wish to share the information in the Professional Development feature on this page.) Skipping stones and water-skiing are also possible because of surface tension.

DIFFERENTIATED INSTRUCTION

- **Support Struggling Students** Have students demonstrate surface tension by drawing several water molecules joined together, in which the positive end of one molecule is adjacent to the negative end of another molecule. Alternatively, some students may benefit from observing or making a three-dimensional model.
- **Support Special Needs Students** Modify this activity to be discussion-based for students with visual or physical limitations.
- **Support Advanced Students** Challenge students to consider the vector nature of surface tension. Surface tension is a force—it is often strong enough to counteract gravity. Like all forces, surface tension can be designated with a vector arrow. Ask students to diagram surface tension using vector arrows and to use these arrows to explain why surface tension only exists at the surface of a liquid.

PROFESSIONAL DEVELOPMENT

Inspire Your Students Consider showing students a picture of a water strider sitting on the surface of a body of water and discuss with them why they think this insect can walk on water. Then provide the following information.

Water striders are small insects with a long, thin body and six long legs. They can be seen rapidly skimming across the surface of calm or slow-moving water. Most insects with a weight similar to that of a water strider would sink in water, but the water strider is able to walk on water as a result of surface tension and several other factors.

- The water strider's legs are covered with thousands of microscopic hairs that repel water and trap air bubbles. The captured air helps them to float on the water's surface.
- The long length, slender structure, and flexibility of its legs helps the insect to spread out and distribute its weight over the large surface area of water and to flow with the movement of the water.

Water and Aqueous Systems

Experience Notebook Ideally, assign the Experience Notebook or Realize Reader for this experience the day before, and then follow up with any of the following suggested instructional strategies to address knowledge gaps and deepen understanding.

Use these strategies to help students make sense of the images and text on the indicated pages, as well as to engage science skills.

- **Water and Hydrogen Bonding** (p. 148) Organize students into groups of four, and direct each group to list as many examples of polar objects as they can. (Possible answers include Earth, magnets, or batteries.) Point out that, generally, if something is polar, it has two ends that are opposite in some way. Have students note the polar ends on the water model diagram.
- **Surface Tension** (pp. 149–150) Help students recall the water drops from the teacher demo at the beginning of this experience. Explain that the water formed drops because of the relatively high surface tension of water. Help students apply the concept of surface tension to the water drops using the diagram on page 149. Then ask student to look at the diagram on page 150 and to find the water drop in the top row that looks most like the water drops on the waxed paper in the demo. Explain that, like the drop on the waxed car in the diagram, the waxed paper was a nonpolar substrate that did not pull very hard on the water molecules. Then have students study the bottom row of the diagram. Call on volunteers to use the information in the diagram to explain why the water droplets spread out when you added the dish detergent.
- **Structure Affects Properties of Ice** (pp. 152–153) After students make their graphs for Question 35, have them write a hypothesis to explain why this trend exists. Call on students to read aloud their hypotheses. Then direct students to extend their graph from 4°C to 0°C. Have students write a hypothesis to explain this new trend, and discuss as a class.
- Have students extend the drawing of solid water on page 153 to show how this structure relates to the snowflake. Remind them that their drawings must show the correct number of hydrogens and oxygens in each hexagon.
- **Aqueous Solutions** (pp. 154–155) Explain that polar substances tend to dissolve in other polar substances, and nonpolar substances tend to dissolve in other nonpolar substances. Instruct students to create two lists: one of substances that dissolve in water and the other of substances that do not. Then direct them to identify patterns [CCC-1] in order to classify each substance as polar or nonpolar. As a class, combine all lists for each type into a single list.
- **Electrolytes and Nonelectrolytes** (pp. 156–157) Ask students how they would know if a sports drink they consumed contained electrolytes. Refer to the nutrition label on page 157. Explain that salts are the electrolytes, which in this case contain positive sodium and potassium ions. These ions are necessary to maintain proper fluid balance in cells, as well as to allow for optimal muscle and nerve function. Remind students that sodium is salt.
- **Hydrates** (pp. 158–159) Before students answer Question 40, have them define *boiling*, *sublimation*, and *efflorescence*. Then ask them to determine whether hydrogen bonds are formed or broken during each of these processes. Challenge students to see whether they can identify the reverse process for each.

ASSESS ON THE SPOT

Present the following scenario: A container with an unknown chemical is pulled from the shelf of the chemistry storeroom. The lid of the container is slightly ajar, and the contents, which should be a powder, have liquefied. Have students write a short explanation about why the powder turned into a liquid. Students should use evidence from the Experience Notebook and other related activities to support their explanations.

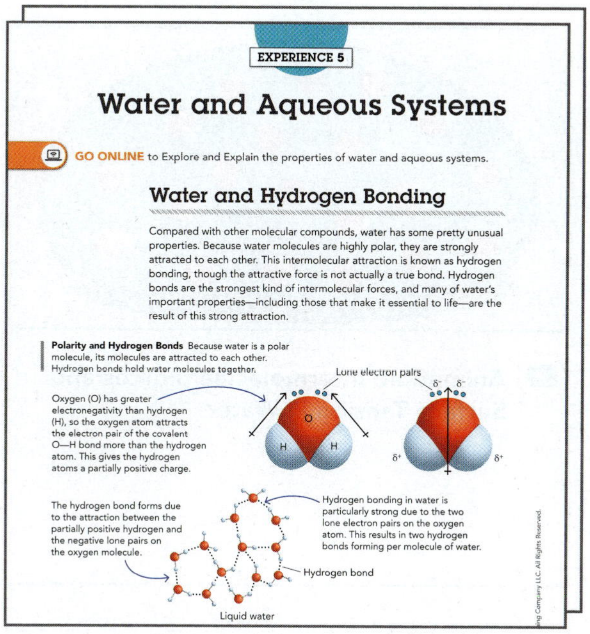

EXPERIENCE 5

Water and Aqueous Systems

GO ONLINE to Explore and Explain the properties of water and aqueous systems.

Water and Hydrogen Bonding

Compared with other molecular compounds, water has some pretty unusual properties. Because water molecules are highly polar, they are strongly attracted to each other. This intermolecular attraction is known as hydrogen bonding, though the attractive force is not actually a true bond. Hydrogen bonds are the strongest kind of intermolecular forces, and many of water's important properties—including those that make it essential to life—are the result of this strong attraction.

Polarity and Hydrogen Bonds Because water is a polar molecule, its molecules are attracted to each other. Hydrogen bonds hold water molecules together.

Experience Notebook, pp. 148–159

eTEXT

ELD SUPPORT

Speaking/Writing Students will work in pairs to clearly explain the effect of a surfactant on surface tension, as discussed on page 150 of the Experience Notebook.

- **Emerging/Beginning** Have partners list and use general words that they associate with surfactants as if they were talking to a younger sibling. Examples include *water drops* and *surface*. The words may be in either oral or written form.
- **Developing/Expanding** Have partners list and use more specialized words that they associate with surfactants as if they were talking to a classmate. Examples include *polar, nonpolar,* and *surface tension*. The words may be in either oral or written form.
- **Bridging** Have partners list and use specific words that they think pertain to a surfactant decreasing surface tension as if they were talking to a teacher. Examples include *wetting* and *hydrogen bonding*. The words should be in both oral and written form.

ADDRESS PRECONCEPTIONS

Students may incorrectly think that a kind of molecule that is different from the interior molecules forms the surface of a volume of water. Remind students that surface tension still exists after you mix the water to redistribute the molecules.

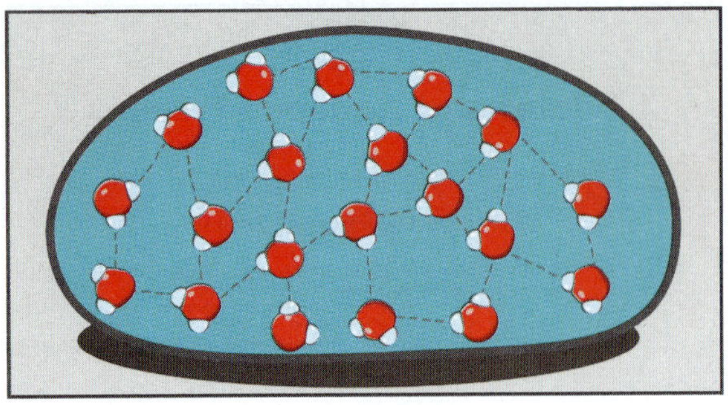

Animation: Intermolecular Forces and Surface Tension in Water

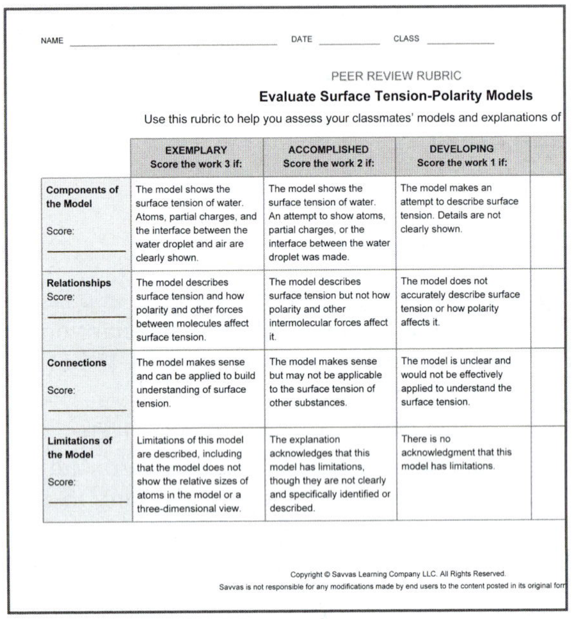

NAME ______ DATE ______ CLASS ______

PEER REVIEW RUBRIC

Evaluate Surface Tension-Polarity Models

Use this rubric to help you assess your classmates' models and explanations of

	EXEMPLARY Score the work 3 if:	**ACCOMPLISHED** Score the work 2 if:	**DEVELOPING** Score the work 1 if:	
Components of the Model Score: ______	The model shows the surface tension of water. Atoms, partial charges, and the interface between the water droplet and air are clearly shown.	The model shows the surface tension of water. An attempt to show atoms, partial charges, or the interface between the water droplet was made.	The model makes an attempt to describe surface tension. Details are not clearly shown.	
Relationships Score: ______	The model describes surface tension and how polarity and other forces between molecules affect surface tension.	The model describes surface tension but not how polarity and other intermolecular forces affect it.	The model does not accurately describe surface tension or how polarity affects it.	
Connections Score: ______	The model makes sense and can be applied to build understanding of surface tension.	The model makes sense but may not be applicable to the surface tension of other substances.	The model is unclear and would not be effectively applied to understand the surface tension.	
Limitations of the Model Score: ______	Limitations of this model are described, including that the model does not show the relative sizes of atoms in the model or a three-dimensional view.	The explanation acknowledges that this model has limitations, though they are not clearly and specifically identified or described.	There is no acknowledgment that this model has limitations.	

Peer Review Rubric Interactive Worksheet

ADDRESS PRECONCEPTIONS

Some students may not understand that polarity affects the surface tension of a substance. Explain that while all liquids have surface tension, water's surface tension is higher than most because the molecules are more polar. The more polar the molecules are, the stronger the surface tension.

Intermolecular Forces and Surface Tension in Water

Animation This animation uses models [SEP-2] to explain that the high surface tension of water is due to strong hydrogen bonding, such that water beads up on nonpolar surfaces but not on polar surfaces. Choose among these strategies as you use the animation:

- Pause the animation at key spots and ask volunteers to summarize the important information presented. If students have difficulty with the concepts presented in any segment, play that part of the animation again. Encourage students to take notes in their science notebooks on keywords and concepts that stand out to them.
- Encourage students to use what they learn in the animation to refine their models of surface tension and polarity in the Modeling activity.

ELABORATE

Evaluate Surface Tension–Polarity Models

Peer Review Rubric Students will use the rubric as a scoring guide to evaluate the models their peers developed in the Modeling activity, Model Surface Tension and Polarity.

- Have students work in small groups to evaluate [SEP-8] the models of the other members in the group, using a separate rubric sheet for each evaluation and clearly identifying the name of each peer on each rubric.
- Remind students that the grade received for this activity is based on how accurate and thoughtfully executed their evaluations are articulated in writing.
- Have advanced students use their completed rubrics to write a detailed, but respectful, recommendation of how each peer can improve their models.

DIFFERENTIATED INSTRUCTION

- **Support Struggling Students** If students struggle with timed tasks, you can reduce the writing load in the Peer Review Rubric activity by assigning another student to write their dictated scoring explanations in their rubrics and/or by providing only two of their peers' models to evaluate.
- **Support Special Needs Students** Review the Peer Review Rubric before students assess their classmates' models and explanations of surface tension. Point out how an exemplary model is different from an accomplished or developing model. Demonstrate how to use the rubric to evaluate the models and explanations.

ASSESS ON THE SPOT

Using a pipette, squirt equal-sized amounts of water and rubbing alcohol side-by-side on a dark surface. As students observe the differing roundedness of the bubbles, have them explain what causes this difference.

PROFESSIONAL DEVELOPMENT

Explaining Phenomena Explain that water's ability to form rounded drops on solid surfaces is due to an exceptionally high surface tension that is produced by an extensive network of hydrogen bonds. As an analogy, describe this scene: A crowd of autograph-seekers surrounds a celebrity. As each person approaches the celebrity as closely as possible, an impermeable circular barrier forms. This barrier will remain intact as long as the net attraction toward the circle's center continues. The process is dynamic. As one person wiggles closer to the celebrity, another is forced to retreat, but the overall shape does not change. Similarly, in a drop of water, attractions between individual molecules may shift, but the overall shape remains constant as molecules continue to be drawn toward a central focal point.

Compare Intermolecular Forces in Fresh and Salt Water

15

Analyzing Data In this activity, students investigate how the presence of salt in water affects surface tension and cohesion. Students interpret graphs [SEP-4] and construct explanations [SEP-6] to describe the relationship between surface tension and salinity, and cohesion and salinity.

- Prompt students to consider the cause-and-effect [CCC-2] nature of the concepts involved. Direct students to examine the diagrams and note the polar nature of the water molecules. Point out that the attraction of the positive end of one water molecule to the negative end of another leads to cohesion, which causes surface tension. Ask students to consider how salt might interact with water and how this interaction affects water's cohesiveness and surface tension.

PROFESSIONAL DEVELOPMENT

Develop Classroom Collaboration Before students begin conversing about the discussion questions at the end of the Analyzing Data activity, have the class brainstorm a list of questions that partners can ask each other. Model some techniques students can use to help partners articulate their ideas. Use prompts such as:

- I like the way to explained ___________, but I think it would be even better if you ___________.
- What evidence led you to that idea?
- What other reasons or evidence did you see?

Note that these questions are neutral and open-ended, and that asking these types of questions is a skill that we develop with practice. Remind students that they should give their partner a few moments to form an answer, and not to interrupt them.

INTEGRATE MATH

The formula for hydrates gives the number of water molecules per formula unit of ionic compound. For example, for $CuSO_4 \cdot 5H_2O$, there are 5 water molecules for every 1 formula unit of $CuSO_4$. **Ask** How many water molecules would be present given the following number of formula units of $CuSO_4$: 2, 5, 10? [10, 25, 50]

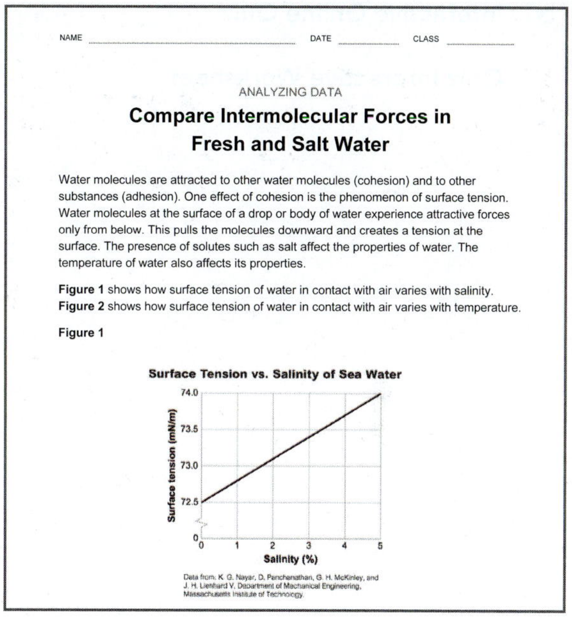

NAME ______________ DATE ________ CLASS ________

ANALYZING DATA

Compare Intermolecular Forces in Fresh and Salt Water

Water molecules are attracted to other water molecules (cohesion) and to other substances (adhesion). One effect of cohesion is the phenomenon of surface tension. Water molecules at the surface of a drop or body of water experience attractive forces only from below. This pulls the molecules downward and creates a tension at the surface. The presence of solutes such as salt affect the properties of water. The temperature of water also affects its properties.

Figure 1 shows how surface tension of water in contact with air varies with salinity.
Figure 2 shows how surface tension of water in contact with air varies with temperature.

Figure 1

Analyzing Data Interactive Worksheet

INTEGRATE THE THREE DIMENSIONS

In the Analyzing Data activity, students construct explanations [SEP-6] to describe the relationship between surface tension and salinity, and cohesion and salinity. Students apply what they learned about the structure and properties of water [PS1.A] to explain how these properties interact with the presence of salt in water and affect [CCC-2] surface tension and cohesion.

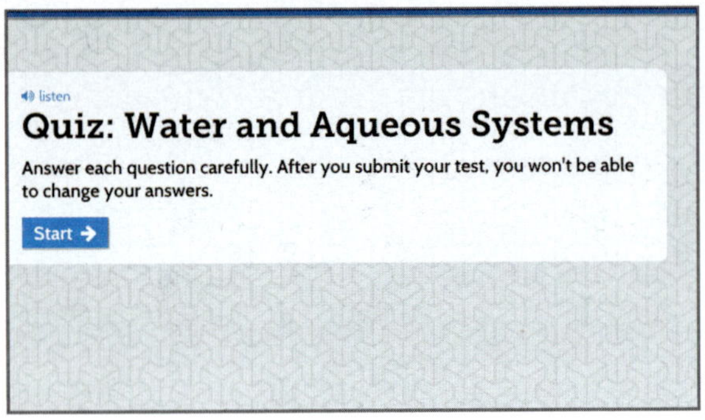

Interactive Online Quiz

Quiz Interactive Worksheet

EVALUATE

Water and Aqueous Systems

Quiz Assign the quiz in online technology-enhanced, auto-graded format or as an editable quiz worksheet. Use the scoring notes and remediation strategies found online to assess students' responses and to provide targeted feedback for each item to remediate well before assigning the summative 3-D Assessment.

REMEDIATION SUGGESTIONS

- **If** students are struggling to explain the relationship between polarity and hydrogen bonding, **then** have them review the Modeling activity, Model Surface Tension and Polarity. Have students review the models on page 148 of the Experience Notebook and paraphrase the relationship.
- **If** students are struggling to explain the relationship between polarity and surface tension, **then** have them review the Modeling activity, Model Surface Tension and Polarity, and their Peer Review Rubrics.
- **If** students struggle to describe why and how density changes with temperature, **then** direct them to reread pages 152–153 in the Experience Notebook. Have students also review the activity, Compare Intermolecular Forces in Fresh and Salt Water.
- **If** students struggle to explain why polar solvents can dissolve polar solutes, **then** direct them to study the images and captions on pages 154 and 155 of the Experience Notebook.

Revisit INVESTIGATIVE PHENOMENON

Support Reflection Students can complete the reflection prompt, where they will unpack and make sense of the Investigative Phenomenon, based on practices and understandings that have been reinforced over the course of this experience.

- Call on students to explain the relationship between polarity and the ability to repel or attract water. Remind students that nonpolar substances have a greater tendency to repel water, and, therefore, the outer layer of a water-repellant jacket must be coated with or made from a nonpolar substance.
- Ask students to describe the second factor that is necessary for a water-repellant jacket, which is the need for the material to be breathable, that is, to allow for the free exchange of gases. Solicit input as to the best way to make material both breathable and water repellant.

Further Develop Your CER Argument Have students add any additional evidence they have collected in this experience. Evidence may include the fact that polar substances like water tend to repel nonpolar substances like wax or oil. Surfactants can decrease surface tension and make water more likely to penetrate a fabric.

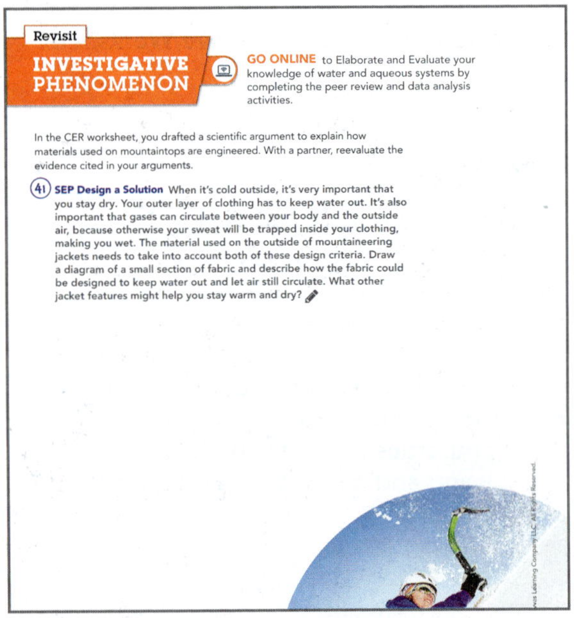

Revisit
INVESTIGATIVE PHENOMENON

GO ONLINE to Elaborate and Evaluate your knowledge of water and aqueous systems by completing the peer review and data analysis activities.

In the CER worksheet, you drafted a scientific argument to explain how materials used on mountaintops are engineered. With a partner, reevaluate the evidence cited in your arguments.

41 **SEP Design a Solution** When it's cold outside, it's very important that you stay dry. Your outer layer of clothing has to keep water out. It's also important that gases can circulate between your body and the outside air, because otherwise your sweat will be trapped inside your clothing, making you wet. The material used on the outside of mountaineering jackets needs to take into account both of these design criteria. Draw a diagram of a small section of fabric and describe how the fabric could be designed to keep water out and let air still circulate. What other jacket features might help you stay warm and dry?

Experience Notebook, p. 160

eTEXT

EXPERIENCE 6

Properties of Solutions

Teacher Background

Experience 6 is an overview of solutions, along with a brief discussion of suspensions and colloids. Students examine the factors that affect solubility, such as temperature, agitation, and pressure. The relationship between solubility and temperature is examined by constructing graphs depicting solubility curves. The mathematical relationship between pressure and temperature is explored by applying Henry's law.

Objectives

- **Investigate the role of temperature and surface area in the formation of solutions.**
- **Develop a model to explain how solutions can become supersaturated.**
- **Construct and interpret graphs depicting solubility curves.**
- **Use Henry's law to discover the relationship between the solubility of a gas and pressure.**
- **Differentiate between solutions, suspensions, and colloids.**

ENGAGE

EVERYDAY PHENOMENON

Does salt dissolve in water?

Use the teacher demo to prompt student discussion about whether salt forms a true solution in water.

Fun With Salt

Engage students with this demonstration of an everyday phenomenon to introduce the concept of solutions, suspensions, and colloids.

Materials various types of salt from the grocery store, such as table salt, rock salt, kosher salt, and sea salt; beakers; stirring rods; water

1. Ask students what type of mixture they think salt will form when added to water.
2. Add small amounts of each salt to separate beakers of water and stir until the salts disappears.
3. Ask students to carefully observe each beaker, especially noting the clarity of the water.
4. Prompt students to explain why some of the mixtures are transparent, whereas others are cloudy.
5. Read aloud the ingredients of each container of salt, and ask if students can find a connection between the ingredients and the appearance of the mixtures. Then share that anti-caking additives are used in table salt, and that because these substances do not dissolve, they make the water cloudy. Salt that lacks these anti-caking agents will be transparent. If some salt settles on the bottom of the beakers, the mixture may eventually settle into distinct layers.

RELATED PHENOMENA

In addition to the teacher demo, Fun With Salt, consider using other phenomena to launch this experience.

- **Solidifying Before Your Eyes** Show students a supersaturated solution of sodium acetate in an Erlenmeyer flask. Add one crystal of sodium acetate. The entire contents of the flask will solidy before students eyes. Discuss with students what they think caused the change.
- **Dissolving Sugar** Give each group a sugar cube and a little packet of granulated sugar. Instruct students to drop each in water and note the time it takes each to dissolve. Have students make quick sketches to show what they think is happening at the molecular level to cause the difference.

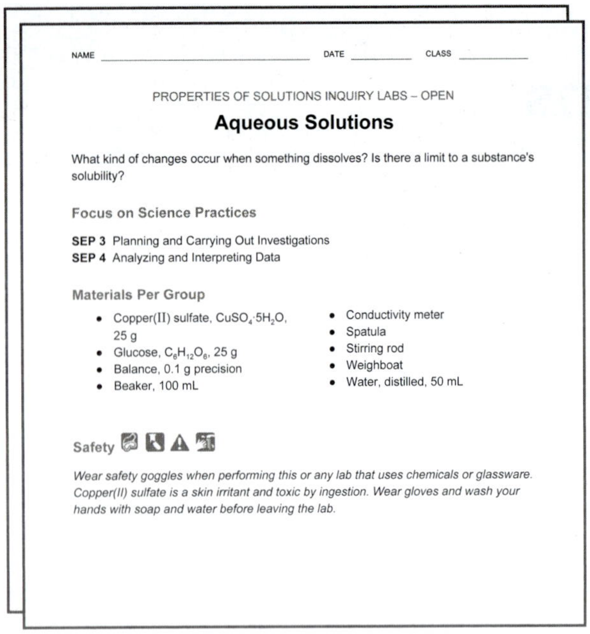

NAME ______________________ DATE __________ CLASS __________

PROPERTIES OF SOLUTIONS INQUIRY LABS – OPEN

Aqueous Solutions

What kind of changes occur when something dissolves? Is there a limit to a substance's solubility?

Focus on Science Practices

SEP 3 Planning and Carrying Out Investigations
SEP 4 Analyzing and Interpreting Data

Materials Per Group

- Copper(II) sulfate, $CuSO_4 \cdot 5H_2O$, 25 g
- Glucose, $C_6H_{12}O_6$, 25 g
- Balance, 0.1 g precision
- Beaker, 100 mL
- Conductivity meter
- Spatula
- Stirring rod
- Weighboat
- Water, distilled, 50 mL

Safety

Wear safety goggles when performing this or any lab that uses chemicals or glassware. Copper(II) sulfate is a skin irritant and toxic by ingestion. Wear gloves and wash your hands with soap and water before leaving the lab.

O/G/S/A Lab Interactive Worksheets

EXPLORE

Aqueous Solutions

Inquiry Lab Students carry out an investigation [SEP-3] to observe the color and conductivity of copper(II) sulfate solutions at different concentrations. They then repeat the investigation using glucose.

Lab Demo Video Watch the Lab Demo Video for advice on materials and preparation.

Choose Your Version Open-ended (O), Guided (G), Shortened (S), Advanced (A)

Materials 25 g copper(II) sulfate, 25 g glucose, balance, 100-mL beaker, conductivity meter, spatula, stirring rod, weighboat, 50 mL distilled water

Expected Outcome The more copper(II) sulfate that is dissolved in the water, the bluer the solution becomes. Glucose doesn't change the color of the solution; however, it is more soluble.

Safety Instruct students to wear safety goggles when performing this or any lab that uses chemicals or glassware. Copper(II) sulfate is a skin irritant and toxic by ingestion. Students should wear gloves and wash their hands with soap and warm water before leaving the lab.

Lab Summary Video Watch the Lab Summary Video for support on connecting the lab investigation to the Investigative Phenomenon.

Dissolution Rate

Interactivity In this activity, students are faced with the challenge that a pharmacist is trying to determine the fastest way to dissolve potassium iodide (KI) in water in an emergency. They learn about the variables the pharmacist will test. They predict which variables increase and decrease dissolving rate, test them, and record their data. Students should apply what they learn in this interactivity when they complete the Modeling activity. **Ask:**

- Which variables decreased the dissolving rate? (low heat, not stirring, and lower surface area)
- How can you relate stirring the potassium iodide in the water to increase the dissolving rate with everyday examples? (Stirring the iodide is similar to stirring the sugar in lemonade or the cocoa powder in hot chocolate to have it dissolve faster.)

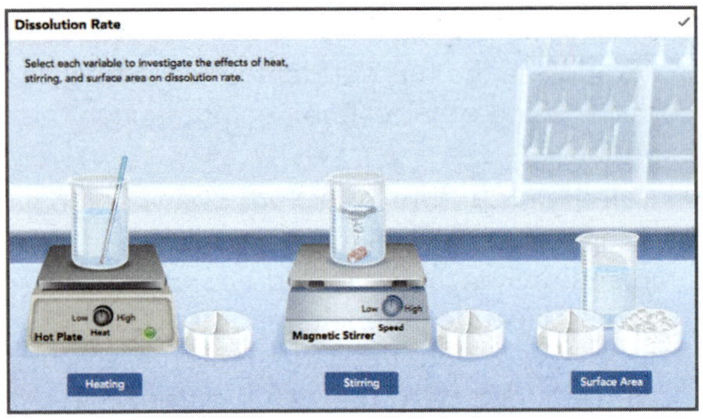

Interactivity: Dissolution Rate

ASSESS ON THE SPOT

After students work through the Dissolution Rate interactivity, ask them how to quickly dissolve instant coffee in water. (Place the instant coffee in a large cup of water with greater surface area and have the water be very hot. Stir constantly.)

CONNECT TO CAREERS

Lab Technician If you visit the doctor, you may be asked to provide a urine sample. One of the first things lab technicians look for is whether the urine is cloudy. Urine should be transparent, and any cloudiness could be a sign of an abnormality, such as a urinary tract infection. Cloudy urine is an example of a colloid. Lab technicians need to have a good understanding of solutions, suspensions, and colloids to properly provide test results to patients.

EXPLAIN

Model Concentration's Effect on Conductivity

Modeling Use this activity after students have had the opportunity to observe and explore the ability of various substances to conduct electricity. Ideally, this would be after students complete the Inquiry Lab. In this activity, students develop models [SEP-2] to explain why a salt solution conducts electricity, but neither the salt nor the water alone conducts electricity. Students should realize that a cause-and-effect relationship [CCC-2] exists between conductivity and solvation.

Choose from these suggested strategies to guide students in deepening their understanding of conductivity.

- **Developing Models** Students do not have to model water or show the battery and light bulb. Students should orient the ions so that positive ions are pointed toward the oxygen in the water molecules and the negative ions are pointed toward the hydrogen in the water molecules. Students might benefit from labeling the electrodes of the conductivity apparatus as positive and negative, enabling them to better understand why the ions are attracted to opposite ends of the solution.
- **Related Examples** Ask students what would happen if a sugar solution were tested for conductivity. (Even though sugar dissolves, it does not form ions, so it would not be conductive.) Then ask students to predict what would happen if sand were added to the beaker of water. (Since sand does not dissolve, it will not be conductive in water.)
- **Address Preconceptions** Remind students that the presence of ions themselves does not enable conductivity. The electrolytes must contain ions that are able to migrate to their respective electrodes. It is worth noting that water only conducts electricity if it contains some dissolved salts; students are often surprised to learn that pure water, a covalent compound, does not conduct electricity.

DIFFERENTIATED INSTRUCTION

- **Support Special Needs Students** If students have physical disabilities that make drawing difficult or impossible, have them work with partners. The students can describe their ideas for the model to the partner, who can then translate the description into a drawing. Or provide a recording device that students can use to record their ideas.
- **Support Struggling Students** For Step 1 of the Modeling activity, instruct students how to draw the individual particles of each of the substances. Begin by instructing students to draw water molecules as individual spheres (the partial positive and negative charges are not necessary in this context). Next, have them diagram the solid substance by drawing individual positive and negative ions that are connected to one another. Finally, instruct them to draw individual positive and negative ions interspersed throughout the water molecules.
- **Support Advanced Students** Challenge students to consider why sports drinks, which are advertised as containing electrolytes, would not cause the light bulb within the indicated conductivity apparatus to light. After students have had time to brainstorm and hypothesize, ask them if sports drinks taste salty. Since they do not, lead students into an understanding of the role concentration plays in conductivity—if the concentration of ions in a solution is too small, a measurable effect may be difficult to observe.

PROFESSIONAL DEVELOPMENT

Explaining Phenomena Electrolytes are essential to all metabolic processes. Sodium and potassium ions control nerve impulse transmission and muscle contraction. If optimum sodium and potassium levels are disturbed, such as sometimes happens with severe diarrhea, serious nervous system problems arise. Loss of consciousness or difficulty maintaining muscle coordination could result. Doctors may recommend that people with severe diarrhea drink sports drinks rather than water in order to replace electrolytes. Sports drinks are a good source of electrolytes because they contain Na^+, K^+ and Ca^{2+}.

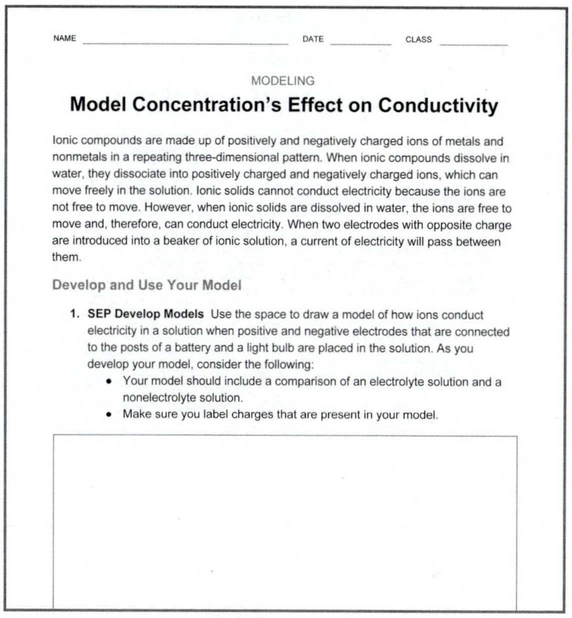
NAME ______ DATE ______ CLASS ______

MODELING

Model Concentration's Effect on Conductivity

Ionic compounds are made up of positively and negatively charged ions of metals and nonmetals in a repeating three-dimensional pattern. When ionic compounds dissolve in water, they dissociate into positively charged and negatively charged ions, which can move freely in the solution. Ionic solids cannot conduct electricity because the ions are not free to move. However, when ionic solids are dissolved in water, the ions are free to move and, therefore, can conduct electricity. When two electrodes with opposite charge are introduced into a beaker of ionic solution, a current of electricity will pass between them.

Develop and Use Your Model

1. **SEP Develop Models** Use the space to draw a model of how ions conduct electricity in a solution when positive and negative electrodes that are connected to the posts of a battery and a light bulb are placed in the solution. As you develop your model, consider the following:
   - Your model should include a comparison of an electrolyte solution and a nonelectrolyte solution.
   - Make sure you label charges that are present in your model.

Modeling Interactive Worksheet

CLASSROOM MODIFICATIONS

Based on your students' abilities and your schedule, you may wish to edit the Model Concentration's Effect on Conductivity activity to make it more open ended.

- **More Open Ended** Before assigning the worksheet, ask students to predict what will occur in the electrolyte and nonelectrolyte solutions. An alternative approach is to allow students to set up their own conductivity apparatus using a flashlight battery, wires with attached alligator clips, and a light bulb. Allow students to discover which of the three solutions conduct electricity before giving them the worksheet. The conductivity apparatus could also be set up by the teacher as a demonstration.

INTEGRATE THE THREE DIMENSIONS

In the Modeling activity, students develop models [SEP-2] of how ions conduct electricity in a solution. They display an understanding that a cause-and-effect relationship [CCC-5] exists between conductivity and concentrations, demonstrating that the structure and interactions of matter at the bulk scale are determined by electrical forces within and between atoms [PS1.A].

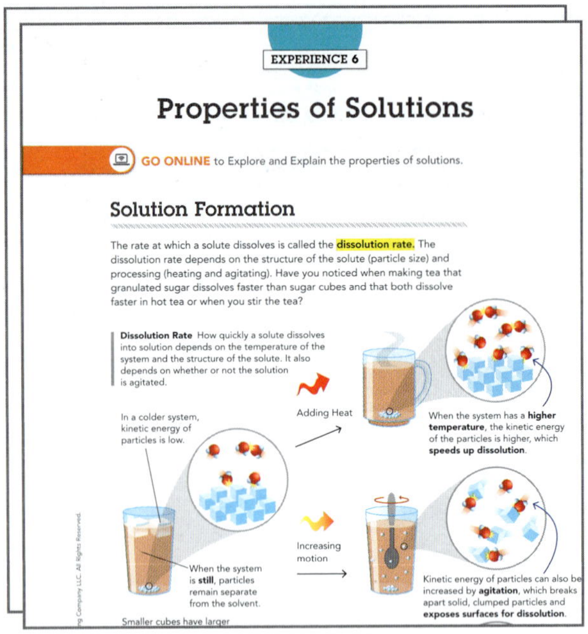
EXPERIENCE 6

Properties of Solutions

GO ONLINE to Explore and Explain the properties of solutions.

Solution Formation

The rate at which a solute dissolves is called the dissolution rate. The dissolution rate depends on the structure of the solute (particle size) and processing (heating and agitating). Have you noticed when making tea that granulated sugar dissolves faster than sugar cubes and that both dissolve faster in hot tea or when you stir the tea?

Experience Notebook, pp. 161–169

eTEXT

SAMPLE PROBLEM SUPPORT

Draw two arrows pointing upwards and label one "pressure" and the other "solubility." Remind students that the pressure decreased in their sample problem, thus the solubility decreased. Viewing these arrows helps students to double-check that their answers for the Sample Problem on page 167 show a solubility that is lower than it was originally.

ELD SUPPORT

Writing Students use familiar general academic and domain-specific words to create clear written text about the solubility curves on pages 163 and 164 of the Experience Notebook.

- **Emerging/Beginning** Have students write two short sentences about the solubility of sodium acetate, using the terms *solubility* and *temperature*.
- **Developing/Expanding** Have students use the terms *solubility*, *temperature*, *increase*, *decrease*, and *varies* to write sentences that summarize the general trend shown in the Solubility Varies with Temperature graph.
- **Bridging** Have students write a comparison of the solubility curves for KNO_3 and $Yb_2(SO_4)_3$ using the terms *solubility*, *function*, *temperature*, *increasing*, and *decreasing*.

Properties of Solutions

Experience Notebook Ideally, assign the Experience Notebook or Realize Reader for this experience the day before, and then follow up with any of the following suggested instructional strategies to fill knowledge gaps and deepen understanding. Alternatively, assign it alongside the Model Concentration's Effect on Conductivity activity as support for the activity. Use these strategies to help students make sense of the images and text on the indicated pages, as well as to engage science skills.

Choose from these suggested strategies to guide students in deepening their understanding of solutions and their properties.

- **Solution Formation** (p. 161) Display these diagrams for the class. Challenge students to discuss with one other person the role of surface area in solution formation. After student discussion, reiterate that both heating and agitation affect surface area, since both processes expose more surfaces of the solute to the solvent. **Ask** What other factors affect the dissolution rate? (structure of solute, area-to-volume ratio)
- **Solubility and Temperature** (pp. 163–164) Interpreting graphs [SEP-4] is a crucial skill. The solubility curve graphs can also be used as a springboard to inquiry. **Ask:**
  a. Why are the solubility curves different for each substance? (because the solubility of the substance at a given temperature depends on how the particles of the substance interact with molecules of the solvent)
  b. Why do some substances become less soluble as the temperature increases? (Solubility decreases at higher temperature when the temperature exceeds the normal boiling point of the substance. Molecules have a greater tendency to escape the solution, decreasing the concentration.)
  c. Why is the solubility of NaCl not affected by temperature? (As temperature increases, the energy needed to break down the crystal lattice and the energy needed to solvate ions is about the same across the entire temperature range.)
  d. What are two possible outcomes if a saturated solution is cooled? (A precipitate forms, or a supersaturated solution forms.)
- **Solubility and Pressure** (p. 166) Encourage students to predict what is present in the headspace above an unopened bottle of a carbonated beverage. Once you establish that the gas within the headspace is CO_2, direct students to rewrite Henry's law in their own words. Challenge students to use this law to explain why opening a bottle of carbonated beverage will cause [CCC-2] it to go flat even if the cap is quickly replaced.
- **Sample Problem** (p. 167) Provide extra Sample Problem practice, while you circulate and help out as needed:
  a. The solubility of a gas in water is 1.2 g/L at 160 kPa. What is the solubility when the pressure of the gas is decreased to 80 kPa? Assume the temperature remains constant. (0.6 g/L)
  b. A gas has a solubility in water of 0.9 g/L at a pressure of 1.1 atm. What pressure is needed to dissolve 3.5 g of the same gas in 1 L of water? Assume the temperature remains a constant 20°C. (4.3 atm)
- **Colloids and Suspensions** (pp. 168–169) Organize students into groups of four, and instruct them to identify additional examples of each type of colloid in the chart on page 169. Instruct students to consider the dispersed phase and dispersion medium, which is analogous to the solute and solvent in a solution.

ASSESS ON THE SPOT

Ask students to classify each of the following mixtures as a solution, suspension, or colloid: (a) a condiment that requires shaking before you can use it, such as salad dressing (suspension); (b) a transparent, but colored beverage, such as lemonade; (solution) (c) clouds (colloid).

INTEGRATE MATH

A sugar cube where each side measures 1 cm will have a total surface area of 6 cm^2. If a sugar cube is cut in half, its surface area will increase. Ask students to calculate the surface area of this cube if it were cut in half (8 cm^2), and then cut in half again (12 cm^2). To help students visualize the concept of surface area, pass out chunks of clay that they can cut in half and measure.

ELABORATE

Ionic Concentration and Conductivity Modeling Rubric

Peer Review Rubric Students use the rubric as a scoring guide to evaluate the models their peers developed in the earlier Modeling activity, Model Concentration's Effect on Conductivity.

- Organize students into groups and have each student evaluate the models of the three other group members, using a separate rubric sheet for each evaluation and clearly identifying the name of each peer on each rubric.
- Give students 10 minutes to review their peers' models. Make it clear to students that they will receive a grade for this activity based on how accurate and thoughtfully executed their evaluations [SEP-8] are articulated in writing.

ASSESS ON THE SPOT

Ask students to diagram what happens when the following substances are added to water: (a) NaCl, (b) $CaCl_2$, (c) $C_6H_{12}O_6$. Then instruct them to predict which substances will conduct electricity. (Both a and b will form an electrolyte because they are ionic, but c will not because $C_6H_{12}O_6$ (glucose) does not form ions in water.)

Solubility and Temperature

Writing About Science In this activity, students identify the pattern [CCC-1] of how the solubility of carbon dioxide decreases with increasing temperature. Students then design a solution [SEP-6] to increase the oxygen concentration when an algal bloom occurs.

- As students are completing this activity, encourage them to consider the cause-and-effect [CCC-2] nature of temperature and solubility for carbon dioxide.
- Students should also consider whether their solutions are practical for large bodies of water.

PROFESSIONAL DEVELOPMENT

Background Notes Hypoxic dead zones can result when algal blooms sink, decompose, and reduce dissolved oxygen concentrations. These processes can increase hypoxia and the death of fish. Increasing concentrations of carbon dioxide, warming lake temperatures, more extreme precipitation, and excess nutrients increase the risk of algal blooms. The density of water is dependent on temperature, and it varies with depth in the water column. Surface waters are typically warmer and less dense. Bottom waters are colder and denser. During the summer, surface waters warm further, and wind and wave action that mixes surface and deep areas of the water decrease. This restricts movement of oxygen and thus increases the likelihood of expanded dead zones.

NAME ____________ DATE ________ CLASS ________

PEER REVIEW RUBRIC

Ionic Concentration and Conductivity Modeling Rubr

Use this rubric to help you assess a classmate's conductive ionic solution mo

	EXEMPLARY Score the work 3 if:	ACCOMPLISHED Score the work 2 if:	DEVELOPING Score the work 1 if:
Components of the Model Score: ______	The model accurately depicts ions moving freely in aqueous solution and interacting with water molecules to conduct electricity.	The model shows that components of a solution are mobile to conduct electricity but is vague on the details.	The model attempts to show how solutions conduct electricity.
Relationships Score: ______	The model describes the relationships between conductivity and the concentrations of ionic solutions.	The model describes the relationships between conductivity and type of substance but not how concentrations affect conductivity.	The model attempts to describe the relationship between how conductivity works and the types of substances that conduct it.
Connections Score: ______	The model makes sense and can be applied to build understanding of conductivity with other substances.	The model makes sense, but it is more specific to solutions only and does not supply scope to extend to general conductivity.	The model attempts to explain conductivity in solutions.
Limitations of the Model Score: ______	Limitations of the model are described, and solutions for improvement are discussed.	The explanation admits the model has limitations, though they are not clearly and specifically identified or described.	The model is presented as perfect as is, and scope for improvement is not considered.

Peer Review Rubric Interactive Worksheet

ADDRESS PRECONCEPTIONS

Students are often familiar with solutions and suspensions, having learned that if settling occurs, a suspension has formed. It is easy to distinguish a solution from a suspension, because nothing settles out in a solution. The concept of a colloid can be challenging for students, however, as they can easily be mistaken for solutions since no settling occurs. Remind students that true solutions are transparent, as the particles are too small to reflect visible light. Since the particle size of colloids is larger, they are able to reflect light, and even though the individual particles are too small to see, the colloid will still have a cloudy appearance—a clear indicator that it is not a solution.

NAME ____________ DATE ________ CLASS ________

WRITING ABOUT SCIENCE

Solubility and Temperature

Use the information provided and information gathered from authoritative sources on your own to answer Questions 1 and 2.

The effect of temperature on the solubility of a substance can depend on the substance's state of matter. The solubilities of liquids and solids can increase or decrease with increasing temperature. However, most gases become less soluble with increasing temperature. For example, carbon dioxide has a solubility of about 2.5 g per 100 g of water at 10°C but only about 0.5 g per 100 g of water at 60°C.

Obtain and Evaluate Information

1. **CCC Patterns** Why does the solubility of carbon dioxide in water decrease with an increase in temperature? Explain what the pattern would look like on a graph.

2. **SEP Design Your Solution** The ocean and other large bodies of water often have dead zones or areas that have very low concentrations of oxygen. Dead zones often occur when algal blooms deplete the area of oxygen. The algal blooms are caused by excess nutrients, such as from fertilizers. Design a solution to increase oxygen concentration in water when an algal bloom occurs to help prevent dead zones. Is your solution practical?

Writing About Science Interactive Worksheet

EVALUATE

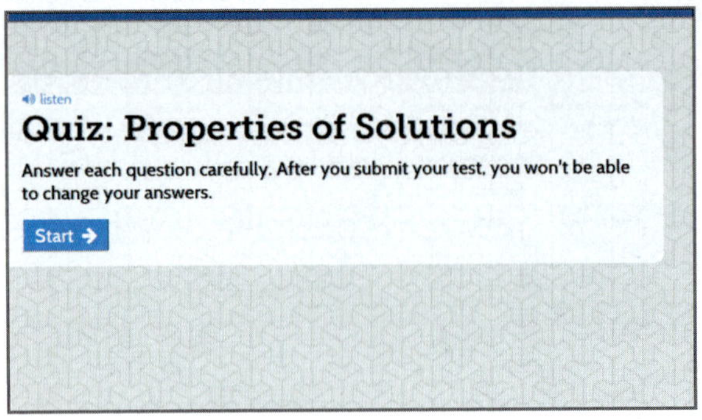

Interactive Online Quiz

Quiz Interactive Worksheet

Properties of Solutions

Quiz Assign the quiz in online technology-enhanced auto-graded format or as an editable quiz worksheet. Use the scoring notes and remediation strategies found online to assess students' responses and to provide targeted feedback for each item to remediate well before assigning the summative 3-D Assessment.

REMEDIATION SUGGESTIONS

- **If** students have trouble explaining the factors that affect solubility, **then** have them revisit the Inquiry Lab. They can also review the information on page 161 of the Experience Notebook. Direct them to list the factors and explain them in their own words.
- **If** students struggle with interpreting solubility and temperature graphs, **then** direct them to study the information on pages 163 and 164 of the Experience Notebook. Direct students to use a ruler to make vertical and horizontal lines on the graphs to make it easier to correlate a specific temperature with a specific solubility. Also, have then revisit the Writing About Science activity.
- **If** students have difficulty in solving Henry's law problems, **then** have them review the definitions and examples on pages 166 and 167 of the Experience Notebook. Suggest that students use an alternate, more conceptual approach. Because solubility and pressure are directly proportional, change in one variable will produce the same amount of change in the other. If solubility doubles, pressure doubles. If the pressure is halved, solubility is halved.

Revisit

INVESTIGATIVE PHENOMENON

GO ONLINE to Elaborate and Evaluate your knowledge of solutions by completing the peer review and writing activities.

In the CER worksheet, you drafted a scientific argument to explain how materials used on mountaintops are engineered. With a partner, reevaluate the evidence cited in your arguments.

50 **SEP Design a Solution** Acute mountain sickness (AMS) is caused by low amounts of oxygen in the bloodstream at high elevation. The decrease in the amount of oxygen at high altitude can be easily corrected by using oxygen tanks and masks. However, simply breathing more oxygen doesn't prevent AMS. Why? Explain using Henry's law and design a solution for emergency treatment of AMS at high altitude.

Experience Notebook, p. 170

eTEXT

Revisit
INVESTIGATIVE PHENOMENON

Support Reflection Students can complete the reflection prompt, where they will unpack and make sense of the Investigative Phenomenon, based on practices and understandings that have been reinforced over the course of the experience.

- Ask students if they have ever visited high altitudes, and, if so, how they adapted to the lower oxygen levels.
- Show students pictures of an oxygen tent or hyperbaric chamber, which are devices designed to deliver oxygen at higher pressures. Ask students to explain how these devices utilize Henry's law.
- Solicit student input as to why it is necessary to not just increase the amount of oxygen but also the amount pressure at which the oxygen is delivered.
- Ask students how they could use what they learned about solutions to design a material for a specific function.

Evaluate and Revise Your CER Argument Have students answer Questions 3 and 4 in the CER activity and re-evaluate the claim they made. Students should add any additional evidence they have collected in this investigation and revise their CER. Discuss how properties of solids can be changed, such as by changing temperature or the size of the solute. **Ask** What are examples of solids that are "designed" in the real world? (Some examples are electronics, fabrics, and furniture.)

EVALUATE

Physical Properties of Materials

3-D Assessment For a summative assessment of Investigation 4, assign the test, which is available online, as an ExamView bank, or as an editable worksheet.

Road Deicers

Performance-Based Assessment Use this Performance-Based Assessment to assess students' mastery of the standards. In this activity, students make predictions about which of three compounds—sodium chloride, calcium chloride, and silicon dioxide—makes the best road deicer. Students plan and conduct an experiment [SEP-3] to test the reactions [PS1.B] of the substances. They analyze data [SEP-4] looking for patterns [CCC-1]. Based on their findings, students recommend which material should be used.

Expected Outcome Students will find that calcium chloride is the most effective road deicer. However, because it costs twice as much, it might not be the most cost effective.

Safety Have students wear safety goggles when performing this or any lab that uses chemicals, heat, or glassware. Calcium chloride and sodium chloride are slightly toxic, and skin and eye irritants. Make sure students wear gloves at all times during the experiment. Remind students to wash their hands thoroughly with soap and warm water before leaving the laboratory.

Experience Notebook (p. 171) After students complete the Performance-Based Assessment, have them complete the reflection prompt in the Experience Notebook.

DIFFERENTIATED INSTRUCTION

Support Struggling Students Struggling students may have difficulty analyzing costs and benefits in the Performance-Based Assessment. It may be helpful to make a bar graph of the three substances to help students better visualize the expense of the materials.

Support Advanced Students Have students additionally test the alternate materials, calcium carbonate and glucose, and evaluate which of the five substances is the best deicer. Students may also wish to conduct research and write a paragraph on the most effective deicer a city or town has used.

How can we produce better foods?

Revisit Anchoring Phenomenon At the end of Investigation 4, have students revisit the Anchoring Phenomenon question about how to produce better foods. Lead a class discussion about the reasons why people produce certain foods (such as better nutrition, coloring, longevity). Prompt students to relate those responses to explain how foods can be produced better.

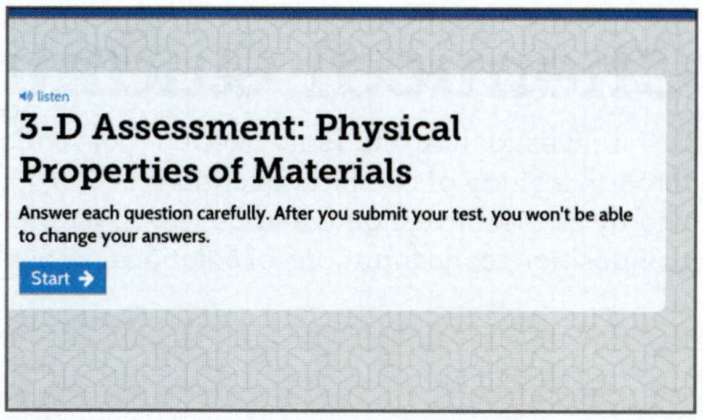

listen

3-D Assessment: Physical Properties of Materials

Answer each question carefully. After you submit your test, you won't be able to change your answers.

Start →

Interactive Online 3-D Assessment

Interactive ExamView 3-D Assessment

3-D Assessment Interactive Worksheet

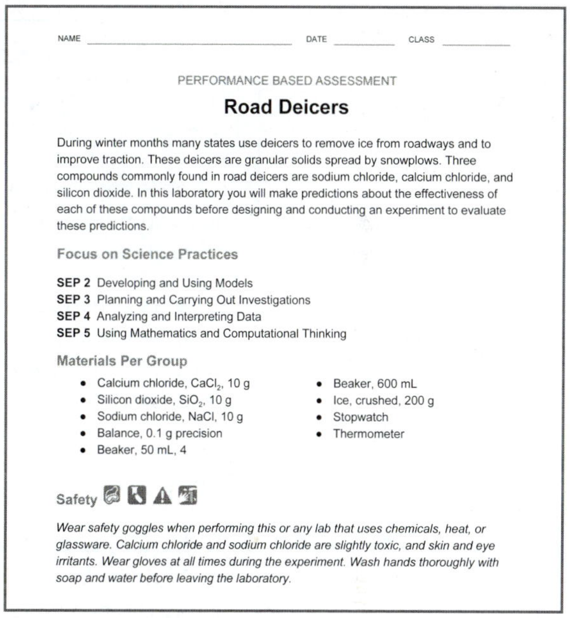

NAME ________ DATE ________ CLASS ________

PERFORMANCE BASED ASSESSMENT

Road Deicers

During winter months many states use deicers to remove ice from roadways and to improve traction. These deicers are granular solids spread by snowplows. Three compounds commonly found in road deicers are sodium chloride, calcium chloride, and silicon dioxide. In this laboratory you will make predictions about the effectiveness of each of these compounds before designing and conducting an experiment to evaluate these predictions.

Focus on Science Practices

SEP 2 Developing and Using Models
SEP 3 Planning and Carrying Out Investigations
SEP 4 Analyzing and Interpreting Data
SEP 5 Using Mathematics and Computational Thinking

Materials Per Group

- Calcium chloride, $CaCl_2$, 10 g
- Silicon dioxide, SiO_2, 10 g
- Sodium chloride, NaCl, 10 g
- Balance, 0.1 g precision
- Beaker, 50 mL, 4
- Beaker, 600 mL
- Ice, crushed, 200 g
- Stopwatch
- Thermometer

Safety

Wear safety goggles when performing this or any lab that uses chemicals, heat, or glassware. Calcium chloride and sodium chloride are slightly toxic, and skin and eye irritants. Wear gloves at all times during the experiment. Wash hands thoroughly with soap and water before leaving the laboratory.

Performance-Based Assessment Interactive Worksheet

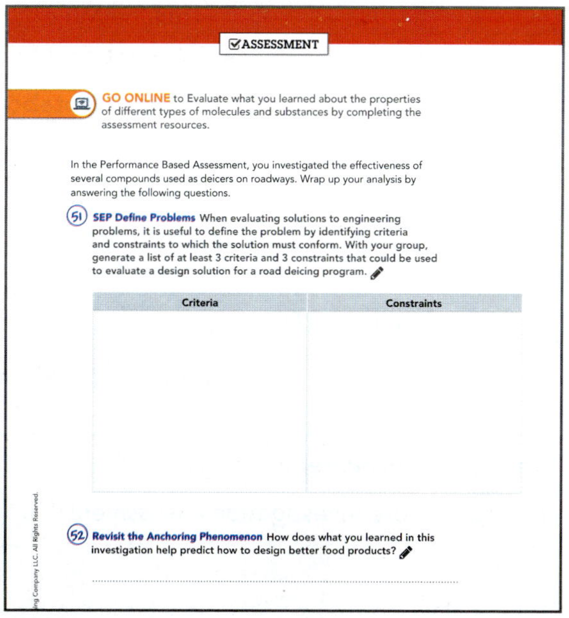

ASSESSMENT

GO ONLINE to Evaluate what you learned about the properties of different types of molecules and substances by completing the assessment resources.

In the Performance Based Assessment, you investigated the effectiveness of several compounds used as deicers on roadways. Wrap up your analysis by answering the following questions.

51 **SEP Define Problems** When evaluating solutions to engineering problems, it is useful to define the problem by identifying criteria and constraints to which the solution must conform. With your group, generate a list of at least 3 criteria and 3 constraints that could be used to evaluate a design solution for a road deicing program.

Criteria	Constraints

52 **Revisit the Anchoring Phenomenon** How does what you learned in this investigation help predict how to design better food products?

Experience Notebook, p. 171

eTEXT

Chemical Quantities

In this investigation, students deepen their understanding of scale, proportion, and quantity [CCC-3] through a study of chemical quantities [PS1.A]. Students apply knowledge of differences in size and energy as they investigate and develop system models of the mole concept, molar relationships, percent composition, concentrations of solutions, as well as other related phenomena.

INVESTIGATIVE PHENOMENON

Why do we quantify matter in different ways?

Explaining Phenomena In order to fully understand the phenomenon of why we quantify matter in different ways, students must calculate and convert matter as well as understand relationships between matter. As students develop the ability to analyze and calculate different types of formulas, they identify patterns in matter and energy.

	EXPERIENCE 1	EXPERIENCE 2
	The Mole Concept **2 days** Students measure matter and count with moles. They use mathematics to convert atoms to moles and find the molar mass of a compound.	**Molar Relationships** **2 days** Students explore the mole–mass relationship. They use mathematics to convert moles to mass and mass to moles. They interpret data on molar mass and density.
CONNECTION TO THE INVESTIGATIVE PHENOMENON	Students construct an explanation of why chemists use moles when dealing with macroscopic quantities and relate that to the phenomenon of quantifying matter in different ways.	Students design a solution for quantities of ingredients in a bread recipe and relate that to the phenomenon of quantifying matter in different ways.
ENGAGE	**Teacher's Guide** Everyday Phenomenon Different Things, Same Unit, p. 156	**Teacher's Guide** Everyday Phenomenon The Self-Inflating Balloon, p. 163
EXPLORE	**Inquiry Lab** Describe Small-scale Matter Using the Mole **Analyzing Data** Counting Atoms in One Gram	**Inquiry Lab** Mole Ratios **Interactivity** Mole Road Map
EXPLAIN	**Claim-Evidence-Reasoning** Discuss the Masses of One Mole **Animation** Moles Are Many **Experience Notebook,** pp. 174–181	**Modeling** Model Molar Mass and Molar Volume **Animation** Introduction to STP **Experience Notebook,** pp. 183–191
ELABORATE	**Discussion Rubric** Critique the Good of the Mole **Writing About Science** Counting Tiny Objects	**Peer Review Rubric** Review Models of Molar Mass and Molar Volume **Analyzing Data** Identify an Element From Its Molar Mass
EVALUATE	**Quiz** The Mole Concept **Experience Notebook** Revisit Investigative Phenomenon, p. 182	**Quiz** Molar Relationships **Experience Notebook** Revisit Investigative Phenomenon, p. 191

*Pacing for Encounter Investigative Phenomenon core instruction is a half-day.

†Pacing for core Investigation Assessment is approximately 1 day.

GOT MORE TIME? Personalize and enhance your instructional plan by assigning the activities with the got-more-time icon, as time allows.

Investigative Phenomenon Video Counting Cranberries*

Modeling Model the Investigative Phenomenon*

Virtual Reality Experience (+)

Experience Notebook, p. 172*

EXPERIENCE 3	EXPERIENCE 4
Percent Composition and Empirical Formulas **2 days** Students use mathematics to calculate percent composition of a compound. They determine empirical, molecular, and chemical formulas.	**Concentrations of Solutions** **2 days** Students carry out an investigation of concentrations of solutions. They use mathematics to calculate molarity and moles of solute in a solution. They design a process for diluting an aqueous solution.
Students obtain information on glucose and fructose and their chemical formulas and use this to refine explanations on quantifying matter in different ways.	Students plan an investigation where they dilute a sports drink into five different dilutions with varying concentrations of sucrose and use this to refine explanations on quantifying matter in different ways.
Teacher's Guide Everyday Phenomenon Roasting a Marshmallow, p. 169	**Teacher's Guide** Everyday Phenomenon Drink Mix Concentration, p. 175
Inquiry Lab Determine an Empirical Formula **Analyzing Data** Assess the Percent Composition in DNA (+)	**Inquiry Lab** Preparation of Solutions **Virtual Lab** Making Dilutions (+)
Modeling Model Percent Composition **Experience Notebook,** pp. 192–201	**Modeling** Model Measures of Concentration **Experience Notebook,** pp. 203–211
Peer Review Rubric Model Percent Composition **Engineering Design Challenge** An Empirical Formula Challenge (+)	**Discussion Rubric** Discuss Molarity and Other Measures of Concentration **Analyzing Data** Solubility and Percent by Mass (+)
Quiz Percent Composition and Empirical Formulas **Experience Notebook** Revisit Investigative Phenomenon, p. 202	**Quiz** Concentrations of Solutions **Experience Notebook** Revisit Investigative Phenomenon, p. 212

INVESTIGATION ASSESSMENT

Performance-Based Assessment Analysis of Basic Copper Carbonate†

3-D Assessment Chemical Quantities†

Experience Notebook Performance-Based Assessment, p. 213; Revisit Anchoring Phenomenon, p. 213†; **Appendix C** Problem Bank, pp. R14–R15

INVESTIGATION 5

Chemical Quantities

Teacher Background

The mole is the fundamental unit used by chemists for quantifying matter. The mole concept underlies much of chemistry and is crucial to understanding how quantities of different substances combine to form compounds. Students must understand that a mole contains exactly 6.02×10^{23} entities. This quantity is known as Avogadro's number. It is commonly used to refer to the mass of a substance containing 6.02×10^{23} particles. The usefulness of the mole is evident when examining empirical formulas, as the subscripts provide the mole ratio of the elements making up a compound. When students can tell you that H_2O is made by combining 2 moles of hydrogen with 1 mole of oxygen, they are making progress in utilizing proportional reasoning.

Learning Progression

In this investigation, students begin by examining Avogadro's number and its relationship to the mole. The mole is used to bridge the atomic and macroscopic domains. A variety of core ideas are integrated—students use their knowledge of the periodic table and atomic structure [PS1.A] to calculate molar mass. A mathematical approach [SEP-5] is utilized as students convert from moles to mass and mass to moles. Computational thinking is used throughout the investigation.

Proportional reasoning takes center stage when students look at Avogadro's hypothesis. By realizing that 22.4 L = 1 mole at STP, students can then readily calculate the moles, and then the mass, of any gas if they know its volume. When students learn how to find empirical and molecular formulas, they realize that chemical formulas are based on mole ratios, providing a great connection to prior concepts and further evidence for the unifying nature of the mole. Examining the percent composition of compounds gives students further exposure to scale, proportion, and quantity [CCC-3]. The concept of molarity provides yet another example of how the mole touches on nearly every aspect of chemistry, as students realize that the mole concept is needed to find the concentration of solutions.

RELATED PHENOMENA

In addition to using the cranberries in the video, consider using other phenomena to launch this investigation.

- **Bottle of Juice** Ask students what unit is used to measure a bottle of fruit juice. Challenge them to state the advantages of selling some products by volume, as opposed to some other method.
- **Container of Vinegar** Share with students that vinegar is 5% acetic acid. Ask students what this number means and why concentration is an important way to quantify certain types of matter.

TAKE IT LOCAL

Ask students to suggest other examples of products they might buy from the store and how they are quantified. Challenge them to suggest reasons why some products are sold by mass, others are sold by volume, and still others are sold by count.

ENCOUNTER

INVESTIGATIVE PHENOMENON

Why do we quantify matter in different ways?

Begin this investigation by introducing the concept of quantitative units, specifically the dozen. Then lead students through the content related to defining and clarifying the mole (Experience 1). After finding the molar mass of compounds, students investigate molar relationships—mass, volume, and density (Experience 2). They use what they learn about the mole to calculate percent composition and empirical formulas (Experience 3). Students then relate the mole to the concentration of solutes in a solution (Experience 4).

Counting Cranberries

Investigative Phenomenon Video Instruct students to watch the video and ask them to share their observations. **Ask** How many cranberries are being harvested? How can you quantify the cranberries? Explain to students that in the footage, you could estimate the number of cranberries using the area of the cranberries floating on the pond, or by the dimensions of the truck bed. Discuss that matter can be quantified in a number of different ways.

Model the Phenomenon

Modeling Have students review the video to develop a model of the phenomenon they observed. Remind students that a model does not have to look like the object or process it represents, but students should be able to use it to explain and/or predict. Have students complete Question 1 of the Modeling worksheet.

Remind students that their understanding of the phenomenon will be incomplete at this stage, but that they will revisit this activity as they learn more. Make sure to provide students with an opportunity to revisit their models throughout the investigation as well as at the end of the investigation for further revision and peer review.

Reflect on the Phenomenon

Experience Notebook Transition to the opener pages for Investigation 5 in the Experience Notebook and discuss the question on the photo, "Why do we quantify matter in different ways?"

If students struggle, then guide them to use what they've learned in the video and the Modeling activity to answer the driving question. Additionally, at the end of each experience, direct students to complete the writing prompt to reflect on the Investigative Phenomenon.

Investigative Phenomenon Video: Counting Cranberries

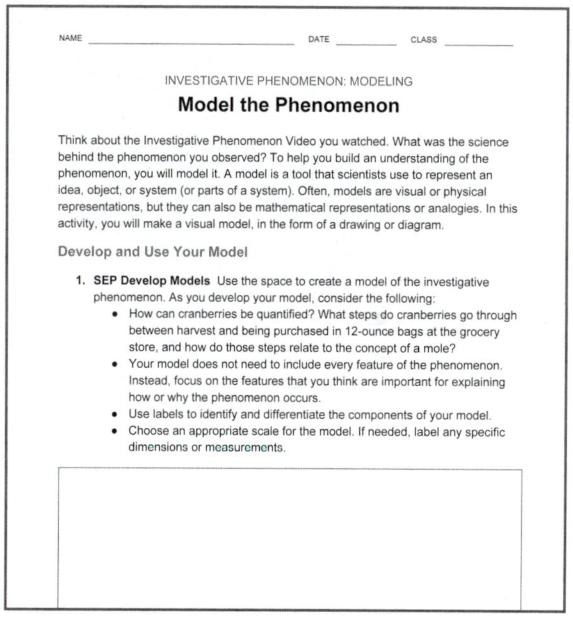

NAME ________ DATE ________ CLASS ________

INVESTIGATIVE PHENOMENON: MODELING

Model the Phenomenon

Think about the Investigative Phenomenon Video you watched. What was the science behind the phenomenon you observed? To help you build an understanding of the phenomenon, you will model it. A model is a tool that scientists use to represent an idea, object, or system (or parts of a system). Often, models are visual or physical representations, but they can also be mathematical representations or analogies. In this activity, you will make a visual model, in the form of a drawing or diagram.

Develop and Use Your Model

1. **SEP Develop Models** Use the space to create a model of the investigative phenomenon. As you develop your model, consider the following:
   - How can cranberries be quantified? What steps do cranberries go through between harvest and being purchased in 12-ounce bags at the grocery store, and how do those steps relate to the concept of a mole?
   - Your model does not need to include every feature of the phenomenon. Instead, focus on the features that you think are important for explaining how or why the phenomenon occurs.
   - Use labels to identify and differentiate the components of your model.
   - Choose an appropriate scale for the model. If needed, label any specific dimensions or measurements.

Modeling Interactive Worksheet

Experience Notebook, pp. 172–173

eTEXT

EXPERIENCE 1

The Mole Concept

Teacher Background

Experience 1 introduces one of the most fundamental concepts in all of chemistry—the concept of the mole. Students begin by exploring the different ways to measure matter, which involve counting, finding mass, and finding volume. Avogadro's number—6.02×10^{23}—will be introduced, and students will discover its relationship to the mole. The importance of the mole as a counting unit is introduced first. Once the conceptual foundation of a mole has been established, students work through problems converting moles to particles and particles to moles, and then investigate how to find the molar mass of both elements and compounds.

Objectives

- **Investigate the three methods used to measure matter—count, mass, and volume.**
- **Develop models of the mole that encompass atoms, molecules, and formula units.**
- **Explain the relationship between the mole and Avogadro's number.**
- **Use Avogadro's number to convert from moles to particles and particles to moles.**
- **Use the periodic table to find the molar mass of elements and compounds.**

RELATED PHENOMENA

In addition to the Different Things, Same Unit teacher demo, consider using other phenomena to launch this experience.

- **Counting Beans** Pass around plastic bags of beans to groups of students. Have them examine the bag for about a minute. Then ask what are some ways to discuss the number of beans in the bag. (Examples include: use the actual number of beans, express as dozens of beans.)
- **Mass of a Dozen** Display three different dozen cartons of eggs: one of small eggs, one of medium eggs, and one of extra large eggs. Point out that each carton has the same number of eggs. But the masses of the cartons of eggs are different. Tell students to think of the eggs as atoms, with each size being a different element. Point out that equal numbers of different kinds of atoms would have different masses too.

ENGAGE

EVERYDAY PHENOMENON

How can you measure matter?

Use this teacher demo to prompt student discussion about specific units of measurement in preparation for learning about the concept of a mole. As students consider new questions about this phenomenon, challenge them to apply their ideas to what they learn in the Inquiry Lab.

Different Things, Same Unit

Engage students with this demonstration of an everyday phenomenon to introduce the concept of the mole.

Materials small beakers containing the following quantities: 32.0 g sulfur, 56.0 g iron; water. Label each beaker with the name of its contents and its mass.

1. **Ask** What do a dozen eggs and a dozen donuts have in common? (A dozen always contains the same number of members—12.)
2. Show the class the labeled beakers of sulfur and iron. **Ask** How are the masses of the two samples related to the information in the periodic table? (The mass of each substance in the beakers is equal to its atomic mass on the periodic table.) Share that you could say each of the beakers contains exactly 1 unit of a pure element (i.e., mole, but do not yet introduce this term).
3. Tell students that in this experience, they will learn about a unit that they can use to count the number of atoms in a sample of matter. Point out that this unit of measurement is one way that we quantify matter. Ask students to identify ways in which they quantify matter. Discuss when scientists might use this information and why they quantify matter in different ways.

EXPLORE

Describe Small-scale Matter Using the Mole

Inquiry Lab In this lab, students perform a series of exercises to conceptualize just how big a chemical mole is [NoS-6]. They carry out an investigation [SEP-3] that highlights why the "counting by weighing" method enabled by the mole is so important when working on very small scales [CCC-3].

Lab Demo Video Watch the Lab Demo Video for advice on materials and preparation.

Choose Your Version Open-ended (O), Guided (G), Shortened (S), Advanced (A)

Materials aluminum foil, navy beans, rice, balance, 4 weighing dishes

Safety Have students wash their hands with soap and warm water after the lab.

Expected Outcome Students are able to better conceive the number and scale conveyed by a chemical mole, and they understand the need to "count by weighing" attributable to the small scales associated with atoms, molecules, and other particles.

Lab Summary Video Watch the Lab Summary Video for support on connecting the lab investigation to the Investigative Phenomenon.

NAME ______________ DATE ________ CLASS ________

THE MOLE CONCEPT INQUIRY LABS – OPEN

Describe Small-scale Matter Using the Mole

How big is a mole? The number is so large, it's almost impossible to imagine. The following activity will help you visualize the size of a mole and better understand its use as a tool to count matter on very small scales, such as the atomic scale.

Focus on Science Practices

SEP 2 Developing and Using Models
SEP 3 Planning and Carrying Out Investigations
SEP 4 Analyzing and Interpreting Data
SEP 5 Using Mathematics and Computational Thinking

Materials Per Group

- Aluminum foil
- Balance, 0.01-g precision
- Navy beans
- Rice
- Weighing Dishes, 4

Procedure

Part A - Counting with the Mole

1. "Counting by weighing" is used in chemistry and other applications to deal with small things. A hardware store, for example, may sell nails in packages of 500. Similarly, the office supply store probably carries boxes that contain 100 paper clips. Do you think someone counts out by hand every nail or paper clip in these products?

O/G/S/A Lab Interactive Worksheets

Counting Atoms in One Gram

Analyzing Data In this activity, students complete a table to show various numbers of carbon atoms and hydrogen atoms, the masses of these atoms, and the mass ratio of carbon to hydrogen to help explain Avogadro's number and how it relates to atomic mass. Students should understand that since a carbon atom has a mass 12 times greater than that of a hydrogen atom, a mole of carbon will have a mass 12 times greater than a mole of hydrogen, even though the number of atoms is the same.

- As students complete the activity, encourage them to identify patterns [CCC-1] in the data. As long as the number of carbon atoms is the same as the number of hydrogen atoms, the carbon atoms will have a mass 12 times greater.
- Remind students that just like a dozen, a mole represents a specific number. If the number of dozens is known, then it is easy to calculate the number of individual parts. In the same way, if the number of moles is known, then the number of individual atoms can easily be calculated.
- Instruct students to use the periodic table anytime they are asked to find the mass of a specific atom.

NAME ______________ DATE ________ CLASS ________

ANALYZING DATA

Counting Atoms in One Gram

A mole is a quantity just like a dozen is. A dozen is a quantity of 12 items. A mole has a quantity of 6.02×10^{23} items. This enormous number is called Avogadro's number. To help explain Avogadro's number and how it relates to atomic mass, complete the table to show various numbers of carbon atoms and hydrogen atoms, the masses of these atoms, and the mass ratio of carbon to hydrogen. Use the first two rows as a guide.

Comparing Carbon Atoms and Hydrogen Atoms

Number of atoms	Carbon		Hydrogen		Mass ratio
	Picture	Mass (amu)	Picture	Mass (amu)	$\frac{Mass\ Carbon}{Mass\ Hydrogen}$
1	O	12	•	1	$\frac{12\ amu}{1\ amu} = \frac{12}{1}$
2	O O	24	••	2	$\frac{24\ amu}{2\ amu} = \frac{12}{1}$
10					
50					

Analyzing Data Interactive Worksheet

ASSESS ON THE SPOT

As students are working through the Analyzing Data activity, ask them to determine the ratio of hydrogen atoms to oxygen atoms in a molecule of water and the mass ratio of oxygen to hydrogen in water. (2:1, 8:1)

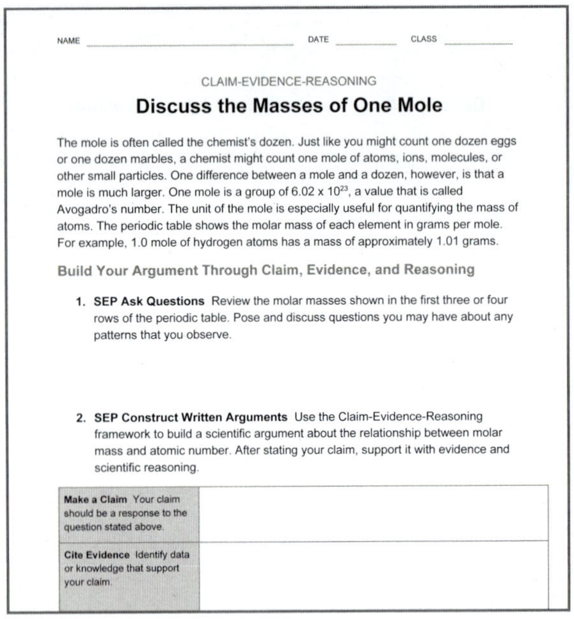
NAME ______ DATE ______ CLASS ______

CLAIM-EVIDENCE-REASONING

Discuss the Masses of One Mole

The mole is often called the chemist's dozen. Just like you might count one dozen eggs or one dozen marbles, a chemist might count one mole of atoms, ions, molecules, or other small particles. One difference between a mole and a dozen, however, is that a mole is much larger. One mole is a group of 6.02×10^{23}, a value that is called Avogadro's number. The unit of the mole is especially useful for quantifying the mass of atoms. The periodic table shows the molar mass of each element in grams per mole. For example, 1.0 mole of hydrogen atoms has a mass of approximately 1.01 grams.

Build Your Argument Through Claim, Evidence, and Reasoning

1. **SEP Ask Questions** Review the molar masses shown in the first three or four rows of the periodic table. Pose and discuss questions you may have about any patterns that you observe.

2. **SEP Construct Written Arguments** Use the Claim-Evidence-Reasoning framework to build a scientific argument about the relationship between molar mass and atomic number. After stating your claim, support it with evidence and scientific reasoning.

Make a Claim Your claim should be a response to the question stated above.	
Cite Evidence Identify data or knowledge that support your claim.	

CER Interactive Worksheet

EXPLAIN

Discuss the Masses of One Mole

Claim-Evidence-Reasoning Use this activity after students have had the opportunity to observe and explore how to count the number of atoms in 1 mole. Ideally, this would be after students complete the Inquiry Lab. In this activity, students investigate the relationship between molar mass and atomic number. Using the periodic table, they make a claim [SEP-7] concerning this relationship and provide evidence for this claim. Finally, students discuss [SEP-8] the reasoning strategy they used in formulating their claim.

- Encourage students to construct models [SEP-2] of the nucleus of an atom that includes the correct number of protons and neutrons. Doing so will make it easier to see the relationship between molar mass and atomic number.
- Remind students that patterns [CCC-1] often have exceptions. Most trends on the periodic table will have exceptions where some elements do not follow the established pattern.

DIFFERENTIATED INSTRUCTION

- **Support Less Proficient Readers** In the CER activity, instead of asking students to read and examine three or four rows on the periodic table, ask them to look at only a few elements in a single row. Have them point out atomic number and then molar mass. Make sure students understand that atomic number refers to number of protons in an atom of that element.
- **Support Struggling Students** Ask students to first find the trend for atomic number and then for atomic mass. To explain why this trend might occur, instruct them to write the number of protons for several successive elements and then write the number of neutrons for these same elements. You may need to remind students that the atomic mass represents the sum of the protons and neutrons in the nucleus. Instruct students to make their claim after examining this data.
- **Support Advanced Students** For the elements that do not follow the overall trend for atomic mass, challenge students to explain why these exceptions might exist. Before they make a claim, instruct students to look up the masses of various isotopes that might exist for these elements. Ask students if there is an isotope that follows the trend for increasing mass and if there is one that provides an exception to the trend. Instruct students to revise their claims in light of this new evidence.

Moles Are Many

Animation In this animation, students explore moles. They identify that a mole is the SI measure for a quantity of a substance and explain why we use the mole as a unit of measurement [SEP-5]. Students also determine its relation to atomic mass.

- Before the animation, have groups brainstorm what they already know about moles. As groups share, make a list on the board that summarizes their responses. Have students review the list after the animation to revise inaccuracies and add new information they learned.
- After the animation, have groups construct an explanation [SEP-6] to describe what a mole is, why it is used, and its relation to atomic mass. Have groups share their explanations with the class.

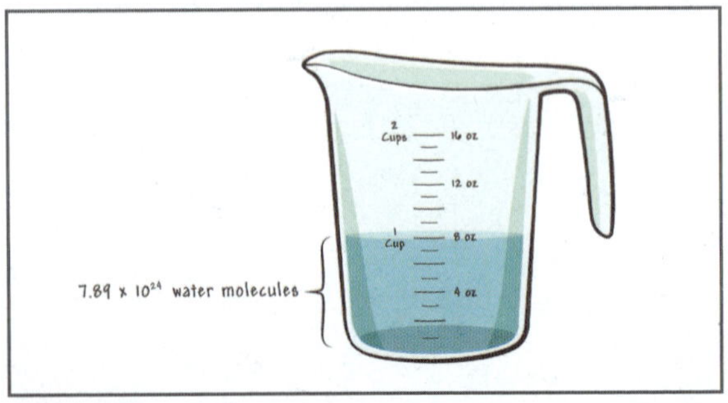

Animation: Moles Are Many

The Mole Concept

Experience Notebook Ideally, assign the Experience Notebook or Realize Reader for this experience the day before, and then follow up with any of the following suggested instructional strategies to fill knowledge gaps and deepen understanding. Alternatively, assign it alongside the Counting Atoms in One Gram activity as support for the activity.

Use these strategies to help students make sense of the images and text on the indicated pages, as well as to engage in science skills.

- **Measuring Matter** (pp. 174–175) Organize students into groups of four, and direct each group to list as many different terms as they can that represent numbers. Using the term *dozen* as an example, instruct students to use the following format: dozen = 12. Then compile a master list with the entire class. (Possible answers include: couple = 2; score = 20; gross = 144.) By familiarizing students with terms that represent numbers, the concept of a mole can be reinforced.
- **Counting With Moles** (pp. 176–177) If students struggle with understanding the meaning of a mole, tell them to develop a mental model [SEP-2] of it. For example, they might visualize a giant egg carton with 6.02×10^{23} depressions for particles. Then as students work through the table, reinforce that a mole represents 6.02×10^{23} particles, which can encompass more than just atoms. A mole of water contains 6.02×10^{23} molecules. Because each molecule contains 3 atoms, a mole of water would actually have three times as many atoms as would a mole of a pure element like copper. A mole of sodium chloride contains 6.02×10^{23} formula units. Because each formula unit contains 2 atoms, a mole of sodium chloride would contain twice the number of atoms as a mole of a pure element.
- **Molar Mass** (p. 179) Call on each student in the class and ask for either the molecular mass or the molar mass while pointing to a specific element on the periodic table. If reporting the molecular mass, students should give an answer with units in amu, but if giving the molar mass, they will need to provide an answer with units of g/mol. The molecular mass of sodium is 23 amu, but its molar mass is 23 g/mol.
- **Molar Mass of Compounds** (p. 180) Pair students and provide each pair with a ball-and-stick model of a molecule (or equivalent). Instruct them to use the model [SEP-2] to determine the number of each type of atom within the molecule. Then ask them to determine the number of moles of each element given 1 mole of the compound [SEP-5]. Direct them to determine the mass of each atom within the molecule, and then the mass of each element within 1 mole of the compound. Adding the masses of each atom within a molecule will yield the molar mass, and adding the masses of each element within a mole will yield the molar mass.
- **Sample Problem** (p. 181) Provide extra Sample Problem practice, while you circulate and help as needed:
  a. Find the molar mass of AlF_3. (84 g/mol)
  b. Find the molar mass of $Fe_3(PO_4)_2$. (358 g/mol)

How Do You Divide Numbers in Scientific Notation?

Virtual Nerd Video Use this video to reinforce how to divide numbers when using scientific notation.

How Do You Use Dimensional Analysis to Convert Units on One Part of a Rate?

Virtual Nerd Video Students can use this video to find and use conversion factors to convert a unit in the rate.

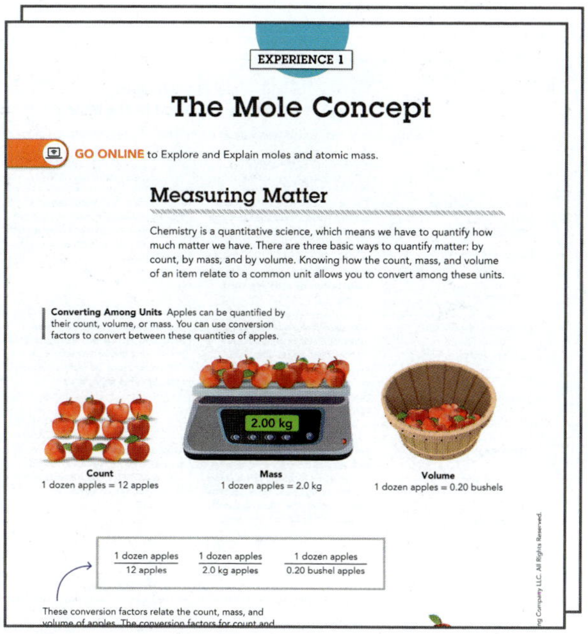
EXPERIENCE 1

The Mole Concept

GO ONLINE to Explore and Explain moles and atomic mass.

Measuring Matter

Chemistry is a quantitative science, which means we have to quantify how much matter we have. There are three basic ways to quantify matter: by count, by mass, and by volume. Knowing how the count, mass, and volume of an item relate to a common unit allows you to convert among these units.

Converting Among Units Apples can be quantified by their count, volume, or mass. You can use conversion factors to convert between these quantities of apples.

Count
1 dozen apples = 12 apples

Mass
1 dozen apples = 2.0 kg

Volume
1 dozen apples = 0.20 bushels

$\frac{1 \text{ dozen apples}}{12 \text{ apples}}$ $\frac{1 \text{ dozen apples}}{2.0 \text{ kg apples}}$ $\frac{1 \text{ dozen apples}}{0.20 \text{ bushel apples}}$

These conversion factors relate the count, mass, and

Experience Notebook, pp. 174–181

eTEXT

SAMPLE PROBLEM SUPPORT

Help students view calculating molar mass as individual parts when solving the problem on page 181. Focus on the atoms separately, and then at the end, put them all together. Students should understand that, looking at mass alone, oxygen should have a higher mass because the mass of 1 mole of oxygen is more than the mass of 1 mole of hydrogen. They can use this to check that their individual calculations are correct.

Virtual Nerd Video: How Do You Divide Numbers in Scientific Notation?

Virtual Nerd Video: How Do You Use Dimensional Analysis to Convert Units on One Part of a Rate?

ADDRESS PRECONCEPTIONS

While most students will have been exposed to scientific notation before now, many students will have trouble conceptualizing its meaning and may see Avogadro's number as little more than a number they enter into their calculator. You can use scientific notation to gain an understanding of Avogadro's number by using the following analogy: Suppose you had 6.02×10^{23} marbles, and for every 10 marbles, you disposed of 9 of them and put 1 aside. If you repeated this process for all of the marbles, the stack formed by putting aside just 1 out of every 10 marbles would only reduce the number of marbles by 1 zero—to 6.02×10^{22}! If you then repeated the procedure for this stack—throwing away 9 and keeping 1—the stack of marbles that remained from keeping just 1 out of every 10 would again only reduce the number of marbles to 6.02×10^{21}.

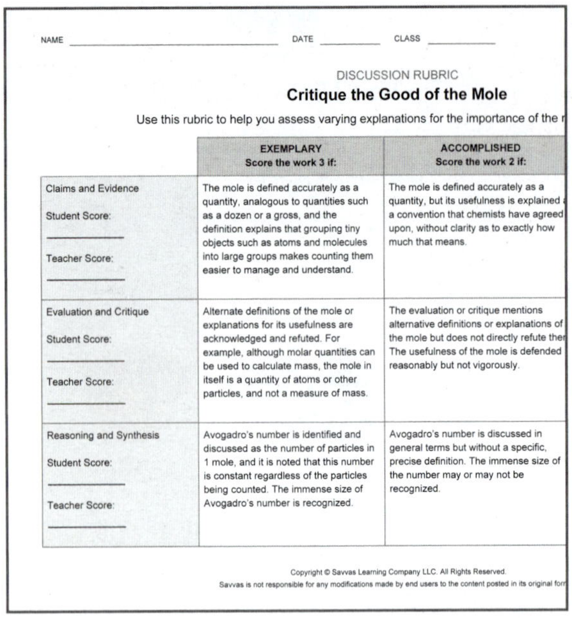

NAME ______________ DATE ________ CLASS ________

DISCUSSION RUBRIC

Critique the Good of the Mole

Use this rubric to help you assess varying explanations for the importance of the r

	EXEMPLARY Score the work 3 if:	ACCOMPLISHED Score the work 2 if:
Claims and Evidence Student Score: ______ Teacher Score: ______	The mole is defined accurately as a quantity, analogous to quantities such as a dozen or a gross, and the definition explains that grouping tiny objects such as atoms and molecules into large groups makes counting them easier to manage and understand.	The mole is defined accurately as a quantity, but its usefulness is explained a convention that chemists have agreed upon, without clarity as to exactly how much that means.
Evaluation and Critique Student Score: ______ Teacher Score: ______	Alternate definitions of the mole or explanations for its usefulness are acknowledged and refuted. For example, although molar quantities can be used to calculate mass, the mole in itself is a quantity of atoms or other particles, and not a measure of mass.	The evaluation or critique mentions alternative definitions or explanations of the mole but does not directly refute ther The usefulness of the mole is defended reasonably but not vigorously.
Reasoning and Synthesis Student Score: ______ Teacher Score: ______	Avogadro's number is identified and discussed as the number of particles in 1 mole, and it is noted that this number is constant regardless of the particles being counted. The immense size of Avogadro's number is recognized.	Avogadro's number is discussed in general terms but without a specific, precise definition. The immense size of the number may or may not be recognized.

Discussion Rubric Interactive Worksheet

ELD SUPPORT

Listening Students work in pairs to demonstrate comprehension of the Discussion Rubric by discussing the importance of the mole in chemistry.

- **Emerging/Beginning** Have student pairs say words or short phrases to answer the first discussion question. Provide substantial support as needed.
- **Developing/Expanding** Have each student say aloud to a partner the answer to the first and second discussion questions, showing thoughtful consideration of the ideas. Provide moderate support.
- **Bridging** Have pairs explain to a second pair the answer to the third discussion question.

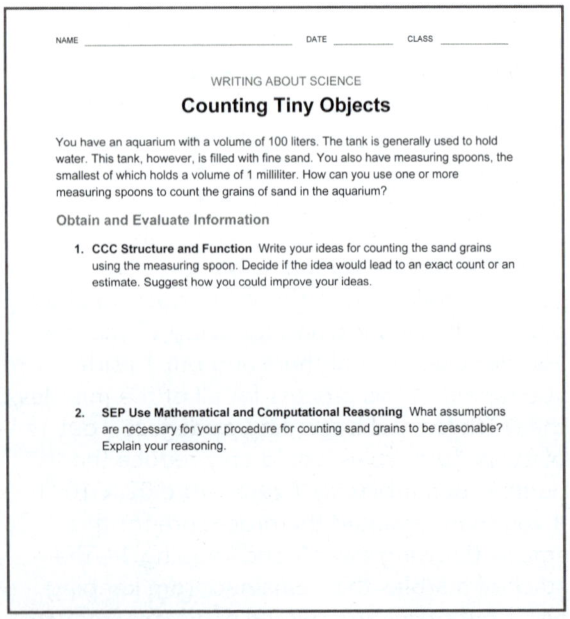

NAME ______________ DATE ________ CLASS ________

WRITING ABOUT SCIENCE

Counting Tiny Objects

You have an aquarium with a volume of 100 liters. The tank is generally used to hold water. This tank, however, is filled with fine sand. You also have measuring spoons, the smallest of which holds a volume of 1 milliliter. How can you use one or more measuring spoons to count the grains of sand in the aquarium?

Obtain and Evaluate Information

1. **CCC Structure and Function** Write your ideas for counting the sand grains using the measuring spoon. Decide if the idea would lead to an exact count or an estimate. Suggest how you could improve your ideas.

2. **SEP Use Mathematical and Computational Reasoning** What assumptions are necessary for your procedure for counting sand grains to be reasonable? Explain your reasoning.

Writing About Science Interactive Worksheet

ASSESS ON THE SPOT

Ask students to provide the following, assuming 1 mole of water (H_2) and 1 mole of hydrogen peroxide (H_2O_2).

- molar mass of each (18 g water; 34 g hydrogen peroxide)
- number of oxygen atoms in each (1 in water; 2 in hydrogen peroxide)
- number of hydrogen atoms in each (2 in water; 2 in hydrogen peroxide)
- total number of atoms in each (3 in water; 4 in hydrogen peroxide)

ELABORATE

Critique the Good of the Mole

Discussion Rubric Lead a class discussion about the usefulness of a mole to measure large quantities with these questions:

- What is a mole, and why is it useful?
- Describe some examples of quantities similar to a mole that are used in daily life. Why are these quantities useful? (Examples include dozens of eggs, reams of copy-machine paper, and ounces or grams of cereal or granola. In these cases, using larger quantities makes counting easier.)
- Do you think chemists could analyze atoms and elements without using moles or molar quantities? Why or why not?
- Iron is denser than hydrogen. Which has more atoms, 1 mole of hydrogen atoms or 1 mole of iron atoms? (The number of atoms is the same.) Which has the greater mass? (iron)

Have small groups of students discuss their ideas. When students have finished their discussion, have them use the rubric to evaluate [SEP-8] their understanding and communication, keeping in mind that they will be assessed on the accuracy of their self-evaluation.

ASSESS ON THE SPOT

Ask How many particles does 1 mole of any substance represent? (6.02×10^{23} representative particles of that substance) How can you convert the number of atoms of any substance to moles? (Multiply the number of atoms by the conversion factor 1 mole/6.02×10^{23} representative particles.)

Counting Tiny Objects

Writing About Science Students are challenged to explain [SEP-6] how they would determine the number of grains of sand in a 100-L aquarium using only a few measuring spoons, the smallest of which holds 1 mL.

- Encourage students to write their ideas individually, even if they think the merit of their idea is questionable.
- Organize students into groups of four, and ask them to discuss their ideas. Circulate among groups to assess understanding. Stop and ask questions, such as: Why did you decide to use an idea that would provide an estimate rather than an exact count? What do you think is the most important factor to consider when deciding whether an idea is reasonable? How is counting grains of sand different from counting atoms?
- Ask students how long it would take to count all of the grains of sand in the aquarium. Then relate this task to the difficulty of counting the number of atoms in a mole.

INTEGRATE MATH

Volume Conversions Students may require a review of volume conversions that are required in the Writing About Science activity. Remind students that the prefix *milli-* represents one-thousandth, so 1 mL represents one-thousandth of a liter. Therefore, 1000 mL = 1 liter. Likewise, the prefix *kilo-* represents 1000, so a kL contains 1000 L, and 100 L could also be represented as 0.1 kL. Finally, because there are 1000 mL in 1 L and 1000 L in 1 kL, then there must be 1,000,000 mL in 1 kL. Encourage students to draw diagrams when attempting to convert volume units within the metric system.

DIFFERENTIATED INSTRUCTION

- **Support Special Needs Students** Help students understand the Writing About Science activity by providing images of a grain of sand, a small pile of sand, a fish aquarium, and a measuring spoon. Guide students to understand the relative size of each of these things.
- **Support Struggling Students** Ask students to think about how the volume of the aquarium tank relates to counting the sand in it. Explain that they should use this volume in their estimation and that they should not be actually hand counting the small grains. If students have difficulty relating counting sand to atoms, they can make a drawing to help visualize it.
- **Support Advanced Students** Have advanced students choose two other types of matter to fill the aquarium in addition to the fine sand. Additional matter may include pieces of rice, marbles, paper clips, or beans. Ask students to describe how they would count the matter and how their procedure is different from or similar to the sand grains and to counting atoms.

PROFESSIONAL DEVELOPMENT

Develop Classroom Collaboration Pose the following challenge to small groups of students: An intermediate school teacher has requested your group's assistance in explaining the mole to her eighth-grade science class, using a creative and entertaining 5-minute animation or a computerized slide show with audio. The presentation should include multiple examples and demonstrate step-by-step calculations that support the examples.

Provide time for groups to share their ideas among group members and come to a consensus about a final idea for the presentation. Then groups can develop their presentations. You may wish to spread this activity over several class periods to allow sufficient time for development and presentations. Students can also work on parts of the activity as homework.

Chemical Quantities (30)

Virtual Reality Experience Students examine the law of conservation of mass and the concept of mole.

INTEGRATE THE THREE DIMENSIONS

In the Writing About Science activity, Counting Tiny Objects, students infer the structure [PS1.A] of an aquarium by using mathematical thinking [SEP-5] to estimate the number of sand grains in the aquarium. They construct explanations [SEP-6] to describe how the method of counting small grains relates to the use of Avogadro's number when referring to the number of atoms or molecules in a sample or counting atoms in a larger sample of matter.

CLASSROOM MODIFICATIONS

Based on your students' abilities and your schedule, you may wish to edit the document to make the Writing About Science activity more open ended or more guided.

- **More Open Ended** Introduce additional equipment, such as a sensitive balance. By recording the mass of a small amount of sand and then counting the grains, students can arrive at a reasonable estimate of the total number of grains in the aquarium. It might be interesting to use both a volume and mass approach, and then compare them.
- **More Guided** Provide students with the metric conversions they will need, such as 1000 mL = 1 L. You can also give each student a small amount of sand to see whether it is feasible to count the grains.

Virtual Reality Experience: Chemical Quantities

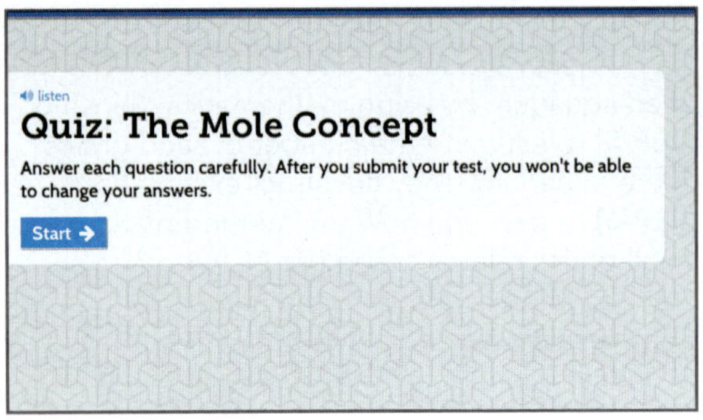

Interactive Online Quiz

Quiz Editable Worksheet

EVALUATE

The Mole Concept

Quiz Assign the quiz in online technology-enhanced, auto-graded format or as an editable quiz worksheet. Use the scoring notes and remediation strategies found online to assess students' responses and to provide targeted feedback for each item to remediate well before assigning the summative 3-D Assessment.

REMEDIATION SUGGESTIONS

- **If** students are struggling to explain why we use the mole as a unit of measurement, **then** prompt them to review the Moles Are Many animation.
- **If** students have difficulty calculating the mass of different atoms, **then** direct them to revisit the Analyzing Data worksheet, Counting Atoms in One Gram.
- **If** students have trouble converting from atoms to moles, **then** tell them to revisit how Avogadro's number defines the number of atoms in a mole. Direct students to page 177 of the Experience Notebook, and instruct them to rework the problems. Also, instruct students to examine the images and captions on pages 176 and 178.
- **If** students struggle with calculating molar mass, **then** direct them to reread the text and work through the problems in the section Molar Mass on page 179 of the Experience Notebook.
- **If** students struggle with how to find the molar mass of a compound, **then** direct them to study the images and captions and work through the problems on pages 180 and 181 of the Experience Notebook.

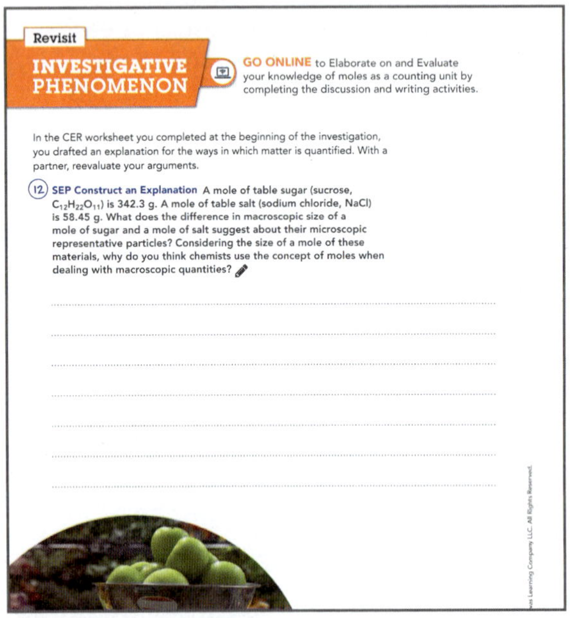
Revisit
INVESTIGATIVE PHENOMENON

GO ONLINE to Elaborate on and Evaluate your knowledge of moles as a counting unit by completing the discussion and writing activities.

In the CER worksheet you completed at the beginning of the investigation, you drafted an explanation for the ways in which matter is quantified. With a partner, reevaluate your arguments.

(12) SEP Construct an Explanation A mole of table sugar (sucrose, $C_{12}H_{22}O_{11}$) is 342.3 g. A mole of table salt (sodium chloride, NaCl) is 58.45 g. What does the difference in macroscopic size of a mole of sugar and a mole of salt suggest about their microscopic representative particles? Considering the size of a mole of these materials, why do you think chemists use the concept of moles when dealing with macroscopic quantities?

Experience Notebook, p. 182

eTEXT

Revisit
INVESTIGATIVE PHENOMENON

Support Reflection Students can complete the reflection prompt, where they will unpack and make sense of the Investigative Phenomenon, based on practices and understandings that have been reinforced over the course of the experience.

- Call on students to explain how the size of microscopic particles can affect their macroscopic representation.
- Measure out a mole of sucrose (342.3 g) and a mole of sodium chloride (58.45 g) and place them side by side to provide a visual representation.
- Call on students to describe how moles are used as a way to quantify matter.
- Prompt students to explain why they think using moles as a way to quantify matter is important.

Refine Your Model Have students answer Question 2 in the Modeling worksheet relating their model to the Investigative Phenomenon. Have students add any evidence they have collected from the activities so far in this investigation. Evidence may include incorporating representative particles and changing how the objects are viewed and grouped to be clearer.

EXPERIENCE 2

Molar Relationships

Teacher Background

Experience 2 continues to develop the mole concept, beginning with a discussion of converting moles to mass and then mass to moles. In the last experience, students learned how to find the molar mass of both elements and compounds. They now use molar mass to make conversions between moles and mass. Although students should be able to convert from particles to moles to mass, the relationship between moles and mass will be the most beneficial to students as they continue throughout this investigation and their study of chemistry in general. Students also investigate the relationship between moles and the volumes of gases and learn how to easily find the density of any gas at STP.

Objectives

- **Convert mole quantities to masses, and mass quantities to moles.**
- **Explain the relationship between moles and volumes of gases at STP.**
- **Calculate the density of a gas at STP, given the molar mass of the gas.**

ENGAGE

EVERYDAY PHENOMENON

Can you inflate a balloon with vinegar and baking soda?

Use this teacher demo to prompt student discussion about finding the number of gas molecules in a balloon.

The Self-Inflating Balloon

Engage students with this demonstration of an everyday phenomenon to introduce the concept of molar volumes of gases.

Materials 250-mL Erlenmeyer flask, sturdy balloon, household vinegar (5% solution of acetic acid), baking soda (sodium bicarbonate), lab spatula, electronic balance

Safety Prompt students to wear safety goggles.

1. Find the mass of an uninflated balloon.
2. Add approximately 100 mL of vinegar to the flask.
3. Using the spatula, fill the balloon until it is half filled with baking soda.
4. Carefully place the balloon over the mouth of the flask, being careful not to allow baking soda to fall into the flask.
5. Once the balloon is attached to the flask, invert the balloon so that the baking soda mixes with the vinegar.
6. After the balloon has stopped inflating, tie it off and remove it from the flask.
7. Drop the balloon. Ask the students to observe its rate of fall and then predict the identity of the gas. (CO_2)
8. Find and record the mass of the CO_2-filled balloon. Have students find the number of CO_2 molecules in the balloon. (Make sure they subtract the mass of the empty balloon first.) Discuss how molecules and mass are needed to quantify the gas-filled balloon and the importance of different methods of quantification.

RELATED PHENOMENA

In addition to The Self-Inflating Balloon teacher demo, consider using other phenomena to launch this experience.

- **Atoms in Graphite Signature** Challenge students to find the number of atoms in their signature made with a pencil. Remind students that pencils do not contain lead, but graphite, which is a form of carbon. Students will need to take the mass of their pencils before and after writing their signature to find the mass of carbon used. (Alternatively, they may take the mass of the paper before and after writing on it.) Once students know the mass of carbon, they can use the molar mass of carbon (12 g/mol) and Avogadro's number to find the number of atoms in their signature.
- **Atoms in Chalk Signature** Challenge students to find the number of atoms in their signature made with chalk. Tell students that chalk is made of calcium carbonate ($CaCO_3$). The procedure will be similar to the previous activity, except they will need to multiply the number of formula units in their signature by 5, since there are 5 atoms in each formula unit of $CaCO_3$.

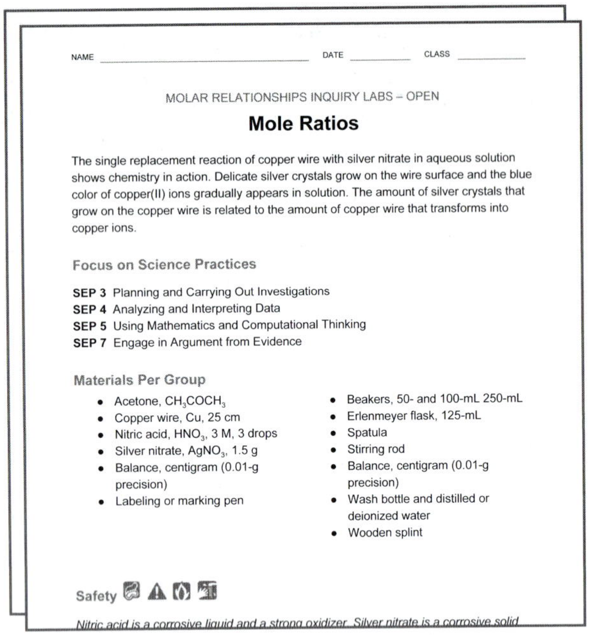
NAME ______________ DATE ________ CLASS ________

MOLAR RELATIONSHIPS INQUIRY LABS – OPEN

Mole Ratios

The single replacement reaction of copper wire with silver nitrate in aqueous solution shows chemistry in action. Delicate silver crystals grow on the wire surface and the blue color of copper(II) ions gradually appears in solution. The amount of silver crystals that grow on the copper wire is related to the amount of copper wire that transforms into copper ions.

Focus on Science Practices

SEP 3 Planning and Carrying Out Investigations
SEP 4 Analyzing and Interpreting Data
SEP 5 Using Mathematics and Computational Thinking
SEP 7 Engage in Argument from Evidence

Materials Per Group

- Acetone, CH_3COCH_3
- Copper wire, Cu, 25 cm
- Nitric acid, HNO_3, 3 M, 3 drops
- Silver nitrate, $AgNO_3$, 1.5 g
- Balance, centigram (0.01-g precision)
- Labeling or marking pen
- Beakers, 50- and 100-mL 250-mL
- Erlenmeyer flask, 125-mL
- Spatula
- Stirring rod
- Balance, centigram (0.01-g precision)
- Wash bottle and distilled or deionized water
- Wooden splint

Safety

Nitric acid is a corrosive liquid and a strong oxidizer. Silver nitrate is a corrosive solid.

O/G/S/A Lab Interactive Worksheets

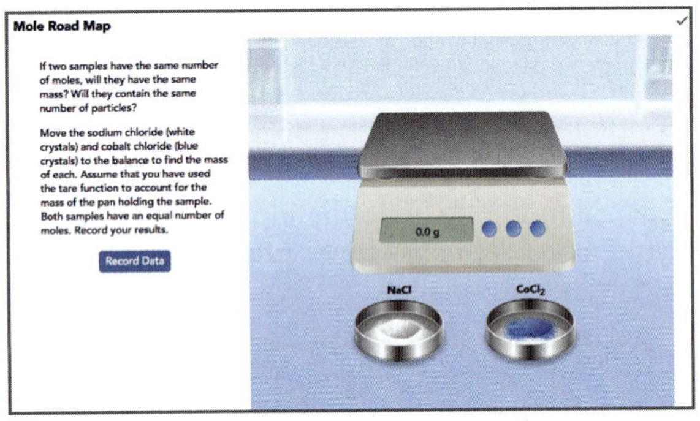

Interactivity: Mole Road Map

INTEGRATE THE THREE DIMENSIONS

In this interactivity, students use mathematical and computational thinking [SEP-5] to determine how to find the number of particles in a salt packet. As students work through each step in the interactivity and convert units, they observe how atoms (and mass) are conserved [CCC-5] in a chemical reaction [PS1.B] as they are converted from one form to another.

EXPLORE

Mole Ratios

Inquiry Lab Students develop an experimental procedure [SEP-3] to determine the molar relationship between silver and copper in the single replacement reaction between copper metal and silver nitrate. Students further see that atoms (and mass) are conserved in a chemical reaction [PS1.B], because matter is not created or destroyed but converted from one form to another. This idea is reflected in the coefficients in balanced chemical equations.

Lab Demo Video Watch the Lab Demo Video for advice on materials and preparation.

Choose Your Version Open-ended (O), Guided (G), Shortened (S), Advanced (A)

Materials 25 cm copper wire; acetone; 3 drops 3*M* nitric acid; 1.5 g silver nitrate; centigram balance; labeling or marking pen; 50-mL, 100-mL, and 250-mL beakers; 125-mL Erlenmeyer flask; spatula; stirring rod; wash bottle with distilled or deionized water; wooden splint

Safety Students must wear chemical splash goggles and chemical-resistant gloves and apron. Chemicals used are corrosive, toxic, and flammable. Tell students to avoid contact with flames and other sources of ignition. Monitor students closely. Remind students to carefully wash their hands with soap and warm water after completing the lab.

Expected Outcome Students see that the mole ratios between components in a balanced chemical reaction, that derive from the coefficients, should be reflected in experimental data.

Lab Summary Video Watch the Lab Summary Video for support on connecting the lab investigation to the Investigative Phenomenon.

ASSESS ON THE SPOT

As students complete the lab, have them write a description of the part of the lab that they struggled with the most. Collect responses and review the most common problems with the entire class the following day.

Mole Road Map

Interactivity In this interactivity, students explore the relationship between mass, moles, and the number of particles in a sample of a substance. Students work with a model [SEP-2] to convert from moles to grams to particles to volume (if a gas). Students first analyze three samples of salt to identify how moles and particles are related. Next, they compare two samples that have the same number of moles to explain whether these samples have the same mass and the same number of particles. Then students determine the volume of a gas from the number of moles of the gas at STP.

Choose among these strategies to engage students with the interactivity:

- Have students work in pairs to complete the activity. Then have pairs work with another pair of students to discuss their understanding of the relationship between mass, moles, and the number of particles in a substance. Have them describe how they could count the number of salt particles in a salt packet.
- Go through the interactivity as a class, allowing students to direct the exploration by calling on individuals and asking them what step to take next. Prompt students to record data and responses to questions as they are modeled and answered throughout the interactivity.

EXPLAIN

Model Molar Mass and Molar Volume

Modeling In this activity, students use data to make graphs that relate mass, moles, and volume to model [SEP-2] the concepts of molar mass and molar volume. Students identify the slope of the graph line formed for each element. Then students apply the concepts of molar mass and molar volume to solve mathematical problems [SEP-5].

- When constructing graphs, make sure students label both axes, give the graph a title, and make the scales on both the *x*- and *y*-axes proportional.
- Remind students that when calculating slope to use the formula rise/run.
- When students are making mole conversions, encourage them to keep in mind scale and proportion [CCC-3]. For example, if they know that 32 g of O_2 is equal to 1 mole and they are asked to find the number of moles in 50 g of O_2, ask students if this amount is more or less than 1 mole. By continually keeping in mind the number of grams in a single mole, students are less likely to make errors when doing calculations. Encourage students to write the definition of molar mass for each substance they are working with. For O_2, direct them to write: 32 g = 1 mole.

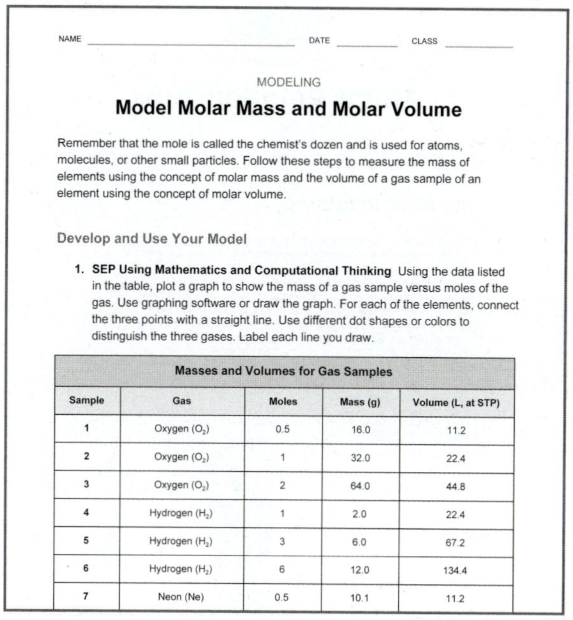

NAME ______ DATE ______ CLASS ______

MODELING

Model Molar Mass and Molar Volume

Remember that the mole is called the chemist's dozen and is used for atoms, molecules, or other small particles. Follow these steps to measure the mass of elements using the concept of molar mass and the volume of a gas sample of an element using the concept of molar volume.

Develop and Use Your Model

1. **SEP Using Mathematics and Computational Thinking** Using the data listed in the table, plot a graph to show the mass of a gas sample versus moles of the gas. Use graphing software or draw the graph. For each of the elements, connect the three points with a straight line. Use different dot shapes or colors to distinguish the three gases. Label each line you draw.

Masses and Volumes for Gas Samples

Sample	Gas	Moles	Mass (g)	Volume (L, at STP)
1	Oxygen (O_2)	0.5	16.0	11.2
2	Oxygen (O_2)	1	32.0	22.4
3	Oxygen (O_2)	2	64.0	44.8
4	Hydrogen (H_2)	1	2.0	22.4
5	Hydrogen (H_2)	3	6.0	67.2
6	Hydrogen (H_2)	6	12.0	134.4
7	Neon (Ne)	0.5	10.1	11.2

Modeling Interactive Worksheet

DIFFERENTIATED INSTRUCTION

- **Support Struggling Students** Instead of students making their own graphs, give them a blank graph with the *x*- and *y*-axes already labeled. When calculating slope, first guide students through a sample problem that they can use as a guide.
- **Support Less Proficient Readers** Read aloud the instructions and questions while students follow along. Before the activity, highlight vocabulary words that some students might struggle with, and direct them to look up the definitions for these terms before they proceed with the activity.
- **Support Special Needs Students** Provide students with a graph that has the *x*- and *y*-axes already labeled and also has the values along these axes. Instead of having them calculate slope, ask them to rank the slopes of the lines of different elements from steepest to shallowest, and then ask them to explain what the slope represents.
- **Support Advanced Students** Ask students to describe how the volume of gases changes under conditions other than STP and how increasing and then decreasing the temperature will affect the volume of a mole of gas. Ask students to describe how increasing and then decreasing the pressure of a gas will affect its molar volume.

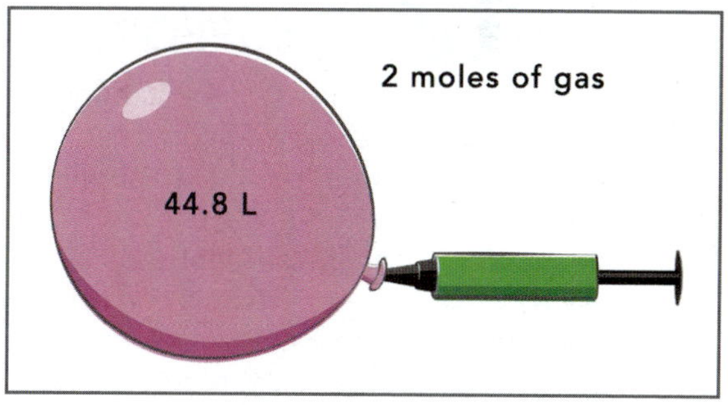

Animation: Introduction to STP

Introduction to STP

Animation In this animation, students are introduced to the concept of standard temperature and pressure (STP). They observe how a balloon changes as it is pumped up with air to understand the relationship between standard temperature and pressure. Students discover that STP is a temperature of 273.15 K and a pressure of 1 atmosphere. They find out that at STP, 1 mole of gas fills a volume of 22.4 L.

- State a goal for students before they watch the animation. Tell students to improve their molar mass and molar volume models from the Modeling activity based on what they learn from the animation.
- Pause the animation after an important concept is presented and ask students to summarize the concept. Ask students to identify temperature and pressure at STP. Then watch that short part again to help students make better sense of that concept.

ELD SUPPORT

Speaking After students view the animation, they work with a partner to engage in conversational exchanges and express ideas about STP using knowledge they have gained from the animation, Introduction to STP.

- **Emerging/Beginning** Students use their own words to ask and answer questions about what they learned about STP in the animation.
- **Developing/Expanding** Students paraphrase the main ideas about STP in the animation.
- **Bridging** Have students complete the Expanding activity. Then, group pairs of students. Have them share their main ideas about STP and discuss how STP relates to the changes in the balloon in the animation.

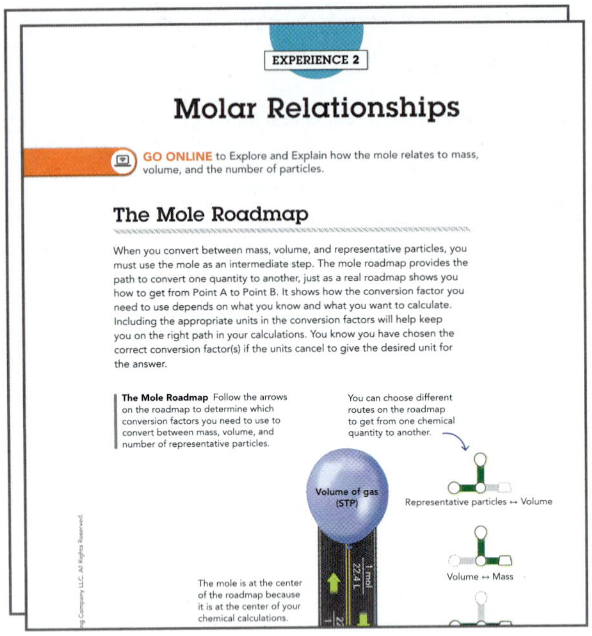
EXPERIENCE 2

Molar Relationships

GO ONLINE to Explore and Explain how the mole relates to mass, volume, and the number of particles.

The Mole Roadmap

When you convert between mass, volume, and representative particles, you must use the mole as an intermediate step. The mole roadmap provides the path to convert one quantity to another, just as a real roadmap shows you how to get from Point A to Point B. It shows how the conversion factor you need to use depends on what you know and what you want to calculate. Including the appropriate units in the conversion factors will help keep you on the right path in your calculations. You know you have chosen the correct conversion factor(s) if the units cancel to give the desired unit for the answer.

The Mole Roadmap Follow the arrows on the roadmap to determine which conversion factors you need to use to convert between mass, volume, and number of representative particles.

Experience Notebook, pp. 183–191

eTEXT

SAMPLE PROBLEM SUPPORT

When converting moles to volume, encourage students to write out the relevant conversion factor before attempting to solve the problem (22.4 L = 1 mole). By having this piece of information in front of them, students are more likely to know if their answer is correct. Encourage students to view these problems conceptually, as opposed to just math problems. Students may choose to draw a container with 1 mole of gas, labeling the container as *22.4 L*. Models such as these can be powerful problem-solving aids.

ADDRESS PRECONCEPTIONS

Students are typically familiar with the concept of volume as it relates to liquids and solids. Both solids and liquids are for the most part incompressible, so their volume is an accurate representation of how much space these substances occupy. Gas molecules themselves, however, take up virtually no space. As gases are cooled, they move more slowly, exerting less pressure, and thus take up less space in flexible containers such as balloons. As gases are heated, they expand as long as they are not constrained by a rigid container. It is important for students to realize that 1 mole of a gas only occupies 22.4 L at STP, and that changing the temperature or pressure of a gas has no effect on the actual size of the molecules, but can have a dramatic effect on the space they take up as they move about.

Molar Relationships (20)

Experience Notebook Ideally, assign the Experience Notebook or Realize Reader for this experience the day before, and then follow up with any of the following suggested instructional strategies to fill knowledge gaps and deepen understanding. Alternatively, assign it alongside the Model Molar Mass and Molar Volume activity as support.

Use these strategies to help students make sense of the images and text on the indicated pages, as well as to engage science skills.

- **The Mole–Mass Relationship** (pp. 184–186) Instruct students to identify the relationship between moles and mass as they are working through conversions [SEP-5]. For example, for the element sodium, have students write: 1 mole Na = 23 g. For a compound such as water, have them write: 1 mole H_2O = 18 g. Having this handy guide in front of them will help students to know whether their answers are reasonable.
- **Avogadro's Hypothesis** (p. 187) Organize students into groups of four and give each group an air-filled ball, such as a volleyball, basketball, or kickball. Instruct them to first find the volume of the ball. (You may need to tell them that the volume of a sphere = $\frac{4}{3}\pi r^3$.) After students have figured out the volume, instruct them to find the number of molecules of air (N_2 and O_2 mostly) within the ball.
- **The Mole–Volume Relationship** (p. 188) Pair students and ask them to find the slope of the line in the graph [SEP-5] in their answer to Question 16, and then ask them to draw a separate graph of a different gas at STP. When students are finished, tell them that the slope of both graphs should be equal to 22.4 L/mol.
- **Sample Problems** (p. 189) If students are struggling to understand the difference between moles and mass, explain that in the types of Sample Problems on pages 185 and 186 of the Experience Notebook, mass is typically given in grams. A mole is the unit of measurement for the number of representative particles. Clearly emphasize that mass is not equivalent to moles. Suggest that students create a spider chart to explore the relationship between the mole, mass, volume, and number of particles. Provide extra Sample Problem practice, while you circulate and help out as needed:
  a. Find the number of moles in 17.1 L of NO_2 at STP. (0.76 mol)
  b. A balloon is filled with 0.75 moles of hydrogen gas (H_2) at STP. What is the volume of the balloon? (16.8 L)
- **Mass and Density** (pp. 190–191) Provide a helium-filled balloon and ask students how to calculate [SEP-5] its density. Its volume can easily be found, but if you attach the string to a piece of tape and then affix it to a balance, it will register a negative reading due to the buoyant force of the air pushing it up. Challenge students to then find the mass of the helium within the balloon using Avogadro's hypothesis (assume STP). Once they find the density by using the formula on page 190, they can then calculate the mass by using the formula $D = M/V$. Remind the students that the density of gases is expressed as g/L, not g/mL, as is usually the case with liquids and solids.

ASSESS ON THE SPOT

Hold up an empty 2-L bottle and ask students to calculate the number of oxygen (O_2) molecules in the bottle. Tell your students that oxygen makes up 21% of the air. Assume STP.

$$(2.0 \text{ L air} \times \frac{1 \text{ mol air}}{22.4 \text{ L}} \times \frac{21 \text{ mol } O_2}{100 \text{ mol air}} \times \frac{6.02 \times 10^{23} \text{ molecules}}{\text{mol}}$$
$$= 1.1 \times 10^{22} \text{ molecules } O_2)$$

INTEGRATE MATH

When calculating density using a formula, students might easily view these types of problems as they would any other math problem. But solving math-related problems in science has an added advantage in that it is often possible to verify an answer by looking at real-world phenomenon. When calculating the density of a gas, students can often verify if their answer is correct by comparing its density to that of air (1.23 g/L). If a gas, like helium, has a lower density than air, it will rise. Always encourage students to check their answers for reasonableness.

PROFESSIONAL DEVELOPMENT

Explaining Phenomena Explain that in many chemical manufacturing processes, reactants are purchased by mass and products are sold by mass. However, point out that processes are set up and designed based on the ratio in which moles of reactants combine with each other to form moles of products. **Ask** If 1 mole of reactant produces 1 mole of product, how can you find the mass of product if you know the mass of the reactant? (Convert the mass of reactant to the number of moles, and then convert that number of moles to the mass of product.)

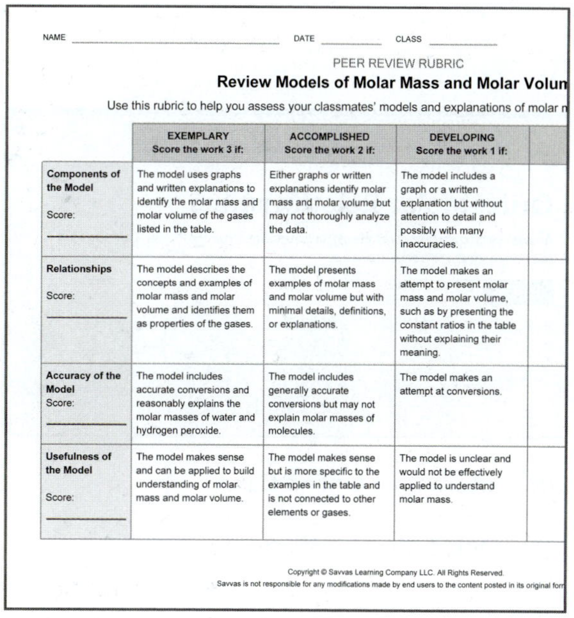

NAME ______ DATE ______ CLASS ______

PEER REVIEW RUBRIC

Review Models of Molar Mass and Molar Volum

Use this rubric to help you assess your classmates' models and explanations of molar m

	EXEMPLARY Score the work 3 if:	ACCOMPLISHED Score the work 2 if:	DEVELOPING Score the work 1 if:
Components of the Model Score: ______	The model uses graphs and written explanations to identify the molar mass and molar volume of the gases listed in the table.	Either graphs or written explanations identify molar mass and molar volume but may not thoroughly analyze the data.	The model includes a graph or a written explanation but without attention to detail and possibly with many inaccuracies.
Relationships Score: ______	The model describes the concepts and examples of molar mass and molar volume and identifies them as properties of the gases.	The model presents examples of molar mass and molar volume but with minimal details, definitions, or explanations.	The model makes an attempt to present molar mass and molar volume, such as by presenting the constant ratios in the table without explaining their meaning.
Accuracy of the Model Score: ______	The model includes accurate conversions and reasonably explains the molar masses of water and hydrogen peroxide.	The model includes generally accurate conversions but may not explain molar masses of molecules.	The model makes an attempt at conversions.
Usefulness of the Model Score: ______	The model makes sense and can be applied to build understanding of molar mass and molar volume.	The model makes sense but is more specific to the examples in the table and is not connected to other elements or gases.	The model is unclear and would not be effectively applied to understand molar mass.

Peer Review Rubric Interactive Worksheet

ELABORATE

Review Models of Molar Mass and Molar Volume

Peer Review Rubric Use the Peer Review Rubric to help students analyze and evaluate the molar mass and molar volume models [SEP-2] and explanations their classmates constructed in the Model Molar Mass and Molar Volume activity.

- Organize students into groups of four, and have each student evaluate the models of the three other members in the group, using a separate rubric sheet for each evaluation and clearly identifying the name of the peer on each rubric.
- Give students 10 minutes to review their peers' models. Make it clear to students that they will receive a grade for this activity based on how accurate and thoughtfully executed their evaluations are articulated in writing [SEP-8].

Identify an Element From Its Molar Mass

Analyzing Data In this activity, students analyze three graphs [SEP-4] of mass versus moles to calculate [SEP-5] the molar masses of the elements. Then students use molar masses and the periodic table to identify each element.

- As students are completing this activity, ask them to review other points on the graphs besides the indicated points. Because each graph is a straight line, point out that students should be able to gather data from any point on the line.
- Ask students to determine the relationship between slope and molar mass. (A steeper slope indicates a higher molar mass.)
- Make sure that students understand the limitations to this model. Any number of compounds will have the same molar mass. Emphasize that without additional information they are only making predictions, and a graph alone cannot be used to determine the identity of a gas.

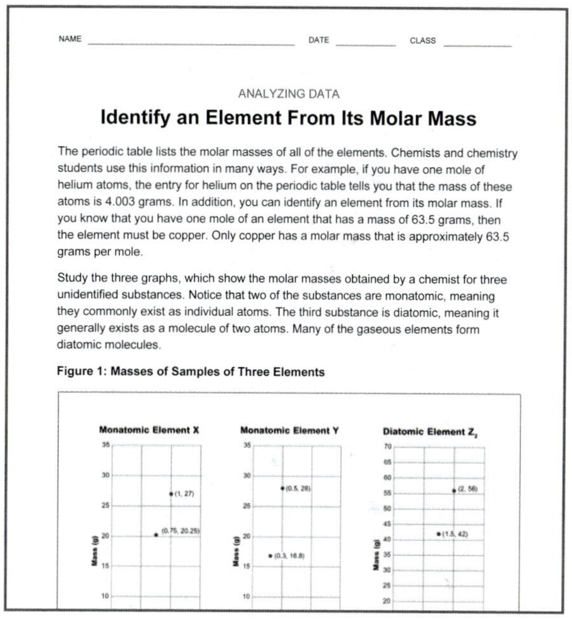

NAME ______ DATE ______ CLASS ______

ANALYZING DATA

Identify an Element From Its Molar Mass

The periodic table lists the molar masses of all of the elements. Chemists and chemistry students use this information in many ways. For example, if you have one mole of helium atoms, the entry for helium on the periodic table tells you that the mass of these atoms is 4.003 grams. In addition, you can identify an element from its molar mass. If you know that you have one mole of an element that has a mass of 63.5 grams, then the element must be copper. Only copper has a molar mass that is approximately 63.5 grams per mole.

Study the three graphs, which show the molar masses obtained by a chemist for three unidentified substances. Notice that two of the substances are monatomic, meaning they commonly exist as individual atoms. The third substance is diatomic, meaning it generally exists as a molecule of two atoms. Many of the gaseous elements form diatomic molecules.

Figure 1: Masses of Samples of Three Elements

Analyzing Data Interactive Worksheet

ASSESS ON THE SPOT

Ask students to construct a graph of molar mass versus moles for the molecule F_2. (1 mole of F_2 will have a mass of 38 g.) If drawn properly, students will be able to determine the molar mass from any point on their line.

CLASSROOM MODIFICATIONS

Based on your students' abilities and your schedule, you may wish to edit the Identify an Element From Its Molar Mass worksheet to make it more open ended or more guided.

- **More Open Ended** Give each group of students an element or compound and then direct them to construct a graph based on the molar mass of their substance. Students can exchange graphs with other groups, and challenge them to determine the identity of the substance.
- **More Guided** Complete the activity as a class. Model how to graph the data and find the slope of the line for Substance X in Question 1 while students follow along. Then guide them through the steps for Substance Y and Substance Z_2. Lead a discussion to answer the remaining questions.

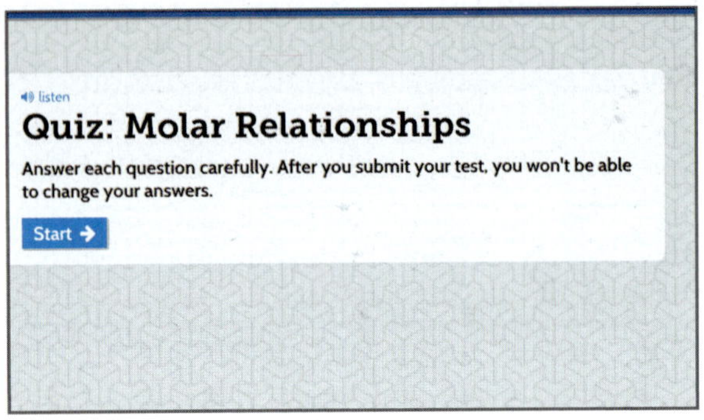

Interactive Online Quiz

Quiz Editable Worksheet

EVALUATE

Molar Relationships

Quiz Assign the quiz in online technology-enhanced, auto-graded format or as an editable quiz worksheet. Use the scoring notes and remediation strategies found online to assess students' responses and to provide targeted feedback for each item to remediate well before assigning the summative 3-D Assessment.

REMEDIATION SUGGESTIONS

- **If** students have difficulty identifying an element from its molar mass, **then** direct them to revisit the Analyzing Data worksheet, Identify an Element From Its Molar Mass.
- **If** students have trouble converting from grams to moles, or moles to grams, **then** review the steps needed to make these conversions, beginning with elements before moving on to compounds. Make sure students know that 1 mole of an element has a mass in grams equal to its atomic mass. Refer students to the mole road map on page 183 of the Experience Notebook. Work through the problems on pages 185–189 with them.
- **If** students struggle with finding the number of moles in a certain volume of gas, **then** direct them to review the text and work through the problems in the section Avogadro's Hypothesis on page 187 of the Experience Notebook. Also, instruct students to examine the images and captions on pages 188 and 190.
- **If** students struggle with how to find the density of a gas, **then** direct them to study the images and captions and work through the problems on page 189 of the Experience Notebook.
- **If** students are struggling to understand the concept of STP, **then** prompt them to review the Introduction to STP animation.

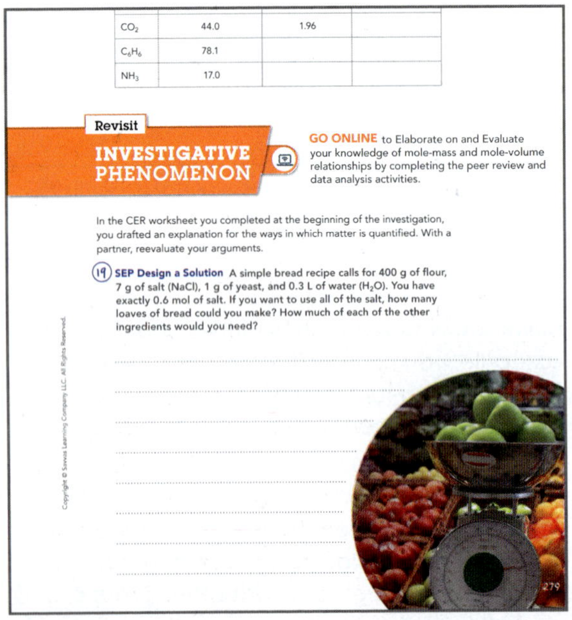

CO_2	44.0	1.96	
C_6H_6	78.1		
NH_3	17.0		

Revisit
INVESTIGATIVE PHENOMENON

GO ONLINE to Elaborate on and Evaluate your knowledge of mole-mass and mole-volume relationships by completing the peer review and data analysis activities.

In the CER worksheet you completed at the beginning of the investigation, you drafted an explanation for the ways in which matter is quantified. With a partner, reevaluate your arguments.

19 **SEP Design a Solution** A simple bread recipe calls for 400 g of flour, 7 g of salt (NaCl), 1 g of yeast, and 0.3 L of water (H_2O). You have exactly 0.6 mol of salt. If you want to use all of the salt, how many loaves of bread could you make? How much of each of the other ingredients would you need?

Copyright © Savvas Learning Company LLC. All Rights Reserved.

279

Experience Notebook, p. 191

eTEXT

Revisit INVESTIGATIVE PHENOMENON

Support Reflection Students can complete the reflection prompt, where they will unpack and make sense of the Investigative Phenomenon, based on practices and understandings that have been reinforced over the course of the experience.

- Remind students that, to solve any problem, the units must be consistent. Before solving, the moles of salt must be converted to grams. Discuss how units are important for quantifying different types of matter and why different units are used.
- To reinforce the concept of proportionality, provide students with a simpler example first. Ask students to describe how many sandwich wraps they could make if they had 12 slices of cheese, 10 lettuce leaves, and 8 tortillas.

Further Develop Your Model Have students add any evidence they have collected in this experience. Allow time for them to make any additional changes based on information they have collected from the activities in this learning experience. Evidence may include the fact that even though gases may have different masses, as long as they have the same volume under the same conditions of temperature and pressure, they will contain the same number of particles. Volume provides another way to quantify matter.

EXPERIENCE 3

Percent Composition and Empirical Formulas

Teacher Background

Experience 3 introduces the concept of percent composition. Percentages are a recurring concept in chemistry, and they have numerous applications. Even though students will have previously studied percentages, some students might benefit from a review of how percentages are calculated. Students explore the percent composition of compounds, so stress that the percentages within a compound must add up to exactly 100%. Students next examine empirical and molecular formulas, which are based on mole ratios. This experience provides students with an excellent opportunity to reinforce proportional reasoning strategies. Even though this experience is heavily math-based, a focus on conceptual understanding will help students to be successful.

Objectives

- **Explain how to find the percent composition of a compound.**
- **Develop models to illustrate the law of definite proportion and law of constant composition.**
- **Find the empirical and molecular formulas for a compound.**
- **Use subscripts within a chemical formula to represent a mole ratio.**

ENGAGE

EVERYDAY PHENOMENON

What percentage of a marshmallow is carbon?

Use this teacher demo to prompt student discussion about percent composition.

Roasting a Marshmallow

Engage students with this demonstration of an everyday phenomenon to introduce the concept of percent composition.

Materials safety goggles, large marshmallows, Bunsen burner, crucible tongs, electronic balance

1. Put on safety goggles and instruct your students to do the same.
2. Find the mass of a marshmallow.
3. Ask students to predict what percentage of a marshmallow is carbon.
4. Holding the marshmallow with the tongs, carefully heat it over the Bunsen burner. Rotate the marshmallow to prevent it from dripping.
5. Heat the marshmallow until it is completely black. At this point, the hydrogen and water will have been driven off, leaving behind carbon. (It may not be possible to burn every bit of the marshmallow, but do the best you can.)
6. After the marshmallow cools, place it on the balance to find the mass of carbon remaining.
7. Prompt students to find the percentage of carbon in the original marshmallow. It can be found by dividing the mass of carbon by the initial mass of the marshmallow. Share with students that this value will only represent a rough estimate, due to unavoidable sources of error. Relate the percentage of carbon in the marshmallow to why we quantify matter in different ways.

RELATED PHENOMENA

In addition to the Roasting a Marshmallow teacher demo, consider using other phenomena to launch this experience.

- **Mass of Bubble Gum** Give each student a piece of bubble gum. Direct them to find the mass of the gum and then chew it for the entire class period. Instruct students to lay the gum aside until the next day, and then find the mass again. Students can then calculate the percentage of sugar in their original piece of bubblegum, as the loss of mass is due to the sugar in the gum being dissolved when chewed.
- **Mass of Popped Corn** Find and record the mass of a container of stovetop popcorn, and then pop the popcorn over a hot plate. After the corn has stopped popping, allow it to cool before finding and recording the mass again. Students can now determine the percentage of water that was in the original kernels, as water is released when popcorn pops.
- **Mass of Water in the Human Body** Share with students that the percentage of water in the human body by mass is approximately 60%. Challenge students to find the mass of water in their body based on this percentage.

NAME ____________________ DATE __________ CLASS __________

PERCENT COMPOSITION AND EMPIRICAL FORMULA INQUIRY LABS – OPEN

Determine an Empirical Formula

Empirical formulas are chemical formulas that show the simplest ratio of elements in a compound. Through experimentation and careful measurements, you can determine the empirical formula of an unknown binary compound. In this lab, your group will be given an unknown binary compound to analyze. Each group's compound has the general formula D_xE_y. When heated, the compound decomposes and E becomes a gas.

$$D_xE_y(s) \rightarrow xD(s) + yE(g)$$

To calculate the empirical formula of a compound, you need to know the percent or mass of each element in the compound. These masses, once converted to moles using molar mass values, reveal the mole ratios of the constituent elements to each other in the compound.

Focus on Science Practices

SEP 3 Planning and Carrying Out Investigations
SEP 4 Analyzing and Interpreting Data
SEP 5 Using Mathematics and Computational Thinking

Materials Per Group

- Unknown Binary Compound in vial, 34 g
- Balance, milligram (0.001-g precision)
- Bunsen burner
- Clay triangle
- Crucible and crucible lid
- Crucible tongs
- Support Stand and ring clamp
- Wire gauze with ceramic center

O/G/S/A Lab Interactive Worksheets

NAME ____________________ DATE __________ CLASS __________

ANALYZING DATA

Assess the Percent Composition in DNA

In the 1940s and 1950s, the X-ray crystallography of Rosalind Franklin, along with work by other scientists, was adding up to a picture of the purpose, structure, and function of DNA. Today, we recognize DNA as the molecule of heredity. It is passed from parents to offspring and determines how the body grows and develops. The structure of DNA consists of many repetitions of small units called nucleotides. Each nucleotide contains one of four different nitrogenous bases—adenine (A), cytosine (C), guanine (G), and thymine (T).

The table shows the percent composition of several samples of DNA. Look for patterns in the data and then respond to the questions.The table shows the percent composition of several samples of DNA. Look for patterns in the data and then respond to the questions.

Nitrogenous Bases in DNA Samples									
		Percent composition by number				Percent Composition by mass			
Sample	Size (number of nitrogenous bases)	Adenine (A)	Cytosine (C)	Guanine (G)	Thymine (T)	Adenine (A)	Cytosine (C)	Guanine (G)	Thymine (T)
1	5600	22.5%	27.5%	27.6%	22.4%	23.2%	23.3%	31.9%	21.6%
2	1400	27.5%	22.4%	27.6%	22.6%	28.1%	18.8%	31.5%	21.5%
3	800	25.5%	24.3%	24.6%	25.6%	26.3%	20.6%	28.4%	24.7%

Analyzing Data Interactive Worksheet

CLASSROOM MODIFICATIONS

Based on your students' abilities and your schedule, you can modify the Analyzing Data activity to be more open ended or more guided.

- **More Open Ended** Have students describe additional samples with varying sizes that they would want to examine for percent compositions. Encourage students to discuss what ways they would change the samples to develop a further understanding of the patterns.
- **More Guided** Give students a diagram of a portion of a strand of DNA and have them count the number of each kind of nucleotide in the strand.

EXPLORE

Determine an Empirical Formula

40

Inquiry Lab Students carry out an investigation [SEP-3] to determine the empirical formula of an unknown binary compound.

Lab Demo Video Watch the Lab Demo Video for advice on materials and preparation.

Choose Your Version Open-ended (O), Guided (G), Shortened (S), Advanced (A)

Materials 34 g Unknown Binary Compound in vial, milligram balance, Bunsen burner, clay triangle, crucible and crucible lid, crucible tongs, support stand and ring clamp, wire gauze with ceramic center

Safety The unknown compounds are toxic if swallowed and harmful if inhaled. Tell students to avoid breathing dust or fumes. Students must wear chemical splash goggles and chemical-resistant gloves and an apron. Make sure that students handle the hot crucible and its lid only with tongs. They should not touch the crucible with their fingers or hands. Monitor students closely and make sure they wash their hands with soap and warm water before leaving the lab.

Expected Outcome Students learn that mass percent data, which can be obtained by heating compounds that decompose into a gaseous product and a solid product, can be used to determine the chemical formula of a compound. Students become familiar with the mathematics and computational thinking needed to convert mass percent data into an empirical formula.

Lab Summary Video Watch the Lab Summary Video for support on connecting the lab investigation to the Investigative Phenomenon.

Assess the Percent Composition in DNA

15

Analyzing Data In this activity, students analyze data [SEP-4] collected from several samples of DNA. They examine the percent composition of the four nucleic acids found in each DNA sample. Students identify patterns [CCC-1] in the data and reflect on the size of the DNA samples, which can contain thousands of nucleic acids.

- As students are completing this activity, ask them to use percentage to find the number of each nucleic acid in one of the samples. Then ask them to compare the sum of these values to the total number of nucleic acids in the sample. (They should be the same.)
- Share with students that each nucleic acid is a compound with a specific formula. Adenine is $C_5H_5N_5$; cytosine is $C_4H_5N_3O$; guanine is $C_5H_5N_5O$; and thymine is $C_5H_6N_2O_2$. Revisit this activity when you discuss formulas and ask whether they represent empirical or molecular formulas.
- Since students have likely taken a biology course previously, this activity provides a good opportunity to connect chemistry to biology. Students will have previously studied DNA, and to see its appearance in chemistry will reinforce the idea that all of the disciplines in science are interrelated.

ASSESS ON THE SPOT

After students complete the Analyzing Data activity, have them complete an exit card and respond to the question: How can the mass of a substance be used to determine the number of atoms, molecules, or ions using moles and mole relationships? Review responses to assess students' understanding.

EXPLAIN

Model Percent Composition

Modeling Use this activity after students have had the opportunity to observe and explore the percent composition in DNA in the Analyzing Data activity. In this activity, students develop models [SEP-2] to explain how elements combine to form compounds. Students construct pie graphs to illustrate the percent composition of compounds. They apply what they have learned by working through several problems related to percent composition. Students use percent composition to find the empirical formula.

- Remind students that when finding percent composition, the percentages of all elements within a compound must add up to 100%. To find the percent of a particular part of the whole, divide the part by the whole.
- Ask students what the subscripts in a formula represent. (There are two possible answers: Subscripts can refer to the number of atoms in a molecule or the number of moles of an element within a mole of the compound. In either case, subscripts represent the ratio of elements within a compound.)
- Share with students that a chemical formula contains the necessary ingredients to make a compound in the correct proportions. To make water, for example, you would need 2 moles of hydrogen for every 1 mole of oxygen.

NAME ______________ DATE ________ CLASS ________

MODELING

Model Percent Composition

When copper and chlorine react, they can form either copper(I) chloride (CuCl) or copper(II) chloride ($CuCl_2$). How can a chemist tell the difference between the two products? One way is to calculate the percent composition of each element in the product. As shown by the chemical formulas, the proportion of atoms of the two elements is 1:1 in copper(I) chloride and 1:2 in copper(II) chloride. Those proportions remain constant regardless of the amount of the compound.

Data on Selected Elements and Compounds		
Element or compound	**Chemical symbol/formula**	**Molar mass (g/mol)**
Copper	Cu	63.55
Chlorine	Cl	35.45
Copper(I) chloride	CuCl	99.00
Copper(II) chloride	$CuCl_2$	134.45
Carbon	C	12.00
Oxygen	O	16.00

Modeling Interactive Worksheet

DIFFERENTIATED INSTRUCTION

- **Support Struggling Students** Instead of asking students to construct their own graphs, give them blank graphs with the circle already drawn. Remind students that the complete circle represents 100% and that each quadrant represents 25%. Help them figure out how to represent each percent as part of the whole circle.
- **Support Less Proficient Readers** You may need to read aloud the instructions for some students. Before the activity, highlight vocabulary words that you know some students might struggle with, such as *percent composition* and *proportion*, and discuss the meanings of these terms before students proceed with the activity.
- **Support Special Needs Students** Some special needs students may benefit from using calculators with large keys that are easier to read. Some could construct their graph in alternative ways, such as by cutting a modeling-clay disk into the correct proportions.
- **Support Advanced Students** Once students have solved for the empirical formula, ask them to come up with several possible molecular formulas for each one. As long as the subscripts maintain the same ratio, any variation of molecular formula is possible, although they may not represent actual compounds. For example, if the empirical formula is N_2O, possible molecular formulas might include N_4O_2, $N_{10}O_5$, or $N_{20}O_{10}$.

PROFESSIONAL DEVELOPMENT

Develop Classroom Collaboration Before students begin conversing about the discussion questions at the end of the Model Percent Composition activity, have the class brainstorm a list of questions that partners can ask each other. Model some techniques students can use to help partners articulate their ideas. Use prompts such as:

- So, I think you are saying __________. Is that right?
- What evidence led you to that idea?
- What other reasons or evidence did you see?

Note that these questions are neutral and open-ended, and that asking these types of questions is a skill that we develop with practice. Remind students that they should give their partner a few moments to form an answer, and not to interrupt them.

INTEGRATE THE THREE DIMENSIONS

In the Model Percent Composition activity, students use mathematical thinking [SEP-5] and apply their knowledge of chemical reactions [PS1.B] to construct and evaluate symbolic models [SEP-2] of chemical compounds. Students use atomic mass to calculate the percent composition of each component element of a compound. As students analyze and interpret data, they should consider how atoms are conserved [CCC-5] during these chemical reactions.

CONNECT TO CAREERS

Genetic Counselor Explain to your students that DNA contains the genetic instructions for making all of the proteins within an organism, which, in turn, determines its specific traits. A good understanding of DNA is necessary for success in any of the medical professions. Recently, several companies have popularized DNA testing as a way to explore your family tree. Genetic counselors are trained to advise families to deal with the implications of genetic disorders or other type of inheritable diseases.

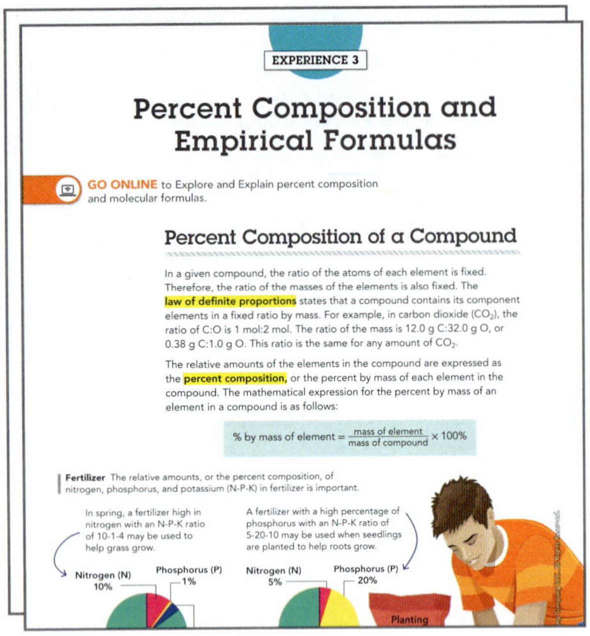

EXPERIENCE 3

Percent Composition and Empirical Formulas

GO ONLINE to Explore and Explain percent composition and molecular formulas.

Percent Composition of a Compound

In a given compound, the ratio of the atoms of each element is fixed. Therefore, the ratio of the masses of the elements is also fixed. The **law of definite proportions** states that a compound contains its component elements in a fixed ratio by mass. For example, in carbon dioxide (CO_2), the ratio of C:O is 1 mol:2 mol. The ratio of the mass is 12.0 g C:32.0 g O, or 0.38 g C:1.0 g O. This ratio is the same for any amount of CO_2.

The relative amounts of the elements in the compound are expressed as the **percent composition,** or the percent by mass of each element in the compound. The mathematical expression for the percent by mass of an element in a compound is as follows:

$$\% \text{ by mass of element} = \frac{\text{mass of element}}{\text{mass of compound}} \times 100\%$$

Fertilizer The relative amounts, or the percent composition, of nitrogen, phosphorus, and potassium (N-P-K) in fertilizer is important.

Experience Notebook, pp. 192–201

eTEXT

ADDRESS PRECONCEPTIONS

Students often have trouble conceptualizing percentages that are greater than 100%. When dealing with percent composition, the sum of the parts can never exceed 100%. However, when dealing with percent increase, there is really no limit as to how high a percentage can go. If a paper towel absorbs its weight in water, we say that it has absorbed 100% of its weight in water. But if a paper towel absorbs twice its weight in water, it will have absorbed 200% of its weight. Remind students that percentages often exceed 100% when referring to the amount of increase, but not when used to refer to the parts that make up a whole.

SAMPLE PROBLEM SUPPORT

Finding the molecular formula is a great exercise in proportional reasoning. Remind students that the ratio of subscripts within an empirical formula must be equal to the ratio in a molecular formula. If there are only two subscripts, this ratio can be found by simply dividing the subscripts. Remind students that to find a molecular formula, it is often necessary to find the empirical formula first.

Virtual Nerd Video: How Do You Divide a Decimal by a Decimal?

Percent Composition and Empirical Formulas

20

Experience Notebook Ideally, assign the Experience Notebook or Realize Reader for this experience the day before, and then follow up with any of the following suggested instructional strategies you desire to fill knowledge gaps and deepen understanding. The experience involves many calculations, which can be challenging for some students, so you may wish to move slowly through the materials, perhaps spreading the discussion over two days. Alternatively, assign it alongside the Model Percent Composition activity as support for the activity.

Use these strategies to help students make sense of the images and text on the indicated pages, as well as to engage science skills.

- **Percent Composition of a Compound** (pp. 192–193) Pair students and give each pair a package of circular tablet candy. Challenge students to find the percent composition of the candy roll by color. Then ask students to write the "formula" for their candy roll, using the first letters of each color as the symbols. (One possible formula is $B_5O_2G_3PVY_3$.)
- **Percent Composition from Chemical Formulas** (pp. 194–195) Before referring students to the caption on page 194, ask them what might cause [CCC-2] an ice cube to sink in water. After soliciting student explanations [SEP-6], instruct them to read about deuterium, which is used to make heavy water. Determine whether students can make the connection between heavy water and sinking ice. Ice made from this heavy form of hydrogen does indeed sink in water.
- **Percent Composition as a Conversion Factor** (pp. 196–197) Organize students into groups of four and give each group the formula for several hydrates, such as $M_gSO_4{\bullet}7H_2O$, $CaCl_2{\bullet}2H_2O$, or $Ba(OH)_2{\bullet}2H_2O$. Alternatively, you may ask students to look at the labels of bottles of chemical hydrates. Challenge each group to find the percentage of water in each hydrate. You might need to tell students that the dot in the hydrate is not a multiplication symbol, but rather represents that water molecules in a hydrate are bound within the crystal lattice of the compound.
- **Empirical Formulas** (pp. 198–199) Remind students that subscripts in a formula represent mole ratios, not mass ratios. A common mistake students sometimes make is forgetting to convert mass to moles before finding an empirical formula.
- **Molecular Formulas** (pp. 200–201) Students often have difficulty understanding why the subscripts in a molecular formula do not need to be reduced to simplest terms, as they do in an empirical formula. Share with students that empirical formulas represent the simplest whole number mole ratios of elements within a compound, whereas molecular formulas represent the compound as it actually exists in nature, which may or may not be in reduced form.
- **Sample Problem** (p. 201) Provide extra Sample Problem practice, while you circulate and help out as needed:
  a. Find the molecular formula for CH if the molar mass of the molecular compound is 78 g/mol. (C_6H_6)
  b. Find the molecular formula (molar mass = 34 g/mol) for a compound formed by combining 1 g of hydrogen with 16 g of oxygen. (H_2O_2)

ASSESS ON THE SPOT

Ask students to provide the empirical formula for the following compounds:

a) H_2O (H_2O)

b) $C_6H_8O_6$ ($C_3H_4O_3$)

c) $C_{100}H_{80}$ (C_5H_4)

d) $C_{12}H_{22}O_{11}$ ($C_{12}H_{22}O_{11}$)

How Do You Divide a Decimal By a Decimal?

Virtual Nerd Video Use this video to reinforce the process for dividing a decimal by a decimal.

ELABORATE

Model Percent Composition

Peer Review Rubric Students use the rubric as a scoring guide to evaluate [SEP-8] the claims their peers developed in the earlier Modeling activity, Model Percent Composition.

- Organize students into groups of four and have each student evaluate the models of the three other members in the group, using a separate rubric sheet for each evaluation and clearly identifying the name of one peer on each rubric.
- Give students 10 minutes to review their peers' models. Make it clear to students that they will receive a grade for this activity based on how accurate and thoughtfully executed their evaluations are articulated in writing.

ASSESS ON THE SPOT

Share with your students that 2% milk contains 2% fat by weight, not volume. Ask students what the weight of fat is in a gallon of milk, which has a mass of 3.9 kg. For an extension, discuss with your students why the fat content is reported as a function of mass, yet milk is always sold by volume.

INTEGRATE MATH

Ratios When using mole ratios to find empirical formulas, it is a good rule of thumb to do very little rounding of the mole values. Share with students that you can safely round 1.99 moles, for example, to 2 moles. Likewise, you can round 1.49 moles to 1.5 moles. When working with ratios, whatever operation is performed on one number in the ratio must be performed on all remaining numbers. So, if the mole ratio is $C_1H_{1.5}$, multiplying both subscripts by 2 will yield an empirical formula of C_2H_3. If no pattern is evident when attempting to find the empirical formula given a set of mole values, encourage students to divide each mole value by the smallest value, which will often lead to a workable solution.

An Empirical Formula Challenge

Engineering Design Challenge In this activity, students are faced with the scenario that their school's electrician has misplaced a year's supply of copper wire. The only other source of copper is in a 500-g bottle of copper chloride hydrate. Students determine if the bottle has enough copper for the electrician's needs. They then have to develop an efficient method to extract the copper from the copper chloride hydrate. Students define the problem [ETS1.A], identify criteria and constraints, and develop a method and possible solutions [ETS1.B] for determining the empirical formula of the copper compound and percent by mass of copper.

Materials 12 cm aluminum wire, 2 g $Cu_xCl_y \bullet zH_2O$, balance, Bunsen burner, crucible, piezoelectric lighter, water, faucet aspirator (optional), 250-mL beaker, Buchner funnel (optional), filter paper (optional), vacuum flask (optional), watch glass

Safety Have students wear safety goggles and gloves while carrying out the investigation. At the end of the lab, they should wash their hands thoroughly with soap and warm water.

Expected Outcome Students use their knowledge of the law of conservation of mass and chemical quantities to determine the percent by mass of copper in a sample of copper chloride hydrate.

Use the following strategies to guide students as they complete indicated steps in the Engineering Design Challenge:

- **Step 2** Copy the chart onto the board, and fill it in as the whole class works together to identify the criteria and constraints. Encourage students to think about what the unknown empirical formula represents and to break it down.
- **Step 3** Provide URLs for some Web sites that students could use for their research.

NAME ______ DATE ______ CLASS ______

PEER REVIEW RUBRIC

Model Percent Composition

Use this rubric to help you assess your classmates' calculations and explanations of the c

	EXEMPLARY Score the work 3 if:	ACCOMPLISHED Score the work 2 if:	DEVELOPING Score the work 1 if:
Components of the Model Score: ______	The model accurately uses calculations and reasoning to justify the identities of the unknown compounds.	The model correctly identifies the unknown compounds, and an attempt is made at the calculations and justification.	The model makes an attempt to identify the unknown compounds.
Relationships Score: ______	The model shows the relationship between molar mass, percent composition, and the identity of an unknown compound.	The model applies the concepts of molar mass and percent composition but without relating them to the elements in compounds.	The model presents molar mass and percent composition in a limited way, without relating them to compounds.
Accuracy of the Model Score: ______	The model presents accurate calculations and shows the steps involved. The pie graphs are accurate.	The model includes generally accurate calculations and makes an attempt to show the steps in obtaining them.	The model includes the results of the calculations without showing the steps involved and includes many inaccurate results or representations.
Usefulness of the Model Score: ______	The model and explanations make sense and can be applied to build understanding of percent composition of compounds.	The model is accurate and reasonable, but explanations are incomplete or omit useful details.	The model is unclear and would not be effectively applied to understand percent composition.

Peer Review Rubric Editable Worksheet

NAME ______ DATE ______ CLASS ______

ENGINEERING DESIGN CHALLENGE

An Empirical Formula Challenge

Your school district's resident electrician has misplaced a year's supply of copper wire. It just so happens that he was about to start work on a long-overdue rewiring project in one of the district's middle schools, where corrosion has led to the failure of several stoves in the cafeteria kitchen. Tomorrow is taco day at the school, and tacos are the students' favorite menu item! Fortunately, the electrician has discovered that the wires that conduct power to the stoves can be fixed by soldering copper at the points where the conducting wires are most corroded. The electrician estimates he will only need about 100 g of copper. The only source of copper in your school district that can be found right away is a 500 g bottle of a copper chloride hydrate compound whose formula has been obscured by water damage to the label. Hydrated compounds have water molecules embedded in their structures that can be removed by gentle heating. Based on the name, which is legible, you know the formula must be $Cu_xCl_y \cdot zH_2O$. The district superintendent has asked your chemistry class to determine whether there is enough copper in the 500-g bottle to provide the electrician with the 100 grams of copper requested. Your class will also have to efficiently remove this copper from the compound, given the information that when aluminum wire is placed in aqueous solutions of copper, the copper plates onto the aluminum wire. Your challenge is to save taco day!

Focus on Engineering Practices

SEP 1 Defining Problems
SEP 3 Planning and Carrying Out Investigations
SEP 6 Designing Solutions

Materials Per Group

- Aluminum wire, 12 cm
- $Cu_xCl_y \cdot zH_2O$, 2 g
- Faucet aspirator, optional
- Beaker, 250 mL

Engineering Design Challenge Interactive Worksheet

ELD SUPPORT

Reading Students work with a partner to analyze the introduction paragraph in the Engineering Design Challenge.

- **Emerging/Beginning** Ask student pairs to use simple words and phrases to summarize the introduction paragraph on the missing copper.
- **Developing/Expanding** Have student pairs write a few sentences outlining questions they have or confusing parts from the introduction paragraph.
- **Bridging** Have student pairs summarize the introduction paragraph in their own words and explain the importance of the problem outlined.

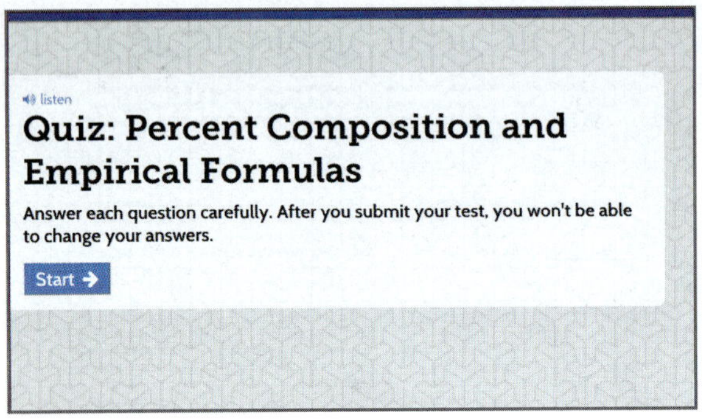

listen

Quiz: Percent Composition and Empirical Formulas

Answer each question carefully. After you submit your test, you won't be able to change your answers.

Start →

Interactive Online Quiz

Quiz Interactive Worksheet

EVALUATE

Percent Composition and Empirical Formulas

Quiz Assign the quiz in online technology-enhanced, auto-graded format or as an editable quiz worksheet. Use the scoring notes and remediation strategies found online to assess students' responses and to provide targeted feedback for each item to remediate well before assigning the summative 3-D Assessment.

REMEDIATION SUGGESTIONS

- **If** students have difficulty modeling percent composition, **then** direct them to revisit the Model Percent Composition worksheet and the corresponding Peer Review Rubric.
- **If** students have trouble calculating percent composition, **then** direct students to pages 192–196 of the Experience Notebook and help them to rework the problems.
- **If** students struggle with finding empirical formulas, **then** prompt them to review the Inquiry Lab and Analyzing Data activity. Students may also benefit from reviewing the problems in the section Empirical Formulas on page 198 of the Experience Notebook.
- **If** students struggle with finding molecular formulas, **then** direct them to study the images and captions and help them work through the problems on pages 200 and 201 of the Experience Notebook.

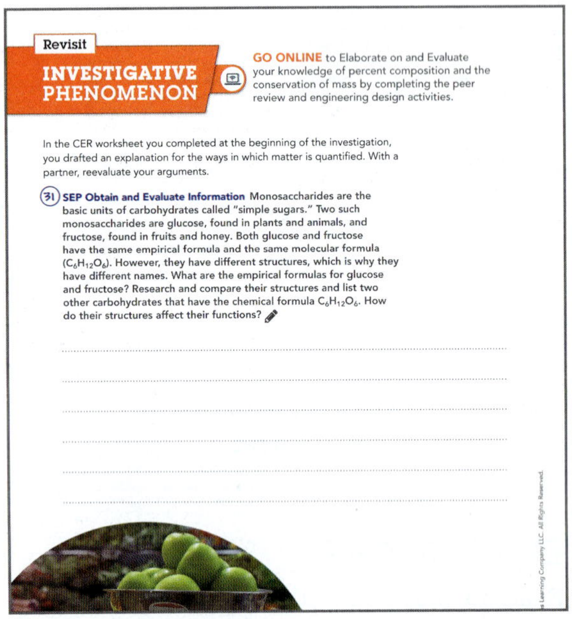

Revisit

INVESTIGATIVE PHENOMENON

GO ONLINE to Elaborate on and Evaluate your knowledge of percent composition and the conservation of mass by completing the peer review and engineering design activities.

In the CER worksheet you completed at the beginning of the investigation, you drafted an explanation for the ways in which matter is quantified. With a partner, reevaluate your arguments.

31 **SEP Obtain and Evaluate Information** Monosaccharides are the basic units of carbohydrates called "simple sugars." Two such monosaccharides are glucose, found in plants and animals, and fructose, found in fruits and honey. Both glucose and fructose have the same empirical formula and the same molecular formula ($C_6H_{12}O_6$). However, they have different structures, which is why they have different names. What are the empirical formulas for glucose and fructose? Research and compare their structures and list two other carbohydrates that have the chemical formula $C_6H_{12}O_6$. How do their structures affect their functions?

Experience Notebook, p. 202

eTEXT

Revisit

INVESTIGATIVE PHENOMENON

Support Reflection Students can complete the reflection prompt, where they will unpack and make sense of the Investigative Phenomenon, based on practices and understandings that have been reinforced over the course of the experience.

- Ask students to explain why empirical formulas are important for quantifying different types of matter.
- Remind students that to find the empirical formula, they must look for the least common multiple of the subscripts. Alternatively, if the numbers are all even, they can just keep dividing by 2. Yet another approach is to keep dividing each subscript by the smallest one.

Further Develop Your Model Have students add any evidence they have collected in this experience to their models. Allow time for them to make any additional changes based on information they have collected from the activities in this learning experience. Evidence may include the use of percentages to help quantify what is in matter. Percentages can be calculated by volume, by mass, or by count. The percent composition of compounds is usually by mass. The percent composition of a mixture of gases, like the atmosphere, however, is by number of molecules.

EXPERIENCE 4

Concentrations of Solutions

Teacher Background

Experience 4 introduces the concept of solution concentration. Since so many chemical reactions take place in a solution, understanding how concentration is determined is of vital importance. The concepts previously introduced in this investigation will form the foundation of this experience, beginning with molarity. Students investigate how to dilute a solution and how to determine solution concentration by measuring the percentage of solute within a specified volume of solvent.

Objectives

- **Find the molarity of a solution.**
- **Investigate how the ratio of solute to solvent affects the concentration of a solution.**
- **Devise a method to make a solution of a specific concentration.**
- **Calculate the percentage of a solution by mass and by volume.**

ENGAGE

EVERYDAY PHENOMENON

How can the concentration of a solution be changed?

Use this teacher demo to prompt discussion about the concentration of solutions.

Drink Mix Concentration

Engage students with this demonstration of an everyday phenomenon to introduce the concept of concentration.

Materials powdered flavored drink mix with sugar, 4 pitchers, measuring spoons, water, stirring spoon, disposable cups

1. Ask students to come up with two methods to make the drink mix that will be twice as concentrated as the regular beverage.
2. After soliciting student input, add twice as much powder to the recommended amount of water in one pitcher. To another pitcher, add the recommended amount of powder to half the amount of water normally used. Allow students or volunteers to sample the flavored drink mix from each pitcher. Both samples should taste the same.
3. Ask students for two methods to make the flavored drink mix that is half as concentrated as the regular beverage.
4. After soliciting student input, add half as much powder to the recommended amount of water in one pitcher. To another pitcher, add the recommended amount of powder to twice as much water as normally used. Allow students or volunteers to sample the flavored drink mix from each pitcher. Both samples should taste the same.
5. After reading the label of the flavored drink mix, ask students to calculate the molarity of each sample, based on the amount of sugar ($C_{12}H_{22}O_{11}$) used in each. Use this lab to further discuss the importance of molarity when quantifying different types of matter.

RELATED PHENOMENA

In addition to the Drink Mix Concentration teacher demo, consider using other phenomena to launch this experience.

- **Compare Dish Detergents** Provide samples of regular and concentrated dish detergent. Demonstrate the amount of suds created by using one drop of each. The concentrated dish detergent should produce more suds than the same amount of regular detergent. Discuss with students what they think causes the difference.
- **Food Color and Water** Ask students to predict how much water 1 drop of food coloring could color. Then add 1 drop of food coloring to a beaker of water. Continue adding water until the food coloring is no longer visible. This demonstration will show how the addition of more solvent will make a solution more dilute.

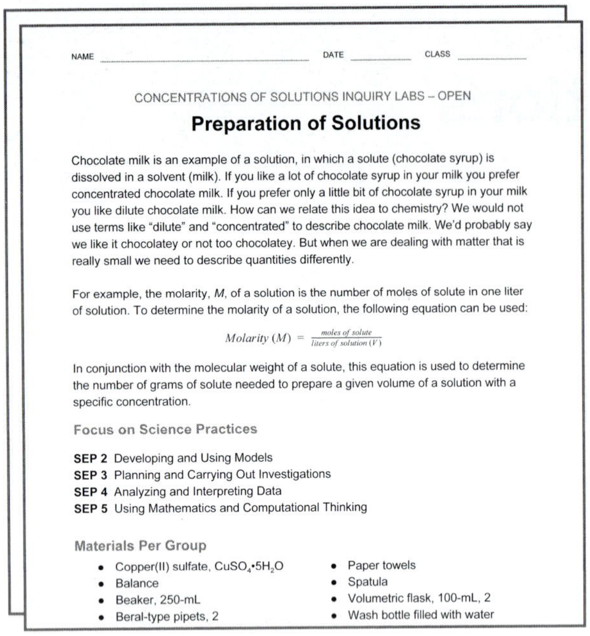
NAME ______________________ DATE ________ CLASS ________

CONCENTRATIONS OF SOLUTIONS INQUIRY LABS – OPEN

Preparation of Solutions

Chocolate milk is an example of a solution, in which a solute (chocolate syrup) is dissolved in a solvent (milk). If you like a lot of chocolate syrup in your milk you prefer concentrated chocolate milk. If you prefer only a little bit of chocolate syrup in your milk you like dilute chocolate milk. How can we relate this idea to chemistry? We would not use terms like "dilute" and "concentrated" to describe chocolate milk. We'd probably say we like it chocolatey or not too chocolatey. But when we are dealing with matter that is really small we need to describe quantities differently.

For example, the molarity, *M*, of a solution is the number of moles of solute in one liter of solution. To determine the molarity of a solution, the following equation can be used:

$$Molarity\ (M) = \frac{moles\ of\ solute}{liters\ of\ solution\ (V)}$$

In conjunction with the molecular weight of a solute, this equation is used to determine the number of grams of solute needed to prepare a given volume of a solution with a specific concentration.

Focus on Science Practices

SEP 2 Developing and Using Models
SEP 3 Planning and Carrying Out Investigations
SEP 4 Analyzing and Interpreting Data
SEP 5 Using Mathematics and Computational Thinking

Materials Per Group

- Copper(II) sulfate, $CuSO_4 \cdot 5H_2O$
- Balance
- Beaker, 250-mL
- Beral-type pipets, 2
- Paper towels
- Spatula
- Volumetric flask, 100-mL, 2
- Wash bottle filled with water

O/G/S/A Lab Interactive Worksheets

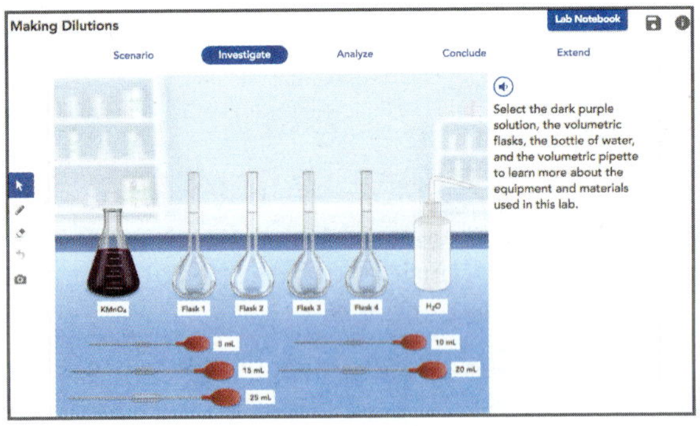

Virtual Lab: Making Dilutions

INTEGRATE THE THREE DIMENSIONS

In the Virtual Lab, students practice making solutions and analyzing chemical reactions [PS1.B] to investigate how concentration affects [CCC-2] the color of a purple potassium permanganate solution. Students use their calculations [SEP-5] to describe their observations throughout the lab. Students explain how dilution is related to atoms being conserved [CCC-5] during chemical reactions.

Virtual Nerd Video: How Do You Use Dimensional Analysis to Convert Units on One Part of a Rate?

EXPLORE

Preparation of Solutions

Inquiry Lab Students prepare a series of solutions of prescribed concentrations in order to learn about the relationship between qualitative descriptions such as "concentrated" and "dilute," and empirical descriptions of solution concentrations based on molarity.

Lab Demo Video Watch the Lab Demo Video for advice on materials and preparation.

Choose Your Version Open-ended (O), Guided (G), Shortened (S), Advanced (A)

Materials 250-mL beaker, copper(II) sulfate, balance, 2 Beral-type pipets, funnel, waterproof marker, paper towels, spatula, 2 100-mL volumetric flasks, wash bottle filled with water, wax pencil or labeling tape, weighing dish

Safety Prompt students to wear chemical splash goggles, chemical-resistant gloves, and a chemical-resistant apron. Copper (II) sulfate is moderately toxic by ingestion and inhalation and is a skin and respiratory irritant.

Expected Outcome Students learn that concentrated solutions have high molarity values and that dilute solutions have (relatively) low molarity values. Moreover, students come to understand that a solution's molarity relates to the molar mass of the solute and that different solutions require different amounts of solids to achieve the same molarity.

Lab Summary Video Watch the Lab Summary Video for support on connecting the lab Investigation to the Investigative Phenomenon.

Making Dilutions

Virtual Lab In this Virtual Lab, students investigate the role of concentration in testing new medicines in the body. They work with solutions of potassium permanganate and observe the effect of heating on solute concentration. Students calculate [SEP-5] the molarity of the solution. After the solution is chilled, crystals form.

- This simulation provides a good example of how the change in solvent concentration affects the concentration of the solution. The concentration of the solution is inversely proportional to the amount of solvent, and directly proportional to the amount of solute.
- Remind students that as solutions are heated, the amount of solute that can be dissolved will generally (but not always) increase. Ask students to devise a model to explain this phenomenon.

How Do You Use Dimensional Analysis to Convert Units on One Part of a Rate?

Virtual Nerd Video Use this video tutorial to reinforce how to use a conversion factor in a rate.

ASSESS ON THE SPOT

As students are working through the Virtual Lab, ask them if they can determine the concentration of 10 g of $KMnO_4$ in 100 mL of water. (0.1*M*) Then ask what the concentration would be if the same amount of solute were dissolved in half as much water. (0.2*M*)

EXPLAIN

Model Measures of Concentration

Modeling Use this activity after students have had the opportunity to observe and explore solution concentration. Ideally, this would be after students perform the Inquiry Lab. In this activity, students use mathematical representations [SEP-5] to model measures of concentration. They evaluate a claim [SEP-8] about concentrations. They use molarity and mass percent to compare and contrast the concentrations of two solutions.

Choose from these suggested strategies to guide students in deepening their understanding of molarity and concentrations:

- Emphasize to students that the two solutes and solutions have the same mass, but the number of moles in the two and their molarities are different due to their molar masses. Make sure students do not get confused between mass and molar mass.
- Encourage students to write their calculations for acetone and sodium chloride in different colors, so they do not get confused between the two.

PROFESSIONAL DEVELOPMENT

Background Notes Inspire your students to think of concentrations of solutions beyond chemistry. One version of brine pickling involves soaking meats, such as beef brisket, in salt water. During this process, salts move into the cells of the meat to equalize sodium chloride concentrations. The cells then absorb water to keep the overall solution concentrations the same. Draw a diagram on the board of a cell and the surrounding solution. Show students how salt and water migrate through the cell wall. Have students research how to brine pickle a meat or vegetable of their choosing. Ask them to write a description of how the food would differ depending on the concentration of the solution it is in. They should also describe how the concentration of the solution would be measured.

INTEGRATE MATH

When working with molarity and concentration, it is often necessary to convert grams to moles, and milliliters to liters. The problems in this experience give students practice in performing these types of conversions. Remind students that if the given mass in a problem is less than the molar mass, there will be less than 1 mole. If the given volume is less than 1000 mL, there will be less than 1 L.

NAME ______________ DATE ________ CLASS ________

MODELING

Model Measures of Concentration

Suppose you are told that 100 grams of sodium chloride (NaCl) are dissolved in 1 liter of water. Do you have enough information to calculate the concentration? The answer depends on how you want the concentration to be measured and how the measurement is to be used.

One way to measure concentration is the mass of solute divided by the volume of solution. A slightly different measure is called percent by mass, which is the mass of solute divided by the mass of solution. Many chemical properties of a solution depend on the distribution of atoms, molecules, or other particles, which are measured in moles. For this reason, chemists often measure concentration in units of molarity (abbreviated M), which is the moles of solute per volume of solution.

Use A Model

1. **SEP Using Mathematics and Computational Thinking** Follow the steps and show your calculations for these two solutions:
   - 100 grams sodium chloride (NaCl) in 1 liter of water
   - 100 grams acetone (C_2H_6O) in 1 liter of water

   Then enter the results in the table.

Concentration	Sodium chloride (NaCl) in water	Acetone (C_2H_6O) in water
Mass per volume		
Percent by mass		
Molarity of solution		

Modeling Interactive Worksheet

ELD SUPPORT

Speaking/Writing After the Modeling activity, have students work in pairs and summarize how they calculated the molarity and mass percent of example solutions and determine through questioning if they have included all relevant steps.

- **Emerging/Beginning** Have students orally describe in their own words how they completed their calculations.
- **Developing/Expanding** Have students write a summary about how they completed their calculations, and then work with their partners to compare their summaries and edit them to reflect their discussion.
- **Bridging** Have students work together to write a summary about how they completed their calculations, based on the data provided. They can then present their summaries to another pair, who should provide feedback and/or missing steps. Pairs should then discuss and incorporate this feedback and information into their summaries.

CONNECT TO CAREERS

Physician Have students conduct research about the career of physician. Point out that physicians must develop knowledge about the concentrations of solutions as they must apply these concepts to develop different types of medicines. With a partner, students should research the career and education requirements to become a physician, as well as identify three facts they find interesting about the career. Students should share their findings in a brief presentation with the class.

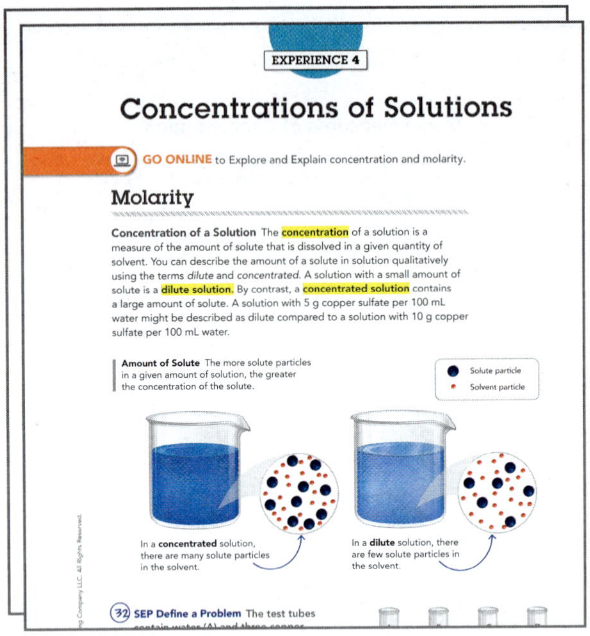

EXPERIENCE 4

Concentrations of Solutions

GO ONLINE to Explore and Explain concentration and molarity.

Molarity

Concentration of a Solution The **concentration** of a solution is a measure of the amount of solute that is dissolved in a given quantity of solvent. You can describe the amount of a solute in solution qualitatively using the terms *dilute* and *concentrated*. A solution with a small amount of solute is a **dilute solution.** By contrast, a **concentrated solution** contains a large amount of solute. A solution with 5 g copper sulfate per 100 mL water might be described as dilute compared to a solution with 10 g copper sulfate per 100 mL water.

Amount of Solute The more solute particles in a given amount of solution, the greater the concentration of the solute.

32 **SEP Define a Problem** The test tubes

Experience Notebook, pp. 203–211

eTEXT

SAMPLE PROBLEM SUPPORT

When solving molarity problems, students can easily make errors, either due to converting units improperly, using grams instead of moles, or not performing the correct mathematical operation. A simple check can ensure that an answer is correct. Instruct students that when finished with a molarity problem, they should always divide the number of moles by the liters of solution. If they get the indicated molarity, they will have solved the problem correctly.

ADDRESS PRECONCEPTIONS

Pure water does not conduct electricity, which can be demonstrated with a conductivity tester. It is the presence of dissolved ions in water that actually makes water conductive. If testing distilled water with a conductivity tester, nothing will happen, but if salt is poured into the water, the bulb will light up. Tap water, which contains dissolved minerals, will normally be conductive as well. These dissolved minerals are typically not harmful, however, because their concentrations are very low.

PhET Simulation: Concentration

PhET Simulation: Molarity

Concentrations of Solutions (20)

Experience Notebook Ideally, assign the Experience Notebook or Realize Reader for this experience the day before, and then follow up with any of the following suggested instructional strategies to fill knowledge gaps and deepen understanding. Alternatively, assign it alongside the Model Measures of Concentration activity as support for the activity. Use these strategies to help students make sense of the images and text on the indicated pages, as well as to engage science skills.

- **Molarity** (pp. 203–205) Organize students into groups of four, and allow 3 minutes for them to provide as many examples as they can of household solutions. (Possible answers include bleach, vinegar, 3% hydrogen peroxide, contact-lens cleaning solution, 70% isopropyl alcohol, and household ammonia.) Ask why none of these solutions are measured using molarity. Share with students that molarity is just one way of expressing the concentration of a solution.
- Remind students that molarity is calculated by dividing moles of solute by liters of solution. A common error is to divide the number of moles by the liters of solvent added, instead of the volume of the final solution. Depending on components, the final volume of the solution may be greater than or less than the volume of solvent added. Flasks designed for preparing solutions have a mark calibrated to the actual solution volume.
- **Sample Problem** (p. 206) Reinforce content by providing these sample problems for students to resolve.
  - a. How many moles of H_2SO_4 are in 50 mL of 0.25*M* H_2SO_4? (0.0125 mol)
  - b. How many grams of NaCl are needed to make 1 L of a 0.75*M* solution? (43.9 g)
- **Dilutions** (pp. 207–209) Ask students how the molarity of a solution changes when it becomes more dilute. Share with students that as solutions become more dilute, their molarity decreases. For an extension, ask students how the pH of a solution is affected by concentration. Add increasing amounts of water to a small amount of acid, measuring the pH as you go. Students may be surprised to learn that the pH decreases as the solution becomes more dilute.
- **Percent Solution** (pp. 210–211) You can dramatically demonstrate the effect of solution concentration by comparing 3% H_2O_2 to 30% H_2O_2. (Note: 30% H_2O_2 will cause severe burns if it comes in contact with skin. Wear gloves and safety goggles, and make sure students wear goggles as well when you are performing this demonstration. Never let students use 30% H_2O_2.) Pour 10 mL of 3% H_2O_2 into a 250-mL Erlenmeyer flask and 10 mL of 30% H_2O_2 into a separate flask. To each flask, add a small amount (about 2–3 g) of KI. You will witness a dramatic reaction with the 30% solution as the H_2O_2 decomposes into water and oxygen, but very little will happen with the 3% solution.

ASSESS ON THE SPOT

The concentration of salt in the oceans is approximately 3.5% by mass. Ask students how much salt is in a kilogram of seawater. (35 g)

Concentration

PhET Simulation Use this simulation to reinforce concepts of molarity and concentration.

Molarity

PhET Simulation Use this simulation to reinforce the relationships between moles, liters, and molarity.

ELABORATE

Discuss Molarity and Other Measures of Concentration

Discussion Rubric Students use the rubric as a scoring guide to evaluate [SEP-8] the calculations [SEP-5] and analyses their peers developed in the Modeling activity, Model Measures of Concentration.

- Organize students in groups of four and have each student evaluate the calculations and analyses of three other group members, using a separate rubric for each evaluation.
- Remind students that student worksheets should show their calculations. If an evaluator finds an incorrect answer on a student's worksheet, the evaluator can check the calculations to point out where the error occurred.
- Tell students to check that any conclusions are based on evidence [SEP-8].

Solubility and Percent by Mass

Analyzing Data In this activity, students investigate how solubility varies with temperature. They examine a graph containing the solubility curves of several different substances and interpret the data [SEP-4] to explain what these curves represent.

- This activity will challenge student thinking in that it is easy to assume that solubility always increases with temperature. Challenge students to construct an explanation [SEP-6] as to why some substances become less soluble as temperature increases.
- Ask students to examine the slope of each line. Challenge them to construct an explanation as to why most of the lines are not straight.
- Ask students to explain at which temperature change did solubility and percent by mass change the most and least for potassium bromide and sodium nitrate.

DIFFERENTIATED INSTRUCTION

- **Support Struggling Students** Ask students to point out a substance on the Analyzing Data solubility curve that is more soluble at higher temperatures and then one that is more soluble at lower temperatures. Ask students what being more or less soluble means.
- **Support Less Proficient Readers** You may need to read aloud the instructions for the Analyzing Data activity. Help students identify and underline the most important words and phrases, such as *solubility*, *percent by mass*, *solute*, and *solution*.
- **Support Special Needs Students** Point out that if the slope of the graph is positive, then more of that substance can be dissolved in hot water than in cold water. Explain that if the slope is negative, the opposite will be true.
- **Support Advanced Students** Show students a picture of mineral buildup in a hot water tank or on a hot water faucet. Challenge them to devise an explanation about why the buildup is greater when hot water is used than when cold water is used.

ASSESS ON THE SPOT

Give each student a notecard. Ask students to write something they found interesting about the Analyzing Data activity and something they still do not clearly understand. Collect the notecards and use the information to help guide a class review before the experience assessment.

NAME ________ DATE ________ CLASS ________

DISCUSSION RUBRIC

Discuss Molarity and Other Measures of Concentr

Use this rubric to help you assess your peers' calculations and analy

	EXEMPLARY Score the work 3 if:	ACCOMPLISHED Score the work 2 if:
Evaluation and Critique Student Score: ____ Teacher Score: ____	Mass per volume, percent per volume, and molarity are accurately calculated. The steps of each calculation are shown, and units are identified.	The measurements of concentration are calculated and recorded with reasonable accuracy, but there are some mistakes due to carelessness or a misapplied formula. Units are generally included.
Reasoning and Synthesis Student Score: ____ Teacher Score: ____	Reasonable and accurate conclusions are drawn about the similarities, differences, and usefulness of the various measures of concentration. The method of calculating concentration is recognized as being essential for evaluating its meaning.	At least one reasonable and accurate conclusion is drawn about the various measures of concentration but without stating that different solutions could have the same concentration measurement.

Discussion Rubric Interactive Worksheet

NAME ________ DATE ________ CLASS ________

ANALYZING DATA

Solubility and Percent by Mass

Solubility is the mass of a solute, such as sodium chloride or glucose, that dissolves in a given mass of a solvent, such as water. Temperature must also be specified for solubility measurements, because solubility varies with temperature for most substances. The graph plots solubility versus temperature for several compounds in 100 g of water.

Percent by mass is another way to quantify the components of a solution. Percent by mass of a solution is the ratio of the masses of the solute and solution.

$$\text{Percent by mass} = \frac{\textit{mass of solute}}{\textit{mass of solution}} \times 100\%$$

Solubility Varies with Temperature

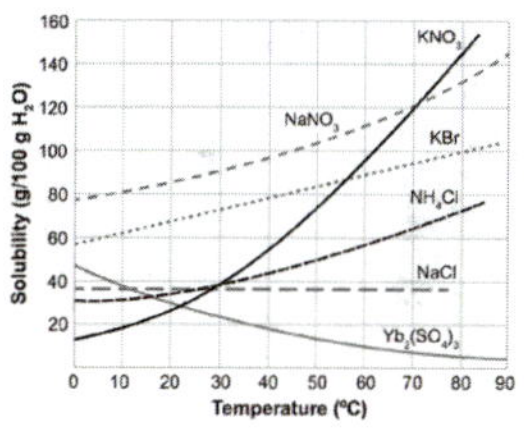

1. **SEP Analyze Data** Use the data in the graph to determine the solubility of

Analyzing Data Interactive Worksheet

CLASSROOM MODIFICATIONS

Based on your students' abilities and your schedule, you can modify the Solubility and Percent by Mass activity to be more open ended or more guided.

- **More Open Ended** Have students test the solubility at different temperatures of one or more of the substances. Instruct students to design their own investigation and carry it out. After performing their experiments, students can then graph their experimental results and compare it to the data on the worksheet graph.
- **More Guided** Walk through the graph with students. Discuss the solutes shown on the graph, and identify which has a solubility that varies the most and least with temperature.

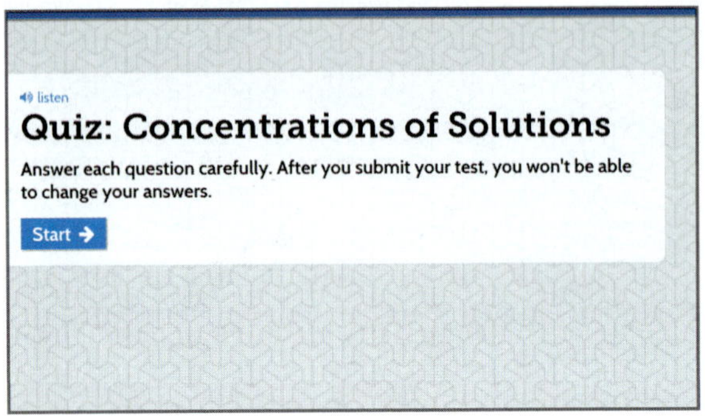

Interactive Online Quiz

Quiz Editable Worksheet

EVALUATE

Concentrations of Solutions

Quiz Assign the quiz in online technology-enhanced, auto-graded format or as an editable quiz worksheet. Use the scoring notes and remediation strategies found online to assess students' responses and to provide targeted feedback for each item to remediate well before assigning the summative 3-D Assessment.

REMEDIATION SUGGESTIONS

- **If** students have difficulty interpreting solubility curves, **then** direct them to revisit the Analyzing Data worksheet, Solubility and Percent by Mass.
- **If** students are struggling to understand how dilutions are used, **then** have them review the Virtual Lab.
- **If** students have trouble finding molarity, **then** instruct them to examine the images and captions on pages 201 and 202 of the Experience Notebook, and help them rework the Sample Problems on pages 203 and 204.
- **If** students struggle with dilutions, **then** direct them to reread the text and, with a partner, rework the problems in the section Dilutions on pages 205–207 of the Experience Notebook.
- **If** students struggle with how to calculate the percentage of a solution, either by mass or volume, **then** direct them to study the images and captions and revisit the problems on pages 208 and 209 of the Experience Notebook.

Revisit INVESTIGATIVE PHENOMENON

Support Reflection Students can complete the reflection prompt, where they will unpack and make sense of the Investigative Phenomenon, based on practices and understandings that have been reinforced over the course of the experience.

- Call on students to describe how diluting a solution changes the molarity of a solution. Ask students to explain how they can apply this concept to adjusting the recipe for lemonade.
- Ask students to explain how to make a dilution of a solution with a known molarity. Ask students how they can quantify different types of matter in solutions and why the process may differ depending on the properties of the matter.

Evaluate and Revise Your Model Have students answer Questions 3, 4, and 5 in the Modeling activity and reevaluate their model based on peer feedback. Students should add any additional evidence they have collected in this investigation. Evidence may include that when finding the concentration of solutions, both mass and volume must be considered. They may also consider other ways of expressing concentration that involve counting, such as parts per million (ppm).

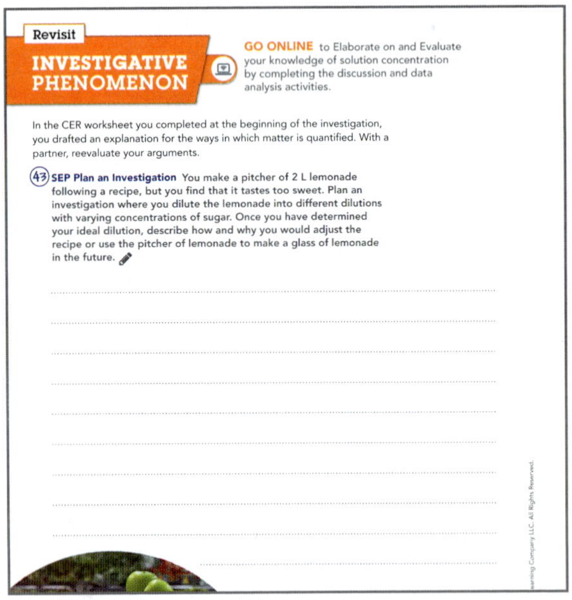
Revisit
INVESTIGATIVE PHENOMENON

GO ONLINE to Elaborate on and Evaluate your knowledge of solution concentration by completing the discussion and data analysis activities.

In the CER worksheet you completed at the beginning of the investigation, you drafted an explanation for the ways in which matter is quantified. With a partner, reevaluate your arguments.

43 **SEP Plan an Investigation** You make a pitcher of 2 L lemonade following a recipe, but you find that it tastes too sweet. Plan an investigation where you dilute the lemonade into different dilutions with varying concentrations of sugar. Once you have determined your ideal dilution, describe how and why you would adjust the recipe or use the pitcher of lemonade to make a glass of lemonade in the future.

Experience Notebook, p. 212

eTEXT

EVALUATE

Chemical Quantities (30)

3-D Assessment For a summative assessment of Investigation 5, assign the 3-D Assessment, which is available online, as an ExamView bank, or as an editable worksheet.

Analysis of Basic Copper Carbonate (40)

Performance-Based Assessment Use this Performance-Based Assessment to assess students' mastery of the standards. In this activity, students carry out an investigation [SEP-3] and determine the empirical formula of an unknown copper carbonate. Students must use a mass-loss approach to determine the percent by mass of CO_2 and a colorimetric approach to determine the mass percent of Cu. In order to complete this investigation, students must be proficient with topics such as the mole, molar mass, molarity, percent composition, and empirical formulas. Students construct an explanation [SEP-6] about whether the chemical reaction [PS1.B] performed in the lab abides by the law of conservation of mass.

Safety Chemicals used in this investigation are toxic and corrosive to eyes and skin tissue and by ingestion and inhalation. Students should wear chemical splash goggles, chemical-resistant gloves, and chemical-resistant aprons. Prompt students to wash their hands with soap and warm water before leaving the laboratory.

Expected Outcome Students determine the experimental mass percents of CO_2 and Cu in a sample of copper carbonate of unknown composition. Students compare their experimentally determined mass percents to the theoretical mass percents, calculated from two potential empirical formulas, to determine the true formula of the sample under investigation.

Experience Notebook (p. 213) After students complete the Performance-Based Assessment, have them complete the reflection prompt in the Experience Notebook.

DIFFERENTIATED INSTRUCTION

- **Support Special Needs Students** Students with attention difficulty may have trouble staying on track for both parts of the Performance-Based Assessment. Have advanced students assist these students on one of the parts and specifically on collecting data.
- **Support Less Proficient Readers** Read the instructions with students who struggle with reading. Review the law of conservation of mass with them and define any other words or phrases that students have difficulty with.

How can we produce better foods? (5)

Revisit Anchoring Phenomenon At the end of Investigation 5, have students revisit the Anchoring Phenomenon question about how we produce better foods. Lead a class discussion and call on students to explain how they can use chemical quantities to improve different foods.

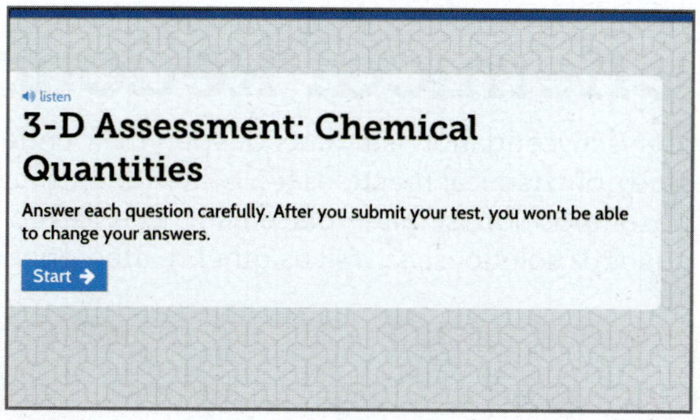
listen
3-D Assessment: Chemical Quantities
Answer each question carefully. After you submit your test, you won't be able to change your answers.
Start

Interactive Online 3-D Assessment

Interactive ExamView 3-D Assessment

3-D Assessment Interactive Worksheet

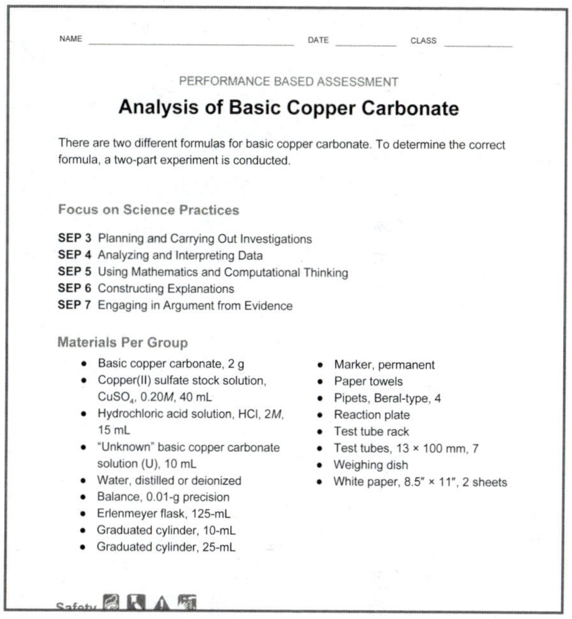
NAME ____ DATE ____ CLASS ____

PERFORMANCE BASED ASSESSMENT

Analysis of Basic Copper Carbonate

There are two different formulas for basic copper carbonate. To determine the correct formula, a two-part experiment is conducted.

Focus on Science Practices

SEP 3 Planning and Carrying Out Investigations
SEP 4 Analyzing and Interpreting Data
SEP 5 Using Mathematics and Computational Thinking
SEP 6 Constructing Explanations
SEP 7 Engaging in Argument from Evidence

Materials Per Group

- Basic copper carbonate, 2 g
- Copper(II) sulfate stock solution, $CuSO_4$, 0.20*M*, 40 mL
- Hydrochloric acid solution, HCl, 2*M*, 15 mL
- "Unknown" basic copper carbonate solution (U), 10 mL
- Water, distilled or deionized
- Balance, 0.01-g precision
- Erlenmeyer flask, 125-mL
- Graduated cylinder, 10-mL
- Graduated cylinder, 25-mL
- Marker, permanent
- Paper towels
- Pipets, Beral-type, 4
- Reaction plate
- Test tube rack
- Test tubes, 13 × 100 mm, 7
- Weighing dish
- White paper, 8.5" × 11", 2 sheets

Safety

Performance-Based Assessment Interactive Worksheet

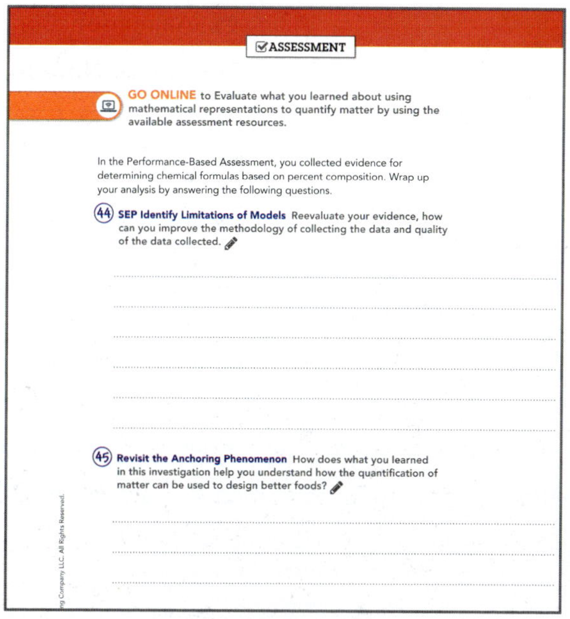
ASSESSMENT

GO ONLINE to Evaluate what you learned about using mathematical representations to quantify matter by using the available assessment resources.

In the Performance-Based Assessment, you collected evidence for determining chemical formulas based on percent composition. Wrap up your analysis by answering the following questions.

44 SEP Identify Limitations of Models Reevaluate your evidence, how can you improve the methodology of collecting the data and quality of the data collected.

45 Revisit the Anchoring Phenomenon How does what you learned in this investigation help you understand how the quantification of matter can be used to design better foods?

Experience Notebook, p. 213

eTEXT

Chemical Reactions

In this investigation, students deepen their understanding of energy and matter [CCC-5] through a study of chemical reactions [PS1.B]. Students investigate and write reaction equations of combination, decomposition, single-replacement, double-replacement, and combustion reactions and reactions in aqueous solutions, as well as other related phenomena.

INVESTIGATIVE PHENOMENON

How is energy obtained from chemical reactions?

Explaining Phenomena In order to fully understand the phenomenon of how energy is obtained from chemical reactions, students must explore how to balance different types of chemical reactions. As students develop the ability to develop models of reactions, analyze and interpret data on what causes reactions, and predict products of reactions, they identify patterns in the reactions.

	EXPERIENCE 1	EXPERIENCE 2
	Modeling Chemical Reactions 2 days Students balance word and chemical equations. They investigate the law of conservation of energy. Students analyze data on what causes reactions.	**Predicting Outcomes of Chemical Reactions** 2 days Students interpret data on different types of reactions. They develop models of the different reactions. They use models to predict the products of reactions.
CONNECTION TO THE INVESTIGATIVE PHENOMENON	Students develop a model for the generation of energy from the reaction of hydrogen and oxygen and relate that to the phenomenon of how energy is obtained from chemical reactions.	Students construct an explanation for the outcome of a potassium hydroxide and carbon dioxide reaction and relate that to the phenomenon of how energy is obtained from chemical reactions.
ENGAGE	**Teacher's Guide** **Everyday Phenomenon** Model a Chemical Reaction, p. 186	**Teacher's Guide** **Everyday Phenomenon** Elephant Toothpaste, p. 192
EXPLORE	**Inquiry Lab** Evaluate Chemical Reactions **Analyzing Data** Analyzing Chemical Reactions +	**Inquiry Lab** Types of Chemical Reactions **Virtual Lab** Reactivity of Metals +
EXPLAIN	**Modeling** Modeling Chemical Reactions **Animation** Bonds Breaking and Forming + **Experience Notebook,** pp. 216–225	**Claim-Evidence-Reasoning** Reaction Reasoning **Experience Notebook,** pp. 227–239
ELABORATE	**Peer Review Rubric** Evaluate Models of Chemical Reactions **Analyzing Data** Balance Combustion Equations	**Discussion Rubric** Classify Reactions and Predict Their Products **Writing About Science** Track the Mass of Reactants and Products +
EVALUATE	**Quiz** Modeling Chemical Reactions **Experience Notebook** **Revisit Investigative Phenomenon,** p. 226	**Quiz** Predicting Outcomes of Chemical Reactions **Experience Notebook** **Revisit Investigative Phenomenon,** p. 240

*Pacing for Encounter Investigative Phenomenon core instruction is a half-day.

†Pacing for core Investigation Assessment is approximately 1 day.

GOT MORE TIME? Personalize and enhance your instructional plan by assigning the activities with the got-more-time icon, as time allows.

Investigative Phenomenon Video Rocket Reaction*

Modeling Model the Investigative Phenomenon*

Authentic Reading Antarctica's Blood Red Waterfall

Virtual Reality Experience

Experience Notebook, p. 214*

EXPERIENCE 3

Reactions in Aqueous Solution

2 days

Students balance net ionic equations. They construct an explanation on solubility and intermolecular forces of a solution. They predict the formation of a precipitate.

Students define a problem on a malfunction of fuel cells and use this to refine explanations of how energy is obtained from chemical reactions.

Teacher's Guide Everyday Phenomenon Clearly a Solid Solution, p. 199

Inquiry Lab Predict Chemical Reactions

Interactivity Cation Meets Anion

Claim-Evidence-Reasoning Predict Whether a Precipitate Will Form

Animation Attractions in Solutions

Experience Notebook, pp. 241–247

Discussion Rubric Discuss Precipitation Predictions

Engineering Design Challenge Water Purification

Quiz Reactions in Aqueous Solution

Experience Notebook Revisit Investigative Phenomenon, p. 248

INVESTIGATION ASSESSMENT

Performance-Based Assessment Identify Evidence of Chemical Reactions†

3-D Assessment Chemical Reactions†

Experience Notebook Performance-Based Assessment, p. 249; Revisit Anchoring Phenomenon, p. 249†; **Appendix C** Problem Bank, pp. R15–R16

Notes:

Chemical Reactions

RELATED PHENOMENA

In addition to energy obtained from chemical reactions, consider using other phenomena to launch this investigation.

- **Acid Rain** Acid rain transformed nearly half of the Black Forest in Germany to blackened skeletal trees by 1984. **Ask** If we wanted to know what chemical reaction caused the acid rain, what are some factors we should consider? Use prompts such as: Why is the rain acidic? What caused the pH to decrease? Is this problem caused by humans or by natural causes? Are there any sources of pollution in the area? Any factories? Explain to students that large areas of the Black Forest were downwind from power plants and factories that burned high-sulfur coal without controlling the emissions. When coal burns, the sulfur in the coal reacts with oxygen in the air. Show students the reactants in equation form: $S + O_2 \rightarrow$? Ask students to predict what product is created. (SO_2 is created as a gas and travels into the atmosphere where it easily combines with water in the clouds.) Show students the reactants in equation form: $SO_2 + H_2O \rightarrow$? Predict what product is created. (H_2SO_3; sulfurous acid)
- **Exploding Gummy Bears** Have students observe a demonstration of exploding gummy bears. Place a gummy bear in a test tube of melted potassium chlorate and observe how the gummy bursts into flames. Provide some background knowledge for students. When the $KClO_3$ is heated, it breaks down into two products, KCl and O_2. When the gummy bear is added, a chemical reaction occurs with the O_2. **Ask** What is the major ingredient in a gummy bear? (sugar or sucrose) The heat causes the sucrose to react with the O_2. Ask students to predict the type of chemical reaction taking place. Can you predict the products of this reaction?

TAKE IT LOCAL

Ask students to brainstorm and list businesses in their community that require chemical reactions to complete certain tasks. Examples may include a bakery, welding company, or hospital. Consider allowing a bit of time for Internet research.

Teacher Background

Introduce this investigation with a discussion about the differences between molecular compounds and ionic compounds and how chemical compounds are represented. Stress that molecular compounds are composed of nonmetallic elements and ionic compounds are composed of a metal cation and an anion. Chemical compounds are represented by chemical formulas that show the kinds and numbers of atoms in each molecule or formula unit. In this investigation, students balance many chemical equations and analyze a variety of data. Some students may benefit from additional support with interpreting and processing the data tables.

While students investigate the various types of chemical reactions, encourage them to analyze how energy is obtained in all these chemical reactions. As you teach Investigation 6, make sure students understand that the coefficients on both sides of the equation do not have to be the same in order for the number of atoms of each type to balance. Convey that if the sums of the coefficients on both sides of a balanced chemical equation are the same number, it is coincidental.

Learning Progression

Throughout this investigation students challenge themselves with building upon their knowledge of chemical reactions [PS1.B]. Students sketch a molecular model [SEP-2] of reactants and products in a skeleton equation. They gain understanding of equations by comparing balanced equations to a sandwich. Students interpret data [SEP-4] on combination and decomposition reactions and identify patterns [CCC-1] concerning the energy for those reactions. They develop balanced-equation models on single-replacement and double-replacement reactions. They engage in arguments from evidence [SEP-7] about ions in aqueous solutions and construct explanations [SEP-6] for why a precipitate forms.

ENCOUNTER

INVESTIGATIVE PHENOMENON

How is energy obtained from chemical reactions?

Introduce this investigation by asking students what the photo shows. Discuss what they know about simple chemical reactions. Then discuss what students know about chemical reactions in everyday forms of transportation, such as cars, and relate that to the chemical reactions of a spacecraft being launched. Students begin this topic by investigating what causes reactions (Experience 1). They further their learning by writing chemical equations for different types of reactions (Experience 2). Finally, they evaluate the formation of a precipitate (Experience 3).

Rocket Reaction

Investigative Phenomenon Video Have students watch the video and discuss what observations they can make about the chemical reactions required to launch a rocket. As students make observations, write them on the board. Call on students to describe how they know that chemical reactions are occurring based on their observations. Then ask students to describe other chemical reactions they think could be used to launch a projectile.

Antarctica's Blood Red Waterfall

Investigative Phenomenon Authentic Reading This reading takes students through the conditions that have combined to cause Antarctica's Blood Falls to pour bright-red water. It allows students to visualize the reaction of how the falls has formed with excess salt, no oxygen, and excess iron. Lead a class discussion about how students think the chemical reactions of the Blood Falls relates to the Investigative Phenomenon on how energy is obtained from chemical reactions. If time allows, assign the worksheet as an in-class assignment or homework.

- For struggling students and less proficient readers, read the article aloud as they follow along. Pause after each paragraph and call on students to briefly summarize the key ideas and details. Have students use a graphic organizer to record their summaries.

Model the Phenomenon

Modeling Have students review the video and Authentic Reading activity to develop a model of the phenomenon they observed. Remind students that a model does not have to look like the object or process it represents, but students should be able to use it to explain and/or predict a phenomenon. Have students complete Question 1 of the Modeling worksheet.

Remind students that their understanding of the phenomenon will be incomplete at this stage, but that they will revisit this activity as they learn more. Make sure to provide students with an opportunity to revisit their models throughout the investigation as well as at the end of the investigation for further revision and peer review.

Reflect on the Phenomenon

Experience Notebook Transition to the opener pages for Investigation 6 in the Experience Notebook. Guide students through a discussion of the questions. Remind them that they should reference the video, Authentic Reading activity, and Modeling activity to answer the questions. Then, as a class, discuss how the reflection questions relate to the Investigative Phenomenon. **Ask** How is energy obtained from chemical reactions?

Investigative Phenomenon Video: Rocket Reaction

Authentic Reading

Authentic Reading Interactive Worksheet

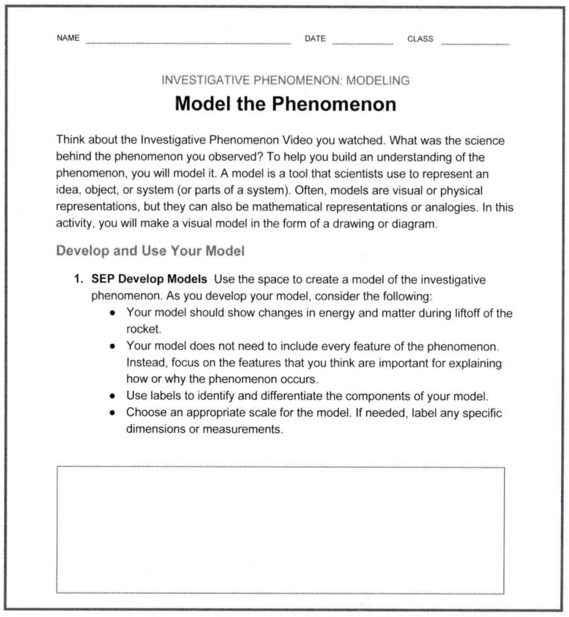

NAME ______ DATE ______ CLASS ______

INVESTIGATIVE PHENOMENON: MODELING

Model the Phenomenon

Think about the Investigative Phenomenon Video you watched. What was the science behind the phenomenon you observed? To help you build an understanding of the phenomenon, you will model it. A model is a tool that scientists use to represent an idea, object, or system (or parts of a system). Often, models are visual or physical representations, but they can also be mathematical representations or analogies. In this activity, you will make a visual model in the form of a drawing or diagram.

Develop and Use Your Model

1. **SEP Develop Models** Use the space to create a model of the investigative phenomenon. As you develop your model, consider the following:
   - Your model should show changes in energy and matter during liftoff of the rocket.
   - Your model does not need to include every feature of the phenomenon. Instead, focus on the features that you think are important for explaining how or why the phenomenon occurs.
   - Use labels to identify and differentiate the components of your model.
   - Choose an appropriate scale for the model. If needed, label any specific dimensions or measurements.

Modeling Interactive Worksheet

Experience Notebook, pp. 214–215

eTEXT

EXPERIENCE 1

Modeling Chemical Reactions

Teacher Background

Experience 1 guides students as they model chemical reactions, starting with word equations. Students write skeleton equations and decode symbols that are used in chemical equations. They use mathematical and computational thinking to practice balancing chemical equations. They analyze relationships between reactants and products and interpret data on what causes reactions, using knowledge of the collision theory. Students may have difficulty accepting the collision theory because they tend to visualize atoms and molecules wedged together with no spaces between them. Remind students of their previous knowledge of the kinetic theory—that all matter is made of tiny particles that are in constant motion, and that between the particles is empty space.

Objectives

- **Write balanced equations for chemical reactions.**
- **Distinguish between endothermic reactions and exothermic reactions.**
- **Explain what causes chemical reactions.**
- **Develop a basic conceptual and mathematical model for the generation of energy from the reaction of two substances.**

RELATED PHENOMENA

In addition to the demo, Model a Chemical Reaction, consider using other phenomena to launch this experience.

- **Hot Versus Cold** Provide a hot pack and a cold pack. Have students feel the two. Discuss the chemical equations for both: cold pack—$NH_4NO_3(s) + H_2O(l) \rightarrow NH_4^+(aq) + NO_3^-(aq)$; hot pack—$CaCl_2(s) + H_2O(l) \rightarrow Ca^{2+}(aq) + 2\ Cl^-(aq)$. Discuss which shows an endothermic reaction and which shows an exothermic reaction.
- **Crime Scene Glow** Slowly mix 500 mL of luminol solution with 500 mL of household bleach solution. Dim the lights and watch as it generates a blue glow. Discuss what caused the reaction and whether it was exothermic or endothermic.

ENGAGE

EVERYDAY PHENOMENON

Does the number of atoms change in a chemical reaction?

Use this teacher demo to prompt student discussion about chemical reactions and equations. As students ask questions about this phenomenon, challenge them to find answers as they complete the Inquiry Lab.

Model a Chemical Reaction (5)

Engage students with this demonstration of an everyday phenomenon to introduce the concept of chemical reactions and how models can be used to illustrate energy in a chemical reaction system.

Materials 100-mL graduated cylinder, 0.1 M copper(II) chloride solution, 400-mL beaker, metric ruler, scissors, 5-cm square piece aluminum foil

Safety Copper(II) chloride solution is an irritant.

1. Add 200 mL of 0.1 M copper(II) chloride solution to a 400-mL beaker.
2. Crumple the foil into a loose ball and place it in the copper solution. Ask students to note any evidence of chemical change. (Students should note that the solution begins to produce gas and that a red-brown precipitate of copper falls to the bottom of the beaker.)
3. Have students write a sentence in their notebooks that describes the chemical reaction. Then explain that students can also model what happens in a chemical reaction using word equations and drawings. Write the skeleton equation for the reaction on the board: $CuCl_2 + Al \rightarrow AlCl_3 + Cu$.

4. Prompt students to begin thinking about balancing equations by asking whether they see a problem with this equation. Lead them to realize that the number of atoms of each element is not the same on both sides of the equation. **Ask** Why do you think that is a problem? (Accept any reasonable answer at this time.) Tell students that they will learn how to solve the problem in the Inquiry Lab.

EXPLORE

Evaluate Chemical Reactions

Inquiry Lab Students carry out an investigation [SEP-3] with bingo chips to build model [SEP-2] molecules, balance chemical equations, label reaction types, and visualize how matter is conserved [CCC-5] in a chemical reaction. They perform two chemical reactions [PS1.B] as a wet lab.

Lab Demo Video Watch the Lab Demo Video for advice on materials and preparation.

Choose Your Version Open-ended (O), Guided (G), Shortened (S), Advanced (A)

Materials bingo chips, small piece aluminum foil, 50 mL 0.05*M* copper(II) chloride solution, 50 mL 1.0*M* copper chloride(II) solution, 50 mL 0.05*M* sodium phosphate solution, 50 mL 0.05*M* sodium phosphate solution, 500 mL distilled or deionized water, 4 100-mL beakers, 50-mL graduated cylinder, stirring rod

Safety Prompt students to wear goggles, gloves, and an apron during this lab. Tell students to allow the charcoal sample to cool before touching or discarding it. Remind them to use a glass stirring rod to stir the liquid; never stir with a thermometer. This lab should be performed in a well-ventilated room. Students should wash their hands thoroughly with soap and warm water before leaving the laboratory.

Expected Outcome Students can properly balance a chemical reaction and identify the reaction type.

Lab Summary Video Watch the Lab Summary Video for support on connecting the lab investigation to the Investigative Phenomenon.

ASSESS ON THE SPOT

Have students reflect on the Inquiry Lab with a quick write, focusing on content rather than grammar and sentence structure. Encourage students to jot down what they learned from using both of the models. Call on students to share their reflections.

Analyzing Chemical Reactions

Analyzing Data In this activity, students analyze data [SEP-4] about the combustion of three samples of steel wool. They calculate [SEP-5] the mass of the oxygen that combined with the steel and the mass of the iron oxide that formed in each reaction. They look for trends [CCC-1] in data and offer explanations [SEP-6] about differences.

- You may wish to begin this activity by first demonstrating the combustion of steel wool. The steel wool can be ignited by using a 9V battery.
- Remind students that a combustion reaction occurs when an element of the compound reacts with oxygen. **Ask** Where did the oxygen come from in this reaction? (air)

NAME ______ DATE ______ CLASS ______

MODELING CHEMICAL REACTIONS INQUIRY LABS – OPEN

Evaluate Chemical Reactions

How do we represent and understand chemical reactions? This lab begins with a bingo chip activity to solidify building molecules, balancing chemical equations, and visualizing how matter is conserved in a chemical reaction. Then you are the scientist in this lab. From a few chemicals to select, perform your own chemical reactions and make observations.

Focus on Science Practices

SEP 2 Developing and Using Models
SEP 4 Analyzing and Interpreting Data
SEP 5 Using Mathematics and Computational Thinking

Materials Per Group

- Bingo chips
- Aluminum foil, small piece
- Copper(II) chloride solution, $CuCl_2$, 0.05 M, 50 mL
- Copper(II) chloride solution, $CuCl_2$, 1.0 M, 50 mL
- Sodium phosphate solution, Na_3PO_4, 0.05 M, 50 mL
- Water, distilled or deionized, 500 mL
- Beakers, 100-mL, 4
- Graduated cylinder, 50mL
- Stirring rod

Safety

Wear safety goggles when performing this or any lab that uses chemicals, heat, or glassware. Allow charcoal sample to cool before touching or discarding it. Use a glass

O/G/S/A Lab Interactive Worksheets

NAME ______ DATE ______ CLASS ______

ANALYZING DATA

Analyzing Chemical Reactions

Steel wool is a good abrasive for scrubbing pots and removing rust. It is made of fine strands of steel wire, the main component of which is iron. Although iron is not generally thought of as a combustible material, steel wool can burn in air, producing iron oxide. This reaction releases energy as heat, causing more of the steel to burn.

A scientist used a 9 V battery to ignite three samples of steel wool in a carefully controlled environment and weighed the samples before and after combustion.

Figure 1 shows the mass of the samples of steel wool before and after combustion. The samples are different grades of steel wool with different strand thicknesses.

Figure 1

Data Table				
Sample	Grade	Strand Thickness (inches)	Initial Mass (g)	Final Mass (g)
1	finest	0.001	112 g	160 g
2	medium coarse	0.003	224 g	320 g
3	extra coarse	0.005	168 g	240 g

1. **Predict** The scientist determines one of the reactants in the reaction is iron, Fe, and that the product produced is an iron oxide, Fe_2O_3. Given that air contains mainly N_2, O_2, H_2O, and CO_2, what do you think is the other likely reactant?

Analyzing Data Interactive Worksheet

CONNECT TO CAREERS

Custodian Custodians maintain areas within and around buildings to ensure that the areas are clean and safe. As a result, custodians deal with chemical reactions every day. They need to have knowledge of the reactants and products of the solutions they use. Drain cleaners, wood-scrubbing chemicals, and solutions that remove permanent marker all produce chemical reactions. Custodians also need to have knowledge of chemical reactions for their own safety and that of others. Have students research the requirements to become a custodian, as well as, the reactants and products of chemical reactions that can occur during a custodian's work.

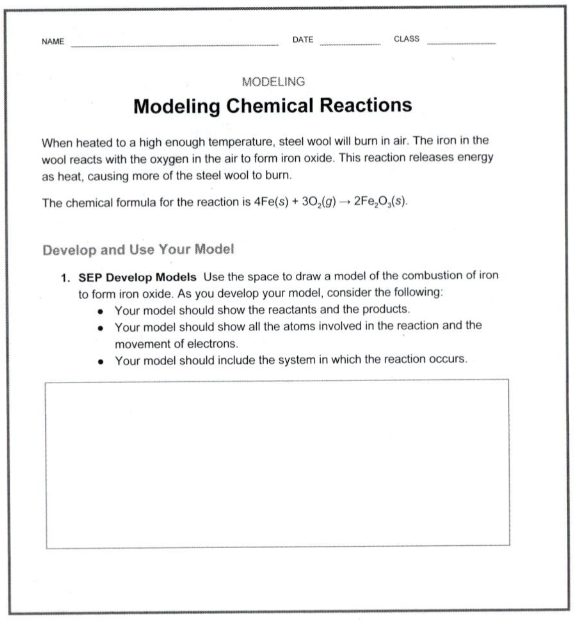

NAME ______ DATE ______ CLASS ______

MODELING

Modeling Chemical Reactions

When heated to a high enough temperature, steel wool will burn in air. The iron in the wool reacts with the oxygen in the air to form iron oxide. This reaction releases energy as heat, causing more of the steel wool to burn.

The chemical formula for the reaction is $4Fe(s) + 3O_2(g) \rightarrow 2Fe_2O_3(s)$.

Develop and Use Your Model

1. **SEP Develop Models** Use the space to draw a model of the combustion of iron to form iron oxide. As you develop your model, consider the following:
   - Your model should show the reactants and the products.
   - Your model should show all the atoms involved in the reaction and the movement of electrons.
   - Your model should include the system in which the reaction occurs.

Modeling Interactive Worksheet

INTEGRATE THE THREE DIMENSIONS

In the Modeling activity, students demonstrate their knowledge of what happens during a chemical reaction [PS1.B] by making a model [SEP-2] in which they identify and describe the relevant components of the reaction. They evaluate [SEP-8] their own models and the model of a classmate. Students also identify changes of energy [CCC-5] within the systems they model.

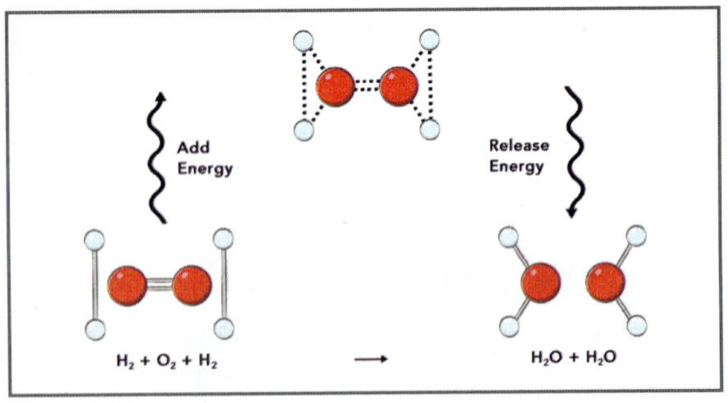

Animation: Bonds Breaking and Forming

Virtual Nerd Video: How Do You Determine if a Graph Represents a Linear, Exponential, or Quadratic Function?

EXPLAIN

Modeling Chemical Reactions

Modeling Use this activity after students have completed the Inquiry Lab in the Explore section of this experience. In this activity, students develop models [SEP-2] to show the chemical reaction [PS1.B] that takes place when steel wool combusts. Their models should show the molecules involved and the movement of electrons. They evaluate [SEP-8] the limitations and strengths of their own models and those of a partner's model.

- Students may choose different formats for their models. Some may choose to make labeled diagrams. Others may make three-dimensional models. Tell students to identify what each part of the model represents.
- After students complete the activity, have them write a short description of the relationship between components, including changes in energy [CCC-5] within the system.

Bonds Breaking and Forming

Animation In this animation, students investigate how a chemical reaction [PS1.B] involves chemical bonds breaking and forming. Students observe a model [SEP-2] of the reaction of hydrogen and oxygen to form water to explore how atoms in reactant molecules rearrange to form product molecules. Students determine that an energy input is required to break bonds in the reactants, and energy is released when new bonds form in the products. Choose among these strategies as you use the animation.

- Make sure that students understand that the rods in the diagrams represent bonds. Point out that some bonds are single bonds and others are double bonds.
- **Ask** What is required to break bonds in the reactants? (an energy input) Reinforce that energy is needed in the breaking and forming of bonds.

How Do You Determine if a Graph Represents a Linear, Exponential, or Quadratic Function?

Virtual Nerd Video Use this video tutorial to reinforce whether a graph represents a linear, quadratic, or exponential function.

Modeling Chemical Reactions

Experience Notebook Ideally, assign the Experience Notebook or Realize Reader the day before and then follow up with any of the following suggested instructional strategies to fill in knowledge gaps and deepen understanding. Alternatively, assign it alongside the Modeling Chemical Reactions activity as support for the activity.

- **Word Equations** (p. 216) Point out that reactants are like the ingredients that are mixed together to make bread. Bread is the product. Write this reaction on the board and have students copy it into their science notebooks: $Fe_2O_3 + H_2 \rightarrow Fe + H_2O$. **Ask** What does the arrow in a word equation mean? (yields or produces) Then invite a volunteer to label the reactants and products in the equation on the board. Keep this equation on the board for additional use. Note to students that the equation is not currently balanced, but it will be referred back to later in order to balance it.
- **Chemical Equations** (pp. 217–219) Write the word *skeleton* on the board. Discuss as a class the context in which students are most familiar with the word. Ask students to write in their science notebooks why an equation without specific amounts would be a skeleton equation. Point out that the equation on the board is a skeleton equation. **Ask** How does a skeleton equation differ from a word equation? (A skeleton equation uses chemical symbols instead of words.)

- **Balancing Equations** (pp. 220–222) Refer to the equation on the board. **Ask** Does this equation follow the law of conservation of mass? (no) Why not? (The number of each kind of atom is not the same on both sides of the equation.) Challenge students to balance to equation in their notebooks. ($Fe_2O_3 + 3H_2 \rightarrow 2Fe + 3H_2O$) Then have students work with partners to take turns writing equations for each other to balance. Encourage pairs to challenge another pair to balance the equations they write and vice versa. The pair that correctly balances the most equations wins.
- **Energy of Reactions** (pp. 223–224) Challenge small groups of students to make a concept map with the phrase *Energy of Reactions* in the center. Allow 5 to 10 minutes for groups to complete their maps. Then have one person from each group communicate [SEP-8] the relationships in their group's map.
- Direct student's attention to the table Average Bond Energies on page 223. **Ask** Which two bonds in the table are strongest? (N triple bond to N, N double bond to O) Which two bonds are weakest? (I single bond to I, H single bond to I)
- **What Causes Reactions?** (p. 225) Remind students that they previously learned about the kinetic theory. Ask volunteers to identify parts of the kinetic theory. Then have student pairs communicate [SEP-8] to each other how the kinetic theory relates to the cause [CCC-2] of a chemical reaction [PS1.B].
- On the board write: *10^{-6} seconds to 10^{6} years*. Ask students what they think the time span refers to. Then tell them that the time required for chemical change to take place may be less than 10^{-6} seconds or more than 10^{6} years. Draw three columns on the board with these headings: *Very fast*, *Average*, and *Very slow*. Call on students to go to the board and add examples of reactions to the columns [CCC-3]. (Examples: Very fast—bleach on a stain; Average—milk spoiling in heat; Very slow—fossilization)

What Is a Coefficient?

Virtual Nerd Video Use this video tutorial to reinforce the definition and use of coefficients.

ASSESS ON THE SPOT

Ask students to write a sentence to answer this question: Why do chemical equations have to be balanced when representing a chemical reaction? (Atoms cannot be created or destroyed, so any atom that is present in the reactants must also be present in the products.)

DIFFERENTIATED INSTRUCTION

- **Support Special Needs Students** Students with visual impairment or who are more tactile learners may benefit from using molecular model kits or foam balls of different sizes to represent atoms of different kinds when they practice balancing equations. Provide a few simple, unbalanced chemical equations and have students use the balls to model balancing the equations.

INTEGRATE MATH

Equality Write on the board a simple math equation without coefficients, such as $20 + 10 = 25 + 5$. **Ask** What does the equal sign tell you about the equation? (The sum of the numbers on one side of the equal sign are the same as the sum of the numbers on the opposite side.) Explain that the arrow in a chemical equation is similar. The mass of matter on one side of the arrow must be the same as the mass on the other side.

Now write a math equation with coefficients; for example, $5x^2 + x = 3x^2 + 2x + 2x^2 - x$. Combine them to show that $5x^2 + x = 5x^2 + x$. Point out that the exponents were not altered; only the coefficients were combined. Explain that, likewise, in a chemical equation, only the coefficient in front of a reactant or product can be changed when balancing an equation.

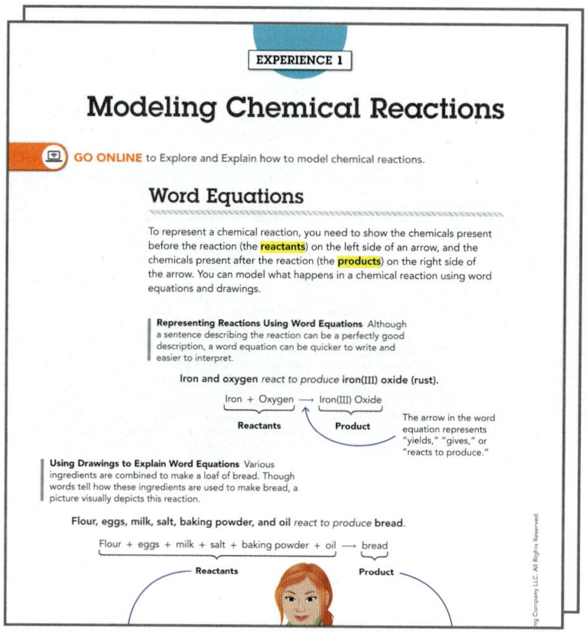

EXPERIENCE 1

Modeling Chemical Reactions

GO ONLINE to Explore and Explain how to model chemical reactions.

Word Equations

To represent a chemical reaction, you need to show the chemicals present before the reaction (the **reactants**) on the left side of an arrow, and the chemicals present after the reaction (the **products**) on the right side of the arrow. You can model what happens in a chemical reaction using word equations and drawings.

Representing Reactions Using Word Equations Although a sentence describing the reaction can be a perfectly good description, a word equation can be quicker to write and easier to interpret.

Iron and oxygen *react to produce* **iron(III) oxide (rust).**

Iron + Oxygen → Iron(III) Oxide

Reactants | Product

The arrow in the word equation represents "yields," "gives," or "reacts to produce."

Using Drawings to Explain Word Equations Various ingredients are combined to make a loaf of bread. Though words tell how these ingredients are used to make bread, a picture visually depicts this reaction.

Flour, eggs, milk, salt, baking powder, and oil *react to produce* **bread**.

Flour + eggs + milk + salt + baking powder + oil → bread

Reactants | Product

Experience Notebook, pp. 216–225

eTEXT

SAMPLE PROBLEM SUPPORT

To give students practice with writing word and skeleton equations, write this information on the board:

Sulfuric acid reacts with solid sulfur to form sulfur dioxide gas and water.

Call on volunteers to go to the board and write a word equation and a skeleton equation for the reaction. (sulfuric acid (*aq*) + sulfur (*s*) → sulfur dioxide (*g*) + water (*l*); $H_2SO_4(aq) + S(s) \rightarrow SO_2(g) + H_2O(l)$)

Virtual Nerd Video: What Is a Coefficient?

ELD SUPPORT

Speaking/Writing Use the following strategies to help students use knowledge of morphology to determine meanings of *endothermic* and *exothermic* on page 224 of the Experience Notebook.

- **Emerging/Beginning** Have students draw pictures to illustrate the meaning of the two words. Then ask them to use their pictures to tell a partner in English or their home language what each word means.
- **Developing/Expanding** Have student pairs write two sentences for each word—one sentence to explain what it means and another to give an example.
- **Bridging** Have pairs write a paragraph that explains how the two terms relate to chemical reactions.

NAME ______________________ DATE __________ CLASS __________

PEER REVIEW RUBRIC

Evaluate Models of Chemical Reactions

Use this rubric to help you assess your classmates' models and explanations of c

	EXEMPLARY Score the work 3 if:	ACCOMPLISHED Score the work 2 if:	DEVELOPING Score the work 1 if:	
Components of the Model Score: ______	All the atoms of the products and reactants are clearly identified. The model shows the movement of electrons and that energy is released.	All the atoms of the products and reactants are identified. An attempt has been made to show the movement of electrons and the release of energy.	An attempt has been made to identify products and reactants. The model describes the reaction under study but does not show energy release or the movement of electrons.	
Limitations of the Model Score: ______	Limitations of this model are described, including that it only represents individual atoms and doesn't show the three-dimensional arrangement of atoms.	The explanation acknowledges that this model has limitations, though they are not clearly and specifically identified or described.	There is no acknowledgment that this model has limitations.	
Revising the Explanation Score: ______	When new reasoning is presented, the model can be used to explain it.	When new evidence is presented, it is considered, and an attempt is made to use the model to explain it.	When new evidence is presented, the model can not really explain it.	

Peer Review Rubric Interactive Worksheet

NAME ______________________ DATE __________ CLASS __________

ANALYZING DATA

Balance Combustion Equations

The general equation for the complete combustion of a hydrocarbon is

$$C_xH_y + \underline{a}\,O_2 \rightarrow \underline{b}\,CO_2 + \underline{c}\,H_2O.$$

1. **SEP Analyze Data** Complete each table to show the number of atoms as you balance each of the following equations for the combustion of hydrocarbons. Use the first reaction and table as an example. First count the atoms on each side of the reaction. As you balance the equation, cross out the original number and add the new number.

reactants		products
$CH_4 + O_2$	→	$CO_2 + H_2O$ (H, O unbalanced)
$CH_4 + 2\,O_2$	→	$CO_2 + H_2O$ (H, O unbalanced)
$CH_4 + 2O_2$	→	$CO_2 + 2H_2O$ (balanced)

C atoms	1	1
H atoms	4	~~2~~ 4
O atoms	~~2~~ 4	~~3~~ 4

reactants products

___ C_2H_6 + ___ O_2 → ___ CO_2 + ___ H_2O

Analyzing Data Interactive Worksheet

CLASSROOM MODIFICATIONS

Based on your students' abilities and your schedule, you can modify the Balance Combustion Equations worksheet to be more open ended or more guided.

- **More Open Ended** Have students make their own data tables and equations to balance. Students should trade their data tables and equations with a classmate and then balance the equations.
- **More Guided** Complete this activity as a class. Provide step-by-step direction and model how to balance the equations as students follow along on their worksheets.

ELABORATE

Evaluate Models of Chemical Reactions

Peer Review Rubric Students use the rubric as a scoring guide to evaluate [SEP-8] their classmates' models and explanations of chemical reactions.

- Organize students in groups of four, and have each member evaluate the models of the other group members. Make sure they use a separate scoring sheet for each student they evaluate.
- Encourage groups to compare the models of all group members and to identify which features made certain models more successful. As a class, compare the features that were identified by each group. Were they similar? How did the features make the models more successful?
- If time allows, you may want to provide students with additional time to revise their models, using the information gathered in the class discussion.

Balance Combustion Equations

Analyzing Data In this activity, students fill out charts showing the number of atoms in the reactants and products of several chemical reactions [PS1.B]. They analyze data [SEP-4] in the charts and use algebra to identify the proportional relationship between carbon and hydrogen atoms in an alkyne hydrocarbon.

- To help students understand how balanced chemical equations are used, ask students to give examples of why a manufacturer might need to use a balanced equation rather than a skeleton equation. (Sample answer: A manufacturer would need to know how much of each reactant to buy to produce a certain amount of product. They would also need to know the exact proportions to use to get the product they want.)

ASSESS ON THE SPOT

Ask students to write a balanced equation for the reaction that occurs when methane (CH_4) burns in oxygen. ($CH_4 + 2O_2 \rightarrow CO_2 + 2H_2O$) Call on volunteers to write their equations on the board. As a class, compare the equations. If any are different, discuss the differences and decide which is correct.

PROFESSIONAL DEVELOPMENT

Explaining Phenomena One reason food spoils, other than microbial activity, is that many foods contain compounds that are highly reactive with oxygen—they oxidize. The oxidation causes the food to become rancid and turn brown. Even though refrigeration slows these reactions, food chemists also rely on compounds called antioxidants to further slow food spoilage. Some fresh foods are natural sources of antioxidants, which give them slightly longer shelf life than those that are low in these compounds. Many processed foods have antioxidants added during the manufacturing process. Encourage interested students to research antioxidants and to make a presentation that explains what antioxidants are, how they work, and what natural and processed foods contain them.

EVALUATE

Modeling Chemical Reactions

Quiz Assign the quiz in online technology-enhanced, auto-graded format or as an editable quiz worksheet. Use the scoring notes and remediation strategies found online to assess students' responses and to provide targeted feedback for each item to remediate well before assigning the summative 3-D Assessment.

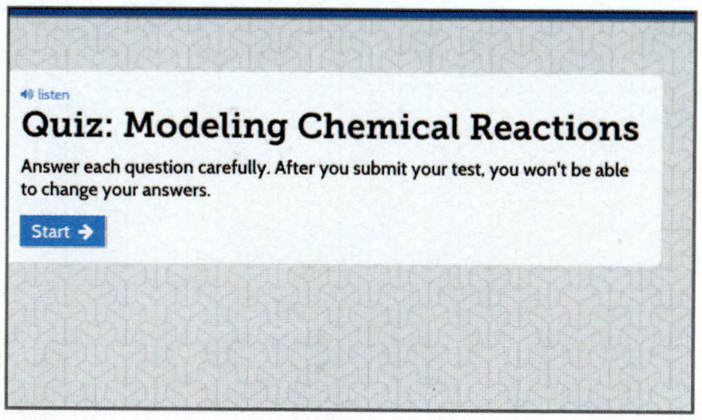

Interactive Online Quiz

Quiz Editable Worksheet

REMEDIATION SUGGESTIONS

- **If** students are struggling to model chemical reactions by writing skeleton equations and balancing equations, **then** have them write the reaction as a word equation first. Students may also want to review the Inquiry Lab, Evaluate Chemical Reactions, to review how chemical reactions are represented.
- **If** students are struggling to balance combustion equations, **then** have them review the Balance Combustion Equations worksheet. Students may also want to reread pages 220–222 in the Experience Notebooks for additional support.
- **If** students are struggling to identify the differences between a balanced and an unbalanced chemical equation, **then** guide them to examine the illustrations of equations throughout the lesson. Have students explain how the illustrations demonstrate the differences between a balanced and an unbalanced chemical equation. Review with students the key steps in writing balanced equations. Have them make a flowchart to describe the best way to subdivide the task.

Revisit INVESTIGATIVE PHENOMENON

Support Reflection Students can complete the reflection prompt, where they will unpack and make sense of the Investigative Phenomenon, based on practices and understandings that have been reinforced over the course of the experience.

- Ask students if they are comfortable explaining the law of conservation of energy and the role energy plays in exothermic and endothermic reactions.
- Have students work with a partner and summarize how energy is required for breaking and forming bonds in a chemical reaction. Then have students relate this to how fuels provide energy that is obtained from chemical reactions.

Refine Your Model Have students answer Question 2 in the Modeling worksheet relating their model to the Investigative Phenomenon. Have students add any evidence they have collected from the activities so far in this investigation. Evidence may include that it takes energy to break bonds and that energy is released when bonds are formed.

Revisit INVESTIGATIVE PHENOMENON

GO ONLINE to Explore a video showing how fuel cells are used on the ISS and to complete a CER interactive worksheet.

13 **SEP Develop a Model** Generating energy requires exothermic reactions. Develop a basic conceptual and mathematical model for the generation of energy from the reaction of hydrogen and oxygen. Your model should be able to predict the average energy released during the reaction and describe where it comes from.

Experience Notebook, p. 226

eTEXT

EXPERIENCE 2

Predicting Outcomes of Chemical Reactions

Teacher Background

In Experience 2, students investigate the five general types of chemical reactions: combination, decomposition, single-replacement, double-replacement, and combustion. Students apply their knowledge from Experience 1 to develop and expand their chemical equation writing skills by predicting the outcomes of different types of chemical reactions. To correctly predict the outcomes of single- and double-replacement reactions, students use the concept of activity series to determine whether one element will displace another element from a compound.

Objectives

- **Identify the five general types of chemical reactions and describe components that are reactants and products in these reactions.**
- **Predict the outcome of certain reactions based on these components, and make a claim about why the reactants react and why the products are formed.**

RELATED PHENOMENA

In addition to the Elephant Toothpaste demo, consider using other phenomena to launch this experience.

- **Water and Electrolysis** Demonstrate the decomposition of water using simple electrolysis. Discuss the outcome of the reaction in relation to the law of conservation of mass.
- **Purple Haze** Show a video clip of the "purple haze" synthesis reaction for the formation of aluminum iodide. Have students attempt to predict the products of the reaction when given the reactants.

ENGAGE

EVERYDAY PHENOMENON

What is the outcome of a decomposition reaction?

Use this teacher demo to prompt student discussion about predicting the outcomes of general types of chemical reactions, using a decomposition reaction as an example.

Elephant Toothpaste

Engage students with this demonstration of an everyday phenomenon to introduce the concept of decomposition reactions as one of the general types of reactions. During the demonstration, challenge students to predict the outcome of this reaction using their qualitative observation skills.

Materials warm water, food coloring, dish soap, 1 package of baker's yeast, 6% hydrogen peroxide, clean 16-ounce plastic bottle, plastic funnel, cup

1. As a class, discuss the definition for a decomposition reaction on page 229 in the Experience Notebook. Write the molecular formula for hydrogen peroxide (H_2O_2) on the board along with the materials list. Ask students to predict which molecular compounds could be produced from the decomposition H_2O_2. (H_2O, O_2)
2. Have students review the term *catalyst* from Experience 1. (A catalyst is a substance that increases the rate of a chemical reaction, but does not go through a chemical change itself.) Explain that baker's yeast acts as a catalyst and that the dish soap and food coloring are only for the visual effect and are not considered reactants in this decomposition reaction.
3. Add 100 mL of 6% hydrogen peroxide followed by 8 drops of food coloring and 15 mL of liquid dish soap into the bottle. Mix well.
4. In a separate small cup, combine the warm water and the package of yeast and mix for about 30 seconds.

5. Pour the yeast/water mixture into the bottle using a plastic funnel. Be aware that the foam produced will overflow the bottle. Tell students that they will learn more about this type of reaction and others in the Inquiry Lab.

EXPLORE

Types of Chemical Reactions

Inquiry Lab In this lab, students carry out an investigation [SEP-3] to perform four different types of reactions, look for evidence of a chemical reaction [PS1.B] in each case, and write the chemical equations for each. Students pick their own chemicals, which are preapproved before beginning.

Lab Demo Video Watch the Lab Demo Video for advice on materials and preparation.

Choose Your Version Open-ended (O), Guided (G), Shortened (S), Advanced (A)

Materials 3 mL 0.5*M* calcium chloride solution, 10 cm copper wire, 2.5 cm magnesium metal ribbon, 5 mL 0.5*M* silver nitrate solution, 1 g sodium bicarbonate, 3 mL 0.5*M* sodium carbonate solution, balance, Bunsen burner, butane safety lighter, cobalt chloride test paper, 10-mL graduated cylinder, 3 Beral-type pipettes, scoop or spatula, 3 13 mm × 100 mm test tubes, test tube clamp, test tube rack, tongs or forceps, wooden splint

Safety Make sure students wear safety goggles and gloves when performing this experiment. They should avoid contact between silver nitrate and skin or clothing as it will readily stain skin and clothing brown. Ethyl alcohol is a flammable liquid and a dangerous fire risk. Addition of denaturant makes the alcohol poisonous—it cannot be made nonpoisonous. This lab should be performed in a well-ventilated room. Make sure students wash their hands thoroughly with soap and warm water before leaving the laboratory.

Expected Outcome Students correctly select the chemicals to perform, identify each reaction, and balance each chemical equation.

Lab Summary Video Watch the Lab Summary Video for support on connecting the lab investigation to the Investigation Phenomenon.

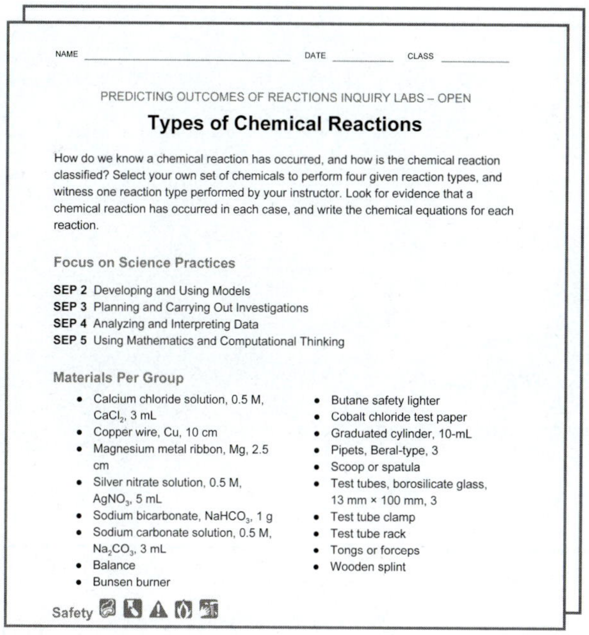

NAME ______ DATE ______ CLASS ______

PREDICTING OUTCOMES OF REACTIONS INQUIRY LABS – OPEN

Types of Chemical Reactions

How do we know a chemical reaction has occurred, and how is the chemical reaction classified? Select your own set of chemicals to perform four given reaction types, and witness one reaction type performed by your instructor. Look for evidence that a chemical reaction has occurred in each case, and write the chemical equations for each reaction.

Focus on Science Practices

SEP 2 Developing and Using Models
SEP 3 Planning and Carrying Out Investigations
SEP 4 Analyzing and Interpreting Data
SEP 5 Using Mathematics and Computational Thinking

Materials Per Group

- Calcium chloride solution, 0.5 M, $CaCl_2$, 3 mL
- Copper wire, Cu, 10 cm
- Magnesium metal ribbon, Mg, 2.5 cm
- Silver nitrate solution, 0.5 M, $AgNO_3$, 5 mL
- Sodium bicarbonate, $NaHCO_3$, 1 g
- Sodium carbonate solution, 0.5 M, Na_2CO_3, 3 mL
- Balance
- Bunsen burner
- Butane safety lighter
- Cobalt chloride test paper
- Graduated cylinder, 10-mL
- Pipets, Beral-type, 3
- Scoop or spatula
- Test tubes, borosilicate glass, 13 mm × 100 mm, 3
- Test tube clamp
- Test tube rack
- Tongs or forceps
- Wooden splint

Safety

O/G/S/A Lab Interactive Worksheets

Chemical Reactions

Virtual Reality Experience Students investigate different types of chemical reactions including single replacement, double replacement, combination, decomposition, and combustion reactions.

Virtual Reality Experience: Chemical Reactions

ASSESS ON THE SPOT

Access student's knowledge about classifying chemical reactions by directing them to answer this question with a written or illustrated example: **Ask** How can you tell the difference between a combination and a decomposition reaction? (A combination reaction forms one product from two or more substances, and a decomposition reaction breaks a single compound into simpler compounds or elements.) If students are having trouble answering the question, draw a Venn diagram on the board for the two reaction types. Complete the diagram as a class. Then ask students to identify the key difference between the two reaction types.

Reactivity of Metals

Virtual Lab In this Virtual Lab, students plan and carry out an investigation [SEP-3] to test the reaction [PS1.B] of unknown metals with cold water, steam, and dilute acid to determine which metal makes the best choice for a ring and to determine the identities of the unknowns. This Virtual Lab should be assigned after a discussion of the activity series of metals on page 232 of the Experience Notebook.

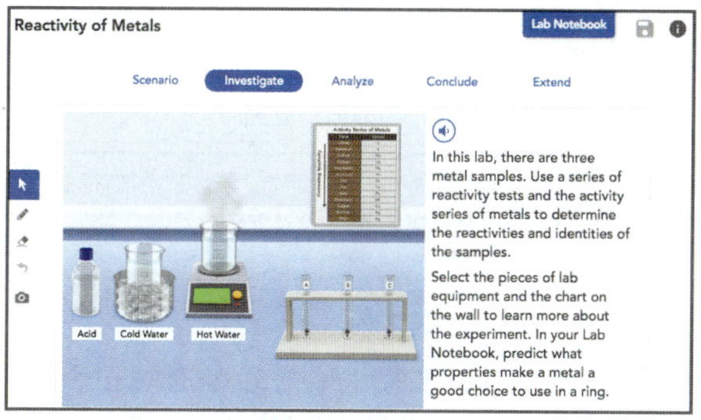

Virtual Lab: Reactivity of Metals

CLASSROOM MODIFICATIONS

Based on your students' abilities and your schedule, you can modify the Reactivity of Metals Virtual Lab to be more open ended or more guided.

- **More Open Ended** Offer students the option to make a presentation about their findings from the lab instead of providing written responses.
- **More Guided** Complete the lab as a class. Alternatively, provide students with completed Procedure Steps 1 and 2. Then have students work with a partner to complete the remaining parts. Review data and responses to prompts as a class.

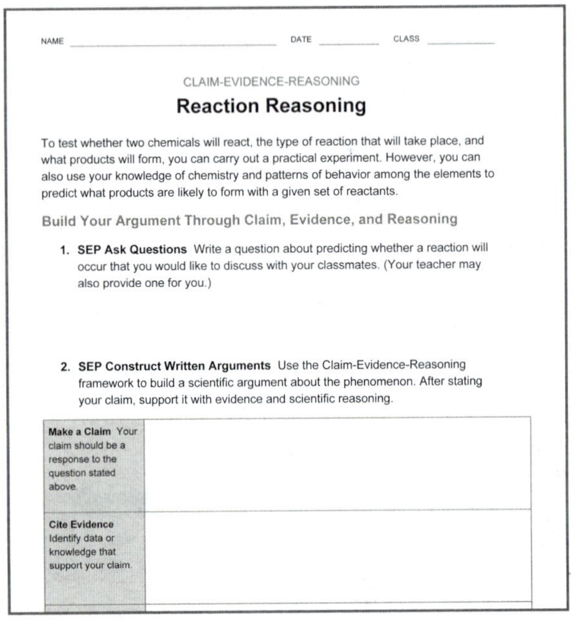

NAME ______ DATE ______ CLASS ______

CLAIM-EVIDENCE-REASONING

Reaction Reasoning

To test whether two chemicals will react, the type of reaction that will take place, and what products will form, you can carry out a practical experiment. However, you can also use your knowledge of chemistry and patterns of behavior among the elements to predict what products are likely to form with a given set of reactants.

Build Your Argument Through Claim, Evidence, and Reasoning

1. **SEP Ask Questions** Write a question about predicting whether a reaction will occur that you would like to discuss with your classmates. (Your teacher may also provide one for you.)

2. **SEP Construct Written Arguments** Use the Claim-Evidence-Reasoning framework to build a scientific argument about the phenomenon. After stating your claim, support it with evidence and scientific reasoning.

Make a Claim Your claim should be a response to the question stated above.	
Cite Evidence Identify data or knowledge that support your claim.	

CER Interactive Worksheet

ELD SUPPORT

Writing In the CER activity, students work in small groups to describe reaction types and to explain why the reactants react and why the products are formed.

- **Emerging/Beginning** Have students write short sentences or phrases describing the energy relationships between combination and decomposition reactions and characteristics that make these reactions different.
- **Developing/Expanding** Have students complete the Emerging activity, and then in teams, take turns sharing responses. All teammates write each answer shared.
- **Bridging** Direct student groups to develop an energy-coupling model to illustrate how the energy products of a decomposition reaction can be used as reactants in a combination reaction. Have students write a description of their model to share with the class.

- Introduce students to the activity series of metals by having them identify which metals in the activity series are most reactive and which are the least reactive. Reinforce that only a metal higher in the activity series will displace another.
- Help students make a connection between the location of the metals on the periodic table and their reactivity as an activity series metal.
- Ask students to develop a list of questions [SEP-1] that must be answered before making a piece of jewelry that would be resistant to everyday wear and tear.

EXPLAIN

Reaction Reasoning

Claim-Evidence-Reasoning In this activity, students ask a question [SEP-1] about reaction types and predict the outcome of a certain reaction. They construct a written argument [SEP-7] about why the reactants change and why the products are formed. Then they evaluate [SEP-8] and revise their arguments after sharing with their classmates. Evidence may include information and patterns [CCC-1] gathered from the periodic table.

- Have students begin the activity independently. Monitor their progress and independent expectations by using proximity control as you walk around the classroom.
- Group students in pairs when they finish their written arguments so that one or more classmates can critique the arguments. Students are to listen closely and record any feedback from their peers.
- Allow students to re-evaluate their evidence and reasoning, and based on the feedback they have received, write an improved draft of their argument.

PROFESSIONAL DEVELOPMENT

Develop Classroom Collaboration Arrange students in small groups to review the improved draft of their CER arguments. Students use talking chips to make sure everyone contributes to the CER discussion.

- Each student receives two talking chips. Ask students to describe how their analysis successfully refuted alternative explanations. Provide time for students to think and ask clarifying questions before they begin the discussion.
- Any student can begin the discussion by placing one of his or her talking chips in the center of the table. Any student with a talking chip continues the discussion by using a talking chip.
- When all chips are used, students collect their own chips and continue the discussion until time is called.

DIFFERENTIATED INSTRUCTION

- **Support Struggling Students** Provide students with general statements that represent the first four types of chemical reactions discussed in this lesson, such as $X + Y \rightarrow XY$ for a combination reaction, $XY \rightarrow X + Y$ for a decomposition reaction, $X + CD \rightarrow XD + C$ for a single-replacement reaction, and $AB + CD \rightarrow AD + CB$ for a double-replacement reaction. Tell students that they can compare actual reactions to these general statements to help them identify the reaction type.

- **Support Advanced Students** When hydrochloric acid (HCl) is dropped on calcium carbonate ($CaCO_3$), a double-replacement reaction occurs. **Ask** What are the products of the reaction? ($CaCl_2$ and H_2CO_3) Neither of these products is a gas, but bubbles of a gas are released as a product. Ask students to identify the gas (CO_2) and what type of reaction could produce this gas. (the decomposition reaction $H_2CO_3 \rightarrow H_2O + CO_2$) Explain that geologists often use this pair of reactions to test rock samples for the presence of limestone, which is formed from the calcium carbonate skeletons of prehistoric corals.

Predicting Outcomes of Chemical Reactions (20)

Experience Notebook Have students read this experience in the Experience Notebook or Realize Reader before class. The following instructional strategies will help students understand and fill any gaps.

Use these strategies to help students make sense of the images and text on the indicated pages, as well as to engage in science practices.

- **Types of Reactions** (p. 227) Direct students' attention to the diagram of the types of reactions. Tell them to refer to this diagram for the notecards and kinesthetic modeling [SEP-2] activities described below. Pass out five notecards and have students make types-of-reactions notecards. One side of the card should have the name and definition of the reaction type, and the other side should have the diagrams of the reactions. They can use these cards for reference throughout the experience.
- **Decomposition Reactions** (p. 229) Have two random students start by holding hands. Have them walk down the aisle of the classroom. Have them let go of each other's hands and return to their seats. Explain how this activity is like the decomposition reaction [PS1.B] of mercury(II) oxide. Have students make a connection with the differences in energy patterns [CCC-1] between combination and decomposition reactions.
- **Single-Replacement Reactions** (p. 231) Have two students join hands and walk down the aisle of the classroom. As they do so, another student takes the place of one of the pairs. Explain how this activity is like the reaction [PS1.B] between potassium and water. Ask students to identify the reactants and products in the reaction with the actors holding hands in the beginning and the end of the activity. (Actors holding hands in the beginning would be water; the actors holding hands at the end would be potassium hydroxide.)
- **Activity Series of Metals** (pp. 232–233) Direct students' attention to hydrogen in the table. Remind students that they learned in Investigation 5 that hydrogen is a nonmetal, even though it is located in Group 1of the periodic table. However, it can be replaced by metals and replace others, so it is included in the table for reference. For this reason, hydrogen is shown in parentheses.
- **Double-Replacement Reactions** (pp. 234–235) Pair two separate groups, partners A-B and C-D. Each student in the groups should model [SEP-2] a different role in the reactants. For example, A partner would represent K in KI, and B partner would represent I. Have partner groups walk down the aisle together and have the B partners switch and hold hands with the C partners. Partner A joins partner D to form new groups, A-D and C-B. Explain how this activity is like the reaction between aqueous solutions of potassium iodide and lead(II) nitrate in a double-replacement reaction to form the yellow precipitate lead(II) iodide. Ask students to identify the products of the reaction with the actors holding hands at the end of the activity. (Actors A-D holding hands in the end would be potassium nitrate, and actors C-B holding hands at the end would be lead(II) iodide.)
- **Combustion Reactions** (pp. 236–237) Direct students' attention to the combustion reaction of methane. Ask students to consider the three things necessary for a fire to burn. (fuel, oxygen, and energy to initiate combustion) Discuss with students the requirements of a gas that might be used to put out a fire. Explain that the gas itself cannot burn or support the combustion of another material. It also must be heavier than air so that it will settle on the fire, depriving it of oxygen. Discuss some specific gases, such as oxygen, methane, helium, and carbon dioxide, for example. Have students research the properties [PS1.A] of these gases to make a claim and provide evidence [SEP-7] about which would be most useful to extinguish a fire.

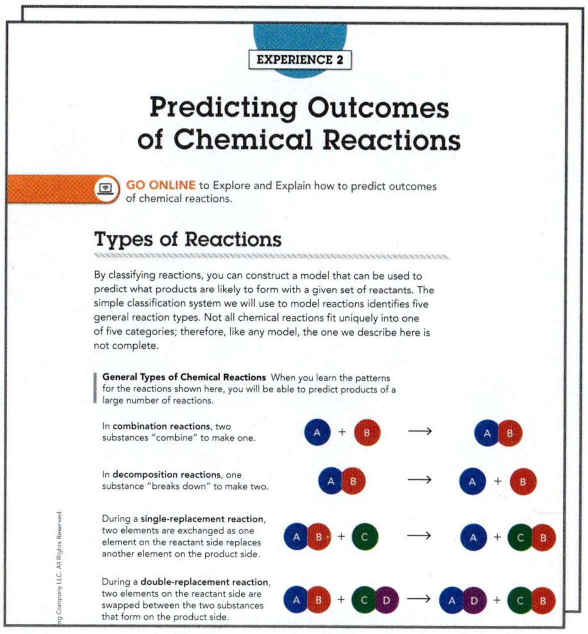
EXPERIENCE 2

Predicting Outcomes of Chemical Reactions

GO ONLINE to Explore and Explain how to predict outcomes of chemical reactions.

Types of Reactions

By classifying reactions, you can construct a model that can be used to predict what products are likely to form with a given set of reactants. The simple classification system we will use to model reactions identifies five general reaction types. Not all chemical reactions fit uniquely into one of five categories; therefore, like any model, the one we describe here is not complete.

General Types of Chemical Reactions When you learn the patterns for the reactions shown here, you will be able to predict products of a large number of reactions.

Experience Notebook, pp. 227–239

eTEXT

ADDRESS PRECONCEPTIONS

Emphasize to students that decomposition consists of one substance forming two or more *different* substances. Students tend to limit decomposition reactions to the decomposition of a compound into its component elements. Explain that a compound can also break down into an element and a compound or two or more compounds. Provide examples of decomposition reaction that result in products other than elements: $2H_2O_2 \rightarrow 2H_2O + O_2$ and $H_2CO_3 \rightarrow H_2O + CO_2$.

SAMPLE PROBLEM SUPPORT

Explain that the balanced chemical equation in the Sample Problem on page 235 is equivalent to the following expanded equation: $1K_2C_3(aq) + 1Ba_1Cl_2(aq) \rightarrow 2K_1Cl_1(aq) + 1Ba_1C_1O_3(aq)$.

Point out to students that by using 1s as coefficients and subscripts, the equation is more difficult to read, thus defeating the purpose of using chemical symbols rather than words to express the events in a chemical reaction.

- **Predicting the Products of Reactions** (pp. 238–239) Use the following review structure to allow students to quiz each other for practice on predicting reactions.
  a. Using notecards, make a set of quiz cards for each of the general types of reactions. Each set should contain six cards. Each card should have the reaction on one side and the reaction type on the other. Adjust the number of cards in each set for classroom size.
  b. Each student gets a card. Tell students to "Stand up, put up a hand, and pair up." Partner A quizzes partner B. Partner B answers.
  c. Partner A praises or coaches. Partners switch roles and trade cards and thank each other. Repeat the steps with the students until enough students have practiced predicting and determining reaction types.

Virtual Nerd Video: What's a Term?

Virtual Nerd Video: How Do You Solve a System of Equations Using the Elimination by Multiplication Method?

What's a Term?

Virtual Nerd Video Use this video tutorial to reinforce the use of the phrase *term* in polynomials.

How Do You Solve a System of Equations Using the Elimination by Multiplication Method?

Virtual Nerd Video Use this video tutorial to reinforce the concept of multiplication in linear equations.

ASSESS ON THE SPOT

Assess students' understanding of how to predict the products of chemical reactions by having them use the activity series table shown on page 232 to answer the following questions.

- What will happen if a piece of iron is placed in a solution of lead (II) nitrate? (Iron will displace lead.)
- What will happen if a piece of aluminum is placed in a solution of calcium chloride? (Nothing will happen because Al will not displace Ca.)

If students have difficulty answering, project or write the activity series table on page 232 on the board. Discuss the information in the table.

ELABORATE

Classify Reactions and Predict Their Products

Discussion Rubric In this activity, students discuss and assess varying explanations [SEP-8] of how to predict the products when the type of reaction [PS1.B] is known. Examples and evidence from the five reaction types should be incorporated into the explanations.

- First, lead a class discussion about the reactions students identified in the Inquiry Lab and how they determined each classification. Then, give students some think time to individually develop their explanations, keeping to the rubric guidelines.
- Organize students into small groups. Tell the groups to stand as each group member discusses his or her explanation. Tell students to sit down when all group members have shared their explanations.
- Have the groups use the rubric to come up with a consensus regarding an explanation.

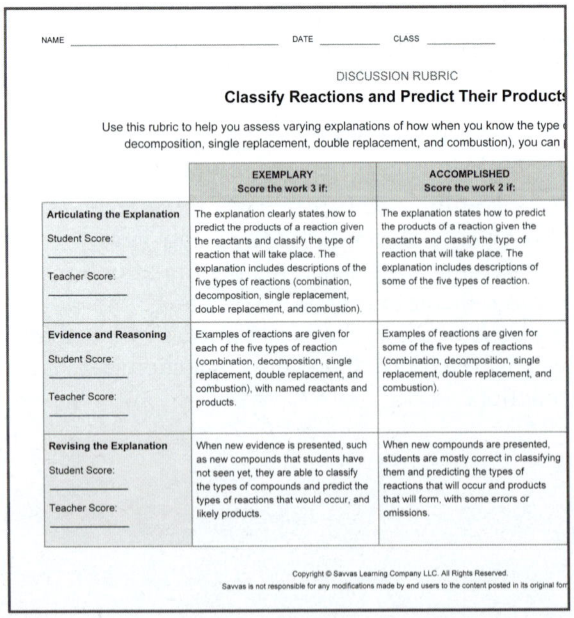

NAME ____ DATE ____ CLASS ____

DISCUSSION RUBRIC

Classify Reactions and Predict Their Products

Use this rubric to help you assess varying explanations of how when you know the type
decomposition, single replacement, double replacement, and combustion), you can

	EXEMPLARY Score the work 3 if:	**ACCOMPLISHED** Score the work 2 if:
Articulating the Explanation Student Score: ____ Teacher Score: ____	The explanation clearly states how to predict the products of a reaction given the reactants and classify the type of reaction that will take place. The explanation includes descriptions of the five types of reactions (combination, decomposition, single replacement, double replacement, and combustion).	The explanation states how to predict the products of a reaction given the reactants and classify the type of reaction that will take place. The explanation includes descriptions of some of the five types of reaction.
Evidence and Reasoning Student Score: ____ Teacher Score: ____	Examples of reactions are given for each of the five types of reaction (combination, decomposition, single replacement, double replacement, and combustion), with named reactants and products.	Examples of reactions are given for some of the five types of reactions (combination, decomposition, single replacement, double replacement, and combustion).
Revising the Explanation Student Score: ____ Teacher Score: ____	When new evidence is presented, such as new compounds that students have not seen yet, they are able to classify the types of compounds and predict the types of reactions that would occur, and likely products.	When new compounds are presented, students are mostly correct in classifying them and predicting the types of reactions that will occur and products that will form, with some errors or omissions.

Discussion Rubric Interactive Worksheet

ASSESS ON THE SPOT

As student groups finish their discussion and generate a consensus, have groups number their members from 1 to 4. Then randomly choose one of the numbers.

- Students with that number will stand up and provide the agree-upon explanation for their group. As each group shares their consensus, write it on the board.
- Have sticky notes ready for each group. As the consensus is being shared, have students write as many ideas about the consensus that they can in the time it takes to share the explanations. Direct students to place the sticky notes on the board for the specific group explanations.
- Collect the sticky notes at the end of the activity to assess for evidence and reasoning skills.

DIFFERENTIATED INSTRUCTION

- **Support Less Proficient Readers** Read aloud the rubric as students follow along. If students are struggling to explain how to predict the outcomes of a chemical reaction, have them make a set of clues for classifying reactions that they can refer to. Have students write clues on sticky notes and attach them to the appropriate locations in the Experience Notebook.
- **Support Advanced Students** Combination reactions are sometimes referred to as synthesis reactions. Have students research the meaning of *synthesis*. Point out that synthesis involves making a final product from other substances, but not all synthesis processes, such as those in photosynthesis, are true combination reactions.

Track the Mass of Reactants and Products

Writing About Science In this writing activity, students construct an explanation [SEP-6] that identifies evidence from a scenario that would suggest that mass is not conserved in a combustion reaction [PS1.B]. After students construct their explanations, focus their attention on the problems scientists face with mass changes during experiments.

- Direct students to look up the combustion reaction of charcoal to assist the construction of their explanation. In their science notebooks, have them draw a model [SEP-2] of the scenario to help them through the thought process.
- If students are having trouble constructing an answer to the Specify Design Criteria question, ask these students what types of problems someone would face when trying to measure the amount of carbon dioxide produced from the burning of a candle.

PROFESSIONAL DEVELOPMENT

Inspire Your Students Show students some NASA images or video clips about the space shuttle program, including some that show the ascent and the three main engines. Use the search phrase *NASA space shuttle era* to find available downloads. The space shuttle program ran for 30 years. During that time, each mission relied on decomposition and displacement reactions to supply the energy needed for launching the space shuttles and their payloads into space.

- Tell students that three Space Shuttle Main Engines and Solid Rocket Boosters provided the thrust to lift the shuttle off the ground for the initial ascent. **Ask** What kind of fuel do you think these huge engines used? Record students answers on the board. Then have small groups of students research online to identify the fuels that were used to propel the main engines. (Fuel for the engines was provided when super-cold hydrogen and liquid oxygen combined. The product of the reaction is mostly water vapor.) Afterward, discuss whether students were surprised to find that a reaction between just two simple gases could lift the shuttle into space.

NAME ________ DATE ________ CLASS ________

WRITING ABOUT SCIENCE

Track the Mass of Reactants and Products

Use the information provided and information gathered from authoritative sources on your own to answer Questions 1 and 2.

Two friends are testing a design for a barbecue that floats on water. They notice that the barbecue sits lower in the water after it has been loaded with charcoal, due to the charcoal's mass. After the charcoal has all been burned, leaving only ash, the barbecue is lower in the water than when it was empty, but not as low as when it was loaded with charcoal. They conclude that the ash must have less mass than the charcoal and wonder where the extra mass has gone.

Obtain and Evaluate Information

1. **SEP Construct Explanations** Explain the reaction that occurred in the barbecue. Describe the evidence that could be observed that would support or refute the law of conservation of mass.

Writing About Science Interactive Worksheet

INTEGRATE THE THREE DIMENSIONS

In the Writing About Science activity, students apply their knowledge about chemical reactions [PS1.B] to construct an explanation [SEP-6] that describes the reaction that occurred in the barbecue. They use patterns [CCC-1] to predict the evidence that could be observed and would support or refute the law of conservation of mass. Then students use this evidence [SEP-7] to describe what precautions scientists should take when performing experiments that produce products that are a different state of matter [CCC-5] than the reactants.

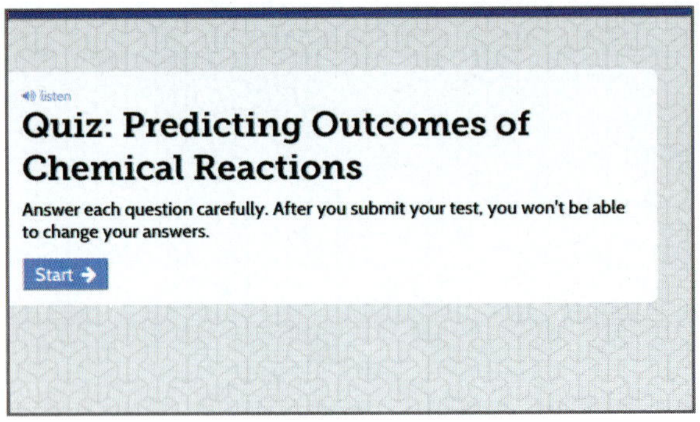
listen

Quiz: Predicting Outcomes of Chemical Reactions

Answer each question carefully. After you submit your test, you won't be able to change your answers.

Start →

Interactive Online Quiz

Quiz Interactive Worksheet

EVALUATE

Predicting Outcomes of Chemical Reactions

Quiz Assign the quiz in online technology-enhanced, auto-graded format or as an editable quiz worksheet. Use the scoring notes and remediation strategies found online to assess students' responses and to provide targeted feedback for each item to remediate well before assigning the summative 3-D Assessment.

REMEDIATION SUGGESTIONS

- **If** students are having trouble predicting the outcome of chemical reactions, **then** have them revisit the CER activity. For additional practice, create a matching assessment showing the types of reactions in one column and the balanced chemical equations in the other column.
- **If** students are having trouble visualizing the process that occurs in each type of chemical reaction, **then** have them review the diagrams on page 227 of the Experience Notebook.
- **If** students are having difficulty determining whether one element will replace another element in a compound, **then** have them view the animation again or refer to page 232 of the Experience Notebook.
- **If** students are having difficulty with the vocabulary in this experience, **then** have students draw a concept map titled *Types of Chemical Reactions*. Have them include all the vocabulary terms in the concept map and ask them to explain how the name of each reaction tells what occurs in the reaction.
- **If** students struggle writing combination reactions, **then** demonstrate how to write a balanced equation for the formation of aluminum chloride ($AlCl_3$) from its elements. ($2Al + 3Cl_2 \rightarrow 2AlCl_3$)

Revisit INVESTIGATIVE PHENOMENON

Support Reflection Students can complete the reflection prompt, where they will unpack and make sense of the Investigative Phenomenon, based on practices and understandings that have been reinforced over the course of the experience.

- Have students discuss in small groups how they could act out the potassium hydroxide reaction from the Investigative Phenomenon. Tell them to decide which students should be the reactants and which students should be the products. Direct students to try to determine the correct reaction type using the kinesthetic activity from the Experience Notebook.
- Suggest to students that they might want to develop a branched flowchart of the five chemical reactions that they can use to eliminate potential reactions. If students have difficulty visualizing the flowchart, start them off by asking if there is a single reactant; if so, the reaction is a decomposition. Have them continue through the five general types of reactions.

Further Develop Your Model Have students add any evidence they have collected in this experience. Allow time for them to make any additional changes based on information they have collected from the activities in this learning experience. Evidence may include the presence or absence of certain reactants to dismiss the reaction type as combustion or decomposition, and the absence of some of the products that are indicative of single- and double-replacement reactions in order to dismiss these reaction types.

Revisit INVESTIGATIVE PHENOMENON

GO ONLINE to Explore and Explain different types of chemical reactions and to complete a CER interactive worksheet.

25 SEP Construct an Explanation Alkaline fuel cells were used by NASA on the space shuttle to convert hydrogen and oxygen gas into electricity, heat, and drinkable water for the astronauts. An alkaline fuel cell uses potassium hydroxide (KOH) as an electrolyte. Because of this, pure oxygen must be used since CO_2 from regular air can "poison" the KOH cell due to the reaction's production of a solid precipitate that blocks the electrode. Construct an explanation for the outcome of the KOH/CO_2 reaction. Predict the reaction type and final product(s).

Experience Notebook, p. 240

eTEXT

EXPERIENCE 3

Reactions in Aqueous Solution

Teacher Background

Experience 3 explores the important chemical reactions that occur in water. Students use what they learn about solubility and intermolecular forces to write and balance net ionic equations. Students predict whether a precipitate will form, using solubility rules for ionic compounds. Students use their knowledge of double-replacement reactions from Experience 2 and apply their ability to balance chemical equations from Experience 1 when they learn how to predict whether a precipitate will form.

Objectives

- **Investigate and explain formation of precipitates using knowledge of solubility and intermolecular forces.**
- **Use evidence to make a claim about whether a reaction will form a precipitate in a chemical reaction.**

ENGAGE

EVERYDAY PHENOMENON

How do substances combine to make new substances in our everyday lives?

Use this teacher demo to prompt student discussion about precipitates in aqueous solutions. Encourage students to record their observations.

Clearly a Solid Solution

Engage students in this demonstration using Epsom salt and laundry detergent to show formation of a precipitate.

Materials Epsom salt (magnesium sulfate), powdered laundry detergent containing sodium carbonate, water, 2 clear plastic cups, food coloring, dropper, measuring spoons

1. Mix a solution of $\frac{1}{2}$ cup of water and 1 teaspoon of powdered laundry detergent in a clear plastic cup. Tell students that powdered laundry detergent contains sodium carbonate (also known as soda ash), which acts as a water softener. The chemical formula for sodium carbonate is Na_2CO_3.
2. In a second cup, mix a solution of 2 tablespoons warm water and 1 tablespoon Epsom salt. Tell students that the chemical formula for Epsom salt is $MgSO_4 \cdot 7(H_2O)$.
3. Add 3 drops of food coloring to the Epsom salt solution.
4. Ask students to make a prediction about what will happen when the Epsom salt solution is added to the laundry detergent solution. Then using the dropper, pick up a few drops of Epsom salt solution and drop it into the laundry detergent solution. Watch as a precipitate forms.
5. Challenge students to write the equation of this reaction ($MgSO_4(aq) + Na_2CO_3(aq) \rightarrow MgCO_3(s) + Na_2SO_4(aq)$) and to draw what is happening at the molecular level. **Ask** What is the precipitate in this reaction? (magnesium carbonate, $MgCO_3$)

RELATED PHENOMENA

In addition to the Clearly a Solid Solution demo, consider using other phenomena to launch this experience.

- **Hard Water and Soft Water** Ask students if they have seen deposits around water faucets. **Ask** How do you think those deposits formed? Test samples of hard water and soft water by adding dish soap to each sample. After shaking each sample with dish soap, soft water will appear clear with many bubbles, and hard water will appear cloudy with few bubbles. **Ask** Why is the water cloudy in the hard water sample? (The soap binds to the calcium and magnesium and forms a precipitate.) What are the benefits of soft water? (Less soap will be used, pipes will not be clogged, and less residue will form on surfaces.)
- **Precipitation Reactions** Precipitation reactions can be extremely visually stimulating because they sometimes start with two clear solutions and the result can be very colorful or cloudy. Look online for videos of precipitation reactions that you can show to students.

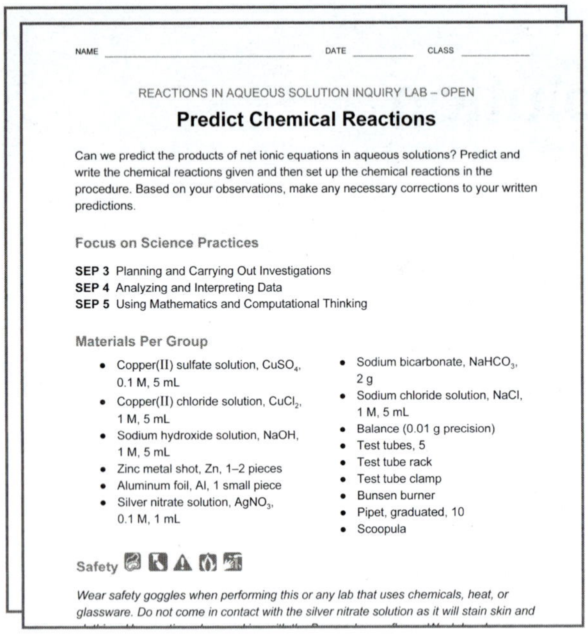
NAME ______ DATE ______ CLASS ______

REACTIONS IN AQUEOUS SOLUTION INQUIRY LAB – OPEN

Predict Chemical Reactions

Can we predict the products of net ionic equations in aqueous solutions? Predict and write the chemical reactions given and then set up the chemical reactions in the procedure. Based on your observations, make any necessary corrections to your written predictions.

Focus on Science Practices

SEP 3 Planning and Carrying Out Investigations
SEP 4 Analyzing and Interpreting Data
SEP 5 Using Mathematics and Computational Thinking

Materials Per Group

- Copper(II) sulfate solution, $CuSO_4$, 0.1 M, 5 mL
- Copper(II) chloride solution, $CuCl_2$, 1 M, 5 mL
- Sodium hydroxide solution, NaOH, 1 M, 5 mL
- Zinc metal shot, Zn, 1–2 pieces
- Aluminum foil, Al, 1 small piece
- Silver nitrate solution, $AgNO_3$, 0.1 M, 1 mL
- Sodium bicarbonate, $NaHCO_3$, 2 g
- Sodium chloride solution, NaCl, 1 M, 5 mL
- Balance (0.01 g precision)
- Test tubes, 5
- Test tube rack
- Test tube clamp
- Bunsen burner
- Pipet, graduated, 10
- Scoopula

Safety

Wear safety goggles when performing this or any lab that uses chemicals, heat, or glassware. Do not come in contact with the silver nitrate solution as it will stain skin and

O/G/S/A Lab Interactive Worksheets

EXPLORE

Predict Chemical Reactions

Inquiry Lab In this lab, students select reactants and predict the outcomes of net ionic reactions [PS1.B] in aqueous solutions and the reaction types. Then they carry out the same chemical reactions and make necessary corrections to the predicted equations and types.

Lab Demo Video Watch the Lab Demo Video for advice on materials and preparation.

Choose Your Version Open-ended (O), Guided (G), Shortened (S), Advanced (A)

Materials 5 mL 0.1*M* copper(II) sulfate solution, 5 mL 1*M* copper(II) chloride solution, 5 mL 1*M* sodium hydroxide solution, 1–2 pieces zinc metal shot, 1 small piece aluminum foil, 1 mL 0.1*M* silver nitrate solution, 2 g sodium bicarbonate, 5 mL 1*M* sodium chloride solution, balance, 5 test tubes, test tube rack, test tube clamp, Bunsen burner, 10 graduated pipettes, Scoopula

Safety Check the students' reactions before they are performed. Goggles, an apron, and gloves are required because students will be working with aqueous solutions. Good ventilation is required because gas is a product in certain reactions.

Expected Outcome Students select reactants and predict the products given the reactant names. After performing the reactions in the lab, students correct any errors in their predicted chemical equations.

Lab Summary Video Watch the Lab Summary Video for support on connecting the lab investigation to the Investigative Phenomenon.

DIFFERENTIATED INSTRUCTION

- **Support Special Needs Students** Encourage struggling students to work in groups or pairs. Allow students to use physical models of compounds to help them visualize the reaction.
- **Support Less Proficient Readers** Before students begin the lab, preview the procedure and questions by reading them aloud while students follow along. Some students may benefit from the opportunity to note their observations and responses to the questions orally while a peer records the information.

ASSESS ON THE SPOT

Write the following chemical equation on the board: $MgSO_4(aq) + Na_2CO_3(aq) \rightarrow MgCO_3(s) + Na_2SO_4(aq)$. Ask students to turn to their neighbors and use the solubility rules to determine the net ionic equation. ($Mg^{2+} + CO_3^{2-} \rightarrow MgCO_3(s)$)

CONNECT TO CAREERS

Wastewater Treatment Plant Chemist
Chemists in wastewater treatment plants use precipitation reactions to clean our drinking water. They also might analyze samples of streams, wastewater, sludge, and other byproducts of the wastewater treatment process. Their goal is to determine whether the wastewater treatment process is effective and to make sure that the treatment plant meets any state or federal regulations. Most of these chemists work in laboratories. They review and record lab data and make recommendations for wastewater treatment. Have students find out what requirements other than a degree in chemistry are required for this career.

Cation Meets Anion

Interactivity This interactivity allows students to carry out an investigation [SEP-3] where they combine anions and cations. They predict which combinations result in precipitates and which do not. Students should ideally use the patterns [CCC-1] they learned in this interactivity to further explain precipitates in the animation Attractions in Solutions. Choose among these suggested strategies as you use the interactivity:

- State a goal for students before they complete the interactivity. For example, tell them, as they complete it, to consider what they want to learn about precipitates.
- Ask students to discuss why certain combinations of anions and cations did not form a precipitate.

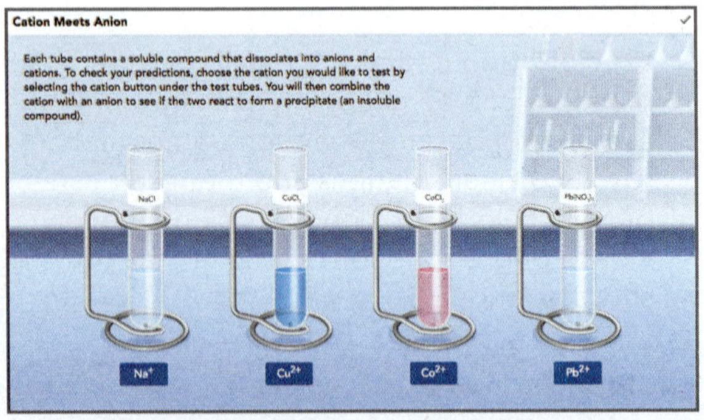

Interactivity: Cation Meets Anion

EXPLAIN

Predict Whether a Precipitate Will Form

Claim-Evidence-Reasoning In this activity, students ask a question [SEP-1] about whether a precipitate will form from a chemical reaction [PS1.B]. They construct a written explanation [SEP-6] about their prediction. Then they evaluate and revise their explanations after sharing with their classmates.

- For Question 1, it may be helpful to provide students with an example of a reaction they would like to explore. Alternatively, you can write examples of reactions on the board and allow students to choose which reaction they would like to investigate. Two examples are barium chloride and sulfuric acid or silver nitrate and hydrochloric acid.
- To assist students who may be having trouble with a claim, have those students determine if the compounds in the reaction are soluble by using the table, Solubility Rules for Ionic Compounds, on page 246 in the Experience Notebook. Once students determine the solubility of the compounds in their investigation, they can then make a claim about whether a precipitate will form.

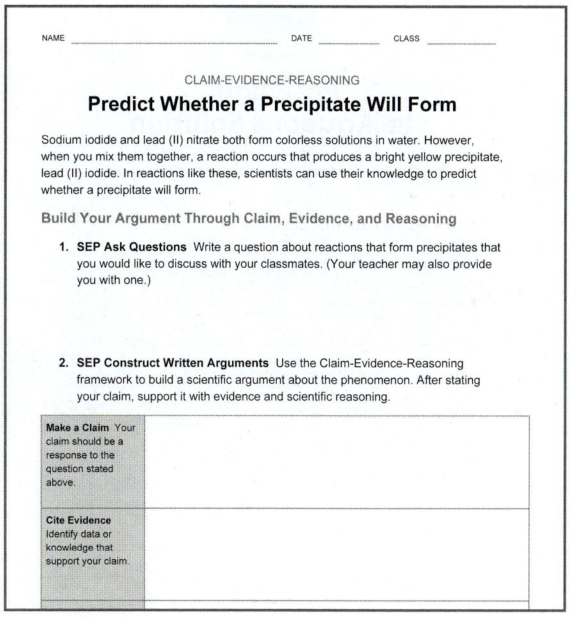

NAME ______ DATE ______ CLASS ______

CLAIM-EVIDENCE-REASONING

Predict Whether a Precipitate Will Form

Sodium iodide and lead (II) nitrate both form colorless solutions in water. However, when you mix them together, a reaction occurs that produces a bright yellow precipitate, lead (II) iodide. In reactions like these, scientists can use their knowledge to predict whether a precipitate will form.

Build Your Argument Through Claim, Evidence, and Reasoning

1. **SEP Ask Questions** Write a question about reactions that form precipitates that you would like to discuss with your classmates. (Your teacher may also provide you with one.)

2. **SEP Construct Written Arguments** Use the Claim-Evidence-Reasoning framework to build a scientific argument about the phenomenon. After stating your claim, support it with evidence and scientific reasoning.

Make a Claim Your claim should be a response to the question stated above.	
Cite Evidence Identify data or knowledge that support your claim.	

CER Interactive Worksheet

ASSESS ON THE SPOT

After students finish the CER activity, ask them to write on a notecard the most confusing point from the activity. This will help you determine which students might need more support and what needs to be addressed in a follow-up lesson to improve students' understanding.

PROFESSIONAL DEVELOPMENT

Science and Engineering Notebooks After students finished their CER worksheets, have them draw a sketch in their science and engineering notebooks of the compounds involved in the CER reaction in which they predicted whether a precipitate would form. Ask students to clearly label all parts of the sketch. Use this as a way for students to reflect on the CER activity and for you to gauge where each student is in his or her understanding.

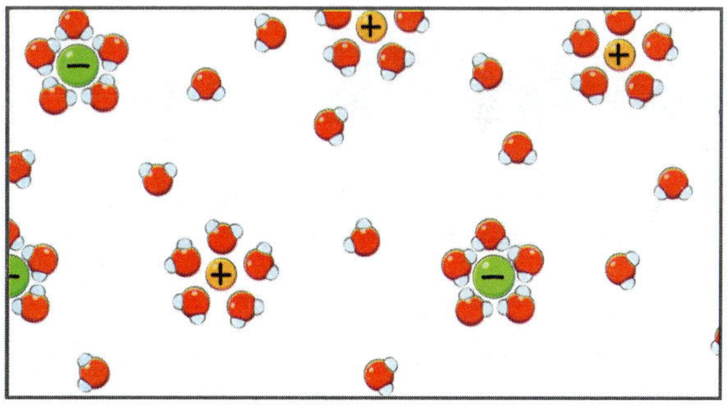

Animation: Attractions in Solutions

Attractions in Solutions

Animation This animation allows students to observe patterns [CCC-1] that help to identify why some substances dissolve in water and others precipitate in water. Students explore the structure [PS1.A] of crystals as they enter water and relate that to how the crystals dissolve. Choose among these suggested strategies as you use the animation.

- Have students write what happened when two precipitating ions met. Students should emphasize that the attraction between the ions was stronger than their attracton to the surrounding water molecules, so they seized and fell to the bottom of the beaker.
- Allow students to draw substances precipitating in water. Make sure students label their drawings accordingly.

ELD SUPPORT

Listening Students work in pairs to demonstrate comprehension of the animation by communicating how ionic compounds react to form precipitates.

- **Emerging/Beginning** Have students ask and answer simple questions about how solubility can be used to predict whether a precipitate will form in a reaction. Provide substantial support as needed.
- **Developing/Expanding** Have students ask and answer questions that demonstrate understanding of the cause-and-effect events shown in the animation.
- **Bridging** Have students ask and answer detailed complex questions about how the structure of crystals aids in their ability to dissolve in water.

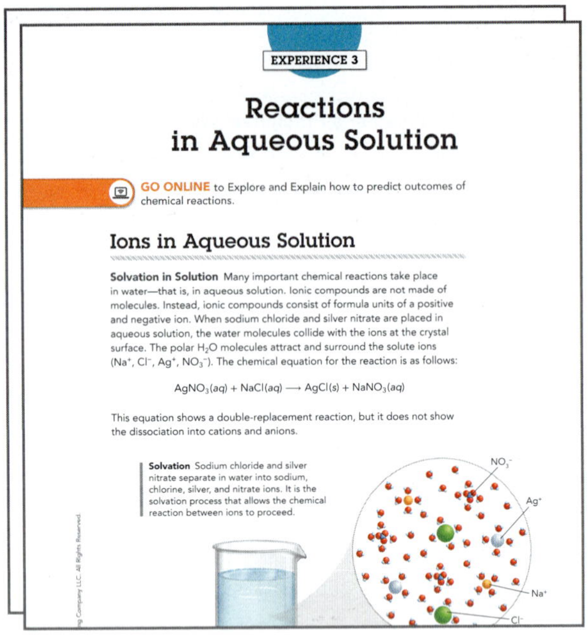

EXPERIENCE 3

Reactions in Aqueous Solution

GO ONLINE to Explore and Explain how to predict outcomes of chemical reactions.

Ions in Aqueous Solution

Solvation in Solution Many important chemical reactions take place in water—that is, in aqueous solution. Ionic compounds are not made of molecules. Instead, ionic compounds consist of formula units of a positive and negative ion. When sodium chloride and silver nitrate are placed in aqueous solution, the water molecules collide with the ions at the crystal surface. The polar H_2O molecules attract and surround the solute ions (Na^+, Cl^-, Ag^+, NO_3^-). The chemical equation for the reaction is as follows:

$$AgNO_3(aq) + NaCl(aq) \longrightarrow AgCl(s) + NaNO_3(aq)$$

This equation shows a double-replacement reaction, but it does not show the dissociation into cations and anions.

Solvation Sodium chloride and silver nitrate separate in water into sodium, chlorine, silver, and nitrate ions. It is the solvation process that allows the chemical reaction between ions to proceed.

Experience Notebook, pp. 241–247

eTEXT

SAMPLE PROBLEM SUPPORT

As a starting point for the problem on page 243, remind students that soluble ionic compounds will break into their constituents, or dissociate, when in water. If needed, have students use physical models to visualize the ionic compounds dissociating. To help students remember that the precipitate will be insoluble, ask students to explain why they are looking for the insoluble substance. (because they are looking for the precipitate, which is insoluble)

Virtual Nerd Video: What Are Equivalent Expressions?

INTEGRATE THE THREE DIMENSIONS

The Experience Notebook uses patterns [CCC-1] of chemical properties [PS1.A] to prompt students to construct and revise an explanation [SEP-6] of reactions in aqueous solution. Students use models [SEP-2] to predict whether a precipitate will form in a chemical reaction [PS1.B].

Reactions in Aqueous Solution

Experience Notebook If possible, have students read this experience in the Experience Notebook or Realize Reader before class. The following instructional strategies will help students understand and fill any gaps. Alternatively, assign it alongside the Predict Whether a Precipitate Will Form CER activity as support for the activity.

Use these strategies to help students make sense of the images and text on the indicated pages, as well as to engage in science practices.

- **Ions in Aqueous Solution** (pp. 241–242) Model an aqueous solution of sodium chloride and silver nitrate with model molecules. Having this visual aid will help students grasp this concept. Allow all students to separate the sodium chloride into sodium and chlorine and the silver nitrate into silver and nitrate. Ask students to pull out the spectator ions, which will help students observe how to balance the net ionic equation.
- **Sample Problem** (p. 242) When writing the complete ionic equation for the reaction [PS1.B] of iron(III) chloride and potassium hydroxide, remind students to write any soluble ionic compounds as individual ions. However, the precipitate formed should be kept as an ionic compound. If students are having trouble, invite them to use the models [SEP-2] to help them visualize the reaction.
- **Solubility and Strength of Intermolecular Forces and Bonds** (pp. 244–245) Have students work in groups to answer Question 29. Ask them how the explanation would change if more sodium and chloride ions were added to the solvation shell model.
- **Formation of a Precipitate** (p. 245) Give students a few minutes to analyze [SEP-4] and complete the table individually and then pair students to discuss their answers. Call on students to share their answers.
- **Predicting the Formation of a Precipitate** (p. 246) Provide students with a list of additional compounds, such as Ag_3PO_4 (insoluble), $PbSO_4$ (insoluble), and KCl (soluble). Have students determine whether the compounds are soluble, using the solubility rules for ionic compounds.
- **Sample Problem** (p. 247) Write and balance the net ionic equation on the board together as a class to answer Question 32. Then pair students to answer Question 33 and go online for additional practice problems.

What Are Equivalent Expressions?

Virtual Nerd Video Use this video tutorial to reinforce the concept of equivalent expressions.

INTEGRATE MATH

Explain to students that when they simplify a mathematical expression or an equation, they combine like terms and write the answer in simplest form. For example, write the following equation on the board: $3x^2 + 4x - 7xy + 2 = 4y + 3x^2 - 7xy$.

Note that crossing out spectator ions from an ionic equation is similar to using inverse operations to solve a mathematical equation. Demonstrate it by crossing out the like terms on the left and right side of the equals sign in the equation. Note that in the mathematical equation, like terms have the same coefficients, the same variable, and the same mathematical signs in front of them.

ELABORATE

Discuss Precipitation Predictions

Discussion Rubric In this activity, students discuss and assess varying explanations [SEP-6] about how to predict whether an ionic compound reaction [PS1.B] will form a precipitate.

- Form small groups of students that have similar claims from the CER activity. Have students work together to discuss their evidence and reasoning. Tell groups to compare their claims, evidence, and reasoning and revise their previous work.
- If any students have claims dissimilar to the claims of other classmates, group them together and have them present their claims, evidence, and reasoning to each other individually.
- After all students have reviewed and revised their claims, have them use the rubric to evaluate themselves. Remind them that for this activity, the accuracy of their self-evaluation is important.

ASSESS ON THE SPOT

Give students 5 minutes to write a 20-word summary of what they learned in their discussion of precipitate predictions. This will reveal what the students think are the key concepts of the lesson. You can use this information to determine if some students are missing the mark.

Water Purification

Engineering Design Challenge Students develop a process of water purification and assess benefits, costs, and whether the process was completely successful. They define the problem of water purification and investigate possible solutions [SEP-6] by conducting research. During their research, students investigate the structure and properties [PS1.A] of sodium carbonate and calcium chloride. Students weigh matter and test the water sample. They evaluate [SEP-8] their solutions.

Materials 50 mL 0.04 M EDTA, 20 g fertilizer, 150 mL 0.1*M* barium nitrate, 5 mL 0.02% sodium rhodizonate solution, 20 g zeolite, graduated Beral-type pipet, 3 g anhydrous calcium chloride, 3 g anhydrous sodium carbonate, balance, 2 150-mL beakers, 3 100-mL beakers, funnel, filter paper, 50-mL graduated cylinder

Safety Students should wear safety goggles and heat-resistant gloves while carrying out the investigation. They should alert you if they break a glass object. At the end of the lab, make sure students wash their hands thoroughly with soap and warm water. Tell students that barium nitrate is toxic by ingestion.

Expected Outcome Students should isolate a precipitate and dissolve a substance by filtration. Then they will determine whether their solution was cost effective.

Use the following strategies to guide students as they complete the indicated steps in the Engineering Design Challenge.

- **Step 2** Students may have difficulty determining the criteria and constraints of the engineering problem. Remind them that criteria are the things that the design must accomplish and that they are derived from the defined problem. Constraints are the limits on materials or resources that affect how the problem can be addressed. If a significant number of students are struggling with these concepts, address the question as a class discussion.
- **Step 3** Remind students that as they research, they should use only reliable Web sites. You may wish to provide a list of pre-approved Web sites.
- **Step 7** You may wish to provide a list of costs for the substances used in the water purification process to help students evaluate their solution, if they cannot find that information during their research.

NAME ______ DATE ______ CLASS ______

DISCUSSION RUBRIC

Discuss Precipitation Predictions

Use this rubric to help you assess varying explanations of how to predict an ionic compound reaction will form a precipitate.

	EXEMPLARY Score the work 3 if:	ACCOMPLISHED Score the work 2 if:
Claims and Evidence Student Score: ______ Teacher Score: ______	The claim clearly explains how to use a solubility table to determine whether an ionic compound is soluble or insoluble and relates solubility to the formation or absence of a precipitate.	The claim explains how to use a solubility table to determine whether an ionic compound is soluble or insoluble. An attempt is made to relate solubility to the presence or absence of a precipitate.
Revising the Explanation Student Score: ______ Teacher Score: ______	When new evidence is presented, such as a new ion that the students have not considered yet, they are able to use the solubility table and theories to predict whether it will precipitate with various counter-ions.	When new evidence or a new ion is presented, it is considered, and an attempt is made to predict if it would precipitate with other ions.

Discussion Rubric Interactive Worksheet

NAME ______ DATE ______ CLASS ______

ENGINEERING DESIGN CHALLENGE

Water Purification

Scientists use chemistry to clean our drinking water. Drinking water can have ions that cause plumbing issues, called "hard water," or contaminants that are harmful to humans. Typical impurities are calcium ions and barium. What could we use to get rid of them, and would it be costly? You will develop a process of water purification and assess benefits, costs, and whether or not the process was completely successful.

Focus on Engineering Practices

SEP 1 Defining Problem
SEP 3 Planning and Carrying Out Investigations
SEP 6 Designing Solutions

Materials Per Group

- EDTA, 0.04 M, 50 mL
- Fertilizer, 20 g
- Barium nitrate, 0.1 M, 150 mL
- Sodium rhodizonate solution, 0.02%, 5 mL
- Zeolite (Ion exchange resin), 20 g
- Beral-type pipet, graduated
- Calcium chloride, anhydrous, $CaCl_2$, 3 g
- Sodium carbonate, anhydrous, Na_2CO_3, 3 g
- Balance, 0.1 g precision
- Beaker, 150 mL, 2
- Beaker, 100 mL, 3
- Funnel
- Filter paper
- Graduated cylinder, 50 mL

Safety

Engineering Design Challenge Interactive Worksheet

CLASSROOM MODIFICATIONS

Based on your students' abilities and your schedule, you may wish to edit the Engineering Design Challenge to make it more open ended or more guided.

- **More Open Ended** Have student groups challenge each other to make a water purification process that is the best for the environment.
- **More Guided** Rather than having students research soil removal, zeolite, chelating agents, and reaction types, provide fact sheets to students with this information.

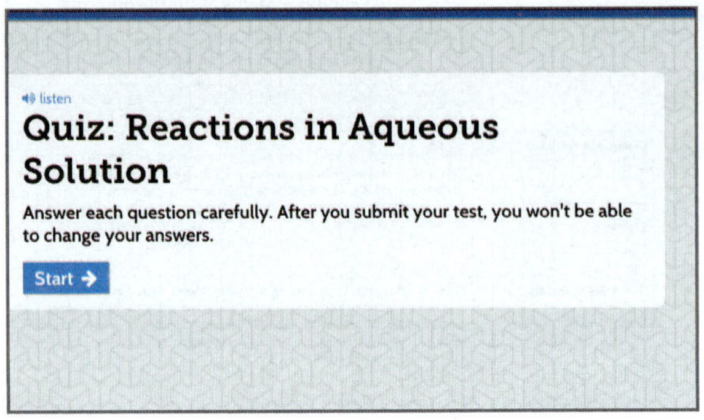

Interactive Online Quiz

Quiz Interactive Worksheet

EVALUATE

Reactions in Aqueous Solution

Quiz Assign the quiz in online technology-enhanced, auto-graded format or as an editable quiz worksheet. Use the scoring notes and remediation strategies found online to assess students' responses and to provide targeted feedback for each item to remediate well before assigning the summative 3-D Assessment.

REMEDIATION SUGGESTIONS

- **If** students struggle with writing and balancing net ionic equations, **then** direct them to reread the section on Ions in Aqueous Solution on page 241 of the Experience Notebook.
- **If** students struggle with solubility and intermolecular forces, **then** direct them to read about solvation shells on page 244 of the Experience Notebook.
- **If** students struggle with predicting the formation of a precipitate, **then** direct them to the CER worksheet they completed.
- **If** students have difficulty predicting the outcome of chemical reactions, **then** direct them back to the Inquiry Lab, Predict Chemical Reactions.
- **If** students have difficulty understanding why substances precipitate in water, **then** direct them back to the Cation Meets Anion animation.

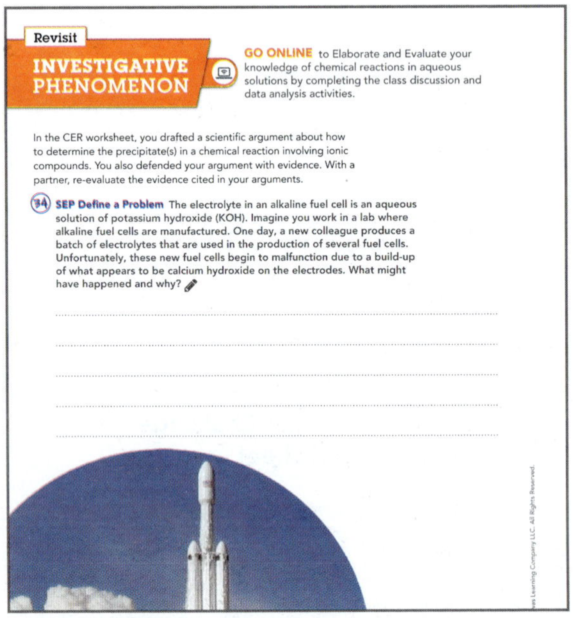

Revisit

INVESTIGATIVE PHENOMENON

GO ONLINE to Elaborate and Evaluate your knowledge of chemical reactions in aqueous solutions by completing the class discussion and data analysis activities.

In the CER worksheet, you drafted a scientific argument about how to determine the precipitate(s) in a chemical reaction involving ionic compounds. You also defended your argument with evidence. With a partner, re-evaluate the evidence cited in your arguments.

34 **SEP Define a Problem** The electrolyte in an alkaline fuel cell is an aqueous solution of potassium hydroxide (KOH). Imagine you work in a lab where alkaline fuel cells are manufactured. One day, a new colleague produces a batch of electrolytes that are used in the production of several fuel cells. Unfortunately, these new fuel cells begin to malfunction due to a build-up of what appears to be calcium hydroxide on the electrodes. What might have happened and why?

Experience Notebook, p. 336

eTEXT

Revisit

INVESTIGATIVE PHENOMENON

Support Reflection Students can complete the reflection prompt, where they will unpack and make sense of the Investigative Phenomenon, based on practices and understandings that have been reinforced over the course of the experience.

- Tell students to reflect on the Inquiry Lab. Have them work in groups and discuss what they understand best and what they could use more help with. Have students answer each other's questions.
- Have students create reflection snowballs. Have each student write on a sheet of paper a key reflection about how energy is obtained from reactions of aqueous solution. Then tell them to crumple the paper. Each student will throw their snowball to the opposite side of the room. Have each student pick up another student's snowball, read it, and then tell how they can use that information to support the Investigative Phenomenon.

Evaluate and Revise Your Model Have students answer Questions 3, 4, and 5 in the Modeling activity and re-evaluate their model based on peer feedback. Students should add any additional evidence they have collected in this investigation. Evidence may include: if a compound is soluble it will not form a precipitate; most carbonates, phosphates, chromates, sulfides, and hydroxides are insoluble; and strong bonds make insoluble substances.

EVALUATE

Chemical Reactions

3-D Assessment For a summative assessment of Investigation 6, assign the 3-D Assessment, which is available online, as an ExamView bank, or as an editable worksheet.

Identify Evidence of Chemical Reactions

Performance-Based Assessment Use this Performance-Based Assessment to assess students' mastery of the standards. In this activity, students carry out an investigation [SEP-3] to determine which solid fills a balloon with gas when reacted with 2*M* acetic acid. Students perform five different test runs on filling a balloon with gas. They record and interpret their data [SEP-4] to compare patterns [CCC-1] in the different chemical reactions [PS1.B]. They use computational thinking [SEP-5] to write balanced chemical equations for each reaction. Students determine if their procedure provided accurate and useful test results and, if not, what specifically caused [CCC-2] the unexpected results.

Safety Acetic acid is corrosive to skin and eyes. Students should wear safety goggles, gloves, and chemical-resistant aprons when working with acetic acid.

Expected Outcome Students should successfully identify the combination that forms a gas and fills the balloon. They should successfully write the full, balanced chemical reaction, predict the products given the reactants, and identify when no reaction has occurred.

Experience Notebook (p. 249) After students complete the Performance-Based Assessment, have them complete the reflection prompt in the Experience Notebook.

DIFFERENTIATED INSTRUCTION

- **Support Struggling Students** Struggling students may have difficulty completing the five different test runs. Complete one of the test runs with the students and discuss with them the potential reaction that occurred.
- **Support Advanced Students** Have advanced students pretend they need to complete this lab with a younger relative. Challenge students to simplify the lab and rework it to be successfully taught to a younger individual.

How can we produce better foods?

Revisit Anchoring Phenomenon At the end of Investigation 6, have students revisit the Anchoring Phenomenon question about how to produce better foods. Lead a class discussion about chemical reactions of foods, both positive and negative. Prompt students to relate those responses to explain how we can produce better foods.

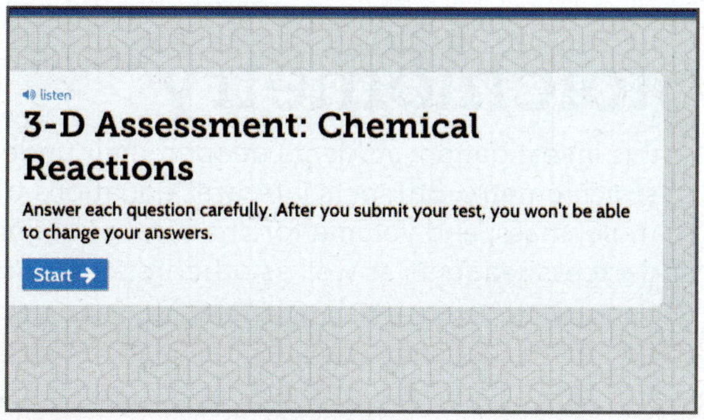
listen

3-D Assessment: Chemical Reactions

Answer each question carefully. After you submit your test, you won't be able to change your answers.

Start →

Interactive Online 3-D Assessment

Interactive ExamView 3-D Assessment

3-D Assessment Interactive Worksheet

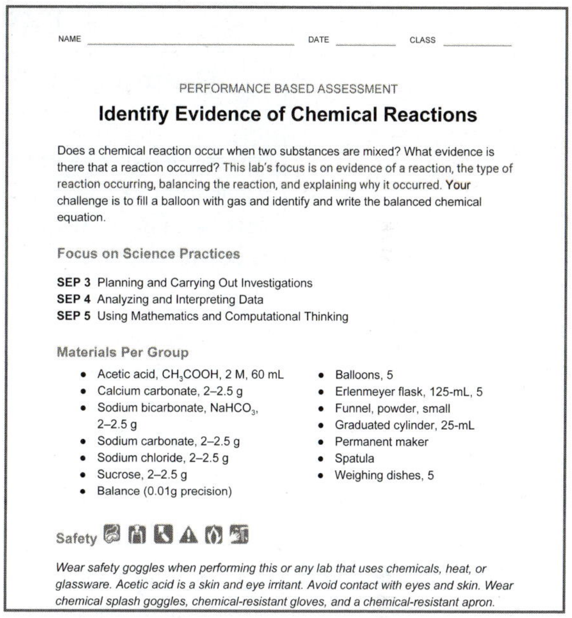
NAME ______ DATE ______ CLASS ______

PERFORMANCE BASED ASSESSMENT

Identify Evidence of Chemical Reactions

Does a chemical reaction occur when two substances are mixed? What evidence is there that a reaction occurred? This lab's focus is on evidence of a reaction, the type of reaction occurring, balancing the reaction, and explaining why it occurred. Your challenge is to fill a balloon with gas and identify and write the balanced chemical equation.

Focus on Science Practices

SEP 3 Planning and Carrying Out Investigations
SEP 4 Analyzing and Interpreting Data
SEP 5 Using Mathematics and Computational Thinking

Materials Per Group

- Acetic acid, CH_3COOH, 2 M, 60 mL
- Calcium carbonate, 2–2.5 g
- Sodium bicarbonate, $NaHCO_3$, 2–2.5 g
- Sodium carbonate, 2–2.5 g
- Sodium chloride, 2–2.5 g
- Sucrose, 2–2.5 g
- Balance (0.01g precision)
- Balloons, 5
- Erlenmeyer flask, 125-mL, 5
- Funnel, powder, small
- Graduated cylinder, 25-mL
- Permanent maker
- Spatula
- Weighing dishes, 5

Safety

Wear safety goggles when performing this or any lab that uses chemicals, heat, or glassware. Acetic acid is a skin and eye irritant. Avoid contact with eyes and skin. Wear chemical splash goggles, chemical-resistant gloves, and a chemical-resistant apron.

Performance-Based Assessment Interactive Worksheet

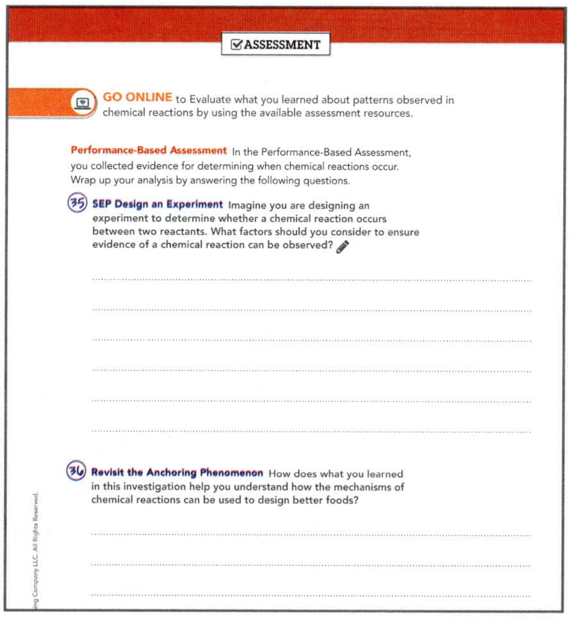
ASSESSMENT

GO ONLINE to Evaluate what you learned about patterns observed in chemical reactions by using the available assessment resources.

Performance-Based Assessment In the Performance-Based Assessment, you collected evidence for determining when chemical reactions occur. Wrap up your analysis by answering the following questions.

35 **SEP Design an Experiment** Imagine you are designing an experiment to determine whether a chemical reaction occurs between two reactants. What factors should you consider to ensure evidence of a chemical reaction can be observed?

36 **Revisit the Anchoring Phenomenon** How does what you learned in this investigation help you understand how the mechanisms of chemical reactions can be used to design better foods?

Experience Notebook, p. 249

eTEXT

INVESTIGATION 7 PLANNER

Stoichiometry

In this investigation, students deepen their understanding of energy and matter [CCC-5] through a study of stoichiometry. Students interpret equations of chemical reactions [PS1.B]. They complete calculations of mole, mass, and volume for chemical equations. Students investigate and determine limiting reagents and excess reagents as well as other related phenomena.

INVESTIGATIVE PHENOMENON

What can make a recipe fail?

Explaining Phenomena In order to fully understand the phenomenon of what can make a recipe fail, students must explore how to quantify reactants and products, which includes how to determine the correct amounts of different ingredients. Students develop the ability to use mathematics and computational thinking to complete chemical equation calculations, analyze and interpret data on reactants, and balance equations. They also identify patterns in the outcomes of reactions.

	EXPERIENCE 1	EXPERIENCE 2
	Quantifying Reactants and Products **2 days** Students explore equations as a recipe. They construct an argument using evidence of how to quantify reactants and products. Students investigate what is conserved according to the law of conservation of mass.	**Chemical Calculations** **2.5 days** Students use mathematical thinking to complete mole–mole, mass–mass, and volume–volume calculations. They investigate a roadmap model for solving stoichiometric problems. Students calculate molecules of a product.
CONNECTION TO THE INVESTIGATIVE PHENOMENON	Students relate scale, proportion, and quantity and explain the amount of ingredients needed to produce three loaves of bread and relate that to the phenomenon of what can make a recipe fail.	Students use data on molar masses to write a balanced chemical equation for making dough. They relate this to the phenomenon of what can make a recipe fail.
ENGAGE	**Teacher's Guide** Everyday Phenomenon The Equation for a Sandwich, p. 210	**Teacher's Guide** Everyday Phenomenon Counting a Year in Milliseconds, p. 217
EXPLORE	**Inquiry Lab** Identify Unknowns Through Stoichiometry **Analyzing Data** Proportional Relationships in Chemical Reactions	**Inquiry Lab** Determination of Reaction Output **Interactivity** Understanding Stoichiometry
EXPLAIN	**Modeling** Put It Together **Experience Notebook,** pp. 252–257	**Modeling** Choose a Practical Unit **Animation** Stoichiometry Calculations **Experience Notebook,** pp. 259–267
ELABORATE	**Peer Review Rubric** Evaluate Put It Together **Writing About Science** Parts and the Whole	**Peer Review Rubric** Evaluate a Practical Unit **Writing About Science** A Scale That Reads Moles
EVALUATE	**Quiz** Quantifying Reactants and Products **Experience Notebook** Revisit Investigative Phenomenon, p. 258	**Quiz** Chemical Calculations **Experience Notebook** Revisit Investigative Phenomenon, p. 268

*Pacing for Encounter Investigative Phenomenon core instruction is a half-day.

†Pacing for core Investigation Assessment is approximately 1 day.

GOT MORE TIME? Personalize and enhance your instructional plan by assigning the activities with the got-more-time icon, as time allows.

Investigative Phenomenon Video When Recipes Go Wrong*

Claim-Evidence-Reasoning Discuss the Investigative Phenomenon*

Virtual Reality Experience

Experience Notebook, p. 250*

EXPERIENCE 3

Limiting Reagent and Percent Yield

2 days

Students compare limiting reagents to limiting ingredients of fish tacos. They analyze and interpret data on mass of products and reactants. They define problems and construct explanations on percent yield and then calculate percent yield.

Students identify the theoretical yield of partial loaves of bread, calculate percent yield, and explain how much of each ingredient is remaining. They use this to refine explanations on what can make a recipe fail.

Teacher's Guide Everyday Phenomenon Stop the Burn, p. 223

Inquiry Lab Formation of Barium Iodate

Virtual Lab Limiting Reagent

Claim-Evidence-Reasoning A Measure of Success

Experience Notebook, pp. 269–277

Discussion Rubric Evaluate Error

Engineering Design Challenge Build a Film Canister Rocket

Quiz Limiting Reagent and Percent Yield

Experience Notebook Revisit Investigative Phenomenon, p. 278

INVESTIGATION ASSESSMENT

Performance-Based Assessment The Stoichiometry of Filling a Balloon†

3-D Assessment Stoichiometry†

Experience Notebook Performance-Based Assessment, p. 279; Revisit Anchoring Phenomenon, p. 279†; **Appendix C** Problem Bank, pp. R17–R19

Notes:

INVESTIGATION 7

Stoichiometry

Teacher Background

Investigation 7 investigates the calculation of quantities in chemical reactions. This investigation differs from others in that it is very abstract and, on the surface, may not seem to connect much to chemistry. Students often get caught up in the math of stoichiometry and lose sight of the reason it is necessary—because mass is neither created nor destroyed in a chemical reaction. Continually encourage students to think of what they are doing mathematically as accounting for mass on one side of the reaction or another. In addition, keep the Investigative Phenomenon, a recipe, in students' minds. Many of the analogies for stoichiometry involve everyday objects, which can help students grasp the math, but may not help students connect the math to chemistry.

Learning Progression

This investigation layers the concept of conservation of mass on top of many of the chemical ideas students have encountered thus far. As students progress through this investigation, they explore different factors that can make a recipe fail by applying mathematical and computational thinking [SEP-5] to consider the proportional relationships [CCC-3] between reactants and products in chemical reactions [PS1.B]. In Experience 1, students begin balancing equations as a way of conserving mass [CCC-5] in the system. In Experience 2, they begin using conversion factors to determine moles, mass, volume, and particles of a reactant or product. In Experience 3, they apply their calculations to determining limiting reactants and percent yield. In this experience, they use the concept of limiting reactant to design [ETS1.C] a rocket and determine the optimal amount of each reactant to launch it efficiently.

RELATED PHENOMENA

In addition to the use of recipes, consider using other phenomena to launch Investigation 7.

- **Hair Dye** Hair dye contains proportioned ingredients that are activated when they are mixed together. Ask students to predict what they think happens if the wrong proportions are mixed. (The wrong proportions in the mixture could lead to the wrong shade.)
- **Air Bag Challenge** Give students a plastic, sandwich-sized zipper bag, vinegar, and baking soda. Challenge them to inflate the bag with the maximum amount of CO_2 gas without breaking the bag. Keep the mass of the system less than 12 g.

TAKE IT LOCAL

Visit a local bakery and ask the bakers to explain the importance of proportions in baking. Note that most bakers use mass (grams) rather than volume (cups) when they bake, because it better allows for scaling the recipe and maintaining correct proportions. Discuss ingredients that have important chemical roles and that students may have worked with in the lab, such as baking soda, salt, and vinegar.

ENCOUNTER

INVESTIGATIVE PHENOMENON

What can make a recipe fail?

Introduce this investigation with the phenomenon of a recipe. For a recipe to be successful, ingredients must be added in the correct proportions to each other. If you know how much of one ingredient you have, you can determine how much you need of others using conversion factors (Experience 1). A balanced chemical equation is a type of recipe, and the act of balancing reactants and products accounts for conservation of mass. A balanced equation tells us how to calculate the amount of reactant needed or to predict the amount of product, using unit conversions and mole ratios (Experience 2). If the proportions of products are not exact, one reactant will run out before the other, thereby limiting the amount of product formed (Experience 3). In addition, all reactions in the real world involve error, which will usually result in a yield of less than 100%.

When Recipes Go Wrong

Investigative Phenomenon Video This short video helps show baking as a set of chemical reactions. For those reactions to produce a successful baked good, they must be added in correct proportion to each other. The same is true of any chemical reaction: reactants will react only in specific proportions to each other, and produce a product in proportion to the amount of reactants.

- Before students watch the video, ask them to describe times they have baked things using a recipe. **Ask:**
  a. What did the recipe look like? What kinds of measurements did it use?
  b. What do you think would have happened if you had added more or less of one of the ingredients?
  c. Have you ever baked something and forgotten one of the ingredients? What happened?
- After students view the video, **Ask:**
  a. When making cookies, what factors could lead to a bad batch of cookies?
  b. How do you think baking with a recipe is similar to a chemical reaction?
  c. Suppose a chemist must produce chemical C using this reaction: A + B → C. What are some factors that might prevent the chemist from making as much chemical C as possible? Think on a molecular level.

Discuss the Phenomenon

Claim-Evidence-Reasoning Have students review the video to help in their understanding of the phenomenon they observed. To help build understanding of the phenomenon, brainstorm a list of questions about the observed phenomenon. Have students complete Question 1 of the CER worksheet and start thinking about the evidence they need to answer their question.

Remind students that their understanding of the phenomenon will be incomplete at this stage, but that they will revisit this activity as they learn more. Make sure to provide students with an opportunity to revisit their CER arguments throughout the investigation as well as at the end of the investigation for further revision and peer review.

Reflect on the Phenomenon

Experience Notebook To get students thinking more deeply about proportions in chemical reactions, write the formulas for sucrose and steviol on the board ($C_{12}H_{22}O_{11}$; $C_{20}H_{30}O_3$). As a class, compare the number of each type of atom in the two compounds. Then tell students to assume that in the process of producing carbon dioxide, the sucrose or steviol is broken down. **Ask** If you break down one of each molecule, do you have the same number of carbon and oxygen atoms to make the carbon dioxide?

Investigative Phenomenon Video: When Recipes Go Wrong

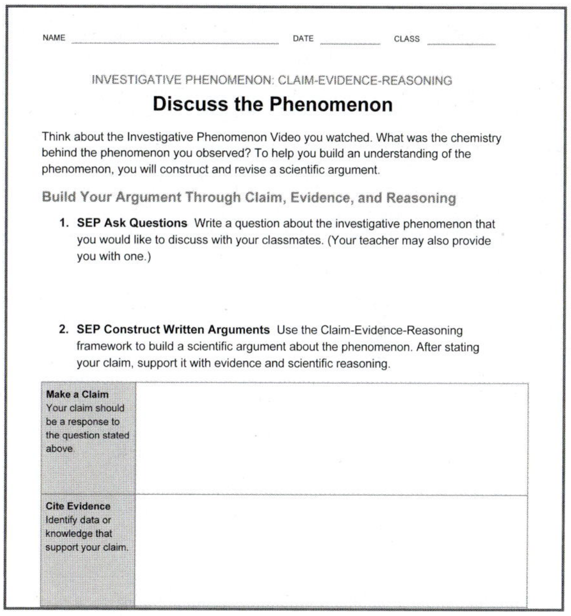

NAME ______ DATE ______ CLASS ______

INVESTIGATIVE PHENOMENON: CLAIM-EVIDENCE-REASONING

Discuss the Phenomenon

Think about the Investigative Phenomenon Video you watched. What was the chemistry behind the phenomenon you observed? To help you build an understanding of the phenomenon, you will construct and revise a scientific argument.

Build Your Argument Through Claim, Evidence, and Reasoning

1. **SEP Ask Questions** Write a question about the investigative phenomenon that you would like to discuss with your classmates. (Your teacher may also provide you with one.)

2. **SEP Construct Written Arguments** Use the Claim-Evidence-Reasoning framework to build a scientific argument about the phenomenon. After stating your claim, support it with evidence and scientific reasoning.

Make a Claim Your claim should be a response to the question stated above.	
Cite Evidence Identify data or knowledge that support your claim.	

CER Interactive Worksheet

Experience Notebook, pp. 250–251

eTEXT

EXPERIENCE 1

Quantifying Reactants and Products

Teacher Background

In Experience 1, students are introduced to the basic mathematics of chemistry by looking at chemical equations as representations of the conservation of mass. You may wish to explain to students that, although stoichiometry may seem more like math than chemistry, it is the underlying "language" of how chemistry works. It is vital for being able to carry out chemical reactions with an understanding of how much reactant is needed and how much product will be produced. Some students may initially be intimidated by the math involved. Give special attention to these students and use hands-on models and real-world examples to help them feel more comfortable with the concepts. Once they have grasped a conservation of mass in a real-life situation or with a model, transition to the more abstract idea of the chemical equation and its coefficients.

Objectives

- **Analyze data on proportionality of reactants and products to predict their stoichiometric ratios in the corresponding chemical equation.**
- **Develop a model that demonstrates conservation of mass in a chemical equation.**
- **Apply mathematical concepts to interpret a chemical equation.**

RELATED PHENOMENA

In addition to the teacher demo, The Equation for a Sandwich, consider using other phenomena to launch this experience.

- **Spotless Pennies** Place old and dirty pennies in a table-salt-and-vinegar solution. See how long it takes before the pennies are clean. Have students quantify the chemical equation of the reaction ($CH_3COOH + NaCl \rightarrow CH_3COONa + HCl$) with a partner in any way they want (atoms, molecules, mass, etc.).
- **Crushed Candy** Show a video of someone crushing candy (such as peppermint candy canes). Have students discuss how the law of conservation of mass is seen in the video.
- **Decomposition of Baking Soda** Have students heat a sample of baking soda in a crucible and examine the mass before and after heating. Ask students to use stoichiometry to prove which chemical reaction occurred:

  $NaHCO_3(s) \rightarrow NaOH(s) + CO_2(g)$

  $2NaHCO_3(s) \rightarrow Na_2CO_3(s) + CO_2(g) + H_2O(g)$

  $2NaHCO_3(s) \rightarrow Na_2O(s) + 2CO_2(g) + H_2O(g)$

  $NaHCO_3(s) \rightarrow NaH(s) + CO(g) + O_2(g)$

  ($2NaHCO_3(s) \rightarrow Na_2CO_3(s) + CO_2(g) + H_2O(g)$ is the correct equation.)

ENGAGE

EVERYDAY PHENOMENON

Is there math in my sandwich?

Use the teacher demo to prompt discussion about proportionality in chemical reactions and the conservation of mass. Encourage students to take notes and add them to their observations during the Inquiry Lab.

The Equation for a Sandwich (5)

Engage students with this demonstration of making sandwiches to introduce the concept of stoichiometry and proportionality in chemical equations.

Materials 6 slices of bread, 9 slices of sandwich meat, 3 slices of cheese, 3 small plates, 1 large plate, scale

1. Place the slices of bread, meat, and cheese on separate plates where students can see them.
2. Ask a volunteer to keep track and add together the masses of the sandwich ingredients. Note to students that each sandwich requires 2 slices of bread, 3 slices of sandwich meat, and 1 slice of cheese.
3. Separately find the mass of each ingredient and tell the volunteer to record the information. Instruct the volunteer to add up the masses of the ingredients and to write the total in a place where students can see it.
4. Ask students to guide you in writing an equation for the sandwich, noting the meaning of coefficients on each ingredient.
5. Ask students to predict the mass of the entire sandwich and to explain their predictions. Guide the discussion to address conservation of mass.
6. Find the mass of the whole sandwich to demonstrate that mass is conserved.

7. Write the equation $2H_2 + O_2 \rightarrow 2H_2O$ on the board. Invite students to describe how this equation is similar to the equation for the sandwich. **Ask:**
   a. How many of each type of atom do we start with?
   b. How many of each type of atom do we end with?
   c. What would you predict to be the mass of the "ingredients" versus the final product?
   d. What does this tell you about conservation of mass in a chemical (or sandwich-making) reaction?

   Use this discussion to transition to the Inquiry Lab. Tell students to keep the concept of conservation of mass in mind as they are doing the lab.

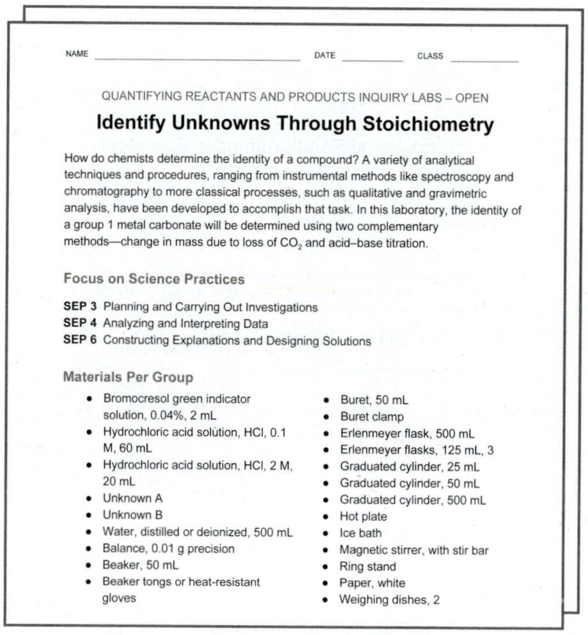

NAME ______ DATE ______ CLASS ______

QUANTIFYING REACTANTS AND PRODUCTS INQUIRY LABS – OPEN

Identify Unknowns Through Stoichiometry

How do chemists determine the identity of a compound? A variety of analytical techniques and procedures, ranging from instrumental methods like spectroscopy and chromatography to more classical processes, such as qualitative and gravimetric analysis, have been developed to accomplish that task. In this laboratory, the identity of a group 1 metal carbonate will be determined using two complementary methods—change in mass due to loss of CO_2 and acid–base titration.

Focus on Science Practices

SEP 3 Planning and Carrying Out Investigations
SEP 4 Analyzing and Interpreting Data
SEP 6 Constructing Explanations and Designing Solutions

Materials Per Group

- Bromocresol green indicator solution, 0.04%, 2 mL
- Hydrochloric acid solution, HCl, 0.1 M, 60 mL
- Hydrochloric acid solution, HCl, 2 M, 20 mL
- Unknown A
- Unknown B
- Water, distilled or deionized, 500 mL
- Balance, 0.01 g precision
- Beaker, 50 mL
- Beaker tongs or heat-resistant gloves
- Buret, 50 mL
- Buret clamp
- Erlenmeyer flask, 500 mL
- Erlenmeyer flasks, 125 mL, 3
- Graduated cylinder, 25 mL
- Graduated cylinder, 50 mL
- Graduated cylinder, 500 mL
- Hot plate
- Ice bath
- Magnetic stirrer, with stir bar
- Ring stand
- Paper, white
- Weighing dishes, 2

O/G/S/A Lab Interactive Worksheets

EXPLORE

Identify Unknowns Through Stoichiometry (40)

Inquiry Lab Students investigate the identity of an unknown Group 1 metal carbonate through gas evolution and titration. This will give them insight into how scientists can learn the identity of unknown substances.

Lab Demo Video Watch the Lab Demo Video for advice on materials and preparation.

Choose Your Version Open-ended (O), Guided (G), Shortened (S), Advanced (A)

Materials 2 mL 0.04% bromocresol green indicator solution, 60 mL 0.1*M* hydrochloric acid solution, 20 mL 2*M* hydrochloric acid solution, Unknown A, Unknown B, 500 mL distilled or deionized water, balance, 50-mL beaker, beaker tongs or heat-resistant gloves, 50-mL buret, buret clamp, 500-mL Erlenmeyer flask, 3 125-mL Erlenmeyer flasks, 25-mL graduated cylinder, 50-mL graduated cylinder, 500-mL graduated cylinder, hot plate, ice bath, magnetic stirrer with stir bar, ring stand, white paper, 2 weighing dishes

Safety Hydrochloric acid solution is toxic and corrosive to eyes and skin tissue. Potassium carbonate is a body tissue irritant. Make sure that students avoid contact of all chemicals with eyes and skin. They should wear chemical splash goggles, chemical-resistant gloves, and a chemical-resistant apron. Tell students to wash their hands thoroughly with soap and warm water before leaving the laboratory.

Expected Outcome The mass lost when CO_2 is released will allow students to determine the molar mass of their assigned Group 1 metal carbonate in Part 1. In Part 2, carbonate acts as a weak base in solution and is neutralized by HCl. The indicator will turn from blue-green to yellow-green when the reaction is complete. The amount of acid used will vary between the metal carbonates.

Lab Summary Video Watch the Lab Summary Video for support on connecting the lab investigation to the Investigative Phenomenon.

CLASSROOM MODIFICATIONS

Based on your students' abilities and your schedule, you may choose the Inquiry Lab to be more advanced or more guided.

- **Advanced Inquiry Lab** Students investigate the identity of an unknown Group 1 metal carbonate through gas evolution and titration.
- **Guided Inquiry Lab** Students investigate the identity of an unknown Group 1 metal carbonate through titration.

ASSESS ON THE SPOT

Tell student groups to discuss the main concepts they have learned in this lab. Then have students write individually in their science notebooks about what they learned and one question they have about the lab. Collect their responses and use them to gauge understanding.

PROFESSIONAL DEVELOPMENT

Background Notes Some students may find it challenging to shift from concrete examples of stoichiometry to the calculations required in the lab, and they may be more focused on balancing numbers than on conservation of mass. Review a similar reaction with them (perhaps one that includes a Group 1 metal carbonate that is not being used), guiding them through thinking about why proportions are important in conserving the total number of atoms, and therefore mass, involved in the reaction.

NAME ______ DATE ______ CLASS ______

ANALYZING DATA

Proportional Relationships in Chemical Reactions

A chemist runs three trials of an experiment to produce ammonia (NH_3) from nitrogen (N_2) and hydrogen (H_2). The unbalanced equation is

$$N_2 + H_2 \rightarrow NH_3$$

The chemist places different amounts of the reactants in a reaction vessel, adjusts some of the conditions such as pressure and temperature, and then records the amounts of the reactants and the products in the table.

Amount of Products and Reactants for $N_2 + H_2 \rightarrow NH_3$

Trial	Original amount (mol)			Final amount (mol)			Change in amount (mol)		
	N_2	H_2	NH_3	N_2	H_2	NH_3	N_2	H_2	NH_3
1	0.345	0.345	0.000	0.335	0.315	0.020			
2	0.102	0.345	0.000	0.032	0.135	0.140			
3	0.345	0.298	0.000	0.305	0.178	0.080			

1. **SEP Use Mathematics** Calculate (in moles) the amount of each reactant that was used up in the reaction and the amount of product that was produced. Record your answers in the table.

Analyzing Data Interactive Worksheet

NAME ______ DATE ______ CLASS ______

MODELING

Put It Together

Aluminum and chlorine gas will react to form aluminum chloride. Atoms of aluminum have three electrons in their outer shell that they easily lose. Chlorine atoms have seven electrons and readily gain one more. Therefore, these two elements combine very easily to form an ionic compound.

Develop and Use Your Model

1. **SEP Develop Models** Use the space to draw a model of chlorine, Cl_2, reacting with aluminum. As you develop your model, consider the following:
   - Your model does not need to include every feature of the reaction. Instead, focus on the features that you think are important for explaining how the molecules combine.
   - Make sure that your model shows that mass is conserved.
   - Use the model to write a balanced equation for the reaction.

Modeling Interactive Worksheet

ELD SUPPORT

Listening/Speaking Students listen and process information and explanations about classmates' models in the Put It Together Modeling activity.

- **Emerging/Beginning** After each classmate presents his or her model, have students state one fact they learned about the model.
- **Developing/Expanding** Have students complete the Emerging activity. Then have students ask at least one question about each model and have their classmates' respond to the question.
- **Bridging** Lead an oral discussion on the ways in which classmates could improve their models. Students should also include an explanation about how they could improve their own models.

Proportional Relationships in Chemical Reactions

Analyzing Data In this activity, students analyze data [SEP-4] they are given from separate trials of an experiment used to produce ammonia from nitrogen and hydrogen. They calculate [SEP-5] the number of moles used in the reaction [PS1.B] and the moles of product that were produced in each trial. Then they make a graph that models [SEP-2] the relationships between the moles of reactant used to the moles of product produced.

- Review with students the role of stoichiometry and proportions in the equation: $2H_2 + O_2 \rightarrow 2H_2O$. **Ask** If you carried out this reaction, what ratio would you expect to find between reactants and products?
- Pair students and tell them to complete the activity together. Then tell the pairs to find another pair to discuss their responses with. As a class, review the balanced equation and discuss how the data reflects the conservation of mass.

DIFFERENTIATED INSTRUCTION

- **Support Special Needs Students** Allow students who are easily distracted to work on their own on the Analyzing Data worksheet, providing guidance when needed. When these students are finished, bring them together to compare the ratios they calculated and to discuss their responses to Question 5.
- **Support Struggling Students** Guide students through setting up and plotting their graphs.
- **Support Advanced Students** Combine this activity with the Modeling activity, inviting students to make a drawn or hands-on model of the production of ammonia. Have students complete a gallery walk of any models students made, and allow peers to circulate and ask each other questions about the models.

EXPLAIN

Put It Together

Modeling In this activity, students model [SEP-2] the reaction [PS1.B] between aluminum and chlorine, and use their models to write a balanced equation for the reaction. They also identify the limitations of their models and consider ways that those limitations could be addressed.

Choose from these suggested strategies to guide students in developing and using their models.

- Pair students to work on their models and to answer Question 2. Remind students that they should each have their own unique model but use their partner for guidance. Tell them to also make a model that shows the reasoning behind their answers to Question 2. Then have students find another partner to discuss the limitations of their models and ideas for revisions.
- You may wish to have students work individually to make their models, write the balanced equation, and answer Question 2. Circulate among students and provide guidance as necessary. Then pair students to discuss the limitations of their models and make suggested revisions.
- If students prefer, allow them to make a hands-on model. Invite other students to engage with the hands-on models and offer thoughts on limitations and revisions of the models.

Quantifying Reactants and Products

Experience Notebook Assign this section of the Experience Notebook or Realize Reader before having students work on any of the activities in the Elaborate portion of this experience. The background knowledge found here is vital for understanding those assignments.

Use the strategies below to help students better understand the content on the indicated pages.

- **Equations as a Recipe** (pp. 252–253) Bring students back to the opening demonstration of sandwich making, and discuss how the sandwich equation is similar to the tricycle equation. Guide students through the Sample Problem. Then pair students and tell them to set up and solve equations [SEP-5] for Questions 3 and 4. Call on pairs to share their equations and solutions with the class.
- **Interpreting Chemical Equations** (pp. 254–255) Review with students the differences between atoms, molecules, moles, mass, volume, and molar mass. Then write and number four simple equations (you may wish to choose some from the online practice problems). Direct students to count off in 4's. Tell students to work with the equation that matches their number, making a model [SEP-2] similar to the chart on page 254, and to show conservation of mass as demonstrated on page 256. Tell students to find a partner with the same number and discuss their work. As a class, discuss any questions students have.
- **What is Conserved?** (p. 256) Again, remind students of the sandwich demonstration. **Ask:**
  a. How did the mass of the ingredients compare to the mass of the sandwich?
  b. How is the sandwich similar to a chemical reaction?
  c. How much CO_2 would be produced (in moles and grams) by burning 36 g of charcoal?
- **Proportionality of Reactants and Products** (p. 257) On the board, write the equation for the reaction of nitrogen and hydrogen to produce ammonia (NH_3), as seen on the student page. Note that in the reaction, 2 moles of ammonia are produced. Direct students to find 2 moles of NH_3 on the Mole Ratio of NH_3:N_2 graph. **Ask** How many moles of nitrogen are needed for this reaction? (one) Point out that the ratio is the same as the coefficients of the formula. Add a 1 before the N_2 in the formula and circle it. Circle the 2 before NH_3 in the product. Then have students find the ratio in the Mass Ratio of NH_3:N_2 graph. Ask students to describe instances in which they would use each of the graphs. Call on pairs to share their answers, and as a class describe how the two graphs are different.

ASSESS ON THE SPOT

Place students in groups of four, and tell them to count off from 1 to 4 within the group. Together, the group should answer this question: Why is the number of grams of reactant equal to the grams of product, but the number of moles may change? Randomly choose a number between 1 and 4, and the student with that number in their group has to share their answer.

Balancing Chemical Equations

PhET Simulation Use this interactive game to help reinforce the concept of balancing chemical equations.

Stoichiometry

Virtual Reality Experience Students learn about stoichiometry, which is based on the concept that atoms are conserved in a chemical reaction and react in a fixed proportion by mass.

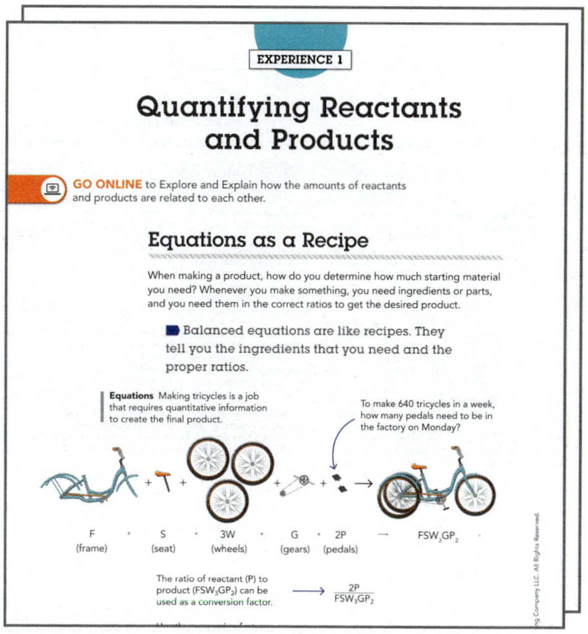
EXPERIENCE 1

Quantifying Reactants and Products

GO ONLINE to Explore and Explain how the amounts of reactants and products are related to each other.

Equations as a Recipe

When making a product, how do you determine how much starting material you need? Whenever you make something, you need ingredients or parts, and you need them in the correct ratios to get the desired product.

Balanced equations are like recipes. They tell you the ingredients that you need and the proper ratios.

Experience Notebook, pp. 252–257

eTEXT

SAMPLE PROBLEM SUPPORT

For the problem on page 253:

- Review the use of coefficients and subscripts with students. **Ask** Why are numbers that were coefficients on the left side subscripts on the right?
- If students are overwhelmed by the number of variables, simplify the problem to $F + 2P + 3W = FP_2W_3$.
- Remind students that the two conversions represent the same ratio. For example, $\frac{3}{4}$ and $\frac{4}{3}$ both represent a 3 of one thing and 4 of another, although the two fractions have different values.

For the problem on page 255:

- Review the importance of setting up equations with units that cancel.
- Review how to find molar mass using the periodic table.
- Call on students to explain how: *a.* relates to the first shaded box, and *b.* relates to the second shaded box, and how the calculations above the bottom shaded box show that mass is conserved.

PhET Simulation: Balancing Chemical Equations

Virtual Reality Experience: Stoichiometry

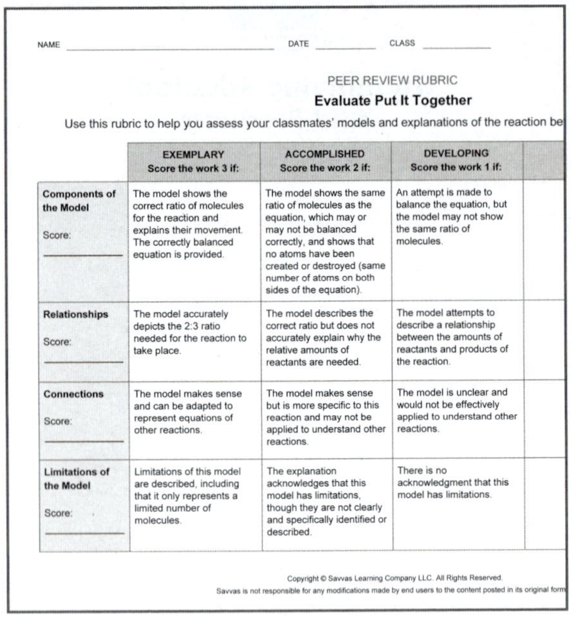

NAME ______ DATE ______ CLASS ______

PEER REVIEW RUBRIC

Evaluate Put It Together

Use this rubric to help you assess your classmates' models and explanations of the reaction be

	EXEMPLARY Score the work 3 if:	ACCOMPLISHED Score the work 2 if:	DEVELOPING Score the work 1 if:
Components of the Model Score: ______	The model shows the correct ratio of molecules for the reaction and explains their movement. The correctly balanced equation is provided.	The model shows the same ratio of molecules as the equation, which may or may not be balanced correctly, and shows that no atoms have been created or destroyed (same number of atoms on both sides of the equation).	An attempt is made to balance the equation, but the model may not show the same ratio of molecules.
Relationships Score: ______	The model accurately depicts the 2:3 ratio needed for the reaction to take place.	The model describes the correct ratio but does not accurately explain why the relative amounts of reactants are needed.	The model attempts to describe a relationship between the amounts of reactants and products of the reaction.
Connections Score: ______	The model makes sense and can be adapted to represent equations of other reactions.	The model makes sense but is more specific to this reaction and may not be applied to understand other reactions.	The model is unclear and would not be effectively applied to understand other reactions.
Limitations of the Model Score: ______	Limitations of this model are described, including that it only represents a limited number of molecules.	The explanation acknowledges that this model has limitations, though they are not clearly and specifically identified or described.	There is no acknowledgment that this model has limitations.

Peer Review Rubric Interactive Worksheet

CONNECT TO CAREERS

Purchasing Manager A purchasing manager is in charge of buying chemical reactants. Reactants are sold by weight or volume, but reactions occur in moles. The purchasing manager must be able to consider purchases in moles as well as conventional units of sale. Tell students to look into the training required for purchasing managers.

ELABORATE

Evaluate Put It Together

15

Peer Review Rubric In this activity, students use the rubric as a scoring guide to evaluate [SEP-8] their classmates' models and explanations of the reaction [PS1.B] between chlorine and aluminum.

- Make a copy of each student's model (include a photo if the student made a physical model rather than a drawing), replacing the students' names with numbers.
- Organize the class into groups of three, give each group a set of three models to critique, and provide each student three blank rubrics. Students should use a separate rubric sheet to evaluate each model. Remind students that the model should reflect conservation of mass [CCC-5] and the proportional relationship [CCC-3] between reactants and products in the reaction, and to consider that in their scoring. Remind them that their participation in the peer review will be assessed on the accuracy and fairness of their evaluations.
- Collect the rubrics. Return students' models, along with the Peer Review Rubrics. Suggest that students make revisions to their models based on the peer reviews. Allow time for students to ask for clarifications from their reviewers.

PROFESSIONAL DEVELOPMENT

Science and Engineering Notebooks Have students use their science notebooks to model and explain a chemical reaction between magnesium and chlorine. Students should write the correct ratio of molecules for the reaction and provide a correctly balanced equation. Have students share their notebooks with a partner so they can critique each other.

DIFFERENTIATED INSTRUCTION

- **Support Less Proficient Readers** For less proficient readers, read aloud the rubric as they follow along. Clarify and/or restate the expectations of the models at the Exemplary, Accomplished, and Developing stages after all of each stage's components are read.
- **Support Special Needs Students** Some students may benefit from completing this activity over multiple days. Alternatively, providing students with special needs with a structured amount of time to complete each step could help keep students focused on the task at hand.

Parts and the Whole

Writing About Science In this activity, students use dimensional analysis to determine the lowest cost option for a one-month supply of ingredients for a company that produces handmade soap. First, students research the role of oil, lye, and water in soap making. They construct an explanation [SEP-6] of how the properties of soap change if too little oil or too little lye is used. Then, students use mathematical thinking [SEP-5] to calculate how much a soap company will spend on ingredients for 20 kg of soap. They connect how calculating ratios for prices for the soap recipe is similar to doing stoichiometric calculations.

- Make sure students research how the sodium hydroxide (lye) is an alkali base and fatty acids make up the oil.
- It may be helpful to define useful terms students can use in their research, such as *saponifcation*, which is the chemical reaction of soap, and *superfatting*, which includes extra fats in the soap mixture.
- To provide additional support for Question 2, lead a class discussion about how to determine how much the company will spend on ingredients for 20 kg of soap. Point out that students first need to determine the minimum amount of each ingredient needed. Next, students should convert the units to determine how many containers of each product are needed from each vendor and then multiply the number of containers by the price per container to find the cost per vendor. Have students analyze their data to determine which vendor provides the lowest price for ingredients.
- After students complete the worksheet, have them work with a partner and review their answers. Then, as a class, have pairs share their answers to check for accuracy.

DIFFERENTIATED INSTRUCTION

- **Support Struggling Students** Some students may have difficultly visualizing the vendor pricing for the soap-making ingredients. Set out physical representations of a gallon, liter, and pound so students can better understand the cost/volume for the prices. For students struggling with conversion factors, remind them that conversion factors should always be oriented so that like units cancel, leaving the desired unit in the numerator. Explain to students that planning the steps of the solution can make the task simpler.
- **Support Advanced Students** Have advanced students conduct the writing task with the addition of the scenario that the small soap company wants to add fragrance and/or coloring to the soap. Students should research other companies and see the amount that is added to a typical bar of soap and the cost.

ASSESS ON THE SPOT

Have students summarize in a paragraph the importance of quantifying reactants and products in soap making. Then have students share their summaries with a partner. Make sure students emphasize that, depending on the amount of soap being produced and the size of the bars, quantities of the ingredients or reactants are quantified in different ways.

NAME ______________ DATE ________ CLASS ________

WRITING ABOUT SCIENCE

Parts and the Whole

A small company produces handmade soap using oil, lye, and water. The recipe they use is:

475 mL of oil + 72.5 g of lye (NaOH) + 177 mL of distilled water → 0.5 kg of soap

Currently the company produces 20 kilograms of soap per month.
Use the information provided and information gathered from authoritative sources on your own to answer Questions 1 and 2.

Obtain and Evaluate Information

1. **CCC Structure and Function** Conduct research to learn about the role of oil, lye, and water in soap making. How would the properties of the product change if too little oil or too little lye is used?

2. **SEP Evaluate** The company has a choice among several vendors to buy their ingredients from. Determine the lowest cost option for the company for a one-month supply of ingredients. The ingredients must be purchased in the amounts listed on the pricing chart. How much will the company spend on ingredients for 20 kilograms of soap? Explain how you made your calculation.

Vendor Pricing for Soap-Making Ingredients

Oil	Cost/Volume	Lye	Cost/Volume	Distilled	Cost/Volume

Writing About Science Interactive Worksheet

INTEGRATE THE THREE DIMENSIONS

In the Writing About Science activity, Parts and the Whole, students quantify the chemical reaction [PS1.B] of soap. They complete calculations [SEP-5] on vendor pricing for the ingredients of the soap-making process. Students relate how making the calculations for the proportions and then converting the units of the ingredients is similar to doing stoichiometric calculations of matter [CCC-5].

EVALUATE

Quantifying Reactants and Products

Quiz Assign the quiz in online technology-enhanced, auto-graded format or as an editable quiz worksheet. Use the scoring notes and remediation strategies found online to assess students' responses and to provide targeted feedback for each item to remediate well before assigning the summative 3-D Assessment.

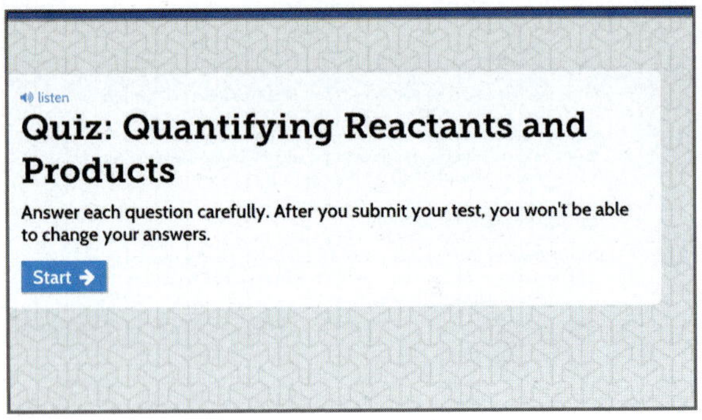

Interactive Online Quiz

Quiz Interactive Worksheet

REMEDIATION SUGGESTIONS

- **If** students are having difficulty converting from grams to moles and moles to grams, **then** lead a class discussion about how to do the calculations using a periodic table.
- **If** students are struggling with the concept of proportionality and chemical equations as a recipe, **then** prompt them to review the Modeling activity, Put It Together. Students can also review the tricycle diagram on page 252 and the Sample Problem on page 253 of the Experience Notebook for additional support.
- **If** students are struggling with the relationship between balanced equations and conservation of mass, **then** have them review the Analyzing Data activity, Proportional Relationships in Chemical Reactions. Students may also want to review the Sample Problem on page 255.
- **If** students are having difficulty understanding how parts can be combined as reactants to make a product, **then** have them return to the Writing About Science activity, Parts and the Whole.

Revisit
INVESTIGATIVE PHENOMENON

Support Reflection Students can complete the reflection prompt, where they will unpack and make sense of the Investigative Phenomenon, based on practices and understandings that have been reinforced over the course of the experience.

- Tell students to write an equation for the loaf of bread. For guidance, they can look at the equation for a tricycle on page 253 of the Experience Notebook. Call on students to share their equations.
- As a class, discuss the ingredients required for three loaves of bread. Further discuss how these particular ingredients are crucial for a bread recipe and how using alternatives that do not have similar properties would make the recipe fail.
- **Ask** Why don't we need to convert the recipe into moles to determine how much we would need? (Because we are multiplying all of the reactants by the same number. The proportions between them don't change; therefore, we can triple all of them and the proportions will remain the same.)

Develop a Draft CER Argument Have students answer Question 2 in the CER worksheet and develop a draft of a CER argument to address the Investigative Phenomenon. Have students add any evidence they have collected from the activities so far in this investigation. Evidence may include the proportional nature of chemical reactions and conservation of mass.

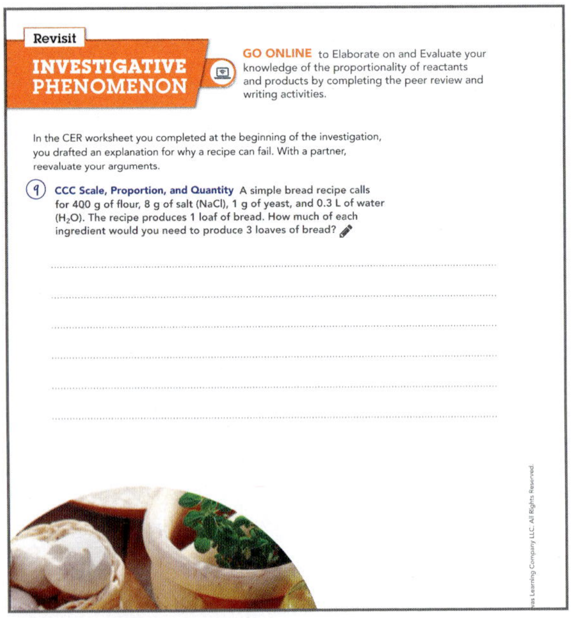

Revisit
INVESTIGATIVE PHENOMENON

GO ONLINE to Elaborate on and Evaluate your knowledge of the proportionality of reactants and products by completing the peer review and writing activities.

In the CER worksheet you completed at the beginning of the investigation, you drafted an explanation for why a recipe can fail. With a partner, reevaluate your arguments.

9 **CCC Scale, Proportion, and Quantity** A simple bread recipe calls for 400 g of flour, 8 g of salt (NaCl), 1 g of yeast, and 0.3 L of water (H_2O). The recipe produces 1 loaf of bread. How much of each ingredient would you need to produce 3 loaves of bread?

Experience Notebook, p. 258

eTEXT

EXPERIENCE 2

Chemical Calculations

Teacher Background

Experience 2 brings the concept of mole ratio to the application of unit conversions in predicting the amount of product in a reaction. Therefore, this experience is largely focused on math in a chemistry context. Students begin with a lab that requires them to calculate the mass of reactants required to produce a given amount of product. They explore the use of units for mass, volume, and moles in an interactivity and a Modeling activity. Finally, they hypothesize about the usefulness of a scale that can measure substances in moles. Becoming adept at unit conversions is necessary for mastering chemistry, so it is important to provide students with a variety of entry points, such as hands-on models, math manipulatives, and opportunities to draw and annotate their own models.

Objectives

- **Use dimensional analysis to determine the mass of reactant required to obtain a given amount of product.**
- **Use the mole ratio in a chemical reaction to relate amounts of participating substances.**
- **Develop and use a model of different units of measurement.**
- **Calculate and communicate data on different units of measurement.**

ENGAGE

EVERYDAY PHENOMENON

Why do we use different types of measurements?

Use the teacher demo to prompt discussion about why we use a variety of types of measurements to describe the world around us.

Counting a Year in Milliseconds

Engage students with this demonstration of an everyday phenomenon to introduce the concept of converting from one unit of measurement to another.

Materials colored pens

1. Explain to students that in chemistry, as in other areas of life, different units of measurement are used in different situations. Emphasize that being able to convert and relate units to each other is an important aspect of chemistry.
2. Tell students that to demonstrate how to convert units, they will help you convert a year into milliseconds. Write *1 year* on the board. Solicit suggestions about how to start the conversion. Ask students to identify a unit of measurement we divide a year into.
3. If one of the students responds with "days," write *1 year × 365 days/1 year*. Use the same color for numbers with year units and a new color for *365 days*. Note for students that the years cancel, and the multiplication gives an answer in days. (A similar equation can be set up if a student responds with "months.")
4. Continue the problem, having students guide you through writing "1 year × 365 days/1 year × 24 hours/1 day × 60 minutes/1 hour × 60 seconds/1 minute × 1000 milliseconds/1 second," being sure to keep numbers with matching units in the same color.

RELATED PHENOMENA

In addition to the Counting a Year in Milliseconds teacher demo, consider using other phenomena to launch this experience.

- **Ideal Omelette** Have students imagine an ideal omelette that they would want to eat or make for someone else. Ask them to discuss the ratio of ingredients used to make the omelette. Have them further discuss why ratios are important here.
- **Let's Make Salt** Show a video of the production of NaCl from sodium metal reacting with chlorine gas. **Ask** Is this how table salt is really made? Why not? Could we make NaCl this way? How would we do it? What ingredients would we need to start with? Work with the students to formulate the equation and write it on the board. Then ask them to balance the equation.

  $$(2Na(s) + Cl_2(g) \rightarrow 2NaCl(s))$$

  Explain that although the balanced equation tells us that 2 particles of Na react with one particle of Cl_2, in reality chemical reactions occur with huge numbers of particles. The word *mole* represents a huge number of particles. Chemists can say 2 moles of Na react with 1 mole of Cl_2 in this reaction.

  Ask If we started with 5.00 grams of Na metal, how many grams of Cl_2 gas should be used to have a "perfect reaction"? In other words, we don't want any leftover Na particles or Cl_2 particles after the reaction is complete. Allow students to brainstorm this problem. Some students may suggest 2.5 grams of Cl_2 as the answer. From this preconception, discuss the different sizes of the particles. Remind students that particles have different sizes and masses. A 2:1 mass ratio does not give us a 2:1 particle ratio. Provide support to help students use a mole-to-mole ratio rather than a gram ratio. Go through the stoichiometric calculation together as a class.

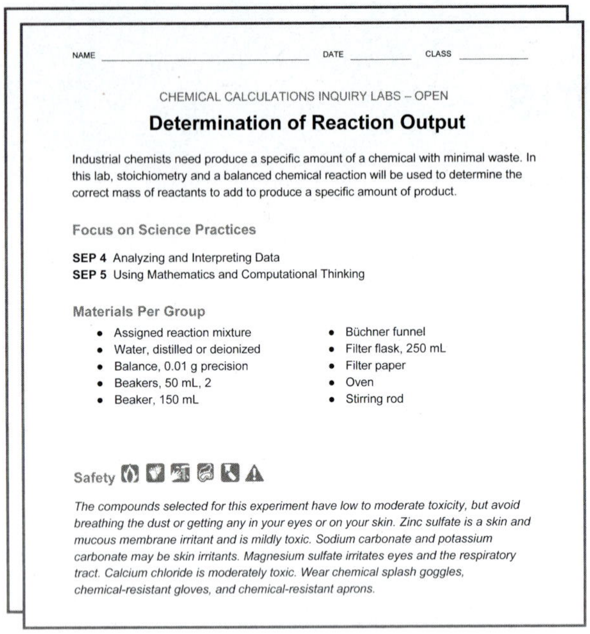

NAME ____________ DATE ________ CLASS ________

CHEMICAL CALCULATIONS INQUIRY LABS – OPEN

Determination of Reaction Output

Industrial chemists need produce a specific amount of a chemical with minimal waste. In this lab, stoichiometry and a balanced chemical reaction will be used to determine the correct mass of reactants to add to produce a specific amount of product.

Focus on Science Practices

SEP 4 Analyzing and Interpreting Data
SEP 5 Using Mathematics and Computational Thinking

Materials Per Group

- Assigned reaction mixture
- Water, distilled or deionized
- Balance, 0.01 g precision
- Beakers, 50 mL, 2
- Beaker, 150 mL
- Büchner funnel
- Filter flask, 250 mL
- Filter paper
- Oven
- Stirring rod

Safety

The compounds selected for this experiment have low to moderate toxicity, but avoid breathing the dust or getting any in your eyes or on your skin. Zinc sulfate is a skin and mucous membrane irritant and is mildly toxic. Sodium carbonate and potassium carbonate may be skin irritants. Magnesium sulfate irritates eyes and the respiratory tract. Calcium chloride is moderately toxic. Wear chemical splash goggles, chemical-resistant gloves, and chemical-resistant aprons.

O/G/S/A Lab Interactive Worksheets

ELD SUPPORT

Speaking In small groups, students discuss how they designed and carried out the precipitate reaction in the Inquiry Lab.

- **Emerging/Beginning** Tell students to use phrases and short sentences to describe simple actions they took, such as "measured 2 grams of reactant."
- **Developing/Expanding** Tell students to take turns asking and answering questions about the Inquiry Lab.
- **Bridging** Have students complete the Expanding activity, using well-articulated comments.

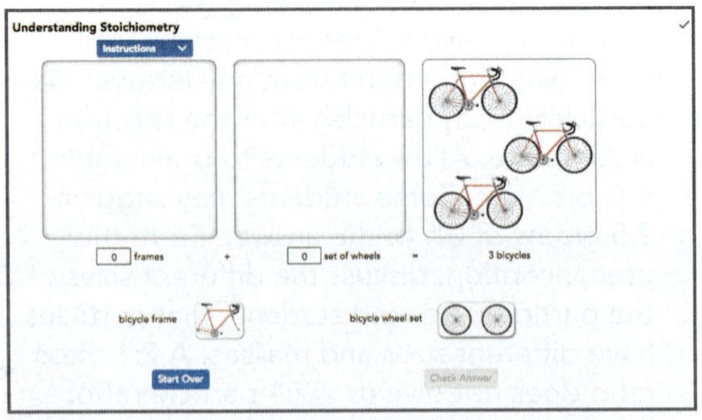

Interactivity: Understanding Stoichiometry

5. When you reach the answer, **ask** Why don't we just use milliseconds or hours to count all of our time?
6. Explain that chemistry has similar units that are more appropriate at certain times. Ask students to describe when they measure in moles and when in grams. How do they covert from one to the other?
7. Tell students that in this experience they will investigate ways to use units in chemistry, particularly in calculations. Transition the conversation to introduce the Inquiry Lab.

EXPLORE

Determination of Reaction Output

Inquiry Lab Students use stoichiometry calculations [SEP-5] to predict the mass of product in a reaction of sodium bicarbonate with heat. They then investigate [SEP-3] the reaction to assess the accuracy of their calculations.

Lab Demo Video Watch the Lab Demo Video for advice on materials and preparation.

Choose Your Version Open-ended (O), Guided (G), Shortened (S), Advanced (A)

Materials assigned reaction mixture (see the online Teacher Support page for possible combinations), distilled or deionized water, balance, 2 50-mL beakers, 150-mL beaker, Büchner funnel, 250-mL filter flask, filter paper, oven, stirring rod

Safety The chemicals in this lab can be moderately toxic and an irritant to the eyes, skin, and respiratory tract. Make sure students wear chemical splash goggles, chemical-resistant gloves, and chemical-resistant aprons and wash their hands thoroughly with soap and warm water after the lab.

Expected Outcome As long as the calculations are accurate and students have good lab technique, their theoretical yield should be very close to their actual yield.

Lab Summary Video Watch the Lab Summary Video for support on connecting the lab investigation to the Investigative Phenomenon.

ASSESS ON THE SPOT

Give students a selection of graphic organizers to choose from, or allow them to make their own. Tell them to devise a concept map that shows how their initial calculations are related to the reaction they carried out in the Inquiry Lab and their actual yield. Invite some students to share their concept maps with the class. Collect students' concept maps and assess gaps in understanding.

PROFESSIONAL DEVELOPMENT

Develop Classroom Collaboration Many students may see the Inquiry Lab (and stoichiometry in general) as a set of math problems, rather than a demonstration of a chemical phenomenon. Keep the chemistry on their radar by emphasizing that stoichiometry is necessary to reflect that matter is conserved in a chemical reaction [PS1.B]. During the Inquiry Lab, encourage groups to track where each type of atom appears in both reactants and products and to compare amounts of and ratios between types of atoms as they balance equations and predict amounts of product.

Understanding Stoichiometry

Interactivity In this interactivity, students use a model [SEP-2] to produce industrial-scale measures of ammonia. They are presented with a few different scenarios, and they choose the appropriate units from a selection provided, considering the scale and proportion [CCC-3] involved.

- Pair students and prompt them to review the first part of the interactivity (about tricycle stoichiometry), making notes and sketches, and recording any questions they have. Tell them to discuss any questions with each other or with another pair. Students should move on to the next section only when they have answered their questions.
- For the second part of the interactivity, tell pairs to have one person complete the first scenario and make choices, while the other person observes and provides hints. Then have students switch roles for the second scenario. They can continue alternating until they have completed all the questions.

EXPLAIN

Choose a Practical Unit

Modeling In this activity, students calculate **[SEP-5]** the mass and volume of a mole of propane and predict how much carbon dioxide is produced during 20 hours of grilling. They make a flowchart model **[SEP-2]** to analyze the relationships between units of moles, mass, and volume, using an amount of propane gas. Then they describe the advantages and disadvantages of using each unit (grams, liters, moles) by itself.

Choose from these strategies to guide students through the activity:

- Students can work in groups of four. Offer them colored pens and paper, and instruct them to create visual models large enough to share with another group. Tell students to take turns presenting their models to the group. After the presentations, students should note any revisions they would like to make to their models.
- Hang the models around the room and let students peruse them. Then, as a class, discuss strengths of different models. Remind students to make notes of any additional revisions they would make to their models.

Stoichiometry Calculations

Animation In this animation, students are guided through the steps of converting between mass and moles to determine the mass or moles of product produced in a reaction **[PS1.B]**.

- Before students view the animation, prepare five problems for students to solve (e.g., "A reacts with B to form C. If you start with 20 g of A, how much C will you get?" Tell them to balance the equation if necessary).
- Watch the animation as a class and make a list of steps for converting from one unit to another.
- Pair students and give the class the first problem to solve. Remind students to follow the conversion steps. Replay the animation for additional support.
- Ask a pair of volunteers to write their solution on the board, and invite classmates to ask questions. Do the same with the four remaining problems.

INTEGRATE MATH

Conversion Ask students to describe how they would calculate the number of students in 8 classes. Explain that they are converting from what they know (the number of classes) to what they do not know (the total number of students). Prompt students to make this familiar conversion by considering proportions and cancelling units:

$$\frac{32 \text{ students}}{1 \text{ class}} \times 8 \text{ classes} = 256 \text{ students}$$

As a class, discuss other everyday examples, and note how they are similar to converting from grams to moles.

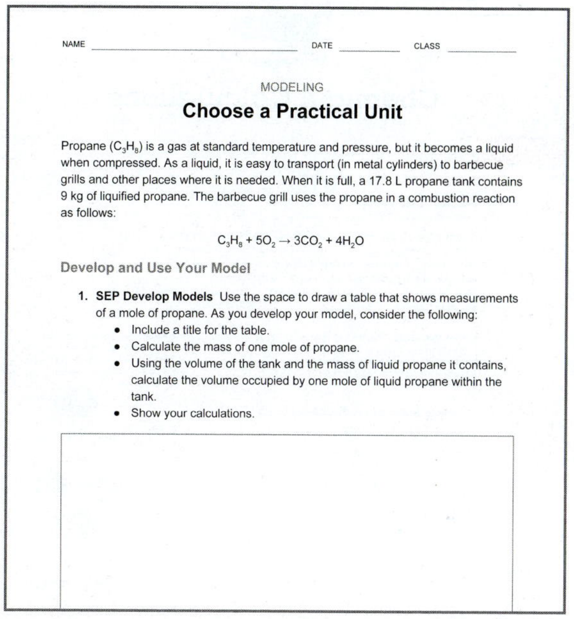

NAME ______ DATE ______ CLASS ______

MODELING

Choose a Practical Unit

Propane (C_3H_8) is a gas at standard temperature and pressure, but it becomes a liquid when compressed. As a liquid, it is easy to transport (in metal cylinders) to barbecue grills and other places where it is needed. When it is full, a 17.8 L propane tank contains 9 kg of liquified propane. The barbecue grill uses the propane in a combustion reaction as follows:

$$C_3H_8 + 5O_2 \rightarrow 3CO_2 + 4H_2O$$

Develop and Use Your Model

1. **SEP Develop Models** Use the space to draw a table that shows measurements of a mole of propane. As you develop your model, consider the following:
   - Include a title for the table.
   - Calculate the mass of one mole of propane.
   - Using the volume of the tank and the mass of liquid propane it contains, calculate the volume occupied by one mole of liquid propane within the tank.
   - Show your calculations.

Modeling Activity Interactive Worksheet

CLASSROOM MODIFICATIONS

Based on your students' abilities and your schedule, you may wish to edit the Choose a Practical Unit worksheet to make it more open ended or more guided.

- **More Open Ended** Allow students to choose from a variety of hydrocarbon fuels. Tell them to research the density of that fuel as a liquid and determine an appropriate-size tank for 20 L of fuel.
- **More Guided** Provide students with a skeletal outline for the flowchart and include areas to place calculations.

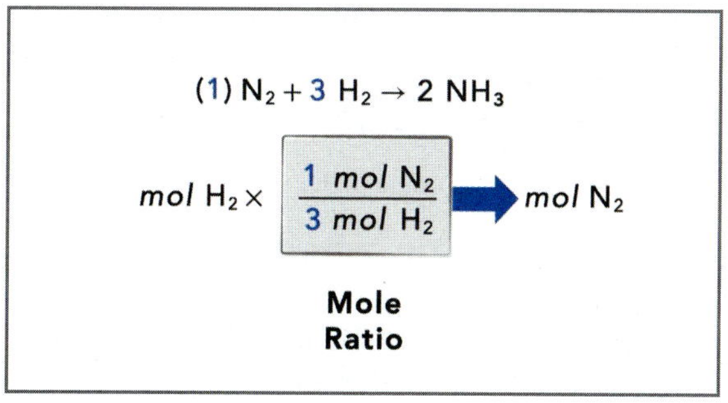

Animation: Stoichiometry Calculations

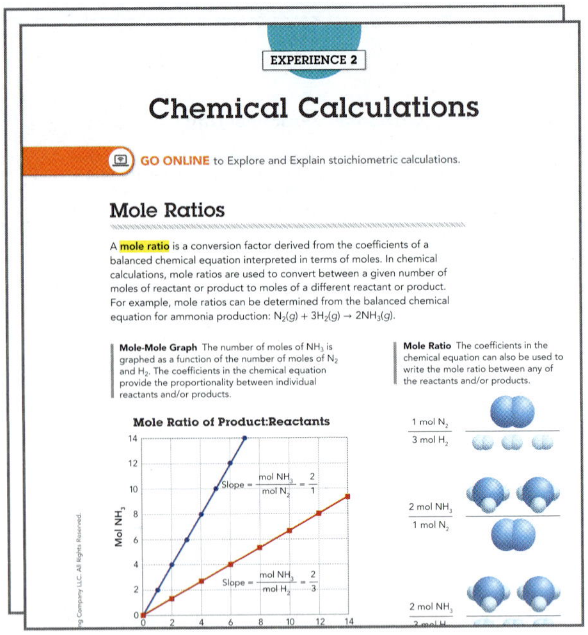

EXPERIENCE 2

Chemical Calculations

GO ONLINE to Explore and Explain stoichiometric calculations.

Mole Ratios

A mole ratio is a conversion factor derived from the coefficients of a balanced chemical equation interpreted in terms of moles. In chemical calculations, mole ratios are used to convert between a given number of moles of reactant or product to moles of a different reactant or product. For example, mole ratios can be determined from the balanced chemical equation for ammonia production: $N_2(g) + 3H_2(g) \rightarrow 2NH_3(g)$.

Mole-Mole Graph The number of moles of NH_3 is graphed as a function of the number of moles of N_2 and H_2. The coefficients in the chemical equation provide the proportionality between individual reactants and/or products.

Mole Ratio The coefficients in the chemical equation can also be used to write the mole ratio between any of the reactants and/or products.

Experience Notebook, pp. 259–267

eTEXT

SAMPLE PROBLEM SUPPORT

Help students with calculating moles of a product by walking through Question 12, part b, on page 261 in the Experience Notebook. The amount of Al_2O_3 is given as 3.7 mol, so that is what you start with. The mole ratio can be found from the balanced equation.

$$3.7 \text{ mol } Al_2O_3 \times \frac{4 \text{ mol Al}}{2 \text{ mol } Al_2O_3} = 7.4 \text{ mol Al}$$

Assist students with calculating the mass of a product by walking through Question 14 on page 263. Start with 5.00 g CaC_2 (given). Find how many grams of C_2H_2 and CaC_2 equal a mole by looking at the atomic mass on the periodic table.

$$5.00 \text{ g } CaC_2 \times \frac{1 \text{ mol } CaC_2}{64.1 \text{ g } CaC_2} \times \frac{1 \text{ mol } C_2H_2}{1 \text{ mol } CaC_2} \times \frac{26.0 \text{ g } C_2H_2}{1 \text{ mol } C_2H_2} = 2.03 \text{ g } C_2H_2$$

Help students with calculating the volume of a product by walking through Question 16 on page 265. Start with 3.86 L CO (given). Make sure students use the conversion factor: 1 mol = 22.4 L.

$$3.86 \text{ L CO} \times \frac{1 \text{ mol CO}}{22.4 \text{ L CO}} \times \frac{1 \text{ mol } O_2}{2 \text{ mol CO}} \times \frac{22.4 \text{ L } O_2}{1 \text{ mol } O_2} = 1.93 \text{ L } O_2$$

Assist students with calculating the molecules of a product by walking through Question 18 on page 267. Start with 6.54 g $KClO_3$ (given). Make sure students use the conversion factor, 1 mol = 6.02×10^{23} molecules.

$$6.54 \text{ g } KClO_3 \times \frac{1 \text{ mol } KClO_3}{122.55 \text{ g } KClO_3} \times \frac{3 \text{ mol } O_2}{2 \text{ mol } KClO_3} \times \frac{6.02 \times 10^{23} \text{ molecules}}{1 \text{ mol } O_2} = 4.82 \times 10^{22} \text{ molecules}$$

Chemical Calculations

Experience Notebook Assign this section of the Experience Notebook or Realize Reader before having students work on any of the activities in the Elaborate portion of this experience. The background knowledge found here is vital for understanding those assignments.

Use the strategies below to help students better understand the content on the indicated pages.

- **Mole Ratios** (p. 259) Return to the sandwich-making demonstration that opened Experience 1. On the board, write the equation for the sandwich (2 slices of bread + 3 slices of meat + 1 slice of cheese = 1 sandwich). Have students make a graph similar to the one on the page using the ratios of sandwich ingredients. Pair students and tell them to write a sentence about what the information in the graph on the page tells them, and invite pairs to share with the class.
- **Mole–Mole Calculations** (pp. 260–261) Ask students to explain why, when given an amount of a substance, the moles of the wanted substance must be in the numerator. Then pair students and direct them to write a mole conversion problem for each of the two equations on page 261. Tell them to swap problems with a neighboring pair, solve them, and then gather as a group of four to discuss.
- **Mass–Mass Calculations** (pp. 262–263) Have students write problems using the ammonium and acetylene reactions. Offer one or two sample problems to be sure students know what the problem should include. Have students swap problems with a neighboring peer to solve. Encourage students to share with the class how they solved the problems.
- **Volume–Volume Calculations** (pp. 264–265) As a class, discuss and list the ways in which volume–volume calculations differ from and are similar to the previous two types of calculations. Remind students how to use a graph to determine the slope of a line. Then pair students and tell them to determine the slopes of the lines of product versus reactant for the formation of nitrogen monoxide on page 265. Call on two different pairs to share their results with the class.
- **A Roadmap for Solving Stoichiometric Problems** (pp. 266–267) Tell students to work individually to make a visual guide or flowchart to explain how to do unit conversions. Tell them the chart must include moles, molecules, volume, and mass. Group students in threes to share their visuals with each other. Tell students to make whatever revisions they would like to their visual. Then have them use their flowchart to work on some of the sample problems online.

DIFFERENTIATED INSTRUCTION

- **Support Less Proficient Readers** Encourage students to review the more graphical parts of each Experience Notebook page first and then take in the text. Tell them to circle words or phrases they do not understand, and then identify explanations in the graphical portions. When reading captions, tell students to match the wording in the caption to what they see in the images on the page.
- **Support Struggling Students** Tell students to review each page and write a two- or three-sentence summary of the information in their own words. Tell them to write annotations for graphs, describing what information the graph is conveying and how it relates to the chemical reaction it is describing. Offer models or manipulatives to any students who are finding the math confusing.

ASSESS ON THE SPOT

- Before students leave class, have them complete an exit card and use what they have learned about stoichiometric calculations to explain the following statement: Stoichiometric calculations are not possible without a balanced equation. (A chemical reaction's mole ratios are derived from the relationships between coefficients in a balanced chemical equation.)

ELABORATE

Evaluate a Practical Unit

Peer Review Rubric Students use the rubric as a scoring guide to evaluate **[SEP-8]** their classmates' explanations of propane units and how to convert between the different units.

- Group students in sets of three. Give each group a large manila envelope and a set of three rubrics. Tell groups to come up with a team name, write it on their envelope, and then put each group member's model inside.
- Have groups exchange envelopes. Tell each group to use a sticky note to assign a number to each model. Have group members collaborate on evaluating the models, using a new, appropriately numbered rubric sheet for each one. When groups are done, tell them to return the models and evaluations to the appropriate team.
- Before students look at their evaluations, ask each team to highlight something they thought was notable about at least one of the models they evaluated. Then tell students to look at their evaluations and make any revisions necessary to their models.

NAME ______ DATE ______ CLASS ______

PEER REVIEW RUBRIC

Evaluate a Practical Unit

Use this rubric to help you assess your classmates' explanations of propane units and how

	EXEMPLARY Score the work 3 if:	ACCOMPLISHED Score the work 2 if:	DEVELOPING Score the work 1 if:	
Components of the Model Score: ______	The model has accurate calculations. Both mass and volume per mole are included.	The model attempts to accurately calculate both the mass and volume per mole.	The model attempts to calculate either mass or volume per mole.	
Relationships Score: ______	The model is used appropriately to calculate relationships with hourly use and CO_2 production.	The model attempts to calculate relationships with both hourly use and CO_2 production.	The model attempts to calculate the relationship with either hourly use or CO_2 production.	
Connections Score: ______	The model makes sense and can be applied to build understanding of other systems in which different measurements are useful.	The model makes sense, but it is more specific to the use of propane and may not be applied to understand other systems of measurement.	The model is unclear and would not be effectively applied to understand other systems of measurement.	
Limitations of the Model Score: ______	Limitations of this model are described, including that different measurements are useful for different industries.	The explanation acknowledges that this model has limitations, though they are not clearly and specifically identified or described.	There is no acknowledgment that this model has limitations.	

Peer Review Rubric Interactive Worksheet

ASSESS ON THE SPOT

Divide the class into groups of three. Give students the reaction for the combustion of propane: $C_3H_8 + 5O_2 \rightarrow 4H_2O + 3CO_2$. Have students discuss what mass of carbon dioxide will be produced if 66 g of propane are used in the reactants. Tell groups to choose one student to write the first step in solving the equation and draw a line under what they have written, without input from group members. Tell a second student to write the second step and draw a line under that. They should not consider what the first student wrote, but only write their assigned step. The third student does the same with the third step. Once all three steps have been written, allow group members to confer until they think they have the correct answer. As a class, discuss the process of solving the problem, and address any questions students have.

A Scale That Reads Moles

Writing About Science In this activity, students conduct research and write about a potential new invention, a scale that can measure moles of a substance. In this scale, the number of moles refers to the number of particles under consideration. For example, if we place 18 g of water on the scale, the reading could be either 1 mole (of water molecules) or 3 moles (total number of H and O atoms).

- Allow students to work either individually or in pairs. Tell them to make notes about ideas that come to mind when they first consider the questions. Then encourage them to review the material they covered in Experiences 1 and 2, keeping the questions in mind and making notes that relate to the questions as they are gathering information. Suggest that they draft their responses from what they can find in the material they are reviewing. If a student feels the need to consult another source, help the student formulate the question to be answered.
- When students have finished writing, organize the class into small groups to discuss their responses. Invite groups to make a drawing, design document, or mock advertisement of their "mole scale" to show the class.

NAME ______ DATE ______ CLASS ______

WRITING ABOUT SCIENCE

A Scale That Reads Moles

A scientist has an idea for a new commercial product that will appeal to chemists and chemistry students. Her idea is to develop a scale that reports the amount of something in moles, instead of grams or other units of mass.

Use the information provided and information gathered from authoritative sources on your own to answer Questions 1 and 2.

Obtain and Evaluate Information

1. **SEP Construct an Explanation** Why would this scale be useful in chemistry?

2. **SEP Evaluate** What are the limitations of the scale? What features might allow it to function?

Writing About Science Interactive Worksheet

INTEGRATE THE THREE DIMENSIONS

In the Writing About Science activity, students use computational thinking **[SEP-5]** to explain why a scale **[CCC-3]** that reports the amount of something in moles would be useful in chemistry. Students should consider how this scale could be used to describe and predict specific chemical reactions **[PS1.B]**. Students evaluate **[SEP-8]** the limitations of the scale and then describe what features might allow it to function.

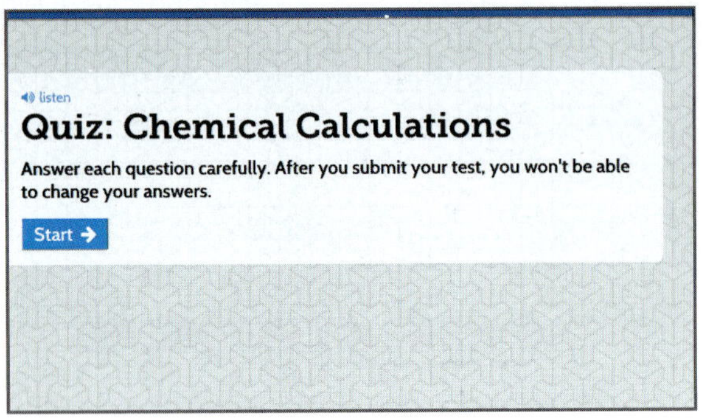

Interactive Online Quiz

Quiz Interactive Worksheet

EVALUATE

Chemical Calculations

Quiz Assign the quiz in online technology-enhanced, auto-graded format or as an editable quiz worksheet. Use the scoring notes and remediation strategies found online to assess students' responses and to provide targeted feedback for each item to remediate well before assigning the summative 3-D Assessment.

REMEDIATION SUGGESTIONS

- **If** students are struggling to describe mole ratios, **then** have them review the first part of the interactivity, Understanding Stoichiometry, in which they build a bicycle and compare the process to making a molecule.
- **If** students are struggling with the process of unit conversion, **then** have them review the second part of the interactivity, Understanding Stoichiometry. Students may also work with a partner and discuss the steps that are confusing when they convert units.
- **If** students are having trouble interpreting the graphs in the Experience Notebook, **then** suggest they make a chart to record *x* and *y* coordinates of the lines at various points to see the mathematical relationship between the two lines.
- **If** students feel overwhelmed by the math and Sample Problems in the Experience Notebook, **then** have them focus on one type of conversion at a time, beginning with moles of a product, and practice problems until they feel confident enough to move on.

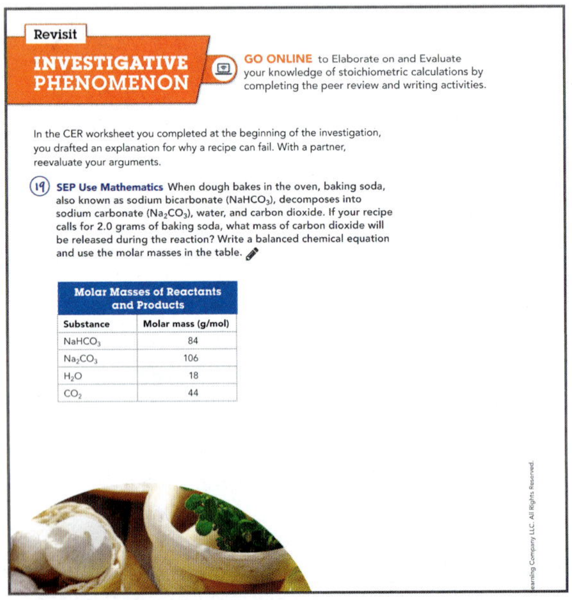
Revisit

INVESTIGATIVE PHENOMENON

GO ONLINE to Elaborate on and Evaluate your knowledge of stoichiometric calculations by completing the peer review and writing activities.

In the CER worksheet you completed at the beginning of the investigation, you drafted an explanation for why a recipe can fail. With a partner, reevaluate your arguments.

(19) **SEP Use Mathematics** When dough bakes in the oven, baking soda, also known as sodium bicarbonate ($NaHCO_3$), decomposes into sodium carbonate (Na_2CO_3), water, and carbon dioxide. If your recipe calls for 2.0 grams of baking soda, what mass of carbon dioxide will be released during the reaction? Write a balanced chemical equation and use the molar masses in the table.

Molar Masses of Reactants and Products

Substance	Molar mass (g/mol)
$NaHCO_3$	84
Na_2CO_3	106
H_2O	18
CO_2	44

Experience Notebook, p. 268

eTEXT

Revisit
INVESTIGATIVE PHENOMENON

Support Reflection Students can complete the reflection prompt, where they will unpack and make sense of the Investigative Phenomenon, based on practices and understandings that have been reinforced over the course of the experience.

- Ask students if they are comfortable completing various chemical calculations that involve moles, volume, and mass.
- Have students work with a partner and summarize how chemical calculations are important in making sure recipes do not fail.

Further Develop Your CER Argument Have students add any evidence they have collected in this experience. Evidence may include the concept that substituting one mass or volume of an ingredient for another may not take into account molar mass and mole ratios of ingredients.

EXPERIENCE 3

Limiting Reagent and Percent Yield

Teacher Background

In Experience 3, students apply their stoichiometric skills to determine the limiting reactant in a reaction, after which they calculate and explain the percent yield. They begin with a hands-on Inquiry Lab followed by a Virtual Lab, both of which explore how the amount of product increases and then flattens out, as one reagent is first limiting and then in excess. The experience continues to review these concepts from a variety of angles, prompting students to complete problems and explain the answers. Finally, students apply the concept of a limiting reactant to the design of a rocket that will be launched using a reaction between baking soda and vinegar. Along the way, be sure that students continue to see the larger picture of the math describing and quantifying a phenomenon that occurs during chemical reactions.

Objectives

- **Explain the concept of limiting reactant and how it affects the amount of product produced in a reaction.**
- **Explain theoretical and actual yield and why the former is usually larger than the latter.**
- **Use computational thinking to predict the grams of product given the grams of reactant.**

ENGAGE

EVERYDAY PHENOMENON

What is the limiting reagent?

Use the teacher demo to prompt discussion about limiting reagents for the reaction that occurs when a candle burns.

Stop the Burn

Engage students with this demonstration of a burning candle in a bell jar to introduce the concept of limiting reactants.

Materials candle, nonflammable surface, bell jar, match

1. Invite a volunteer to write on the board the balanced combustion equation that occurs when a candle burns: $2\ C_{18}H_{38} + 55\ O_2 \rightarrow 36\ CO_2 + 38\ H_2O$.
2. Place the candle on the nonflammable surface and light it. Allow it to burn for a minute or two to demonstrate that it continues to burn.
3. Place the bell jar over the burning candle. Have students observe the candle until the flame goes out.
4. Point to the combustion equation on the board and ask what two reactants must be available for the candle to burn. Explain that when the bell jar was placed over the candle, the amount of oxygen became limited. Not enough oxygen was available to react with all of the candle wax. Explain that oxygen was a limiting reagent and that students will learn more about limiting reagents in the Inquiry Lab.
5. Ask students what they think the result would be if a cake batter had an insufficient amount of an ingredient.

RELATED PHENOMENA

In addition to Stop the Burn teacher demo, consider using other phenomena to launch this experience.

- **Cakes with More or Less** Write this reaction that occurs in cake batter: baking soda + cream of tartar + water → carbon dioxide. Tell students that this reaction is what causes cake to rise: the CO_2 produces bubbles in the batter. Discuss how using more or less of baking soda or cream of tartar that is called for in the recipe would affect the resulting cake.
- **Tickets to a Show** Present this scenario: You want to buy as many tickets as you can to an upcoming show. The tickets are $15 and you have $50. **Ask** How many tickets can you buy? Explain that the money is the limiting reactant, even though you will have some left over. If the show were sold out except for two tickets, the tickets would be limiting.

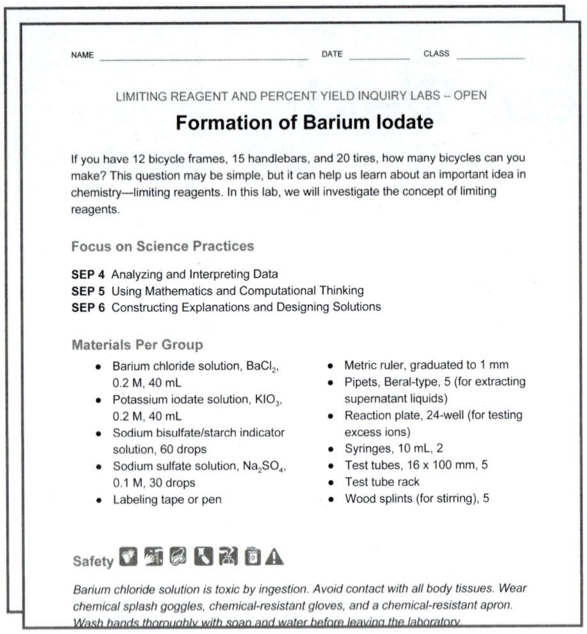

NAME ______________ DATE ________ CLASS ________

LIMITING REAGENT AND PERCENT YIELD INQUIRY LABS – OPEN

Formation of Barium Iodate

If you have 12 bicycle frames, 15 handlebars, and 20 tires, how many bicycles can you make? This question may be simple, but it can help us learn about an important idea in chemistry—limiting reagents. In this lab, we will investigate the concept of limiting reagents.

Focus on Science Practices

SEP 4 Analyzing and Interpreting Data
SEP 5 Using Mathematics and Computational Thinking
SEP 6 Constructing Explanations and Designing Solutions

Materials Per Group

- Barium chloride solution, $BaCl_2$, 0.2 M, 40 mL
- Potassium iodate solution, KIO_3, 0.2 M, 40 mL
- Sodium bisulfate/starch indicator solution, 60 drops
- Sodium sulfate solution, Na_2SO_4, 0.1 M, 30 drops
- Labeling tape or pen
- Metric ruler, graduated to 1 mm
- Pipets, Beral-type, 5 (for extracting supernatant liquids)
- Reaction plate, 24-well (for testing excess ions)
- Syringes, 10 mL, 2
- Test tubes, 16 x 100 mm, 5
- Test tube rack
- Wood splints (for stirring), 5

Safety

Barium chloride solution is toxic by ingestion. Avoid contact with all body tissues. Wear chemical splash goggles, chemical-resistant gloves, and a chemical-resistant apron. Wash hands thoroughly with soap and water before leaving the laboratory.

O/G/S/A Lab Interactive Worksheets

EXPLORE

Formation of Barium Iodate

Inquiry Lab In this lab, students vary the amounts of either Ba^{2+} or IO_3^- to evaluate limiting reagents and how the mole ratio **[SEP-5]** between the reactants **[PS1.B]** plays a role.

Lab Demo Video Watch the Lab Demo Video for advice on materials and preparation.

Choose Your Version Open-ended (O), Guided (G), Shortened (S), Advanced (A)

Materials 40 mL 0.2*M* barium chloride solution, 40 mL 0.2*M* potassium iodate solution, 60 drops sodium bisulfate/starch indicator solution, 30 drops 0.1*M* sodium sulfate solution, labeling tape or pen, metric ruler, 5 Beral-type pipets (for extracting supernatant liquids), 24-well reaction plate (for testing excess ions), 2 10-mL syringes, 5 16 × 100 mm test tubes, test tube rack, 5 wood splints (for stirring)

Safety Tell students that barium chloride solution is toxic by ingestion and that they should avoid contact with all body tissues. Students should wear chemical splash goggles, chemical-resistant gloves, and a chemical-resistant apron. Remind students to wash their hands thoroughly with soap and warm water before leaving the laboratory.

Expected Outcome In Stage 1, when the volume of barium exceeds that of the iodate, the barium will be in excess and the height of the precipitate will be greater. In Stage 2, students will need to conclude to hold the volume of barium constant. The barium will remain in excess until the volume of iodate is twice that of barium.

Lab Summary Video Watch the Lab Summary Video for support on connecting the lab investigation to the Investigative Phenomenon.

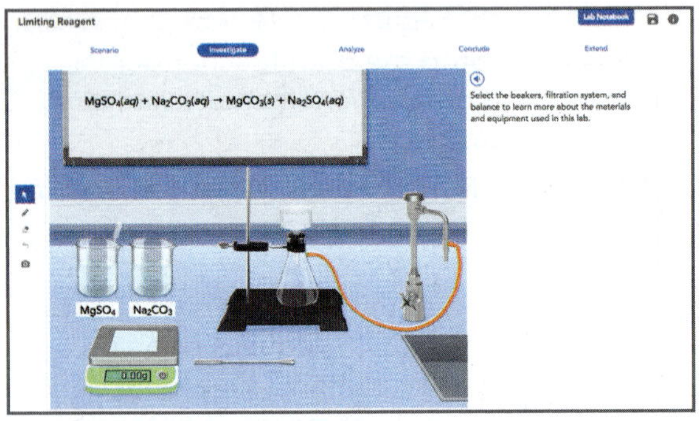

Virtual Lab: Limiting Reagent

Limiting Reagent

Virtual Lab In this Virtual Lab, students investigate **[SEP-3]** the concept of gold in the ocean and whether dissolved gold can be changed into solid gold. They explore the reaction **[PS1.B]** between magnesium sulfate and sodium carbonate by analyzing data **[SEP-4]** on a graph generated by the choices they make in the lab.

- Using a projector, demonstrate the lab to students, asking them to draw parallels between this Virtual Lab and the Inquiry Lab they carried out earlier. Then tell students to work on their own to complete the lab, making notes in their science notebooks.
- When students have finished, pair them to discuss their results and conclusions. Tell pairs to compose a paragraph that summarizes the key points in this lab and relates this lab to the previous one.

CLASSROOM MODIFICATIONS

Based on your students' abilities and your schedule, you may wish to edit the Virtual Lab to be more open ended or more guided.

- **More Open Ended** Instead of providing a procedure for determining how adding different amounts of magnesium sulfate to sodium carbonate affects the mass of solid magnesium carbonate that formed, have students determine that on their own.
- **More Guided** Provide students with a data table with the data filled in for $MgSO_4$ added (mL) and $MgCO_3$ produced (g). Define the relationship between the two and discuss it with students.

ASSESS ON THE SPOT

Tell students to write a short journal entry in their science notebooks that explains what they did and learned in the Inquiry and Virtual Labs. Collect the notebooks entries and review them to gauge understanding.

INTEGRATE MATH

Unit Conversions As students are working their way through the Virtual Lab, tell them to calculate the number of moles of each reactant being used at each point and the mass of product produced. Have them make a graph of moles of Na versus moles of NaCl produced. Tell them to determine the point in the lab at which moles of reactant have reached the proper ratio so that all of the reactant is used up. Remind them to make notes and do these calculations in their science notebooks.

EXPLAIN

A Measure of Success

Claim-Evidence-Reasoning In this activity, students construct an explanation [SEP-6] about the percent yield of a decomposition reaction [PS1.B] of potassium chlorate ($KCLO_3$). Students should support their claims with observed evidence and scientific reasoning.

- Review the concepts of theoretical, actual, and percent yield from the Inquiry and Virtual Labs. Give everyday examples, such as a cookie recipe that claimed to yield 30 cookies but only produced 28.
- Emphasize to students that their CERs should include calculations and explanations of how error arises. Remind them that experimental error is different from human error.
- You may wish to select some peers in the class to answer questions for students who are stuck or intimidated by the math. You could allow these peers to help their classmates one-on-one, or consult with them in small groups where students can ask questions and hear responses to their peers' questions as well.

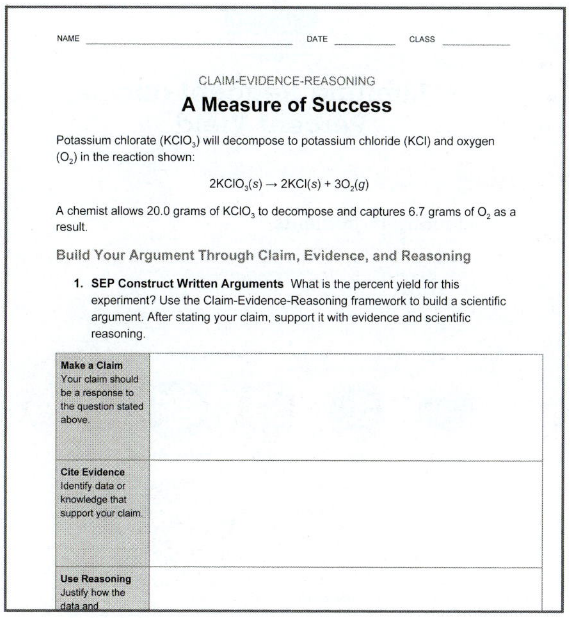
NAME ________ DATE ________ CLASS ________

CLAIM-EVIDENCE-REASONING

A Measure of Success

Potassium chlorate ($KClO_3$) will decompose to potassium chloride (KCl) and oxygen (O_2) in the reaction shown:

$$2KClO_3(s) \rightarrow 2KCl(s) + 3O_2(g)$$

A chemist allows 20.0 grams of $KClO_3$ to decompose and captures 6.7 grams of O_2 as a result.

Build Your Argument Through Claim, Evidence, and Reasoning

1. **SEP Construct Written Arguments** What is the percent yield for this experiment? Use the Claim-Evidence-Reasoning framework to build a scientific argument. After stating your claim, support it with evidence and scientific reasoning.

Make a Claim Your claim should be a response to the question stated above.	
Cite Evidence Identify data or knowledge that support your claim.	
Use Reasoning Justify how the data and	

CER Interactive Worksheet

PROFESSIONAL DEVELOPMENT

Science and Engineering Notebooks Throughout this experience, encourage students to use their science notebooks to record problem-solving techniques, make sketches, and use writing to connect concepts. Prompt students to consider how the concepts of mole ratio and theoretical yield are connected. Remind students that this experience involves many types of calculations. Tell them to make a chart or table to keep track of the types of calculations and examples of each. Point out that this type of chart will be very useful for them when solving problems.

ELD SUPPORT

Selecting Language Resources In pairs, students provide written responses affirming their general understanding about the percent yield of a reaction in the CER activity.

- **Emerging/Beginning** Have students make a list of words and phrases that are specific to the concepts in the CER activity. Tell them to discuss meanings of these words and phrases, using context and word cognates to help them with vocabulary they are uncertain about.
- **Developing/Expanding** Have students make a list of words and phrases they know that relate to the percent yield of a reaction. Tell them to review meanings of each phrase and discuss how they might use it to support their CER.
- **Bridging** Challenge students to use scientific and academic language by giving them a word limit for sections on their CER. Encourage them to use concise phrasings that convey complex ideas to support their CER.

Limiting Reagent and Percent Yield

Experience Notebook Assign this section of the Experience Notebook or Realize Reader before having students work on any of the activities in the Elaborate portion of this experience. The background knowledge found here is vital for understanding those assignments.

Use the strategies below to help students better understand the content on the indicated pages.

- **Limiting Ingredients** (p. 269) Prompt students to think about limiting factors by applying them to scenarios they have already encountered in this investigation—tricycles, recipes, and any demonstrations you have done. Then shift to chemical equations. Provide students with a few reactions with 1:1 molar ratios. Ask students to tell you the limiting reactant and explain why it is limiting.
- **Limiting and Excess Reagents** (p. 270) Review the bicycle model. Then pair students and tell them to refer to the diagram for the production of ammonia to determine the limiting and excess reactant, and how much excess reactant there is in these two scenarios:

  a. start with 10 moles of N_2 and 10 moles of H_2

  b. start with 6 moles of N_2 and 5 moles of H_2
- **Mass of Products and Reactants** (p. 271) As a class, review mole–mass conversions. Explain to students that they can apply these calculations to scenarios such as the ones they were given for the previous page. Have students work in pairs to determine the limiting and excess reactants in these scenarios:

  a. start with 14 g of N_2 and 14 g of H_2

  b. start with 42 g of N_2 and 8 g of H_2

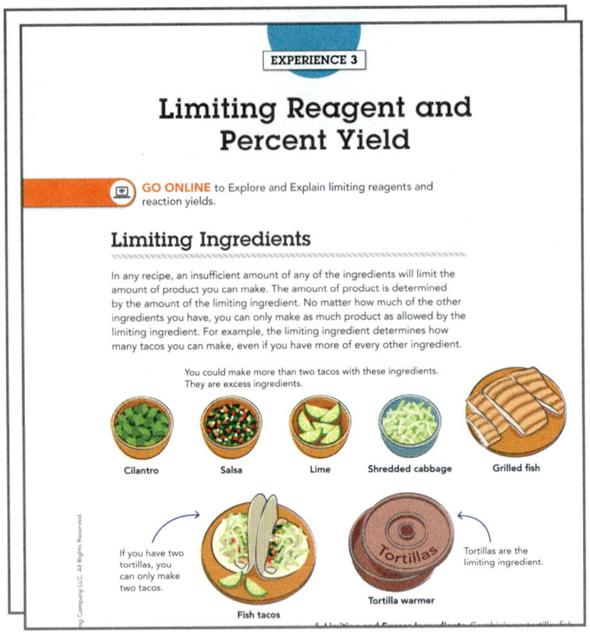
EXPERIENCE 3

Limiting Reagent and Percent Yield

GO ONLINE to Explore and Explain limiting reagents and reaction yields.

Limiting Ingredients

In any recipe, an insufficient amount of any of the ingredients will limit the amount of product you can make. The amount of product is determined by the amount of the limiting ingredient. No matter how much of the other ingredients you have, you can only make as much product as allowed by the limiting ingredient. For example, the limiting ingredient determines how many tacos you can make, even if you have more of every other ingredient.

Experience Notebook, pp. 269–277

eTEXT

SAMPLE PROBLEM SUPPORT

When taking students through the Sample Problems in the Experience Notebook, introduce each with a real-life example. Work the computation visually, using tricycles, and then introduce the chemical reaction. With each new calculation, refer to the previous problem(s) to show how each new problem builds on what was done in the previous one.

Make a visual model of the reaction and use circles and arrows to show how parts of the equation are related to the atoms and molecules in the reaction. Color-code the model if possible.

Virtual Nerd Video: How Do You Figure Out a Percent From a Part to Whole Ratio?

PhET Simulation: Reactants, Products, and Leftovers

CONNECT TO CAREERS

Food Chemist Food chemists are professionals who specialize in developing recipes by considering quantities and proportions of chemicals. Explain that many of the packaged foods students may eat every day contain flavor mixtures and chemicals that affect how the food looks and tastes. A food chemist will often test many different proportions of ingredients to see how changes in the chemistry affect the food product. Tell students to choose one processed food and to research what kind of knowledge a chemist developing that food would need.

- **Sample Problem Support** (pp. 273 and 276) If students have difficulty with part b of Question 24 on page 273, walk them through it. Explain that they should start with 2.7 moles of C_2H_4 (given) and multiply that by the ratio of moles of H_2O over moles of C_2H_4 from the balanced equation (2/1).

  $$2.7 \text{ mol } C_2H_4 \times \frac{2 \text{ mol } H_2O}{1 \text{ mol } C_2H_4} = 5.4 \text{ mol } H_2O$$

  If students have trouble with calculating theoretical yield on page 276, walk them through Question 27. Begin with 84.8 g Fe_2O_3 (given). Find how many grams of Fe_2O_3 and Fe equal a mole by using the atomic mass on the periodic table.

  $$84.8 \text{ g } Fe_2O_3 \times \frac{1 \text{ mol } Fe_2O_3}{159.7 \text{ g } Fe_2O_3} \times \frac{2 \text{ mol Fe}}{1 \text{ mol } Fe_2O_3} \times \frac{55.8 \text{ g Fe}}{1 \text{ mol Fe}} = 59.3 \text{ g Fe}$$

- **Percent Yield** (pp. 274–277) Return to the bicycle model. Have students describe the theoretical yield if you have 12 frames, 24 pedals, and 36 wheels. Then have them describe what the actual yield would be if a friend comes along and takes two of the pedals for a project of his or her own. Pair students and tell them to review the Sample Problem on page 277, and explain how they would calculate and explain the percent yield of tricycles. Ask pairs for their answers and discuss any questions students have.

DIFFERENTIATED INSTRUCTION

- **Support Special Needs Students** To help students integrate the mathematical concepts, have them work through a practice problem in pairs, using colored pens or pencils. Practice problem: A reaction with a calculated yield of 9.23 g produced 7.89 g of product. What is the percent yield of the reaction? (85.5%)
- **Support Less Proficient Readers** Encourage students to first focus on the graphic on page 270 of the Experience Notebook. Tell them to write or say aloud an explanation of what the graphic is showing. Then tell them to look through the text for phrases that describe the graphic, using the image to support their understanding.
- **Support Advanced Students** Invite students to choose one of the online problems and make a 3-D model of it, which they can then present to classmates or use as a peer tutor to support students who are more challenged by the material.

ASSESS ON THE SPOT

As students work on practice problems, take a quick survey using hand signals to gauge understanding.
Thumbs up = I've got this.
Thumbs down = I'm frustrated and confused.
Hand flat, palm down = I'm ok, but have questions.
Work with frustrated students while having those who gave thumbs up answer questions for others.

How Do You Figure Out a Percent From a Part to Whole Ratio?

Virtual Nerd Video Use this video tutorial to reinforce word problems, ratios, and percentages.

Reactants, Products, and Leftovers

PhET Simulation Use this interactive game to help reinforce the concept of limiting and excess reagents.

ELABORATE

Evaluate Error

Discussion Rubric In this activity, students discuss [SEP-8] why percent yield is different from theoretical yield. Then they use the rubric as a scoring guide to assess their evaluation of theoretical yield compared to actual yield.

- Have students work in groups of three or four. Give groups 5 minutes to discuss the questions below.
  a. Why percent yield is usually less than theoretical yield
  b. What might cause percent yield to be higher than theoretical yield
  c. Why experimental error and uncertainties always occur in scientific experiments
  d. The difference between human and experimental error
- After the discussions, each student should write the group's answers as they understand them. Then they can use the rubric to assess their own understanding.

NAME ______________ DATE ________ CLASS ________

DISCUSSION RUBRIC

Evaluate Error

Use this rubric to help you assess your evaluation of theoretical yield compared

	EXEMPLARY Score the work 3 if:	ACCOMPLISHED Score the work 2 if:
Claims and Evidence Student Score: ____ Teacher Score: ____	Percent yield is clearly described, and multiple sources of experimental error, which can lead to differences between the expected and actual yield, are identified.	Percent yield is described, and at least one source of experimental error is identified.
Evaluation and Critique Student Score: ____ Teacher Score: ____	Argument acknowledges that there is always some experimental error in scientific experiments.	Argument acknowledges experimental error but may not discuss its universal existence.
Reasoning and Synthesis Student Score: ____ Teacher Score: ____	Expert-acknowledged sources of error are used to enhance the discussion. It is understood that scientists are not always negligent if errors occur, and that experimental errors are not the same as the kind of errors caused by negligence; what seem to be experimental errors may even lead to new discoveries.	While logical sources of error are discussed, there is a belief that experimental error comes from inept scientists.

Discussion Rubric Interactive Worksheet

Build a Film Canister Rocket

Engineering Design Challenge In this activity, students apply their knowledge of chemical reactions [PS1.B], stoichiometry, and conservation of mass [CCC-5] to design [ETS1.C] and launch a film canister rocket 1 m high using a specific ratio of reactants as fuel.

Materials 5 g sodium bicarbonate, 15 mL vinegar per trial, balance, film canister with cap, manila folder, meterstick, scissors, spatula, tape or glue, timer, large tray, weighing dish or paper, colored markers (optional), paper clips (optional), tissue paper (optional)

Expected Outcome The highest-launching rockets will have a large ratio between the rocket's weight and the mass of baking soda.

Safety Sodium bicarbonate may be harmful if swallowed. Instruct students to wear chemical splash goggles, chemical-resistant gloves, and a chemical-resistant apron. Make sure students wash their hands thoroughly with soap and warm water before leaving the laboratory.

Use the following strategies to guide students as they complete steps in the Engineering Design Challenge.

Step 1 When defining the problem, encourage students to include all of the information they must discern. For example, how much will the rocket weigh? How much fuel is needed to launch that weight of rocket? Their definition of the problem may include more than one step or problem to solve.

Step 3 Remind students to use authoritative sources and to keep a record of all of their sources.

Step 4 Remind uncertain students that they should do their best to get their design correct but should also expect to have to make adjustments and do several trials. They do not have to get the perfect design on their first try.

NAME ______________ DATE ________ CLASS ________

ENGINEERING DESIGN CHALLENGE

Build a Film Canister Rocket

Design and launch a film canister rocket that will fly at least one meter into the air using a specific ratio of reactants as fuel. Combine your knowledge of chemical reactions, stoichiometry, and the law of conservation of mass to create and analyze your rocket.

Focus on Engineering Practices

SEP 1 Asking Questions and Defining Problems
SEP 3 Planning and Carrying Out Investigations
SEP 6 Constructing Explanations and Designing Solutions

Materials Per Group

- Sodium bicarbonate, $NaHCO_3$, 5 g
- Vinegar, 15 mL per trial
- Balance, 0.1 g precision
- Film canister with cap
- Manila folder
- Markers, colored (optional)
- Meter stick
- Paper clips (optional)
- Scissors
- Spatula
- Tape or glue
- Timer
- Tissue paper (optional)
- Tray, large
- Weighing dish or paper

Safety

Sodium bicarbonate may be harmful if swallowed. Wear chemical splash goggles, chemical-resistant gloves, and a chemical-resistant apron. Wash hands thoroughly with soap and water before leaving the laboratory. Please follow all laboratory safety guidelines.

Engineering Design Challenge Interactive Worksheet

ASSESS ON THE SPOT

Tell student groups that their task at the end of this experience is to come up with a question that will stump you. Divide students into small groups or use the groups that were working together on the Engineering Design Challenge. Explain that each group must come up with a question and the answer to it, and then pose their question to you. Then have groups ask their questions. You may wish to introduce this activity at the end of the previous class period or at the beginning of this one, to help students start thinking of questions to pose.

INTEGRATE THE THREE DIMENSIONS

In the Engineering Design Challenge, students conduct an investigation [SEP-3] to determine the correct ratio [CCC-3] of ingredients to design [ETS1.C] and launch a film canister rocket 1 m high. Students consider the proportional nature of chemical reactions [PS1.B] and how it governs the amount of product produced, and therefore, the amount of fuel that will be required to launch the rocket.

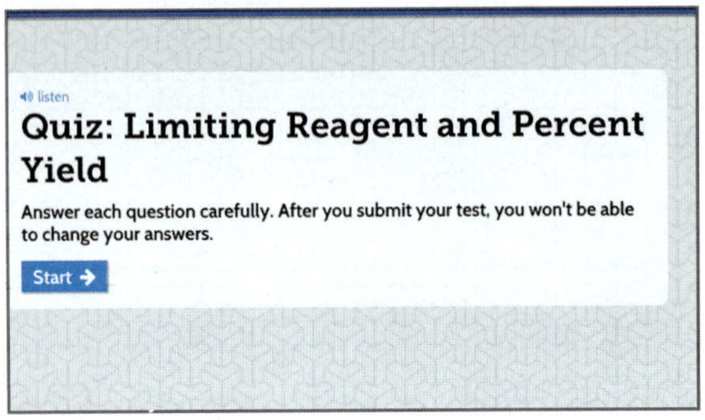

Interactive Online Quiz

Quiz Interactive Worksheet

EVALUATE

Limiting Reagent and Percent Yield

Quiz Assign the quiz in online technology-enhanced, auto-graded format or as an editable quiz worksheet. Use the scoring notes and remediation strategies found online to assess students' responses and to provide targeted feedback for each item to remediate well before assigning the summative 3-D Assessment.

REMEDIATION SUGGESTIONS

- **If** students are struggling to revise their explanations about the percent yield of a reaction, **then** tell them to review their Experience Notebooks and labs for additional support.
- **If** students are struggling with the concepts of limiting reactant in the Experience Notebook, **then** tell them to review the Inquiry and Virtual Labs to connect their reactions with the graphs that they made.
- **If** students are challenged by the CER and Discussion Rubric, **then** tell them to review the Sample Problems and page 275 in the Experience Notebook.
- **If** students are struggling to design a rocket that will fly a meter in the Engineering Design Challenge, **then** refer them to the Experience Notebook to consider the effect of having vinegar as the limiting reactant versus baking soda.

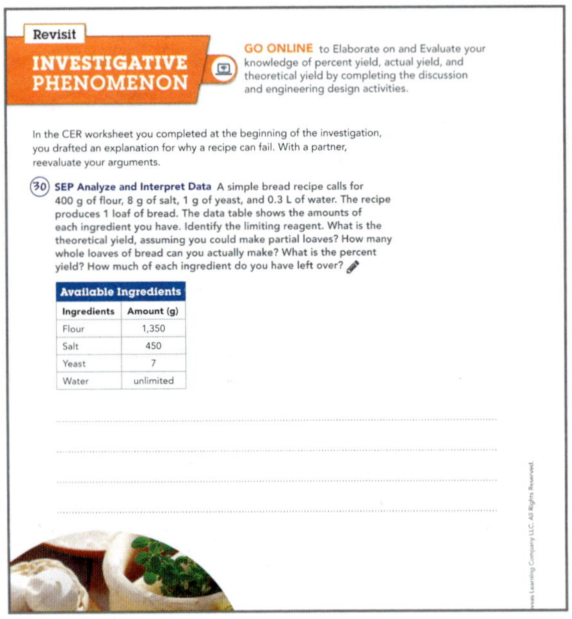
Revisit
INVESTIGATIVE PHENOMENON

GO ONLINE to Elaborate on and Evaluate your knowledge of percent yield, actual yield, and theoretical yield by completing the discussion and engineering design activities.

In the CER worksheet you completed at the beginning of the investigation, you drafted an explanation for why a recipe can fail. With a partner, reevaluate your arguments.

30 **SEP Analyze and Interpret Data** A simple bread recipe calls for 400 g of flour, 8 g of salt, 1 g of yeast, and 0.3 L of water. The recipe produces 1 loaf of bread. The data table shows the amounts of each ingredient you have. Identify the limiting reagent. What is the theoretical yield, assuming you could make partial loaves? How many whole loaves of bread can you actually make? What is the percent yield? How much of each ingredient do you have left over?

Available Ingredients

Ingredients	Amount (g)
Flour	1,350
Salt	450
Yeast	7
Water	unlimited

Experience Notebook, p. 278

eTEXT

Revisit

INVESTIGATIVE PHENOMENON

Support Reflection Students can complete the reflection prompt, where they will unpack and make sense of the Investigative Phenomenon, based on practices and understandings that have been reinforced over the course of the experience.

- Ask students how comfortable they are determining limiting reagents. On the board, work through a few more examples solving for the unknown limiting reagent. Ask students to tie in how limiting reagents are determined in recipes.
- Have students summarize differences between calculating theoretical and percent yield. Make sure students have a complete grasp of the two different yields.

Evaluate and Revise Your CER Argument Have students answer Questions 3 and 4 in the CER activity and re-evaluate the claim they made. Students should add any additional evidence they have collected in this investigation and revise their CER. Evidence may include a limiting reactant shift in the recipe as the result of the change, or errors in measurement that result in less of the product than expected.

EVALUATE

Stoichiometry

3-D Assessment For a summative assessment of Investigation 7, assign the 3-D Assessment, which is available online, as an ExamView bank, or as an editable worksheet.

The Stoichiometry of Filling a Balloon

Performance-Based Assessment Use this Performance-Based Assessment to assess students' mastery of the standards. In this activity, students determine the amount of sodium bicarbonate to add to acetic acid to produce a specific amount of carbon dioxide gas. Students use mathematical and computational thinking [SEP-5] to calculate the mass of sodium carbonate needed to produce certain moles of carbon dioxide gas and to calculate moles of acetic acid used in their experiment. They identify patterns [CCC-1] and interpret their data [SEP-4]. They use the results to determine which reactant is the limiting reagent and which is in excess in the reaction [PS1.B]. They design a solution [SEP-6] for how to measure the amount of carbon dioxide produced in the reaction to determine whether the reaction went to completion. They construct an explanation on how the experiment would be changed if it were carried out with a different substance instead.

Safety Acetic acid is a skin and eye irritant. Make sure students avoid contact with eyes and skin. Students should wear chemical splash goggles, chemical-resistant gloves, and a chemical-resistant apron. Remind students to wash their hands thoroughly with soap and warm water before leaving the laboratory.

Expected Outcome The balloon size should increase fairly uniformly for flasks 1–4 and then stay constant. It may be hard to tell the difference between flasks 3, 4, 5, and 6. The limiting reagent is sodium bicarbonate for the first three flasks and acetic acid for the remaining three.

Experience Notebook (p. 279) After students complete the Performance-Based Assessment, have them complete the reflection prompt in the Experience Notebook.

DIFFERENTIATED INSTRUCTION

- **Support Struggling Students** Struggling students may have difficulty completing the stoichiometry math involved in the Performance-Based Assessment. Have an advanced student help them with the parts they are having difficulty on.
- **Support Advanced Students** Have advanced students add an additional flask (flask 7) to their lab. This flask should be greater than flask 6, which has 0.036 theoretical moles of carbon dioxide produced. Alternatively, advanced students can expand upon the design of the solution by listing criteria and constraints.

How can we produce better foods?

Revisit Anchoring Phenomenon At the end of Investigation 7, have students revisit the Anchoring Phenomenon question about how to produce better foods. Lead a class discussion about limiting ingredients (reagents) of food dishes. Prompt students to relate those responses to explain how foods can be produced better.

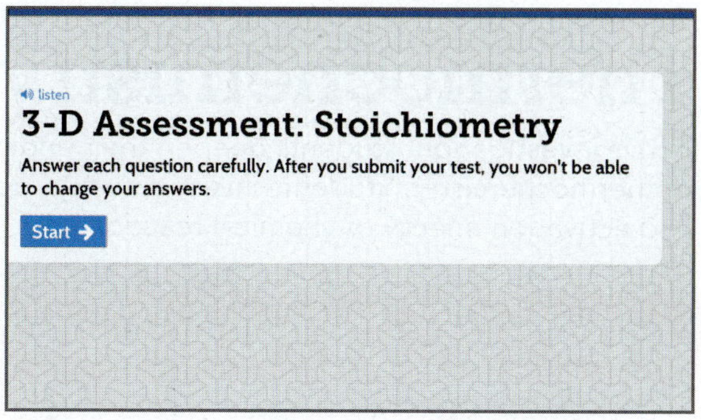
listen
3-D Assessment: Stoichiometry
Answer each question carefully. After you submit your test, you won't be able to change your answers.
Start →

Interactive Online 3-D Assessment

Interactive ExamView 3-D Assessment

3-D Assessment Interactive Worksheet

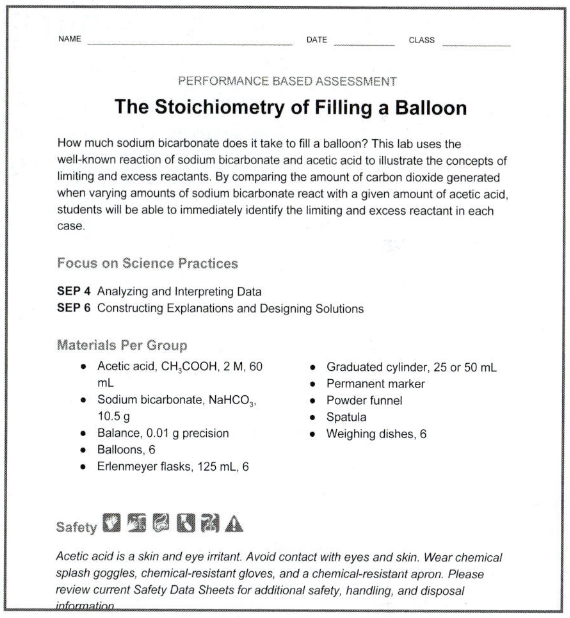
NAME ______ DATE ______ CLASS ______

PERFORMANCE BASED ASSESSMENT

The Stoichiometry of Filling a Balloon

How much sodium bicarbonate does it take to fill a balloon? This lab uses the well-known reaction of sodium bicarbonate and acetic acid to illustrate the concepts of limiting and excess reactants. By comparing the amount of carbon dioxide generated when varying amounts of sodium bicarbonate react with a given amount of acetic acid, students will be able to immediately identify the limiting and excess reactant in each case.

Focus on Science Practices

SEP 4 Analyzing and Interpreting Data
SEP 6 Constructing Explanations and Designing Solutions

Materials Per Group

- Acetic acid, CH_3COOH, 2 M, 60 mL
- Sodium bicarbonate, $NaHCO_3$, 10.5 g
- Balance, 0.01 g precision
- Balloons, 6
- Erlenmeyer flasks, 125 mL, 6
- Graduated cylinder, 25 or 50 mL
- Permanent marker
- Powder funnel
- Spatula
- Weighing dishes, 6

Safety

Acetic acid is a skin and eye irritant. Avoid contact with eyes and skin. Wear chemical splash goggles, chemical-resistant gloves, and a chemical-resistant apron. Please review current Safety Data Sheets for additional safety, handling, and disposal information.

Performance-Based Assessment Interactive Worksheet

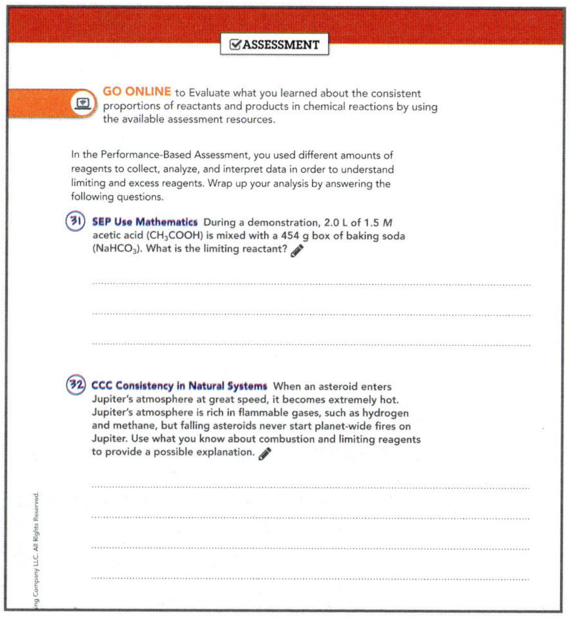
ASSESSMENT

GO ONLINE to Evaluate what you learned about the consistent proportions of reactants and products in chemical reactions by using the available assessment resources.

In the Performance-Based Assessment, you used different amounts of reagents to collect, analyze, and interpret data in order to understand limiting and excess reagents. Wrap up your analysis by answering the following questions.

31 **SEP Use Mathematics** During a demonstration, 2.0 L of 1.5 *M* acetic acid (CH_3COOH) is mixed with a 454 g box of baking soda ($NaHCO_3$). What is the limiting reactant?

32 **CCC Consistency in Natural Systems** When an asteroid enters Jupiter's atmosphere at great speed, it becomes extremely hot. Jupiter's atmosphere is rich in flammable gases, such as hydrogen and methane, but falling asteroids never start planet-wide fires on Jupiter. Use what you know about combustion and limiting reagents to provide a possible explanation.

Experience Notebook, p. 279

eTEXT

INVESTIGATION 8 PLANNER

Thermochemistry

In this investigation, students deepen their understanding of energy and matter [CCC-5] through a study of thermochemistry. Students investigate and develop system models [CCC-4] of collisions, enthalpy, and activation energy of chemical reactions [PS1.B] as well as other related phenomena.

INVESTIGATIVE PHENOMENON

Why do you get hot when you exercise?

Explaining Phenomena In order to fully understand the phenomenon of why we get hot when we exercise, students must investigate heat flow of a system. As students develop the ability to analyze and model enthalpy of reactions and heat during phase changes, they identify patterns in matter and energy.

	EXPERIENCE 1	EXPERIENCE 2
	Energy in Chemical Bonds **2.5 days** Students construct explanations of collisions in reactions. They develop a model of the flow of energy between a system and its surroundings. They use data on bond enthalpies and estimate change in enthalpy. Students model enthalpy diagrams.	**Enthalpies of Formation and Reaction** **2 days** Students investigate Hess's law. They sketch enthalpy diagrams and find the standard enthalpy of formation. Students design a solution for formulating a new compound to be used in a heat pack. They use mathematics to calculate the standard enthalpy of reaction.
CONNECTION TO THE INVESTIGATIVE PHENOMENON	Students formulate a balanced chemical equation for the combustion reaction that takes place during exercise and sketch an enthalpy diagram and relate that to the phenomenon of why we get hot when we exercise.	Students use data to determine the standard enthalpy of the combustion reaction that takes place during exercise and relate that to the phenomenon of why we get hot when we exercise.
ENGAGE	**Teacher's Guide** Everyday Phenomenon Sugar Cube Fireworks, p. 234	**Teacher's Guide** Everyday Phenomenon Thermite Reaction, p. 240
EXPLORE	**Inquiry Lab** The Thermodynamics of Hand Warmers **Virtual Lab** Temperature Changes in Chemical Reactions +	**Inquiry Lab** Hess's Law and the Combustion of a Metal **Analyzing Data** Energy in Reactions +
EXPLAIN	**Modeling** Energy Changes in Reactions **Experience Notebook,** pp. 282–289	**Claim-Evidence-Reasoning** Compare Heats of Formation **Animation** Bond Energy and Enthalpy + **Experience Notebook,** pp. 291–297
ELABORATE	**Discussion Rubric** Representations of Energy Changes **Engineering Design Challenge** Flameless Heating Systems +	**Discussion Rubric** Bond Type and Changes in Enthalpy **Writing About Science** Energy Input for the Rusting of Iron +
EVALUATE	**Quiz** Energy in Chemical Bonds **Experience Notebook** Revisit Investigative Phenomenon, p. 290	**Quiz** Enthalpies of Formation and Reaction **Experience Notebook** Revisit Investigative Phenomenon, p. 298

*Pacing for Encounter Investigative Phenomenon core instruction is a half-day.

†Pacing for core Investigation Assessment is approximately 1 day.

GOT MORE TIME? Personalize and enhance your instructional plan by assigning the activities with the got-more-time icon, as time allows.

Investigative Phenomenon Video The Color of Heat*

Modeling Model the Investigative Phenomenon*

Virtual Reality Experience ⊕

Experience Notebook, p. 280*

EXPERIENCE 3

Enthalpy in Changes of State

2 days

Students explore heat during phase changes. They construct an explanation related to the molar enthalpy of fusion. They complete heat of fusion and vaporization phase-change calculations. They graph data on changes of state and predict enthalpy of vaporization.

Students construct an explanation for how sweating can help cool the body during exercise and use that to refine explanations on why we get hot when we exercise.

Teacher's Guide Everyday Phenomenon Fire From Ice, p. 246

Inquiry Lab The Heat of Melting Ice

Interactivity Heat of Fusion ⊕

Modeling Enthalpy Diagrams for Phase Changes

Animation Energy Changes in Changes of State ⊕

Experience Notebook, pp. 299–305

Peer Review Rubric Enthalpy Diagrams for Phase Changes

Writing About Science Enthalpy of Reaction vs. Phase Change ⊕

Quiz Enthalpy in Changes of State

Experience Notebook Revisit Investigative Phenomenon, p. 306

INVESTIGATION ASSESSMENT

Performance-Based Assessment Enthalpy of a Neutralization Reaction†

3-D Assessment Thermochemistry†

Experience Notebook Performance-Based Assessment, p. 307; Revisit Anchoring Phenomenon, p. 307†; **Appendix C** Problem Bank, pp. R19–R20

Notes:

INVESTIGATION 8

Thermochemistry

Teacher Background

Students should start this investigation with an understanding of heat energy and the laws that govern heat flow. Investigation 8 goes into more detail on how heat energy interacts with chemical bonds through reactions. The concept of enthalpy (heat flow at constant pressure) is introduced for the first time here. Students will learn how to draw an enthalpy diagram for exothermic and endothermic reactions, calculate enthalpy change using a variety of methods, and investigate enthalpy changes for physical processes such as dissolution and phase changes.

Before beginning this investigation, read through the four main ways to find ΔH (change in enthalpy) introduced in this investigation. Students will find ΔH from bond energies, thermochemical equations (including equations for the dissolution of solutes), systems of chemical equations, and enthalpies of formation. Each method is useful for solving different types of problems, and you should be aware of the similarities and differences between them. It is also important to ensure that students have a good qualitative understanding of the differences between exothermic and endothermic reactions and how enthalpy changes can be observed in the physical world.

Learning Progression

In the beginning of this investigation, students use bond energy to calculate the change in enthalpy for chemical reactions [PS1.B] and learn how to represent enthalpy changes using an energy diagram [PS3.D]. Next, students investigate how Hess's law allows for the calculation of enthalpy change for any reaction by using any other combination of reactions, as long as the starting point and end point are the same. Finally, students explore how state changes are accompanied by changes in enthalpy, and how the magnitude of these changes can give us clues about the intermolecular forces [PS3.C] between particles. Throughout this investigation, students make models [SEP-2] of heat transfer in chemical reactions and refine those models through discussion and experimentation. They determine how energy moves between system [CCC-4] and surroundings and how scientists describe those flows of energy [CCC-5] quantitatively.

Students gather and analyze lab data [SEP-4] to help them make rational claims to explain heat change in chemical reactions. They determine how to write out explanations [SEP-6] using an underlying model of enthalpy change that they develop through several hands-on experiences.

RELATED PHENOMENA

In addition to body heat from exercise, consider using other phenomena to launch this investigation.

- **Energy Production in an Engine** Show students an Internet video of a demonstration of how engines work. Find a video that explains the different strokes of the engine—the intake, compression, power, and exhaust. Use this video to discuss topics such as different types of energy (potential energy stored in chemicals versus kinetic energy), interaction between the system versus surroundings, and heat transfer.
- **Fireplace Chemistry** When a log burns in a fireplace, many interesting thermochemical reactions are taking place. Discuss the thermochemistry and energy flows that occur when wood burns.

TAKE IT LOCAL

Ask students if they know what the Calorie numbers shown on food labels actually represent. Have them look at a food label from a food item at a local grocery store. Discuss how much energy 1 Calorie is. Ask students if Calories from different sources (protein, carbohydrates, fats) contain different amounts of energy.

ENCOUNTER

INVESTIGATIVE PHENOMENON

Why do you get hot when you exercise?

Introduce this investigation by asking students why they feel so warm when they exercise. Everyone has felt their body temperature increase when they exert themselves. This can prompt students to wonder where that energy comes from and what kinds of chemical processes produce it. Students begin this topic by investigating heat in systems and surroundings (Experience 1). They further their learning by exploring heat summation (Experience 2). Finally, they explain energy in evaporation (Experience 3).

The Color of Heat

Investigative Phenomenon Video Students can view the video as a class. Tell them to note any new facts they learn as they watch. Tell students that thermography uses cameras to detect infrared radiation given off by an object. The resulting image is a thermogram. In a thermogram, the brighter colors (red, orange, yellow) indicate warmer temperatures; purple and blue colors indicate cooler temperatures.

- **Ask** What processes in the body cause it to emit or transfer heat? (Every cell in the body produces heat as a product of cellular oxidation. The amount of heat produced depends on the location of the cell in the body and the activity taking place. Muscle cells will produce more heat when they are being used than when they are at rest.)
- What did you observe happen to the surface as a result of the hand resting on it? (A hand shape image appeared on the surface.) What caused the change? (Heat was transferred from the hand to the surface.)

Finally, ask students to record some questions about thermograms that they would like to investigate.

Model the Phenomenon

Modeling Have students review the video to develop a model of the phenomenon they observed. Remind students that a model does not have to look like the object or process it represents, but students should be able to use it to explain and/or predict. Make sure students consider the inputs and outputs of the heat transfer. Have students complete Question 1 of the Modeling worksheet.

Remind students that their understanding of the phenomenon will be incomplete at this stage, but that they will revisit this activity as they learn more. Make sure to provide students with an opportunity to revisit their models throughout the investigation as well as at the end of the investigation for further revision and peer review.

Reflect on the Phenomenon

Experience Notebook Transition to the opener pages for Investigation 8 in the Experience Notebook and discuss the question on the photo, "Why do you get hot when you exercise?"

If students struggle, then guide them to use what the have learned in the video and the Modeling activity to answer the driving question. Additionally, at the end of each experience, direct students to complete the writing prompt to reflect on the Investigative Phenomenon.

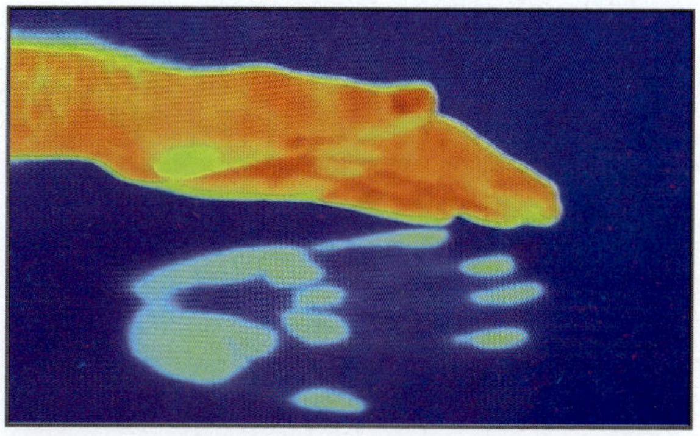

Investigative Phenomenon Video: The Color of Heat

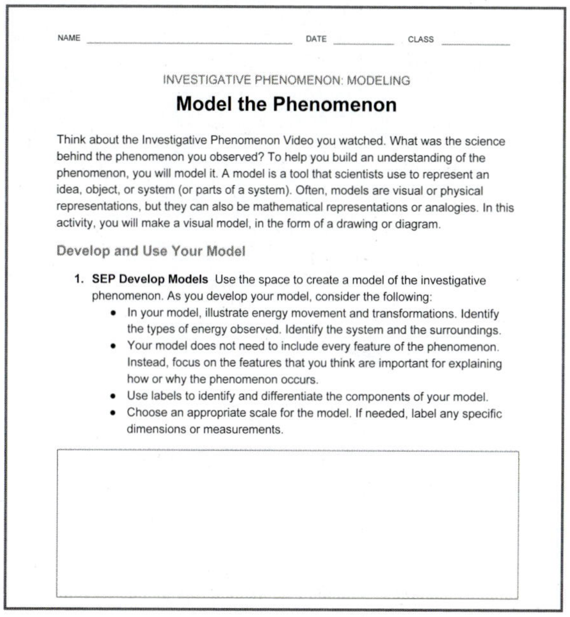

NAME ______ DATE ______ CLASS ______

INVESTIGATIVE PHENOMENON: MODELING

Model the Phenomenon

Think about the Investigative Phenomenon Video you watched. What was the science behind the phenomenon you observed? To help you build an understanding of the phenomenon, you will model it. A model is a tool that scientists use to represent an idea, object, or system (or parts of a system). Often, models are visual or physical representations, but they can also be mathematical representations or analogies. In this activity, you will make a visual model, in the form of a drawing or diagram.

Develop and Use Your Model

1. **SEP Develop Models** Use the space to create a model of the investigative phenomenon. As you develop your model, consider the following:
   - In your model, illustrate energy movement and transformations. Identify the types of energy observed. Identify the system and the surroundings.
   - Your model does not need to include every feature of the phenomenon. Instead, focus on the features that you think are important for explaining how or why the phenomenon occurs.
   - Use labels to identify and differentiate the components of your model.
   - Choose an appropriate scale for the model. If needed, label any specific dimensions or measurements.

Modeling Interactive Worksheet

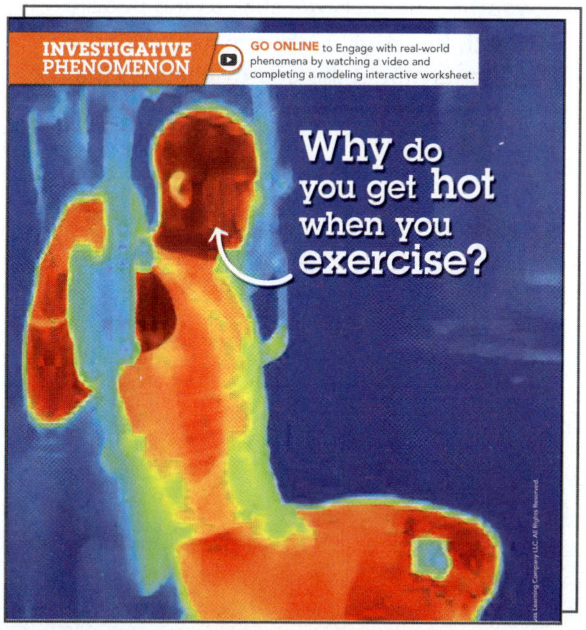

Experience Notebook, pp. 280–281

eTEXT

EXPERIENCE 1

Energy in Chemical Bonds

Teacher Background

In this experience, students learn how scientists measure and describe the energy of chemical bonds and how that energy changes during chemical reactions. Students learn to calculate the enthalpy change for a reaction using bond enthalpies and thermochemical equations. They explore heat changes in chemical reactions through several hands-on experiments. Students also create and analyze models that represent how energy changes as chemical bonds are broken and formed.

Objectives

- **Explain how molecules must collide with each other with sufficient energy and in the correct orientation for a chemical reaction to take place.**
- **Represent energy changes in exothermic and endothermic reactions using an enthalpy diagram.**
- **Calculate enthalpy of reaction from bond energies and molar enthalpy of reaction data.**

ENGAGE

EVERYDAY PHENOMENON

How much energy is in the chemical bonds inside a sugar cube?

Use the teacher demo to help students understand how the energy in chemical bonds can be released during a chemical reaction.

Sugar Cube Fireworks

Engage students with this demonstration of the energy in the chemical bonds of an everyday substance (sugar) and how that energy can be released in a chemical reaction.

Materials sugar cube, wide-mouth test tube, ring stand and clamp, Bunsen burner, approximately 15 g of potassium chlorate

Safety Molten potassium chlorate is extremely reactive. This demonstration should be done under a fume hood with the sash lowered. All participants and observers should wear full chemical splash goggles.

1. Ask students to estimate the number of Calories in a single sugar cube. (A sugar cube has about 10 Calories.)
2. Have students calculate the number of sugar cubes required to meet an average person's daily caloric requirements. (2000 Calories /10 Calories per cube = 200 sugar cubes)
3. Explain that you are going to release some of the energy in the chemical bonds inside a single sugar cube through a chemical reaction.
4. Add about 15 g of potassium chlorate to a wide-mouthed test tube. Clamp the tube to the stand at an angle so that you can heat the base of the tube without heating its mouth. Be sure the mouth of the test tube is not pointing toward anyone.
5. Wait for the potassium chlorate to melt and then remove the heat from the test tube.

RELATED PHENOMENA

In addition to the Sugar Cube Fireworks teacher demo, consider using other phenomena to launch this experience.

- **Hook and Loop** Use a set of hook-and-loop catch game toys to demonstrate collision theory. The balls will only stick to the loop side of the paddle and must have sufficient energy to stay stuck after colliding. Have students to explain what factor determines whether the balls will stick to the paddle.
- **Match Reaction** Light a match and have students model the energy changes that occur in this chemical reaction.

6. Drop a single sugar cube into the test tube, making sure it falls into the molten potassium chlorate. As the sugar in the cube is oxidized, it will release a large amount of heat and light.
7. Discuss how scientists describe this release of energy using enthalpy. Use the discussion and demo to segue to the Inquiry Lab and to the Investigative Phenomenon about why we get hot when we exercise.

EXPLORE

The Thermodynamics of Hand Warmers

50

Inquiry Lab Students investigate **[SEP-3]** the energy changes that accompany the dissolution of common laboratory salts in water and apply the results to design a hand warmer that is reliable, safe, and inexpensive.

Lab Demo Video Watch the Lab Demo Video for advice on materials and preparation.

Choose Your Version Open-ended (O), Guided (G), Shortened (S), Advanced (A)

Materials 15 g ammonium chloride, 15 g calcium chloride, 15 g sodium chloride, 15 g sodium hydroxide, distilled or tap water, balance, 250-mL beaker, 100-mL graduated cylinder, heat-resistant gloves, magnetic stirrer and stir bar or stirring rod, paper towels, solution vessel (two nested polystyrene cups), support stand and ring clamp, digital thermometer, timer or stopwatch, weighing dishes

Safety Calcium chloride and ammonium chloride are slightly toxic. Sodium hydroxide is highly corrosive. Make sure students wear chemical safety glasses, heat-resistant gloves, and a chemical-resistant apron. Instruct students to use a magnetic stirrer and stir bar, or a glass stirring rod to stir the liquid; never stir with a thermometer. Make sure students wash their hands thoroughly with soap and warm water before leaving the laboratory.

Expected Outcome Based on temperature measurement results, students determine that dissolution of NaOH and $CaCl_2$ releases heat energy, whereas dissolution of NaCl and NH_4Cl absorbs heat energy from the surrounding environment. Then they explain the results, based on differences in the strength of ionic bonds in the solid compounds, intermolecular water forces, and interactions between ions and water molecules in solution. Finally, students propose the design of hand warmers using a solution of $CaCl_2$ in water, and instant cold packs using aqueous NH_4Cl.

Lab Summary Video Watch the Lab Summary Video for support on connecting the lab investigation to the Investigative Phenomenon.

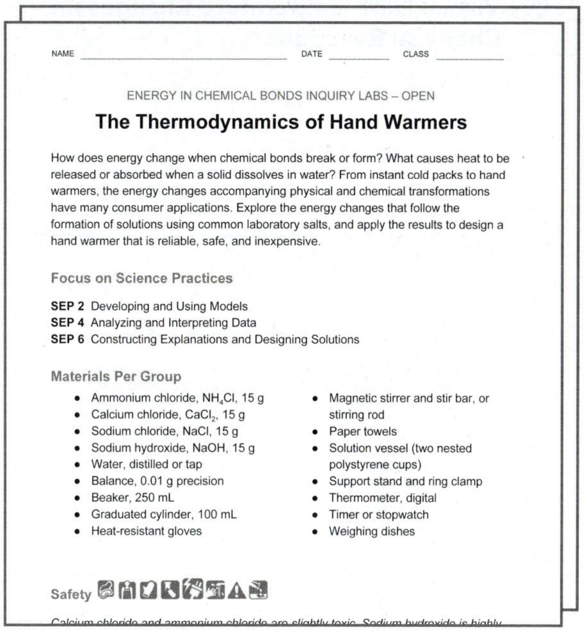

NAME ______ DATE ______ CLASS ______

ENERGY IN CHEMICAL BONDS INQUIRY LABS – OPEN

The Thermodynamics of Hand Warmers

How does energy change when chemical bonds break or form? What causes heat to be released or absorbed when a solid dissolves in water? From instant cold packs to hand warmers, the energy changes accompanying physical and chemical transformations have many consumer applications. Explore the energy changes that follow the formation of solutions using common laboratory salts, and apply the results to design a hand warmer that is reliable, safe, and inexpensive.

Focus on Science Practices

SEP 2 Developing and Using Models
SEP 4 Analyzing and Interpreting Data
SEP 6 Constructing Explanations and Designing Solutions

Materials Per Group

- Ammonium chloride, NH_4Cl, 15 g
- Calcium chloride, $CaCl_2$, 15 g
- Sodium chloride, NaCl, 15 g
- Sodium hydroxide, NaOH, 15 g
- Water, distilled or tap
- Balance, 0.01 g precision
- Beaker, 250 mL
- Graduated cylinder, 100 mL
- Heat-resistant gloves
- Magnetic stirrer and stir bar, or stirring rod
- Paper towels
- Solution vessel (two nested polystyrene cups)
- Support stand and ring clamp
- Thermometer, digital
- Timer or stopwatch
- Weighing dishes

Safety

O/G/S/A Lab Interactive Worksheets

ASSESS ON THE SPOT

Remind students that dissolving salts in water is not a chemical reaction. **Ask** How is the dissolution process similar to a chemical reaction? (It involves the "breaking" of ionic bonds and the making of solvent–solute interactions.) How is the dissolution process different from a chemical reaction? (In the dissolution process, no new substances are formed, and you can recover the original compounds through purely physical changes, such as boiling.)

CONNECT TO CAREERS

Chef A chef needs knowledge of the heat flow of a system. Heat lamps are used in restaurants to keep food warm before it is delivered to customers. A chef attempts to prevent heat from flowing rapidly from the hot food to the cold countertop. When plating a meal, a chef must consider what type of dish it will go on and the heat flow of that meal to the dish. The chef considers whether to use ceramic, wood, plastic, or glass and the benefits and drawbacks of each. Encourage students to find out what training and skills a chef must have.

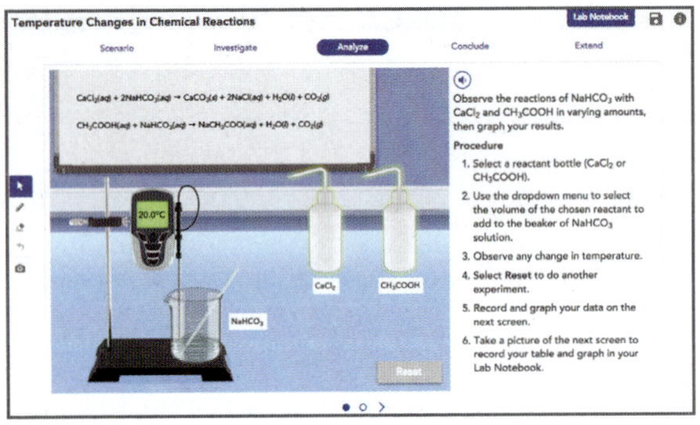

Virtual Lab: Temperature Changes in Chemical Reactions

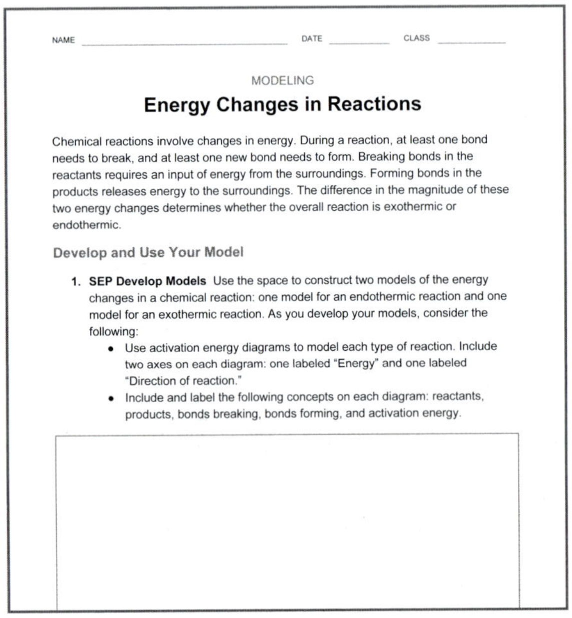

NAME ______________ DATE ________ CLASS ________

MODELING

Energy Changes in Reactions

Chemical reactions involve changes in energy. During a reaction, at least one bond needs to break, and at least one new bond needs to form. Breaking bonds in the reactants requires an input of energy from the surroundings. Forming bonds in the products releases energy to the surroundings. The difference in the magnitude of these two energy changes determines whether the overall reaction is exothermic or endothermic.

Develop and Use Your Model

1. **SEP Develop Models** Use the space to construct two models of the energy changes in a chemical reaction: one model for an endothermic reaction and one model for an exothermic reaction. As you develop your models, consider the following:
   - Use activation energy diagrams to model each type of reaction. Include two axes on each diagram: one labeled "Energy" and one labeled "Direction of reaction."
   - Include and label the following concepts on each diagram: reactants, products, bonds breaking, bonds forming, and activation energy.

Modeling Interactive Worksheet

ELD SUPPORT

Writing Have students work in groups of three to write a summary of the prominent features of the energy-change models they made in the Modeling activity.

- **Emerging/Beginning** Have students make a bulleted list of the important features from the model. They should use short, complete sentences and key words.
- **Developing/Expanding** Have students write a short summary paragraph of the important features of their model and how it can be used to describe a chemical reaction.
- **Bridging** Have students write a paragraph that summarizes the most important parts of the energy-change model and why those parts are important to scientists.

DIFFERENTIATED INSTRUCTION

- **Support Struggling Students** Some students may struggle with setting up the calculations involved in the Inquiry Lab without some additional scaffolding. As students are working on the lab and waiting for the solutions to change temperature, circulate around the room and show them an example calculation for finding heat of reaction from the temperature change of the water.
- **Support Advanced Students** Real hand warmers use a different, nonaqueous reaction to produce heat. This is usually the reaction between iron filings and oxygen from the atmosphere to produce various iron oxides (rust). Have students explain why this reaction might be more difficult to measure and why a nonaqueous reaction would be a good idea for a hand warmer.

Temperature Changes in Chemical Reactions (20)

Virtual Lab In this lab, students are introduced to heat engines and examples of these machines used in everyday objects, such as car engines and electricity-generated turbines. Then students observe how heat is released and absorbed in chemical reactions [PS1.B], and they examine how the amount of reactant affects the temperature change by analyzing and interpreting data [SEP-4].

Expected Outcome Students identify the difference between endothermic and exothermic reactions and determine whether heat is a reactant or product in each reaction. Students use evidence to support their explanation about why the amount of heat absorbed or released during a reaction can be affected by adding more reactant.

- As a brief review, ask students to volunteer one new thing that they have learned so far about exothermic and endothermic reactions. Write student contributions on the board or other place where all students can see.
- Explain to students that they will be investigating three reactants to determine how temperature change is affected when the amount of reactant varies.
- When students finish the lab, lead a class discussion and have students explain how they think heat engines can be impacted by temperature changes.

PROFESSIONAL DEVELOPMENT

Explaining Phenomena Some students may struggle to understand how a reaction that is endothermic (going "uphill") can happen spontaneously. These "uphill" reactions can happen because the endothermic process is offset by an increase in system entropy. If a reaction produces a large enough increase in entropy, it can proceed on its own—even when it is endothermic.

EXPLAIN

Energy Changes in Reactions (15)

Modeling In this activity, students develop models [SEP-2] of the energy change in a chemical reaction [PS1.B]. Students make models of both exothermic and endothermic reactions. You may want to provide students with specific reactions to reference when making and discussing their models.

- Ask students to label the bonds breaking and the bonds forming sections of their models to help reinforce that bond breaking is always endothermic and bond forming is always exothermic.
- Have students compare the total bond energy of the reactants to the activation energy for their reaction. **Ask** Why can the activation energy for the reaction never be greater than the total bond energy of the reactants? (At most, you would have to break every bond in the reactants to form the activated complex.) How should this be represented in your model? (The distance from the x-axis to the reactants should be greater than or equal to the distance from the reactants to the activated complex.)

Energy in Chemical Bonds

Experience Notebook Assign the Experience Notebook or Realize Reader before following up with the various activities in this experience. Use these strategies to help students make sense of the images and text on the indicated pages, as well as to engage science skills.

- **Bond Enthalpy** (pp. 285–286) Remind students that bond formation is always exothermic and bond breaking is always endothermic, regardless of the overall value of ΔH. Every enthalpy diagram for a reaction starts by adding energy to break bonds and ends with releasing energy by forming new bonds. Have students write a short explanation [SEP-6] of why this must be true.
- **Activation Energy** (p. 287) You can use a roller coaster as an analogy to help students better understand activation energy [PS3.A]. As the cars of the roller coaster are pulled to the top of the first hill, energy is added to the system from an outside source. After the cars go over that first hill, the rest of the ride happens spontaneously. Even in endothermic reactions, the activated complex is at the energetic "high point" of the entire process.
- Further explain the activation energy barrier by relating it to a hill covered in snow. Tell students to suppose that they are rolling a large snowball up the hill. When they get to the top of the hill, they will push the snowball over the top. Explain that when they first begin to move the snowball, only a few students are needed to move it because they are moving it over flat ground. But as they begin moving up the hill, more students must join to continue moving the snowball. **Ask** What would happen if not enough students were available to push the snowball to the top of the hill? (The snowball would not go over the hill.) How is the least number of students needed to push the snowball over the top of the hill analogous to the activation energy of a reaction? (The activation energy is the minimum amount of energy needed for the reactants to form products.)
- **Representations of Enthalpy** (p. 288) Review the diagram with students. **Ask** What two ways are changes in enthalpy represented in the diagram? (arrows and an algebraic equation to the side of the chemical equation) How do these representations differ between endothermic and exothermic reactions? (Endothermic arrows point upward; exothermic arrows point downward. The ΔH for an endothermic reaction is positive, and for an exothermic reaction it is negative.)
- Help students remember the correct sign for ΔH by thinking of themselves as the reaction system [CCC-4]. If they give off energy [CCC-5] to the surroundings (in an exothermic process), they will lose energy and, therefore, have a negative change in enthalpy. If they gain energy [PS3.B] from the surroundings (in an endothermic process), they have a positive change in enthalpy.
- **Sample Problem** (p. 289) Provide extra Sample Problem practice, while you circulate and help out as needed.
    a. The average bond enthalpy for C=O bonds is 799 kJ/mol and for C-H bonds is 413 kJ/mol. Using these values and the values from the table on page 285, calculate [SEP-5] the overall change in enthalpy for the following reaction: $CH_4 + 2\ O_2 \rightarrow CO_2 + 2\ H_2O$. Is the reaction exothermic or endothermic? (–818 kJ/mol_{rxn}, therefore exothermic)
    b. Calculate the amount of heat released when 3.56 mol of ammonia is produced from nitrogen gas and hydrogen gas according to this reaction: $N_2 + 3H_2 \rightarrow 2NH_3 + 92.4$ kJ. (164 kJ of heat is released.)

ASSESS ON THE SPOT

Ask students to connect the collision theory illustration on page 282 of the Experience Notebook with their energy-change models by adding the reactants, products, and activated complex from the illustration to their model. Circulate around the room and check that students place the molecules from the illustration in the correct places on their energy-change models.

INTEGRATE THE THREE DIMENSIONS

In the Modeling activity, students develop two models [SEP-2] of energy changes in a chemical reaction [PS1.B]. They construct explanations [SEP-6] about how the models represent the flow of energy [CCC-5] between the reaction system and the surroundings for an endothermic and exothermic reaction. They optimize their models by taking into account criteria and limitations.

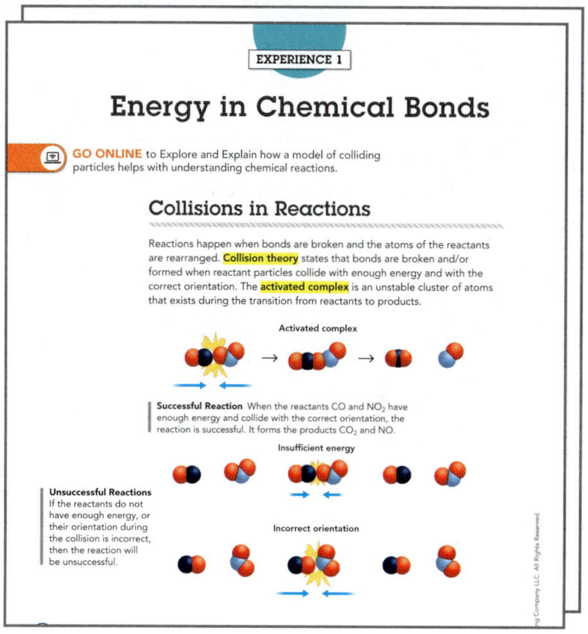

Experience Notebook, pp. 282–290

eTEXT

SAMPLE PROBLEM SUPPORT

Order of operations is extremely important to remember when performing bond-energy calculations, such as for the problem on page 289. Students may get the wrong answer when they simply type the entire problem into their calculator after setting it up. Remind students to calculate the entire reactants side of the equation and record their answer. Next, calculate the entire products side, and record this number before subtracting the two sides. This will help avoid mistakes with the order of operations and can help students track down errors that might have occurred in the middle of their calculations.

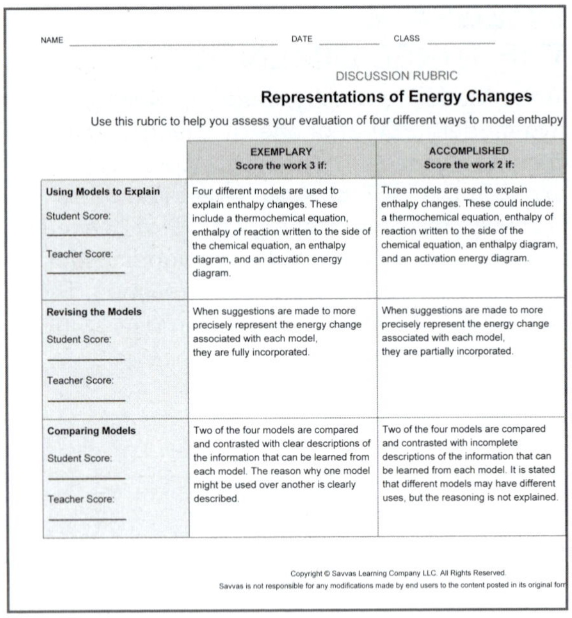

NAME ______ DATE ______ CLASS ______

DISCUSSION RUBRIC

Representations of Energy Changes

Use this rubric to help you assess your evaluation of four different ways to model enthalpy

	EXEMPLARY Score the work 3 if:	ACCOMPLISHED Score the work 2 if:
Using Models to Explain Student Score: ______ Teacher Score: ______	Four different models are used to explain enthalpy changes. These include a thermochemical equation, enthalpy of reaction written to the side of the chemical equation, an enthalpy diagram, and an activation energy diagram.	Three models are used to explain enthalpy changes. These could include: a thermochemical equation, enthalpy of reaction written to the side of the chemical equation, an enthalpy diagram, and an activation energy diagram.
Revising the Models Student Score: ______ Teacher Score: ______	When suggestions are made to more precisely represent the energy change associated with each model, they are fully incorporated.	When suggestions are made to more precisely represent the energy change associated with each model, they are partially incorporated.
Comparing Models Student Score: ______ Teacher Score: ______	Two of the four models are compared and contrasted with clear descriptions of the information that can be learned from each model. The reason why one model might be used over another is clearly described.	Two of the four models are compared and contrasted with incomplete descriptions of the information that can be learned from each model. It is stated that different models may have different uses, but the reasoning is not explained.

Discussion Rubric Interactive Worksheet

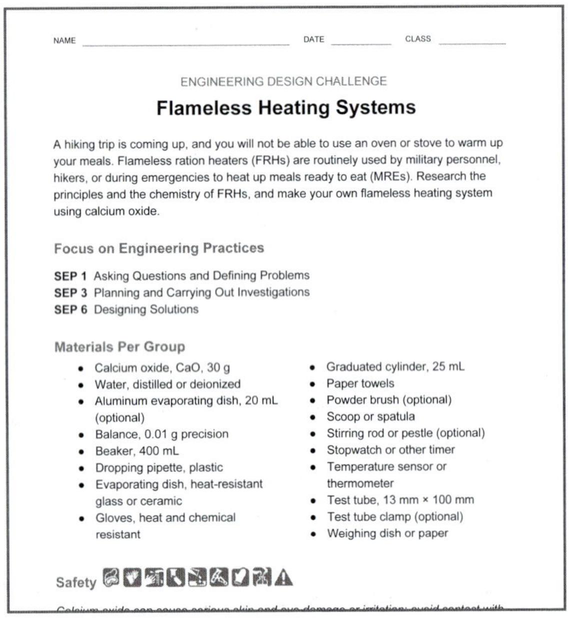

NAME ______ DATE ______ CLASS ______

ENGINEERING DESIGN CHALLENGE

Flameless Heating Systems

A hiking trip is coming up, and you will not be able to use an oven or stove to warm up your meals. Flameless ration heaters (FRHs) are routinely used by military personnel, hikers, or during emergencies to heat up meals ready to eat (MREs). Research the principles and the chemistry of FRHs, and make your own flameless heating system using calcium oxide.

Focus on Engineering Practices

SEP 1 Asking Questions and Defining Problems
SEP 3 Planning and Carrying Out Investigations
SEP 6 Designing Solutions

Materials Per Group

- Calcium oxide, CaO, 30 g
- Water, distilled or deionized
- Aluminum evaporating dish, 20 mL (optional)
- Balance, 0.01 g precision
- Beaker, 400 mL
- Dropping pipette, plastic
- Evaporating dish, heat-resistant glass or ceramic
- Gloves, heat and chemical resistant
- Graduated cylinder, 25 mL
- Paper towels
- Powder brush (optional)
- Scoop or spatula
- Stirring rod or pestle (optional)
- Stopwatch or other timer
- Temperature sensor or thermometer
- Test tube, 13 mm × 100 mm
- Test tube clamp (optional)
- Weighing dish or paper

Safety

Engineering Design Challenge Interactive Worksheet

CLASSROOM MODIFICATIONS

Based on your students' abilities and your schedule, you can modify the Engineering Design Challenge to be more open ended or more guided.

- **More Open Ended** Have students research different compounds to use in their heating systems. Allow students to test the amount of heat that each releases when dissolved in water to decide which chemical to use in their final design.
- **More Guided** Provide students with a flameless heater and have them improve on the design instead of developing an original design. Direct them to describe what the current design does well and what it could do better before suggesting any changes.

ELABORATE

Representations of Energy Changes

Discussion Rubric Students use the rubric to assess themselves during a discussion about the different ways to model enthalpy changes for a reaction.

- Tell students that they will be evaluating themselves on their contribution to the class discussion. Their comments should be precise and complete.
- Discuss as a class four different models that can be used to model enthalpy changes: a thermochemical equation, enthalpy of reaction written to the side of the chemical equation, a simple enthalpy diagram, and an enthalpy diagram that includes the activation energy. Have students compare and contrast the different models and identify the value of each.
- Then direct students to use the Discussion Rubric to assess their evaluation.

ASSESS ON THE SPOT

Provide students with an unlabeled enthalpy diagram and have them label the *x*- and *y*-axes, the energy of the reactants and products, the activation energy, and the overall change in enthalpy (ΔH) for the reaction. Finally, have them indicate whether the reaction is exothermic or endothermic. Collect their responses and review them to determine whether any additional time should be spent on this topic before moving forward.

Flameless Heating Systems

Engineering Design Challenge In this activity, students design and build a meal-heating system that uses an exothermic reaction as the source of heat.

Materials 30 g calcium oxide, distilled or deionized water, 20-mL aluminum evaporating dish (optional), balance, 400-mL beaker, plastic dropping pipette, glass or ceramic heat-resistant evaporating dish, heat- and chemical-resistant gloves, 25-mL graduated cylinder, paper towels, powder brush (optional), scoop or spatula, stirring rod or pestle (optional), stopwatch or other timer, temperature sensor or thermometer, 13 mm x 100 mm test tube, test tube clamp (optional), weighing dish or paper

Safety Calcium oxide can cause serious skin and eye damage or irritation. Tell students to avoid contact with their skin and eyes. Calcium oxide may cause respiratory irritation so students should avoid breathing dust or fumes. Make sure students wear chemical splash goggles, chemical- and heat-resistant gloves, and a chemical-resistant apron. Remind students to wash hands thoroughly with soap and warm water before leaving the laboratory.

Expected Outcome Students will design and build a flameless heating system using the reaction between calcium oxide and water. Adding water to calcium oxide dropwise will generate calcium hydroxide and a large amount of heat. This heat can be used to heat a small volume of water or semisolid food.

- Provide a few MREs with flameless ration heaters so students can analyze current designs and suggest improvements. Allow students to perform tests on the heaters to determine how much heat they produce and what percentage of that heat is actually transferred to the meal.
- Ask students to research whether compounds other than calcium oxide could be used in a ration heater. Have them suggest pros and cons of using these other compounds. Factors to consider may be toxicity, price, and long-term stability.
- Have students draw an enthalpy diagram for this reaction to reinforce the usefulness of this model when describing energy changes in chemical reactions [PS3.D].

EVALUATE

Energy in Chemical Bonds

Quiz Assign the quiz in online technology-enhanced, auto-graded format or as an editable quiz worksheet. Use the scoring notes and remediation strategies found online to assess students' responses and to provide targeted feedback for each item to remediate well before assigning the summative 3-D Assessment.

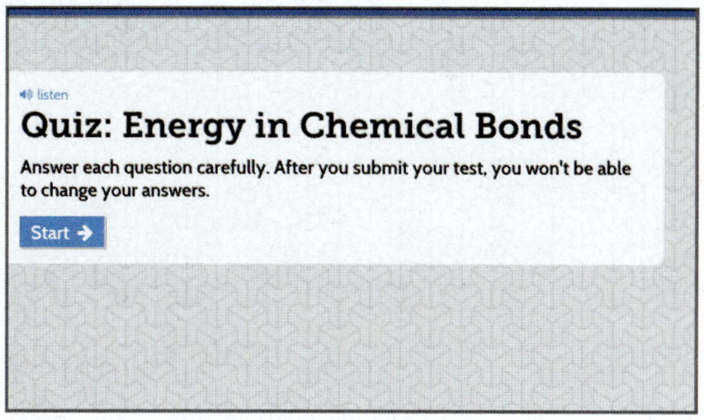

Interactive Online Quiz

Quiz Interactive Worksheet

REMEDIATION SUGGESTIONS

- **If** students have trouble explaining collision theory, **then** have them review the illustration on page 282 of the Experience Notebook and write a short summary in their own words of the key components of a successful reaction.
- **If** students are struggling with drawing and interpreting energy change diagrams for chemical reactions, **then** have them review the models they made in the Energy Changes in Reactions Modeling activity and assign them a few more practice reactions to model.
- **If** students are unable to calculate enthalpy change based on thermochemical equations or bond energy, **then** have them review the Sample Problem on page 289 of the Experience Notebook and assign a few more practice problems as needed.

Revisit INVESTIGATIVE PHENOMENON

Support Reflection Students can complete the reflection prompt where they will unpack and make sense of the Investigative Phenomenon, based on practices and understandings that have been reinforced over the course of the experience.

- Ask students whether they are comfortable identifying endothermic and exothermic reactions from energy change diagrams and ΔH values.
- Have students describe the differences between endothermic and exothermic processes using the idea of system and surroundings. Have students further describe endothermic and exothermic reactions that occur when they exercise.
- Work through a few sample calculations to find change in enthalpy from bond energy and from thermochemical equations.

Refine Your Model Have students answer Question 2 in the Modeling worksheet, relating their model to the Investigative Phenomenon. Have students add any evidence they have collected from the activities so far in this investigation. Evidence may include that heat energy can be released when chemical bonds are formed.

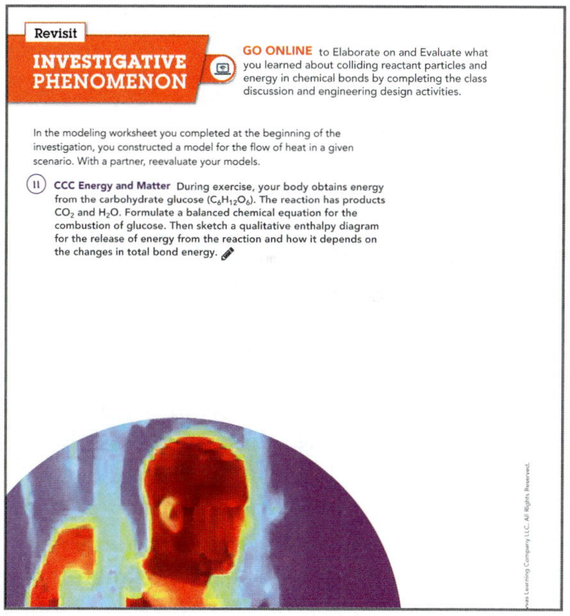
Revisit INVESTIGATIVE PHENOMENON

GO ONLINE to Elaborate on and Evaluate what you learned about colliding reactant particles and energy in chemical bonds by completing the class discussion and engineering design activities.

In the modeling worksheet you completed at the beginning of the investigation, you constructed a model for the flow of heat in a given scenario. With a partner, reevaluate your models.

11 **CCC Energy and Matter** During exercise, your body obtains energy from the carbohydrate glucose ($C_6H_{12}O_6$). The reaction has products CO_2 and H_2O. Formulate a balanced chemical equation for the combustion of glucose. Then sketch a qualitative enthalpy diagram for the release of energy from the reaction and how it depends on the changes in total bond energy.

Experience Notebook, p. 290

eTEXT

EXPERIENCE 2

Enthalpies of Formation and Reaction

Teacher Background

In this experience, students learn that the change in enthalpy for a chemical reaction is always the same, regardless of the path the reaction takes. This understanding, known as Hess's law, allows for several new ways to calculate enthalpy change. Students first learn how to find the change in enthalpy for a reaction by adding two or more other chemical reactions and their enthalpy changes. Next, they learn how to use standard enthalpies of formation to determine the change in enthalpy for a reaction by looking at the elements in each compound. Finally, students learn how to use the enthalpy of solution to calculate the amount of heat released when a given amount of solute is dissolved in water.

Objectives

- **Explain how Hess's law can be used to calculate the change in enthalpy for a chemical reaction using any number of intermediate compounds.**
- **Calculate the change in enthalpy for a reaction using the sum of a system of chemical equations or a table of enthalpies of formation.**
- **Calculate the change in enthalpy for a dissolution process using molar enthalpy of solution.**

RELATED PHENOMENA

In addition to the Thermite Reaction teacher demo, consider using other phenomena to launch this experience.

- **Burning Gas** Demonstrate the formation of water from its elements by burning a small amount of hydrogen gas in a test tube. In order to produce the hydrogen gas, place a few pieces of zinc in a test tube. Add 15 mL of 3.0*M* hydrochloric acid. Light a wooden splint and gently insert it into the mouth of the test tube. Have students explain the water droplets that form inside the test tube.
- **Reaching the Summit** Draw a mountain and two paths starting at the same location at the bottom of the mountain to the same point at the top of the mountain—one path is straight to the top and the other is long and indirect with a number of changes in direction. Discuss how the distances traveled on the two paths differ, but the change in altitude is the same.

ENGAGE

EVERYDAY PHENOMENON

How much heat is released when aluminum oxide is formed?

Use this teacher demo to help students understand how Hess's law can be used to determine the change in enthalpy for a reaction.

Thermite Reaction

Engage students with this demonstration of the energy released when several familiar substances react under the right conditions.

Materials 3 g aluminum powder, 9 g iron oxide powder, fireworks sparkler (metal ones work best), ceramic crucible (or flower pot), sand

Safety This reaction releases a great deal of heat, light, and smoke. It should be performed under a fume hood with the sash lowered or outside behind a safety shield. Ensure that all participants and observers wear full chemical splash goggles and stand several feet back from the demonstration.

1. Ask students to predict how much heat is released from a reaction between aluminum and rust. These two substances are familiar and stable, so most students may assume the reaction will not release much energy.
2. Show students the aluminum powder and iron oxide powder and explain that they are, indeed, quite stable chemicals (even when mixed together). Mix together the two substances. Fill the crucible with sand and form a small depression in the center of the sand to hold the reaction mixture.
3. Place the sparkler in the center of the reaction mixture. Ensure that it is deep enough that the sparkler flame will touch the reaction mixture, not just the sparkler's handle.

4. Light the sparkler and step back from the reaction. (Once the sparker flame touches the reaction mixture, it will provide enough energy to overcome the high activation energy for this reaction. A large amount of heat and light will be released.)
5. Lead a class discussion about how to predict the energy released in this reaction. Tell students that they will find out how to do this in the Inquiry Lab.

EXPLORE

Hess's Law and the Combustion of a Metal

Inquiry Lab Students carry out an investigation [SEP-3] to calculate [SEP-5] how much heat energy is released during the combustion of magnesium in air. They apply Hess's law as an indirect method to determine the heat of combustion of magnesium from the heat of reaction of less hazardous reactions that also involve this metal.

Lab Demo Video Watch the Lab Demo Video for advice on materials and preparation.

Choose Your Version Open-ended (O), Guided (G), Shortened (S), Advanced (A)

Materials 60 mL 1*M* hydrochloric acid, 7-cm strip magnesium ribbon, 0.4 g magnesium oxide, balance, small-scale calorimeter, digital thermometer or temperature sensor, forceps, 25- or 50-mL graduated cylinder, metric ruler, scissors, spatula, stirring rod, wash bottle and water, weighing dish

Safety Remind students to wear safety goggles, chemical-resistant gloves, and a lab coat when performing this lab. Hydrochloric acid is toxic by ingestion and corrosive to skin and eyes. Magnesium metal is a flammable solid. Tell students not to handle magnesium metal with bare hands. This lab should be performed in a well-ventilated room. Make sure students wash their hands thoroughly with soap and warm water before leaving the laboratory.

Expected Outcome The enthalpy of formation of MgO results from combining the enthalpies of reaction between Mg and HCl and between MgO and HCl. The enthalpy of formation of MgO has a negative sign, indicating that this is an exothermic reaction.

Lab Summary Video Watch the Lab Summary Video for support on connecting the lab investigation to the Investigative Phenomenon.

ASSESS ON THE SPOT

As students complete the Inquiry Lab, have them write a short summary of what they did in the lab and what they learned. Collect these responses and review them to be sure students understood why they were doing each part of the lab and what the overall result of the lab showed.

DIFFERENTIATED INSTRUCTION

- **Support Less Proficient Readers** Some students may have difficulty reading the procedure in the Inquiry Lab. Read it with them. Additionally, some students may need help setting up the system of equations used in the lab to find the final heat of combustion of magnesium. Provide support by printing the reactants and products of each reaction onto cards so that students can manipulate them to set up the system of equations properly and cancel out the substances that show up on both sides of the reaction arrow.
- **Support Advanced Students** Ask advanced students to explain why using Hess's law for a reaction such as the combustion of magnesium is often much easier than measuring the heat of reaction directly. Help students understand the crucial role that indirect observation has in chemistry and investigations into reactions that are very fast, dangerous, or difficult to measure.

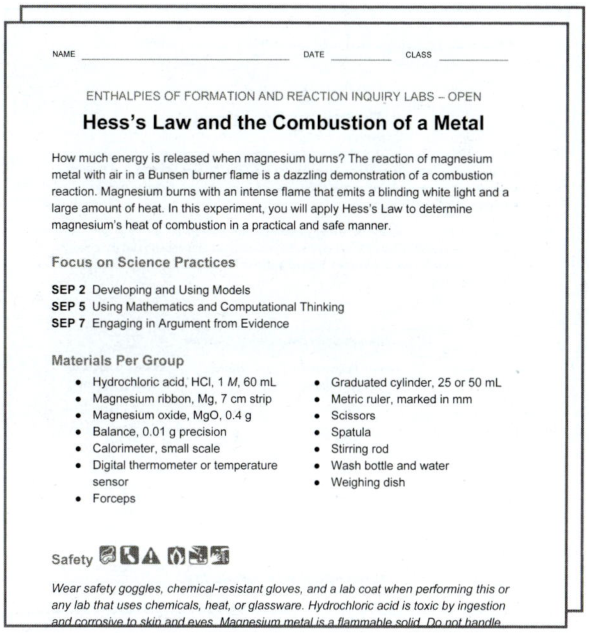

NAME ________ DATE ______ CLASS ______

ENTHALPIES OF FORMATION AND REACTION INQUIRY LABS – OPEN

Hess's Law and the Combustion of a Metal

How much energy is released when magnesium burns? The reaction of magnesium metal with air in a Bunsen burner flame is a dazzling demonstration of a combustion reaction. Magnesium burns with an intense flame that emits a blinding white light and a large amount of heat. In this experiment, you will apply Hess's Law to determine magnesium's heat of combustion in a practical and safe manner.

Focus on Science Practices

SEP 2 Developing and Using Models
SEP 5 Using Mathematics and Computational Thinking
SEP 7 Engaging in Argument from Evidence

Materials Per Group

- Hydrochloric acid, HCl, 1 *M*, 60 mL
- Magnesium ribbon, Mg, 7 cm strip
- Magnesium oxide, MgO, 0.4 g
- Balance, 0.01 g precision
- Calorimeter, small scale
- Digital thermometer or temperature sensor
- Forceps
- Graduated cylinder, 25 or 50 mL
- Metric ruler, marked in mm
- Scissors
- Spatula
- Stirring rod
- Wash bottle and water
- Weighing dish

Safety

Wear safety goggles, chemical-resistant gloves, and a lab coat when performing this or any lab that uses chemicals, heat, or glassware. Hydrochloric acid is toxic by ingestion and corrosive to skin and eyes. Magnesium metal is a flammable solid. Do not handle

O/G/S/A Lab Interactive Worksheets

INTEGRATE THE THREE DIMENSIONS

In the Inquiry Lab, students plan and carry out an investigation [SEP-3] to gather data about energy changes in the system [CCC-5] during the combustion of magnesium in air. They use data collected to calculate [SEP-5] the heat of reaction for the combustion reaction [PS1.B].

CONNECT TO CAREERS

Solar Thermochemist The new field of solar thermochemistry blends solar energy research with thermochemistry to produce new and exciting processes for materials production. Solar thermochemists use the extremely high amounts of energy in concentrated solar rays to catalyze reactions that can produce jet fuel from organic waste products and algae, among other things. These new types of reactions are both environmentally friendly and promise to be economically viable.

NAME ____________ DATE ________ CLASS ________

ANALYZING DATA

Energy in Reactions

Bond dissociation energy is a measure of the strength of a covalent bond. These values can be used to estimate changes in energy for reactions.The standard heat of formation is the change in enthalpy during the formation of one mole of a substance from its elements in their standard states.

Figure 1 shows the average bond energies for several covalent bonds. They are averages because the actual bond energy for a particular bond depends on the specific molecule where the bond is located. **Figure 2** shows the standard heats of formation for some molecules.

Figure 1

Average Bond Dissociation Energies			
Bond	**Bond dissociation energy (kJ/mol)**	**Bond**	**Bond dissociation energy (kJ/mol)**
H–H	432	O=O	498
I–I	151	H–Cl	427
H–I	295	O–H	467
Cl–Cl	243		

Figure 2

Standard Heats of Formation at STP			
Substance	$\Delta H_f°$ (kJ/mol)	Substance	$\Delta H_f°$ (kJ/mol)

Analyzing Data Interactive Worksheet

NAME ____________ DATE ________ CLASS ________

CLAIM-EVIDENCE-REASONING

Compare Heats of Formation

The strength of a covalent bond in a molecular compound can be estimated by determining how much energy is needed to break the bond. The lattice energy for an ionic compound can be used to estimate the strength of the ionic bonds in the compound. The standard heat of formation of a substance is the change in enthalpy that occurs when one mole of a substance is formed from pure elements in their standard states.

Build Your Argument Through Claim, Evidence, and Reasoning

1. **SEP Ask Questions** Write a question about bond energy and heats of formation that you would like to discuss with your classmates. (Your teacher may also provide you with one.)

2. **SEP Construct Written Arguments** Use the Claim-Evidence-Reasoning framework to build a scientific argument about bond energy and heats of formation (for example, comparing a molecular and ionic substance). After stating your claim, support it with evidence and scientific reasoning.

Make a Claim Your claim should be a response to the question stated above.	
Cite Evidence Identify data or knowledge that support your claim.	

CER Interactive Worksheet

ELD SUPPORT

Speaking Have student pairs justify the relationship between bond type and heat of formation for the CER activity.

- **Emerging/Beginning** Have students express opinions with familiar modal expressions, such as *can*.
- **Developing/Expanding** Have students express opinions with a variety of modal expressions, such as *possibly/likely* and *could/would*.
- **Bridging** Have students express opinions with nuanced modal expressions, such as *possibly/potentially* and *certainly/absolutely*.

Energy in Reactions

Analyzing Data Students calculate [SEP-5] the change in enthalpy for several chemical reactions [PS1.B] using bond energies. They compare their answers to the heats of formation for these compounds. This process will help them understand that the change in enthalpy for the formation of these compounds is the same, regardless of the chemical path taken.

- All of the bond dissociation energies shown in Figure 1 are positive, whereas heats of formation can be positive or negative. **Ask** Why are all bond energies shown as positive numbers? (Energy is always required to break chemical bonds.) Why are some heats of formation positive and some are negative? (Some elements exist as molecules in their standard states. If a heat of formation is positive, more energy is required to break these standard state bonds than is given off when the final compound is formed.)
- Once all of the calculations are complete, organize students into small groups and have each student explain how they arrived at their answers. This procedure will give students an opportunity to teach the material to their peers and may help some students understand the material more completely.

EXPLAIN

Compare Heats of Formation

Claim-Evidence-Reasoning In this activity, students construct an explanation [SEP-6] about the relationship between bond energy [CCC-5] and heat of formation. They share their claims with each other to refine them and develop a final evidence-backed statement.

- You may want to provide students with an example question to get them started on this assignment. For example, you may want to ask: Based on their macroscopic properties, would you predict that NaCl or H_2O has higher bond energy?
- Have students look up the heat of formation of several ionic and covalent compounds and see whether they can identify a pattern [CCC-1]. They should notice that large covalent compounds have very high heats of formation, but small ionic compounds seem to have higher heats of formation than smaller covalent compounds.

Bond Energy and Enthalpy

Animation In this animation, students observe several reactions [PS1.B] and the energy changes associated with each reaction. As chemical bonds are broken, energy [CCC-5] is absorbed. Energy is released when chemical bonds are formed. Some reactions have an overall increase in bond energy (endothermic), whereas others have a decrease in bond energy (exothermic).

- Pair students to watch the animation. Encourage them to pause the animation and take notes or make sketches of what they see in the animation. Have students add their thoughts about how they might be able to use the ideas to improve their explanations about the relationship between bond energy and heat of formation.
- You could also watch the animation as a class. Pause it after an important concept is presented, and ask students how the concept applies to the explanations they have written.

ASSESS ON THE SPOT

After students watch the animation, ask them to write three facts they learned and describe how they can use the information as evidence to support their explanations about the relationship between bond energy and heat formation. Collect the fact sheets from students and review for accuracy. Clarify concepts that students do not understand.

Enthalpies of Formation and Reaction

Experience Notebook Assign the Experience Notebook or Realize Reader before following up with the various activities in this experience. Use these strategies to help students make sense of the images and text on the indicated pages, as well as to engage science skills.

- **Hess's Law** (p. 291) If students have a hard time understanding Hess's law, try explaining using a bank account as an analogy. Two accounts start with \$100 each. In the first account, all of the money is spent in one check. In the second, \$20 is deposited first but then the owner spends \$60 twice. In both cases, the bank account balance ends up at zero.
- **Heat Summation** (p. 292) Explain the following to students: When adding chemical reactions [PS1.B], anything that shows up on both sides of the reaction arrow will cancel out. If the coefficients of any compound do not match, you can multiply the entire reaction (and all coefficients) by any number. If you do this, you also must multiply ΔH for that reaction by the same number. You can also flip any reversible reactions if necessary. In this case, you must also flip the sign of ΔH.
- **Standard Enthalpy of Formation** (p. 293) Students may get into the habit of ignoring the state symbols in chemical reactions [PS1.B]. Remind them that, when using standard enthalpies of formation, the state symbol is extremely important. Liquid water and solid water have different ΔH values, as shown in the table.
- **Standard Enthalpy of Reaction** (p. 294) The formula for standard enthalpy of reaction using enthalpies of formation is slightly different than that used in bond energies. For bond energies, it is broken bonds (reactants) minus formed bonds (products). This is because bond energy tables are written with positive values. Be sure students know the difference between the two methods of calculating ΔH.
- **Sample Problem** (pp. 295 and 297) Provide extra Sample Problem practice, while you circulate and help out as needed.

  a. Given the following reaction and enthalpy of formation data.
  $C_6H_{12}O_6(s) + 6\ O_2(g) \rightarrow 6\ CO_2(g) + 6\ H_2O(l)$
  $\Delta H^\circ_f\ C_6H_{12}O_6(s) = -1276$ kJ/mol
  $\Delta H^\circ_f\ CO_2(g) = -393.5$ kJ/mol
  $\Delta H^\circ_f\ H_2O(l) = -285.8$ kJ/mol
  What is the change in enthalpy for the reaction given above? (–2800 kJ)

  b. When potassium hydroxide (KOH) is added to water, the following reaction takes place.
  $KOH(s) \rightarrow K^+(aq) + OH^-(aq) + 43$ kJ/mol
  How much heat is released when 7.45 mol of KOH is dissolved in water? (–320 kJ)

How Do You Multiply Decimals?

Virtual Nerd Video Use this video tutorial to reinforce how to multiply decimals.

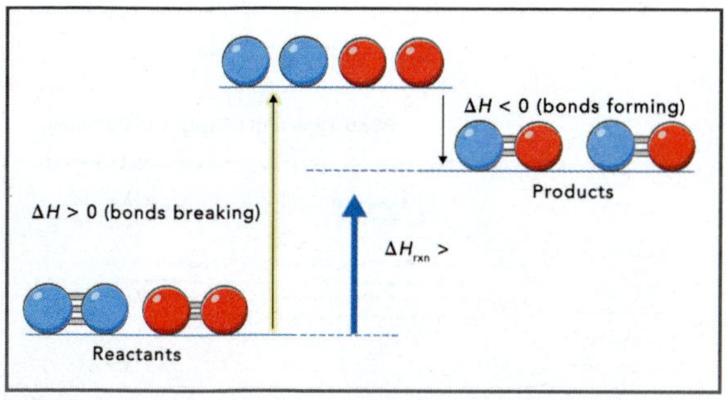

Animation: Bond Energy and Enthalpy

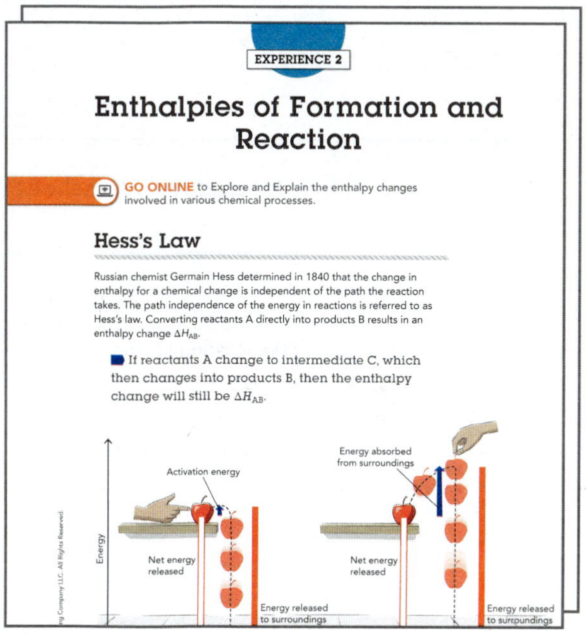

Experience Notebook, pp. 291–297

eTEXT

SAMPLE PROBLEM SUPPORT

Thermochemical calculations can get somewhat complex, even if the actual math skills being used are elementary. Students most often make mistakes because they get lost in the problem or overlook some small detail. Encourage students to use an entire sheet of paper for each problem they work on. This extra room can help them keep track of each part of the problem more easily. You may also want to encourage students to use different colors for the reactants and products side of the problem to help them keep those straight.

Virtual Nerd Video: How Do You Multiply Decimals?

NAME ______ DATE ______ CLASS ______

DISCUSSION RUBRIC

Bond Type and Changes in Enthalpy

Use this rubric to help you assess your explanation about the effect of bond type on

	EXEMPLARY Score the work 3 if:	ACCOMPLISHED Score the work 2 if:
Claims and Evidence Student Score: ______ Teacher Score: ______	The claim evaluates the bond type of each substance and describes evidence that quantifies the amount of energy associated with breaking or forming bonds.	The claim evaluates the bond type of each substance, but the evidence is not related to the breaking or forming of bonds.
Evaluation and Critique Student Score: ______ Teacher Score: ______	Alternative explanations for differences in the energy associated with breaking or forming different types of bonds are identified and actively refuted using evidence.	The evaluation or critique mentions alternative explanations but does not actively refute them.
Reasoning and Synthesis Student Score: ______ Teacher Score: ______	When new evidence or reasoning is presented, it is incorporated into the explanation.	When new evidence or reasoning is presented, it is considered, and an attempt is made to incorporate it into the explanation.

Discussion Rubric Interactive Worksheet

NAME ______ DATE ______ CLASS ______

WRITING ABOUT SCIENCE

Energy Input for the Rusting of Iron

Use the information provided and information gathered from authoritative sources on your own to answer Questions 1 and 2.

Rusting is a chemical reaction between iron metal and oxygen gas that naturally occurs when moisture is present. The reaction changes iron from a shiny, gray metal to the dull, red iron oxide. Recall that every reaction has a minimum amount of energy that is required to allow the reaction to proceed. Where does the energy come from to begin the rusting reaction?

Obtain and Evaluate Information

1. **SEP Evaluate Information** Assume the simplified chemical equation for rusting is $4Fe(s) + 3O_2(g) \rightarrow 2Fe_2O_3(s)$. What bonds must break during the formation of rust? What bonds must form during the formation of rust?

2. **SEP Construct an Explanation** Energy is needed to start the reaction of iron with oxygen to form rust. Rusting can even occur at room temperature. Where does the energy required to break the bonds in the reactants come from?

Writing About Science Interactive Worksheet

CLASSROOM MODIFICATIONS

Based on your students' abilities and your schedule, you can modify the Writing About Science activity to be more open ended or more guided.

- **More Open Ended** Remind students that the term *rusting* can refer to the oxidation of many different metals. Have students select an oxidation reaction for any common metal for their writing instead of requiring them to write about the properties of iron. Aluminum, titanium, and copper are all metals that form oxides and "rust".
- **More Guided** Provide each group of students with a specific chemical reaction between iron, oxygen, and water to investigate. This can help focus the research to help students use their time more efficiently.

PROFESSIONAL DEVELOPMENT

Background Notes Hess's law is an example of a state function. The overall change in enthalpy for any reaction is dependent only on the initial and final states of the system. Chemistry also has path functions (calculations that depend on the intermediate as well), but most thermochemical equations are state functions. This can make it much simpler to find the change in energy for a complex system—only the initial and final states of the system have an impact on the result.

ELABORATE

Bond Type and Changes in Enthalpy

Discussion Rubric Students assess their own explanation about the effect of bond type on changes in enthalpy.

- Lead a class discussion about how different bond types and bond energies [CCC-5] can impact the heat of formation and heat of reaction for different compounds. Students should use their CER worksheet to help them frame their discussion. Start the discussion with the whole class before breaking students into smaller groups to complete the rubric.
- Ask students to write the differences between ionic and covalent bonds and explain why each difference may or may not contribute to the differences in heat of formation seen for each compound.

Energy Input for the Rusting of Iron

Writing About Science In this activity, students construct an explanation [SEP-6] of the chemical and energetic changes that take place when iron rusts. They research chemical reactions [PS1.B] that produce rust and explain how rusting can be exothermic, even if there is no visible sign of heat being given off.

- You can use a chemical hand warmer to demonstrate the exothermic nature of iron rusting. Cut open a used hand warmer to show students the iron powder inside. **Ask** Why does the iron in this hand warmer give off heat so much faster than the iron in a rusty nail or fence? (The powder has much greater surface area, allowing more of the iron to react with the oxygen in the air and speeding up the reaction.)
- Have students calculate [SEP-5] the change in enthalpy for their rusting reaction using a table of standard heats of formation.
- Have students find other chemical equations that they could combine to find the change in enthalpy for their rust reaction, assuming they could not measure it directly.
- Consider giving students extra credit for coming up with the largest system of chemical reactions that still adds up to the correct final equation.

ASSESS ON THE SPOT

Ask students to draw an energy change diagram for their rusting reaction with the energy of the reactants, energy of the products, and activation energy all labeled clearly. Have students draw another energy change diagram for the enthalpy of formation reaction for their product. Students should show that the overall change in enthalpy for both reactions is the same.

EXPERIENCE 2 ASSESSMENT

EVALUATE

Enthalpies of Formation and Reaction

Quiz Assign the quiz in online technology-enhanced, auto-graded format or as an editable quiz worksheet. Use the scoring notes and remediation strategies found online to assess students' responses and to provide targeted feedback for each item to remediate well before assigning the summative 3-D Assessment.

REMEDIATION SUGGESTIONS

- **If** students have a hard time understanding how Hess's law can be used to find the change in enthalpy for a reaction, **then** have them review Hess's Law and the Combustion of a Metal Inquiry Lab. Have students explain Hess's law in their own words.
- **If** students have difficulty understanding the relationship between bond energy and heat of formation, **then** have them return to the CER activity, Compare Heats of Formation.
- **If** students are struggling to calculate change in enthalpy using heats of formation or heats of solution, **then** have them review the Sample Problem on page 297 of the Experience Notebook and assign a few additional practice problems for students to work on.

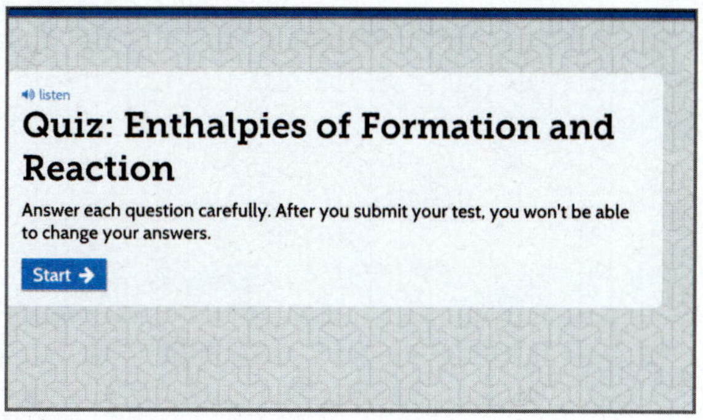

Interactive Online Quiz

Quiz Interactive Worksheet

Revisit INVESTIGATIVE PHENOMENON

Support Reflection Students can complete the reflection prompt, where they will unpack and make sense of the Investigative Phenomenon, based on practices and understandings that have been reinforced over the course of the experience.

- Ask students to explain Hess's law in their own words, and ensure that they understand how it is used in thermochemical equations. Have students apply Hess's law to the process of people exercising.
- Work through a sample enthalpy calculation using a system of chemical equations and make sure students are comfortable manipulating these equations to find ΔH.
- Have students calculate ΔH for a reaction using a table of heats of formation and be sure they can calculate enthalpy change for a reaction using this method.
- Ask students if they are comfortable finding the change in enthalpy for a dissolution process if they are given the enthalpy of solution for a compound.

Further Develop Your Model Have students add any evidence they have collected in this experience. Allow time for them to make any additional changes based on information they have collected from the activities in this learning experience. Evidence may include the technique of calculating reaction enthalpy change from a system of equations or from heats of formation.

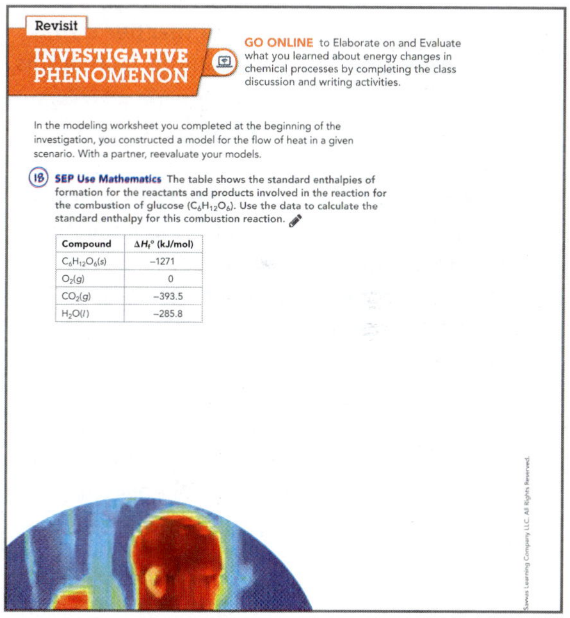
Revisit INVESTIGATIVE PHENOMENON

GO ONLINE to Elaborate on and Evaluate what you learned about energy changes in chemical processes by completing the class discussion and writing activities.

In the modeling worksheet you completed at the beginning of the investigation, you constructed a model for the flow of heat in a given scenario. With a partner, reevaluate your models.

18 **SEP Use Mathematics** The table shows the standard enthalpies of formation for the reactants and products involved in the reaction for the combustion of glucose ($C_6H_{12}O_6$). Use the data to calculate the standard enthalpy for this combustion reaction.

Compound	$\Delta H_f°$ (kJ/mol)
$C_6H_{12}O_6(s)$	−1271
$O_2(g)$	0
$CO_2(g)$	−393.5
$H_2O(l)$	−285.8

Experience Notebook, p. 298

eTEXT

EXPERIENCE 3

Enthalpy in Changes of State

Teacher Background

In this experience, students learn how enthalpy changes when a substance transitions between solid, liquid, and gas. Students learn how to interpret a heating curve for a given substance and how to calculate the change in enthalpy for any type of state change. They learn how enthalpies of fusion and vaporization can be used to understand the relative strengths of the intermolecular forces that hold solids, liquids, and gases together.

Objectives

- **Understand how and why substances change in enthalpy when transitioning between physical states.**
- **Calculate the change in enthalpy for state changes between solid, liquid, and gas.**
- **Describe the link between state change enthalpies and the strength of intermolecular forces.**

ENGAGE

EVERYDAY PHENOMENON

Can ice water be used to start a fire?

Use this teacher demo to help students understand that freezing is always an exothermic process as new intermolecular bonds are formed.

Fire From Ice

Engage students with this demonstration of the energy that is released when a substance is frozen.

Materials paraffin wax, wide-mouthed test tube, ring stand and clamp, beaker full of ice water, Bunsen burner, chemical splash goggles, lab apron, gloves

Safety This demonstration produces a flame and should be conducted under a fume hood with the sash lowered. Be mindful that the test tube may break from heat stress. All participants and observers should wear full chemical splash goggles and stand a few feet back from the demonstration.

1. Ask students whether freezing is an exothermic or endothermic process.
2. Shave 2–4 g of paraffin wax into the bottom of the test tube and clamp the tube so the top is angled away from any observers.
3. Heat the wax until it melts and begins to boil. As this is happening, discuss how melting and boiling are both endothermic processes.
4. Allow the wax to continue boiling for about 30 seconds to generate wax vapor near the mouth of the test tube.
5. Remove the heat from the test tube and immediately raise the beaker of ice water around the bottom of the tube. Note that this will likely cause the test tube to break due to heat stress.
6. As the wax in the test tube freezes, it will release enough heat to ignite the wax vapor formed near the mouth of the test tube. This should create a small flame.
7. Lead a class discussion to explain that freezing is exothermic. Explain that freezing must be exothermic due to the formation of intermolecular bonds. Then connect the discussion with the opposite change of state that students investigate in the Inquiry Lab.

RELATED PHENOMENA

In addition to the Fire From Ice teacher demo, consider using other phenomena to launch this experience.

- **Comparing Enthalpy of Fusion** Melt a sample of tin using a cast iron pot and a Bunsen burner. Have students compare the enthalpy of fusion of tin with that of water. This will demonstrate to students that some substances have much higher enthalpies of fusion than water.
- **Comparing Enthalpies of Vaporization** Place a few drops of a volatile organic compound on a lab bench, and place the same amount of water beside it. Have students note how quickly and easily the volatile compound evaporates, even at room temperature, to demonstrate low enthalpy of vaporization.

EXPLORE

The Heat of Melting Ice

Inquiry Lab In this lab, students carry out an investigation [SEP-3] to determine how much energy is required to melt ice. They determine the energy required to melt ice using calorimetry and the effect of an ionic compound on the freezing temperature of water.

Lab Demo Video Watch the Lab Demo Video for advice on materials and preparation.

Choose Your Version Open-ended (O), Guided (G), Shortened (S), Advanced (A)

Materials ice cubes, 30 g sodium chloride, distilled water, balance, 500-mL beaker, calorimeter (2 nested polystyrene cups), 250-mL Erlenmeyer flask, 100-mL graduated cylinder, paper towels, spatula, stirring rod, support stand and ring clamp, 2 16 mm × 100 mm test tubes, test tube clamp, thermometer, timer or stopwatch, weighing dishes/paper

Safety Make sure students wear safety goggles when performing this lab. They should use a glass stirring rod to stir the liquid; never stir with a thermometer. Remind students to wash their hands thoroughly with soap and warm water before leaving the laboratory.

Expected Outcome The energy required to melt ice will be determined using a calorimeter, and its value will be close to the expected 334 J/g. Changes in temperature of water in a calorimeter will be used to determine the amount of heat absorbed by melting ice cubes. The cooling curve of water will be used to determine that the freezing point of water is approximately 0°C. Dissolution of sodium chloride will lower the freezing temperature of water.

Lab Summary Video Watch the Lab Summary Video for support on connecting the lab investigation to the Investigative Phenomenon.

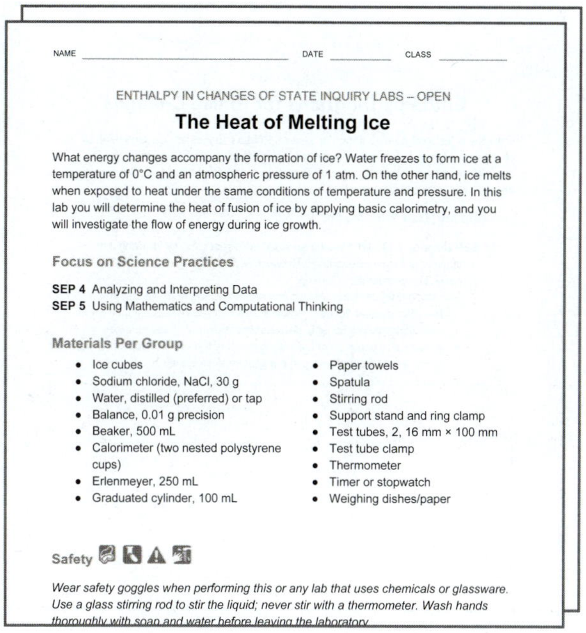

NAME ______ DATE ______ CLASS ______

ENTHALPY IN CHANGES OF STATE INQUIRY LABS – OPEN

The Heat of Melting Ice

What energy changes accompany the formation of ice? Water freezes to form ice at a temperature of 0°C and an atmospheric pressure of 1 atm. On the other hand, ice melts when exposed to heat under the same conditions of temperature and pressure. In this lab you will determine the heat of fusion of ice by applying basic calorimetry, and you will investigate the flow of energy during ice growth.

Focus on Science Practices

SEP 4 Analyzing and Interpreting Data
SEP 5 Using Mathematics and Computational Thinking

Materials Per Group

- Ice cubes
- Sodium chloride, NaCl, 30 g
- Water, distilled (preferred) or tap
- Balance, 0.01 g precision
- Beaker, 500 mL
- Calorimeter (two nested polystyrene cups)
- Erlenmeyer, 250 mL
- Graduated cylinder, 100 mL
- Paper towels
- Spatula
- Stirring rod
- Support stand and ring clamp
- Test tubes, 2, 16 mm × 100 mm
- Test tube clamp
- Thermometer
- Timer or stopwatch
- Weighing dishes/paper

Safety

Wear safety goggles when performing this or any lab that uses chemicals or glassware. Use a glass stirring rod to stir the liquid; never stir with a thermometer. Wash hands thoroughly with soap and water before leaving the laboratory.

O/G/S/A Lab Interactive Worksheets

PROFESSIONAL DEVELOPMENT

Meaningful Uses of Technology The Inquiry Lab works much better if you have access to electronic temperature probes and data logging software. Have students generate a plot of temperature versus time using this software to more accurately determine the freezing point of water. You can also have classes combine their data to get a more accurate result.

ASSESS ON THE SPOT

After students complete the lab, ask them to write a short paragraph that summarizes their findings and to qualitatively relate what they learned during the lab. Students should note that the enthalpy of fusion of water is very large and positive, indicating that water molecules are very strongly attracted to one another.

Heat of Fusion

Interactivity In this interactivity, students are given various metal samples and are asked to predict which sample will melt first. They then melt each sample and watch as their temperatures move along the heating curve.

- **Ask** Do all of the metals have the same slope on the heating curve when going from solid to liquid? (No, some are steeper than others.) What is the relationship between the specific heat capacity of the metals and the slope of the heating curve? (The substances with higher heat capacities have shallower slopes, indicating more heat is required to increase their temperature.) What else is different about each heating curve? (The flat regions are different lengths, indicating that different amounts of energy are required to change phases.)

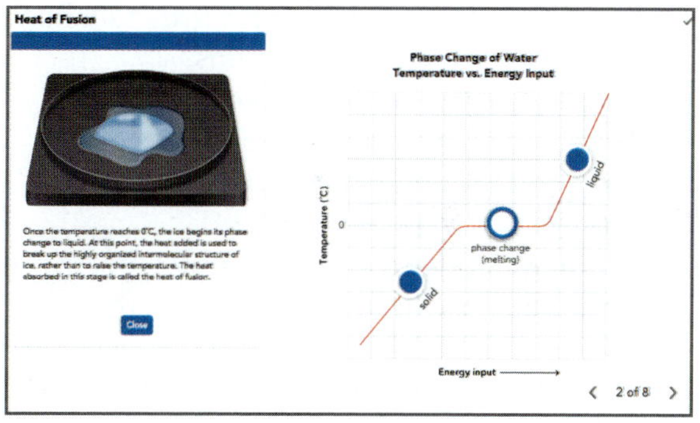

Interactivity: Heat of Fusion

INTEGRATE THE THREE DIMENSIONS

As students complete the Heat of Fusion interactivity, they see how the properties of different compounds can affect [CCC-2] the way those compounds absorb and release heat energy [PS3.D]. By allowing students to manipulate the interactivity, they can identify patterns [CCC-1] in the data and analyze [SEP-4] the heating curves to gain a better understanding of how a substance's properties impact its enthalpy of fusion.

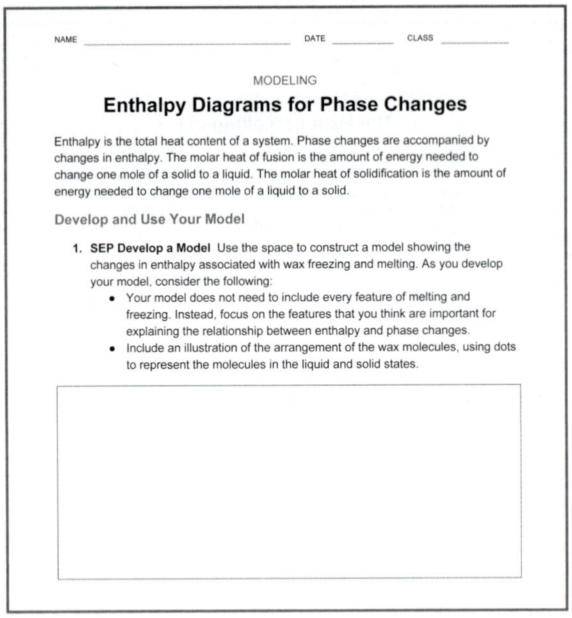
NAME ______________ DATE ________ CLASS ________

MODELING

Enthalpy Diagrams for Phase Changes

Enthalpy is the total heat content of a system. Phase changes are accompanied by changes in enthalpy. The molar heat of fusion is the amount of energy needed to change one mole of a solid to a liquid. The molar heat of solidification is the amount of energy needed to change one mole of a liquid to a solid.

Develop and Use Your Model

1. **SEP Develop a Model** Use the space to construct a model showing the changes in enthalpy associated with wax freezing and melting. As you develop your model, consider the following:
   - Your model does not need to include every feature of melting and freezing. Instead, focus on the features that you think are important for explaining the relationship between enthalpy and phase changes.
   - Include an illustration of the arrangement of the wax molecules, using dots to represent the molecules in the liquid and solid states.

Modeling Interactive Worksheet

ELD SUPPORT

Speaking Have students work in pairs to plan and deliver a short oral presentation of their heating diagram models they drew for the Modeling activity.

- **Emerging/Beginning** Have students make one or two slides to present their models. Encourage them to write notecards to help them deliver their presentations.
- **Developing/Expanding** Have students deliver their presentations using bullet points to prompt their memory but without reading directly from prepared notes.
- **Bridging** Students should prepare presentations without reading from their slides or prepared notes and should include some interactive element, such as allowing time for questions.

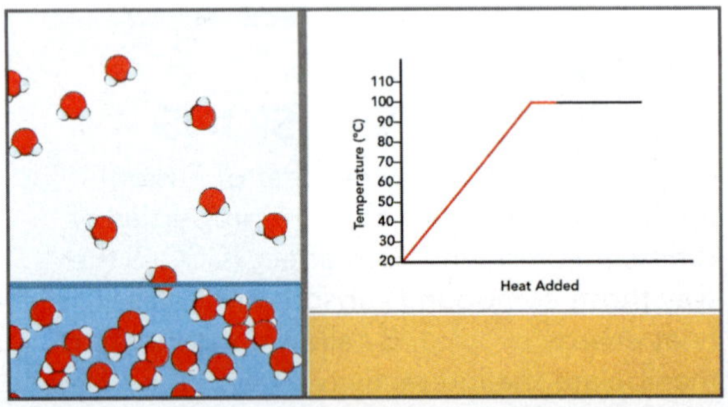

Animation: Energy Changes in Changes of State

EXPLAIN

Enthalpy Diagrams for Phase Changes

Modeling In this activity, students construct models [SEP-2] of the changes in enthalpy as wax freezes and melts. They use their models to predict the amount of energy needed for a particular phase change.

- Before students begin to work on their models, lead a class discussion about the behavior of wax as it transitions from solid to liquid. Students should know that wax increases in temperature as it is heated and that the temperature of a substance remains constant as it undergoes a phase change.
- Have students work with a partner for Questions 4 and 5. When students are finished, have each pair share how they would improve or refine their models.

DIFFERENTIATED INSTRUCTION

- **Support Struggling Students** Some students may require a framework for their models in order to get started. Lead a class discussion about how the models should be developed. Alternatively, provide students with a model that they can label while the components of the model are discussed.
- **Support Less Proficient Readers** Have students work in pairs to complete the worksheet. Encourage them to use a think-aloud strategy before they begin to answer Question 1. They should think-aloud about what their model should show, what the parts should be, and the parts connect to the other parts. As one partner talks, the other partner can take notes.

Energy Changes in Changes of State

Animation In this animation, students are shown what happens at the molecular level when a liquid boils and becomes a gas. As the temperature of the liquid increases, the particles that make up the liquid move more quickly. At a certain point, the molecules gain enough kinetic energy to overcome their intermolecular attractions and spread apart to become a gas.

- Consider showing this animation more than once. Before the first showing, ask students to focus on the motions of the water molecules and describe how they change as the temperature increases toward the boiling point. Before the second viewing, ask students to look at the heating curve and describe what is happening to the particles in the flat portion of the curve.
- After viewing the animation, organize the class into groups of three or four students and have them write a short summary of the key observations they made from the animation. After a few minutes, have one volunteer from each group share their observations with the class and discuss them.

ASSESS ON THE SPOT

Give each student a blank heating curve for a generic substance. Have students draw a picture of the molecules at each point along the curve, using arrows to represent the kinetic energy of the particles (longer arrows represent more kinetic energy). (Students should show the kinetic energy of the molecules increasing in the sloped part of the curve but staying constant as the substance transitions between states.) Collect the drawings and review them to be sure students understand the connection between the heating curve and motions of the particles.

Enthalpy in Changes of State

Experience Notebook Assign the Experience Notebook or Realize Reader before following up with the various activities in this experience. Use these strategies to help students make sense of the images and text on the indicated pages, as well as to engage science skills.

- **Heat During Phase Changes** (p. 299) Point out that the temperature on the heating curve shown does not increase during melting or vaporization, even though the application of heat to the sample is constant. **Ask** What is happening to the heat energy in the flat portions of the heating curve? (The energy is being used to break intermolecular bonds.)
- **Enthalpy of Fusion and Solidification** (p. 300) Write the equation shown on the page on the board and call on students to explain what it means. Then ask why the amounts of heat are the same.
- **Sample Problem** (p. 301) Provide extra Sample Problem practice, while you circulate and help out as needed.
  a. What is the heat required to melt 8.97 g of water at its melting point? (2.99 kJ)
  b. How much heat is required to melt a 10.00 g ice cube that is at −10.00°C? The specific heat capacity of ice is 2.108 kJ/kg°C. (Add heat to raise the ice to 0°C and then melt the ice, 3.546 kJ)
- **Enthalpy of Vaporization and Condensation** (p. 302) Point out to students that the enthalpy of vaporization is typically much greater than the enthalpy of fusion for a given substance. This is because the liquid–gas phase transition requires the molecules to become much more spread apart (and therefore much more weakly bonded) than the solid–liquid transition.
- **Sample Problem** (p. 303) Provide extra Sample Problem practice, while you circulate and help out as needed.
  a. How much water, in grams, can be converted to steam at its boiling point when 45 kJ of heat is added? (20.0 g)
  b. How much heat is required to boil 18.0 g of water that is at 40.0°C? The specific heat capacity of water is 4.19 kJ/kg°C. (Add heat to raise water to 100°C and then boil the water, 45.2 kJ)
- **Structure and Changes of State** (p. 304) Display the Enthalpy of Vaporization diagram but hide the captions on the right of the diagram. **Ask** What does the term *dispersion force* mean in the top middle of the diagram? (attraction between molecules caused by the electron motion on one molecule affecting the electron motion on the other molecule) How does that compare to the force of the hydrogen bond on the right? (The hydrogen bond is a stronger force.) How would you describe the trend shown in the bottom row of the diagram? (Molecules with a larger radius have greater enthalpy.) Then have students read the captions for the diagram in their texts.
- **Evaporation** (p. 305) Before students read this section, remind them that evaporation is a physical change from a liquid state to a gas (vapor). **Ask** On a molecular level, what is the difference between liquid water and water vapor? (In the vapor phase, the water molecules are farther apart and not as strongly attracted to each other.) What must happen for a liquid to change into a gas? (Energy must be added to overcome the attraction.) Is evaporation endothermic or exothermic? (endothermic)

Thermochemistry

Virtual Reality Experience Students explore how the energy of the same set of atoms varies when the atoms are together in a molecule and when they exist separately as individual atoms.

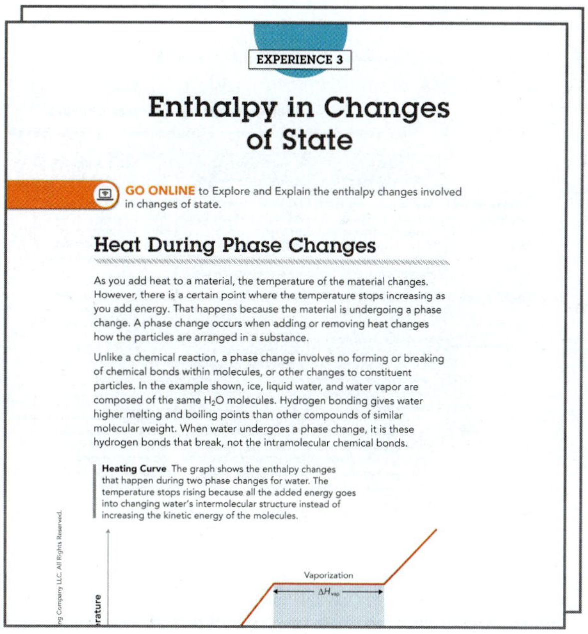
EXPERIENCE 3

Enthalpy in Changes of State

GO ONLINE to Explore and Explain the enthalpy changes involved in changes of state.

Heat During Phase Changes

As you add heat to a material, the temperature of the material changes. However, there is a certain point where the temperature stops increasing as you add energy. That happens because the material is undergoing a phase change. A phase change occurs when adding or removing heat changes how the particles are arranged in a substance.

Unlike a chemical reaction, a phase change involves no forming or breaking of chemical bonds within molecules, or other changes to constituent particles. In the example shown, ice, liquid water, and water vapor are composed of the same H_2O molecules. Hydrogen bonding gives water higher melting and boiling points than other compounds of similar molecular weight. When water undergoes a phase change, it is these hydrogen bonds that break, not the intramolecular chemical bonds.

Heating Curve The graph shows the enthalpy changes that happen during two phase changes for water. The temperature stops rising because all the added energy goes into changing water's intermolecular structure instead of increasing the kinetic energy of the molecules.

Experience Notebook, pp. 299–305

eTEXT

SAMPLE PROBLEM SUPPORT

Point out to students that state change problems do not always start or end at the phase transition temperature. In these cases, first use the specific heat capacity for the substance to determine the heat required to heat or cool the substance to the phase transition point. Then add this heat to the heat required for the phase transition. Because a substance will have different heat capacities in the different phases of matter, keep track of where you are in the problem. Using different colors of ink for each phase can help with these more complex problems.

PBL CONNECTION

Assign the PBL worksheet. Ask the following questions to get students to connect their knowledge to the PBL worksheet.

- Why do recipes differ when different amounts of ingredients are used?
- How can heat change a recipe when its ingredients are cooked?
- How can you determine the number of kilocalories in a serving?
- Why might the number of Calories change when different ingredients are used to make the same recipe?

Virtual Reality Experience: Thermochemistry

NAME ______________________ DATE __________ CLASS __________

PEER REVIEW RUBRIC

Enthalpy Diagrams for Phase Changes

Use this rubric to help you assess your classmate's enthalpy diagrams for ph

	EXEMPLARY Score the work 3 if:	ACCOMPLISHED Score the work 2 if:	DEVELOPING Score the work 1 if:	
Components of the Model Score: ______	Two states of matter (solid and liquid) are labeled on the diagram. The enthalpy change for each phase change is visually represented.	Two states of matter (solid and liquid) are labeled on the diagram, but the enthalpy change for one or both of the phase changes is not clearly represented.	The model includes labels of enthalpy changes and two states of matter (solid and liquid), but the relationship between the two is not clear.	
Relationships Score: ______	The model shows that the enthalpy increases as the state changes from a solid to a liquid and decreases from a liquid to a solid. It also clearly shows that the same magnitude of change in enthalpy occurs for both state changes.	The model shows that the enthalpy increases as the state changes from a solid to a liquid but does not show the decrease in enthalpy from a liquid to a solid.	The model does not clearly show how a change in enthalpy relates to a phase change.	
Connections Score: ______	The model makes sense, and some aspects can be extended to other phase changes or the phase changes of other substances.	The model makes sense but cannot be extended to other phase changes or the phase changes of other substances.	The model is unclear and could not be effectively applied to other phase changes or the phase changes of other substances.	

Peer Review Rubric Interactive Worksheet

NAME ______________________ DATE __________ CLASS __________

WRITING ABOUT SCIENCE

Enthalpy of Reaction vs. Phase Change

Use the information provided and information gathered from authoritative sources on your own to answer the question.

Intramolecular forces hold atoms together in a molecule. They are stronger than the intermolecular forces, which hold molecules close to each other in solids and liquids.

The heat of reaction for the decomposition of water in the liquid state is 285.8 kJ/mol. The molar heat of vaporization for water is 40.7 kJ/mol. In other words, seven times more energy is required to break up a mole of water molecules into hydrogen gas and oxygen gas than is required to convert a mole of liquid water to water vapor.

Obtain and Evaluate Information

1. **SEP Construct an Explanation** Use scientific reasoning to provide an explanation for the difference between the energy needed to split water molecules into hydrogen and oxygen gases and the energy needed to convert liquid water into vapor.

Writing About Science Interactive Worksheet

CLASSROOM MODIFICATIONS

Based on your students' abilities and your schedule, you can modify the Enthalpy of Reaction vs. Phase Change writing activity to be more open ended or more guided.

- **More Open Ended** Allow students to present their findings in any format they wish, including a visual presentation, video, poster, or oral report, instead of requiring them to write their answers in a document. If you choose to allow students to select their own method of delivering the information, give them a rubric that you will use to evaluate their assignment to ensure that they have answered the questions appropriately and completely.
- **More Guided** Provide students with a list of acceptable sources for their research and give them a few key words or phrases to use in their search.

ELABORATE

Enthalpy Diagrams for Phase Changes

Peer Review Rubric In this activity, students assess classmates' enthalpy diagrams from the Enthalpy Diagrams for Phase Changes Modeling activity. Students should use the rubric to provide constructive feedback on their peers' models and help them come up with a more refined diagram.

- Provide students with an example of an accurate heating curve that they can compare their models against. Encourage students to identify at least one thing that their peers' model did better than the heating curve you provided.
- After students finish their reviews, lead a short class discussion to identify the most important parts of the heating curve model and explain why each of those parts is critical for conveying information about a given substance.

ASSESS ON THE SPOT

Give students 5 minutes to draw a flowchart that summarizes the enthalpy changes involved when a substance undergoes a phase change. Tell them they can use symbols, colors, and their own words.

PROFESSIONAL DEVELOPMENT

Develop Classroom Collaboration Have students work in groups to explain how to determine the amount of energy absorbed or released in a chemical or physical process. Give each group 60 seconds to explain, (orally, pictorially, or in writing) how to use molar heats to determine the quantity of heat absorbed by a melting solid and the quantity of heat released when a liquid solidifies. (The molar heat of fusion should be used to determine the energy absorbed by a melting solid and the molar heat of solidification should be used to determine the energy released by a solidifying liquid.)

Enthalpy of Reaction vs. Phase Change

Writing About Science Students construct an explanation [SEP-6] for the extreme difference in the energy required to decompose water into its constituent elements and the energy needed to convert liquid water into a gas.

- Ionic compounds have enthalpies of fusion that are directly related to Coulomb's law: the size and charge of the ions in the compound determine the strength of the forces between particles. Have students make a graph of enthalpy of fusion versus atomic radius for several alkali metal chlorides (LiCl, NaCl, and KCl) to illustrate this relationship.
- Water has an extremely high enthalpy of vaporization for a molecule of its size. This is one of the unique properties that makes water critical for life. Ask students why a high enthalpy of vaporization would be an important characteristic for a substance that makes up the vast majority of the human body.

EVALUATE

Enthalpy in Changes of State

Quiz Assign the quiz in online technology-enhanced, auto-graded format or as an editable quiz worksheet. Use the scoring notes and remediation strategies found online to assess students' responses and to provide targeted feedback for each item to remediate well before assigning the summative 3-D Assessment.

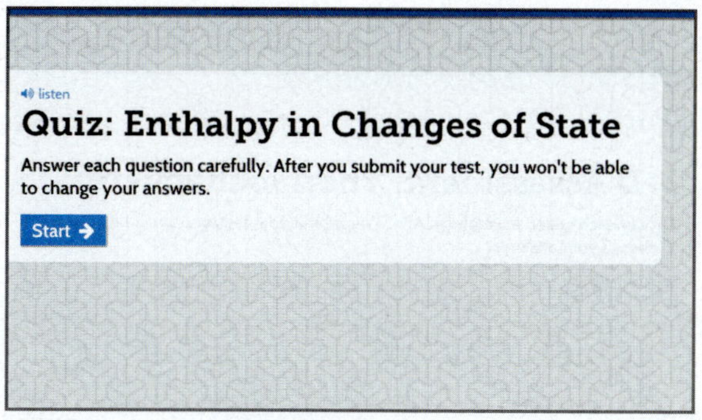

Interactive Online Quiz

Quiz Interactive Worksheet

REMEDIATION SUGGESTIONS

- **If** students struggle with reading a heating curve and explaining what is happening in each section, **then** have them review the Energy Changes in Changes of State animation.
- **If** students are having a hard time calculating enthalpy changes for state transitions, **then** have them review the Sample Problems on pages 301 and 303 of the Experience Notebook and assign a few more practice problems as needed.
- **If** students struggle to understand the link between state change enthalpy and intermolecular forces of attraction, **then** have them review the graphic on page 304 of the Experience Notebook and summarize the key points from it in their own words.

Revisit INVESTIGATIVE PHENOMENON

Support Reflection Students can complete the reflection prompt, where they will unpack and make sense of the Investigative Phenomenon, based on practices and understandings that have been reinforced over the course of the experience.

- Ask students to describe in their own words what happens to a substance as it absorbs heat and transitions from solid to liquid and gas.
- Work through a sample enthalpy of state change calculation with the class, and ensure that they are comfortable solving these problems on their own.
- Have students predict the enthalpy of vaporization for several compounds based on their intermolecular forces of attraction.
- Ask students to use what they have learned in this experience to explain why exercise causes our bodies to become warmer.

Evaluate and Revise Your Model Have students answer Questions 3, 4, and 5 in the Modeling activity and reevaluate their model based on peer feedback. Students should add any additional evidence they have collected in this investigation. Evidence may include the fact that water requires a great deal of energy to evaporate, explaining how sweat is able to remove heat from our bodies during exercise.

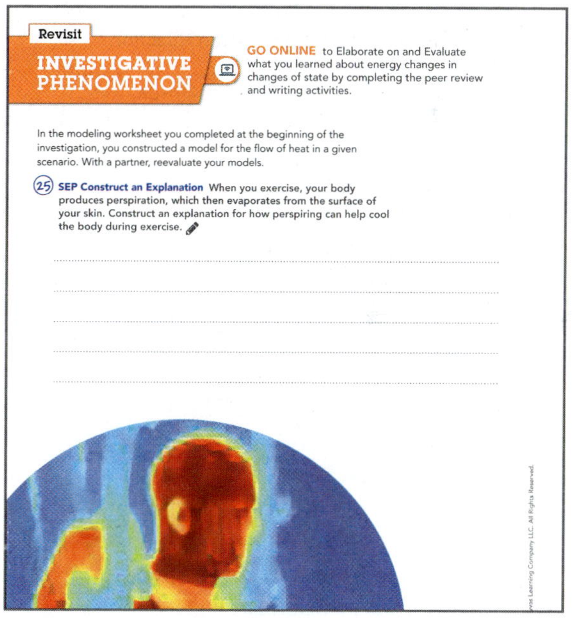
Revisit
INVESTIGATIVE PHENOMENON

GO ONLINE to Elaborate on and Evaluate what you learned about energy changes in changes of state by completing the peer review and writing activities.

In the modeling worksheet you completed at the beginning of the investigation, you constructed a model for the flow of heat in a given scenario. With a partner, reevaluate your models.

25 **SEP Construct an Explanation** When you exercise, your body produces perspiration, which then evaporates from the surface of your skin. Construct an explanation for how perspiring can help cool the body during exercise.

Experience Notebook, p. 306

eTEXT

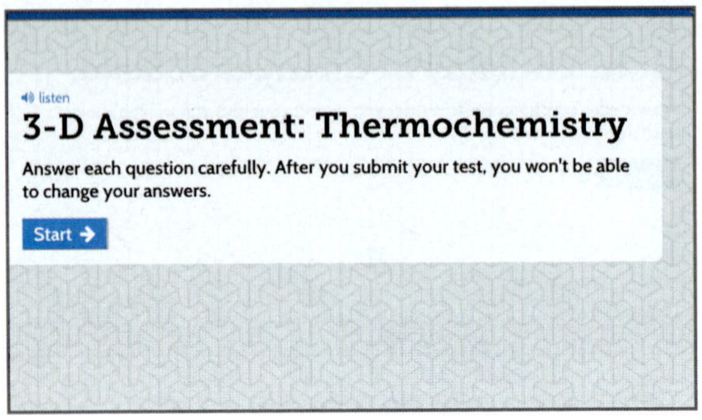

Interactive Online 3-D Assessment

Interactive ExamView 3-D Assessment

3-D Assessment Interactive Worksheet

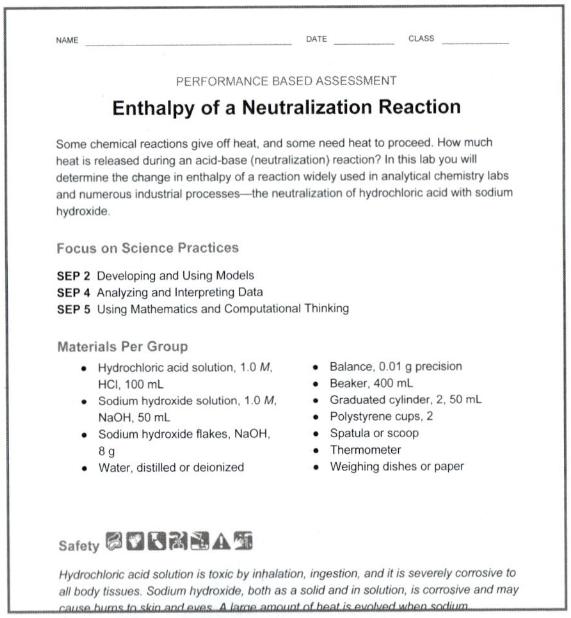

NAME ______ DATE ______ CLASS ______

PERFORMANCE BASED ASSESSMENT

Enthalpy of a Neutralization Reaction

Some chemical reactions give off heat, and some need heat to proceed. How much heat is released during an acid-base (neutralization) reaction? In this lab you will determine the change in enthalpy of a reaction widely used in analytical chemistry labs and numerous industrial processes—the neutralization of hydrochloric acid with sodium hydroxide.

Focus on Science Practices

SEP 2 Developing and Using Models
SEP 4 Analyzing and Interpreting Data
SEP 5 Using Mathematics and Computational Thinking

Materials Per Group

- Hydrochloric acid solution, 1.0 *M*, HCl, 100 mL
- Sodium hydroxide solution, 1.0 *M*, NaOH, 50 mL
- Sodium hydroxide flakes, NaOH, 8 g
- Water, distilled or deionized
- Balance, 0.01 g precision
- Beaker, 400 mL
- Graduated cylinder, 2, 50 mL
- Polystyrene cups, 2
- Spatula or scoop
- Thermometer
- Weighing dishes or paper

Safety

Hydrochloric acid solution is toxic by inhalation, ingestion, and it is severely corrosive to all body tissues. Sodium hydroxide, both as a solid and in solution, is corrosive and may cause burns to skin and eyes. A large amount of heat is evolved when sodium

Performance-Based Assessment Interactive Worksheet

EVALUATE

Thermochemistry

3-D Assessment For a summative assessment of Investigation 8, assign the 3-D Assessment, which is available online, as an ExamView bank, or as an editable worksheet.

Enthalpy of a Neutralization Reaction

Performance-Based Assessment Use this Performance-Based Assessment to assess students' mastery of the standards. In this activity, students carry out an investigation [SEP-3] to determine the enthalpy of a neutralization reaction [PS1.B] involving hydrochloric acid and sodium hydroxide. They record volume, mass, mole, temperature, heat release, and enthalpy of neutralization data for the reaction. They interpret the data [SEP-4] and classify the reaction as endothermic or exothermic. Students develop models [SEP-2] by writing the balanced equations for the reactions. They use mathematical thinking [SEP-5] to calculate moles of sodium hydroxide added, temperature change [CCC-7], heat release, and enthalpy of dissolution. They construct explanations and write observations about the results.

Safety Hydrochloric acid solution is toxic by inhalation and ingestion, and it is severely corrosive to all body tissues. Sodium hydroxide, both as a solid and in solution, is corrosive and may cause burns to skin and eyes. A large amount of heat is evolved when sodium hydroxide is added to water. Make sure students wear chemical splash goggles, chemical-resistant gloves, and a chemical-resistant apron or a lab coat.

Expected Outcome The calculated enthalpy of neutralization of a HCl solution with aqueous NaOH is approximately −63 kJ/mol. By combining this enthalpy value and the enthalpy of dissolution of solid NaOH in water, students will indirectly determine the enthalpy of neutralization of HCl solution with solid NaOH.

Experience Notebook (p. 306) After students complete the Performance-Based Assessment, have them complete the reflection prompt in the Experience Notebook.

DIFFERENTIATED INSTRUCTION

- **Support Struggling Students** Struggling students may have difficulty with the Performance-Based Assessment that is focused on mathematical calculations. Walk through the calculations in Question 1, for Part 1 of the experiment. This will provide struggling students with additional support to complete the calculations for Part 2 of the experiment correctly on their own.
- **Support Advanced Students** Have advanced students write three pieces of information they gained from this lab. Then have them write two ways they could extend this lab further on enthalpies.

Revisit

ANCHORING PHENOMENON

How can we produce better foods? (5)

Experience Notebook At the completion of Investigation 8, revisit the Anchoring Phenomenon question and have students think about the ways chemistry is crucial for producing better foods. Have students think about their favorite meal and write the flow of energy into and out of that system. Then have students write how that meal can be produced to improve the flow of energy. Have students discuss their ideas in small groups. Ideas from this class discussion will be further explored in the Problem-Based Learning Experience.

The Chemistry of Cooking and the Properties of Baked Goods (40)

Problem-Based Learning Experience At the completion of Investigation 8 students prepare a pamphlet about baking with substitutions for people with allergies or health concerns.

- For Part 1 of the activity, you may wish to provide students with acceptable Web sites that they can use for their research. Use the search phrase *baking with substitutes for ingredients* to find sites that you can choose from. You can also search for substitutions for specific ingredients by using the phrase *ingredient substitutes in baking.*
- In Part 2 of the activity, students test several versions of their recipe. Consider working as a class to complete Part 2, Steps 5–7 and then have each group test a different recipe in step 8. Students can individually complete Steps 9 and 10.
- For Part 3, students can work independently. Consider having them complete this part at home.
- Before students begin Part 3, review the difference between *calorie* and *Calorie*. Point out that for this worksheet, *kilocalorie* is used rather than *Calorie,* which is often used when discussing the stored energy in foods.

PROFESSIONAL DEVELOPMENT

Support Language Demands in Science While students are researching the science of baking substitutes and making their leaflet, remind them to use appropriate scientific language. Encourage students to ask you if they have questions about how to properly use vocabulary. Circulate among students and encourage them to use precise language and be concise with their ideas. Emphasize that scientists have to find a balance between conveying complex ideas to the community in understandable terms and still being scientifically accurate and incorporating proper vocabulary.

Storyline 2 (90)

Benchmark 3-D Assessment For a summative assessment of Storyline 2, assign the Benchmark 3-D Assessment, which is available online, as an ExamView bank, or as an editable worksheet.

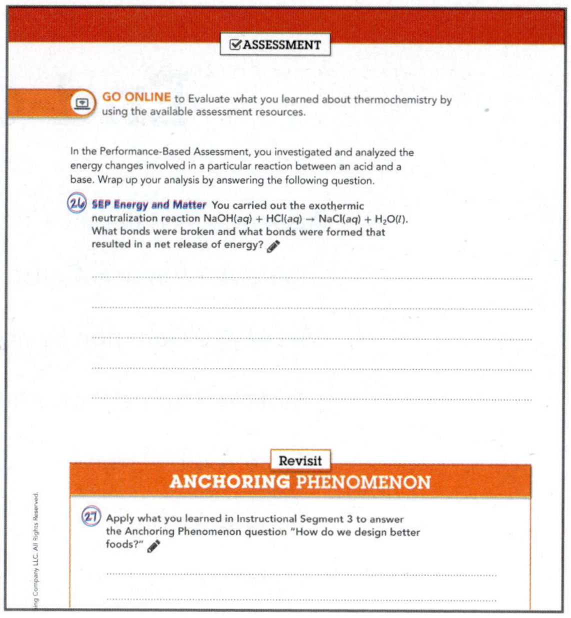

ASSESSMENT

GO ONLINE to Evaluate what you learned about thermochemistry by using the available assessment resources.

In the Performance-Based Assessment, you investigated and analyzed the energy changes involved in a particular reaction between an acid and a base. Wrap up your analysis by answering the following question.

26 **SEP Energy and Matter** You carried out the exothermic neutralization reaction $NaOH(aq) + HCl(aq) \rightarrow NaCl(aq) + H_2O(l)$. What bonds were broken and what bonds were formed that resulted in a net release of energy?

Revisit ANCHORING PHENOMENON

27 Apply what you learned in Instructional Segment 3 to answer the Anchoring Phenomenon question "How do we design better foods?"

Experience Notebook, p. 307

eTEXT

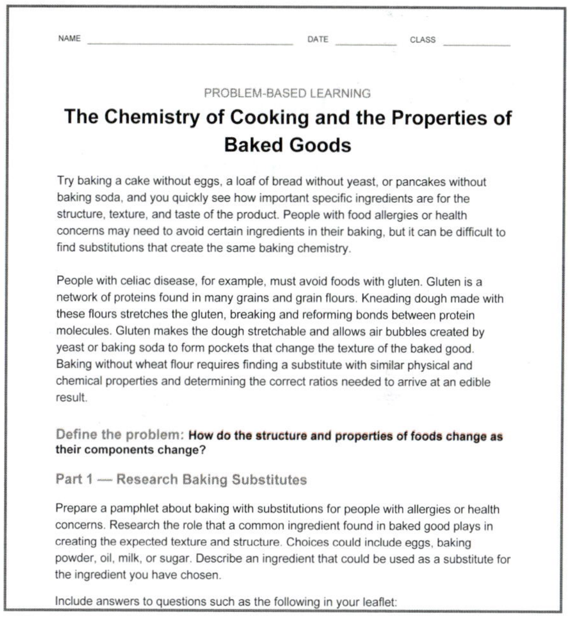

NAME ______ DATE ______ CLASS ______

PROBLEM-BASED LEARNING

The Chemistry of Cooking and the Properties of Baked Goods

Try baking a cake without eggs, a loaf of bread without yeast, or pancakes without baking soda, and you quickly see how important specific ingredients are for the structure, texture, and taste of the product. People with food allergies or health concerns may need to avoid certain ingredients in their baking, but it can be difficult to find substitutions that create the same baking chemistry.

People with celiac disease, for example, must avoid foods with gluten. Gluten is a network of proteins found in many grains and grain flours. Kneading dough made with these flours stretches the gluten, breaking and reforming bonds between protein molecules. Gluten makes the dough stretchable and allows air bubbles created by yeast or baking soda to form pockets that change the texture of the baked good. Baking without wheat flour requires finding a substitute with similar physical and chemical properties and determining the correct ratios needed to arrive at an edible result.

Define the problem: **How do the structure and properties of foods change as their components change?**

Part 1 — Research Baking Substitutes

Prepare a pamphlet about baking with substitutions for people with allergies or health concerns. Research the role that a common ingredient found in baked good plays in creating the expected texture and structure. Choices could include eggs, baking powder, oil, milk, or sugar. Describe an ingredient that could be used as a substitute for the ingredient you have chosen.

Include answers to questions such as the following in your leaflet:

Problem-Based Learning Experience Interactive Worksheet

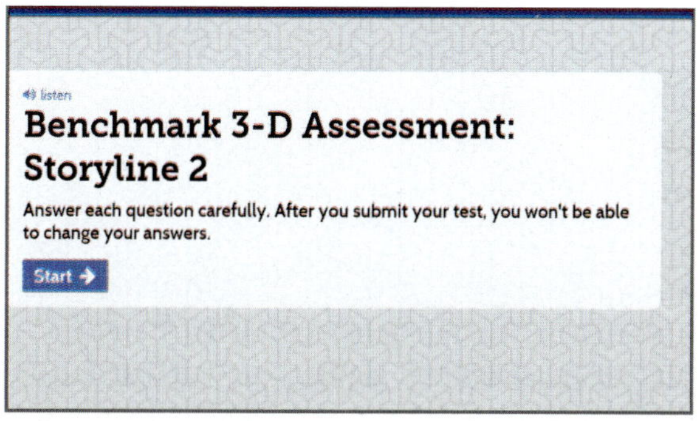

Interactive Benchmark 3-D Assessment

End-of-Book Resources

APPENDIX A REFERENCE TABLES

TABLE A.1	
PHYSICAL CONSTANTS	
Atomic mass unit	1 amu = 1.6605×10^{-24} g
Avogadro's number	$N = 6.02 \times 10^{23}$ particles/mol
Gas constant	$R = 8.31$ L•kPa/(K•mol)
Ideal gas molar volume	$V_m = 22.4$ L/mol
Masses of subatomic particles	
Electron (e^-)	$m_e = 0.000549$ amu $= 9.1094 \times 10^{-28}$ g
Proton (p^+)	$m_p = 1.00728$ amu $= 1.67262 \times 10^{-24}$ g
Neutron (n^0)	$m_n = 1.00867$ amu $= 1.67493 \times 10^{-24}$ g
Speed of light in a vacuum	$c = 3.00 \times 10^8$ m/s

TABLE A.2					
COMMON SYMBOLS AND ABBREVIATIONS					
α	alpha rays	GWP	global warming potential	mm	millimeter
β	beta rays	H	enthalpy	mol	mole
γ	gamma rays	ΔH_f	heat of formation	mp	melting point
Δ	change in	h	hour	n^0	neutron
δ+, δ−	partial ionic charge	h	Planck's constant	n	number of moles
λ	wavelength	Hz	hertz	n	principal quantum number
π	pi bond	J	joule		
σ	sigma bond	K	kelvin	P	pressure
ν	frequency	K_a	acid ionization constant	p^+	proton
amu	atomic mass unit	K_b	base ionization constant	Pa	pascal
(*aq*)	aqueous solution	K_{eq}	equilibrium constant	R	ideal gas constant
atm	atmosphere	K_w	ion product constant for water	S	entropy
bp	boiling point			s	second
°C	degree Celsius	kcal	kilocalorie	(*s*)	solid
c	speed of light in a vacuum	kg	kilogram	STP	standard temperature and pressure
cm	centimeter	kPa	kilopascal		
E	energy	L	liter		
e^-	electron	(*l*)	liquid	T	temperature
EFM	empirical formula mass	M	molarity	$t_{1/2}$	half-life
fp	freezing point	m	meter	V	volume
G	Gibbs free energy	m	mass	v	velocity
g	gram	m	molality	Z_{eff}	effective nuclear charge
(*g*)	gas	mL	milliliter		

Reference Tables R1

TABLE A.3

SOME PROPERTIES OF THE ELEMENTS

Element	Symbol	Atomic number	Atomic mass	Melting point (°C)	Boiling point (°C)	Density (g/cm^3) (gases at STP)	Oxidation numbers
Actinium	Ac	89	(227)	1050	3200	10.07	+3
Aluminum	Al	13	26.98154	660.37	2467	2.6989	+3
Americium	Am	95	243	994	2607	13.67	+3, +4, +5, +6
Antimony	Sb	51	121.75	630.74	1587	6.691	−3, +3, +5
Argon	Ar	18	39.948	−189.2	−185.7	0.0017837	
Arsenic	As	33	74.9216	817	613	5.73	−3, +3, +5
Astatine	At	85	(210)	302	337	—	
Barium	Ba	56	137.33	725	1640	3.5	+2
Berkelium	Bk	97	(247)	986	—	14.78	
Beryllium	Be	4	9.01218	1278	2970	1.848	+2
Bismuth	Bi	83	208.9804	271.3	1560	9.747	+3, +5
Bohrium	Bh	107	(264)	—	—	—	
Boron	B	5	10.81	2075	3675	2.34	+3
Bromine	Br	35	79.904	−7.2	58.78	3.12	−1, +1, +5
Cadmium	Cd	48	112.41	320.9	765	8.65	+2
Calcium	Ca	20	40.08	839	1484	1.55	+2
Californium	Cf	98	(251)	900	—	14	
Carbon	C	6	12.011	3550	4827	2.267	−4, +2, +4
Cerium	Ce	58	140.12	799	3426	6.657	+3, +4
Cesium	Cs	55	132.9054	28.40	669.3	1.873	+1
Chlorine	Cl	17	35.453	−100.98	−34.6	0.003214	−1, +1, +5, +7
Chromium	Cr	24	51.996	1907	2672	7.18	+2, +3, +6
Cobalt	Co	27	58.9332	1495	2870	8.9	+2, +3
Copernicium	Cn	112	(277)	—	—	—	
Copper	Cu	29	63.546	1083.4	2567	8.96	+1, +2
Curium	Cm	96	(247)	1340	—	13.51	+3
Darmstadtium	Ds	110	(269)	—	—	—	
Dubnium	Db	105	(262)	—	—	—	
Dysprosium	Dy	66	162.50	1412	2562	8.550	+3
Einsteinium	Es	99	(252)	—	—	—	
Erbium	Er	68	167.26	159	2863	9.066	+3
Europium	Eu	63	151.96	822	1597	5.243	+2, +3
Fermium	Fm	100	(257)	—	—	—	
Flerovium	Fl	114	(289)	—	—	—	
Fluorine	F	9	18.998403	−219.62	−188.54	0.00181	−1
Francium	Fr	87	(223)	27	677	—	+1
Gadolinium	Gd	64	157.25	1313	3266	7.9004	+3
Gallium	Ga	31	69.72	29.78	2204	5.904	+3
Germanium	Ge	32	72.59	937.4	2830	5.323	+2, +4
Gold	Au	79	196.9665	1064.43	2856	19.3	+1, +3
Hafnium	Hf	72	178.49	2227	4602	13.31	+4
Hassium	Hs	108	(265)	—	—	—	
Helium	He	2	4.00260	−272.2	−268.934	0.0001785	
Holmium	Ho	67	164.9304	1474	2695	8.795	+3
Hydrogen	H	1	1.00794	−259.14	−252.87	0.00008988	−1, +1
Indium	In	49	114.82	156.61	2080	7.31	+1, +3
Iodine	I	53	126.9045	113.5	184.35	4.93	−1, +1, +5, +7
Iridium	Ir	77	192.22	2410	4130	22.42	+3, +4
Iron	Fe	26	55.847	1535	2750	7.874	+2, +3
Krypton	Kr	36	83.80	−156.6	−152.30	0.003733	
Lanthanum	La	57	138.9055	921	3457	6.145	+3
Lawrencium	Lr	103	(262)	—	—	—	+3
Lead	Pb	82	207.2	327.502	1740	11.35	+2, +4
Lithium	Li	3	6.941	180.54	1342	0.534	+1
Livermorium	Lv	116	(293)	—	—	—	
Lutetium	Lu	71	174.967	1663	3395	9.840	+3
Magnesium	Mg	12	24.305	648.8	1107	1.738	+2
Manganese	Mn	25	54.9380	1244	1962	7.32	+2, +3, +4, +7

R2 Appendix A

TABLE A.3 (cont.)

SOME PROPERTIES OF THE ELEMENTS

Element	Symbol	Atomic number	Atomic mass	Melting point (°C)	Boiling point (°C)	Density (g/cm³) (gases at STP)	Oxidation numbers
Meitnerium	Mt	109	(278)	—	—	—	
Mendelevium	Md	101	257	—	—	—	+2, +3
Mercury	Hg	80	200.59	−38.842	356.58	13.55	+1, +2
Molybdenum	Mo	42	95.94	2617	4612	10.22	+6
Moscovium	Mc	115	(289)	—	—	—	
Neodymium	Nd	60	144.24	1021	3068	6.90	+3
Neon	Ne	10	20.179	−248.67	−246.048	0.0008999	
Neptunium	Np	93	(237)	640	3902	20.25	+3, +4, +5, +6
Nickel	Ni	28	58.69	1453	2732	8.902	+2, +3
Nihonium	Nh	113	(286)	—	—	—	
Niobium	Nb	41	92.9064	2468	4742	8.57	+3, +5
Nitrogen	N	7	14.0067	−209.86	−195.8	0.0012506	−3, +3, +5
Nobelium	No	102	(259)	—	—	—	+2, +3
Oganesson	Og	118	(294)	—	—	—	
Osmium	Os	76	190.2	3045	5027	22.57	+3, +4
Oxygen	O	8	15.9994	−218.4	−182.962	0.001429	−2
Palladium	Pd	46	106.42	1554	2970	12.02	+2, +4
Phosphorus	P	15	30.97376	44.1	280	1.82	−3, +3, +5
Platinum	Pt	78	195.08	1772	3627	21.45	+2, +4
Plutonium	Pu	94	(244)	641	3232	19.84	+3, +4, +5, +6
Polonium	Po	84	(209)	254	962	9.32	+2, +4
Potassium	K	19	39.0982	63.25	760	0.862	+1
Praseodymium	Pr	59	140.9077	931	3512	6.64	+3
Promethium	Pm	61	(145)	1168	2460	7.22	+3
Protactinium	Pa	91	231.0359	1560	4027	15.37	+4, +5
Radium	Ra	88	(226)	700	1140	5.5	+2
Radon	Rn	86	(222)	−71	−61.8	0.00973	
Rhenium	Re	75	186.207	3180	5627	21.02	+4, +6, +7
Rhodium	Rh	45	102.9055	1966	3727	12.41	+3
Roentgenium	Rg	111	(272)	—	—	—	
Rubidium	Rb	37	85.4678	38.89	686	1.532	+1
Ruthenium	Ru	44	101.07	2310	3900	12.41	+3
Rutherfordium	Rf	104	(261)	—	—	—	
Samarium	Sm	62	150.36	1077	1791	7.520	+2, +3
Scandium	Sc	21	44.9559	1541	2831	2.989	+3
Seaborgium	Sg	106	(263)	—	—	—	
Selenium	Se	34	78.96	217	684.9	4.79	−2, +4, +6
Silicon	Si	14	28.0855	1410	2355	2.33	−4, +2, +4
Silver	Ag	47	107.8682	961.93	2212	10.50	+1
Sodium	Na	11	22.98977	97.81	882.9	0.971	+1
Strontium	Sr	38	87.62	769	1381	2.63	+2
Sulfur	S	16	32.06	112.8	444.7	2.07	−2, +4, +6
Tantalum	Ta	73	180.9479	2996	5425	16.654	+5
Technetium	Tc	43	(98)	2172	4877	11.50	+4, +6, +7
Tellurium	Te	52	127.60	449.5	989.8	6.24	−2, +4, +6
Tennessine	Ts	117	(294)	—	—	—	
Terbium	Tb	65	158.9254	1356	3123	8.229	+3
Thallium	Tl	81	204.383	303.5	1457	11.85	+1, +3
Thorium	Th	90	232.0381	1750	4790	11.72	+4
Thulium	Tm	69	168.9342	1545	1947	9.321	+3
Tin	Sn	50	118.69	231.968	2270	7.31	+2, +4
Titanium	Ti	22	47.88	1660	3287	4.54	+2, +3, +4
Tungsten	W	74	183.85	3410	5660	19.3	+6
Uranium	U	92	238.0289	1132.3	3818	18.95	+3, +4, +5, +6
Vanadium	V	23	50.9415	1890	3380	6.11	+2, +3, +4, +5
Xenon	Xe	54	131.29	−111.9	−107.1	0.005887	
Ytterbium	Yb	70	173.04	819	1194	6.965	+2, +3
Yttrium	Y	39	88.9059	1522	3338	4.469	+3
Zinc	Zn	30	65.38	419.58	907	7.133	+2
Zirconium	Zr	40	91.22	1852	4377	6.506	+4

Reference Tables R3

TABLE A.4

ELECTRON CONFIGURATION OF THE ELEMENTS

Element		Sublevels																		
		1s	2s	2p	3s	3p	3d	4s	4p	4d	4f	5s	5p	5d	5f	6s	6p	6d	7s	7p
1	Hydrogen	1																		
2	Helium	2																		
3	Lithium	2	1																	
4	Beryllium	2	2																	
5	Boron	2	2	1																
6	Carbon	2	2	2																
7	Nitrogen	2	2	3																
8	Oxygen	2	2	4																
9	Fluorine	2	2	5																
10	Neon	2	2	6																
11	Sodium	2	2	6	1															
12	Magnesium	2	2	6	2															
13	Aluminum	2	2	6	2	1														
14	Silicon	2	2	6	2	2														
15	Phosphorus	2	2	6	2	3														
16	Sulfur	2	2	6	2	4														
17	Chlorine	2	2	6	2	5														
18	Argon	2	2	6	2	6														
19	Potassium	2	2	6	2	6		1												
20	Calcium	2	2	6	2	6		2												
21	Scandium	2	2	6	2	6	1	2												
22	Titanium	2	2	6	2	6	2	2												
23	Vanadium	2	2	6	2	6	3	2												
24	Chromium	2	2	6	2	6	5	1												
25	Manganese	2	2	6	2	6	5	2												
26	Iron	2	2	6	2	6	6	2												
27	Cobalt	2	2	6	2	6	7	2												
28	Nickel	2	2	6	2	6	8	2												
29	Copper	2	2	6	2	6	10	1												
30	Zinc	2	2	6	2	6	10	2												
31	Gallium	2	2	6	2	6	10	2	1											
32	Germanium	2	2	6	2	6	10	2	2											
33	Arsenic	2	2	6	2	6	10	2	3											
34	Selenium	2	2	6	2	6	10	2	4											
35	Bromine	2	2	6	2	6	10	2	5											
36	Krypton	2	2	6	2	6	10	2	6											
37	Rubidium	2	2	6	2	6	10	2	6			1								
38	Strontium	2	2	6	2	6	10	2	6			2								
39	Yttrium	2	2	6	2	6	10	2	6	1		2								
40	Zirconium	2	2	6	2	6	10	2	6	2		2								
41	Niobium	2	2	6	2	6	10	2	6	4		1								
42	Molybdenum	2	2	6	2	6	10	2	6	5		1								
43	Technetium	2	2	6	2	6	10	2	6	5		2								
44	Ruthenium	2	2	6	2	6	10	2	6	7		1								
45	Rhodium	2	2	6	2	6	10	2	6	8		1								
46	Palladium	2	2	6	2	6	10	2	6	10										
47	Silver	2	2	6	2	6	10	2	6	10		1								
48	Cadmium	2	2	6	2	6	10	2	6	10		2								
49	Indium	2	2	6	2	6	10	2	6	10		2	1							
50	Tin	2	2	6	2	6	10	2	6	10		2	2							
51	Antimony	2	2	6	2	6	10	2	6	10		2	3							
52	Tellurium	2	2	6	2	6	10	2	6	10		2	4							
53	Iodine	2	2	6	2	6	10	2	6	10		2	5							
54	Xenon	2	2	6	2	6	10	2	6	10		2	6							
55	Cesium	2	2	6	2	6	10	2	6	10		2	6			1				
56	Barium	2	2	6	2	6	10	2	6	10		2	6			2				
57	Lanthanum	2	2	6	2	6	10	2	6	10		2	6	1		2				
58	Cerium	2	2	6	2	6	10	2	6	10	1	2	6	1		2				
59	Praseodymium	2	2	6	2	6	10	2	6	10	3	2	6			2				

R4 Appendix A

TABLE A.4 (cont.)

ELECTRON CONFIGURATION OF THE ELEMENTS

Element		Sublevels																		
		1s	2s	2p	3s	3p	3d	4s	4p	4d	4f	5s	5p	5d	5f	6s	6p	6d	7s	7p
60	Neodymium	2	2	6	2	6	10	2	6	10	4	2	6			2				
61	Promethium	2	2	6	2	6	10	2	6	10	5	2	6			2				
62	Samarium	2	2	6	2	6	10	2	6	10	6	2	6			2				
63	Europium	2	2	6	2	6	10	2	6	10	7	2	6			2				
64	Gadolinium	2	2	6	2	6	10	2	6	10	7	2	6	1		2				
65	Terbium	2	2	6	2	6	10	2	6	10	9	2	6			2				
66	Dysprosium	2	2	6	2	6	10	2	6	10	10	2	6			2				
67	Holmium	2	2	6	2	6	10	2	6	10	11	2	6			2				
68	Erbium	2	2	6	2	6	10	2	6	10	12	2	6			2				
69	Thulium	2	2	6	2	6	10	2	6	10	13	2	6			2				
70	Ytterbium	2	2	6	2	6	10	2	6	10	14	2	6			2				
71	Lutetium	2	2	6	2	6	10	2	6	10	14	2	6	1		2				
72	Hafnium	2	2	6	2	6	10	2	6	10	14	2	6	2		2				
73	Tantalum	2	2	6	2	6	10	2	6	10	14	2	6	3		2				
74	Tungsten	2	2	6	2	6	10	2	6	10	14	2	6	4		2				
75	Rhenium	2	2	6	2	6	10	2	6	10	14	2	6	5		2				
76	Osmium	2	2	6	2	6	10	2	6	10	14	2	6	6		2				
77	Iridium	2	2	6	2	6	10	2	6	10	14	2	6	7		2				
78	Platinum	2	2	6	2	6	10	2	6	10	14	2	6	9		1				
79	Gold	2	2	6	2	6	10	2	6	10	14	2	6	10		1				
80	Mercury	2	2	6	2	6	10	2	6	10	14	2	6	10		2				
81	Thallium	2	2	6	2	6	10	2	6	10	14	2	6	10		2	1			
82	Lead	2	2	6	2	6	10	2	6	10	14	2	6	10		2	2			
83	Bismuth	2	2	6	2	6	10	2	6	10	14	2	6	10		2	3			
84	Polonium	2	2	6	2	6	10	2	6	10	14	2	6	10		2	4			
85	Astatine	2	2	6	2	6	10	2	6	10	14	2	6	10		2	5			
86	Radon	2	2	6	2	6	10	2	6	10	14	2	6	10		2	6			
87	Francium	2	2	6	2	6	10	2	6	10	14	2	6	10		2	6		1	
88	Radium	2	2	6	2	6	10	2	6	10	14	2	6	10		2	6		2	
89	Actinium	2	2	6	2	6	10	2	6	10	14	2	6	10		2	6	1	2	
90	Thorium	2	2	6	2	6	10	2	6	10	14	2	6	10		2	6	2	2	
91	Protactinium	2	2	6	2	6	10	2	6	10	14	2	6	10	2	2	6	1	2	
92	Uranium	2	2	6	2	6	10	2	6	10	14	2	6	10	3	2	6	1	2	
93	Neptunium	2	2	6	2	6	10	2	6	10	14	2	6	10	4	2	6	1	2	
94	Plutonium	2	2	6	2	6	10	2	6	10	14	2	6	10	6	2	6		2	
95	Americium	2	2	6	2	6	10	2	6	10	14	2	6	10	7	2	6		2	
96	Curium	2	2	6	2	6	10	2	6	10	14	2	6	10	7	2	6	1	2	
97	Berkelium	2	2	6	2	6	10	2	6	10	14	2	6	10	9	2	6		2	
98	Californium	2	2	6	2	6	10	2	6	10	14	2	6	10	10	2	6		2	
99	Einsteinium	2	2	6	2	6	10	2	6	10	14	2	6	10	11	2	6		2	
100	Fermium	2	2	6	2	6	10	2	6	10	14	2	6	10	12	2	6		2	
101	Mendelevium	2	2	6	2	6	10	2	6	10	14	2	6	10	13	2	6		2	
102	Nobelium	2	2	6	2	6	10	2	6	10	14	2	6	10	14	2	6		2	
103	Lawrencium	2	2	6	2	6	10	2	6	10	14	2	6	10	14	2	6	1	2	
104	Rutherfordium	2	2	6	2	6	10	2	6	10	14	2	6	10	14	2	6	2	2	
105	Dubnium	2	2	6	2	6	10	2	6	10	14	2	6	10	14	2	6	3	2	
106	Seaborgium	2	2	6	2	6	10	2	6	10	14	2	6	10	14	2	6	4	2	
107	Bohrium	2	2	6	2	6	10	2	6	10	14	2	6	10	14	2	6	5	2	
108	Hassium	2	2	6	2	6	10	2	6	10	14	2	6	10	14	2	6	6	2	
109	Meitnerium	2	2	6	2	6	10	2	6	10	14	2	6	10	14	2	6	7	2	
110	Darmstadium	2	2	6	2	6	10	2	6	10	14	2	6	10	14	2	6	9	1	
111	Roentgenium	2	2	6	2	6	10	2	6	10	14	2	6	10	14	2	6	10	1	
112	Copernicium	2	2	6	2	6	10	2	6	10	14	2	6	10	14	2	6	10	2	
113	Nihonium	2	2	6	2	6	10	2	6	10	14	2	6	10	14	2	6	10	2	1
114	Flerovium	2	2	6	2	6	10	2	6	10	14	2	6	10	14	2	6	10	2	2
115	Moscovium	2	2	6	2	6	10	2	6	10	14	2	6	10	14	2	6	10	2	3
116	Livermorium	2	2	6	2	6	10	2	6	10	14	2	6	10	14	2	6	10	2	4
117	Tennessine	2	2	6	2	6	10	2	6	10	14	2	6	10	14	2	6	10	2	5
118	Oganesson	2	2	6	2	6	10	2	6	10	14	2	6	10	14	2	6	10	2	6

Reference Tables R5

TABLE A.5

COMMON POLYATOMIC IONS

Charge	Name	Formula	Charge	Name	Formula
1−	Chlorate	ClO_3^-	2−	Carbonate	CO_3^{2-}
	Chlorite	ClO_2^-		Chromate	CrO_4^{2-}
	Cyanide	CN^-		Dichromate	$Cr_2O_7^{2-}$
	Dihydrogen phosphate	$H_2PO_4^-$		Oxalate	$C_2O_4^{2-}$
	Ethanoate	CH_3COO^-		Peroxide	O_2^{2-}
	Hydroxide	OH^-		Silicate	SiO_3^{2-}
	Hydrogen carbonate	HCO_3^-		Sulfate	SO_4^{2-}
	Hydrogen sulfate	HSO_4^-		Sulfite	SO_3^{2-}
	Hydrogen sulfite	HSO_3^-		Thiosulfate	$S_2O_3^{2-}$
	Hypochlorite	ClO^-			
	Nitrate	NO_3^-	3−	Phosphate	PO_4^{3-}
	Nitrite	NO_2^-		Phosphite	PO_3^{3-}
	Perchlorate	ClO_4^-			
	Permanganate	MnO_4^-	1+	Ammonium	NH_4^+
	Thiocyanate	SCN^-			

TABLE A.6

SOLUBILITIES OF COMPOUNDS AT 25°C

	ethanoate	bromide	carbonate	chlorate	chloride	hydroxide	iodide	nitrate	oxide	perchlorate	phosphate	sulfate	sulfide
aluminum	S	S	X	S	S	I	S	S	I	S	I	S	d
ammonium	S	S	S	S	S	X	S	S	X	S	S	S	S
barium	S	S	I	S	S	S	S	S	sS	S	I	I	d
calcium	S	S	I	S	S	S	S	S	sS	S	I	sS	I
copper(II)	S	S	X	S	S	I	S	S	I	S	I	S	I
iron(II)	S	S	I	S	S	I	S	S	I	S	I	S	I
iron(III)	S	S	X	S	S	I	S	S	I	S	I	sS	d
lithium	S	S	sS	S	S	S	S	S	S	S	sS	S	S
magnesium	S	S	I	S	S	I	S	S	I	S	I	S	d
potassium	S	S	S	S	S	S	S	S	S	S	S	S	S
silver	sS	I	I	S	I	X	I	S	I	S	I	sS	I
sodium	S	S	S	S	S	S	S	S	S	S	S	S	S
strontium	S	S	I	S	S	S	S	S	S	S	I	I	I
zinc	S	S	I	S	S	I	S	S	I	S	I	S	I

Key: S = soluble
sS = slightly soluble
I = insoluble
d = decomposes in water
X = no such compound

R6 Appendix A

TABLE A.7

SI UNITS AND EQUIVALENTS

Quantity	SI unit	Common equivalents
Length	meter (m)	1 meter = 1.0936 yards
		1 centimeter = 0.39370 inch
		1 inch = 2.54 centimeters
		1 mile = 5280 feet
		= 1.6093 kilometers
Volume	cubic meter (m^3)	1 liter = 10^{-3} m^3
		= 1.0567 quarts
		1 gallon = 4 quarts
		= 8 pints
		= 3.7854 liters
		1 quart = 32 fluid ounces
		= 0.94635 liter
Temperature	kelvin (K)	1 kelvin = 1 degree Celsius
		°C = $\frac{5}{9}$(°F − 32)
		K = °C + 273.15
Mass	kilogram (kg)	1 kilogram = 1000 grams
		= mass weighing 2.2046 pounds
		1 amu = 1.66057×10^{-27} kilograms
Time	second (s)	1 hour = 60 minutes
		1 hour = 3600 seconds
Energy	joule (J)	1 joule = 1 kg•m^2/s^2 (exact)
		1 joule = 0.2390 calorie
		1 calorie = 4.184 joules
Pressure	pascal (Pa)	1 atmosphere = 101.3 kilopascals
		= 760 mm Hg (Torr)
		= 14.70 pounds per square inch

Reference Tables R7

The experiments in this program have been carefully designed to minimize the risk of injury. However, safety is also your responsibility. The following rules are essential for keeping you safe in the laboratory. The rules address pre-lab preparation, proper laboratory practices, and post-lab procedures.

Pre-Lab Preparation

1. Read the entire procedure before you begin. Listen to all of your teacher's instructions. When in doubt about a procedure, ask your teacher.
2. Do only the assigned experiments. Only do experiments when your teacher is present and has given you permission to work.
3. Know the location and operation of the following safety equipment: fire extinguisher, fire blanket, emergency shower, and eye wash station.
4. Know the location of emergency exits and escape routes. To make it easy to exit quickly, do not block walkways with furniture. Keep your work area orderly and free of personal belongings, such as coats and backpacks.
5. Protect your clothing and hair from chemicals and sources of heat. Tie back long hair and roll up loose sleeves when working in the laboratory. Avoid wearing bulky or loose-fitting clothing. Remove dangling jewelry. Wear closed-toe shoes at all times in the laboratory.

Proper Laboratory Practices

6. Even with well-designed and tested laboratory procedures, an accident may occur while you are working in the lab. Report any accident, no matter how minor, to your teacher.
7. Wear chemical splash goggles at all times when working in the laboratory. These goggles are designed to protect your eyes from injury. While working in the lab, do not rub your eyes, because chemicals are easily transferred from your hands to your eyes.

⚠ If, despite these precautions, a chemical gets in your eye, remove any contact lenses and immediately wash your eye with a continuous stream of lukewarm water for at least 15 minutes.

8. Always use the minimal amounts of chemicals specified for an experiment to reduce danger, waste, and cleanup.
9. Never taste any chemical used in the laboratory, including food products that are the subject of an investigation. Treat all items as though they are contaminated with unknown chemicals that may be toxic. Keep all food and drink that is not part of an experiment out of the laboratory. Do not eat, drink, or chew gum in the laboratory.

⚠ If you accidentally ingest a substance, notify your teacher immediately.

10. Don't use chipped or cracked glassware. Don't handle broken glass. If glassware breaks, tell your teacher and nearby classmates. Discard broken glass as instructed by your teacher.

⚠ If, despite these precautions, you receive a minor cut, allow it to bleed for a short time. Wash the injured area under cold, running water and notify your teacher. More serious cuts or puncture wounds require immediate medical attention.

11. Do not handle hot glassware or equipment. You can prevent burns by being aware that hot and cold equipment can look exactly the same.

⚠ If you are burned, immediately run cold water over the burned area for several minutes until the pain is reduced. Cooling helps the burn heal. Ask a classmate to notify your teacher.

12. Recognize that the danger of an electrical shock is greater in the presence of water. Keep electrical appliances away from sinks and faucets to minimize the risk of electrical shock. Be careful not to spill water or other liquids in the vicinity of an electrical appliance.

R8 Appendix B

⚠ If, despite these precautions, you spill water near an electrical appliance, stand back, notify your teacher, and warn other students in the area.

13. Report any chemical spills immediately to your teacher. Follow your teacher's instructions for cleaning up spills. Warn other students about the identity and location of spilled chemicals.

⚠ If, despite these precautions, a corrosive chemical gets on your skin or clothing, notify your teacher. Then wash the affected area with cold running water for several minutes.

Post-Lab Procedures

14. Dispose of chemicals in a way that protects you, your classmates, and the environment. Always follow your teacher's directions for cleanup and disposal. Clean your small-scale reaction surface by draining the contents onto a paper towel. Then wipe the surface with a damp paper towel and dry the surface completely. Dispose of the paper towels in the waste bin.

15. Wash your hands thoroughly with soap and water before leaving the laboratory.

A Materials Safety Data Sheet (MSDS) for a chemical describes any safety issues. A diagram summarizes risks related to flammability, health, and reactivity. A number scale indicates the level of risk.

0 Low
1 Slight
2 Moderate
3 High
4 Extreme

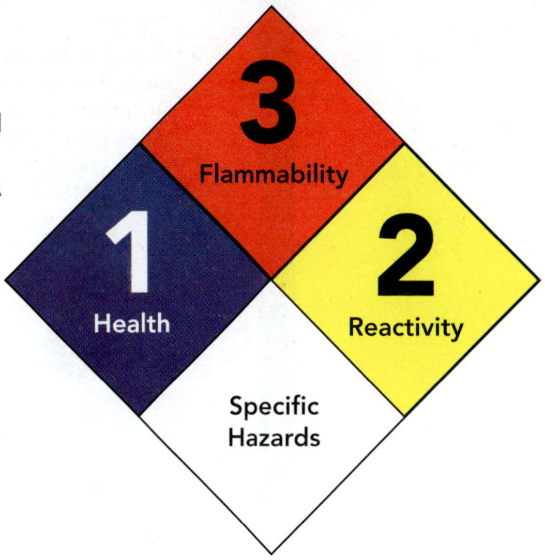

Safety Procedures

Take appropriate precautions when any of the following safety symbols appears in an experiment.

Eye Safety Wear safety goggles.

Clothing Protection Wear a lab coat or apron when using corrosive chemicals or chemicals that can stain clothing.

Skin Protection Wear plastic gloves when using chemicals that can irritate or stain your skin.

Broken Glass Do not use chipped or cracked glassware. Do not heat the bottom of a test tube.

Open Flame Tie back hair and loose clothing. Never reach across a lit burner.

Flammable Substance Do not have a flame near flammable materials.

Corrosive Substance Wear safety goggles, an apron, and gloves when working with corrosive chemicals.

Poison Don't chew gum, drink, or eat in the laboratory. Never taste a chemical in the laboratory.

Fume Avoid inhaling substances that can irritate your respiratory system. Use a fume hood whenever possible.

Thermal Burn Do not touch hot glassware or equipment.

Electrical Equipment Keep electrical equipment away from water or other liquids.

Sharp Object To avoid a puncture wound, use scissors or other sharp objects only as intended.

Disposal Dispose of chemicals only as directed.

Hand Washing Wash your hands thoroughly with soap and water.

Safety in the Lab R9

Investigation 1

1. Water vapor molecules contain higher kinetic energy and higher thermal energy than water molecules in a liquid.
2. One limitation of Model 2 is that it does not show the chemical bonds that exist within the molecule. The lines extending outward from the carbon atom in Model 1 represent the chemical bonds, or binding forces, between the atoms.
3. The system takes in thermal energy from the surroundings, causing an increase in kinetic energy of molecular particles. Both the thermal and kinetic energy increased as the phase changed since the particles are moving around more freely. The particles are no longer held together by attractive forces. So, the end product is most likely in the gaseous phase.
4. Protons, neutrons and electrons; the relative mass of protons and neutrons is similar. Electrons have almost negligible mass compared to that of protons and neutrons. Protons and neutrons are located in the center of the atom (nucleus); electrons are located in a cloud around the nucleus.
5.

Particle	Symbol	Relative charge
Electron	e^-	1–
Proton	p^+	1+
Neutron	n^0	0

6. a. 4 electrons, 4 protons
   b. 17 electrons, 17 protons
   c. 27 electrons, 27 protons
7. Matter is anything that has mass and volume. Element is the simplest form of matter that has a unique set of properties.
8. a. Atomic number = 20; Mass number = 40
   b. Atomic number = 14; Mass number = 28
   c. Atomic number = 44; Mass Number = 101
9. 19 protons; 19 electrons

APPENDIX C PROBLEM BANK

INVESTIGATION 1

1. Compare the kinetic and thermal energy of water vapor molecules to the kinetic and thermal energy of liquid water molecules.
2. Compare the two molecular models for the compound methane. Identify one limitation that Model 2 has in displaying the structure of the molecule. What do the lines that extend outward from the atom in Model 1 represent?

Model 1 Model 2

3. The model shows a liquid substance undergoing a phase change. Describe how energy moves within the system and how the energy and attractive forces of the particles change as the phase changes. Which phase is the end product most likely in?

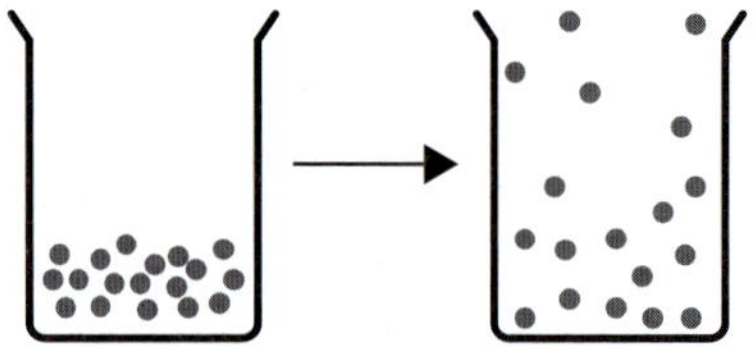

4. List the three main subatomic particles. Describe their relative masses and locations within an atom.
5. Complete the table.

Particle	Symbol	Relative charge
Electron		
		1^+
	n^0	

6. Determine the number of electrons and protons for these elements.
   a. Be
   b. Cl
   c. Co
7. What is the difference between matter and element?
8. Determine the atomic number and mass number for these elements.
   a. $^{40}_{20}Ca$
   b. $^{28}_{14}Si$
   c. $^{101}_{44}Ru$
9. Potassium has an atomic number of 19. How many protons and electrons are in a neutral potassium atom?
10. What are isotopes? Do isotopes differ chemically? Why or why not?
11. Calculate the number of protons, electrons, and neutrons for these elements.
    a. $^{23}_{11}Na$
    b. $^{88}_{38}Sr$
12. Magnesium has three isotopes with the following atomic masses and relative abundance: 23.985 amu (78.99%), 24.986 amu (10.00%), and 25.982 amu (11.01%). Calculate the atomic mass of magnesium as a weighted average.

10. Isotopes of an element have different numbers of neutrons. They are chemically similar because the number of protons and electrons, which are responsible for chemical behavior, remain the same.
11. a. protons = 11; electrons = 11; neutrons = 12
    b. protons = 38; electrons = 38; neutrons = 50
12. 24.305 amu

13. Uranium has three naturally occurring isotopes: uranium-238, uranium-235, and uranium-234. The atomic mass for uranium is 238.028 amu. Which of these three isotopes is most abundant? Explain.

14. What is the frequency of radiation with a wavelength of 5×10^{-10} m?

15. What is the wavelength of radiation with a frequency of 5.2×10^{7}/s? Is it closer to red or blue light?

16. What is the frequency of radiation that has a wavelength of 510 nm? What is the energy of a single photon of this light?

17. What is the frequency of radiation that has a wavelength of 750 nm? What is the energy of a single photon of this light?

18. What is the electron configuration for the following?
   a. He
   b. Si
   c. As
   d. Kr

19. Write the electron configuration for the following atoms. How many unpaired electrons are present for each atom?
   a. nitrogen
   b. calcium
   c. sodium

20. Write the electron configuration for iodine (I). Then draw the electron dot structure for iodine.

21. Draw the electron dot structure for each element.
   a. Sr
   b. Sn
   c. Te

INVESTIGATION 2

1. What is the difference in the way Mendeleev ordered the elements in his periodic table and the modern periodic table?

2. Identify the element in each description.
   a. Group 3, row 5
   b. column 6, Period 4
   c. metalloid in row 2
   d. 3rd column of p-block, Period 4

3. Based on their position in the periodic table, state which atom in each pair has the larger atomic radius.
   a. potassium, rubidium
   b. magnesium, aluminium
   c. bromine, iodine
   d. oxygen, nitrogen

4. Choose the species that has the larger atomic radius in the following pairs.
   a. chlorine atom and chloride ion
   b. sodium atom and sodium ion
   c. sodium ion and potassium ion
   d. oxide ion and sulfide ion

5. Element X has 13 protons.
   a. To which group and period does X belong?
   b. Is X a metal, nonmetal, or metalloid?
   c. How many valence electrons does an atom of element X have?
   d. What is the effective nuclear charge experienced by the valence electrons of atom X?

6. The table shows two sets of ionization energies. One set is made up of elements in Group 1A. The other set is made up of elements in Group 7A.
Explain which set of values may be assigned to which group.

First Ionization Energy (kJ/mol) Set 1	First Ionization Energy (kJ/mol) Set 2
1681	1312
1251	520
1140	496
1008	419

7. Explain how ionization energy and electron affinity are basically measures of energy of opposite processes, but they both generally increase from left to right in a period.

8. Explain the trend that both atomic radius and ionic radius increase going down a group in the periodic table.

13. U-238; the atomic mass is closer in value to 238 than 235 or 234.

14. 6×10^{17}/s

15. 5.8 m; closer to red light

16. Frequency = 5.8×10^{18}/s
Energy = 3.9×10^{-15} J

17. Frequency = 4.167×10^{14}/s
Energy = 2.76×10^{-19} J

18. a. $1s^2$
   b. $1s^2\,2s^2\,2p^6\,3s^2\,3p^2$
   c. $1s^2\,2s^2\,2p^6\,3s^2\,3p^6\,3d^{10}\,4s^2\,4p^3$
   d. $1s^2\,2s^2\,2p^6\,3s^2\,3p^6\,3d^{10}\,4s^2\,4p^6$

19. a. $1s^2\,2s^2\,2p^3$, 3 unpaired electrons
   b. $1s^2\,2s^2\,2p^6\,3s^2\,3p^6\,4s^2$, 0 unpaired electrons
   c. $1s^2\,2s^2\,2p^6\,3s^1$, 1 unpaired electron

20. [Kr] $4d^{10}\,5s^2\,5p^5$; 

21. a. 
   b. 
   c. 

Investigation 2

1. Mendeleev ordered the elements by atomic mass, not by atomic number.

2. a. yttrium (Y)
   b. chromium (Cr)
   c. boron (B)
   d. arsenic (As)

3. a. rubidium
   b. magnesium
   c. iodine
   d. nitrogen

4. a. chloride ion
   b. sodium atom
   c. potassium ion
   d. sulfide ion

5. a. Group 3A; third period
   b. metal
   c. 3
   d. +3

6. Set 1 belongs to Group 7A elements, as the values are high. Set 2 belongs to Group 1A elements. An electron is more difficult to remove from an atom with many valence electrons (Group 7A), as that atom tends to gain, not lose, electrons.

7. Ionization energy is the energy it takes to lose electrons, whereas electron affinity is the energy released when an atom gains electrons. An atom is less likely to lose an electron and more likely to gain one moving from left to right across a period, because of effective nuclear charge.

8. These measurements are from the nucleus to the outermost layer of electrons in the atom or ion. As the number of electron shells increases with each element going down a group, both atomic and ionic radii increase.

9. Group 1 elements reach noble gas configuration after 1 valence electron is removed. Removing a second electron breaks the stable noble gas configuration, requiring much more energy. Group 2 elements' second ionization energy is lower because the elements have 2 valence electrons and removing the second results in a noble gas configuration.

10. Electronegativity is a value that relates to how strongly an element attracts an electron. Noble gases naturally satisfy the octet rule, so they have no need to attract electrons.

Investigation 3

1. a. Li^+ b. Cl^- c. S^{2-} d. Mg^{2+}

2. a. 

b. 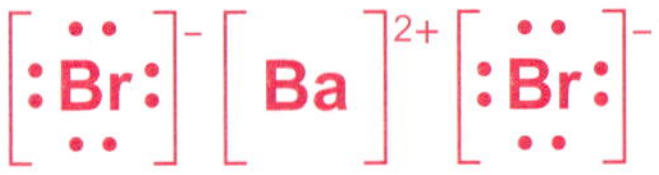

c. 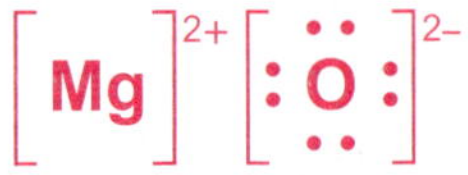

3. 6

4. a. no b. yes c. yes d. no

5. The model states that the valence electrons in a metallic solid do not remain with their atom's nuclei and are free to move about the solid. So, heat and electricity can flow through them easily.

6. Electrons are shared to allow each atom to complete its octet. In some bond situations, more than two electrons need to be shared in order to provide both atoms with eight valence electrons.

7. Ionic bonds form when metallic atoms transfer one or more electrons to a nonmetallic atom. Covalent bonds form when two nonmetallic atoms share two or more electrons between them.

8. a. polar b. nonpolar c. polar d. nonpolar

9. a. 2 b. 1 c. 0 d. 0

10. a. 4 b. 3 c. 3 d. 2

11. a. 

b. 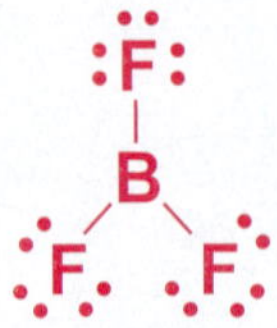

c. 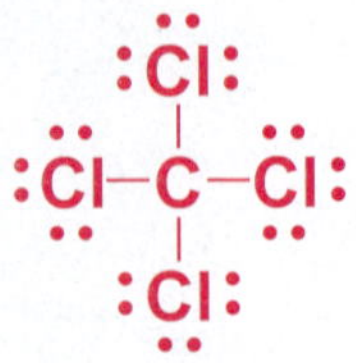

9. Explain why the second ionization energy for elements in Group 1 is significantly higher than the second ionization energy for Group 2.

10. Explain why noble gases do not have electronegativity values.

INVESTIGATION 3

1. For each element, write its symbol and charge as an ion.
   a. lithium
   b. chlorine
   c. sulfur
   d. magnesium

2. Draw the electron dot structure for each compound.
   a. KCl
   b. $BaBr_2$
   c. MgO

3. Atoms can gain or lose electrons to become stable ions. How many valence electrons are present in an oxygen atom?

4. Do the following properties apply to ionic compounds?
   a. low melting points
   b. conduct electricity in aqueous solution
   c. form crystalline solids
   d. conduct electricity in solid form

5. Metals such as gold, silver, and copper have high thermal and electrical conductivity. How does the "sea of electrons" model explain these properties?

6. Explain why some covalent bonds contain multiple pairs of shared electrons.

7. Using the terms "share" and "transfer," describe the difference between an ionic and a covalent bond.

8. Based on electronegativity values, are the covalent bonds in each of these compounds polar or nonpolar?
   a. H_2O
   b. O_2
   c. HCl
   d. H_2

9. How many unshared pairs are present in each molecule?
   a. H_2S
   b. NH_3
   c. BF_3
   d. CCl_4

10. Based on their valence electrons, how many atoms of chlorine are expected to bond with each of the following elements?
   a. carbon
   b. nitrogen
   c. aluminum
   d. sulfur

11. Draw the electron dot structure for each of the following compounds.
   a. H_2O
   b. BF_3
   c. CCl_4

12. Considering the intermolecular forces that may be present, predict whether each compound would have a relatively low or relatively high melting point.
   a. H_2O
   b. CO_2
   c. BF_3
   d. NaCl

13. Does each molecule exhibit hydrogen bonding?
   a. H_2O
   b. H_2S
   c. CH_4
   d. NH_3

14. Identify each compound as ionic or molecular.
   a. CaO
   b. CS_2
   c. LiF
   d. PCl_3

15. Name the ionic compounds that form from their ions in these solutions.
   a. Ba^{2+} and Cl^-
   b. Mg^{2+} and O^{2-}
   c. Li^+ and P^{3-}
   d. Be^{2+} and I^-

12. a. high b. low c. low d. high

13. a. yes b. no c. no d. yes

14. a. ionic b. molecular c. ionic d. molecular

15. a. barium chloride
   b. magnesium oxide
   c. lithium phosphide
   d. beryllium iodide

16. Name the molecular compounds formed when these nonmetals combine.
   a. one atom of carbon and one atom of oxygen
   b. one atom of silicon and four atoms of chlorine
   c. one atom of boron and three atoms of fluorine
   d. two atoms of phosphorus and five atoms of sulfur

17. Write the formula for the ionic compound that forms from
   a. lithium and nitrogen.
   b. strontium and bromine.
   c. aluminum and oxygen.
   d. potassium and fluorine.

18. Write the formula for the covalent compounds.
   a. nitrogen triiodide
   b. sulfur hexafluoride
   c. trinitrogen heptachloride
   d. phosphorus pentabromide

INVESTIGATION 4

1. Solid particles exhibit only ______ motion. As heat is added and the sample becomes a liquid, ______ motion is added, and upon its change to gas, ______ motion is added.

2. The strength of intermolecular forces directly impacts the physical properties of materials. What type of solid is described in each statement?
   a. typically soft; low melting points
   b. charges are present; high melting points
   c. a network of atoms; strong; typically highest of all melting points
   d. properties vary widely; tend to be conductive and malleable

3. In terms of energy and pressure, explain what occurs when gas in a rigid container is heated.

4. Identify each phase change described.
   a. liquid to gas
   b. solid to gas
   c. gas to liquid
   d. solid to liquid

5. Use the phase diagram for water to answer the following questions.

Phase Diagram for Water

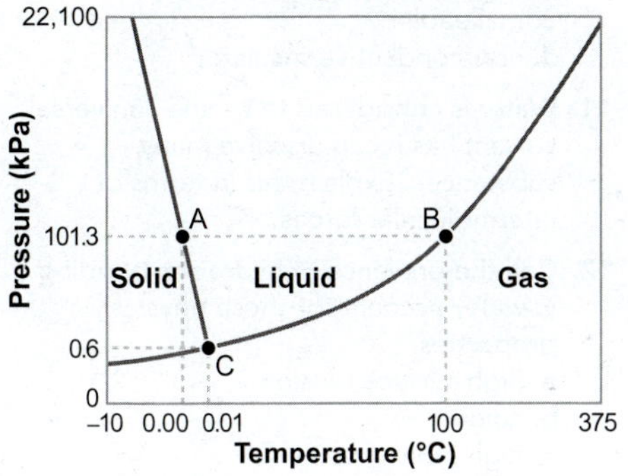

   a. What phase is present at 90°C and 50 kPa?
   b. What process occurs when water at 0.5 kPa and –5°C goes to 10 kPa and 50°C?
   c. What is significant about water at 101.3 kPa and 0°C?

6. Explain the difference between evaporation and boiling in terms of the energy involved.

7. You are provided with two white, crystalline solids. Suggest at least two tests that could be performed to determine which is molecular and which is ionic.

8. Predict whether an ionic or molecular compound forms when the following elements combine:
   a. sodium and bromine
   b. carbon and fluorine
   c. magnesium and oxygen
   d. chlorine and iodine

9. The strength of a bond between two ions increases with the charge on each ion, and decreases as the ions' radii increase. Using this information, predict which compound in each pair should have a higher melting point.
   a. sodium chloride (NaCl) vs. potassium chloride (KCl)
   b. sodium chloride (NaCl) vs. barium chloride ($BaCl_2$)

16. a. carbon monoxide
   b. silicon tetrachloride
   c. boron trifluoride
   d. diphosphorus pentasulfide

17. a. Li_3N b. $SrBr_2$
   c. Al_2O_3 d. KF

18. a. NI_3 b. SF_6
   c. N_3Cl_7 d. PBr_5

Investigation 4

1. vibrational; rotational; translational

2. a. molecular b. ionic
   c. covalent d. metallic

3. As heat is added, the gas particles gain energy and their speed increases. This results in more collisions with the container, which causes an increase in pressure.

4. a. vaporization b. sublimation
   c. condensation d. melting

5. a. vapor (gas) b. sublimation
   c. normal melting point

6. While both are a change from liquid to gas, evaporation results from only some particles having enough kinetic energy to break free of the surface tension forces. Boiling occurs when all particles have enough kinetic energy to break free of those forces.

7. Multiple answers possible. Dissolve each in water to find which one conducts electricity (ionic). Heat a small sample of each to find which melts at a low temperature (molecular). Determine the hardness (molecular typically low hardness/soft).

8. a. ionic b. molecular
   c. ionic d. molecular

9. a. NaCl (charges are the same, but the ionic radius of K is larger than Na)
   b. $BaCl_2$ (radii are essentially the same, but Ba is 2+ and Na is 1+)

10. a. metal
b. nonmetal
c. metal
d. nonmetal

11. Water is a polar compound (with positively and negatively-charged ends). Most ionic compounds will dissolve because they contain ions that are more attracted to water's charges than to each other. Polar compounds have charged ends and may bond more strongly with water than themselves and dissolve. Nonpolar compounds have no charged ends and typically do not dissolve well, if at all, in water.

12. a. yes
b. no
c. yes
d. yes
e. no

13. Surfactant particles disrupt the order of the hydrogen bonding between water molecules, creating a less-ordered surface.

14. A nonelectrolyte is a compound that does not break apart into ions in a solution and will not conduct electricity. Only a portion of a weak electrolyte's particles split apart when it dissolves, so only a few ions are weakly conductive. In a strong electrolyte, all particles split apart into ions when dissolved and the solution is highly conductive.

15. unsaturated

16. Dissolve the maximum amount of solute at a given temperature. Heat the solution and add additional solute so that it dissolves. Slowly cool the solution. The supersaturated solution contains more solute than would normally dissolve at that temperature.

17. increases; decreases

18. a. heterogeneous
b. homogeneous
c. heterogeneous
d. homogeneous
e. heterogeneous

Investigation 5

1. a. They have the same number of particles.
b. 0.75 mol H_2
c. 3.0 mol SnO_2
d. 0.66 mol FeO

2. No, sodium is the smaller of the two elements and will occupy less space.

3. It allows chemists to determine the approximate number of atoms in a sample of a substance, which helps to determine the ratio of substances involved in chemical reactions.

4. One mole of hydrogen peroxide and hydrogen chloride have the same number of molecules. They differ by having different molar masses, because the masses of the elements that make up the molecules are different.

5. 66 grams

10. Identify whether each property describes a metal or a nonmetal.
a. high luster
b. brittle
c. malleable
d. non-conductive/insulator

11. Water is considered to be the "universal solvent" as it can dissolve many substances. Explain this in terms of intermolecular forces.

12. Can the presence of hydrogen bonding in water account for these physical properties?
a. high surface tension
b. color
c. high boiling point
d. density as a solid being less than as a liquid
e. being a non-conductor

13. How does the addition of a surfactant reduce the surface tension of water?

14. What is the difference between a non-electrolyte, a weak electrolyte, and a strong electrolyte?

15. The solubility of barium hydroxide in water is 4.68 g/100 mL at 25°C. If a mixture of 2.50 g barium hydroxide in 100 mL of water is prepared, will it be unsaturated, saturated, or supersaturated?

16. Describe the process of preparing a supersaturated solution.

17. The solubility of a gas in a liquid ______ as the pressure over a solution increases. The solubility of the same gas ______ as the temperature of the solvent increases.

18. Determine whether each of the following is a homogeneous or heterogeneous mixture.
a. pepperoni pizza
b. white vinegar
c. crunchy peanut butter
d. warm maple syrup
e. beach sand

INVESTIGATION 5

1. For each pair listed, which has more particles?
a. 1 mol OCl_2 or 1 mol H_2O
b. 0.5 mol O_2 or 0.75 mol H_2
c. 1.5 mol SnO or 3.0 mol SnO_2
d. 0.33 mol Fe_2O_3 or 0.66 mol FeO

2. Does one mole of sodium, Na, have the same volume as one mole of bromine, Br?

3. How does the concept of the mole help chemists?

4. Explain how a mole of hydrogen peroxide (H_2O_2) and a mole of hydrogen chloride (HCl) are the same but different.

5. If one mole of an unknown substance is 200.59 g/mol, what is the mass of 0.33 mol of the substance?

6. If you had one mole of avocados, then how many avocados would you have?

7. A chemist has 3.45×10^{22} molecules of P_2O_5. How many grams of P_2O_5 does the scientist have?

8. Calculate the number of moles of each substance.
a. 5.45×10^{26} particles of methane, CH_4
b. 3.22×10^{23} atoms of xenon, Xe
c. 9.6×10^{23} formula units of sodium chloride, NaCl

9. How many moles of hydrogen atoms are in 7.10 mol of H_2O?

10. How many moles of oxygen atoms are in 3.60 mol of SiO_2?

11. What is the molar mass of molecular oxygen, O_2?

12. What is the molar mass of barium chloride, $BaCl_2$?

13. What is the molar mass of $CaCO_3$?

14. What is the molar mass of SF_6?

15. Calculate the number of moles of each substance.
a. 6.00 g oxygen, O_2
b. 450.0 g of iron(III) oxide, Fe_2O_3
c. 45.5 g of calcium chloride, $CaCl_2$

R14 Appendix C

6. 6.02×10^{23} avocados

7. 5.54 g P_2O_5

8. a. 905 mol CH_4
b. 0.535 mol Xe
c. 1.6 mol NaCl

9. 14.2 mol hydrogen

10. 7.20 mol oxygen

11. 31.998 g/mol

12. 208.23 g/mol

13. 100.086 g/mol

14. 152.048 g/mol

15. a. 0.188 mol O_2
b. 2.818 mol Fe_2O_3
c. 0.410 mol $CaCl_2$

16. Which has more atoms: 2.5 mol of calcium carbonate, $CaCO_3$, or 3.5 mol of calcium hydroxide, $Ca(OH)_2$?

17. How many grams is 2.50 mol of H_2O?

18. How many atoms is 0.750 mol of Na_3PO_4?

19. How many moles are present in 20.0 g of NO_2?

20. How many formula units are in 171 g of lithium nitride, Li_3N?

21. How many molecules are in 550.0 g of palladium(IV) oxide, PdO_2?

22. How many formula units are in 0.472 mol of iron(III) bromide, $FeBr_3$?

23. How many ions of fluoride are in 410.0 g of uranium(VI) fluoride, UF_6?

24. What is molar volume of a gas?

25. How does the number of particles of nitrogen in a balloon at STP compare to the number of particles of oxygen in a different balloon at STP with the same volume?

26. A compound contains 85.63% carbon and 14.37% hydrogen. What is the empirical formula of the compound?

27. Glucose has the formula $C_6H_{12}O_6$. What is the percent composition of each element?

28. How many moles of sodium fluoride are needed to make 500.0 mL of 3.5*M* solution?

29. How many grams of ethanol, CH_3CH_2OH, are needed to make 1.00 L of a 3.50*M* solution?

30. What is the concentration of the these solutions?
    - a. 3.5 mol HBr in 500 mL of water
    - b. 0.0750 mol NaCl in 250.0 mL of water
    - c. 1.95 mol $AgNO_3$ in 1.2 L of water
    - d. 0.500 mol NH_3 in 2.5 L of water

INVESTIGATION 6

1. In the following reactions, what is/are the reactant(s)?
    - a. $C_6H_{12}O_2 + 8O_2 \rightarrow 6CO_2 + 6H_2O$
    - b. $2H_2O_2 \rightarrow 2H_2O + O_2$
    - c. $BaO + H_2O \rightarrow Ba(OH)_2$

2. In the following reaction, what is(are) the product(s)?
    - a. $CaCO_3 + 2HCl \rightarrow CO_2 + CaCl_2 + H_2O$
    - b. $N_2 + O_2 \rightarrow 2NO$
    - c. $2SO_2 + O_2 \rightarrow 2SO_3$

3. In the following reaction, what is(are) the reactant(s)?
   Potassium bromate, $KBrO_4$, decomposes into potassium bromide, KBr, and oxygen, O_2.

4. In the following reaction, what is the solid?
   $AgNO_3(aq) + NaCl(aq) \rightarrow AgCl(s) + NaNO_3(aq)$

5. What is the skeleton equation for these reactions?
    - a. magnesium oxide, MgO, and water to produce magnesium hydroxide, $Mg(OH)_2$
    - b. aqueous phosphoric acid, H_3PO_4, and aqueous sodium hydroxide, NaOH, to produce aqueous sodium phosphate, Na_3PO_4, and water
    - c. methane, CH_4, and oxygen, O_2, to produce carbon dioxide, CO_2, and water, H_2O

6. What is the skeleton equation for the decomposition of aqueous hydrogen peroxide, H_2O_2, into liquid water and gaseous oxygen, O_2, as catalyzed by potassium iodide, KI?

7. What are the coefficients in the following reactions?
    - a. __ Fe_2O_3 + __ $H_2O \rightarrow$ __ $Fe(OH)_3$
    - b. __ C_2H_4 + __ $O_2 \rightarrow$ __ CO_2 + __ H_2O

8. What is the balanced equation for the synthesis of sodium bromate, $NaBrO_3$, from oxygen, O_2, and sodium bromide, NaBr?

9. What is the balanced equation for the combustion of ethanol, C_2H_6O, and oxygen, O_2, to produce carbon dioxide, CO_2, and water?

10. When lithium chloride, LiCl, is dissolved in water, there is a steep rise in the temperature of the water. Based on this evidence, is the dissolution of lithium chloride endothermic, exothermic, or neither? Explain.

16. 3.5 mol $Ca(OH)_2$

17. 45.0 g H_2O

18. 3.61×10^{24} atoms

19. 0.435 mol NO_2

20. 2.11×10^{24} formula units of Li_3N

21. 2.393×10^{24} molecules of PdO_2

22. 2.84×10^{23} formula units of $FeBr_3$

23. 4.209×10^{24} ions of fluoride

24. The volume occupied by one mole of gas at standard temperature and pressure

25. The two balloons would have the same number of particles.

26. CH_2

27. 40.0% C, 6.7% H, and 53.3% O

28. 1.8 mol NaF

29. 161 g of CH_3CH_2OH

30. a. 7.0*M* HBr b. 0.300*M* NaCl
    c. 1.6*M* $AgNO_3$ d. 0.20*M* NH_3

Investigation 6

1. a. $C_6H_{12}O_2$ and O_2 b. H_2O_2
   c. BaO and H_2O

2. a. CO_2, $CaCl_2$, and H_2O
   b. NO c. SO_3

3. Potassium bromate

4. AgCl

5. a. $MgO + H_2O \rightarrow Mg(OH)_2$
   b. $H_3PO_4(aq) + NaOH(aq) \rightarrow Na_3PO_4(aq) + H_2O(l)$
   c. $CH_4 + O_2 \rightarrow CO_2 + H_2O$

6. $H_2O_2(aq) \xrightarrow{KI} H_2O(l) + O_2(g)$

7. a. 3 b. 2

8. $3O_2 + 2NaBr \rightarrow 2NaBrO_3$

9. $C_2H_6O + 3O_2 \rightarrow 2CO_2 + 3H_2O$

10. Exothermic. The increase in the solution's temperature shows that heat is released by the reaction.

11. 146 kJ/mol

12. 2,223 kJ/mol

13. 509 kJ/mol is released

14. The two chemicals react in such a way that the energy of the new compound is greater than the energy of the initial reactants. This is because the products have a higher bond energy than the reactants, so energy is absorbed from the surroundings.

15. Combination or synthesis

16. Decomposition

17. $4Li(s) + O_2(g) \rightarrow 2Li_2O(s)$

18. Sodium is higher on the activity series than hydrogen. This means that it has a greater tendency to replace a less active element.

19. a. Li   b. H
 c. Na   d. Cl

20. $2FeCl_3(aq) + 3Na_2CO_3(aq) \rightarrow Fe_2(CO_3)_3(s) + 6NaCl(aq)$

21. These are examples of combustion reactions, or the combustion of a hydrocarbon with oxygen, that result in the formation of carbon dioxide and water.

22. $2Na(s) + Cl_2(g) \rightarrow 2NaCl(s)$

23. $Pb^{2+}(aq) + 2I^-(aq) \rightarrow PbI_2(s)$

24. There is not enough water to form a solvation shell around all of the sodium and acetate ions present in a solution. Therefore, some of the ions precipitate out in the form of solid sodium acetate.

25. $BaSO_4(s) + H_2O(l)$

26. $CO_2(g) + H_2O(l)$

27. Na^+ and Cl^-

28. $Mg^{2+}(aq) + CO_3^{2-}(aq) \rightarrow MgCO_3(s)$

29. a. Precipitate   b. No precipitate
 c. No precipitate   d. Precipitate

30. The bonds between the ions in the precipitate are stronger than the intermolecular attractions between the water of a solvation shell and the ions of the precipitate.

11. How much energy is required to break apart one mole of single-bonded oxygen atoms?

12. How much energy is needed to break the necessary bonds in the formation of water based on the following reaction?

$2H_2 + O_2 \rightarrow 2H_2O$

13. How much energy is released or absorbed in the formation of water based on the following reaction?

$2H_2 + O_2 \rightarrow 2H_2O$

14. An emergency ice pack is made of a pouch containing a chemical inside a large pouch containing a different chemical. When the inner pouch is broken, the solution cools drastically. In terms of bond energy, what is happening?

15. This reaction is an example of what type of chemical reaction?

$2KCl + 3O_2 \rightarrow 2KClO_3$

16. This reaction is an example of what type of chemical reaction?

$2B(OH)_3 \rightarrow B_2O_3 + 3H_2O$

17. Write a balanced equation for the synthesis of solid lithium oxide, Li_2O, from solid lithium, Li, and gaseous oxygen, O_2.

18. In this single replacement reaction, why does one sodium replace hydrogen?

$2Na(s) + 2HCl(aq) \rightarrow 2NaCl(aq) + H_2(g)$

19. For each pair listed, which element is the most reactive?
a. Mg or Li
b. H or Al
c. Na or K
d. Br or Cl

20. A precipitate of iron (III) carbonate, $Fe_2(CO_3)_3$, forms in the reaction of sodium carbonate, Na_2CO_3, and iron (III) chloride, $FeCl_3$. Write a balanced chemical reaction for this reaction.

21. What reactants and/or products do the following reactions have in common?
$CH_4(g) + 2O_2(g) \rightarrow CO_2(g) + 2H_2O(l)$
$2C_2H_6(g) + 7O_2(g) \rightarrow 4CO_2(g) + 6H_2O(l)$
$C_4H_8(g) + 6O_2(g) \rightarrow 4CO_2(g) + 4H_2O(l)$

22. Write the balanced reaction that occurs between solid sodium, Na, and gaseous chlorine, Cl_2.

23. Write the net ionic equation for the reaction between aqueous lead (II) nitrate, $Pb(NO_3)_2$, and aqueous sodium chloride, NaCl, to produce solid lead (II) iodide, PbI_2, and aqueous sodium chloride, NaCl.

24. Some hand warmers use a solution of sodium acetate and water. When triggered, solid sodium acetate forms. Why is some of the sodium acetate not dissolved in the water?

25. Complete the equation.

$Ba(OH)_2(aq) + H_2SO_4(aq) \rightarrow$

26. Complete the equation.

$C_2H_2(g) + O_2(g) \rightarrow$

27. In the net ionic equation for the reaction between aqueous hydrochloric acid, HCl, and aqueous sodium hydroxide, NaOH, what are the spectator ions?

28. Write the net ionic equation for the reaction between aqueous magnesium chloride, $MgCl_2$, and aqueous potassium carbonate, K_2CO_3.

29. Identify which of these ions will combine to form a precipitate.
a. Pb^+ and Cl^-
b. Ba^{2+} and OH^-
c. Na^+ and CO_3^{2-}
d. Pb^{2+} and I^-

30. Why do precipitate compounds not have a solvation shell?

INVESTIGATION 7

1. Balance the equation.
   $Fe + Cl_2 \longrightarrow FeCl_3$
2. Why is it so important to balance equations? Use a specific law to justify your response.
3. The balanced equation for the formation of water is given:

   $2H_2 + O_2 \longrightarrow 2H_2O$

   How many moles of water are produced when 4.5 mol of O_2 fully react?
4. Reinterpret the following equation in terms of volumes of each gas at STP.

   $2N_2(g) + O_2(g) \longrightarrow 2N_2O(g)$
5. What is a mole ratio? Why is it important?
6. In order to produce 40 mol of NO_2 gas, how many moles of oxygen gas are needed? The balanced equation is given.

   $2NO(g) + O_2(g) \longrightarrow 2NO_2(g)$
7. The unbalanced equation for the combustion of propane gas is given.

   $C_3H_8 + O_2 \longrightarrow CO_2 + H_2O$

   Balance the equation and determine the mole ratio of oxygen gas to carbon dioxide.
8. Using the equation for the combustion of propane, determine the number of molecules of CO_2 produced if the reaction uses and fully consumes 3.4 mol of C_3H_8?

   $C_3H_8 + O_2 \longrightarrow CO_2 + H_2O$
9. Your friend's favorite superhero is a man that is able to change shape. In one episode, the hero turns into a very large dinosaur. Explain, using conservation of mass, why this super power is possible or not.
10. The reaction for the formation of ammonia (NH_3) is shown:

    $N_2 + 3H_2 \longrightarrow 2NH_3$

    Suppose you start with 2 mol of N_2 at 300.0 K and 0.70 atm. Your classmate tries to determine the amount of ammonia gas produced and comes up with 89.6 L of ammonia. Is this calculation correct? Explain your answer.
11. This is the equation for the formation of sodium hydroxide:

    $Na_2O(s) + H_2O(l) \longrightarrow 2NaOH(aq)$

    How many moles of H_2O are needed to produce 4.5 L of NaOH?
12. Would you ever need more than two conversion factors to convert between volume, mass, and/or factors representative? Explain your answer.
13. The equation for the formation of calcium nitrate is given. Assume that you have 30.1 g of HNO_3.

    $Ca(OH)_2(aq) + 2HNO_3(aq) \longrightarrow 2H_2O(l) + Ca(NO_3)_2(aq)$

    a. How many grams of $Ca(OH)_2$ are needed to fully react with the HNO_3?
    b. Assuming that both reactants are fully consumed and there is no excess left, how many liters of H_2O are produced in this reaction?
14. The unbalanced equation that results in the formation of aluminum sulfate is given.

    $Al(OH)_3 + H_2SO_4 \longrightarrow Al_2(SO_4)_3 + H_2O$

    a. Balance the equation.
    b. Determine mole ratio of H_2O to $Al_2(SO_4)_3$.
    c. If 50.6 g of H_2O was produced during this reaction, how many grams of aluminum sulfate was produced?
15. How many representative particles of NF_3 are formed when 30 L of N_2 at STP is consumed in the following reaction?

    $N_2 + 2F_3 \rightarrow 2NF_3$
16. Magnesium oxide is produced from magnesium and oxygen gas. The unbalanced equation is given.

    $Mg(s) + O_2(g) \longrightarrow MgO(s)$

    a. Balance the equation.
    b. How many grams of MgO are produced if a total of 40.5 L of oxygen gas at STP reacts with magnesium?

Investigation 7

1. $2Fe + 3Cl_2 \rightarrow 2FeCl_3$
2. Balancing an equation ensures that the law of conservation of mass is being followed. It ensures that moles of all elements on both sides of the equation are equal.
3. 9.0 mol H_2O
4. 44.8 L of N_2 reacts with 22.4 L of O_2 to form 44.8 L of N_2O
5. It is a ratio determined from the coefficients of a balanced chemical equation. It is used to convert between the moles of reactants or products.
6. 20 mol oxygen
7. $C_3H_8 + 5O_2 \rightarrow 3CO_2 + 4H_2O$; 5 mol O_2 : 3 mol CO_2
8. 6.1×10^{24} molecules CO_2
9. A dinosaur is much more massive than a person. Without the superhero taking in something else to increase his mass, he cannot simply become a massive dinosaur, as that violates the law of conservation of mass.
10. No. The calculation is incorrect. For a gas, 1 mol = 22.4 L only at STP conditions. This reaction is occurring at non-STP conditions and, therefore, the calculation is incorrect.
11. 4.5 mol H_2O
12. No. All of these calculations require two conversion factors. The first is from the original unit to moles. The second is from moles to the final unit.
13. **a.** 17.7 g $Ca(OH)_2$ **b.** 10.7 L H_2O
14. **a.** $2Al(OH)_3 + 3H_2SO_4 \rightarrow Al_2(SO_4)_3 + 6H_2O$
    b. 6:1
    c. 1.60×10^2 g $Al_2(SO_4)_3$
15. 2×10^{24} particles
16. **a.** $2Mg(s) + O_2(g) \rightarrow 2MgO(s)$
    b. 146 g of MgO

17. a. 33.1 g NaCl
b. 6.34 L CO_2
c. 1.70×10^{23} molecules of H_2O
d. 36.4 g HCl

18. 1.3 L N_2

19. a. 2.01×10^4 g NO
b. 6.70×10^3 mol HNO_2

20. 68.0 g H_2O_2

21. 144 g potassium superoxide

22. No. This is not a violation of the conservation of mass. All of the mass that has reacted is conserved. The mass that is "lost" may be explained through impurities, human error, or an incomplete reaction. It did not simply disappear.

23. Compound B

24. 92.5%

25. Because the mole ratio of A and B is provided, it is simple to determine the limiting reagent. Compound B has a molar mass of 200 g/mol. We have 100 g of compound B or 0.5 moles. Compound A has a molar mass of 100 g/mol. We have 1 mol of this substance. However, we need 3 moles of compound A to form 1 mole of compound C. We have 33% of compound A needed to form one mole of compound C, and 50% of the compound B needed to form one mole of compound C. Therefore, compound A is the limiting reactant.

26. a. oxygen b. 90.1%

27. a. $C_7H_{16}(l) + 11O_2(g) \rightarrow 7CO_2(g) + 8H_2O(g)$
b. n-heptane is the limiting reagent.
c. 335.5 g H_2O

28. a. Sulfuric acid b. 92.1%

17. The balanced equation for the reaction of sodium carbonate and hydrochloric acid is given.

$Na_2CO_3 + 2HCl \longrightarrow CO_2 + H_2O + 2NaCl$

Assume that you start with 30.0 g of Na_2CO_3.
a. How many grams of NaCl can be produced?
b. At STP, how many liters of CO_2 are produced?
c. How many molecules of H_2O are produced?
d. What is the minimum mass of HCl needed in order for all of the Na_2CO_3 to be fully consumed?

18. Carbon monoxide reacts with nitrogen monoxide to form carbon dioxide and nitrogen.

$2NO(g) + 2CO(g) \longrightarrow 2CO_2(g) + N_2(g)$

Suppose you start with 3.6 g of NO and perform the reaction at STP conditions. How many liters of N_2 are produced from this reaction?

19. The density of nitric oxide, a highly corrosive mineral acid, is 1.51 g/cm^3. It is involved in the following reaction:

$4NO + O_2 + 2H_2O \longrightarrow 4HNO_2$

Suppose you start with 13.3 L of liquid nitric oxide.
a. How many grams of NO do you have?
b. How many moles of HNO_2 can be produced if all of the NO reacts?

20. Decomposition of hydrogen peroxide results in water and oxygen gas. How many grams of hydrogen peroxide are needed to produce 1.20×10^{24} molecules of oxygen gas? The unbalanced equation is provided.

$H_2O_2(l) \longrightarrow H_2O(l) + O_2(g)$

21. Water vapor reacts with potassium superoxide to form oxygen and potassium hydroxide.

$4KO_2(s) + 2H_2O(g) \longrightarrow 3O_2(g) + 4KOH(s)$

How many grams of potassium superoxide were consumed in the reaction if 34.0 L of oxygen gas is produced at STP from this reaction?

22. The conservation of mass states that matter is conserved in chemical reactions. Does having a percent yield <100% violate this law? Explain your answer.

23. Consider this equation.

$2A + 3B \longrightarrow 5C$

What is the limiting reactant if you have 20 moles of compound A and 25 moles of compound B?

24. A reaction predicted to make 94.5 g of HCN actually produced about 87.4 g of HCN. What is the percent yield?

25. In a reaction, compounds A and B react to form compound C. You are given 100 g of both compounds. Compound A has a molar mass of 100 g/mol, while compound B has a molar mass of 200 g/mol. Is it possible to determine which one is the limiting reagent from the information given? Explain your answer.

$3A + B \longrightarrow C$

26. In a reaction, 24.0 g of diboron hexahydride reacts with 40.0 L of oxygen to form diboron trioxide at STP. The balanced equation is shown.

$B_2H_6(g) + 3O_2(g) \longrightarrow 3H_2O(l) + B_2O_3(s)$

a. Which reagent is the limiting reagent?
b. Assume that the reaction produces 37.6 g of B_2O_3. What is the percent yield?

27. In a reaction, 233.0 g of n-heptane (C_7H_{16}) is combusted with 540.0 g of oxygen. The skeletal equation is shown.

$C_7H_{16}(l) + O_2(g) \longrightarrow CO_2(g) + H_2O(g)$

a. What is the balanced equation?
b. What is the limiting reagent?
c. How many grams of water are produced?

28. In a reaction, 30.5 g of sulfuric acid reacts with 51.6 g of calcium fluoride to form hydrogen fluoride and calcium sulfate. The balanced equation is shown.

$H_2SO_4(l) + CaF_2(s) \longrightarrow 2HF(g) + CaSO_4(s)$

a. What is the limiting reagent?
b. What is the percent yield if 39.0 g of $CaSO_4$ is produced?

29. In a reaction at STP, 58.6 L of chlorine gas reacts with 89.5 g of sodium hydroxide to form laundry bleach (NaClO) as shown in the equation.

$Cl_2(g) + 2NaOH(aq) \longrightarrow NaClO(aq) + NaCl(aq) + H_2O(l)$

a. Which is the limiting reagent?
b. How many grams of NaClO are produced?

30. Suppose that the actual yield of NaClO from the given equation is only 56.3 g. What is the percent yield?

$Cl_2(g) + 2NaOH(aq) \longrightarrow NaClO(aq) + NaCl(aq) + H_2O(l)$

31. A sample of 7.40 g of aluminum oxide was prepared. Assuming all of the starting reagents were consumed, how many grams of aluminum were needed to create this compound? An unbalanced equation is provided.

$Al + O_2 \longrightarrow Al_2O_3$

INVESTIGATION 8

1. Explain why the rate of a reaction increases when the temperature increases.
2. Why is activation energy required even when the enthalpy of the reaction is negative?
3. What is an activated complex? How does it relate to the activation energy?
4. Your friend argues that when sunlight is absorbed by trees, the trees reduce some of the energy present in the universe. Using the concept of a system and its surroundings, how would you correct your friend?
5. When energy is absorbed by a system, what happens to the surrounding temperature? What happens when energy is released?
6. Suppose that reactant A reacts to form product B and releases –300 kJ of heat. However, it is later discovered that there is an intermediate C that is formed before product B. The enthalpy change from A to C is –150 kJ of heat. Does the discovery of this intermediate require us to determine a new heat of reaction for $A \longrightarrow B$?
7. Compare the chemical potential energy of the reactants and the products:
   a. exothermic reaction
   b. endothermic reaction
8. Identify each of the reactions as exothermic or endothermic.
   a. combustion of propane to produce carbon dioxide and water
   b. decomposition of sodium hydrogen carbonate by applying heat
   c. synthesis of salt (NaCl) through the combination of sodium and chlorine
9. Suppose a combustion reaction of propane was performed with excess oxygen. How many kcal of energy are produced when 36.2 g of C_3H_8 is burned?

   $C_3H_8(g) + 5O_2(g) \longrightarrow 3CO_2(g) + 4H_2O(g) + 526\text{ kcal}$
10. Suppose that sulfuric acid is dissolved in water. The reaction is shown.

   $H_2SO_4(aq) \longrightarrow H^+(aq) + HSO_4^-(aq)$

   $\Delta H_{soln} = -71.76\text{ kJ/mol}$

   How does this reaction change the temperature of the water?
11. Describe Hess's law. What does it allow us to determine?
12. The heat of fusion of aluminum is 10.79 kJ/mol. How much heat is released when 13.3 g Al changes from a liquid state to a solid state at the freezing point?
13. At 0°C, does H_2O exist as solid ice, liquid water, or both?
14. Calculate the amount of heat required to change 75.0 g of liquid mercury to a gas. The heat of vaporization of mercury is 55.229 kJ/mol.

29. a. NaOH is the limiting reagent.
    b. 83.3 g of NaClO is produced.

30. 67.6%

31. 3.92 g Al

Investigation 8

1. A reaction is dependent on the rate at which reactant molecules collide with one another. The higher the temperature, the higher the velocity of the molecules. This means that more molecules will interact with each other in a shorter amount of time.
2. The enthalpy of a reaction represents the change in energy in the system due to the reaction. If this is negative, then energy is released in the reaction. However, a certain amount of energy is still needed to initiate the reaction. Once the reaction is started, energy released by the reaction keeps the reaction going.
3. An activated complex is an intermediate between the reactants and products at which energy is at the highest point along the reaction path. The activation energy is the difference between the energy of the reactants and the energy of the activated complex.
4. Remind him that the total energy in the universe is always conserved. If he defines the trees as the system and the rest of the universe as the surroundings, then the system has gained heat while the surroundings have lost some heat. However, the total overall heat in the universe remains conserved.
5. When energy is absorbed into a system the surrounding temperature decreases. When energy is released, the surrounding temperature increases.
6. No. Because of the path independence, which states that no matter what path is taken, it will still require the same energy change from reactant A to product B. Whatever the number of intermediates is, the final enthalpy change will be the same.
7. a. The chemical potential energy is higher in the reactants than the products.
   b. The chemical potential energy is higher in the products than the reactants.
8. a. Exothermic b. Endothermic
   c. Exothermic
9. 431 kcal
10. The dissolution of sulfuric acid is exothermic. For this reason, it will increase the temperature of the water.
11. Hess's law states that if you add two or more thermochemical equations to a final equation, you can also summate their heats of reaction to find out the overall heat of reaction. This allows us to determine the heat of a reaction indirectly if we know the heat of reaction of the sub-reactions.
12. 5.30 kJ
13. Both. This is the state at which solid and liquid phases are at equilibrium and therefore coexist.
14. 20.673 kJ

15. a. 34.0 kJ **b.** 37 kJ

16. The cold pack reaction is endothermic. The hot pack reaction is exothermic.

17. Acetone requires less energy to break the surface of the liquid and enter the gas phase than water. There is more attraction between water molecules than there is between acetone molecules. Both compounds would absorb heat from the surroundings, but the acetone would vaporize more quickly.

18. Temperature will increase.

19. a. 66.7 kJ **b.** 25.1 kJ **c.** 2.99 kJ

20. 36.52 kJ

21. 638.3 kJ

22. 9.0 kJ

23. exothermic; −290 kJ

24. 250 kJ

25. 1 atm of pressure and 298.15 K

26. Chlorine has a higher enthalpy of vaporization than oxygen, which has a higher heat of vaporization than hydrogen. Stronger bonds require more heat to break, and Cl_2 has stronger bonds than O_2, which has stronger bonds than H_2.

27. 3.335×10^5 kJ

28. 256.0 kJ

29. Neither; they are the same.

30. Alcohol has a low heat of vaporization and evaporates from the skin quickly. The energy transfered from the skin to the alcohol causes the cooling effect on the skin.

15. Calculate the quantity of energy gained or lost in the following reactions.
a. 5.66 mol of water condensing at 100°C
b. 0.90 mol of water freezing at 0°C

16. A cold pack contains two sealed bags. When the cold pack is squeezed, these bags break and their compounds intermix, leading to a chemical reaction. Would you expect this reaction to be exothermic or endothermic? How about for a hot pack?

17. The heat of vaporization of water is 40.7 kJ/mol while the heat of vaporization of acetone is 31.3 kJ/mol. Explain what these values mean about the structure of these molecules and what would happen if the surroundings of these chemicals were heated up.

18. The enthalpy of a solution for sodium hydroxide is −44.5 kJ/mol. If this compound is dissolved in water, how will the temperature of the water change?

19. What is the amount of heat required to vaporize 30.0 g of these compounds?
a. water (ΔH_{vap}40.1 kJ/mol)
b. ethanol C_2H_6O (ΔH_{vap}38.6 kJ/mol)
c. nitrogen N_2 (ΔH_{vap}2.79 kJ/mol)

20. How much heat is lost when 109.5 g of water freezes to form solid ice? The heat of fusion of water is −6.01 kJ/mol.

21. How much heat is released during the decomposition of 6.5 mol of H_2O_2? Enthalpy of reaction is −196.4 kJ.

$$2H_2O_2 \longrightarrow 2H_2O + O_2$$

22. How much energy is required to turn 45 g of liquid nitrogen into a gas? The heat of vaporization of liquid nitrogen (N_2) is 6.1 kJ/mol.

23. Calculate the heat absorbed when 3.6 mol of $CaCl_2$ is dissolved in water. The heat of solution is −80 kJ/mol. Is this reaction exothermic or endothermic?

24. Consider these equations:

$2A + 2B \longrightarrow 3C$ −200 kJ/mol

$C + E \longrightarrow F$ −150 kJ/mol

Calculate the enthalpy of the combined reaction using Hess's law.

25. What are the conditions of the surroundings required to define the standard enthalpy of a system?

26. Describe the relative values of enthalpy of vaporization of chlorine (Cl_2), oxygen (O_2), and hydrogen (H_2). Explain your answer.

27. How much heat must be added to a 1,000-kg piece of ice in order for it to melt? Assume that the temperature is at 0°C exactly. The heat of fusion of water is 6.01 kJ/mol.

28. The equation for the formulation of HCN is shown.

$$CH_4(g) + NH_3(g) \longrightarrow HCN(g) + 3H_2(g)$$

Given the equations, calculate the total ΔH for the following reaction to form HCN.

$N_2(g) + 3H_2(g) \longrightarrow 2NH_3(g)$
$\Delta H = -91.8$ kJ

$C(s) + 2H_2(g) \longrightarrow CH_4(g)$
$\Delta H = -74.9$ kJ

$2C(s) + H_2(g) + N_2(g) \longrightarrow 2HCN(g)$
$\Delta H = 270.3$ kJ

29. Which is greater: the quantity of heat absorbed by a vaporizing liquid, or the quantity of heat released when the vapor condenses?

30. When isopropyl alcohol is placed on the skin, the alcohol evaporates and there is a cooling sensation on the skin. Skin has an average temperature of 37°C and the boiling point of isopropyl alcohol is 82.5°C. The heat of vaporization of isopropyl alcohol is 45.2 kJ/mol. Explain this phenomenon in terms of the heat of vaporization.

R20 Appendix C

GLOSSARY

A

activated complex: an unstable cluster of atoms that exists during the transition from reactants to products (282)

activation energy: the minimum energy colliding particles must have in order to react (287)

activity series: a list of elements in order of decreasing activity (232)

actual yield: the amount of product that forms when a reaction is carried out in the laboratory (275)

allotropes: different molecular forms of an element in the same physical state; graphite and diamond are allotropes of the element carbon (139)

amorphous solid: a solid that lacks an ordered internal structure; rubber, plastic, and asphalt are examples (122)

anion: any atom or group of atoms with a negative charge (58)

aqueous solution: a solution in which water is the solvent (154)

atom: the smallest particle of an element that retains its identity in a chemical reaction (6)

atomic emission spectrum: the pattern formed when light passes through a prism or diffraction grating to separate it into the different frequencies of light it contains (22)

atomic number: the number of protons in the nucleus of an atom of an element (13)

atomic orbital: a mathematical expression describing the probability of finding an electron at various locations; usually represented by the region of space around the nucleus where there is a high probability of finding an electron (28)

atomic radius: one half the distance between the nuclei of two atoms of the same element when the atoms are joined (56)

average atomic mass: the weighted average of the masses of the isotopes of an element; also called atomic mass (18)

Avogadro's hypothesis: any two samples of gas with an equal number of particles will have the same volume when they are held at the same pressure and temperature (187)

Avogadro's number: the number of representative particles contained in one mole of a substance; equal to 6.02×10^{23} (176)

B

binary compound: a compound composed of only two elements (99)

bond enthalpy: the amount of energy needed to break the bonds of one mole of a substance (285)

C

cation: any atom or group of atoms with a positive charge (58)

change in enthalpy (ΔH): the heat absorbed or released by a reaction at constant pressure (284)

chemical formula: an expression that indicates the number and type of atoms present in the smallest representative unit of a substance (99)

chemical potential energy: energy stored in the chemical bonds of a substance (9, 223)

chemical symbol: a one- or two-letter representation of an element (6)

coefficients: whole numbers that appear in front of chemical formulas in a balanced chemical equation (221)

collision theory: a theory that states that bonds are broken when molecules collide with enough energy to break bonds in reactants and with the correct orientation to form bonds that make products (225, 282)

Glossary **R21**

colloid: a heterogeneous mixture containing particles, called the dispersed phase, that are spread throughout another substance, called the dispersion medium (168)

combination reaction: a chemical change in which two or more substances react to form a single new substance (228)

combustion reaction: a chemical change in which an element or a compound reacts with oxygen, often producing energy in the form of heat and light (236)

complete ionic equation: an equation that shows dissolved ionic compounds as dissociated free ions (242)

concentrated solution: a solution that contains a large amount of solute (203)

concentration: measure of the amount of solute that is dissolved in a given quantity of solvent, usually expressed in moles/L or molarity (203)

condensation: the changing from a gas to a liquid (126)

covalent bond: a bond formed by the sharing of electrons between atoms (81)

covalent network solids: solids consisting of networks of atoms held together by covalent bonds; they are very hard and tend to have the highest melting points of all solids (121, 139)

crystal: a solid consisting of particles arranged in an orderly, repeating, three-dimensional pattern called a crystal lattice (122)

crystal lattice: an orderly, repeating, three-dimensional pattern of many ions, atoms, or molecules (72)

D

decomposition reaction: a chemical change in which a single compound breaks down into two or more products (229)

density: the ratio of the mass of an object to its volume (190)

deposition: the changing from a gas directly to a solid without passing through the liquid state (126)

dilute solution: a solution with a small amount of solute (203)

dipole interactions: the intermolecular attractions between oppositely charged regions of polar molecules (92)

dislocation: a defect or irregularity within a crystal structure (146)

dispersion forces: attractions between molecules caused by the electron motion on one molecule affecting the electron motion on the other through electrical forces; these are the weakest interactions between molecules (91)

dissolution rate: the rate at which a solute dissolves (161)

double covalent bond: a bond made by two shared pairs of electrons (84)

double-replacement reaction: a chemical change involving an exchange of positive ions between two compounds (234)

ductility: the ability to be drawn into wires (142)

E

effective nuclear charge (Z_{eff}): the net positive nuclear charge experienced by an electron in an atom (53)

efflorescence: the loss of water by a hydrate (158)

electrical conductivity: the ability of a material to conduct electricity (143)

electrolyte: a compound that conducts electric current when dissolved in an aqueous solution or in the molten state (156)

electron: a negatively charged subatomic particle (12)

electron affinity: the energy change when an atom gains an electron (61)

electron configuration: the arrangement of electrons of an atom in its ground state into various orbitals around the atom's nucleus (33)

electron dot structure: a notation that depicts valence electrons as dots around the atomic symbol of the element (39)

electronegativity: a measure of the ability of an atom to attract electrons when the atom is in a compound (86)

R22 Glossary

element: the simplest form of matter that has a unique set of properties; an element cannot be broken down into simpler substances by chemical means (6)

empirical formula: the chemical formula of a compound that gives the lowest whole-number ratio of the atoms or moles of elements in a compound (198)

endothermic: a term describing processes that absorb energy from the surroundings (224)

energy: the capacity to move, do work, change matter, or produce heat (9)

energy levels: the specific energies an electron in an atom or other system can have (24)

enthalpy diagram: a representation of the relative internal energy of a system undergoing a chemical change (285)

enthalpy of reaction: the total change in energy for a reaction (286)

evaporation: vaporization that occurs at the surface of a liquid that is not boiling (128)

excess reagent: any reactant that is not used up in a reaction (270)

exothermic: a term describing processes that release net energy to the surroundings (224)

F

fluid: any substance that flows; both liquids and gases are fluids (118)

G

gas pressure: the result of forces between the molecules of a gas with each other and a container's walls (114)

group: a vertical column of elements in the periodic table; the constituent elements of a group have similar chemical and physical properties (46)

H

heat: the energy transferred from one object to another because of a temperature difference between the objects (283)

Henry's law: at a given temperature, the solubility of a gas in a liquid is directly proportional to the pressure of the gas above the liquid (166)

Hess's law of heat summation: if you add two or more thermochemical equations to give an overall equation, you can also add the enthalpies of reaction to give the overall enthalpy of reaction (292)

heterogeneous mixture: a mixture that does not have a uniform composition (168)

homogeneous mixture: a mixture that has a uniform appearance and composition (168)

hydrate: a solid, typically crystalline compound that contains water molecules as an integral part of its structure (158)

hydrocarbon: a compound composed of hydrogen and carbon (236)

hydrogen bonds: intermolecular forces in which a hydrogen covalently bonded to a very electronegative atom is also weakly bonded to an unshared electron pair of another electronegative atom from a second molecule (93)

hypoxic zones: areas in the ocean where the oxygen concentration is so low that animal life suffocates (164)

I

internal energy: the total energy contained in a system (284)

ion: an atom or group of atoms that has a positive or negative charge (58)

ionic bond: an electrostatic attraction that holds oppositely charged ions together (70)

ionic compound: an electrically neutral compound made of cations and anions (70)

ionic solids: solids that consist of positively and negatively charged ions held together by ionic bonds with relatively strong attractions and resulting in high melting points and hardness (121)

ionization energy: the energy required to remove an electron from an atom in its gaseous state (59)

Glossary R23

isotopes: atoms of the same element that have the same atomic number but different atomic masses due to a different number of neutrons (16)

K

kinetic energy: the energy of an object's motion (9, 112)

kinetic theory: a theory explaining the states of matter, based on the concept that all matter consists of tiny particles that are in constant motion (112)

L

law of conservation of energy: in any chemical or physical process, energy is neither created nor destroyed (223)

law of conservation of mass: in any chemical reaction, the mass of the products is always equal to the mass of the reactants (220, 256)

law of constant composition: any sample of a compound will be made up of the same elements in the same ratio (194)

law of definite proportions: a compound contains its component elements in a fixed ratio by mass (192)

limiting reagent: the reactant that determines the amount of product that can be formed (270)

luster: the way light interacts with a material's surface (143)

M

macroscopic property: a characteristic of matter that is large enough to see, handle, or measure without magnification (10)

main group elements: elements in Groups 1, 2, and 13 to 18 of the periodic table that display a wide range of physical and chemical properties (48)

malleability: the ability to be hammered or pressed into shapes (142)

mass number: the total number of protons and neutrons in the nucleus of an atom (15)

matter: anything that has mass and occupies space (6)

melting point: the temperature at which a solid becomes a liquid (132)

metal: one of a class of elements that are good conductors of heat and electric current; metals tend to be ductile, malleable, and shiny (47)

metallic bond: the electrostatic attraction between the free-floating valence electrons and the positively charged metal cations (77)

metallic solids: solids formed via strong metallic bonds and having highly variable properties dependent on electron arrangement (121)

metalloid: an element that tends to have properties that are similar to those of metals and nonmetals (47)

molar enthalpy of condensation: the heat released by one mole of a gaseous substance as it condenses at its normal boiling point (302)

molar enthalpy of fusion: the heat absorbed by one mole of a solid substance as it melts to a liquid at constant temperature (300)

molar enthalpy of solidification: the heat released by one mole of a liquid substance as it solidifies at constant temperature (300)

molar enthalpy of solution: the enthalpy change caused by the dissolution of one mole of a substance (296)

molar enthalpy of vaporization: the heat absorbed by one mole of a liquid substance as it vaporizes at constant temperature (302)

molar mass: the mass of one mole of a substance (178)

molar volume: the volume of one mole of a gas at STP; 22.4 L/mol for any ideal gas (187)

molarity: molar concentration; the number of moles of solute dissolved in one liter of solution (204)

mole: the amount of a substance that contains 6.02×10^{23} representative particles of that substance (176)

mole ratio: a conversion factor derived from the coefficients of a balanced chemical equation interpreted in terms of moles (259)

R24 Glossary

molecular formula: the chemical formula of a compound that is either the same as its experimentally determined empirical formula or a simple whole-number multiple of its empirical formula (200)

molecular solids: solids held together by the relatively weak dipole-dipole intermolecular forces; tend to be soft and have low melting points (121)

molecule: a neutral group of atoms held together by one or more covalent bonds (81)

monoatomic ion: a single atom with a positive or negative charge (97)

N

net ionic equation: an equation for a reaction in solution that shows only the particles directly involved in a chemical change (242)

neutron: a subatomic particle with no charge and a mass of about 1 amu; found in the nucleus of an atom (12)

nonelectrolyte: a compound that does not conduct electric current when dissolved in an aqueous solution or in the molten state (156)

nonmetal: an element that tends to be a poor conductor of heat and electric current; nonmetals generally have properties opposite to those of metals (47)

nonpolar covalent bond: a bond in which the electrons are shared equally (87)

nucleus: the tiny, dense central portion of an atom, composed of protons and neutrons (12)

O

octet rule: a general rule that atoms tend to form bonds so that each atom has eight electrons in its valence shell (68)

P

percent by mass: the ratio of the masses of solute to solution, expressed as a percentage (210)

percent by volume: the ratio of the volumes of solute to solution, expressed as a percentage (210)

percent composition: the percent by mass of each element in a compound (192)

percent yield: the ratio of the actual yield to the theoretical yield for a chemical reaction expressed as a percentage; a measure of the efficiency of a reaction (275)

period: a horizontal row of elements in the periodic table (46)

periodic law: when the elements are arranged in order of increasing atomic number, there is a periodic repetition of their physical and chemical properties (46)

periodic table: an arrangement of elements in which the elements are separated into groups based on a set of repeating properties (14)

phase change: the changing from one state of matter to another (125)

phase diagram: a graph that describes the conditions of temperature and pressure at which a substance exists as a solid, liquid, or gas (134)

point defect: a defect or irregularity within a crystal that occurs at a point in the lattice (145)

polar covalent bond: a bond in which electrons are not shared equally between the atoms (87)

polyatomic ion: a group of atoms that is covalently bonded together and has a positive or negative charge (98)

potential energy: the energy stored in a system (9)

products: substances produced in a chemical reaction (216)

proton: a positively-charged subatomic particle found in the nucleus of an atom (12)

Q

quantum: the amount of energy needed to move an electron from one energy level to another (24)

quantum mechanical model: the modern description, primarily mathematical, of the behavior of electrons in atoms (28)

Glossary R25

R

reactants: substances present at the start of a reaction (216)

reaction rate: the speed at which reactants become products (225)

representative particle: the species present in a substance; usually atoms, molecules, or formula units (176)

rotation: the movement of a body in a circular path around a fixed point (117)

S

saturated solution: a solution that contains the maximum amount of solute for a given quantity of solvent at a constant temperature and pressure (162)

single covalent bond: a bond made by one shared pair of electrons (84)

single-replacement reaction: a chemical change in which one element replaces a second element in a compound (231)

skeleton equation: a chemical equation that does not indicate the relative amounts of the reactants and products (217)

solubility: the amount of solute that dissolves in a given quantity of a solvent at a specified temperature and pressure to produce a saturated solution (162)

solubility curve: a graph of solubility as a function of temperature (163)

solute: the dissolved particles; usually ions, but also polar molecules (154)

solvation: the process of ion capture by a solvent (154)

solvation shell: a layer of solvent particles surrounding a solute species in a solution (244)

solvent: the dissolving medium in a solution (154)

spectator ion: an ion that is not directly involved in a reaction (242)

spin: a quantum mechanical property of electrons that may be thought of as clockwise or counterclockwise orientation (34)

standard enthalpy of formation: the change in enthalpy that accompanies the formation of one mole of the compound from its elements, with all substances in their standard states (293)

standard enthalpy of reaction: the change in enthalpy when one mole of matter undergoes a chemical reaction at standard conditions (294)

standard state: the stable form of a substance at a temperature of 25°C and a pressure of 100 kPa, which may be a solid, liquid, or gas (293)

standard temperature and pressure (STP): the standard set of conditions used for comparing properties of different gases; corresponds to a temperature of 0°C and approximately atmospheric pressure at sea level (100 kPa) (113)

stoichiometry: the calculation of quantities in chemical reactions (254)

sublimation: the changing from a solid directly to a gas without passing through the liquid state (126)

supersaturated solution: a solution that contains more solute than it can theoretically hold at a given temperature (165)

surface tension: an inward force that tends to minimize the surface area of a liquid; it causes the surface to behave as if it were a thin skin (149)

surfactant: a substance that reduces surface tension (150)

surroundings: everything in the universe outside of the system (10, 283)

suspension: a heterogeneous mixture from which particles settle out upon standing (168)

system: a part of the universe on which you focus your attention (10, 283)

T

theoretical yield: the amount of product that could form during a reaction calculated from a balanced chemical equation; it represents the maximum amount of product that could be formed from a given amount of reactant (275)

thermal conductivity: the ability of a material to conduct heat (143)

R26 Glossary

thermal energy: the total kinetic energy of the atoms of a substance (9)

thermochemical equation: a chemical equation that includes the enthalpy change (288)

translation: the shift of a body from one point in space to another (117)

triple covalent bond: a bond made by three pairs of shared electrons (84)

V

valence electron: an electron in the outermost or highest occupied energy level of an atom (38)

van der Waals forces: the two weakest intermolecular attractions—dispersion interactions and dipole forces (91)

vapor pressure: a measure of the force exerted by a gas above a liquid in a sealed container; a dynamic equilibrium exists between the vapor and the liquid (130)

vaporization: the changing from a liquid to a gas (126)

vibration: the rapid back-and-forth movement of an object in a fixed place (117)

VSEPR theory (valence-shell electron-pair repulsion theory): a theory that states that bonding pairs of electrons and unshared valence electron pairs repel each other and push each other as far away as possible to minimize the electrostatic repulsion between them; these repulsions result in specific three-dimensional shapes (88)

Glossary R27

INDEX

A

B

C

D

F

G

H

I

K

L

M

N

Q

R

S

T

U

X

Y

Notes

Notes

Notes

Notes

Notes

Solid (▪C)
Liquid (●Br)
Gas (●He)
Not applicable; not found in nature (×Tc)

Main-Group Elements

- Alkali metals
- Alkaline earth metals
- Other metals
- Metalloids
- Nonmetals
- Halogens
- Noble gases

Transition Elements

- Transition metals
- Inner transition metals

Key (example cell): 13 (Atomic number), 26.982 (Atomic mass†), Element classification, Al (Element symbol), Phase at STP, $[Ne]3s^23p^1$ (Electron configuration), Aluminum (Element name)

†*The atomic masses in parentheses refer to the longest lived or most important isotope of radioactive elements.*

	1 1A	2 2A	3 3B	4 4B	5 5B	6 6B	7 7B	8 8B	9 8B	10 8B	11 1B	12 2B	13 3A	14 4A	15 5A	16 6A	17 7A	18 8A
1	1 H 1.008 $1s^1$ Hydrogen																	2 He 4.003 $1s^2$ Helium
2	3 Li 6.94 $[He]2s^1$ Lithium	4 Be 9.0122 $[He]2s^2$ Beryllium											5 B 10.81 $[He]2s^22p^1$ Boron	6 C 12.011 $[He]2s^22p^2$ Carbon	7 N 14.007 $[He]2s^22p^3$ Nitrogen	8 O 15.999 $[He]2s^22p^4$ Oxygen	9 F 18.998 $[He]2s^22p^5$ Fluorine	10 Ne 20.180 $[He]2s^22p^6$ Neon
3	11 Na 22.990 $[Ne]3s^1$ Sodium	12 Mg 24.305 $[Ne]3s^2$ Magnesium											13 Al 26.982 $[Ne]3s^23p^1$ Aluminum	14 Si 28.085 $[Ne]3s^23p^2$ Silicon	15 P 30.974 $[Ne]3s^23p^3$ Phosphorus	16 S 32.06 $[Ne]3s^23p^4$ Sulfur	17 Cl 35.45 $[Ne]3s^23p^5$ Chlorine	18 Ar 39.948 $[Ne]3s^23p^6$ Argon
4	19 K 39.098 $[Ar]4s^1$ Potassium	20 Ca 40.078 $[Ar]4s^2$ Calcium	21 Sc 44.956 $[Ar]3d^14s^2$ Scandium	22 Ti 47.867 $[Ar]3d^24s^2$ Titanium	23 V 50.942 $[Ar]3d^34s^2$ Vanadium	24 Cr 51.996 $[Ar]3d^54s^1$ Chromium	25 Mn 54.938 $[Ar]3d^54s^2$ Manganese	26 Fe 55.845 $[Ar]3d^64s^2$ Iron	27 Co 58.933 $[Ar]3d^74s^2$ Cobalt	28 Ni 58.693 $[Ar]3d^84s^2$ Nickel	29 Cu 63.546 $[Ar]3d^{10}4s^1$ Copper	30 Zn 65.38 $[Ar]3d^{10}4s^2$ Zinc	31 Ga 69.723 $[Ar]3d^{10}4s^24p^1$ Gallium	32 Ge 72.630 $[Ar]3d^{10}4s^24p^2$ Germanium	33 As 74.922 $[Ar]3d^{10}4s^24p^3$ Arsenic	34 Se 78.971 $[Ar]3d^{10}4s^24p^4$ Selenium	35 Br 79.904 $[Ar]3d^{10}4s^24p^5$ Bromine	36 Kr 83.798 $[Ar]3d^{10}4s^24p^6$ Krypton
5	37 Rb 85.468 $[Kr]5s^1$ Rubidium	38 Sr 87.62 $[Kr]5s^2$ Strontium	39 Y 88.906 $[Kr]4d^15s^2$ Yttrium	40 Zr 91.224 $[Kr]4d^25s^2$ Zirconium	41 Nb 92.906 $[Kr]4d^45s^1$ Niobium	42 Mo 95.95 $[Kr]4d^55s^1$ Molybdenum	43 Tc (98) $[Kr]4d^55s^2$ Technetium	44 Ru 101.07 $[Kr]4d^75s^1$ Ruthenium	45 Rh 102.906 $[Kr]4d^85s^1$ Rhodium	46 Pd 106.42 $[Kr]4d^{10}$ Palladium	47 Ag 107.868 $[Kr]4d^{10}5s^1$ Silver	48 Cd 112.414 $[Kr]4d^{10}5s^2$ Cadmium	49 In 114.818 $[Kr]4d^{10}5s^25p^1$ Indium	50 Sn 118.710 $[Kr]4d^{10}5s^25p^2$ Tin	51 Sb 121.760 $[Kr]4d^{10}5s^25p^3$ Antimony	52 Te 127.60 $[Kr]4d^{10}5s^25p^4$ Tellurium	53 I 126.904 $[Kr]4d^{10}5s^25p^5$ Iodine	54 Xe 131.293 $[Kr]4d^{10}5s^25p^6$ Xenon
6	55 Cs 132.905 $[Xe]6s^1$ Cesium	56 Ba 137.327 $[Xe]6s^2$ Barium	71 Lu 174.967 $[Xe]4f^{14}5d^16s^2$ Lutetium	72 Hf 178.49 $[Xe]4f^{14}5d^26s^2$ Hafnium	73 Ta 180.948 $[Xe]4f^{14}5d^36s^2$ Tantalum	74 W 183.84 $[Xe]4f^{14}5d^46s^2$ Tungsten	75 Re 186.207 $[Xe]4f^{14}5d^56s^2$ Rhenium	76 Os 190.23 $[Xe]4f^{14}5d^66s^2$ Osmium	77 Ir 192.217 $[Xe]4f^{14}5d^76s^2$ Iridium	78 Pt 195.084 $[Xe]4f^{14}5d^96s^1$ Platinum	79 Au 196.967 $[Xe]4f^{14}5d^{10}6s^1$ Gold	80 Hg 200.592 $[Xe]4f^{14}5d^{10}6s^2$ Mercury	81 Tl 204.38 $[Xe]4f^{14}5d^{10}6s^26p^1$ Thallium	82 Pb 207.2 $[Xe]4f^{14}5d^{10}6s^26p^2$ Lead	83 Bi 208.980 $[Xe]4f^{14}5d^{10}6s^26p^3$ Bismuth	84 Po (209) $[Xe]4f^{14}5d^{10}6s^26p^4$ Polonium	85 At (210) $[Xe]4f^{14}5d^{10}6s^26p^5$ Astatine	86 Rn (222) $[Xe]4f^{14}5d^{10}6s^26p^6$ Radon
7	87 Fr (223) $[Rn]7s^1$ Francium	88 Ra (226) $[Rn]7s^2$ Radium	103 Lr (262) $[Rn]5f^{14}7s^27p^1$ Lawrencium	104 Rf (267) $[Rn]5f^{14}6d^27s^2$ Rutherfordium	105 Db (268) $[Rn]5f^{14}6d^37s^2$ Dubnium	106 Sg (269) $[Rn]5f^{14}6d^47s^2$ Seaborgium	107 Bh (270) $[Rn]5f^{14}6d^57s^2$ Bohrium	108 Hs (269) $[Rn]5f^{14}6d^67s^2$ Hassium	109 Mt (278) $[Rn]5f^{14}6d^77s^2$ Meitnerium	110 Ds (281) $[Rn]5f^{14}6d^97s^1$ Darmstadtium	111 Rg (280) $[Rn]5f^{14}6d^{10}7s^1$ Roentgenium	112 Cn (285) $[Rn]5f^{14}6d^{10}7s^2$ Copernicium	113 Nh (286) $[Rn]5f^{14}6d^{10}7s^27p^1$ Nihonium	114 Fl (289) $[Rn]5f^{14}6d^{10}7s^27p^2$ Flerovium	115 Mc (289) $[Rn]5f^{14}6d^{10}7s^27p^3$ Moscovium	116 Lv (293) $[Rn]5f^{14}6d^{10}7s^27p^4$ Livermorium	117 Ts (294) $[Rn]5f^{14}6d^{10}7s^27p^5$ Tennessine	118 Og (294) $[Rn]5f^{14}6d^{10}7s^27p^6$ Oganesson

Elements 104–118 are the transactinide elements.

Lanthanide series

57 La 138.905 $[Xe]5d^16s^2$ Lanthanum	58 Ce 140.116 $[Xe]4f^15d^16s^2$ Cerium	59 Pr 140.908 $[Xe]4f^36s^2$ Praseodymium	60 Nd 144.242 $[Xe]4f^46s^2$ Neodymium	61 Pm (145) $[Xe]4f^56s^2$ Promethium	62 Sm 150.36 $[Xe]4f^66s^2$ Samarium	63 Eu 151.964 $[Xe]4f^76s^2$ Europium	64 Gd 157.25 $[Xe]4f^75d^16s^2$ Gadolinium	65 Tb 158.925 $[Xe]4f^96s^2$ Terbium	66 Dy 162.500 $[Xe]4f^{10}6s^2$ Dysprosium	67 Ho 164.930 $[Xe]4f^{11}6s^2$ Holmium	68 Er 167.259 $[Xe]4f^{12}6s^2$ Erbium	69 Tm 168.934 $[Xe]4f^{13}6s^2$ Thulium	70 Yb 173.045 $[Xe]4f^{14}6s^2$ Ytterbium

Actinide series

89 Ac (227) $[Rn]6d^17s^2$ Actinium	90 Th 232.038 $[Rn]6d^27s^2$ Thorium	91 Pa 231.036 $[Rn]5f^26d^17s^2$ Protactinium	92 U 238.029 $[Rn]5f^36d^17s^2$ Uranium	93 Np (237) $[Rn]5f^46d^17s^2$ Neptunium	94 Pu (244) $[Rn]5f^67s^2$ Plutonium	95 Am (243) $[Rn]5f^77s^2$ Americium	96 Cm (247) $[Rn]5f^76d^17s^2$ Curium	97 Bk (247) $[Rn]5f^97s^2$ Berkelium	98 Cf (251) $[Rn]5f^{10}7s^2$ Californium	99 Es (252) $[Rn]5f^{11}7s^2$ Einsteinium	100 Fm (257) $[Rn]5f^{12}7s^2$ Fermium	101 Md (258) $[Rn]5f^{13}7s^2$ Mendelevium	102 No (259) $[Rn]5f^{14}7s^2$ Nobelium